THE PERSONNEL MANAGEMENT PROCESS

WENDELL L. FRENCH

UNIVERSITY OF WASHINGTON

THE PERSONNEL MANAGEMENT PROCESS

Human Resources Administration and Development

FOURTH EDITION

HOUGHTON MIFFLIN COMPANY   Boston

Dallas   Geneva, Illinois   Hopewell, New Jersey
Palo Alto   London

To my wife and parents

Printed in the U.S.A.

Library of Congress Catalog Card No.: 77-073992

ISBN: 0-395-25529-5

Contents

Preface

This book reflects what I believe are the two human imperatives in modern organizations: (1) enhancing the quality of organizational life in a psychological and sociological sense; and (2) increasing organizational, group, and personal effectiveness. By "effectiveness" I include such matters as productivity, efficiency, creativity, and vitality. These two major imperatives can be opposite, complementary, or highly reinforcing. The challenge is that, at a time in history when the first imperative is more and more salient, the second is no less compelling. As a matter of fact, the pressures to accommodate both are increasing, and it is vital that contemporary organizations find ways to enhance them. One implication is clear: There is a growing need for all organizational members —managers, professionals, team leaders, team members—to know more about and be more skilled in the "people" aspects of management and organization in order to channel the two imperatives in an optimally synergetic way.

Two features of this book are particularly important. One is a general systems view of organizations. This view permits examination of personnel management as a dynamic network of processes, systems, and conditions that affect all organizations and the people in them in profound ways. Another feature of the book is its extensive application of contemporary behavioral science theory, research, and practice to the management of certain critical organizational processes, including job design, staffing, training and development, appraisal, compensation, leadership, organizational justice, and collective bargaining.

The fourth edition includes new or expanded attention to such matters as human resources planning, behaviorally anchored rating scales, flextime, the compressed workweek, management by objectives, career ladders, integrative bargaining, final-offer arbitration, and organization development. The topic of women and minorities in management receives additional attention in this edition, and the increasingly pervasive impact of federal legislation is evident throughout the book.

I wish to express my gratitude to the many instructors, students, and managers who made helpful suggestions for the improvement of the book from the first edition through the fourth. Robert J. Solomon of the College of William and Mary; Louis V. Imundo, Jr., of Wright State University; Randall S. Schuler of Pennsylvania State University; Paul Shaffer of Washington State University; Herb Heneman of the University of Wisconsin; and Mark Wallace of the University of Kentucky provided many helpful suggestions for the fourth edition. Michael Moore of Michigan State University contributed a number of very helpful suggestions. I am also indebted to Sheila Adams and Charles Fay who provided some important library research for the fourth edition while working on their doctorates at the University of Washington. I am also grateful to Helene S. Tanimoto, librarian at the Industrial Relations Center, University of Hawaii, Honolulu, and to Gail Bartholomew and Janet Domiano, librarians at the Maui Community College Library, Kahului, for their excellent assistance and cooperation. My wife Marjorie provided all of the typing services for the fourth edition and made many helpful editorial suggestions.

Thomas Patten of Michigan State University, George Milkovitch of the University of Minnesota, Tom Atchison of San Diego State College, Paul Johnson of Purdue University, Sam Aertker of the University of Alaska, Robert Zawacki of the University of Colorado, Colorado Springs, and John Dittrich of the University of Kentucky were particularly helpful with extensive comments relative to the third edition. Robert Roser of Chaffey College, William Switzer of the University of Puget Sound, Floyd Paulk of Oklahoma's Central State University, David Van Fleet of the University of Akron, Clyde Schrickel of Wright State University, Stephen Miller of California State University at Hayward, William Oberg of Michigan State, Robert Finn of the University of Georgia, Charles Phillips of Boise State College, Samuel Roberto of Massachusetts Bay Community College, Donald Bolon of Ohio University, Richard Sylvester of California State University, Fullerton, and D. W. Jarrell of Drexel University all made helpful comments on a questionnaire in preparation for the third edition. Paul Zingale of the University of Maine also provided a number of helpful suggestions. Carol Summer provided excellent typing service for the third edition.

Wilmar Bernthal of the University of Colorado, William G. Scott of the University of Washington, Lane Tracy of Ohio University, and E. Frank Harrison of Illinois State University provided comprehensive suggestions for the second edition. Helpful questionnaire responses relative to preparation for the second edition were received from Arthur Elkins of the University of Massachusetts, Gerald Foster of the University of Denver, Raymond Hilgert of Washington University, William Keown of the University of Oklahoma, Elizabeth Lanham of the University of Texas, Frank Paine of the University of Maryland, and George Strother of the University of Wisconsin. Nona Pedersen and Margaret Trudo provided major typing and duplicating services for the second edition.

John Hennessey of Dartmouth College, Joseph W. Towle of Washington University, and Lee Danielson of the University of Michigan read and commented on most, or all, of the manuscript for the first edition and made many valuable suggestions. A number of people who were then graduate students at the University of Washington and have since moved on to various significant academic and industrial positions also made many helpful comments on the first edition. These people include John Buckley, C. Thomas Cherian, Alvar Elbing, James Garrison, Chester Sorenson, and Burke Williams. My wife Marjorie provided most of the typing for the first edition.

To all of these people I am most grateful. Any deficiencies, of course, I accept as my responsibility.

W. L. F.

THE PERSONNEL
MANAGEMENT PROCESS

1

PART 1
A DEFINITION AND HISTORY OF PERSONNEL MANAGEMENT

1. A Definition and an Overview

2. A History of Modern Personnel Management

Chapter 1 begins our study of personnel management with a definition and a brief overview of the subject. It also lists various challenging problems in the administration of human resources that are faced by our contemporary organizations. The second chapter presents a brief history of personnel management and describes some highlights in the development of modern philosophy and practice.

CHAPTER 1
A DEFINITION AND
AN OVERVIEW

Personnel management is the recruitment, selection, development, utilization of, and accommodation to human resources by organizations. The human resources of an organization consist of all individuals, regardless of their roles, who are engaged in any of the organization's activities. An organization may be a manufacturing firm, an insurance company, a governmental agency, a hospital, a university, a labor union, a ski resort, a public school system, a church, or an airline. It may be small or large, simple or complex. It may be a model of longevity like the Hudson's Bay Company (incorporated in 1670), or it may be here today and gone tomorrow like the campaign organization of a defeated political candidate.

A MAJOR SUBSYSTEM OF ORGANIZATIONS

Since the recruitment, selection, development, utilization of, and accommodation to people are integral aspects of any organized effort, personnel management is inherent in all organizations, whether or not there is a department by that name. Personnel management is a major component of the broad managerial function and has roots and branches extending throughout and beyond each organization. As such, it is more than the management of people by supervisors, and it also is more than the "personnel" responsibilities assigned to a particular manager or department. As I will explain later in more detail, *personnel management is a major, pervasive subsystem of all organizations.*

THE EFFECTIVENESS OF PERSONNEL MANAGEMENT

The effectiveness of the personnel management subsystem can be evaluated in terms of its contribution to the effectiveness with which an organization attains its particular goals. In an automobile manufacturing firm with the primary objective of producing passenger cars at a profit, personnel management may be considered effective to the degree that it contributes to this objective. On the other hand, if a nonprofit hospital has the objective of producing the highest quality of care within the limits of available financial resources, personnel management will be effective to the extent that it contributes to this objective.

The measurement of effectiveness in achieving objectives, however, is an extremely difficult matter. Typically, not only must several objectives be considered simultaneously, but it is important to think about both short- and long-range goals and about the health and viability of the enterprise. Thus, the broad concept of organizational effectiveness needs to be considered in analyzing and evaluating personnel management in organizations.

A FREQUENTLY MISUNDERSTOOD AND UNDERMANAGED FUNCTION

A good deal of misunderstanding exists about the nature of personnel management, partly because of the almost universal emergence of personnel departments in organizations with, say, two hundred or more employees and the understandable tendency to think of personnel management in departmental terms. From my experience, this misunderstanding appears frequently in communications among managers, among members of the academic community, and in the literature. Sometimes the subject of personnel management is approached solely from the standpoint of the personnel department, despite the fact that all managers at all levels of the organization are deeply involved in the management of human resources. Sometimes the situation is reversed, with the subject being approached solely from the standpoint of effective supervision, while the roles of

personnel specialists and top managers are ignored. Either approach glosses over the highly complex nature of personnel management and overlooks its interdependence with other broad managerial functions.

Widespread lack of understanding and knowledge about effective personnel management likewise exists, particularly in the many organizations in which the top managers have had little or no systematic exposure to managerial concepts and theory. This is more likely to be the case in smaller organizations than in larger ones, because the latter usually have more resources for management development and can be more selective in terms of managerial knowledge and experience. Furthermore, the management of people presents an extraordinary number of problems for management's concern, including those that are psychological, social, philosophical, ethical, and physiological. In a sense, then, the management of human resources is a formidable area for study. Paradoxically, we all deal with other people so much that we are frequently smug about our knowledge of human behavior—and managers consequently resist examining the assumptions under which they manage others.

The complex nature of personnel management is also evident in the frustration that personnel specialists sometimes experience in attempting to explain and justify their respective roles. Frequently this frustration is compounded by the assignment of unrelated and extraneous functions to the personnel department, making it difficult to develop an overall rationale for that unit. Then, too, a good deal of frustrating dialogue may result from a lack of appreciation on the part of personnel specialists and others that *the broad personnel managerial function must be the joint effort of all managers within the organization.*

Related to this problem, a tendency on the part of many personnel specialists to attempt to install various programs without adequate organizational diagnosis also adds to confusion and misunderstanding. This creates an image of personnel management as a field of fad and fashion imposed on reluctant managers and on an even more reluctant work force. But it is not fair to level this criticism solely at personnel specialists—managers in general are often prone to promote and/or support new programs without assessing their relevance or the likely impact.

Another, but less important, difficulty is the lack of standardization in terminology. In this book, *personnel management* and *human resources administration* are intended to be synonymous with *personnel and industrial relations, personnel and labor relations,* and *personnel and employee relations.* Similarly, when I refer to the *personnel department,* I intend the same meaning conveyed by longer terms such as the *personnel and labor relations department.*[1] This book focuses on the very broad human resources function of general administration.

It should not be inferred that problems in personnel management are new. Every organization from the beginning of human history has been required to concern itself in some fashion with the selection, utilization, and development of people. Of course, the personnel philosophy and methods in ancient times were often crude and barbarous. History abounds with examples of exploitation and suppression, including slavery, and of the degrading and dysfunctional consequences, including apathy, sabotage, and revolution. Unfortunately, illustrations of gross suppression are still apparent

in various parts of the world. In the United States where, relatively speaking, freedom and opportunity are almost without bounds, less than full utilization of minority groups in organizational life is a problem that has confronted the American people for a long time, and it still requires much attention. Lack of full opportunity for women employees is a major inequity that only now is beginning to be corrected.

In general, however, human resources unquestionably have become more effectively managed over the centuries, although it is apparent that not every problem in personnel management has disappeared. New problems have emerged, and old problems have taken on new aspects that require new solutions. In addition, many of the assumptions underlying traditional personnel practices are now being seriously questioned.

SALIENT TRENDS AFFECTING PERSONNEL MANAGEMENT

A number of trends on the contemporary scene are making effective personnel management even more important than in past decades. Here are some of the more salient ones:

○ *People are better educated.* This means that they are more likely to question prevailing practices and assumptions, that they want more voice in matters pertaining to their work lives, and that they want to use their abilities.

○ *Federal legislation in the United States has prohibited discrimination in the work situation on the basis of race, color, national origin, religion, sex, or age.* This has meant and will continue to mean dramatic changes in the field of personnel management.

○ *International competition among organizations is becoming more intense.* There are many reasons for this, of course, including competition for

---

[1] The American Society for Personnel Administration *Handbooks of Personnel and Industrial Relations* use the acronym PAIR to abbreviate "personnel and industrial relations." Dale Yoder and Herbert G. Heneman, Jr., *ASPA Handbook of Personnel and Industrial Relations,* Volumes I–VIII (Washington, D.C.: The Bureau of National Affairs, 1974–1977). I prefer to use *personnel* or *personnel management.*

resources, a wide sharing of technology, satellite communications, and the jet airplane—all of which accelerate the tempo of events.

○ *Technological innovation is intensifying.* This is occurring because of intensified competition and other reasons, and means that rapid changes in many organizations will occur. Many jobs, procedures, and organizational structures can and will become obsolete overnight. These changes will place heavy demands on personnel management.

○ *There is a heightened awareness of the fragility of the ecological system and the interdependency of people and their surroundings.* Consequently, there must be more efficient and careful practices in organizations including more attention to health and safety, work rules pertaining to disposal, and such matters as how working hours affect traffic and pollution control.

○ *The world is now aware that the supply of energy and natural resources is not inexhaustible.* Thus, there will be intensified demands for efficiency and innovation, as well as for new forms of energy.

○ *There is a growing trend toward collective action on the part of previously nonunionized groups.* We are seeing more frequent instances of unionization and strike action on the part of such groups as nurses, government employees, teachers, and even physicians and professional athletes. This is bound to mean increased attention to personnel practices across all segments of the work force.

○ *There is more concern about the quality of work life in general.* This will create heightened attention to human needs and development and to the kinds of work climates that humans create for each other.

All these trends will intensify the need for effective personnel management in all its facets.

SOME CONTEMPORARY PROBLEMS

The following questions typify the tremendously challenging human problems faced by the modern manager, some of which are influenced directly by the trends just mentioned. In a large measure, these are problems in personnel management, although they are inseparably linked to other problems in general management as well. They grow out of fundamental concerns that managers, employees, and the public have about organizational effectiveness and efficiency; these questions in turn stem from anxieties about such matters as the cost and quality of goods and services, the ability of organizations to compete domestically and internationally and/or to survive, and the equitable treatment of all workers and the quality of work life. Concerns about equitable treatment, as reflected in government legislation, have produced some of the most critical questions and problems on this list, at least for the near future. Other concerns that speak to the broader questions of motivation and performance are in danger of receiving less management attention, in the rush to comply with laws pertaining to nondiscrimination.

SOCIAL RESPONSIBILITY

○ How meaningful is work and a career to most people? How does this square with their expectations and aspirations?

○ To what extent should an organization be concerned with the quality of work life?

○ How much responsibility should a business organization assume for remedying cultural and educational deficiencies among applicants from disadvantaged groups?

○ How can a balance be struck between affirmative action and the avoidance of reverse discrimination?

° What is the relationship, if any, between the ecological impact of a factory and effective personnel management within that plant?

JOB DESIGN AND WORK RULES

° To what extent are job enlargement and job enrichment associated with motivation? Who wants their jobs enriched? What are the consequences of job enrichment efforts?

° What are the different forms of employee participation, and do the various forms decrease or increase effective control by management?

° What requirements does the federal government place on organizations relative to the safety and health of employees, and what has been the impact of these requirements?

° How useful is the matrix type of organization, and what is its impact on people's careers?

° What assumptions about people underlie various kinds of work rules?

° How useful/dysfunctional is the four-day, forty-hour workweek?

° Does flexitime work? Under what circumstances?

° Does the sharing of one job by two people make sense? When?

° Can women handle all jobs traditionally held by men and vice versa? What are the implications for job redesign?

STAFFING

° What selection devices discriminate against minorities, and in what way?

° What are the merits of such devices as stress interviews and personality tests?

° What subtle forms of discrimination occur in organizations?

° What are the implications of federal legislation requiring equal opportunity for women in matters of promotion and compensation? What are the implications for training? For conflict resolution? For benefits and work rules?

° What should management's responsibilities be in the case of a possible need to lay off part of the work force? How should members of minority groups be treated in a layoff situation?

° Can the "assessment center" be used to assist organizational members in career development as well as in selection for promotion? How?

° Should all job openings be advertised within an organization? What are the merits of promoting from within versus employing from the outside?

LEADERSHIP AND SUPERVISION

° Does effective leadership vary with different situations? What are these contingencies?

° Can effective leadership be learned?

° Can leadership functions be shared among members of a work team?

° What is the impact of group norms on team and organizational effectiveness?

° Which leadership styles do various organization improvement strategies reinforce?

ORGANIZATIONAL JUSTICE

° What is the nature of "fair" treatment; how is it related to various organizational outcomes?

° How tough should management be in matters of discipline?

° To what extent do concepts of fairness vary by subcultures?

° Should an organization have a formalized grievance procedure?

° What personnel devices are used to enhance equity in the organization?

° What are the advantages and disadvantages in the use of an organizational ombudsman in the administration of corrective justice?

PERFORMANCE APPRAISAL

° How successful are various merit-rating approaches?

° How do subordinates react to appraisal interviews? How do supervisors conducting the interviews react?

° How effective is criticism as a motivating factor?

° What does a performance appraisal system do to a subordinate's self-concept and attitude toward the organization?

° Are management-by-objectives techniques participative, or are these techniques really autocratic?

COMPENSATION AND REWARD

° How useful is money as a motivator?

° How do monetary payments interact with nonfinancial rewards?

° What is the impact of using across-the-board adjustments versus merit pay?

° What are the consequences of allowing salaries for beginning jobs to rise at a faster rate than salaries for positions involving more length of service and/or responsibility?

° What are the results of profit sharing and other kinds of incentive plans?

° How practical is the notion of a "cafeteria type" of fringe benefit program?

° What are the salary administration implications of federal regulations about equal pay for women for equal work?

COLLECTIVE BARGAINING

° Why do people join unions?

° What can an organization do and not do during a unionization campaign?

° What are the implications of growing collective action by nurses, teachers, and government employees?

° What are the implications of the apparently growing phenomenon of union members refusing to support agreements made by negotiating committees?

° Are there viable alternatives to traditional power bargaining?

° To what extent should an organization rely on arbitration and dispute settlement to resolve conflicts?

° Do public employees have the right to strike? Should they have this right?

EMPLOYEE TRAINING AND DEVELOPMENT

° How effective are contemporary techniques in management development? How does one know? Are human-relations training programs effective?

° What are the conditions under which T-group or laboratory training are related to organizational effectiveness? What are the different forms of laboratory training?

° How can an organization assess training needs?

ORGANIZATION DEVELOPMENT

° What are some of the various contemporary organizational improvement strategies; how do they differ?

° What is the nature of emerging organization development (OD) programs? Under what circumstances are they successful?

° What are the consequences of legitimizing the expression of feelings and attitudes in the work environment?

° What role should the personnel department play in organization improvement?

° How much competition within an organization is healthy? At what point does such competition become dysfunctional to both individuals and the organization?

° How can interdepartmental conflict be managed effectively?

° What is the impact of various personnel techniques on organizational climate and vice versa?

° What diagnostic techniques of relevance to personnel management can be learned from the field of organization development?

These are the kinds of problems with which the discipline or study of modern personnel management must be concerned. Undoubtedly, you can add significant problems and questions from your own experience. Some of these questions will be answered directly in this book; others will be restated to acknowledge additional complexity; still others may be answered only indirectly.

While generalized conclusions or implications about many matters are presented in the various chapters, the intent of this book is not to provide pat answers. The intent is to provide a frame of reference and an awareness of the more significant variables (popularly referred to as *contingencies*) that operate in effective and ineffective human resources management. In addition, sufficient theory and research are presented so that the reader will be better equipped to anticipate and solve personnel problems in particular settings. Thus, I hope to enhance perspective and judgment in contrast to providing "cookbook recipes" for successful personnel management.

SUMMARY

Personnel management is the recruitment, selection, development, utilization of, and accommodation to human resources by organizations. It is part of the general management function and is a central, pervasive subsystem of all organizations. The effectiveness of personnel management needs to be assessed in terms of organizational effectiveness, which includes organizational goal attainment and organizational health and viability.

Departmentalizing some aspects of personnel management has resulted in much misunderstanding about the function. In addition, a good deal of misunderstanding stems from the relative recency of education and research in management, from a tendency to initiate programs without adequate organizational diagnosis, and from problems of terminology and semantics.

As a central management function, and as a field of study, contemporary personnel management is faced with many challenging problems centering on social responsibility, job design and work rules, staffing, leadership style, organizational justice, performance appraisal, compensation and reward, collective bargaining, employee training and development, and organization development. These challenges, intensified by significant changes in the United States and abroad, have thrust personnel management onto center stage.

REVIEW AND DISCUSSION QUESTIONS

1. Define personnel management.

2. What is the difference between personnel management and the personnel department?

3. What trends and/or events are intensifying the need for more effective personnel management?

4. As you see it, what are the most critical "people" problems faced by the organizations with which you are familiar?

SUPPLEMENTAL REFERENCES

Foulkes, Fred K., "The Expanding Role of the Personnel Function," *Harvard Business Review*, 53:71–84 (March–April 1975).

Mills, Ted, "Human Resources—Why the New Concern?" *Harvard Business Review*, 53:120–134 (March–April 1975).

Myer, Herbert E., "Personnel Directors Are the New Corporate Heroes," *Fortune*, 93:84–88ff. (February 1976).

CHAPTER 2
A HISTORY OF MODERN PERSONNEL MANAGEMENT

Modern personnel management has evolved from a number of significant and interrelated developments dating from the beginning of the Industrial Revolution. An exhaustive history would trace such matters as the evolution of workers' associations from ancient times, the vast changes in educational opportunity in recent years and their impact on the total labor force, developments in managerial education, the evolution of the corporation and an urban society, changes in employers' attitudes and assumptions about employees, and other social, economic, and political developments of the twentieth century and before. This book, however, will concentrate on relatively recent developments unique to the management of human resources in the United States,[1] although it will cite a number of illustrations from the British Isles. In short, the history of American personnel management is inseparable from the evolution of the American culture and its broader context. All that can be done in this chapter is to identify and discuss some of the highlights. (See the Appendix for a more complete chronological listing of significant events in the history of personnel management in the United States.)

THE INDUSTRIAL REVOLUTION

The Industrial Revolution appeared almost simultaneously with the intellectual, scientific, and political revolutions of the seventeenth and

[1] Matters of historical interest in personnel management that are part of ancient history are exemplified by workers' unions and strikes, which can be traced to ancient Rome and Egypt. Louis reports that there were eight craft guilds in Rome as early as the seventh century B.C.: ''. . . flute players, gold-smelters, smiths, dyers, cordwainers, curriers, brass-workers, and potters.'' See Paul Louis, *Ancient Rome at Work* (New York: Alfred A. Knopf, Inc., 1927), p. 48. Ward writes of a strike of slave masons working on an Egyptian temple in B.C. 1100. See C. Osborne Ward, *The Ancient Lowly* (Washington: W. H. Lowdermilk & Company, 1899), II, p. 82.

eighteenth centuries. The Industrial Revolution consisted essentially of the development of machinery, the linking of power to machines, and the consequent establishment of factories in which a large number of people were employed—all resulting in a tremendous increase in the productive power of people.

The factory gradually replaced the "putting out" or "cottage" system in which merchants furnished raw materials to the cottage of a worker and family and paid cash for the completion of the product. This decline of the cottage system was largely due to the ability of factory owners to pay a family higher wages than could be earned in home manufacture, primarily because of the speed of machines and the efficiencies gained through a further subdivision of labor.[2] Although specialization by crafts in terms of the "end product" had been in existence throughout recorded history, a major shift to specialization in terms of subaspects of the final product had now occurred.

DIVISION OF LABOR

Adam Smith has given us a graphic picture of this further subdivision of labor in his *Wealth of Nations*, published in 1776. It concerns the manufacture of pins.

. . . One man draws out the wire, another straightens it, a third cuts it, a fourth points it, a fifth grinds it at the top for receiving the head; to make the head requires two or three distinct operations; to put it on is a peculiar business, to whiten the pins is another; it is even a trade by itself to put them into the paper; the important business of making a pin is, in this manner, divided into about eighteen distinct operations, which in some manufactories, are performed by distinct hands, though in others the same man will sometimes perform two or three of them. . . .[3]

Workers were no longer obliged to perform one minute function and then go on to another as they had done in the relative quiet of small shops or in their own homes. They now operated a complex machine that performed a minute task with great rapidity, and they were surrounded by other workers similarly operating machines. Rather than being skilled in a number of tasks, they now specialized in one task.

Some advantages of this division of labor were discussed by Charles Babbage in his *On the Economy of Machinery and Manufactures,* first published in 1832. One advantage was a shortened learning period for apprentices, "If . . . instead of learning *all* the different processes for making a needle, for instance, his attention be confined to one operation, the portion of time consumed unprofitably at the commencement of his apprenticeship will be small. . . ."[4] Babbage also perceived that such division of labor reduced the waste in raw materials, achieved savings through more effective placement of workers, produced economies through a differential wage scale based on skill level, saved time by not requiring workers to switch from task to task, gained efficiencies stemming from the workers' familiarization with special tools, and stimulated workers' inventions pertaining to tools and methods.[5] It should be noted, however, that disadvantages of this division of labor are contemporary managerial problems.

Regarding placement according to a hierarchy of skills, Babbage stated, ". . . we . . . avoid the loss arising from the employment of an accomplished mathematician in performing the lowest processes of arithmetic."[6] With respect to worker innovations, he said:

[2] Andrew Ure, *The Philosophy of Manufactures,* 2nd ed. (London: Charles Knight, 1835).
[3] Adam Smith, *An Inquiry into the Nature and Causes of the Wealth of Nations* (London and Toronto: J.M. Dent & Sons, Ltd., 1910), I, p. 5.

[4] Charles Babbage, *On the Economy of Machinery and Manufacturers,* 4th ed. (London: Charles Knight, 1835), p. 170.
[5] Ibid., pp. 169–176.
[6] Ibid., p. 201.

Figure **2-1** Rates of wages in the cotton factories of England, of the different countries on the continent, and of the United States

Country	Quantity of raw cotton consumed	Hours worked per week	Average wages	
			s.	d.
England	240,000,000	69	11	0
America	77,000,000	78	10	0
France	74,000,000	72–84	5	8
Prussia	7,000,000	72–90	–	–
Switzerland	19,000,000	78–84	4	5
The Tyrol	12,000,000	72–80	4	0
Saxony	5,000,000	72	3	6
Bonn in Prussia	–	94	2	6*

*Factory Commission Report, Part I., D. 2, p. 44.

From Andrew Ure, *The Philosophy of Manufactures*, 2nd ed. (London: Charles Knight, 1835), p. 373.

When each process, by which any article is produced, is the sole occupation of one individual, his whole attention being devoted to a very limited and simple operation, improvements in the form of his tools, or in the mode of using them, are much more likely to occur to his mind, than if it were distracted by a greater variety of circumstances. Such an improvement in the tool is generally the first step towards a machine. If a piece of metal is to be cut in a lathe, for example, there is one particular angle at which the cutting-tool must be held to insure the cleanest cut; and it is quite natural that the idea of fixing the tool at that angle should present itself to an intelligent workman.[7]

These observations by Babbage anticipated, in a number of ways, the *scientific management movement* of a half century later.

CONDITIONS IN THE FACTORY

With the factory came a type of regimented behavior that stemmed from the interdependence of tasks and positions. Obviously, this regimentation was not new, since for centuries the erection of buildings, the construction of canals, and military operations, for example, had required a great deal of coordinated effort. But the factory did create substantial changes from cottage manufacture, agricultural pursuits, and small shop life. Clearly it was necessary to start and stop work at the same time and to establish rigorous working rules applicable to large numbers of people. In addition, a more extensive hierarchy of officials appeared in contrast to cottage manufacture, including the owner, managers, superintendents, and foremen. The social distance between factory hand and owner was now far greater than was the case between the journeymen and master craftsmen of the Middle Ages. Most employees in the factories worked long hours at low pay under conditions of extremes in temperature, dust, noise, and other discomforts, although it should not be assumed that conditions in agriculture or the small shops were much better.

As shown in Figure 2-1, around 1835, workers were employed an average of seventy-eight hours per week in the United States and sixty-nine hours in England. These were literally sunrise-to-sunset hours; in the winter months, employees undoubtedly went to work long before light and returned home after dark.

[7] Ibid., pp. 173–174.

Figure 2-2   The British Factories Regulation Act, *circa* 1835

The new Factories Regulation Act applies to all cotton, wool, flax, tow, hemp, or silk-mills, of which the machinery is driven by steam-engines or water-wheels. Where the machinery is moved by animal power, the act does not apply, nor to bobbin-net lace factories.

No child can be employed at all before it is nine years old.

No child younger than eleven must work more than forty-eight hours in any one week, or more than nine hours in any one day.

After the 1st March, 1835, this restriction extends to children under twelve; and after the 1st March, 1836, to children under thirteen.

To render these restrictions effective, no child must remain on any pretence more than nine hours a day in any working apartment of the factory.

Persons under eighteen years of age must not work more than sixty-nine hours in a week, or twelve in a day; nor at all between half-past eight o'clock at night and half-past five o'clock in the morning.

Children under nine may be employed in silk-mills.

One hour and a half must be allowed for meals to all young persons, but that time is exclusive of the nine or twelve hours' work.

Two entire holidays and eight half-holidays are to be allowed to all young persons who are under the restrictions.

Every child restricted to forty-eight hours' labour in the week must attend a school for at least two hours a day, for six days out of the seven. The mill-owner is not allowed to continue in his employment any child who does not regularly attend school as above stated; for which purpose he must be certified every week of the child's attendance by the teacher.

From Andrew Ure, *The Philosophy of Manufactures*, 2nd ed. (London: Charles Knight, 1835), pp. 358–359.

Practices were frequently unethical by today's standards. For example, in England, a frequent practice was to raise prices charged to employees in the "master's shop" (called the "company store" in American history) to offset declining prices of products manufactured by the particular factory. As a corrective device, Babbage recommended that employees oversee the operations of the store:

Wherever the workmen are paid in goods, or are compelled to purchase at the master's shop, much injustice is done to them, and great misery results from it. . . . If the object be solely to procure for his workmen better articles, it will be more effectually accomplished by the master confining himself to supplying a small capital, at a moderate rate of interest; leaving the details to be conducted by a committee of workmen, in conjunction with his own agent, and the books of the shop to be audited periodically by the men themselves.[8]

CHILD LABOR

Child labor in the factories was common. One of the worst abuses of the Industrial Revolution in the British factory was the use of the "parish apprentice," a child who had come under the jurisdiction of the Poor Law authorities because of the impoverishment of her or his parents. The authorities, ". . . eager to rid themselves of the burden of the child's maintenance, virtually sold it, under indentures for a period of years, to a factory owner, who was experiencing a shortage of labour for the running of the new machines."[9]

To cite a further illustration, investigation of English coal mines in the early 1800s found that the adult miners were working from nine to eleven hours a day and that children were working sometimes from fourteen to fifteen hours a day. Some of these children were only

[8] Babbage, *Economy of Machinery and Manufactures*, p. 309.

[9] G.D.H. Cole, *A Short History of the British Working-Class Movement* (London: George Allen & Unwin, Ltd., 1948), pp. 23–24.

four or five years of age. In 1829, boys of age seven and upward were reported employed in suburban Philadelphia factories from dawn until 8 P.M.[10] However, around 1835, the British Factories Regulation Act prohibited the employment of children under nine years of age and restricted the working hours of persons between ages thirteen and eighteen to sixty-nine hours per week. (See Figure 2-2.)

CONSEQUENCES OF THE INDUSTRIAL REVOLUTION

Economically, the Industrial Revolution resulted in great increases in output and in the accumulation of goods and capital. In turn, business and commerce were greatly accelerated. Owners and entrepreneurs often did well, but the average citizen fared poorly in comparison with today's workers in terms of purchasing power and working conditions. Labor was considered a commodity to be bought and sold, and the prevailing political philosophy of laissez faire resulted in little action by governments to protect the lot of the workers.

THE EMERGENCE OF FREE COLLECTIVE BARGAINING

It was inevitable that associations of wage earners would arise to protect themselves against some of the abuses of the Industrial Revolution and to improve their lot in life. Trade or labor unions spread from factory to factory. The first recorded strike in the American history of artisans occurred in 1786 and was called by the Philadelphia Journeymen Printers

because of a wage cut.[11] In 1799 the Philadelphia Journeymen Cordwainers (shoemakers) attempted to bargain collectively with their employers, an attempt that resulted in a lockout and then a negotiated settlement between the union and the employer association.

THE CONSPIRACY DOCTRINE AND ITS OVERTHROW

In 1806 the Cordwainers in Philadelphia were found guilty of criminal conspiracy to raise wages. Similarly, because of the number of violent strikes, the English Parliament passed a series of laws in 1799 and 1800, known as the Combination Laws, that declared trade unions to be illegal. In 1842, however, in the *Commonwealth* v. *Hunt* case, the Massachusetts Supreme Court overturned the "conspiracy doctrine" in the United States. The court ruled that labor combinations were not criminal per se and that labor organizations could have honorable as well as destructive objectives. Combinations must have a criminal or unlawful aspect to be illegal, the court held.[12]

After the *Commonwealth* v. *Hunt* decision, the right to organize and bargain collectively was gradually established. It would be almost one hundred years, however, before legislation would affirm the right of workers to organize and bargain collectively.

LABOR VIOLENCE

Considerable violence characterized many of the strikes of the second half of the nineteenth

---

[10] Gilbert Stone, *A History of Labour* (London: George G. Harrap & Company, Ltd., 1921), p. 300; and John R. Commons, et al., *History of Labour in the United States* (New York: The Macmillan Company, 1926), I, p. 182.

[11] Earlier concerted activity among American workers has been reported, however. In 1636 a group of fishermen in Maine protested against their wages being held. In 1741 a municipal regulation in New York City on the price of bread resulted in a strike of bakers. See Sanford Cohen, *Labor in the United States* (Columbus, Ohio: Charles E. Merrill Books, Inc., 1960), p. 70.

[12] Cohen, *Labor in the United States*, p. 449.

century. As a vivid example, during the Civil War the "Molly Maguires," a secret society of Irish miners in the anthracite fields, carried out terroristic activities including beatings and murders of employers. Not until ten of the leaders were executed in 1876 did their activities subside.[13]

As further evidence of the violence of this period, in 1886 four people were killed by police while striking for an eight-hour day at the McCormick Reaper Works in Chicago. At a resulting protest meeting in Haymarket Square in Chicago, a bomb was thrown into the ranks of police. Seven police officers and four workers were killed in the ensuing melee.[14]

SUPPORT OF COLLECTIVE BARGAINING DURING WORLD WAR I

World War I gave impetus to governmental support of collective bargaining. The National War Labor Board of that period established "Works Councils," which consisted of elected representatives from the various departments, in factories. As a wartime emergency measure, employers were required to meet with these representatives to discuss grievances, wages, hours, and working conditions. Although many of these councils continued after the war, many were dissolved by employers, and all were opposed by the American Federation of Labor on the grounds that they were company-dominated.

EARLY TWENTIETH-CENTURY LEGISLATION

In 1914 the Clayton Act had been passed exempting unions from the provisions of the Sherman Act (antimonopoly). The Clayton Act limited the use of injunctions in labor disputes and made picketing and other union activities legal. The courts, however, tended to negate the provisions of the Clayton Act, and in 1932 the Norris-LaGuardia Act essentially prohibited the use of injunctions in labor disputes. That act also made the "yellow-dog" contract unenforceable. The yellow-dog contract was an agreement between management and a worker under which the latter agreed not to join a union as a condition of employment.

Six years prior to the Norris-LaGuardia Act, the Railway Labor Act (1926) had been passed, establishing collective bargaining for the railways, outlawing "company unions" in that industry, and providing grievance and arbitration procedures. In 1933, with the passage of the National Industrial Recovery Act, for the first time in the history of the United States most workers in interstate commerce were given the right to organize and bargain collectively. Subsequently, the NIRA was declared unconstitutional, but its labor provisions were then written into the Wagner Act of 1935.

THE SCIENTIFIC MANAGEMENT MOVEMENT

Another development of far-reaching significance to personnel management is the *scientific management* movement. The most famous name associated with this movement is that of Frederick W. Taylor.[15] Taylor started his experiments in the steel industry in the Midvale and

---

[13] Ibid., p. 86.

[14] Ibid., p. 91. See also *Business Week*, May 6, 1961, pp. 90–91, for discussion of labor's attitude about the length of the workweek seventy-five years after the Haymarket Square riot. For other interesting incidents in the history of the reduction in working hours, see O.L. Harvey, "The 10 Hour Day in Philadelphia Navy Yard: 1835–36," *Monthly Labor Review*, 85:258–260 (March 1962).

[15] Frederick Taylor was influenced by Capt. Henry Metcalf, who had developed a simplified cost accounting system at the Frankford Arsenal around 1881. See "Famous Firsts," *Business Week*, Dec. 25, 1965, p. 74. It should be noted that some of the principles of scientific management were anticipated a century earlier by James Watt, Jr., and Matthew Boulton, Jr., in their management of the Soho Engineering Foundry near Birmingham, England. See L. Urwick, *The Golden Book of Management* (London: Newman Neame, Ltd., 1956), pp. 1–5. See also previous references to Charles Babbage.

Bethlehem plants in 1885. Around 1878, Taylor had developed what he called "the four great underlying principles of management": (1) "the development of a true science"; (2) "the scientific selection of the workmen"; (3) "his [the worker's] scientific education and development"; and (4) "intimate friendly cooperation between the management and the men."[16]

Taylor's first principle involved the systematic observation, classification, and tabulation of job activities as they were typically carried out, and then the simplification of the tasks to be done based on an analysis of motions, material, and equipment. This scientific method was to be substituted for the trial-and-error methods under which foremen and workers had been operating for centuries. The second principle had to do with selecting people with the skills and capacities necessary to carry out effectively the now efficiently organized job. The third principle involved training and was to be a substitute for the centuries-old practice of permitting people to choose their own work methods and to train themselves as best they could. The fourth principle concerned an "almost equal division of the work and the responsibility between the management and the workmen." It emphasized planning by management and worker-management cooperation as well as a provision for the worker to share financially on the basis of increased efficiency.[17] Compensation was based on a straight piecework system.

Through the use of his four principles, Taylor was able to increase efficiency in the handling of pig iron at the Bethlehem Steel Company to such a point that a worker could handle about 42.5 long tons per day in contrast to the 12.5 long tons per worker per day that had been the prevailing standard. Other experiments at Bethlehem, aimed at improving the efficiency of people shoveling ore, coke, limestone, sand, coal, and other kinds of material, also resulted in drastic improvements in efficiency and in greatly reduced costs.

Although the major emphasis of Taylor's scientific management was on the planning and simplification of tasks, he by no means forgot the worker involved. Many critics of Taylor and the scientific management movement have implied that he ignored the humanitarian and motivational aspects of the worker's role. Not only did he stress the desirable consequences of sharing economic gains with employees, but he also stressed the importance of individual recognition for superior performance. In addition, he stressed the need for a developmental attitude toward employees. Taylor strongly recommended that, when workers failed to respond to initial training, they should not be "brutally" discharged but given more time or transferred to work for which they were better suited. He also noted the value of workers' ideas and anticipated the modern suggestion system by recommending cash bonuses for adopted suggestions.[18]

Taylor was also interested in the social aspects of work, although his opinions of group effort were quite negative. He believed that ". . . when men work in gangs, their individual efficiency falls almost invariably down to, or below, the level of the worst man in the gang. . . ."[19] He saw little good emerging from the social interaction within work groups.

---

[16] Frederick Winslow Taylor, *The Principles of Scientific Management* (New York: Harper & Bros., 1919) (copyright 1911), pp. 21–37, 130.

[17] Taylor, *Principles of Scientific Management*, pp. 37, 39.

[18] Ibid., pp. 39, 128. The statement for which Taylor probably has been criticized most is as follows: "Now one of the very first requirements for a man who is fit to handle pig iron as a regular occupation is that he shall be so stupid and so phlegmatic that he more nearly resembles in his mental make-up the ox than any other type. The man who is mentally alert and intelligent is for this very reason entirely unsuited to what would, for him, be the grinding monotony of work of this character." See Frederick W. Taylor, *Scientific Management* (New York: Harper & Brothers, 1947), p. 59.

[19] Taylor, *Principles of Scientific Management*, pp. 72, 73.

Taylor's efforts were strongly resisted by organized labor, and even Congress prohibited the use of scientific management principles in the Watertown Arsenal. Taylor had strong and influential champions over the years, however, including James Dodge, president of the Link-Belt Company,[20] and lawyer Louis Brandeis, who was later appointed to the Supreme Court.[21]

Among the contemporaries of Taylor who extended his concepts were the Gilbreths and Henry Gantt. Frank Gilbreth made extensive use of motion pictures of tasks being performed in order to analyze body movements, and from these studies he formulated laws of efficient motion. This analytical approach to efficiency in industry was a forerunner of industrial engineering and the development of more effective automatic machinery.[22] Lillian Gilbreth worked closely with her husband and is credited with one of the early books relating the principles of scientific management to the field of psychology.[23]

Henry Gantt worked for six years as Frederick Taylor's assistant at Midvale and Bethlehem. One of his innovations was a "task and bonus" wage system that removed the penalties under Taylor's wage system. Taylor's plan had provided that workers be paid very low piece rates until they reached standards based on time-and-motion study. When the standard was reached, a high piece rate was paid. Under Gantt's plan, the worker was paid a guaranteed hourly rate, a bonus of 20 percent if he or she reached the standard output, and a high piece rate for output above standard. Further, the foreman received a bonus for each worker who was successful.[24] Another innovation by Gantt was the Gantt chart, which proved highly useful as a scheduling aid.[25]

In general, the scientific management movement emphasized the importance of management planning down to the smallest details in the operations of the factory. This careful planning of all operations of an enterprise, along with careful selection and systematic training of workers, undoubtedly has resulted in much higher production in business and industry than would have been otherwise possible.[26] Many of the assumptions in this movement, however, including those about group relationships, job design, and incentives have been seriously questioned in recent years. They are currently the focal point of considerable theorizing and research.

EARLY INDUSTRIAL PSYCHOLOGY
MUNSTERBERG'S CONTRIBUTIONS

Early industrial psychology seemed to focus on improvements in selling techniques, but researchers in industrial psychology were also interested in a more effective matching of workers' abilities with jobs.[27] In 1913 Hugo

[20] See Urwick, Golden Book of Management, pp. 40–43. For another biographical sketch of Taylor's, see John Dos Passos, "The Prophet of the Stop-Watch," in U. S. A. (New York: Harcourt, Brace & Co., 1936).
[21] "Milestones of Management," Business Week, Reprint Series, p. 5, 1964.
[22] See Frank B. Gilbreth, Motion Study (New York: D. Van Nostrand Company, 1911).
[23] Lillian M. Gilbreth, The Psychology of Management (New York: The Macmillan Company, 1914). For a brief history of the distinguished career of Lillian Gilbreth, see Daniel A. Wren, "In Memoriam: Lillian Moller Gilbreth (1878–1972)," Academy of Management Journal, 15:7–8 (March 1972).

[24] For a brief description of these plans, see "Milestones of Management," pp. 18–19. Incentive plans were not new to the scientific management movement, although scientific management gave considerable impetus to their use. In 1832, Babbage was recommending profit sharing, and reported various profit-sharing systems in use in Cornish mines and on English whaling and fishing ships. Babbage, Economy of Machinery and Manufactures, pp. 253–259.
[25] "Milestones of Management," p. 18.
[26] A parallel development was the introduction of the assembly-line technique into the automobile industry by Henry Ford in the decade before World War I.
[27] For an accounting of the early beginnings of industrial psychology, see B. Von Haller Gilmer, Industrial Psychology (New York: McGraw-Hill Book Company, 1961), pp. 18–19.

Munsterberg's book, *Psychology and Industrial Efficiency*, described experiments in selecting streetcar motormen, ship's officers, and telephone switchboard operators. Munsterberg was a world-famous experimental psychologist at Harvard University whose interests extended beyond his prolific laboratory experimentation and scholarly publication to writing sensational articles in the Sunday newspapers and popular magazines on such subjects as temperance, hypnosis, and detecting lies.[28]

Munsterberg's contributions to industrial management were particularly notable with respect to the analysis of jobs in terms of their mental and emotional requirements and in terms of the development of testing devices. In his book *Psychology and Industrial Efficiency*, Munsterberg described his experiments with the Boston Elevated Railway Company. Indemnity payments for accidents imposed by courts on the electric railways had sometimes amounted to 13 percent of the gross earnings of the companies, and officials were eager to reduce these costs in addition to reducing the associated suffering and hardships. After testing motormen with a fairly elaborate mechanical device, Munsterberg reported a "far-reaching correspondence between efficiency in the experiment and efficiency in actual service."[29] His book, however, did not provide much information about the actual validation of his testing device.

Another of Munsterberg's experiments was in the telephone industry, where many switchboard operators were susceptible to fatigue and nervous breakdown. Through various kinds of tests, including those of space perception, intelligence, and dexterity, Munsterberg found that the better performers on the tests were also the better performers as rated by the company.

Consequently, according to Munsterberg, the tests proved to be valuable aids in the selection of telephone operators.[30]

In commenting on the problem of monotony, Munsterberg stressed the importance of the individual worker's needs and motivations:

. . . no one ought to underestimate the importance of higher motives, intellectual, aesthetic, and moral motives, in their bearings on the psychological impulses of the laborer. If these higher demands are satisfied, the whole system gains a new tonus, and if they are disappointed, the irritation of the mental machinery may do more harm than any break in the physical machine at which the man is working.[31]

Munsterberg did not talk a great deal about the social aspects of work, but he did notice certain social phenomena:

. . . various factories . . . have changed the positions of the workmen so that conversations become more difficult or impossible. The result reported seems to be everywhere a significant increase in production . . . the help which is rendered by the feeling of social co-operation, on the other hand, is not removed by the mere abstaining from speaking. Interesting psychopedagogical experiments have, indeed, demonstrated that working in a common room produces better results than isolated activity.[32]

Thus, both Munsterberg and Taylor were concerned with the selection of employees, with the individual worker's feelings and aspirations, and to a certain extent with the effects of social structure on productivity, although they reach somewhat different conclusions about the latter.

These early relationships between scientific management and industrial psychology were not entirely coincidental. For example, Munsterberg, although stating that "those followers of Frederick W. Taylor who have made almost a religion out of his ideas have certainly often exaggerated the practical applicability of the new

---

[28] "Famous Firsts: Measuring Minds for Jobs," *Business Week*, January 29, 1966, p. 60.
[29] Hugo Munsterberg, *Psychology and Industrial Efficiency* (Boston: Houghton Mifflin Company, 1913), pp. 63–75.

[30] Ibid., Chapter 10.
[31] Ibid., p. 190.
[32] Ibid., pp. 209–210.

theories . . . ," was also convinced that ". . . the principles of the new theory will prove to be of lasting value."[33] His writings clearly suggest that he felt the two emerging fields were complementary.

OTHER DEVELOPMENTS

Tests for measuring differences among people in terms of aptitude and mental ability were extensively developed about this time. For example, the test known as Test 1-A, a forerunner of our present mental alertness tests, was developed by 1917. By this time, Hugo Munsterberg and Edison D. Woods had also evolved the concept of statistical validity relative to the use of tests. Both had early recognized the importance of comparing test scores with criteria of success as a way of determining predictive validity, that is, the extent to which a test predicted success or lack of it.[34]

Along with developments in testing and psychological experiments in improving the work situation during the pre–World War I period, there were developments in checking references, in the use of rating sheets for interviewers, and in the comparison of applicant ratings with ratings of successful people. World War I gave further impetus to the testing movement. The Army Alpha and the Army Beta intelligence tests were developed. In addition to intelligence tests, other kinds of tests evolved rapidly after World War I, including tests of aptitude, trade, interest, and personality.

PERSONNEL ADMINISTRATION
THE FEDERAL CIVIL SERVICE

The Civil Service Commission established by the Pendleton Act of 1883 undoubtedly has had a major impact on the development of personnel administration in the United States. Patterned after the British civil service system, the Pendleton Act provided competitive examinations for admission into public service, relative security of tenure for appointees, protection of appointees from discharge for refusing to engage in politics, prohibition of political activity, encouragement of a nonpartisan approach to appointments, and a commissioner to administer the Act.[35]

The major impact of the Act was to foster employees' appointment and progression in federal service on the basis of merit. A secondary result over the years has been the stimulation of progressive personnel policies and practices in governmental agencies, including state governments, with a resulting impact on business and industrial organizations. For example, by 1890 the Civil Service Commission was developing forerunners of general intelligence tests and trade tests and, by 1900, was developing entrance criteria for the majority of positions within its purview.

Although there were no full-time personnel officers in federal departments and bureaus by the end of the century, "appointment clerks" frequently assisted in the central administration of the major governmental subdivisions. These officials kept records, reviewed documents, and proposed recommendations for their superiors on matters pertaining to employment, promotion, demotion, transfer, leaves, and separations.[36]

PERSONNEL SPECIALISTS IN PRIVATE INDUSTRY

Between 1900 and 1920, concurrently with developments in scientific management, industrial psychology, and the federal Civil Service, a

---

[33]Ibid., pp. 49–50.
[34]Gilmer, *Industrial Psychology*, pp. 21–22.

[35]Paul P. Van Riper, *History of the United States Civil Service* (Evanston, Ill.: Row, Peterson and Company, 1958), pp. 96–112.
[36]Ibid., pp. 136–149.

number of specialists emerged in companies to assist with such matters as employment, welfare, rate setting, safety, training, and health. Collectively, these specialists were the forerunners of the modern personnel department, which today typically includes several specialized personnel activities. Probably giving impetus to the emergence of such specialists was the publication of a number of books between 1899 and 1912 in Great Britain and the United States that included chapters on such topics as "The Selection of Employees," "Profit Sharing," "Discipline," and "Provision for Health and Safety." (See the Appendix.)

EMPLOYMENT AGENTS   By 1900 a few employment agents or clerks were beginning to be found in companies. For example, an employment department at the B.F. Goodrich Company started about this time.[37] Companies had found that efficiencies could be gained by centralizing part of the employment function.

SOCIAL OR WELFARE SECRETARIES   Industry was also beginning to employ staff members called "social secretaries" or "welfare secretaries" at about the turn of the century. These secretaries were employed to help with financial, housing, medical, recreational, educational, and other matters.[38] This development had its origin in philanthropy, welfare work, the "social gospel" movement, and the papal encyclicals, all of which were trying to improve the lot of the workers, particularly the poor and otherwise disadvantaged. Welfare work was defined as consisting of ". . . voluntary efforts on the part of employers to improve, with the existing industrial system, the conditions of employment

in their own factories."[39]   Following the emergence of the social secretary in the United States in 1889, Rowntree's in Great Britain employed a "lady Social Secretary" in 1891 to work with women employees. The results were so satisfactory that by 1905 the firm had added a man with a university M.A. degree "to perform a like service for men."[40]

LABOR DEPARTMENT SPECIALISTS   A development that appears to have emerged more slowly than the welfare department was the organization of the labor department. About 1901, a labor department was formed at the National Cash Register Company, a company of approximately four thousand employees, with responsibility for responding to complaints from members of the unionized work force and for monitoring working conditions and wage policies. Two years later, citing the National Cash Register experience, a strong argument for the creation of labor departments was published in *Engineering Magazine*, recommending that such departments be given "full authority to settle all questions that the men and foremen cannot settle," and that it be involved in supervising the wage system, in foremen's meetings, and in improving working conditions.[41]

WAGE AND PENSION ADMINISTRATORS   Another development around the turn of the century was the rate-fixing department which employed

[37] Henry Eilbirt, "The Development of Personnel Management in the United States," *Business History Review*, 30:352 (Autumn 1959).
[38] Ibid., pp. 348–349.

[39] E. Dorothea Pround, *Welfare Work* (London: G. Bell and Sons, Ltd., 1916), p. 5. Additional significant efforts in employee welfare can be traced back as far as the period 1800–1828, when Robert Owen greatly improved the working and living conditions of the employees in the textile mills in Scotland that he managed. See Urwick, *Golden Book of Management*, pp. 5–9. In this book Robert Owen is called "the pioneer of personnel management."
[40] Ian McGivering, "Sketchbook of Business Scientists—Personnel Management," *Scientific Business*, 2:222 (August 1964).
[41] C.V. Carpenter, "The Working of a Labor Department in Industrial Establishments," *Engineering Magazine*, 25:1–9 (April 1903).

wage or rate clerks. These departments were established to set wage rates based on time-and-motion study.[42] Similarly, administrators were required to manage the growing number of pension and insurance plans that existed in many railways and labor organizations.[43]

SAFETY SPECIALISTS AND COMPANY PHYSICIANS In 1902 the state of Maryland passed the first workmen's compensation law in the United States, but it was subsequently declared unconstitutional. After the United States Supreme Court upheld the 1911 workmen's compensation laws of Washington, Wisconsin, California, and New Jersey, the occupation of safety specialist became very common in industry. These laws required employers to pay for lost time and injuries resulting from occupational accidents, and industrial firms obviously wanted to reduce claims against themselves. Thus, the safety specialist became an important person in industry.[44] As a parallel development, physicians were employed by companies to insure that employees would be assigned jobs suited to their physical qualifications.[45]

TRAINING SPECIALISTS Formal training programs were emerging around the turn of the century, many in the area of sales training. In 1894 the National Cash Register Company formed a corporate school that focused on both selling and broad aspects of business administration.[46] The emergence of safety programs undoubtedly stimulated the need for formal training programs in the area of safety as well.

THE PERSONNEL DEPARTMENT Some grouping of specialized personnel activities had occurred at least by the 1880s. For example, the Baltimore and Ohio Railroad's "Relief Department," a relief association that employees might join on a voluntary basis, consisted of three sections: a relief department to assist members incapacitated because of illness or accident, a pension department to assist those retiring due to age or ill health, and a savings and loan department to assist workers in purchasing homes.[47] According to a 1923 book, the U.S. Steel Company created a "Bureau of Safety, Sanitation, and Welfare" in 1911 and the International Harvester Company established a "Department of Industrial Relations" in 1918. The same source refers to a "Sociological Department" in the Ford Motor Company that combined medical, welfare, safety, and legal aspects, and to a "Department of Industrial Relations" in B. Kuppenheimer and Company that included the following subdivisions: "Health, education, and safety," "Employment," "Education," "Grievances and Discipline," "Wage and rate setting," "Negotiations," and "Lunch Service and Recreation."[48] As a general guide, however, 1912 is considered the approximate date of emergence of the modern personnel department.[49]

[42] See F.W. Taylor, "Shop Management," *Transactions, American Society of Mechanical Engineers,* 24:1399–1404 (1903).

[43] William F. Willoughby, *Workingman's Insurance* (New York: Thomas Y. Crowell & Company, 1898), p. 282.

[44] The United States was slow in passing workmen's compensation laws in comparison to a number of European countries. Germany passed such a law in 1883, and Austria, Norway, Switzerland, and England had such laws by 1898. Ibid., pp. 332–333.

[45] Thomas G. Spates, *Human Values Where People Work* (New York: Harper & Bros., 1960), p. 73.

[46] "Famous Firsts: How Personnel Relations Was Born," *Business Week,* June 26, 1965, pp. 92–94.

[47] Willoughby, *Workingman's Insurance,* pp. 286–287.

[48] Louis A. Boettiger, *Employee Welfare Work: A Critical and Historical Study* (New York: The Ronald Press Company, 1923), pp. 127–133.

[49] Eilbirt, "Development of Personnel Management," p. 352. The word *personnel* began to appear in its modern connotation around 1909. The term appeared as a major item in the index of the Civil Service Commission report of that year, and in 1910 the Secretary of Commerce and Labor used the term in a major heading in his annual report. See Van Riper, *History of the Civil Service,* p. 197. Henry Metcalf established a "Bureau of Personnel Administration" in 1920, and the first comprehensive textbook in the field, *Personnel Administration,* by Tead and Metcalf appeared. See Spates, *Human Values Where People Work,* p. 7.

Basically, then, various combinations of several positions were the forerunners of the modern personnel department: the employment agent, the social or welfare secretary, the labor department specialist, the wage or rate clerk, the pension administrator, the safety director, the company physician, and the training specialist.

THE HUMAN RELATIONS MOVEMENT

In 1923, in collaboration with the National Research Council and the Massachusetts Institute of Technology, the Western Electric Company started experiments at its Hawthorne Works in Chicago in an attempt to find out what the effects of illumination were on workers and their output. Vannevar Bush and Joseph Barker were the original investigators on the project. In one experiment, production went up when the lighting was improved. Paradoxically, in another experiment, production went up when the lighting was severely reduced. After three years of experimentation with "illogical" results, the researchers concluded that in a situation involving people, it was impossible to change one condition (the lighting) without affecting other variables. Vannevar Bush suggested that social scientists be brought into the inquiries and withdrew from the project when it became clear that morale and motivation were the important factors.[50] Professor Elton Mayo and his colleagues, F.J. Roethlisberger, T. North Whitehead, and others at the Harvard Business School subsequently became identified with the project and conducted research continuing into the early 1930s.[51]

Inquiry and experimentation by the social scientists led to the conclusion that productivity was a function of the extent to which the group became a team and cooperated wholeheartedly and spontaneously. This cooperation and enthusiasm seemed to be related to the interest of the supervisor and experimenters in the work group, the lack of coercion, and the participation permitted the workers in changes that would affect them.[52] Fundamentally, then, the researchers came to view the industrial organization as a social system. In the researchers' words:

The study of the bank wiremen showed that their behavior at work could not be understood without considering the informal organization of the group and the relation of this informal organization to the total social organization of the company. The work activities of this group, together with their satisfactions and dissatisfactions, had to be viewed as manifestations of a complex pattern of interrelations. In short, the work situation of the bank wiring group had to be treated as a social system; moreover, the industrial organization of which this group was a part also had to be treated as a social system.[53]

[50] For mention of the role of Vannevar Bush and Joseph Barker, see Rensis Likert, *Developing New Patterns of Management*, reprinted from American Management Association, General Management Series No. 82, 1956.
[51] As early as 1924, Mayo was presenting papers urging concern for a "psychology of the total situation," which he believed "basic to a psychology of management." See Elton Mayo, "The Basis of Industrial Psychology," *Bulletin of the Taylor Society*, 9:249–259 (December 1924). Mayo was associated with the Wharton School of the University of Pennsylvania from 1923 to 1926. Earlier, he had held several posts in Australia, including Professor of Psychology at the University of Queensland. Mayo came to Harvard University in 1926.
[52] For detailed reports of these experiments, see F.J. Roethlisberger and W.J. Dickson, *Management and the Worker* (Cambridge, Mass.: Harvard University Press, 1939); T. North Whitehead, *The Industrial Worker*, I–II (Cambridge, Mass.: Harvard University Press, 1938); and G.A. Pennock, "Industrial Research at Hawthorne and Experimental Investigation of Rest Periods, Working Conditions, and Other Influences," *Personnel Journal*, 8:296–309 (February 1930). G.A. Pennock was a superintendent at the Hawthorne Works under whom the experiments were conducted between 1924 and 1933. See Howard W. Johnson, "The Hawthorne Studies: The Legend and the Legacy," in Eugene L. Cass and Frederick G. Zimmer, eds., *Man and Work in Society* (New York: Van Nostrand Reinhold Company, 1975), p. 274.
[53] Roethlisberger and Dickson, *Management and the Worker*, p. 551.

Although mentioned or quoted less often, the use of nondirective interviewing as an important tool in personnel management was an outgrowth of the Hawthorne experiments. Effective listening in interviews by the experimenter seemed to be dependent upon reflecting the feeling expressed and avoiding arguments, taking sides, or moralizing.[54] Not only did this type of interview have salutary effects on the morale of employees, but the researchers discovered that surface complaints and grievances were rarely the real problems. An outgrowth of this successful experience in interviewing led to the recommendation that Western Electric establish an employee-counseling program, which was subsequently put into effect. Fifty-five counselors were employed in the Hawthorne plant by 1948. However, the overall effort did not flourish at Hawthorne and in the broader company, and by 1955 the number of counselors at Hawthorne was down to eight.[55]

This focus on group behavior and workers' feelings as being associated with productivity and morale characterized much of the research and theorizing in the human relations movement for the next two decades. Although the scientific management movement and early industrial psychology emphasized the proper design of tasks, selection and training of employees, and individual incentives, the human relations movement was mainly concerned with the informal, spontaneous behavior of work groups and the sentiments, interactions, and attitudes of employees. The scientific management movement was mainly concerned with the organization as a technical-economic system; the human relations movement viewed the organization as a social system.

THE BEHAVIORAL SCIENCES AND GENERAL SYSTEMS THEORY

The "behavioral sciences" are essentially the social and biological sciences pertaining to the study of human behavior. The term was coined about 1949 and grew out of a meeting of scientists who were considering ". . . whether a sufficient body of facts exists to justify developing an empirically tenable general theory of behavior."[56] Therefore, the phrase was adopted

. . . first, because its neutral character made it acceptable to both social and biological scientists, and, second, because we foresaw a possibility of someday seeking to obtain financial support from persons who might confound social science with socialism.[57]

Subsequent meetings of the original scientists included the disciplines of anthropology, economics, history, physiology and mathematical biology, medicine and psychiatry, sociology, social psychology, and psychology.

Recent contributions from the behavioral sciences to the study of personnel management have come mainly from sociology, industrial psychology, social psychology, and organizational psychology, and a great deal of relevant research cuts across these disciplines. It should be noted, however, that general systems theory, which has had a major impact on this book, has emerged largely from such fields as biology, physics, and cybernetics as well as from sociology, although a wide number of branches of study have utilized, and elaborated upon, the concepts. In addition, a substantial body of research relevant to personnel management incorporates concepts from organization theory and organizational behavior, disciplines that also draw extensively from the behavioral sciences.

The behavioral science approach, as it relates

[54] Elton Mayo, *The Social Problems of an Industrial Civilization* (Boston: Harvard University, 1945), pp. 73–74.
[55] Johnson, "Hawthorne Studies: Legend and Legacy," pp. 273–277. See also Carl R. Rogers, *Counseling and Psychotherapy* (Boston: Houghton Mifflin Company, 1942), p. 8.

[56] James G. Miller, "Toward a General Theory for the Behavioral Sciences," *American Psychologist*, 10:513 (1955).
[57] Ibid.

to the study of management, is essentially an outgrowth of the human relations studies of the previous decades, but it includes a wider disciplinary base and is concerned with a much wider range of problems. For example, contemporary behavioral scientists are concerned with the impact of different methods of pay on individual performance, with the effects of different styles in leadership and of different philosophies on total organizational performance, with job design and its relationship to human satisfaction and development, with the impact of different appraisal systems, and with the dynamics of different organization improvement strategies. The preponderant method of research makes use of data obtained from employees and managers in living organizations rather than data obtained in controlled experiments separated from an organizational context, although there have been some experimental studies of considerable significance to personnel management.

Since this book will extensively relate contemporary behavioral science theory and research to the various personnel processes, it would be redundant to mention specific studies here. It should be pointed out, however, that the foci of the studies of those modern behavioral scientists who are interested in organizations, and the implicit or explicit values underlying their writings, range across a wide spectrum. Some scholars/researchers are interested in two-person or small-group dynamics; some are interested in the total organization; some are mainly interested in the external forces that shape events within the organization. Some are interested in developing hypotheses and testing them; some are conceptualizers or model builders; others are interested in acting as consultants or "change agents" in organizations. Some play different roles at different times.

In general, those aspects of contemporary behavioral science that focus on management and

organization can be grouped in terms of methodology as follows:

A. Empirical research
   1. Field studies
   2. Experimental simulations
   3. Laboratory experiments
   4. Computer simulations [58]
B. Program- or action-oriented research
C. Theory or model building, or both

Most behavioral scientists are probably involved in at least two of these major categories. Most scholars in the eclectic fields of personnel management, organizational behavior, and organizational theory probably draw from the results of all three approaches, including one or more of the subaspects of the empirical research category. The chapters that follow will utilize studies emerging from all these methodological approaches.

THE SOCIAL LEGISLATION OF THE 1960s AND 1970s

Since a good deal of attention will be paid throughout this book to the impact of federal legislation, Presidential Executive Orders, administrative rulings, and court decisions of the 1960s and 1970s on personnel management, they will not be dealt with in any detail here. However, it is abundantly clear that today's personnel management practices and today's organizations are being and will be dramatically influenced by the Equal Pay Act of 1963, the Civil Rights Act of 1964, the Age Discrimination in Employment Act of 1967, the Occupational Safety and Health Act of 1970, the Employee Retirement Income Security Act of 1974,

[58] These four categories are drawn from W.W. Cooper, H.J. Leavitt, and M.W. Shelly, II, eds., *New Perspectives in Organization Research* (New York: John Wiley & Sons, 1964), pp. 535–541.

and a wide range of administrative and court decisions and orders of these two decades.

SUMMARY

Modern personnel management has emerged from nine interrelated sources in particular: (1) rapid technological change and a drastically increased specialization of labor associated with the Industrial Revolution, (2) the emergence of free collective bargaining, (3) the scientific management movement, (4) early industrial psychology, (5) governmental personnel practices growing out of the establishment of a Civil Service Commission, (6) the emergence of personnel specialists and various groupings of these specialists into personnel departments, (7) the human relations movement, (8) the behavioral sciences and general systems theory, and (9) the social legislation of the 1960s and 1970s. These constitute the main historical roots of the philosophy and practice of personnel management in today's organizations.

REVIEW AND DISCUSSION QUESTIONS

1. What effect did the Industrial Revolution have upon personnel management?

2. What were the important legislative and judicial landmarks in the history of the labor movement in the United States?

3. What were the origins of the modern personnel department?

4. Discuss the similarities and differences in approach and philosophy between the scientific management movement and early industrial psychology.

5. In what way were these movements different from or similar to the human relations movement?

6. What was the contribution of the Pendleton Act of 1883 to personnel management?

7. What is meant by *the behavioral sciences?* How did the term originate? What are the major methodological categories within the behavioral sciences that relate to the study of organizations and management?

SUPPLEMENTAL REFERENCES

Commons, John R., et al., *History of Labour in the United States, 1896–1932* (New York: The Macmillan Company, 1935), III, Chapter 17.

Dyer, Henry, *The Evolution of Industry* (London: Macmillan & Company, 1895), pp. 66–67.

Eitington, Julius E., "Pioneers of Management: Personnel Management," *Advanced Management—Office Executive*, 2:16–19 (January 1963).

"Employment Management, Its Research Scope," *Employment Management Series No. 1*, Bulletin No. 5, Federal Board for Vocational Education, January 1920.

Etz, Donald V., "Han Fei Tzu: Management Pioneer," *Public Administrative Review,* 24:36–38 (March 1964).

Ginzberg, Eli, and Hyman Berman, *The American Worker in the Twentieth Century: A History Through Autobiographies* (New York: Free Press of Glencoe, Inc., 1963).

Hayes, Carlton J.H., *A Political and Cultural History of Modern Europe* (New York: The Macmillan Company, 1932), I, 55–58.

Hoagland, John H., "Historical Antecedents of Organization Research," in W.W. Cooper, H.J. Leavitt, M.W. Shelly, II, eds., *New Perspectives in Organization Research* (New York: John Wiley & Sons, Inc., 1964), pp. 27–34.

Landsberger, Henry A., "The Behavioral Sciences in Industry," *Industrial Relations,* 7:8–19 (October 1967).

Ling, Cyril C., *The Management of Personnel Relations: History and Origins* (Homewood, Ill.: Richard D. Irwin, Inc., 1965).

Linton, Ralph, *The Tree of Culture* (New York: Alfred A. Knopf, Inc., 1955), pp. 103–114.

Lynch, Edmund C., "Walter Dill Scott: Pioneer Industrial Psychologist," *Business History Review*, 42:149–170 (Summer 1968).

Mayo, Elton, *The Human Problems of an Industrial Civilization* (Cambridge, Mass.: Harvard University, 1933), Chapter 3.

Miller, Frank B., and Mary Ann Coghill, *The Historical Sources of Personnel Work* (Ithaca, N.Y.: New York State School of Industrial and Labor Relations, Cornell University, 1961), Bibliography Series No. 5.

Milton, Charles R., *Ethics and Expediency in Personnel Management: A Critical History of Personnel Philosophy* (Columbia, S.C.: University of South Carolina Press, 1970).

Owen, Robert, *A New View of Society and Other Writings* (London: J.M. Dent and Sons, Ltd., 1927).

Sarton, George A., *A History of Science* (Cambridge, Mass.: Harvard University Press, 1952), Chapter 2.

Scott, Walter Dill, *Increasing Human Efficiency in Business* (New York: The Macmillan Company, 1914).

Spates, Thomas G., *Man and Management: The Spiritual Content of Business Administration—Our Legacy from Ancient Greece* (New Haven, Conn.: Privately published, 1965).

———, "The Scope of Modern Personnel Administration," *Reading Course in Executive Technique* (New York: Funk & Wagnalls Company, 1948), Book I, Section III, p. 4.

Tead, Ordway, and Henry C. Metcalf, *Personnel Administration* (New York: McGraw-Hill Book Company, 1920).

Ward, C. Osborne, *The Ancient Lowly* (Chicago: Charles H. Kerr & Company, 1970), I, 140–143.

Wrege, Charles D., "Solving Mayo's Mystery: The First Complete Account of the Origin of the Hawthorne Studies—The Forgotten Contributions of C.E. Snow and H. Hibarger," in R.L. Taylor, M.J. O'Connell, R.A. Zawacki, and D.D. Warrick, eds., *Academy of Management Proceedings*, Proceedings of the Thirty-Sixth Annual Meeting of the Academy of Management, Kansas City, Missouri, August 11–14, 1976, pp. 12–14.

PART 2
A PROCESS-SYSTEMS MODEL AND MAJOR CONTINGENCIES

3. A Process-Systems Model of the Organization

4. The Model Applied to Personnel Management

5. Major Contingencies: Authority, Structure, and Technology

Part 2 is essentially organization theory relevant to an understanding and analysis of personnel management. Using systems theory, in particular, Chapter 3 develops a theoretical model of the organization, a procedure that in turn permits the development of the model for visualizing personnel management in Chapter 4.

Chapter 5 discusses some major contingencies in personnel management including authority relationships, organizational structure, and technology. Relevant concepts such as line-and-staff, mechanistic, and organic systems are also discussed.

CHAPTER 3
A PROCESS-SYSTEMS MODEL OF THE ORGANIZATION

A *process-systems approach,* which provides a convenient way of studying personnel management, utilizes the models described in this chapter.[1] These models provide for (1) a description of personnel management as a *dynamic subaspect of the total management process* and as an integral part of all subdivisions of an organization; (2) an analysis of the *interdependence* between the various aspects of personnel management and between personnel management and other managerial processes; and (3) an analysis of the ecology of personnel management. In this context *ecology* refers to the rela-

tionship between the various personnel processes and their environments, including organizational climate and governmental regulations. A start will be made toward the development of these models by next defining *process* and *system.*

THE CONCEPT OF PROCESS
A DEFINITION OF PROCESS

The word *process* is used extensively in the literature of many disciplines. For example, authors in management theory write about the decision-making process, the planning process, the collective-bargaining process, and the administrative process. Authors in the physical sciences talk about chemical, biological, and physical processes. Authors in the social

[1] A model has been defined as ". . . a symbolic representation of a perceptual phenomenon." See Gordon Hearn, *Theory Building in Social Work* (Toronto: University of Toronto Press, 1958), p. 10. Just as it is useful for the architect to build miniature models of a proposed building, so it is useful for the student of management to build conceptual models of such abstract matters as organization.

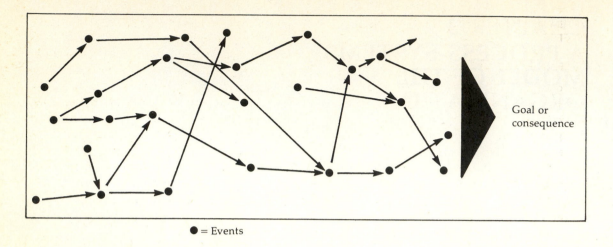

● = Events

Figure **3-1**   Process as a flow of events

sciences refer to social, psychological, and economic processes.

In general, the concept of *process* may be defined as *an identifiable flow of interrelated events moving toward some goal, purpose, or end.* In this definition, *flow* implies movement through time and in the direction of a result. *Interrelated* implies interaction within the process and between events. *Events* are activities, happenings, or changes, which may be major or minor. *Goal* suggests a human objective, while *purpose* suggests either human objectives or objectives in a philosophical sense. *End* implies some conclusion or consequence that may not necessarily be sought or planned. Thus, a process may, or may not, have consequences intended by people. (See Figure 3-1 for an illustration of process.)

EXAMPLES AND CHARACTERISTICS OF
PROCESSES

An example of a process in nature is the erosion of mountain peaks. Another example is the process of photosynthesis in green plants.

A familiar example of a process in personnel management is the staffing process, a flow of events that results in the continuous filling of positions within the organization. This flow is composed of such events as recruitment, interviews, decisions to hire, transfers, and promotions. (Since each of these occurrences can also be considered a process, the scope of a process is an arbitrary matter depending upon the point of view of the perceiver.) Some processes, such as staffing and planning, are common to all organizations, although others, such as the care of patients in hospitals, are unique to certain kinds of organizations.

It should be noted that a process usually, if not always, involves events that are simultaneously events in one or more other processes. For example, a decision to offer a particular initial salary is an event in the financial management process as well as in the staffing process. Since most events probably have more than one consequence, one of the key tasks in management is to channel and control events so that they have desired or anticipated rather than dysfunctional consequences.

SYSTEM DEFINED AND CONTRASTED WITH PROCESS

A DEFINITION OF SYSTEM

The concept of *system* has been defined and utilized by many authors in cybernetics, biology, physics, psychology, sociology, economics, management, and a variety of other basic and applied fields. Hall and Fagen define system as ". . . a set of objects together with relationships between the objects and between their attributes."[2] Bertalanffy defines systems as "sets of elements standing in interaction."[3] Kast and Rosenzweig define system as "an organized, unitary whole composed of two or more interdependent parts, components, or subsystems and delineated by identifiable boundaries from its environmental suprasystem."[4] Thus, all the definitions of system denote interdependency or interaction of components or parts, and an identifiable wholeness or gestalt.

The definition of system that follows is consistent with these definitions, but it will be enlarged to include the concept of process and the relationship between system and process. A *system* is a particular linking of interrelated and interdependent components having a facilitating effect, or an intended facilitating effect, on the carrying out of one or more processes.

In this definition *particular* suggests that System₁ may be different in some respects from System₂, although both may be contributing to the carrying out of similar processes. In addition, a given component of one system may be identical to a component in another system, or it may be very different. The *components* of a system may be devices, raw materials, techniques, procedures, plans, policies, rules, and/or people. The phrase *interrelated and interdependent* signifies that interdependency among components is a major aspect of a system. *Facilitating effect* suggests that systems are ordinarily designed (or they evolve) as a means of carrying out or regularizing processes. *Intended* is used to imply that (1) mistakes may be made in the design of a system so that it works at cross-purposes with planned consequences or in opposition to the survival of an organism or organization, and (2) a system can be in a static condition.

The reader will also note that this definition, since it incorporates the concept of process, includes the important idea that a system is goal-, consequence-, or end-oriented. (From a managerial standpoint, systems are designed to achieve goals.) And finally, in the context of this definition, *carrying out* means unfolding or progressive development. (See Figure 3-2 for an illustration of system.)

EXAMPLES OF SYSTEMS

An example of a system is the electrical wiring, terminals, sockets, bulbs, and switches that facilitate the processes of power distribution and electrical wiring in a building. The components installed in one room might be considered a *subsystem*, and the total electrical power network in a community, a *suprasystem*.

Thus, the definition of a system is always a relative matter, as is the definition of a process. It should be noted, however, that a system can be static (in the above illustration, the system is static and the interdependencies of the components are only potential until the switches are turned on), whereas by definition, a process is always dynamic (the power distribution process involves a flow of electricity that activates the lights).

---

[2] A.D. Hall and R.E. Fagen, "Definition of System," *General Systems: Systems Theory,* I (1956), p. 18.
[3] Ludwig von Bertalanffy, *General Systems Theory* (New York: George Braziller, 1968), p. 38.
[4] Fremont E. Kast and James E. Rosenzweig, *Organization and Management: A Systems Approach,* 2nd ed. (New York: McGraw-Hill Book Company, 1974), p. 101.

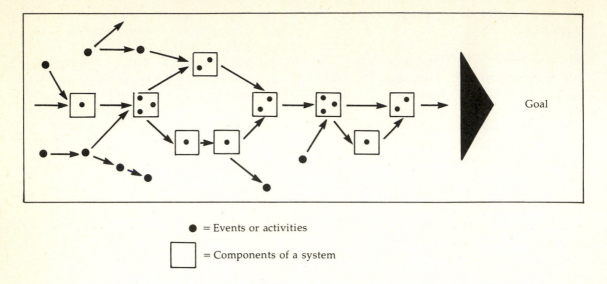

● = Events or activities

☐ = Components of a system

Figure **3-2**   System as a linkage of components facilitating a process

The passenger transportation system of an airline, designed to facilitate the process of transporting passengers at high speed between airports, provides those of us who frequently travel by air with a vivid example of systems and related subsystems. Such a system encompasses a number of subsystems or components including (1) the aircraft; (2) the mobile ground support equipment and procedures for fuel, maintenance, passenger and baggage loading and unloading, food, and sanitation; (3) the people who operate the system, including the aircraft crews; and (4) the passengers and their luggage. A breakdown in any one of those subsystems becomes quickly evident and has an immediate impact on the other subsystems.

The interdependence and interface with other systems is also readily apparent in the above example—interdependence with the weather reporting and prediction system, with the flight planning and control system, with the baggage transfer system between airlines, with the passenger terminal, and with the linking freeways. Although the plane could not land on such a short runway, one can readily visualize the chaos and confusion that would occur if a jumbo jet, nearly out of fuel and food, landed sixty miles away from its destination at a small airport where there was one telephone, one restroom, an occasional taxi, and a short-order lunch counter. It would be immediately evident that the system components that had made an emergency landing were out of joint with the systems of the host airport and community.

To use an example of a system from personnel management, the employment process in a given firm is facilitated by a unique linkage of people, policies, and devices and procedures for hiring employees such as application blanks, tests, a series of interviews, and reference checks. In all likelihood, the employment systems of various firms will differ in some respects, including the way their components are arranged and the design of some devices used. The people involved, of course, will also differ from each other. On the other hand, some aspects of the systems may be identical; e.g., two firms may be using the same proficiency

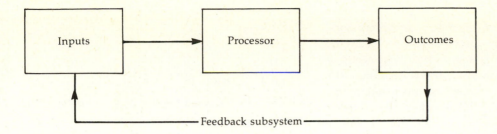

Figure **3-3**   Simple diagram of a system

test to select employees for a particular job.

The example of an employment system is, of course, a subsystem relative to the broader personnel management system of the organization. And the total organization itself or any of its subunits such as divisions or departments can be considered systems.

SOME CHARACTERISTICS OF SYSTEMS

A system in operation (in process) includes a flow of *inputs* (energy, materials, or information, or all three), a *processor* or *transforming mechanism* (a machine or the technical-human component doing the work), and a flow of *outputs* or outcomes (the product or services, and waste). (See Figure 3-3.) In the case of the power distribution system described earlier, electricity is the input; the wires, outlets, sockets, and bulbs constitute the processor; and illumination is one output.

A system may also include a mechanism for *feedback*. A common illustration is the thermostat coupled to a furnace. When the temperature in a room drops to a predetermined minimum, the thermostat activates the furnace; when the temperature rises to a predetermined maximum, the thermostat sends a signal to the furnace, where a mechanism shuts off the fuel or power supply.

Optner specifies some additional character-

istics of systems by differentiating between "structured" and "incompletely structured" systems. A *structured system* has highly regulated inputs, is essentially free from disturbance, and has outputs within highly predictable limits. Examples are hydraulic and electrical systems. In contrast, an *incompletely structured* system has inputs that are variable in terms of quality and quantity; it is subject to considerable disturbance; and it has less predictable outputs. It would appear that the less structured a system, the more probable the existence of unsystematized processes. An example of an incompletely structured system would be an industrial enterprise or any system involving people.[5] Thus, the airline transportation system described earlier is an incompletely structured system, although probably manifesting a much higher degree of structure than a school system or a research laboratory.

Comparable to the concepts of structured versus unstructured systems is the notion of an *open system* in contrast to a *closed system*. In general, organizations are essentially open systems in that they exist in a highly interdependent relationship of exchange with their environment, a relationship that includes the

[5] Stanford L. Optner, *Systems Analysis for Business Management* (Englewood Cliffs, N.J.: Prentice-Hall, Inc., 1960), pp. 3–9.

utilization of a wide variety of inputs, the ability to make improvements in the processors, and the capability of modifying or changing outputs in order to adapt to external needs or demands. As is implied in this definition, the more the managers view the organization as a closed system, the less the enterprise can adapt to changing conditions, and the more it will be subject to *entropy*, i.e., running down. In the case of the furnace, which is much more a closed system than is an organization, the thermostat provides a degree of openness to the environment that permits the system to conserve energy or fuel when additional heat is not required for human comfort. So, again, the degree of openness of a system is a relative matter, as is the complexity of the mechanism for feedback.[6]

The area where one system comes into contact with another is called an "interface." Across this boundary occur the transactions involving the inputs and outputs, which may include "the transfer of energy, material objects, men, money, and information."[7] How these interfaces are managed can have a major impact on the health and vitality of either system.

Implicit in this discussion are some differences that should be noted between natural systems and social systems. Organizations, as social systems, tend to have less evident structures and less defined boundaries (and are thus more open) than natural systems such as trees, animals, or machines. Organizations are also socially contrived (they are made, not born) and tend to be goal-oriented. It is important to keep these differences in mind, lest we fall into the trap of considering organizations perfectly

analogous to biological organisms or other natural systems.[8]

FAYOL'S CONCEPTS

To continue toward the development of models that can be useful in understanding and examining personnel management, we next turn to the concepts developed in France by Henri Fayol. From the time of the writings of Fayol in the early 1900s, authors in the field of managerial theory have stressed certain managerial activities common to the manager's job, i.e., ". . . planning, organization, command, coordination, control. . . ."[9] In recent years, a typical list of activities utilized by theorists of the "Fayol school," who have retained Fayol's categories with only minor modifications, includes planning, organizing, staffing, controlling, coordinating, and directing.[10] These activities will be called "administrative processes" in the models of the organization and the manager's job to be discussed below.

Briefly, *planning* includes the establishment of goals and objectives and the determination of activities and resources needed to achieve these objectives. *Organizing* includes the building of an organizational structure, dividing up the total job into departments, divisions, sections, jobs, and so forth. *Staffing* refers to securing people with the appropriate skills and placing

[6] For a discussion of open-system theory, see Daniel Katz and Robert L. Kahn, *The Social Psychology of Organizations* (New York: John Wiley & Sons, 1966), Chapters 1 and 2.

[7] Charles R. Deckert, "The Development of Cybernetics," *The American Behavioral Scientist*, 8:19 (June 1965).

[8] For additional discussion of the differences between social and natural systems, see David Silverman, *The Theory of Organizations* (New York: Basic Books, Inc., 1971), pp. 27, 61–62, 67–68, 119–120; and Katz and Kahn, *Social Psychology of Organizations*, pp. 33–34.

[9] Henri Fayol, *General and Industrial Management*, Constance Storrs, trans. (London: Sir Isaac Pitman and Sons, 1949. First published, 1916), p. 3.

[10] The "Fayol school" has also been labeled "the management process school," "the traditional school," and "the universalist school." See Harold Koontz, "The Management Theory Jungle," *Journal of the Academy of Management*, 4:175–176 (December 1961).

them properly. *Controlling* is the process of evaluating performance throughout the organization in comparison to desired standards and of taking steps to bring performance in line with expectations. *Coordinating* refers to maintaining proper interrelationships between various segments of the enterprise. *Directing* is typically defined as the process of getting people to carry out the activities of the organization. The reader will note that the concepts of staffing and directing are major aspects of what we have labeled *personnel management,* although personnel management includes other important processes ordinarily not included in the categories of staffing and directing.

THE CONCEPT OF ORGANIZATIONAL RESOURCES

One additional concept—*managing organizational resources*—is necessary for the development of our models. In Chapter 1, personnel management was defined in terms of the management and development of human resources, but obviously human resources are only one of several kinds used by the organization. Clearly, other important resources must be effectively utilized, including materials, money, markets, and technical knowledge.

Converting the concept of managing organizational resources into process terminology, we use the terms *resource procurement and utilization processes* or, more simply, *operational processes.* These operational processes can be called the "personnel management process," the "financial management process," the "materials and production management process," the "marketing management process," and the "research, development, and engineering management process."[11]

TOWARD A MODEL OF THE ORGANIZATION

Using the concepts of process, system, administrative processes, and operational processes, the organization may be defined as follows: An *organization* is an essentially person-directed and multiple-goal-oriented network of interacting administrative and operational processes and corresponding facilitating systems and is immersed in a broader network of processes and systems with which it interacts.

This definition recognizes several important characteristics of organizations that, although set forth as theoretical propositions, seem to reflect some realities of enterprise life.

1. An organization is *essentially person-directed* in that human planning and direction, whether efficient or not, are its major characteristics. The organization is only *essentially* directed by people, however, since, as an "open" system, it may be affected by a network of external environmental processes over which organizational members have little or not control. In addition, an organization is an "incompletely structured" system, a condition implying that there are some internal processes less structured than others and that some may not be directed by people, at least at a conscious level. Further, some processes may be moving in a direction contrary to enterprise goals.

2. In general, organizations are adaptive systems in that they are in a relationship of continuous exchange with, and coping with, their environments.

3. As implied, organizations exist in a highly interdependent state with other systems. (The current emphasis on ecology is a belated recognition of this fact.)

4. Most, if not all, organizations are directed

---

[11] In the above context, the word *function* could be used synonymously with the word *process.* But although the concept

tends to focus on the grouping of similar activities, it does not emphasize flow and interdependence.

toward the attainment of multiple goals. Multiple goals increase the complexity of the network of organizational processes and systems.

5. There can be no organization without a network of systems. Systems are essential for channeling processes in the direction of, and toward the fulfillment of, enterprise goals.

6. The organization is a complex network of interdependent flows of events having to do with human planning, organizing, coordinating, and controlling of the procurement and utilization of various human and nonhuman resources.

Thus, we can conceptualize two major types of processes interacting in a highly interdependent way: (1) administrative processes, i.e., planning, organizing, coordinating, and controlling; and (2) operational processes, i.e., personnel management, financial management, materials and production management, marketing management, and research, development, and engineering management. Although the second category is roughly the rationale for the departmentalization of many industrial firms, it includes processes that by definition cannot be completely departmentalized. Both categories overlap each other, however, and cannot be considered mutually exclusive.[12] (See Figure 3-4 for a rough diagrammatic representation. The processes are shown as intersecting in order to suggest interdependence.)

7. Any organization will possess a unique fabric of processes and systems. It would seem unlikely for the flows of events described above and the quality and quantity of the available resources external to, and within, any two organizations to be identical.

8. An organization can be considered a sociotechnical system since its technical and human aspects are highly interdependent. It is also a system existing in a highly interdependent state with other systems.

9. Any major organizational process will have events occurring in common with other processes. Therefore, systems designed to facilitate major processes are likely to have components that are also components of other systems.

10. Changes in the inputs or the processing of one organizational subsystem are likely to have an impact on the operation of one or more other subsystems.

11. Although individual executives and departments may be assigned to focus on, or specialize in, the design and administration of particular systems, managers and subunits tend to exist in a highly interdependent relationship.

12. The people who manage the organization tend to be planners and actors in a fairly extensive network of systems. They may have one task in one system, a different task in another, etc.

13. In general, the task of top management is to crystallize the definition of enterprise goals, assemble resources, visualize the processes essential to the attainment of these goals, and design, direct, and control the network of facilitating systems, including feedback systems.

14. An organizational issue will be the degree of openness and participation in the management of the human resources subsystems. The scope of participation of the nonmanagerial members in the design and administration of the various systems will be a function of a number of forces, including the technology used in the particular enterprise, the prevailing philosophy of management, and cultural norms.

Perhaps the following illustration about forest management will serve to dramatize some of the concepts used above. This illustration applies the terminology of *process* and *systems* to a

---

[12] There are, of course, other ways to subdivide the totality of an organization. Katz and Kahn, for example, refer to five basic subsystems: (1) "production or technical," (2) "supportive," (3) "maintenance," (4) "adaptive," and (5) "managerial." See Katz and Kahn, *Social Psychology of Organizations*, pp. 39–43.

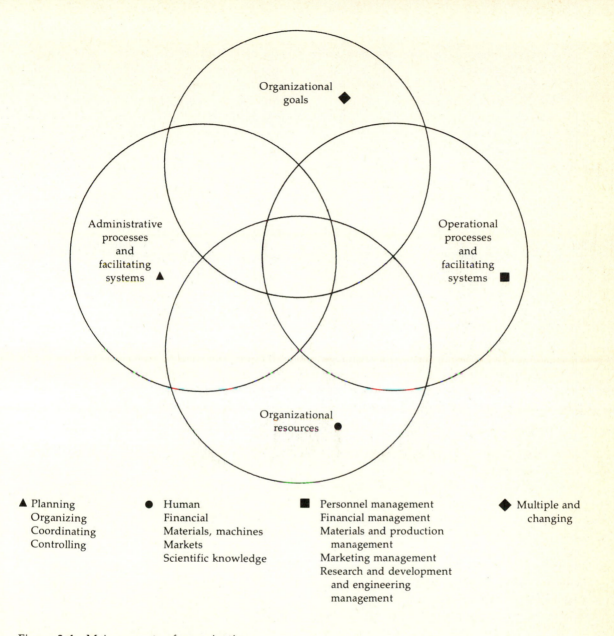

Figure **3-4**   Major aspects of organization

description of forest management, a discipline in which concepts of interdependence and ecology are very apparent.

The management of a forest (a complex, natural system) typically involves many goals—for example, the outputs of tree and plant products; the furnishing of recreational areas, water supply, and conservation; soil conservation; production and protection of wild life; the cultivation of grass for the grazing of domesticated animals; and the care of streams for the production and conservation of fish life. Thus, the management of a forest requires systematic administration and control of a highly complex network of interacting processes, including tree, plant, animal, fish, bird, insect, fungus, and virus growth, and other processes involving fire and erosion. All must be maintained or controlled in some kind of equilibrium that will maximize the attainment of multiple goals.

The interdependence of trees, low vegetation, and deer presents a typical forest-management problem. If the tree growth in the forest is too dense, shrubs and grasses will be choked out, and the deer, dependent upon these for food, will be unable to survive. On the other hand, if trees are selectively cut and conditions become more favorable for the growth of shrubs and other low vegetation, the deer population will rapidly multiply. Eventually, unless checked in some way, the deer may exceed the food supply provided by grasses and shrubs and, before starving, will eat the young tree growth necessary for replenishing the timber crop. Thus, it becomes the task of forest management to devise subsystems to control various overlapping processes and to maintain a dynamic equilibrium appropriate to the attainment of the pre-established multiple goals.

While I have cautioned against overreliance on drawing analogies between organizations and natural systems (although when we add humans to the management of a forest we have really inserted a social system into a natural

one), the above illustration has many aspects that parallel the management of contemporary organizations. In particular, concepts like nurturance, growth, climate, interdependence, equilibrium, and goals come to one's mind as extremely important relative to the management of our modern social systems.

SUMMARY

In this chapter, the concept of process has been described and contrasted with that of system. Both concepts have been integrated with concepts relating to general administrative processes and the resources of an enterprise as a step toward developing a model of the organization. In addition, concepts pertaining to systems theory, including notions of closed and open systems, structured and incompletely structured systems, feedback, and interface have been discussed. These concepts and the organizational model, in turn, provide for the development of a model of personnel management and a framework for analysis that will be the focus of the next chapter.

REVIEW AND DISCUSSION QUESTIONS

1. Using *process* as defined in this chapter, what are some common processes that can be observed in nature?

2. What additional processes can you visualize in an organization? What systems are used to facilitate these processes?

3. How would you relate the concepts in this chapter to home management?

4. What is the difference between a structured and an incompletely structured system? Between a closed and an open system? Can you give some illustrations?

5. What is meant by *ecology* from the standpoint of (a) biology, (b) the study of organizations, (c) the study of administrative and operational processes?

6. Discuss *interface* and *feedback* as these terms could apply to organizations.

SUPPLEMENTAL REFERENCES

Allport, Floyd, *Theories of Perception and the Concept of Structure* (New York: John Wiley & Sons, Inc., 1955), pp. 469ff.

Baker, Frank, ed., *Organizational Systems: General Systems Approaches to Complex Organizations* (Homewood, Ill.: Richard D. Irwin, Inc., 1973).

Bertalanffy, Ludwig von, *General System Theory* (New York: George Braziller, 1968).

———, "The Theory of Open Systems in Physics and Biology," *Science*, 111:23–28 (January 13, 1950).

Boulding, Kenneth E., "General Systems Theory—The Skeleton of Science," *Management Science*, Vol. 2, No. 3 (April 1956), pp. 197–208.

Chin, Robert, "The Utility of System Models and Developmental Models for Practitioners," in Warren G. Bennis, Kenneth D. Benne, and Robert Chin, eds., *The Planning of Change*, 2nd ed. (New York: Holt, Rinehart and Winston, 1969), p. 300.

Cooper, Robert, and Michael Foster, "Socio-technical Systems," *American Psychologist*, 26:467–474 (May 1971).

DeGreene, Kenyon B., ed., *Systems Psychology* (New York: McGraw-Hill Book Company, 1970).

Duncan, Otis D., "Social Organization and the Ecosystem," in Robert E. Faris, ed., *Handbook of Modern Sociology* (Chicago: Rand McNally & Company, 1964), pp. 36–45.

Forrester, Jay W., *Industrial Dynamics* (New York: John Wiley & Sons, Inc., 1961).

French, Wendell, "Processes Vis-a-Vis Systems: Toward a Model of the Enterprise and Administration," in Frank Baker, ed., *Organizational Systems: General Systems Approaches to Complex Organizations* (Homewood, Ill.: Richard D. Irwin, Inc., 1973), pp. 425–437.

Gagne, Robert M., et al., *Psychological Principles in System Development* (New York: Holt, Rinehart and Winston, Inc., 1962).

Johnson, Richard A., Fremont E. Kast, and James E. Rosenzweig, *The Theory and Management of Systems*, 3rd ed. (New York: McGraw-Hill Book Company, 1973).

Kohler, Wolfgang, *Gestalt Psychology* (New York: Horace Liveright, 1929).

Koontz, Harold, and Cyril O'Donnell, *Management: A Book of Readings* (New York: McGraw-Hill Book Company, 1972).

Lewin, Kurt, *Field Theory in Social Science* (New York: Harper & Brothers, 1951), p. 57.

Miller, E.J., and A.K. Rice, *Systems of Organization* (New York: Tavistock Publications, 1967), Chapter 1.

Murphy, Gardner, *Personality: A Bio-Social Approach to Origins and Structure* (New York: Harper & Brothers, 1947), pp. 1–37.

Optner, Stanford L., *Systems Analysis for Business and Industrial Problem Solving* (Englewood Cliffs, N.J.: Prentice-Hall, Inc., 1965).

Petersen, James, "Lessons from the Indian Soul: A Conversation with Frank Waters," *Psychology Today* (May 1973), pp. 63–64.

Presthus, Robert V., "Toward a Theory of Organizational Behavior," *Administrative Science Quarterly*, 3:50 (June 1958).

Roethlisberger, F.J., and William J. Dickson, *Management and the Worker* (Cambridge, Mass.: Harvard University Press, 1956) (Copyright 1939), p. 557.

Scott, William G., "Organization Theory: An Overview and an Appraisal," *Journal of the Academy of Management*, 4:15–20 (April 1961).

Seckler-Hudson, Catheryn, "Major Processes of Organization and Management," in Harold Koontz and Cyril O'Donnell, *Readings in Management* (New York: McGraw-Hill Book Company, 1959), p. 22.

Storey, John H., *The Web of Life* (New York: The Devin-Adair Company, 1954).

CHAPTER 4
THE MODEL APPLIED
TO PERSONNEL
MANAGEMENT

The process-systems approach can now be applied specifically to personnel management, which has been described thus far as a broad operational process inherent in all organizations. An examination of organizations in general suggests that this broad process can be divided into a number of interdependent subprocesses vital to the existence of most enterprises.

Some of these processes in personnel management can be described in a straightforward manner. Some are much more complicated, in reality being complex constellations of subprocesses. Each personnel process, however, is a complex flow of events that has certain unique ends or objectives differentiating it from the others.

In process-systems terminology, *personnel management* is the diagnosis and planning,

coordinating, and controlling of a network of organizationwide processes and facilitating systems pertaining to leadership, justice determination, task specialization, staffing, performance appraisal, training and development, compensation and reward, collective bargaining, and organization development. Each will be described briefly here and then analyzed in detail in subsequent chapters. (See Figure 4.1 for a diagrammatic representation.)

These processes tend to be found, in some form or another in most, if not all, kinds of organizations. Partial exceptions to this universality, however, can be found in the processes of compensation and reward and collective bargaining. Some organizations, for example, depend entirely upon voluntary nonpaid help, and many organizations are not involved in formal collective bargaining with unions. On the

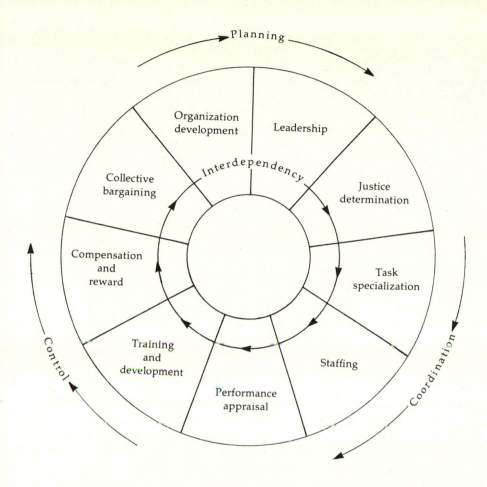

Figure **4-1**   The major personnel management processes in organizations

other hand, some aspects of compensation and reward, such as the allocation of privileges or the granting of recognition, will occur in volunteer organizations; and institutions such as churches will have compensation plans for a core of full- or part-time staff members, or both. Further, some elements of collective action may be seen in many organizations that are not unionized. For example, a faculty council of a school may make demands pertaining to working conditions that resemble those made in more traditional union-management relationships. Thus, the various personnel management processes may be more universally found than might appear at first glance.

An attempt has been made in this chapter to define the various personnel subprocesses in descriptive rather than normative terms in order to stress their universal nature. Thus, the process may be in existence even though the system designed to facilitate it may be inadequate or neglected and the consequence less than optimum. The existence of a process says nothing about the effectiveness of its management. For example, by handling their own recruitment and hiring, production managers may be thwarting the career aspirations of people in other departments and creating serious wage inequities relative to other units.

It should also be noted that the following discussion of each process uses illustrations of procedures and devices (system components) that may not be in existence in some organizations, although they tend to be widely found in the United States. In particular, some of the devices alluded to may not be found in certain other countries.

In short, much of our terminology in American management may be "culture-bound." Thinking through the *process* that a particular device is designed to facilitate, however, should tend to minimize this cultural bias. For example, an organization may not be using a formal plan called "job evaluation," but there may be a flow of events that results in a ranking of jobs in terms of relative financial worth, which can be considered a definition of the salary administration technique of job evaluation.

THE LEADERSHIP PROCESS

The *process of leadership* is an interactive flow of events comprising the "development and maintenance of role structure and goal direction necessary for effective group performance."[1] Leadership is a complex matter involving the traits and behavior of the leader, the characteristics and behavior of subordinates, group skills and behavior, the traits and behavior of the leader's

[1] Adapted from Ralph M. Stogdill, *Handbook of Leadership* (New York: The Free Press, 1974), p. 411.

superior, the goals of the organization, and the entire network of personnel subprocesses. I will take the point of view that effective leadership is situational but that research seems to point toward a certain optimal mix of behaviors that has been found effective in a high percentage of situations. Leadership will be discussed in Chapter 7.

THE JUSTICE-DETERMINATION PROCESS

The *process of justice determination* is a flow of organizational events that allocates rewards and penalties to organizational members in proportion to their relative contribution and that corrects mistakes in such allocations. The administration of equity and justice is a matter that occupies a good deal of the time and energy of every manager. As in the age-old definition of justice, "equal treatment under the law," people working in organizations expect treatment based upon reasonable policies and rules applicable to the entire group of which they are part. Since most employees also have some concept of the importance of being treated as individuals as well as members of a group, what is just or fair becomes an exceedingly complex question—one with which all managers must deal.

In addition to being concerned with the substance of the decisions on human resources, people in organizations also tend to be concerned with the *procedures* used for determining what is equitable or fair. Further, they are concerned with the kind and quality of the avenues of appeal open to them. Thus, both the quality of treatment and the procedures used in this treatment are important, and any discussion of organizational justice must include some emphasis on substantive and procedural matters pertaining to discipline, layoffs, transfers, promotions, privileges, work schedules, and wages. This complex subject will be discussed in Chapter 8.

THE TASK-SPECIALIZATION PROCESS

The *task-specialization process* is a flow of events through which the total task to be done is divided and through which the nature of individual jobs is determined. To some extent this process is synonymous with *designing the organization* or with the traditional management concept of *organizing*. Of the various personnel processes we will be discussing, this one is probably the least specially identified with personnel management. Yet so much of personnel management is a direct reflection of this process that it is almost impossible to present a thorough treatment of the subject without some analysis of this flow of events. In addition, more and more personnel specialists, as well as line managers, are becoming interested in the organizational and human consequences of job design.

In general, the task-specialization process consists of a sequence of events and activities as follows: (1) the determination of organizational objectives; (2) organizational planning, including design of the organization and jobs based on the tools, machines, and the systems technology to be used in achieving the enterprise's goals; (3) the communication of job design to members of the organization through the use of such devices as job descriptions and performance standards and through training and example; (4) the determination of human qualifications required on these jobs (job specifications); and (5) the establishment of work rules. Although each of these activities or events tends to stem from the preceding one, there is considerable reciprocal interdependence. The task-specialization process will be analyzed and discussed in Chapters 9 and 10.

THE STAFFING PROCESS

The *staffing process* is a complex network of events that results in the continuous assignment of human resources to the various jobs throughout the organization. In one sense, it is a flow of people into, and out of, the various jobs in the organization. The process typically includes the following activities: human resources planning, authorization for staffing, developing sources of applicants, applicant evaluation, employment decisions and offers, induction and orientation, transfers, demotions, promotions, and separations. Some of the devices commonly used in the systems designed to facilitate this broad process are staffing charts, application blanks, interviews, tests, reference checks, and performance appraisal devices. The staffing process will be analyzed and discussed in Chapters 11 through 14.

THE PERFORMANCE APPRAISAL PROCESS

The *process of performance appraisal* is the continuous evaluation of the contribution of individuals and groups within the organization. Such evaluations are constantly being made for a variety of purposes, including selection, correction, training, pay increases, promotions, discipline, and transfers. Appraisals may vary from highly subjective, almost subconscious evaluations to highly systematized reviews focusing on specific behavior. This process will be discussed in Chapter 15. Although the communication and discussion of performance appraisal is an integral part of the training and development process, the communication of appraisal is also inseparable from the appraisal process itself, and will also be discussed in Chapter 15. Management by objectives will also be a part of that discussion.

THE TRAINING AND DEVELOPMENT PROCESS

The *training and development process* is a complex amalgamation of many subprocesses aimed at increasing the capability of individuals and groups to contribute to organizational goal attainment. Included in this flow of events are the determination of training and development needs, skill training, professional and management development, employee counseling, and the dialogue surrounding performance appraisal (the latter to be discussed in the chapter on performance appraisal). Training and development will be discussed in Chapters 16–17.

THE COMPENSATION AND REWARD PROCESS

The *process of compensation and reward* is a flow of events that determines the level, forms, and differentials of financial rewards, fringe benefits, and nonfinancial rewards received by each member of the organization. Typically found in this complex process are mechanisms for assessing competitive wages in the external labor market, for job evaluation, for the establishment of wage rates and/or salary ranges for different job categories, and for decision-making processes to establish salaries or wages according to differential performance. In addition, there will usually be extra payments for shift work, overtime, or "call-in" work. There may also be some efforts directed to the stimulation of individual or group performance, or both, through incentive systems, profit sharing, or bonuses. The provision of vacations, holidays, and other fringe benefits may also be considered important parts of the compensation and reward process. These and other matters will be described and analyzed in greater detail in Chapters 19–21. Nonfinancial rewards such as intrinsic job satisfaction, recognition, privileges, and status are also significant aspects of

this broad process and will be discussed in these chapters and elsewhere.

THE COLLECTIVE-BARGAINING PROCESS

The *collective-bargaining process* can be thought of as a complex network of events in the unionized organization, a process that serves to determine wages and fringe benefits, hours, and working conditions and that introduces a unique kind of transactional relationship between two institutions, the union and the employer.[2] Not only does this flow of events have the purpose of reconciling the conflicting demands and requirements of both parties, but it is assumed to have broader social purposes, including minimizing labor strife and facilitating the flow of commerce.

Certain aspects of the collective-bargaining process will be emphasized. Stressed, in particular, will be the process that culminates in the formation of a union, i.e., the unionization process; prenegotiation strategies and tactics; negotiations between the union and management on wages, hours, and working conditions; and the process of administering the agreement, including avenues of appeal and grievance and arbitration proceedings. The collective-bargaining process will be discussed in Chapters 22–25.

THE ORGANIZATION DEVELOPMENT PROCESS

Organization development is a new concept that is beginning to have a major impact on a significant number of organizations in the United States and abroad. Although this concept has a specific and unique meaning, which will be

---

[2] *Union* is used in a broad sense to include those professional organizations that bargain with employees over a variety of matters but do not call themselves unions.

discussed in Chapter 26, the process will be defined here in general terms as a complex network of events that enhances the ability of organizational members to manage the culture of their organization, to be effective in solving problems, and to assist their organization in adapting to the external environment. In its more precise meaning, organization development (OD) is a specific strategy for planned organizational improvement and is of considerable contemporary importance and interest to practicing managers and to scholars throughout the world.

THE FRAMEWORK OF THE CHAPTERS

The following framework will be utilized to a varying extent when analyzing the previously mentioned processes in the chapters that follow. To avoid redundancies, however, this pattern will not be followed in each instance.

1. *Current practice and problems* Reference will be made to typical or frequently found designs of the various personnel systems in modern organizations. Further, there will be some discussion of problems faced by today's managers in the administration of these systems.

2. *Relationship to other organizational processes and facilitating systems* An analysis will be made of the degree of interrelationship between the various personnel processes and other broad management processes. The impact of a change in the design of one subsystem upon other subsystems will also be discussed.

3. *Impact of environment* Personnel management is affected by forces both internal and external to the organization, i.e., the environment within which various flows of events (processes) take place. For example, the managerial philosophy of the top executives in an enterprise, together with the attitudes of supervisors and their behavior toward subordinates,

will have a major impact on the effectiveness of the various personnel subsystems. Further, the nature of the organization's technology will affect such matters as work rules and the kind and degree of employee participation that is feasible. And both law and custom will have a major impact on personnel management.

Thus, while the emphasis in many chapters will be on processes and systems, the *conditions* or *environment* of effective personnel management will also be stressed. A complex spectrum of forces needs to be examined in a particular organization at a given point in time in order to determine which personnel practices will be effective and which will not. Of particular consequence are the following:

a. Community and societal customs and attitudes

b. Federal and state law

c. Technology and science

d. Union-management relations

e. Managerial philosophy and behavior

f. Skills and capabilities of the human resources in the organization and available in the labor market

4. *Effect on need fulfillment* Personnel systems affect the fulfillment of human needs in various ways. Since the extent to which fulfillment of need is thwarted or augmented has consequences in terms of employees' performance, the impact on people of various designs in personnel systems is a significant subject of inquiry.

5. *Diagnosis and participation in systems design* Above and beyond the intrinsic merits of a particular system, *the way the organization goes about diagnosing the need for creating or modifying a particular personnel system or subsystem will have an impact on need fulfillment as well as ease of implementation of that system.* As Scott Myers states it,

. . . a management system is considered effective when the people whose job performance is influenced by the system:

1. Understand its purpose
2. Agree with its purpose
3. Know how to use it
4. Are in control of it
5. Can influence its revision
6. Receive timely feedback from it.[3]

Questions such as the following are vital, and they are all too frequently ignored in personnel management: Who determines that there is a problem requiring a different or modified personnel system? Who should be involved in the diagnosis of the problem? What diagnostic procedure will be used? How broad a diagnosis of the organization will occur? What range of solutions will be examined? Who will be involved in the design of the system? The mode of installing new personnel systems frequently seems to be one of selling the idea at the top level of the organization and unilateral change in policy or practice, without adequate diagnosis of organizational strengths and weaknesses and without the participation of those affected.

6. *Authority and accountability* Additional understanding of personnel management can be derived from analyzing the various kinds of authority exercised by managers over the different components of personnel systems and from analyzing the degree to which managers tend to be held accountable for the successful administration of each system and its components. Accountability refers to the extent to which an individual is held responsible for a particular outcome or final result, regardless of the type of authority he or she may be able to exercise. For example, safety managers may be held accountable for reducing accidents in a manufacturing plant, but they will need to rely mainly on their expertise (personal authority in contrast to formal authority) and ability to obtain cooperation in accomplishing this end. Ideally, safety managers are held jointly accountable along with manufacturing directors and other executives. However, their role in safety management is unique.[4]

7. *Validity and reliability of systems* A central question in personnel systems and subsystems is the question of *validity*, i.e., to what degree do the systems contribute to organizational goals and organizational effectiveness? *Reliability*, on the other hand, is the extent to which a particular system or component produces consistent results. If a particular system lacks reliability, its validity will be correspondingly affected, although reliability in itself is no guarantee of validity. Thus it is important to ascertain both.

While validity is the central question, it is extremely difficult to measure, and for several reasons. In the first place, organizations typically have several overriding goals, and their attainment represents some balance that is judged optimal.[5] Although corporate goals are frequently reported in terms of profit objectives, even a superficial probing finds most business executives talking about the production of a particular kind and quality of goods or

[3] M. Scott Myers, *Every Employee a Manager* (New York: McGraw-Hill Book Company, 1970), p. 126.

[4] In the dual accountability situation, Schleh recommends that both managers involved should receive full credit for the accomplishment of objectives. See Edward C. Schleh, *Management by Results* (New York: McGraw-Hill Book Company, 1961), pp. 63, 212.

[5] Optimum connotes best in terms of all things considered. See Stanford L. Optner, *Systems Analysis for Business and Industrial Problem Solving* (Englewood Cliffs, N.J.: Prentice-Hall, Inc., 1965), p. 93. Although the terms *optimize* and *maximize* relative to goal attainment will be used frequently in this book, March and Simon's "satisficing" hypothesis is also relevant. According to these authors, "Most human decision-making . . . is concerned with the discovery and selection of satisfactory alternatives . . ." rather than ". . . optimal alternatives." See James G. March and Herbert A. Simon, *Organizations* (New York: John Wiley & Sons, Inc., 1958), pp. 140–141. Also, for a discussion of goal definition, see David Silverman, *The Theory of Organizations* (New York: Basic Books, Inc., 1971), pp. 1–12.

services at a profit. Most managers of any type of organization are very conscious of the importance of satisfying certain customer or client needs if they are to satisfy their own. Further, executives are increasingly developing a concern about both the short- and long-run consequences of management practices as they relate to the depletion or development of the human resources within the organization. Thus, the criteria used to measure the effectiveness of a given personnel system will inevitably be a complex matter.

Second, determining the validity of a given personnel system is difficult since many variables will be impinging on the effectiveness of a system at a given time. For example, the relationship between a change in the employee selection system and subsequent changes in profits can be largely obscured by changes in pricing policy, changes in production techniques, or changes in competitors' practices. We will, however, try to develop a rationale for approaching the validity problem in connection with some topics. In many instances, validity becomes a matter of judgment after the impact of a particular policy or procedure is measured, or estimated, relative to each of several organizational goals in turn. As a practical matter, in most organizational research these goals will usually be subgoals; it is much easier to make a case for cause-and-effect relationships when using intermediate criteria such as turnover or supervisory ratings of employee performance. A judgment still needs to be made, however, as to the relationship between such intermediate criteria and more *ultimate criteria* such as organizational survival, profits, return on investment, or satisfaction of participants.[6]

---

[6] The concept of ultimate criteria is intended to be synonymous with Rensis Likert's "end result variables" such as "level of productivity," "level of scrap loss," "level of share of the market," "level of profits," and "current value of investment in human organization." Likert refers to causal, intervening, and end result variables. See Rensis Likert, *The*

8. *Utility and consequences of systematization* Part of the validity question has to do with the utility and consequences of the *degree* of systematization. While systematization can produce desirable consequences such as predictability, focus, and coordination with other activities, systematization can also dampen innovativeness, create excessive dependence on procedures, and give people a sense of being stifled by the organization. Thus, processes can be oversystematized as well as undersystematized, and the optimum degree of systematization becomes an important question in personnel management. This question will be examined when it seems particularly pertinent relative to certain personnel systems.

SUMMARY

Personnel management has been described as the planning, coordinating, and controlling of a network of subprocesses and facilitating subsystems pertaining to the recruitment, selection, utilization, development of, and accommodation to human resources. The following subprocesses have been suggested as comprising the most vital aspects of personnel management: leadership, justice determination, task specialization (job and organization design), staffing, performance appraisal, training and development, compensation, collective bargaining, and organization development. Each of these significant subprocesses lends itself to description and analysis in a number of important dimensions, including a description of the design of systems typically employed to facilitate these subprocesses, the nature of the diagnosis made before systems design, the extent of employee involvement in system design, the interrelationship of each of the various subprocesses, the relationship of each to broader

---

Human Organization: Its Management and Value (New York: McGraw-Hill Book Company, 1967), pp. 228–229.

management processes, and the validity of various devices and systems commonly used.

This framework will be utilized in analyzing the various personnel management processes in the following chapters.

REVIEW AND DISCUSSION QUESTIONS

1. Briefly describe the major personnel management processes identified in this chapter.

2. Which of these processes are *not* found in all types of organizations? In a family?

3. From your experience, what additional personnel processes do you see that might be used to supplement or revise the classification scheme of this chapter?

4. Referring back to one of the processes you described in question 1, describe this process in *systems* terminology. How did the two statements differ?

5. What is meant by *validity* and *reliability* of personnel systems?

6. What is meant by *accountability?* Can you think of other illustrations of accountability that do not involve formal authority? Can you give some illustrations of joint accountability?

7. What is your reaction to Scott Myers' list of six criteria for system effectiveness?

SUPPLEMENTAL REFERENCES

Etzioni, Amitai, *Modern Organizations* (Englewood Cliffs, N.J.: Prentice-Hall, Inc., 1964), pp. 1–19.

Katz, Daniel, and Robert Kahn, "The Concept of Organizational Effectiveness," in *The Social Psychology of Organizations* (New York: John Wiley & Sons, Inc., 1966), pp. 149–170.

Mott, Paul E., *The Characteristics of Effective Organizations* (New York: Harper and Row, 1972), Chapter 2.

Smith, Patricia C., "Behaviors, Results, and Organizational Effectiveness: The Problem of Criteria," in Marvin D. Dunnette, ed., *Handbook of Industrial and Organizational Psychology* (Chicago: Rand McNally College Publishing Company, 1976), pp. 745–775.

Yuchtman, Ephraim, and Stanley E. Seashore, "A System Resource Approach to Organizational Effectiveness," *American Sociological Review*, 32:891–903 (December 1967).

CHAPTER 5
MAJOR CONTINGENCIES: AUTHORITY, STRUCTURE, AND TECHNOLOGY

The student of personnel management needs to be aware of the wide diversity among modern organizations in terms of authority relationships, organizational structure, and technology used. These dimensions are major contingencies in the management of human resources within an enterprise. Personnel systems are affected by these variables, and perhaps to a lesser extent, these variables are affected by the way various personnel systems are designed and administered. (By *contingency* is meant the complex way in which two or more variables interact to produce particular outcomes. A contingency approach focuses on several phenomena simultaneously rather than just two.)

First I will distinguish between power and authority and examine different types of authority relationships that can exist in organizations. Then I will turn to a description of sev-

eral types of organizational structures, followed by a description of various major types of organizations in terms of the technology used. Finally, the concepts of organic and mechanistic systems will be described to highlight the interdependence between the type of organization and the way personnel administration is carried out.

POWER AND AUTHORITY

Power and authority are aspects of organizational life that are very real to organizational members and that have a major impact on a wide variety of organizational phenomena including communications and control patterns, the quality of interpersonal relationships, and job satisfaction. Power is a broad concept that is not necessarily confined to an organizational context, while authority is usually defined in organizational terms.

According to Weber, "Power . . . is the probability that one actor within a social relationship will be in a position to carry out his own will despite resistance. . . ."[1] *Formal authority*, or the *authority of position*, on the other hand, is institutionalized power, or more specifically, the institutionalized right to apply rewards or negative sanctions to the behavior of others. As Simon states it, "The most important sanctions of managers over workers in industrial organizations are (a) power to hire and fire, (b) power to promote and demote, and (c) incentive rewards."[2]

This kind of authority is inherent in a position or office, but it tends to be limited by codes of behavior that may be stated policy or which may be implicit organizational norms. Formal authority may also be limited by the power of unions or by previous or anticipated subordinate response. With respect to subordinate response, in what has been referred to as the "acceptance theory of authority," Barnard states that there are orders ". . . which are clearly unacceptable, that is, which certainly will not be obeyed; there is another group somewhat more or less on the neutral line . . . and a third group unquestionably acceptable."[3] Furthermore, there is a wide range of behaviors, short of refusal, that are utilized by unwilling subordinates. As Presthus says, "There are so many degrees of compliance, ranging all the way from enthusiasm to resignation, that outright rejection of an order becomes a gross and unlikely alternative, particularly among highly socialized . . . members of an organiza-

tion."[4] Thus, formal authority tends not to be absolute, and subordinate resistance to authority can be manifested in many ways short of outright refusal to carry out an order or request.

In a thoughtful review of the literature, Peabody has concluded that most theorists tend to recognize two other major kinds of authority in addition to formal authority, the authority of competence and the authority of person. *Authority of competence* includes ". . . possession of experience and appropriate technical skills by the superior . . ." that ". . . enhances the acceptance of his formal authority by his subordinates."[5] The *authority of person*, on the other hand, refers to "knowledge of the human aspects of administration" and "the ability to mediate individual needs."[6] In short, the authority of person rests on identifiable human relations skills. (A kind of personal authority frequently referred to in the literature is *charismatic authority*, which is seen as consisting of magical qualities ascribed to certain leaders.[7] Charisma appears to be a function of both "bold and imaginative acts of leadership" and the emotional needs of the followers.[8])

One other concept of authority, functional authority, will conclude our delineation of kinds of authority. *Functional authority* is of two types: (1) formal authority exercised outside of one's own department but over specialized activities in other parts of the organization, and (2) authority stemming from the interdependence of a position with other positions in the system. Almost universally, an in-

[1] Max Weber, *The Theory of Social and Economic Organization* (New York: Oxford University Press, 1947), p. 152.
[2] Herbert A. Simon, "Authority," in Conrad M. Arensberg et al., *Research in Industrial Human Relations* (New York: Harper & Brothers, 1957), p. 104.
[3] Chester I. Barnard, *The Functions of the Executive* (Cambridge, Mass.: Harvard University Press, 1960), pp. 168–169.

[4] Robert V. Presthus, "Toward a Theory of Organizational Behavior," *Administrative Science Quarterly*, 3:57 (June 1958).
[5] Robert L. Peabody, "Perceptions of Organizational Authority: A Comparative Analysis," *Administrative Science Quarterly*, 6:470 (March 1962).
[6] Ibid., pp. 467, 472. These are statements by Warren Bennis and Robert Presthus as cited by Peabody.
[7] Weber, *Theory of Social and Economic Organization*, p. 328.
[8] Daniel Katz and Robert L. Kahn, *The Social Psychology of Organizations* (New York: John Wiley & Sons, 1966), pp. 318–319.

Figure **5-1**   Scale of authority: the personnel manager

	Decision made by
No authority	**1a.** The personnel manager's superior, with one or two others, but without the personnel manager. **1b.** The personnel manager's superior. **1c.** Others, with neither the superior nor the personnel manager.
Joint or shared authority	**2.** Joint decision among the personnel manager, his superior, and others. **3.** Joint decision between the personnel manager and superior. **4.** The personnel manager and others, without the superior. **5.** The personnel manager plus one other person without the superior.
Unilateral authority	**6.** The personnel manager.

cumbent of a position is dependent upon the collaboration of persons in other positions who can exercise some control by the withholding of their cooperation or by threats to do so.

In actual practice, these various kinds of authority are not mutually exclusive, and the distinctions between them are not precise. In the example of accountability given in Chapter 4, the safety director who is held accountable for an effective safety program exercises personal and competent authority stemming from his or her knowledge and capabilities, plus functional authority stemming from recognition by others that the lack of a safety program would have a serious impact on the whole organization. As an illustration of functional authority, he or she may have the right to declare a piece of machinery inoperative if, upon inspection, it is found to be dangerous.

Furthermore, authority is frequently shared in the sense that many decisions are made jointly. For example, Figure 5-1 shows an authority scale that was used in a study of the functional authority exercised by corporate personnel directors. This research indicated that the exercise of authority by the personnel directors in the sample was joint or shared in a large majority of personnel decision areas—i.e., many decisions were typically made in consultation between the personnel director and one or more other executives.[9]

Both *the way the organization goes about designing personnel systems* and the resulting system itself can augment one kind of authority over another. For example, a decision made unilaterally by top management to lower the mandatory retirement age, or to change the hours of work, is an application of formal authority. On the other hand, a clear statement by a personnel director to department heads about the problems created by a strict seniority system in granting pay raises to production workers, accompanied by a request for comments as to the advantages and disadvantages of moving to a compensation plan that would acknowledge differential performance as well as seniority, would signal a willingness to exercise a kind of joint functional authority and a desire to tap the personal authority of key supervisors.

[9] Wendell French and Dale Henning, "The Authority-Influence Role of the Functional Specialist in Management," *Journal of the Academy of Management*, 9:187–203 (September 1966).

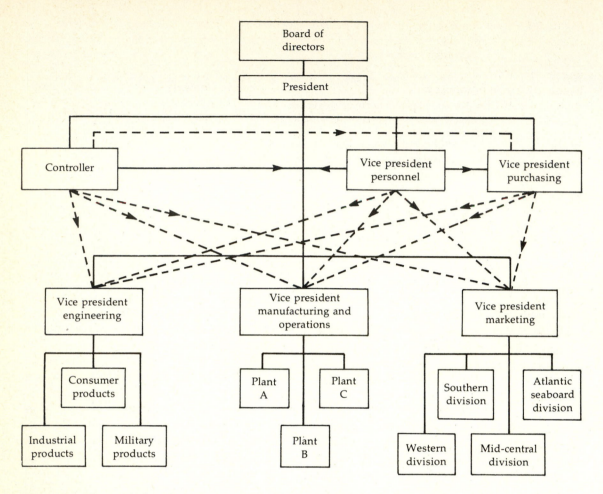

Figure **5-2**   Functional organization combining other forms

Once a new or revised personnel system is implemented, the degree of unilateral decision making versus the kind of shared decision making encouraged by that system will augment or diminish different kinds of authority. To illustrate, a management by objectives program can encourage a substantial amount of real give and take between peers (the exercise of authority of competence and authority stemming from interdependence) and between subordinates and their supervisors (a diminution of formal authority and increase in the exercise of personal authority and authority of competence) providing these features are built into the system and there is widespread commitment to them.

It is obvious, of course, that attitudes and behavior on the part of top management about how authority should be exercised will have a major impact on the design of personnel systems. A top management philosophy dedicated to extensive consultation and joint decision making will tend to extend such a style to the design of personnel systems. A more authoritarian philosophy will tend to produce personnel policies and practices that tend to focus on control. However, an incongruity can occur by attempting to introduce a "democratic" personnel system into a basically "autocratic" organization, or vice versa, with predictable tensions resulting.

STRUCTURE

Structure is another major contingency in personnel management. By *structure* is meant ". . . the established pattern of relationships among the components or parts of the organization."[10] Figure 3-3 in Chapter 3, an illustration of the arrangement of systems components, and Figure 5-2, an organization chart, both depict structure, although in a highly oversimplified and abbreviated way.

Organizational charts tend to portray structure in terms of major groupings of subsystem components and in terms of approximate formal authority relationships. For example, in Figure 5-2, one can infer that a vice president is in charge of all manufacturing and that managers in each of three manufacturing plants report to her or him. Such a diagram is intended to be reflective of the *formal organization*, i.e., the *planned* pattern of relationships.

Traditional organization charts, however, tell us little or nothing about the *informal organization*, that is, they do not reflect the unplanned or unofficial relationships that exist between positions, whether vertically, laterally, or diagonally across organizational subunits. For example, the pyramidal chart does not necessarily show the relationships that may exist between people in terms of communication net-

works, the exercise of power and influence, and sociometric choice. In addition, the traditional organization chart gives little recognition to the complex network of processes and systems as described in Chapters 3 and 4. However, organizational charts do give us useful insight into gross relationships between system components.[11]

LINE AND STAFF

In traditional managerial literature, the concept of staff typically refers to auxiliary, service, or supportive units that are not directly involved with the end product of the organization. Thus personnel and accounting departments are likely to be labeled *staff*, and manufacturing and sales departments are likely to be labeled *line*. The word *staff* also frequently has the connotation of advice giving, or authority of a technically competent nature as described earlier. However, it can also have the connotation of formal authority exercised over a specialized activity. In contrast, the word *line* frequently has the connotation of command, or unilateral formal authority exercised downward to the people represented by the lower boxes on the organization chart.

The diagonal and horizontal dotted lines in Figure 5-2 from the controller, Vice president personnel, and Vice president purchasing to the other major subunits are drawn to suggest these staff relationships. In reality, however, to have a clear understanding of the authority exercised by these various executives would require a detailed analysis of their roles with respect to a wide variety of subsystems and as to what

---

[10] Fremont E. Kast and James E. Rosenzweig, *Organization and Management: A Systems Approach* (New York: McGraw-Hill Book Company, 1974), p. 170.

[11] In process-systems terminology, the formal organization is comprised of planned systems, while the informal organization is comprised of spontaneously emerging processes—e.g., the emergence of feelings and attitudes, and the development of norms and friendship and avoidance patterns.

kinds of authority—formal, technical, personal, or shared or unilateral—were being exercised.

Thus, while these concepts of line and staff have utility, it is important to recognize their limitations. These terms can be dysfunctional in the sense that they oversimplify the real relationships that may exist in terms of authority, influence, and control. Further, the concepts tend to focus on departmentalization and underplay the high degree of interdependence between the major operational systems in the organization, as well as between subunits. In addition, departments traditionally called "line" in some instances become "staff" under differing organizational forms, as in the project form of organization to be discussed later. Perhaps the most serious deficiency in these concepts is that they gloss over the fact that most managers exercise the several forms of authority on nearly a daily basis, and in different degrees depending upon circumstances.

Conflict will emerge regardless of terminology if the various executives in an organization have differing perceptions about the legitimacy of the use of authority by others. Line-staff conflict can and frequently does occur. For example, conflict is likely to emerge if the manufacturing executive sees no need for specialized, functional controls to be exercised in a subunit, or if the personnel executive is precipitous in the exercise of functional authority in contrast to relying on the authority of competence and authority of person.

FUNCTIONAL ORGANIZATION

The term *functional organization* (not to be confused with functional authority) in terms of structure refers to the subdivision of an organization on the basis of similarity of activity. To some extent this form is utilized by most, if not all, organizations.

Figure 5-2 indicates that a number of special-ized activities such as engineering, manufacturing, marketing, accounting, purchasing, and personnel are grouped into separate departments. It should be stressed again, however, that a department specializing in the management of a particular resource is typically not the total system related to that particular resource. For example, the personnel department is a major component of the human resources system but it is not the total personnel system. Similarly, the controller's office does not represent the total financial management system. (Departments can be considered subsystems, however, in the sense that they can be analyzed in terms of inputs, processing mechanisms, and outputs.)

SUBDIVISION BY OTHER CRITERIA

Major segments of the organization may also be divided on the basis of product line or service performed, by categories of client or customer served, by technology used, by geographical area, or by various combinations of these types of subdivisions. Organizations may also be subdivided on the basis of process or work flow. These various forms of subdivision may occur at the level immediately below the chief executive or may occur two or more levels below. Figure 5-2 shows a hypothetical organization subdivided on a functional basis at the level below the president, and on the basis of both geographical area and type of customers served at the second level. Figure 5-3 shows an organization subdivided on a product basis, a subdivision that is also partially oriented to type of technology used. (The dotted lines suggest policy direction by a functional executive.) Figure 5-4 shows a department subdivided on the basis of work flow.

Typically, large organizations utilize two or more of these forms of subdivision, and almost always include a functional subdivision of some

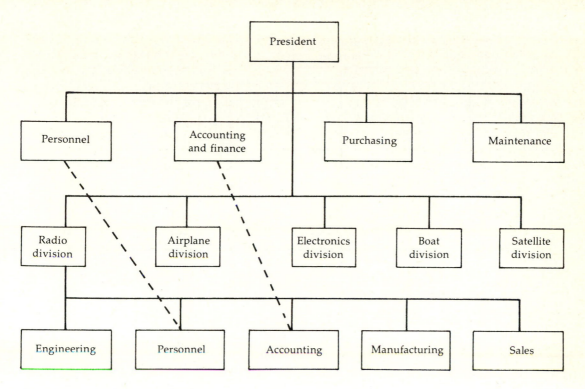

Figure **5-3**   Product organization

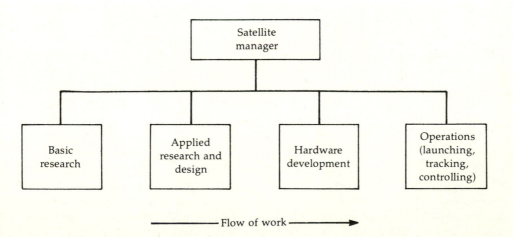

Figure **5-4**   Process or work-flow organization

This illustration is based on data from pp. 164–165 in *Managing Large Systems: Organizations for the Future* by Leonard R. Sayles and Margaret K. Chandler (New York: Harper & Row, 1971).

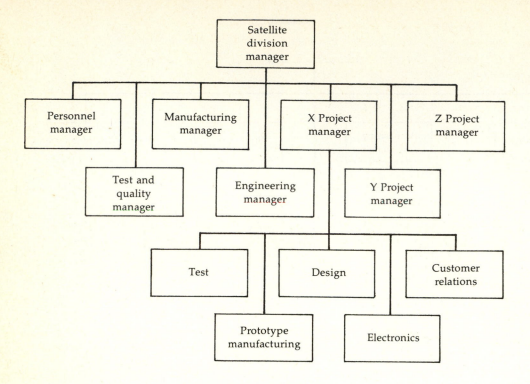

Figure **5-5**   Project organization (intermix or aggregate form)

kind (similarity of activity). Staff departments are almost universally found in large organizations and typically report to the chief executive.

PROJECT AND MATRIX ORGANIZATIONS

The project (sometimes called "task force" or "program") form of organization has been particularly evident in recent years in the aerospace industry and in other highly technical industries, especially those involved in government work. As an organizational form, however, project management has existed for years, perhaps for centuries, in such industries

as construction and the theater, and in the military establishment.[12]

In terms of organizational charts, project organizations typically resemble a combination of functional and product organizations. (See Figure 5-5.) It should be noted that the project manager ordinarily reports to the chief executive or the head of a major unit along with the functional executives.

A project organization typically has three characteristics. One, it usually features the formation of teams from diverse functional speci-

[12] See Albert K. Wickesberg, *Management Organization* (New York: Appleton-Century-Crofts, 1966), p. 84.

alties to work on particular products or end items. Two, the projects have a temporary nature. Thus, the organizational subunits reporting to project managers are *temporary systems*. Three, the project form is typically used as an extension of, and complementary to, the functional form of organization.

The central purpose of the project form of organization is to provide a high degree of coordination and a high degree of visibility to a particular task. It is especially relevant to unique or one-time undertakings of a highly complex nature that require frequent and close coordination of the work of diverse specialists.[13]

Project organizations can exist in a number of forms. Middleton, for example, distinguishes between individual, staff, intermix, and aggregate project organizations.

An *individual* project organization consists of only one person—the project manager. He exercises project control through the functional departments performing all the work on the project. No activities or personnel (except clerical support) report directly to him.

In a *staff* project organization, the project manager is provided a staff to exercise control through activities such as scheduling, task and funds supervision, and change control, and to carry out any functions unique to the project, like testing or site activation. Functional departments still perform the primary tasks of engineering, procurement, and manufacturing.

An *intermix* project organization is established when some of the primary functions are removed from functional departments and are assigned to report directly to the project manager, along with staff functions.

Under an *aggregate* organization, all departments

and activities required to accomplish a project report directly to the project manager.[14]

Thus project organizations can be differentiated along several dimensions including the number of personnel involved, the percentage of people assigned "permanently" to the project in contrast to those loaned for a short period, and the responsibilities assigned to the project manager in contrast to the functional executives.

Although the specific roles of the project manager relative to the functional manager will vary under the different forms of project management outlined above, Cleland describes a typical delineation of responsibilities.

The project manager:

1. Unifies the project affairs such that the customer is satisfied.

2. Establishes the funding, scheduling, and performance standards for the project.

3. Acts as the focal point for customer contact in the company.

4. Resolves any conflict that threatens to disrupt the project activities.

The functional manager:

1. Provides functional facilitation to this as well as the other projects in the organization.

2. Prescribes *how* the day-to-day projects will be supported.

3. Maintains an existing capability in terms of the state-of-the-art in the particular function.[15]

In a sense, then, some functional departments become as much staff departments under a project form of organization as they are line. For example, the engineering department becomes heavily involved in supportive or service relationships to various project managers.

[13] See John M. Stewart, "Making Project Management Work," *Business Horizons*, 8:54–68 (Fall 1965). For more on task forces see Robert A. Luke, "Temporary Task Forces: A Humanistic Problem Solving Structure," in W. Warner Burke, ed., *Contemporary Organization Development: Conceptual Orientations and Interventions* (Washington, D.C.: NTL Institute for Applied Behavioral Science, 1972), pp. 149–167.

[14] C.J. Middleton, "How to Set Up a Project Organization," *Harvard Business Review*, 45:75 (March-April 1967).
[15] David I. Cleland, "Understanding Project Management," reprint from *Manage*, Vol. 19, No. 9 (1967).

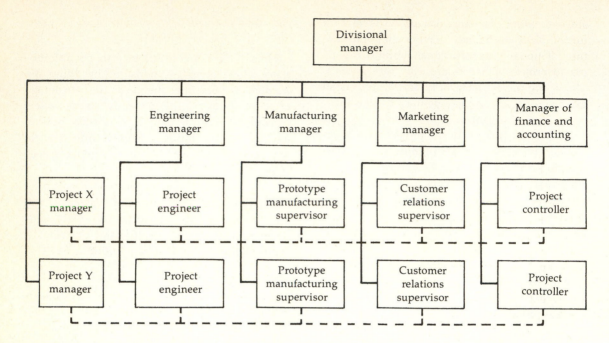

Figure **5-6**   Matrix organization

Dashed and solid lines connote situation of joint reporting.

The term *matrix organization* is essentially synonymous with project organization, except that the concept is frequently used to convey the notion of an organization being continuously involved with many small projects in contrast to a few major ones. Thus, new groups are formed and disbanded, and people are assigned and reassigned with greater frequency. In short, under this meaning the matrix organization is a fluid form of project organization.

A second way in which the concept of matrix organization is used is to connote the idea that the majority of the members assigned to a project continue to report to a functional executive along with the project manager. Thus, under this form of organization most of the members have two superiors for the life of the project. (See Figure 5-6 for an organization chart depicting these joint reporting relationships.)

PROBLEMS WITH PROJECT MANAGEMENT

While the project form of organization has a number of advantages, several personnel management issues emerge:

1. What is the impact on employees of the frequent forming and disbanding of project teams?

2. What can top management do to facilitate team formation?

3. How does the use of a project or matrix form of organization relate to the long-range career development of the employees affected?

4. In situations involving two superiors, who reviews performance matters, who writes the performance report, and who makes decisions about salary administration, and what are the consequences?

5. Does the project management form of organization call for different leadership skills than the functional form of organization?

Some research is beginning to emerge that has a bearing on such questions. It seems that the project form of organization does, indeed, create some unique personnel problems. For example, in a study of an aerospace firm, the attitudes of engineers in three project subunits were compared with the attitudes of engineers in a functional subunit, and it was found that the project engineers were (1) more anxious about a possible loss of employment, (2) more frustrated about "make work" assignments, (3) more anxious about possible career setbacks, and (4) more anxious about their personal development.[16]

Some additional disadvantages of the project form of organization have been noted by Sayles and Chandler. From their observations at the National Aeronautics and Space Administration (NASA), at NASA contractor sites and at a number of British and Japanese organizations, they concluded that project organizations, in contrast to the functional form, tended to limit the experience gained by employees, that there was little exchange of knowledge with similar units outside of the project and a resultant tendency to "reinvent the wheel," and that there was a relatively high degree of fluctuation in work force levels and skill-mix. Conversely, the functional organization provided less visibility to a given project, lack of a focal point and diffused responsibility relative to projects of a multidisciplinary nature, and required

more accommodation to a wider range of interests of the various specialists.[17]

Thus, it would appear necessary to use different personnel approaches for each of the organizational forms to minimize unique disadvantages and to reinforce advantages. For example, in the project form of organization it would appear wise to devote more resources to training and the exchange of information between units, and to career planning and development, than in other forms of organization. Similarly, the use of team-building techniques, as part of a broader OD effort (see Chapter 26), could assist teams in faster and more efficient starts as well as in surfacing career development issues. As another example, in the matrix organization, appraisal of the performance of a given subordinate ideally would require a three-way dialogue among the two supervisors involved and the subordinate.

TECHNOLOGY AS A MAJOR CONTINGENCY

Technology, which is a reflection of the total task to be done, is also a major contingency in personnel management. By *technology* I mean tools, machines, procedures, production processes, and technical knowledge. Joan Woodward, in her study of firms in South Essex, England, has identified eleven different production systems in the manufacturing organizations she studied. As will be discussed later, these different types of technologies were associated with differences in organizational structure and with differences in leadership style, communications, and procedures.

The different production systems that Woodward found were as follows:

---

[16] Clayton Reeser, *Some Problems Perceived as Causes for Frustrations and Anxieties by Subordinates in Project Form Organizations* (Unpublished dissertation, University of Washington, Graduate School of Business Administration, 1968). For a summary of this study see Clayton Reeser, "Some Potential Human Problems of the Project Form of Organization," *Academy of Management Journal*, 12:459–467 (December 1969).

[17] Leonard R. Sayles and Margaret K. Chandler, *Managing Large Systems: Organizations for the Future* (New York: Harper & Row, 1971), p. 185.

I. Integral Products
   A. Unit and small-batch production
      1. Production of units to customer's requirements
      2. Production of prototypes
      3. Fabrication of large equipments in stages
      4. Production of small batches to customer's orders
   B. Large-batch and mass production
      5. Production of large batches
      6. Production of large batches on assembly lines
      7. Mass production
II. Dimensional Products (Process Production)
      8. Intermittent production of chemicals in multi-purpose plants
      9. Continuous flow production of liquids, gases, and crystalline substances
III. Combined Systems
      10. Production of standardized components in large batches subsequently assembled diversely
      11. Process production of crystalline substances, subsequently prepared for sale by standardized production methods.[18]

As Woodward notes, categories 1–9 form a scale in terms of chronological development and in terms of technical complexity. The manufacture of unit items according to the specification of the customer is seen by Woodward as one of the oldest and technically least complex forms of manufacture, while continuous flow production is described as "the most advanced and most complicated." The latter type, however, permits the greatest control and the greatest degree of certainty in reaching goals.[19]

Other organizational attributes that, in Woodward's study, appear to be associated with differing systems of production are shown

in Figure 5-7. The number of levels of supervision tended to increase from unit or small batch production to large batch and mass production and to process manufacture. Furthermore, the span of control of the chief executives of these three major organizational categories tended to vary in the same way, although the span of control at middle-management levels varied in the opposite direction.

In addition, the ratio of indirect workers to production employees increased with technical complexity. Similarly, the ratio of supervisory to nonsupervisory personnel increased markedly from the system 1 to the system 9 end of the scale. However, different characteristics were found relative to the number of employees controlled by first-level supervisors. The average number controlled varied from a low of fourteen in the case of unit production to a high of fifty-six in mass production, but the number dropped to eighteen in the case of intermittent process industries and to eleven in continuous flow process industries.[20]

In the same study it was also found that there was a tendency for firms with low labor costs to spend the most amount of money per employee on welfare and service programs. In addition, these were the firms that were the most likely to have well-developed personnel departments.[21]

In short, a number of organizational attributes of both a structural and a personnel policy nature were associated with the type of production or technological system used. Prescriptions about managerial policies and practices, therefore, need to be highly situational and, in particular, need to be accommodated to the realities of the technological system

[18] Joan Woodward, *Industrial Organization: Theory and Practice* (London: Oxford University Press, 1965), p. 39. These categories are direct quotations.
[19] Ibid., p. 40.

[20] Ibid., p. 61.
[21] Ibid., p. 55. For research that supports much of Joan Woodward's studies but obtains different results on some dimensions, see Peter M. Blau, Cecilia M. Falbe, William McKinley, and Phelps K. Tracy, "Technology and Organization in Manufacturing," *Administrative Science Quarterly*, 21:20–40 (March 1976).

Figure 5-7 Summary of Joan Woodward's findings: organizational characteristics associated with type of technology in British firms

	Unit and small batch production				Large batch and mass production			Process production	
	1	2	3	4	5	6	7	8	9
	Units to customer requirements	Prototypes	Large equipment in stages	Small batches to customer order	Large batches	Large batches on assembly lines	Mass production	Intermittent production of chemicals in multi-purpose plants	Continuous flow production of liquids, gases, and crystalline substances
Age of technology	Older				$\longrightarrow$			More advanced	
Complexity of technology	Less				$\longrightarrow$			High	
Complexity of management	Less				High			Less	
Control and certainty in reaching goals	Less				$\longrightarrow$			More	
Paperwork	Less				High			Less	
Pressure, stress	Less				High			Less	
Number of supervision levels	Low				Medium			High	
Span of control of chief executive	Lower				$\longrightarrow$			Higher	
Span of control of middle manager	Higher				$\longleftarrow$			Lower	
Span of control of first-level supervisors	Low				High			Low	
Ratio of indirect to production workers	Lower				$\longrightarrow$			Higher	
Ratio of supervisory to non-supervisory personnel	Lower				Higher			Highest	
Labor costs	High				High			Low	
Expenditures for employee welfare and services	Lower				$\longrightarrow$			Higher	
Employment of personnel specialists	Less likely				$\longrightarrow$			More likely	
Use of top management committees	Unusual				$\longrightarrow$			Typical	
Use of college graduates	Less				$\longrightarrow$			More	
Type of management system	Organic				Mechanistic			Organic	

Adapted from *Industrial Organization: Theory and Practice* by Joan Woodward, published by Oxford University Press, 1965, Chapters 3–4.

in use. This does not mean that the organizational characteristics of different technologies as found by Woodward are as they should be; in fact, Woodward concluded that the large-batch and mass-production industries, with fewer personnel specialists, needed such specialists even more than did the process industries. What it does suggest is that there needs to be a search in each instance for the optimal fit between the technological system, the structural system, and the personnel system.

MECHANISTIC AND ORGANIC SYSTEMS

The contrasting concepts of mechanistic and organic systems are useful in highlighting the reciprocal relationship between personnel systems and types of organizations. These concepts are useful typologies that include a number of dimensions, including authority, structure, leadership style, and communications, and an indirect reference to technology. The concepts of mechanistic and organic systems also lead into the Chapter 7 discussion of leadership and organizational climate (the latter term will be defined in Chapter 7), and the discussion of organization development in Chapter 26.

Burns and Stalker describe these two major types of managerial systems—mechanistic and organic—as located at opposite ends of a continuum, rather than as a dichotomy. Some firms may have features of both or may oscillate between the two forms, depending upon circumstances. Thus, the concepts are not mutually exclusive.[22] From my experience, however, I frequently see organizations or subunits having constellations of characteristics that tend to resemble one system in contrast to the other.

The mechanistic form of organization is seen as particularly appropriate to conditions that are fairly stable, and has the following major characteristics:[23]

1. A high degree of task specialization and functionalization.

2. Precise delineation of responsibilities and methods to be used. (From my experience, high emphasis on developing written job descriptions might be symptomatic of this characteristic.)

3. A high degree of reliance on each level of the managerial hierarchy to coordinate activities, to provide controls, and to facilitate communications.

4. A tendency for the top of the hierarchy to be conservative about dispensing knowledge about overall company matters. (Burns and Stalker cite an illustration of a chief executive of an organization who reviewed and controlled *all* incoming and outgoing correspondence.)

5. A high degree of reliance on vertical interactions between superiors and subordinates, with activities mainly governed by these vertical interactions. (From my experience, these interactions tend to be a telling-reporting relationship: "I'll tell you what to do; you tell me what you did.")

6. Strong emphasis on company loyalty and obedience to superiors.

7. More importance attached to internal (local) in contrast to general (cosmopolitan)[24] knowledge, skill, and experience.

Another characteristic not explicit in Burns and Stalker's model, although perhaps implicit, that

[22] Tom Burns and G.M. Stalker, *The Management of Innovation* (London: Social Science Paperbacks, 1961), pp. 119–125.

[23] Ibid., pp. 119–120. In a number of respects the mechanistic form of organization is highly comparable to the pure bureaucratic form of organization described by Weber, who believed it to be ". . . capable of attaining the highest degree of efficiency. . . ." See Max Weber, *The Theory of Social and Economic Organization*, pp. 333–336.

[24] See Chapter 18 for Gouldner's definition of "locals" and "cosmopolitans."

I believe to be a salient characteristic of a mechanistic system is:

8. A one-to-one leadership style, with most exchanges between superiors and subordinates occurring in a two-person interaction, with little or no attention to group processes or to the informal organization. (I have seen some organizational subunits, for example, in which the supervisor has never held a joint meeting with key subordinates, and I have seen many organizations where little attempt is made to manage group processes.)

The *organic* form of organization, on the other hand, is seen by Burns and Stalker as particularly appropriate to rapidly changing conditions, and it has the following characteristics: [25]

1. A continuous assessment of tasks as to their relevance to the overall mission of the organization through interaction of a lateral, diagonal, and vertical nature.

2. A network of authority, control, and communication stemming more from expertise pertaining to a particular task or problem than from the "omniscience" of the chief executive and successive levels of the hierarchy. (From my experience, a "task-force" problem-solving orientation is frequently evident in these kinds of relationships.)

3. Communications more of a consultative, informative, and advice-giving nature than of a command or decision-relaying nature, with an emphasis on consensus in decision making.

4. Emphasis on commitment to the tasks of the organization and its survival and growth, in contrast to an emphasis on loyalty and obedience. (I interpret this as not denigrating loyalty to superiors but as an increased emphasis on overall mission.)

5. More emphasis attached to expertise, and more value placed on affiliations that are relevant to the technical or commercial milieu in which the firm is operating (cosmopolitan) in contrast to internal (local) skill and knowledge; a high appreciation of special knowledge and experience particularly relevant to contributing to the overall mission of the organization.

And finally, a characteristic not made explicit by Burns and Stalker but central, I believe, to a truly organic system:

6. A team leadership style involving relatively frequent meetings of a superior and key subordinates in which consultation and frequent use of consensus are evident, as well as attention to the dynamics of group interaction. (Major emphasis is placed on the effectiveness of work teams and between-team cooperation.)

Thus, the organic organization is much more of an open system than is the mechanistic form, in the sense that the individuals and subunits in the organization are much more inclined to seek inputs from any internal and external sources that will assist in enhancing effectiveness. In addition, in the organic system there is a heightened emphasis on technical, personal, and functional authority in contrast to the emphasis on formal authority in the mechanistic system. Therefore, we are likely to see different approaches to the design and administration of personnel systems in these two forms. Job design will be different, staffing will be different, performance appraisal will be different, leadership style will be different.

There is some evidence that these two types of organizations tend to be associated with differing forms of technology. As shown in Figure 5-7, Woodward found that successful manufacturing firms of the large-batch production range tended to be mechanistic organizations,

---

[25] Burns and Stalker, *Management of Innovation*, pp. 119–125. Bennis uses the term *organic-adaptive* in describing a comparable form of organization. See Warren Bennis, "Organizations of the Future," *Personnel Administration*, 30:6–19 (September-October 1967).

while successful firms of the unit and small-batch production and of the process production types tended to be organic systems. We interpret this to mean, for example, that a successful assembly-line type of operation may require much more delineation of responsibilities and reliance on formal authority than would be appropriate in prototype manufacturing or in a petroleum refinery.

Further, organizations may require different mixes of these characteristics. For optimal effectiveness, an assembly-line manufacturing type of organization may require a relatively mechanistic way of operating at the production level but an organic mode at the top-management level, with gradations in between. In a military organization, planning may be an organic function but field operations mechanistic. More research on some of these contingencies will be cited in Chapter 7.

SUMMARY

In conclusion, it is evident that organizations differ widely in terms of authority and power relationships, structure, technology, degree of temporariness of subunits, informal relationships, system openness, and participation. I take the point of view that all these variables are manageable but that the shape of one variable tends to be a powerful determiner of the others. If one wanted to create a truly organic manufacturing department out of a mechanistic assembly-line operation, for example, it would require changes in production technology, reporting relationships, leadership style, communications patterns, and structure. Thus, in designing, or modifying personnel systems, we need to be aware of these interrelationships and not assume we can simply "plug in" programs and expect them to work. There probably is no best design for a given personnel system in the abstract, but in specific circumstances there

may be an optimal design that takes into account a number of contingencies, including technology, structure, authority relationships, and desired organizational "type." Action research as described in the chapter on "The Organization Development Process" is one method of searching for optimal designs.

REVIEW AND DISCUSSION QUESTIONS

1. Describe the different types of authority that may exist in organizations.

2. What is the usefulness, and what are the deficiencies, of the traditional organization chart?

3. What is meant by staff and line? In what ways might these concepts be dysfunctional?

4. What is meant by (a) functional organization, (b) product organization, (c) project organization, and (d) matrix organization?

5. According to Woodward's research, what are some organizational characteristics that seem to vary according to type of technology used?

6. What are the differences between organic and mechanistic systems? Under which circumstances does one form seem more appropriate than the other?

7. Why are matters of authority, structure, and technology relevant to personnel management?

8. From your experience, describe an organization that seems to have moved too far in the organic direction, or too far in the mechanistic direction. Why have you reached these conclusions?

SUPPLEMENTAL REFERENCES

Carzo, Rocco, and John N. Yanouzes, *Formal Organization: A Systems Approach* (Homewood, Ill.: Richard D. Irwin and The Dorsey Press, 1967).

Cleland, David I., and William R. King, *Systems, Organizations, Analysis, Management: A*

Book of Readings (New York: McGraw-Hill Book Company, 1969).

Dalton, Gene W., Louis B. Barnes, and Abraham Zaleznik, *The Distribution of Authority in Formal Organizations* (Boston: Graduate School of Business Administration, Harvard University, 1968).

Filley, Alan C., and Robert J. House, *Managerial Success and Organizational Behavior* (Glenview, Ill.: Scott, Foresman and Company, 1969).

Form, William H., "Technology and Social Behavior of Workers in Four Countries: A Sociotechnical Perspective," *American Sociologist Review*, 37:727–738 (December 1972).

Goodman, Richard A., *Organizational Effects Upon Manpower Utilization in Research and Development* (St. Louis: Department of Economics, Washington University, 1967).

Kast, Fremont E., and James E. Rosenzweig, *Contingency Views of Organization and Management* (Chicago: Science Research Associates, 1973).

Koontz, Harold, and Cyril O'Donnell, *Management: A Book of Readings,* 3rd ed. (New York: McGraw-Hill Book Company, 1972).

Litterer, Joseph A., *Organizations: Structure and Behavior*, Vol. I, 2nd ed. (New York: John Wiley & Sons, 1969).

Lorsch, Jay W., and John J. Morse, *Organizations and Their Members: A Contingency Approach* (New York: Harper & Row, 1974).

Miles, Matthew B., "On Temporary Sytems," in Matthew B. Miles, ed., *Innovation in Education,* (New York: Teachers College, Columbia University, 1964), pp. 437–490.

Mohr, Lawrence B., "Organizational Technology and Organizational Structure," *Administrative Science Quarterly*, 16:444–459 (December 1971).

Morse, John J., and Jay W. Lorsch, "Beyond Theory Y," *Harvard Business Review*, 48:61–68 (May-June 1970).

Perrow, Charles, *Organizational Analysis: A Sociological View* (Belmont, Calif.: Wadsworth Publishing Co., 1970).

Seiler, John A., *Systems Analysis in Organizational Behavior* (Homewood, Ill.: Richard D. Irwin, and The Dorsey Press, 1967).

Silverman, David, *The Theory of Organizations* (New York: Basic Books, Inc., 1971), pp. 14–38.

Taylor, James C., *Technology and Planned Organiational Change* (Ann Arbor: The University of Michigan, Institute for Social Research, 1971).

Thompson, Victor A., *Modern Organization* (New York: Alfred A. Knopf, 1961).

Weber, Max, *The Theory of Social and Economic Organization* (New York: Oxford University Press, 1967), pp. 328–341.

3

PART 3
BEHAVIORAL-SCIENCE CONCEPTS AND ASSUMPTIONS

Part 3 examines some dimensions of organizational life that pervade the domain of personnel management.

Chapter 6 discusses the complex and interrelated topics of motivation, productivity, and worker satisfaction. Chapter 7 focuses on leadership and the idea of an organizational climate. Chapter 8 deals with the important topic of organizational justice and the organizational consequences of unfair or inequitable treatment.

CHAPTER 6
MOTIVATION, SATISFACTION, AND PRODUCTIVITY

This chapter will summarize certain aspects of contemporary theory and research pertaining to motivation and satisfaction and their relationship to productivity, and it briefly will comment on the significance of other dimensions such as group attitudes and technology. What managers believe to be true about these matters, of course, greatly affects the design and administration of personnel systems.

INDIVIDUAL DIFFERENCES

Some aspects of personnel management, such as hiring, promotion decisions, and training, are largely based on the premise that people differ significantly from one another. It is well documented that people differ in terms of intellectual abilities, temperament, motor skills, interests, attitudes, level of aspiration, available energy, education, training, and experience.[1] Managers regularly make decisions about the selection, utilization, and development of people based on this knowledge, and organizational members routinely adjust their own behavior to accommodate differences among peers. The individual characteristics of organizational members clearly can determine organizational success, average performance, or failure.

THE NEED HIERARCHY

While individual differences undoubtedly establish the limits on human performance, motivation is also clearly a powerful determinant

[1] See, for example, John O. Crites, *Vocational Psychology* (New York: McGraw-Hill Book Company, 1969).

of human behavior. It is fairly widely accepted that a good deal of motivation has its origins in certain basic needs that are common to people. These needs pertain to physiological requirements, security (or safety), belonging and affection, esteem, integration (or wholeness), and self-actualization. This list is essentially a composite of the items set forth by Abraham H. Maslow and Walter C. Langer. Both of these men were influenced by the theories and a list of needs developed by Henry Murray[2] and by their extensive experiences as clinicians. Maslow, in particular, has been identified in recent years with the development of need theory.[3]

PHYSIOLOGICAL NEEDS

The physiological needs (or drives) are easily recognized: the need for food, water, oxygen,

elimination of body wastes, sleep and relaxation, sex and muscular activity. The expression or satisfaction of many of these needs is socially determined or socially modified. For example, the obtaining and eating of food and the gratification of the need for sex are controlled by many laws and customs.

SECURITY OR SAFETY NEEDS

The need for security includes avoidance of harm from the physical environment. Thus, people require shelter, protective clothing, warmth, and ways of defending themselves. These needs probably give rise also to desires for job security, fair treatment, and predictability, without which the physical environment appears threatening. The needs connected with security or safety, of course, overlap with the physiological needs. The need for shelter, for example, is at once a security need and a physiological need.

BELONGING AND AFFECTION NEEDS

All normal human beings seem to have strong needs to relate to other people. These needs can be categorized as needs for affiliation, affection, nurture, and cooperation.

The need for affiliation refers to the need for companionship and association with other people. Human beings seek the company of other people, whether it be through the medium of small, informal groups, or through that of larger, more formal organizations.

The need to love and be loved—or to express affection and receive it—also seems to be a universal social need, as does the need to nurture other people. The latter is most vividly expressed in the desire to protect the infant or child, although it is also evident in the desire to protect the weak and helpless of any age.

The need for cooperation may be one of the strongest human needs, at least when com-

---

[2] Murray divided needs into viscerogenic (primary) needs and psychogenic (secondary) needs. In the latter category were listed some twenty-seven needs, including needs for acquisition, conservance, order, retention, construction, superiority, achievement, recognition, exhibition, inviolacy, infavoidance, defendance, counteraction, dominance, deference, similance, autonomy, contrarience, aggression, abasement, blamavoidance, affiliation, rejection, nurturance, play, succurance, cognizance, and exposition. Henry A. Murray, *Explorations in Personality* (New York: Oxford University Press, 1938), pp. 76–83.

[3] A.H. Maslow, *Motivation and Personality*, 2nd ed. (New York: Harper & Brothers, 1970), Chapters 3–7, and Walter C. Langer, *Psychology and Human Living* (New York: D. Appleton-Century Company, 1943), Chapters 3–8. Abraham Maslow, a psychoanalyst, psychologist, and anthropologist, in a 1942 address to a psychoanalytic society, first presented his basic ideas on motivation, which were, in Maslow's words, ". . . an effort to integrate into a single theoretical structure the partial truths I saw in Freud, Adler, Jung, D.M. Levy, Fromm, Hovney and Goldstein." (Maslow, *Motivation and Personality*, 2nd ed., p. xi.) He also acknowledges the writings of Henry Murray, Gordon Allport, Carl Rogers, and others. See A.H. Maslow, *Motivation and Personality* (New York: Harper & Brothers, 1954), p. xi. Walter Langer was a Boston psychoanalyst and psychologist. Alderfer has reformulated the Maslow hierarchy into three basic needs called "existence needs," "relatedness needs," and "growth needs." See C.P. Alderfer, "An Empirical Test of a New Theory of Human Needs," *Organizational Behavior and Human Performance*, 4:142–175 (1969).

bined with the need for affiliation. As Elton Mayo stated: "Man's desire to be continuously associated in work with his fellows is a strong, if not the strongest human characteristic."[4]

ESTEEM NEEDS

People require self-esteem and the esteem of others. Self-esteem (or self-respect) comprises feelings of competence, autonomy, independence, dominance, achievement, acquisition, and retention. These needs may be an outgrowth of the more basic physiological and safety needs.

The need for esteem from others includes the need for recognition and acclamation, attention, appreciation, prestige, and status. These needs obviously overlap with the needs for belonging and affection. Of particular importance to individuals is the esteem of reference groups, that is, the groups of which they consider themselves a part or to which they aspire. As Whiting Williams observed years ago after talking to workers in many industries, "the prime influence on all of us today is our wish to enjoy the feeling of our worth as persons among other persons."[5]

INTEGRATION OR WHOLENESS NEEDS

People have a need to maintain an integrated and consistent picture of themselves and their world. This need gives rise to a desire for knowledge and understanding. The need for integration can also be thought of as a need to avoid inconsistencies within one's personality, the need to resolve conflict, the need to feel fairly and justly treated, and the need to make order out of disorganized or chaotic situations.

The latter need gives rise to the propensity of most people to accept some kind of leadership and organization, without which the resulting chaos becomes intolerable.

THE SELF-ACTUALIZATION, BECOMING, OR GROWTH NEED

Maslow postulates a need for self-actualization, which he describes as ". . . man's desire for self-fulfillment, namely, . . . the tendency for him to become actualized in what he is potentially. This tendency might be phrased as the desire to become more and more what one idiosyncratically is, to become everything that one is capable of becoming."[6]

In a sense, this need is a culmination or a composite of the others. For example, major dimensions of this need are probably drives toward accomplishment, competence, and autonomy. Implicit in the writings of Argyris is the theme that the formalized apects or organizations typically frustrate expression of this need. However, Argyris also observes that not all organizations suppress drives toward self-actualization, and that not all individuals wish psychological success.[7]

THE INTERRELATIONSHIP OF NEEDS

Maslow postulates that the needs listed previously are organized into what he calls ". . . a

[4] Elton Mayo, *The Social Problems of an Industrial Civilization* (Boston: Harvard University, 1945), p. 111.
[5] Whiting Williams, *Mainsprings of Men* (New York: Charles Scribner's Sons, 1925), p. 147.
[6] Maslow, *Motivation and Personality*, 2nd ed., p. 46. In another work, Maslow suggests that the terms *becoming* and *growth* may be more descriptive than *self-actualization*. See A.H. Maslow, *Toward a Psychology of Being* (Princeton, N.J.: D. Van Nostrand Company, 1962), pp. iii–iv, 146. The self-actualization need was considered the most important to managers in a survey of managers in many different countries. See Mason Haire, Edwin E. Ghiselli, and Lyman W. Porter, "Cultural Patterns in the Role of the Manager," *Industrial Relations*, 2:108–117 (February 1963).
[7] Chris Argyris, *Understanding Organizational Behavior* (Homewood, Ill.: The Dorsey Press, 1960), pp. 10–18, and *Integrating the Individual and the Organization* (New York: John Wiley & Sons, Inc., 1964), p. 67.

hierarchy of relative prepotency." That is, once the physiological and security needs of a person are satisfied with sufficient frequency, the "higher" needs, such as esteem and self-actualization, emerge with greater predominance. In the case of self-actualization, Maslow states that "the clear emergence of these needs usually rests upon some prior satisfaction of the physiological, safety, love and esteem needs." Thus, Maslow theorizes that the various needs are interrelated, with the maximum expression of need for accomplishment and growth emerging with the satisfaction of the more basic needs. He acknowledges, however, that there can be reversals in this hierarchy. A particularly notable exception is the martyr who is willing to give up everything in the service of a particular ideal or value.[8]

RESEARCH SUPPORT FOR THE NEED HIERARCHY THEORY

Research has long shown that people tend to interpret the world in terms of their least satisfied needs. Stagner reported two studies in which hungry people perceived a large proportion of ambiguous figures projected onto a screen as food items or instruments, such as knives and forks. Well-fed people reported a smaller percentage of hunger-related items.[9] The hungry people were unconsciously searching for ways to satisfy an unfulfilled need. This gives some support to the notion that, consciously or not, people tend to give their least satisfied needs the highest priority.

However, in a review of the research, Porter, Lawler, and Hackman have concluded that, while there is strong evidence that the activation of higher-order needs depends on the satisfaction of the security and existence needs, there is little evidence that the higher-order

needs act in a hierarchical way. It appears that people may be motivated by several higher-order needs simultaneously. Further, they conclude that, while satisfaction of lower-order needs tends to reduce motivation to seek outcomes that will satisfy those needs, at least temporarily, the self-actualization or growth needs do not act this way. Once activated, self-actualization seems to be an insatiable and growing need, unless, as Porter et al. state it, there is ". . . a threat to the satisfaction of the person's lower-level needs."[10] This argues that managers should pay attention simultaneously to a wide range of human needs.

THE UNIVERSALITY OF NEEDS

Although the previous lists of needs is derived from American culture, it probably applies in large part to all cultures. Certainly the assumptions Leighton has drawn from anthropology, psychology, and psychiatry about people in general would suggest that this list is universally applicable.[11] Furthermore, a study by Haire et al. found that managers in a wide variety of cultures believed that managers had these needs and that they were important.[12] It is probable, however, that the importance attached to the satisfaction of different needs varies from culture to culture.[13]

[8]Maslow, *Motivation and Personality*, 2nd ed., p. 38.
[9]Ross Stagner, *Psychology of Industrial Conflict* (New York: John Wiley & Sons, Inc., 1956), p. 25. See also Langer, *Psychology and Human Living*, pp. 54–55.
[10]Lyman W. Porter, Edward E. Lawler III, and Richard Hackman, *Behavior in Organizations* (New York: McGraw-Hill Book Company, 1975), pp. 43–45. See also John P. Campbell and Robert D. Pritchard, "Motivation Theory in Industrial and Organizational Psychology," in Marvin D. Dunnette, ed., *Handbook of Industrial and Organizational Psychology* (Chicago: Rand McNally College Publishing Company, 1976), pp. 96–100; and Douglas T. Hall and Khalil E. Nougaim, "An Examination of Maslow's Need Hierarchy in an Organizational Setting," *Organizational Behavior and Human Performance*, 3:12–35 (February 1968).
[11]See Alexander H. Leighton, *Human Relations in a Changing World* (New York: E. P. Dutton & Co., 1949), pp. 76–79.
[12]Haire, Ghiselli, and Porter, "Cultural Patterns," pp. 108–117.
[13]See Muzafer Sherif and Carolyn Sherif, *An Outline of Social Psychology*, rev. ed. (New York: Harper & Brothers, 1956), p. 379.

McCLELLAND'S RESEARCH

Although we will rely on Maslow's hierarchy formulation throughout the book, the work of McClelland and others relative to the need for achievement (*n* Ach), the need for affiliation (*n* Aff), and the need for power (*n* Pow) is receiving sufficient attention so that most students of personnel management will want to have some knowledge of these concepts. McClelland and colleagues, focusing on a narrower subset of Murray's list of needs, have made substantial progress in defining and measuring these more specific needs. (Overlap with the Maslow-Langer list is apparent. For example, the *n* Aff is an aspect of the need for belonging, and *n* Ach and *n* Pow are aspects of the esteem and self-actualization needs.)

Using stories told by respondents in taking the Thematic Apperception Test (TAT), McClelland and coinvestigators found that themes pertaining to achievement, affiliation, and power appeared with considerable frequency but that the mix varied from person to person. That is, one person may say a good deal about power, very little about affiliation, and a moderate amount about achievement, while another person may express a different pattern.

Theoretically, these responses are projections of needs that are aroused by certain stimuli. According to Campbell et al., using *n* Ach as an example, "the achievement motive is viewed as a relatively stable disposition . . . to strive for achievement or success. The motive is presumed not to operate until it is aroused by certain situational cues or incentives, which signal the individual that certain behaviors will lead to feelings of achievement. . . ." This emergence of needs, in turn, is presumed to be associated with behavior.[14] For example, based

on our interpretation of the theory, the person experiencing a high need for affiliation and a low need for achievement will tend to seek ways of enhancing association with others, perhaps at the expense of completing tasks. A person with high power, high achievement, and low affiliation needs may be perceived as ambitious, hard driving, and a "loner."

Early research by McClelland on entrepreneurial business managers found that this group displayed more achievement motivation than other identifiable groups and that this motivation was associated with certain behaviors. More specifically, the entrepreneur-manager was found to behave in the following ways:

1. . . . He likes situations in which he takes personal responsibility for finding solutions to problems. . . .

2. Another characteristic . . . is his tendency to set moderate achievement goals and to take "calculated risks. . . ."

3. The man . . . wants concrete feedback as to how well he is doing.[15]

These findings led McClelland and co-researchers to investigate whether *n* Ach and its corresponding behaviors could be increased. They theorized that while motives were associated with typical behavior, both motives and behavior were subject to modification. The following are the results of a pilot program in a U.S. company to test the theory:

The sessions lasted only a week and consisted largely of teaching 16 participants (1) about the achievement motive—what it was and how research had shown it to be important for entrepreneurship,

---

[14] John P. Campbell, Marvin D. Dunnette, Edward Lawler III, and Karl E. Weick, Jr., *Managerial Behavior, Performance, and Effectiveness* (New York: McGraw-Hill Book Company, 1970), p. 351. For research on the relationship between TAT responses and behavior see David C. McClelland, *The Achieving Society* (Princeton, N.J.: D. Van Nostrand Company, 1961). Author Andreski believes labels like *n* Ach are "pseudomathematical decorations" and that some social scientists are motivated by *n* Bam, "the need to bamboozle." Stanislov Andreski, *Social Sciences as Sorcery* (London: Andre Deutsch, 1972), as reviewed in *Time*, September 25, 1972, p. 71.

[15] David C. McClelland, "Business Drive and National Achievement," *Harvard Business Review*, 40:104–105 (July-August 1962).

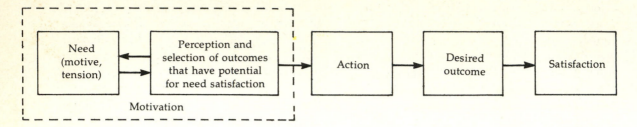

Figure **6-1**   Basic ingredients of motivation

and (2) how to think, talk, act, and perceive the world like a person with a high need for achievement.

The 16 participants were carefully matched with other executives from the company of comparable age, length of service with the company, job type, salary level, and so forth, who had attended one of the regular executive development courses given by the company. We did a careful follow-up study two years later to find out which group of men had done better in the company subsequent to training. Unfortunately we lost some of the original participants in our course through illness or resignation from the company, but the 11 remaining had clearly done better on the average—been promoted faster—than their matched controls.[16]

The results of this pilot project were encouraging enough for the researchers to conduct a ten-day residential program for heads of small businesses in India, with promising results.

MOTIVATION BASED ON NEEDS

Needs are the basic motivators in human behavior. Individuals appear to be compelled by inner urges to find ways to satisfy their needs. As Maslow states it, "Man is a perpetually wanting animal."[17]

Figure 6-1 diagrams the basic ingredients of motivation. The individual has needs (we will consider motives and tensions as synonymous with needs); he or she perceives alternative goals or outcomes which have the potential to satisfy these needs; activity occurs; and if the desired outcome is achieved, satisfaction results. *Motivation*, which we will define as the propensity to act in the direction of a particular outcome or set of outcomes, is a function of both needs and the perceived probability that those needs will be met.[18] Whether the felt need or the perception of some outcome that has potential for need satisfaction arises first is probably a "chicken-or-egg" matter. Needs affect perception, as we have seen earlier, and perceptions can serve to arouse needs.

EXPECTANCY (V-I-E) THEORY

Of considerable interest to contemporary researchers is expectancy theory, which appears simple at first glance but is extremely complex when one digs beneath the surface. This

[16] David C. McClelland, "Achievement Motivation Can Be Developed," *Harvard Business Review*, 43:10 (November-December 1965). See also David C. McClelland and David H. Burnham, "Power is the Great Motivator," *Harvard Business Review*, 54:100–110 (March-April 1976).

[17] A.H. Maslow, "A Theory of Human Motivation," *Psychological Review*, 50:370 (July 1943).

[18] Vroom defines motivation as ". . . the amount of task-related effort exerted by a person. . . ." Victor H. Vroom, *Work and Motivation* (New York: John Wiley & Sons, 1964), p. 193. Atkinson and Feather define motivation as a "disposition to strive for a certain kind of satisfaction." J.W. Atkinson and N.T. Feather, *A Theory of Achievement Motivation* (New York: John Wiley & Sons, 1966), pp. 12–13.

theory is further complicated by different authors ascribing different meanings to the various basic terms as research and conceptualizing has proceeded. (I have arbitrarily selected a few sources for a brief description of the theory, including one of the earliest formulations, that of Vroom.[19])

Expectancy theory includes the concepts of valence, expectancy, and instrumentality. Vroom postulates that ". . . the force on a person to perform an act . . . ," i.e., one's degree of motivation, is a product of "valence" times "expectancy."[20] That is, the motivational force (F) equals expectancy (E) times valence (V), or in symbolic form,

$$F = E \times V$$

Valence is a person's affective response toward a particular outcome, either positive or negative, and the degree of preference or aversion. Valence is usually scored with small positive or negative numbers from zero, e.g., from +3 to −3. For example, a person can have a high positive preference for the outcome of promotion (+3), or a mild aversion to the outcome (−1), or the valence could be zero if the person is indifferent to a promotion. Expectancy, on the other hand, is the ". . . momentary belief concerning the likelihood that a particular act will be followed by a particular outcome."[21] Expectancy is "an action-outcome association."[22] Expectancy is usually scored from zero (complete uncertainty as to the outcome of the behavior) to 1 (complete certainty as to the outcome). Using these numbers, the maximum motivational force relative to a given outcome would be +3.0 and the lowest (highest aversion) would be −3.0. Thus, in a hypothetical illustration, a person may have a high preference for a promotion (V = +3), but see little likelihood of the behavior of working hard resulting in that outcome (E = .1) and the motivational force will be low (F = +.3). In contrast, if changing jobs is perceived as almost totally certain to produce promotion (E = .9), the motivational force will be high to seek a change (F = +2.7).

But motivation is not that simple. Since there are usually several outcomes for a given behavior, valences and expectancies are scored and multiplied together for each outcome and then totaled. In the following fictional situation illustrated by Figure 6–2, a person is trying to decide whether to work very hard or coast along at an average pace. A promotion is very much desired (V = +3) but is not seen as likely in the present situation, even with hard work (E = .1). The possibility of recognition from the boss is mildly desirable (V = +1) and more certain than not (E = .6), but approval of peers (really disapproval) is seen as somewhat undesirable (V = −1) and fairly likely to occur if one works hard (E = .5). On the other hand, there is an incentive payment system, and the higher pay would be quite desirable (V = +2), and is perceived to be a certain outcome of hard work (E = 1.0). Working at a slower pace would result in more peer approval (V = +2) but very little change in the boss's attitude (E = .5). However,

[19] This discussion is largely based on Victor H. Vroom, *Work and Motivation* (New York: John Wiley & Sons, 1964); George Graen, "Instrumentality Theory of Work Motivation," *Journal of Applied Psychology Monograph*, 53:1–25 (April 1969), part 2; Edward E. Lawler III, *Pay and Organizational Effectiveness: A Psychological View* (New York: McGraw-Hill Book Company, 1971), pp. 19–24; Campbell, Dunnette, Lawler, and Weick, *Managerial Behavior*, pp. 344–345; Porter, Lawler, and Hackman, *Behavior in Organizations*, pp. 56–57; Joe Kelly, *Organizational Behaviour*, rev. ed. (Homewood, Ill.: Richard D. Irwin, Inc., 1974), pp. 286–292; and Campbell and Pritchard, "Motivation Theory" in Dunnette, *Handbook of Industrial and Organizational Psychology*, pp. 63–130. The latter includes an overview of both "process" and "content" themes of motivation.

[20] Vroom, *Work and Motivation*, p. 18.

[21] Ibid., p. 17.

[22] Ibid., p. 18.

Figure **6-2** Analysis for predicting motivation in a fictional situation, including the concepts of valence and expectancy

Behavior	Outcomes	Valence (+3 to −3)	Expectancy (.00 to 1.00)	V × E
Working hard	Promotion	+3	.1	+ .3
	Recognition from boss	+1	.6	+ .6
	Approval of peers	−1	.5	− .5
	Higher pay	+2	1.0	2.0
				$F = \Sigma\,(E \times V) = +2.4$
Working at average pace	Promotion	+3	0	0
	Recognition from boss	+1	.5	.5
	Approval of peers	+2	.5	1.0
	Higher pay	+2	.2	.4
				$F = \Sigma\,(E \times V) = +1.9$

while higher pay is to be desired, the expectancy is very low ($E = .2$) without hard work. In this fictional situation, the outcome of higher pay through the incentive system is both attractive and certain through hard work, and produces sufficient motivational force for "working hard" to be the more likely behavior chosen ($F = +2.4$), according to the model, in contrast to coasting ($F = +1.9$).

As implied earlier, different authors define basic terms of the V-I-E model in different ways. For example, in the above illustration, which I believe is consistent with the description of the expectancy model provided by Porter, Lawler, and Hackman,[23] "outcomes" are promotion, recognition, peer approval, and higher pay. In other explanations of the model, a distinction is made between first- and second-level outcomes, with the first-level outcome frequently considered to be level of performance while second-level outcomes would be pay, promotion, etc. (See Figure 6-3.)

The concept of "instrumentality" is also frequently included in these more elaborate models. Instrumentality theory hypothesizes that the attitudes of a person toward some outcome is a function of how that outcome is perceived as instrumental in producing various other outcomes. According to Vroom, instrumentality "is an outcome-outcome association."[24] Instrumentality is frequently scored like the coefficient of correlation, from +1.0 to −1.0. The usual interpretation of instrumentality is the degree to which a first-level outcome (level of performance) is instrumental in obtaining secondary outcomes such as higher pay or promotion. In such a model, expectancy is frequently used as the likelihood of

[23] Porter, Lawler, and Hackman, *Behavior in Organizations*, pp. 56–57.

[24] Vroom, *Work and Motivation*, p. 18.

Figure **6-3**   Analysis for predicting motivation in a fictional situation, adding the concepts of first- and second-level outcomes and instrumentality

Behavior (level of effort)	Expectancy (.00 to 1.00)	First-level outcome (level of performance)	Instrumentality (+1 to −1.0)	Second-level outcome	Valence (+3 to −3)	V × I
Working hard	.90	High performance	+ .1	Promotion	+3	.3
			+ .6	Recognition from boss	+1	.6
			+ .5	Approval of peers	−1	−.5
			+1.0	Higher pay	+2	2.0

$$\Sigma\, V\, I = 2.4$$
$$F = E \times \Sigma\, V\, I = 2.16$$

Behavior (level of effort)	Expectancy (.00 to 1.00)	First-level outcome (level of performance)	Instrumentality (+1 to −1.0)	Second-level outcome	Valence (+3 to −3)	V × I
Working at average pace	.80	Medium performance	.0	Promotion	+3	.0
			+ .5	Recognition from boss	+1	.5
			+ .5	Approval of peers	+2	1.0
			+ .2	Higher pay	+2	.4

$$\Sigma\, V\, I = 1.9$$
$$F = E \times \Sigma\, V\, I = 1.52$$

the level of effort resulting in a certain level of performance.

Figure 6-3 provides an example of a fictional situation using the additional variable of instrumentality and making a distinction between first- and second-level outcomes. In this illustration, level of performance is considered a first-level outcome, and pay, promotion, recognition, and peer approval are considered secondary outcomes. In Figure 6-3 instrumentality is multiplied by valence for each outcome and then totaled, with the overall sum multiplied by the expectancy. This analysis, I believe, is consistent with the description of the model as described by Campbell and Pritchard.[25] The re-

sults of the analysis of the fictional situation in Figure 6-3 are comparable to the results in Figure 6-2, with the difference arising from the addition of a variable, "level of performance." The reader will note that "instrumentality" in Figure 6-3 is essentially synonymous with "expectancy" as used in Figure 6-2, but in both instances Vroom's conceptualizing of expectancy as an "action-outcome association" has been retained.

One implication of expectancy theory, if valid, is that managers need to have a fairly good understanding of the valences employees ascribe to different outcomes, and they need to

[25] Campbell and Pritchard, "Motivation Theory," pp. 75–84. Another interpretation of instrumentality views variables such as salary and promotion as first-level outcomes instrumental in producing secondary outcomes such as food, shelter, or status.

be able to show subordinates how those outcomes might be achieved. For example, if employee Nancy Green is highly interested in promotion (high positive valence), and promotion is seen as being important for satisfying her status and self-actualization needs (instrumentality), her supervisor needs to be able to describe what opportunities might occur given appropriate levels of performance. Another implication is that management needs to examine the certainties with which various behaviors produce different outcomes. If management preaches hard work and sacrifice as the route to high performance, which in turn is supposed to lead to pay increases and promotions, but practice demonstrates to employees that what really counts is length of service and not rocking the boat (low expectancy of hard work having a positive payoff), the motivation of those with higher-income and promotion goals will be seriously impaired.

RESEARCH SUPPORT FOR EXPECTANCY THEORY

The use of expectancy theory in research obviously requires obtaining a considerable amount of data from research subjects including what optional behaviors they are considering, what outcomes they see as resulting from various behaviors, what valences are associated with those outcomes, and their perceptions of the degree of instrumentality one outcome has for another. Using this approach, researchers have typically found positive correlations of approximately .25 when the valence, expectancy, and instrumentality scores have been combined and related to effort as a criterion.[26] That is,

the higher the predicted motivation based on valence, expectancy, and instrumentality scores, the higher the measured effort. Although these correlations are not high, they give sufficient credibility to the theory for extensive research to continue along this avenue.

THE CONSEQUENCES OF FRUSTRATION

A person who is frustrated in attempts to attain some desired outcome will either aim for alternative desired outcomes that hold promise for satisfaction of needs or will exercise some kind of defensive behavior in an attempt to assuage feelings, i.e., to reduce the tension.[27] The term *defense mechanism* is typically used to describe such behavior.[28]

There has been some research on defensive behavior as a consequence of frustration in the organizational setting. For example, in a study of eighty-two employees—nurses, secretaries, mental health aides, and custodial and clerical workers in several organizations including a mental health facility, a local utility company, and national insurance company—Spector found that frustration can have extremely dysfunctional consequences in terms of organizational goals. Such self-reported behaviors as interpersonal arguments or trying to hurt someone, complaining about the boss or organization to outside people, ignoring the boss, considering quitting, purposely damaging or defacing equipment, doing work incorrectly,

---

[26] Campbell and Pritchard, "Motivation Theory," p. 91. For a critique of expectancy theory, including a discussion of the problem of measurement and the theory's essentially hedonistic approach as viewed by the authors, see Edwin A. Locke, "Personnel Attitudes and Motivation," in Mark R. Rosenzweig and Lyman W. Porter, eds., *Annual Review of Psychology,* 26:457–465 (1975). For a review of instrumentality

theories, see T.R. Mitchell and A. Biglan, "Instrumentality Theories: Current Uses in Psychology," *Psychological Bulletin,* 76:432–454 (1971).

[27] Maslow defines frustrations as a "threatening deprivation." See Maslow, *Motivation and Personality,* 2nd ed., p. 106.

[28] Argyris defines a defense mechanism as ". . . any sequence of behavior in response to a threat whose goal is to maintain the present state of the self against threat. . . ." Chris Argyris, "Personality and Organization," in David A. Hampton, Charles E. Summer, and Ross A. Webber, *Organizational Behavior and the Practice of Management* (Glenview, Ill.: Scott, Foresman and Company, 1968), p. 140.

taking undeserved breaks, or using drugs appeared with alarming frequency.[29]

EMPLOYEES' SATISFACTION AND DISSATISFACTION

Defense mechanisms, then, are dissatisfactions acted out in nonproductive and, frequently, highly costly ways. Let us now turn to a more detailed examination of worker satisfaction and dissatisfaction and of some of the implications for management.

FACTORS IN SATISFACTION

A number of studies have been made over the years that have asked workers what job factors are the most important to them in terms of job satisfaction or dissatisfaction. These studies are of particular interest in determining what satisfiers (goals or outcomes) the worker seeks from the organizational environment and what dissatisfactions are likely to result in defensive behavior.

Herzberg and his co-researchers have summarized sixteen of these studies, in which large groups of employees ranked the importance of various factors for job satisfaction. These groups of employees, which were considered comparable by the researchers, represented some eleven thousand employees in many occupations in the United States and the United Kingdom. Averaging the rankings across the sixteen studies, the researchers found the various job factors to be ranked in the following way, from highest to lowest: security; job interest; opportunity for advancement; appreciation from supervisor, company and management; intrinsic aspects of the job (excluding ease);

wages; supervision (including "consideration," "fairness," "encouragement," etc.); social aspects of the job; working conditions (excluding hours); communication; hours; ease; and benefits.[30]

Logic suggests that these factors are probably not mutually exclusive. For example, opportunity for advancement is probably not independent of attitudes about wages, and feelings about wages are not likely to be entirely independent of appreciation from supervision. Job security is obviously basic to ongoing wages as well as to the other factors. (Later I will discuss further the interdependence and/or overlap of such factors.)

Further, instrumentality theory would suggest that pay is much more important than indicated by the review by Herzberg et al. As Lawler has concluded ". . . it would seem that pay should, in most instances, be rated high in importance because of its assumed ability to satisfy a large variety of needs." This was demonstrated in Lawler's review of forty-nine studies, including studies both before and after 1957, that found pay to be ranked about third highest among factors in importance to employees, in contrast to the findings of Herzberg et al.[31]

HERZBERG'S MOTIVATION-HYGIENE THEORY

Based on the survey cited previously and on later research, Frederick Herzberg and colleagues have developed a motivation-hygiene

---

[29] Paul Spector, "Relationships of Organizational Frustration with Reported Behavioral Reactions of Employees," *Journal of Applied Psychology,* 60:635–637 (October 1975).

[30] Frederick Herzberg et al., *Job Attitudes, Review of Research and Opinion* (Pittsburgh: Psychological Service of Pittsburgh, 1957), pp. 43–47. Job security also ranked highest in a study made in India. See Paros Noth Singh and Robert J. Wherry, Sr., "Ranking of Job Factors by Factory Workers in India," *Personnel Psychology,* 16:29–33 (Spring 1963). Job security does not appear as a major factor in the Herzberg et al. study of accountants and engineers, however. This could be explained in terms of the prevailing industrial environment in which rank-and-file employees are more subject to layoff than are professional and managerial employees. The latter groups probably have more job mobility as well.

[31] Lawler, *Pay and Organizational Effectiveness,* pp. 38–42.

theory of worker satisfaction and dissatisfaction. This theory has stimulated a great deal of research as well as controversy and is essentially as follows:

1. The Motivators

   a. Some job factors, when present to a positive degree, increase satisfaction from work and motivation toward superior effort and performance.

   b. When absent, these factors do not lead to dissatisfaction.

   c. These factors reflect a need for personal growth and are directly related to the job.

2. The Hygiene Factors

   a. These factors, to the degree they are absent, increase worker dissatisfaction with their jobs.

   b. When present, these factors serve to prevent job dissatisfaction but do not result in positive satisfaction and motivation.

   c. These factors reflect a need for the avoidance of unpleasantness and are related to the context of the job, that is, its environment.[32]

Herzberg et al. tested this theory in a study of engineers and accountants in several different firms. Respondents were asked to discuss the times "you felt exceptionally good or exceptionally bad about your present job or any other job you have had." Supplemental questions were used to probe various ramifications of the responses. Responses were then coded by factor, by duration of time the attitude persisted, and by other dimensions. Figure 6-4 summarizes the basic results.[33]

The conclusions drawn by Herzberg et al. were that achievement, recognition for achievement, work itself, responsibility, and advancement were key factors in increasing job satisfaction and motivation of engineers and accountants in their sample. These were the things respondents tended to cite as "good" things. Although salary was also reported to be significant in job satisfaction, the researchers typically report this factor as a hygiene factor. Among the hygiene factors, that is, factors the absence of which leads to dissatisfaction but which tend not to contribute to satisfaction and motivation, were company policy and administration, technical supervision, salary, working conditions, and interpersonal relations. These were the things people tend to cite as "bad" things.[34]

Although the notion of hygiene versus motivating factors is a highly useful construct and although the results of the research seem generally plausible, the research reports can be criticized on at least three grounds. First, although the researchers go to considerable lengths to document the interrelationships among the various factors, their summaries frequently do not emphasize these interdependencies. Second, a number of the factors appear to be associated with *both* satisfaction and dissatisfaction; for example, the importance of salary in both satisfaction and dissatisfaction seems to be given less weight than the results of the research warrant. The latter may be partly because the research reports emphasized

---

[32] Frederick Herzberg, Bernard Mausner, and Barbara Snyderman, *The Motivation to Work,* 2nd ed. (New York: John Wiley & Sons, Inc., 1959); and Frederick Herzberg, *Work and the Nature of Man* (Cleveland: The World Publishing Company, 1966).

[33] Herzberg, *Work and the Nature of Man,* pp. 92–95; and Herzberg, Mausner, and Snyderman, *The Motivation to Work,* pp. 20–54.

[34] Herzberg, Mausner, and Snyderman, *The Motivation to Work,* pp. 59–62, 70–74. For studies reaching similar conclusions, see Frank Friedlander and Eugene Walton, "Positive and Negative Motivations toward Work," *Administrative Science Quarterly,* 9:194–207 (September 1964); G. Halpern, "Relative Contributions of Motivator and Hygiene Factors to Overall Job Satisfaction," *Journal of Applied Psychology,* 50:198–200 (June 1966); and P. Weissenberg and L. W. Gruenfeld, "Relationship Between Job Satisfaction and Job Involvement," *Journal of Applied Psychology,* 52:469–473 (December 1968).

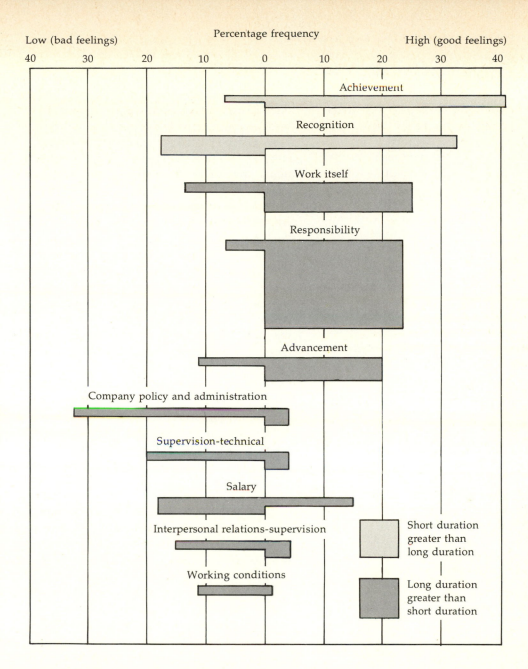

Low (bad feelings)   Percentage frequency   High (good feelings)

40   30   20   10   0   10   20   30   40

Achievement

Recognition

Work itself

Responsibility

Advancement

Company policy and administration

Supervision-technical

Salary

Interpersonal relations-supervision

Working conditions

Short duration greater than long duration

Long duration greater than short duration

Figure 6-4   Comparison of satisfiers and dissatisfiers

From Frederick Herzberg, Bernard Mausner, and Barbara Snyderman, *The Motivation to Work* (New York: John Wiley & Sons, 1959), p. 81. Used with permission. The authors explain this figure as follows: ". . . the distance from the neutral area shows the percentage frequency with which each factor occurred in the high job-attitude sequences and in the low job-attitude sequences. The width of the boxes represents the ratio of long-range to short-range attitude effects; the wider the box, the more frequently this factor led to a long-range job attitude change. The factors of recognition and achievement are shaded . . . to indicate that the width of their boxes portrays a reversal of the long-range ratio. The attitude effects of both of these factors were substantially more short-range."

the factors that produced statistically significant differences between the satisfaction and dissatisfaction sequences, while salary, which appeared with considerable frequency in both sequences, did not produce this result.[35] (See Chapter 19 for further discussion of motivators and hygiene factors, with particular reference to salaries.)

OTHER FACTORS IN SATISFACTION AND DISSATISFACTION

Age appears to be a factor in job satisfaction. A number of early studies indicated that younger workers expressed considerable job satisfaction, that morale went down during the first few years of work, and that it then rose steadily with age. The lowest point seemed to be when workers are in their twenties.[36] A more recent study confirms these findings, with the exception that the sixteen-to-twenty age group was slightly more dissatisfied than workers in their twenties.[37] (See Figure 6-5).

Those twenty and below are in a period of uncertainty regarding job choice and job security, and this may explain their dissatisfactions. A high percentage of workers in their twenties are experiencing the emotional and financial pressures of starting homes and families, and their discontent at work might be caused by these concerns. The higher satisfactions of later years may be related to the fact that people have either reconciled themselves to their occupational choices or moved into more desirable jobs.

Occupational level also seems to be related to job satisfaction. It has long been observed that the higher the level of the job in terms of the organizational hierarchy, the greater the satisfaction. Gilmer, for example, found that professional people had the highest degree of job satisfaction, salaried workers came next, and factory workers were the least satisfied with their jobs.[38] A more recent study found a similar ranking occurring when people were asked, "What type of work would you try to get into if you could start all over again?" Seventy-five to over 90 percent of the people in different professional groups said they would choose a similar occupation, but 43 percent of white-collar workers, 41 percent of skilled auto workers, and only 16 percent of unskilled auto workers would choose similar occupations. Only 24 percent of a cross section of blue-collar workers would choose similar work again.[39] These results can be interpreted in terms of salary, opportunity for self-actualization, status, other correlates of rank, or combinations of these factors.

Similar results are shown in the study summarized in Figure 6-5. In this study, on the average, the professional, technical, and managerial group had the lowest proportion of dissatisfied people, followed by structure work occupations, machine trades, clerical and sales, and service occupations. Here we see the level of dissatisfaction higher among certain white-collar occupations—clerical and sales—than in

[35] For research that did not support the two-factor theory, see Robert J. House and Lawrence A. Widgor, "Herzberg's Dual Factor Theory of Job Satisfaction and Motivation: A Review of the Evidence and a Criticism," *Personnel Psychology*, 20:369–389 (Winter 1967); Hanafi M. Soliman, "Motivation-Hygiene Theory of Job Attitudes," *Journal of Applied Psychology*, 54:452–461 (October 1970). Others have criticized the research on the grounds that (a) a possible defensiveness on the part of respondents may lead them to blame their environments for unhappy occurrences rather than their own lack of achievement, and (b) replication of the research using other methodologies has not confirmed the two-factor theory. See the review by Marvin D. Dunnette in *Administrative Science Quarterly*, 12:170–173 (June 1967); and H.R. Bobbitt, Jr., and Orlando Behling, "Defense Mechanisms as an Alternate Explanation of Herzberg's Motivator-Hygiene Results," *Journal of Applied Psychology*, 56:24–27 (February 1972).
[36] Herzberg et al., *Job Attitudes*, pp. 5, 6.
[37] Neal Q. Herrick, "Who's Unhappy at Work and Why," *Manpower*, U.S. Department of Labor, 4:2–7 (January 1972).
[38] B. Von Haller Gilmer, *Industrial Psychology* (New York: McGraw-Hill Book Company, Inc., 1961), p. 200.
[39] Angus Campbell and Philip E. Converse, eds., *The Human Meaning of Social Change* (New York: Russell Sage Foundation, 1972), p. 182.

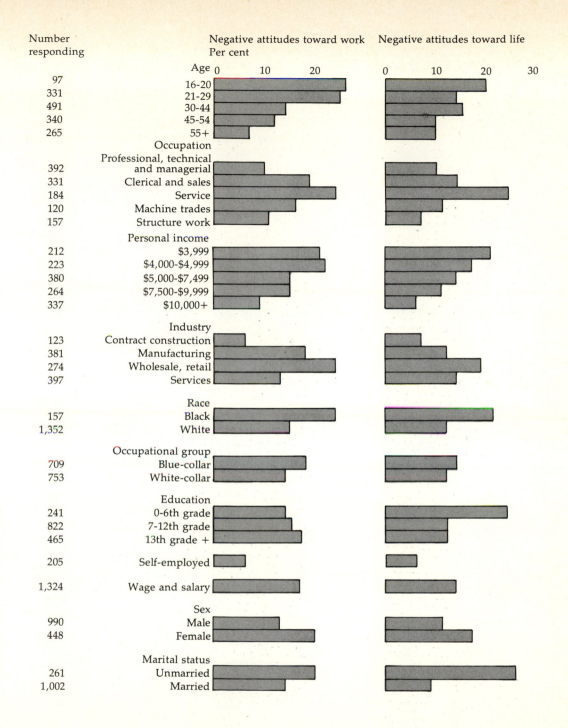

Number responding		Negative attitudes toward work Per cent	Negative attitudes toward life

Figure **6-5** Percentage of workers with negative attitudes toward work and life

Figure **6-6**   Mean job satisfaction by occupational group

Occupational group [1]	Mean job satisfaction [2]
Professional and technical (N= 323)	25
Managers, officials, and proprietors (N= 319)	19
Sales (N= 112)	11
Craftsmen and foremen (N= 270)	8
Service workers, except private household (N= 238)	−11
Clerical (N= 364)	−14
Operatives (N= 379)	−35
Nonfarm laborers (N= 72)	−42

[1] The following categories have been omitted due to small numbers of cases: farmers and farm managers, farm laborers, and private household workers.
[2] Mean values in this table are based on a 28-question measure of overall job satisfaction. A higher numeric score indicates greater job satisfaction. The mean of this measure in 1973 was −2; its standard deviation was 84.

From U.S. Department of Labor, "Job Satisfaction: Is There a Trend?" *Manpower Research Monograph*, No. 30, 1974, p. 10.

skilled blue-collar occupations such as machine trades and construction work. When sales people are separated from the clerical category, however, we see that job satisfaction in the selling occupations is much higher than in the clerical occupations (see Figure 6-6).

It should be noted that differentials in satisfaction occur within the managerial group as well. In a study of nearly two thousand managers, Porter found lower and middle managers significantly more dissatisfied than top executives with respect to the satisfaction of their needs for "esteem," "autonomy," and "self-actualization." Deficiencies in need fulfillment increased progressively from the top to the bot-

tom of the managerial hierarchy.[40] A study by Edel produced comparable results.[41]

There is some evidence to show that the higher the general personality adjustment, the higher the job satisfaction, and vice versa, although it is difficult to tell from the research summaries to what extent the degree of adjustment or maladjustment is a function of the job.[42] No doubt general emotional and social adjustment does affect job satisfaction, but probably the relationship is circular. That is, the poorly adjusted worker may not receive much reward from the job environment in terms of interpersonal relationships, and in turn, this lack of reward serves to reinforce the maladjustment.

Race and sex are also factors in job satisfaction. In a nationwide sample of 1,500 workers (see Figure 6-5) black workers under age thirty were "far and away the most dissatisfied with their jobs." The third most dissatisfied group was women age twenty-nine or under. (The second most dissatisfied group was workers age twenty-nine or under who had some college education.) In general, blacks were found to be more dissatisfied with their jobs than were whites, and females were more dissatisfied than males. The likely explanation for these data is that blacks and females have less job and pay opportunity than white males.

EXTREME DISSATISFACTION NOT GENERAL

In general, people do not dislike work per se. In the study summarized in Figure 6-5, 13 percent of white-collar workers and 17 percent of blue-collar workers expressed negative attitudes to-

[40] Lyman W. Porter, "Job Attitudes in Management: I. Perceived Deficiencies in Need Fulfillment as a Function of Job Level," *Journal of Applied Psychology*, 46:375–384 (December 1962).
[41] Eugene C. Edel, "A Study in Managerial Motivation," *Personnel Administration*, 29:31–38 (November-December 1966).
[42] See Herzberg et al., *Job Attitudes*, pp. 17–20.

ward their jobs.[43] Thus, a large majority were not dissatisfied.

Further confirming the conclusion that extreme dissatisfaction is not general is a survey of 1,114 persons in which it was found that more than two-thirds (69 percent) would continue working at their present or a different job even if they did not need the money. Fifty-nine percent of the women respondents would continue, and 74 percent of the men would continue in employment. Examination of the data by age groupings, however, indicates that as people come closer to retirement age their willingness to relinquish employment for a guaranteed income increases.[44]

These data are hardly grounds for complacency, however. After comparing 1969–1970 data with 1972–1973 data on various indices evaluating working conditions in America, Quinn and Shepard concluded that it was ". . . comforting to think that at least matters are not getting any worse, but there remains the question of why they are not getting any better . . . knowledge that the sky is not really falling should not breed complacency. More sobering is the question of why the sky is not any higher than it used to be."[45]

THE RELATIONSHIP BETWEEN SATISFACTION AND PERFORMANCE

Thus far I have discussed how motivation is based on needs, some of the consequences of

unfilled needs, the kind and extent of employee satisfactions and dissatisfactions that occur in contemporary organizations, and a little about Herzberg's motivation-hygiene theory. I now wish to focus more directly on this question: What is the relationship between satisfaction and productivity? Certainly the removal of serious dissatisfactions is a worthy organizational and social goal, and an important objective in personnel management. But what about the relationship of satisfaction to other organizational goals such as productivity or efficiency? The answer to this is complex.

RESEARCH FINDINGS

Theory and research suggest that focusing solely on satisfying workers will not result in high productivity. Summarizing a decade or more of research by the Survey Research Center at the University of Michigan, Kahn states unequivocally ". . . that the two do not necessarily go together." He states further ". . . employees in highly productive work groups were no more likely than employees in the low-producing groups to be satisfied with their jobs. . . ."[46]

An exhaustive, critical study by Herzberg et al. reached a somewhat similar conclusion. Out of twenty-six studies that the author found to focus on the question of the relationships between productivity and job attitudes, fourteen showed that workers with positive job attitudes had higher productivity than those with negative attitudes. In nine studies productivity and job attitudes were not related, and in three studies workers with positive job attitudes showed poorer records of production than those

[43] Herrick, *Who's Unhappy at Work and Why*, pp. 3–4.
[44] Angus Campbell, Philip E. Converse, and Willard L. Rodgers, *The Quality of American Life* (New York: Russell Sage Foundation, 1976), pp. 291–292.
[45] Robert P. Quinn and Linda J. Shepard, *The 1972–73 Quality of Employment Survey* (Ann Arbor, Mich.: Survey Research Center, Institute for Social Research, The University of Michigan, 1974), pp. 260–262. Somewhat more pessimistic conclusions are drawn by the study by the Department of Health, Education, and Welfare, *Work in America* (Cambridge, Mass.: M.I.T. Press, 1973).

[46] Robert L. Kahn, "Productivity and Job Satisfaction," *Personnel Psychology*, 13:275, 277 (Autumn 1960). See also William F. Dowling, "Conversation with George C. Homans," *Organizational Dynamics*, 4:40 (Autumn 1975).

with negative attitudes.[47] Although Herzberg and his colleagues point out the low correlations obtained in the studies examining the relationship between productivity and positive attitudes, they conclude that ". . . there are enough data to justify attention to attitudes as a factor in improving the worker's output."[48]

Their later research tended partially to confirm this. In the study cited earlier, when workers were asked to talk about the times they felt unusually good or bad about their jobs, in more than 60 percent of the descriptions, respondents stated that their job performance moved in the direction of the attitude expressed. That is, if it was a good incident they were describing, they also reported that their performance was enhanced; if it was a bad one, performance was adversely affected.[49]

Turnover and absenteeism appear to be associated with job dissatisfaction. In a review of research studies, Porter and Steers concluded that there was ". . . very strong evidence that overall job satisfaction represents an important force in the individual's participation decision." While there was strong evidence that dissatisfaction was associated with turnover, the authors concluded that there was at least "preliminary evidence" that dissatisfaction was also a significant factor in absenteeism.[50] Thus, there are clear economic reasons for management to be concerned with job satisfaction. Although not all turnover or absenteeism can or should be prevented, it is obvious that at some level both can be extremely costly to an organization.

SITUATIONS OF INVERSE RELATIONSHIP

There can be inverse relationships between productivity and satisfaction. The reaction of most people forced to work under threat of dire consequences is readily imagined. They might produce, but under such circumstances they would certainly not be pleased or well satisfied with their productivity. For a short period of time, dissatisfaction might well be associated with higher productivity.

Then, too, logic suggests that a high degree of job satisfaction does not necessarily result in high productivity. It is possible to imagine an absurd situation in which the employer goes so far in furnishing pleasures and comforts for the workers that there is practically no productivity. Under such an arrangement the workers might very well express a great deal of satisfaction with their jobs, particularly if it were possible for them to be creative and constructive off the job or to use the job for furthering certain private objectives. A benevolent and nondemanding job environment might well provide opportunities for employees to run their own small businesses at the expense of the employer. Thus, it is possible for satisfactions to be obtained through the attainment of personal goals that may not necessarily coincide with those of the organization.[51]

---

[47] Herzberg et al., *Job Attitudes,* p. 99.
[48] Ibid., 103.
[49] Herzberg, Mausner, and Snyderman, *The Motivation to Work,* pp. 84–88.
[50] Lyman W. Porter and Richard M. Steers, "Organizational, Work, and Personal Factors in Employee Turnover and Absenteeism," *Psychological Bulletin,* 80:151–176 (August 1973).

[51] The following note appeared on the bulletin board of the Cleveland Auto Dealers, 1954:

"Due to increased competition and a keen desire to remain in business, we find it necessary to institute a new policy— effective immediately.

"We are asking that somewhere between starting and quitting time, and without infringing too much on the time usually devoted to Lunch Periods, Coffee Breaks, Rest Periods, Story Telling, Ticket Selling, Vacation Planning and the Re-Hashing of Yesterday's T.V. Programs, each employee endeavor to find some time that can be set aside and known as the 'Work Break.'

"To some this may seem a radical innovation, but we honestly believe the idea has great possibilities. It can conceivably be an aid to steady employment, and it might also be a means of assuring regular pay checks.

"While the adoption of the Work Break plan is not compul-

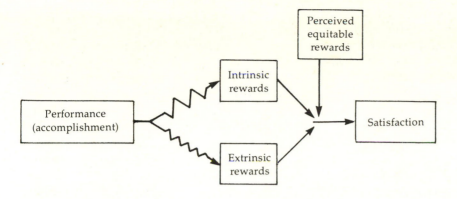

Figure 6-7 The performance-reward-satisfaction model

From Edward E. Lawler III, and Lyman W. Porter, "The Effect of Performance on Job Satisfaction," *Industrial Relations*, 7:23 (October 1967). Used with permission.

SATISFACTION NOT A CAUSAL FACTOR

Thus, it would appear to be a fallacy to focus on satisfaction as a causal factor in performance. As Lawler and Porter see it, the relationship may be the reverse: The level of performance may be a causal factor in job satisfaction, with intrinsic and extrinsic rewards as reinforcing variables. *Intrinsic rewards* are such rewards as "the feeling of having accomplished something worthwhile." *Extrinsic rewards* are pay, promotion, status, and so forth. As shown in Figure 6-7, performance may lead to rewards that in turn produce satisfaction. Perception of equity is also shown as a relevant variable, since satisfaction may to a certain extent be a function of level of rewards in relationship to the rewards given others. (The chapter on Organizational Justice will treat the subject of equity in some detail.) The wavy lines between performance and rewards suggest that the relationship is typically imperfect.[52]

NEED-PATH-GOAL HYPOTHESIS

Georgopoulos et al. state the relationship between productivity and satisfaction in this way: ". . . motivation depends upon (a) the particular needs of the individual as reflected in the goals toward which he is moving, and (b) his perception regarding the relative usefulness of productivity behavior as an instrument, or a path to the attainment of these goals."[53] Thus, if productivity is perceived as a pathway to achieving need-satisfying goals, high productivity is likely to be the consequence, an interpretation that also takes into account the situation in which the worker's goal may be the reduction of tension from fear. If high productivity is not so perceived, or is perceived as hindering the achievement of other need-satisfying goals, such as group membership or approval, the worker is not likely to be a high producer.

In most situations, the employee strives toward attaining a complex mixture of goals, all of

---

sory, it is hoped that each employee will find enough time to give the plan a fair trial. . . ."
[52] Edward E. Lawler III, and Lyman W. Porter, "The Effect of Performance on Job Satisfaction," *Industrial Relations*, 7:20–28 (October 1967).

[53] See Basil S. Georgopoulos, Gerald M. Mahoney, and Nyle W. Jones, Jr., "A Path-Goal Approach to Productivity," *Journal of Applied Psychology*, 41:345–346 (December 1957).

which may not be entirely compatible, in order to reach some kind of satisfactory equilibrium. Thus, the employee may work toward the enterprise's goals only up to the point at which such striving begins to interfere with other important goals.

LAW OF EFFECT AND OPERANT CONDITIONING

The need-path-goal concept and the concepts of valence, expectancy, and instrumentality are consistent with a principle with which psychologists have long been acquainted, the *Law of Effect*.[54] The essence of the Law of Effect is that behavior that results in the satisfaction of needs tends to be repeated, while behavior that does not result in need satisfaction or that results in the withdrawal of satisfactions—punishment for example—tends not to be repeated. Thus, if management provides adequate rewards for productivity, such activity will be reinforced and probably repeated. The more immediate the reward, the greater the reinforcement. On the other hand, if management does not provide adequate rewards for productive behavior, or if the rewards are too remote, people will learn to devote more effort to attaining goals that provide more satisfaction. In short, performance is to a great extent a function of what behavior gets rewarded.

However, to digress with a philosophical note, while it is clear to me that the reinforcement of desired behavior is necessary for effective organized effort, and that it universally occurs, to me it would not seem wise to embrace operant conditioning as a complete explanation for behavior in organizations nor as a unilateral management tool—nor any single theory of motivation, for that matter. Major issues to me are whether reinforcement patterns (or any strategies of motivation) are open and above board,

whether they can be modified by organizational participants and whether dissent is encouraged, and whether inner states of feelings, perceptions and choice have relevance. I believe that people can, people do, and people will make choices. The latter conditions would seem to be denied by some operant conditioning adherents, among whom B.F. Skinner is the best known. (For further discussion of operant conditioning in the context of incentive systems, see Chapter 21.)[55]

GROUP ATTITUDES AND PRODUCTIVITY

So far we have emphasized motivation, performance, and satisfaction as these relate to individuals. What is the impact of the group? Research suggests that the peer work group is a powerful factor on all three dimensions.

A number of studies have demonstrated that groups of workers, in concert, can defend themselves against what the group considers unreasonable or unfair performance standards. For example, the Hawthorne experiments of the late 1920s and early 1930s found that workers in the bank wiring observation room had a standard for output considerably below that set officially by management and that this norm was enforced by pressure from the group.[56] Another example of restriction in output comes from a study in the English coal mines, where it was found that members of a work group, newly assigned to an exceptionally dirty and undesira-

---

[54] E.L. Thorndike, *Animal Intelligence* (New York: Macmillan and Company, 1911).

[55] For a general discussion of operant conditioning, see Walter R. Nord, "Beyond the Teaching Machine," in Walter R. Nord, ed., *Concepts and Controversy in Organizational Behavior*, 2nd ed. (Pacific Palisades, Calif.: Goodyear Publishing Company, 1976), pp. 151–174. For the classic debate on some of these issues surrounding operant conditioning, see Carl R. Rogers and B.F. Skinner, "Some Issues Concerning the Control of Human Behavior: A Symposium," *Science*, 124:1057–1066 (November 1956).

[56] See F.J. Roethlisberger and William J. Dickson, *Management and the Worker* (Cambridge, Mass.: Harvard University Press, 1939).

ble job, slowed down the entire mine operation by restricting their output.[57]

In another study, Patchen found work groups to have a great deal of control over productivity. In general, the higher the standards of performance established informally by work groups, the higher the production of those groups, the less the absenteeism and tardiness, and the less the tendency to leave the job early.[58]

A study by Seashore indicated that the members of a very cohesive group would nearly conform to the standards set by the group whether the standards were high or low, but the groups that lacked cohesiveness tended to have considerable variation in productivity among members. A high degree of cohesiveness seemed to lead to high productivity when the attitude of the group toward the company was favorable. If there were good relationships between management, union, and the employee, the cohesive group would set high standards of performance. If not, a cohesive group tended to have a much lower than average level of productivity.[59]

It also appears that some defensive behavior affecting productivity is directed against loss of need satisfaction from within the group, in contrast to defensive behavior aimed at management. A study of a manufacturing firm by Zaleznik and co-researchers documented this phenomenon. The department they were studying was found to consist of a number of friendship groups that the researchers categorized as "regulars," "deviants," and "isolates." The regulars shared certain values, such as mutual generosity, helpfulness, loyalty to the group, and friendliness and tended to hold production to the minimum expected by manage-

ment. The informal leaders of these groups were more concerned with maintaining these values and the group's social life than they were in attaining organizational goals. It was the regulars who expressed the greatest degree of job satisfaction.

The small groups that did not completely accept the values of the regulars but emphasized saving, individual resourcefulness, personal advancement, and seriousness tended to be the highest producers. These groups were called "deviants" by the researchers. The deviants showed signs of resenting their lack of membership in the regular groups, and their high productivity was interpreted by the researchers as partly a means of getting even with the regulars. Isolates, i.e., workers who belonged to neither regular nor deviant groups, tended to be low producers. Both the deviants and the isolates tended to express less job satisfaction than the regulars.[60]

Thus, research suggests that the degree of job satisfaction and productive efficiency are to some extent functions of both internal group behavior and managerial practice. The study by Zaleznik et al. further suggests that productive efficiency and worker satisfaction do not necessarily exist simultaneously.

IMPORTANCE OF TECHNOLOGY IN PRODUCTIVITY

Another major variable in productivity should be emphasized—the technical know-how of the people in the organization and the technology utilized. A survey of the research by Argyle et al. emphasizes this fact: "It may be concluded that differences produced by wage incentives, method study, and the use of automatic equipment are far greater than those caused by social

[57] Herzberg, et al., *Job Attitudes*, p. 124.
[58] Martin Patchen, "Supervisory Methods and Group Performance Norms," *Administrative Science Quarterly*, 7:275–294 (December 1962).
[59] Kahn, "Productivity and Job Satisfaction," 13:285; and Herzberg et al., *Job Attitudes*, p. 139.

[60] A. Zaleznik, C.R. Christensen, F.J. Roethlisberger, *The Motivation, Productivity, and Satisfaction of Workers* (Boston: Harvard University, Graduate School of Business Administration, 1958).

factors."[61] These conclusions were drawn from the observation that differences in group productivity ranging from 7 to 15 percent were related to changes in supervisory practice, while differences in group productivity of 20 to 200 percent were associated with wage incentive systems and improved methods and equipment.[62]

It should be recognized, however, that the higher gains produced by incentive systems and improved methods and equipment did not necessarily exclude group or supervision factors. Without an analysis of the extent of change in group or supervision variables in any given technological change situation, or analysis of the extent of such change between various studies of the results of technological change, one cannot be certain as to what part these variables may have played in productivity gains. Furthermore, many high gains are obviously a function of the extent to which an organization has fallen behind in its technology. It may be that supervisory practices tend to move forward at a relatively uniform rate, while there is a much higher variability in adopting technological innovations between organizations. But even the cautious estimate of a 7 to 15 percent gain in productivity due to improved supervisory practices is of great practical importance to managers and suggests the imperative need for managerial attention to the proper utilization of both people and technology and to their proper integration.

WORKERS' SATISFACTION—A WORTHWHILE OBJECTIVE?

Both research and logic suggest that focusing on satisfying workers' needs outside of the context of the goals of the enterprise might result in more satisfied employees but would not necessarily motivate employees beyond a minimum degree in the direction of the enterprise's goals. According to the Law of Effect, if the rewards people receive are not related to constructive activity, or if people are inadequately rewarded for constructive performance, minimum performance will be reinforced, and people will tend to seek additional need satisfaction in extraneous ways.

On the other hand, research and logic also suggest that considerable attention to human needs in the work situation is imperative for high levels of motivation and for minimizing dysfunctional behaviors, such as excessive turnover, absenteeism, apathy, work stoppages, and other defense mechanisms. Furthermore, managers in our culture are increasingly committed to the objective of providing as much satisfaction and human development in the work situation as is consistent with the goals of the enterprise. Many aspects of employees' welfare, of course, are regulated by public policy and are imposed on organizations.

Then, too, practice and research are beginning to demonstrate ways of increasing human satisfaction *within the context of productive work*. Even more optimistically, it is beginning to appear that the congruency between realization of individual needs and attainment of the enterprise's goals can be enhanced in such a way as to maximize the attainment of the organization's goals over the long pull. In my opinion, human satisfactions and organizational goals can be made highly congruent, and it is in management's own interests to make them so.

SUMMARY

An examination of theory and research on motivation, satisfaction, and productivity in organizations suggests that the following conclusions, although tentative, are warranted:

[61] Michael Argyle, Godfrey Gardner, and Frank Cioffi, "Supervising Methods Related to Productivity, Absenteeism, and Labor Turnover," *Human Relations*, 11:24 (1958).
[62] Ibid., pp. 23–40.

1. People differ along many dimensions, including those of mental and motor ability, interests, level of aspiration, personality, energy, training, and experience. Ability is clearly a factor in performance.

2. Needs for self-actualization and personal growth are probably latent in most people, but substantial expression of such needs depends upon some reasonable level of satisfaction with respect to physiological requirements and security needs.

3. Individual and group defensive behavior, including turnover and absenteeism, tends to occur when needs are unfulfilled.

4. Motivation depends upon worker perceptions of the likelihood of needs being satisfied. In more complex terms, motivation is a function of worker perceptions of the valences and expectancies of various outcomes, including the instrumentality of these outcomes in producing desired secondary outcomes.

5. A wide range of interrelated extrinsic and intrinsic job factors contribute to differing states of job satisfaction and motivation. These variables are interrelated, and their degree of presence or absence is "added" together by individuals in some subjective and complex way.

6. A number of extrinsic job factors (e.g., working conditions and job security) probably contribute more to job dissatisfaction if absent than to job satisfaction and motivation if present beyond some optimal level.

7. A number of intrinsic job factors (e.g., responsibility and challenging, interesting work), when present, are probably major contributors to job satisfaction. When intrinsic factors are absent, dissatisfaction tends to focus on extrinsic factors.

8. Salary appears to be both a motivator and a dissatisfier. When financial compensation is consistent with accomplishment, recognition,

advancement, and the nature of the job, it acts interdependently with these factors as motivator and satisfier. Compensation probably also acts as a partial inducement toward undertaking more demanding tasks and risks. When salary is inconsistent with the above factors, it serves as a dissatisfier to high performers.

9. Age, occupational level, general personality adjustment, race and sex tend to be factors in job satisfaction. The direction and extent of job satisfaction or dissatisfaction associated with such variables warrants our concern.

10. Dissatisfaction with work per se is not general. However, an inference can be drawn from the research that many people wish more challenging work, at least to the extent that such work is associated with other desirable outcomes such as higher pay.

11. Satisfaction is not the central causal factor in productivity; satisfaction is an *outcome* associated with performance and rewards. However, perception of *potential* satisfaction resulting from job performance is important in motivation.

12. Productivity and satisfaction are not necessarily correlated. Consistent with the Law of Effect, if productivity is perceived as a means of achieving need-satisfying goals, high productivity will probably result.

13. Both technology and human factors are major, interdependent factors in productivity and organizational effectiveness.

Finally, in addition to selecting, utilizing, and developing the most qualified people and the most appropriate technology, management's challenge is twofold: (1) to create an organizational environment in which nonproductive and costly defensive behavior is minimized, and (2) to create an organization in which people have an opportunity to give expression to their higher needs through successful accomplishment.

The creation of these conditions requires a re-examination of many of our basic assumptions about people and the management of people. Some of our traditional assumptions and some newer, emerging assumptions will be examined under the topics of leadership and organizational climate in the next chapter, and under the topics of organizational justice and job design in the chapters that follow.

REVIEW AND DISCUSSION QUESTIONS

1. What are the basic ideas of Maslow's theory of a hierarchy of needs?

2. What behaviors did McClelland find as characteristic of entrepreneurial business managers?

3. In motivation theory, what does *valence* mean? *Expectancy? Instrumentality?*

4. Where has pay tended to rank in studies of how workers rank various job factors? How would you explain this?

5. According to Herzberg, what job factors are motivators and what ones are hygiene factors? What have been some of the criticisms of Herzberg's research?

6. In examining Herrick's study of job satisfaction, what combination of age, sex, occupation, race, and other conditions would seem to be associated with the highest degree of job dissatisfaction? With job satisfaction?

7. Discuss the relationship between satisfaction and (a) productivity, and (b) performance.

8. Discuss the relative merits of trying to improve organizational performance via the "people" route versus the technological route.

9. How widespread is dissatisfaction with work? What data can you cite to defend your answer?

10. In jobs that you have held, what aspects have been the most satisfying to you? The most dissatisfying?

SUPPLEMENTAL REFERENCES

Alderfer, C.P., *Existence, Relatedness, and Growth: Human Needs in Organizational Settings* (New York: The Free Press, 1972).

Alexander, Franz, and Helen Ross, *Dynamic Psychiatry* (Chicago: University of Chicago Press, 1952), Chapter 1.

Argyris, Chris, *Integrating the Individual and the Organization* (New York: John Wiley & Sons, Inc., 1964).

———, *Understanding Organizational Behavior* (Homewood, Ill.: The Dorsey Press, 1960).

Atkinson, John W., *An Introduction to Motivation* (Princeton, N.J.: D. Van Nostrand Company, 1964).

Berger, Chris J., "Reliability and Validity of Expectancy Theory Constructs," in Robert L. Taylor, Michael J. O'Connell, Robert A. Zawacki, and D.D. Warrick, eds., *Academy of Management Proceedings,* Proceedings of the 36th Annual Meeting of the Academy of Management, Kansas City, Missouri, August 11–14, 1976, pp. 74–78.

Broedling, Laurie A., "Relationship of Internal-External Control to Work Motivation and Performance in an Expectancy Model," *Journal of Applied Psychology*, 60:65–70 (February 1975).

Cooley, Charles H., *Social Organization* (New York: Charles Scribner's Sons, 1909).

Davis, Keith, "A Law of Diminishing Returns in Organizational Behavior?" *Personnel Journal*, 54:616–619 (December 1975).

Dubin, Robert, R. Alan Hedley, and Thomas C. Taveggia, "Attachment to Work," in Robert Dubin, ed., *Handbook of Work, Organization, and Society* (Chicago: Rand McNally College Publishing Company, 1976), pp. 281–341.

Dunnette, Marvin D., *Personnel Selection and Placement* (Belmont, Calif.: Wadsworth Publishing Company, 1966).

Dyer, Lee, and Donald F. Parker, "Classifying Outcomes in Work Motivation Research: An

Examination of the Intrinsic-Extrinsic Dichotomy," *Journal of Applied Psychology*, 60:455–458 (August 1975).

Freud, Sigmund, "Psychopathology of Everyday Life," in A.A. Brill, *The Basic Writings of Sigmund Freud* (New York: The Modern Library, 1938), pp. 35–178.

Friedlander, Frank, "Motivations to Work and Organizational Performance," *Journal of Applied Psychology*, 50:143–152 (April 1966).

Gomberg, William, "Job Satisfaction: Sorting Out the Nonsense," *AFL/CIO American Federationist*, June 1973, pp. 14–19.

Goodwin, Leonard, *Do The Poor Want to Work?* (Washington, D.C.: The Brookings Institution, 1972).

Homans, George C., *The Human Group* (New York: Harcourt Brace & Co., 1950), p. 1.

Hunt, John W., and Peter N. Saul, "The Relationship of Age, Tenure, and Job Satisfaction: Males and Females," *Academy of Management Journal*, 18:690–702 (December 1975).

Levinson, Harry, "What Work Means to a Man," *Think*, 30:8–11 (January–February, 1964).

Lewin, Kurt, *Field Theory in Social Science* (New York: Harper & Brothers, 1951).

Locke, Edwin A., "The Nature and Causes of Job Satisfaction," in Marvin D. Dunnette, ed., *Handbook of Industrial and Organizational Psychology* (Chicago: Rand McNally College Publishing Company, 1976), pp. 1297–1349.

Maier, Norman R.F., *Psychology in Industrial Organizations*, 4th ed. (Boston: Houghton Mifflin Company, 1973).

Maslow, A.H., "Preface to Motivation Theory," in *Psychosomatic Medicine: Experimental and Clinical Studies*, (Baltimore: The Williams and Wilkins Co., 1947), 5. The Committee on Problems of Neurotic Behavior, Division of Anthropology and Psychology, National Research Council.

Matsui, Tamao, and Takeshi Osawa, "Relations between Supervisory Motivation and the Consideration and Structure Aspects of Supervisory Behavior," *Journal of Applied Psychology*, 60:451–454 (August 1975).

Memiroff, Paul M., and David L. Ford, Jr., "A Contingency Approach to Task Effectiveness and Human Fulfillment in Organizations: An Empirical Test of a Conceptual Model," *Krannert Graduate School of Industrial Administration Paper Series*, Purdue University, Paper No. 512, May 1975.

Milutinovich, Jugoslav S., and Angelos A. Tsaklanganos, "The Impact of Perceived Community Prosperity on Job Satisfaction of Black and White Workers," *Academy of Management Journal*, 19:49–65 (March 1976).

Monhardt, Philip J., "Job Orientation of Male and Female College Graduates in Business," *Personnel Psychology*, 25:361–368 (Summer 1972).

Murphy, Gardner, *Personality: A Biosocial Approach to Origins and Structure* (New York: Harper & Brothers, 1947).

Patchen, Martin, *Participation, Achievement, and Involvement on the Job* (Englewood Cliffs, N.J.: Prentice-Hall, Inc., 1970).

Petrock, Frank, and Victor Gamboa, "Expectancy Theory and Operant Conditioning: A Conceptual Comparison," in Walter R. Nord, ed., *Concepts and Controversy in Organizational Behavior*, 2d ed. (Pacific Palisades, Calif.: Goodyear Publishing Company, 1972), pp. 175–187.

Porter, Lyman W., and Edward E. Lawler, III, "What Job Attitudes Tell about Motivation," *Harvard Business Review*, 46:118–126 (January–February 1968).

Reif, William E., "Intrinsic versus Extrinsic Rewards: Resolving the Controversy," *Human Resource Management*, 14:2–10 (Summer 1975).

Reinharth, Leon, and Mahmoud A. Wahba, "Expectancy Theory As a Predictor of Work Motivation, Effort Expenditure, and Job Performance," *Academy of Management Journal*, 18:520–537 (September 1975).

Schmidt, F.L., "Implications of a Measurement Problem for Expectancy Theory Research," *Organizational Behavior and Human Performance,* 10:243–251 (1973).

Schwab, Donald P., and Larry L. Cummings, "Theories of Performance and Satisfaction: A Review," *Industrial Relations,* 9:408–430 (October 1970).

Sheppard, Harold L., and Neal Q. Herrick, *Where Have All the Robots Gone? Worker Dissatisfaction in the '70's* (New York: The Free Press, 1972).

Sims, Henry P., Jr., "Intrinsic and Extrinsic Expectancies as Causes of Satisfaction and Performance," in Robert L. Taylor, Michael J. O'Connell, Robert A. Zawacki, and D.D. Warrick, eds., *Academy of Management Proceedings,* Proceedings of the 36th Annual Meeting of The Academy of Management, Kansas City, Missouri, August 11–14, 1976, pp. 118–121.

Strauss, George, "Workers: Attitudes and Adjustments," in Jerome M. Rosow, ed., *The Worker and the Job* (Englewood Cliffs, N.J.: Prentice-Hall, Inc., 1974), pp. 73–98.

Sullivan, Harry Stack, *The Interpersonal Theory of Psychiatry* (New York: W.W. Norton and Company, Inc., 1953).

U.S. Department of Labor, *Job Satisfaction: Is There a Trend?* (Washington, D.C.: U.S. Department of Labor, Manpower Research Monograph No. 30, 1974).

Wanous, John P., "A Causal-Correlational Analysis of the Job Satisfaction and Performance Relationship," *Journal of Applied Psychology,* 59:139–144 (April 1974).

White, Robert W., "Motivation Reconsidered: The Concept of Competence," *Psychological Review,* 66:297–333, No. 5 (1959).

Wild, Ray, "Job Needs, Job Satisfaction, and Job Behavior of Women Manual Workers," *Journal of Applied Psychology,* 54:157–162 (April 1970).

Wolf, Martin G., "Need Gratification Theory: A Theoretical Reformulation of Job Satisfaction/Dissatisfaction and Job Motivation," *Journal of Applied Psychology,* 54:87–94 (February 1970).

CHAPTER 7
LEADERSHIP PATTERNS AND ORGANIZATIONAL CLIMATE

After summarizing the history of theory and research on leadership and hundreds of studies, Stogdill provides a definition of leadership to which I will subscribe in this chapter. This definition is applicable both to initially unstructured groups and to established groups.

Leadership is defined as the initiative and maintenance of structure in expectation and interaction . . . The leader plays an active part in development and maintenance of role structure and goal direction, necessary for effective group performance.[1]

It is implicit that effective group performance is defined in the context of effective organizational functioning and that effective leadership is causally linked to optimal organizational effectiveness. The reader will note, however,

that this definition does not say that the leader provides all the "initiative and maintenance of structure in expectation and interaction." As Kerr says, "The research literature does *not* require that guidance and good feelings be provided by the hierarchical superior; it is only necessary that they somehow be provided."[2]

Although I consider leadership behavior to be a major causal force in organizational effectiveness, this chapter will take the point of view that optimum effectiveness in leadership can take place only in an appropriate total organizational climate. Effective leadership is a complex matter involving the traits and behavior of the leader, the characteristics and behavior of individual subordinates and the subordinate group,

[1] Ralph M. Stogdill, *Handbook of Leadership* (New York: The Free Press, 1974), p. 411.

[2] Steven Kerr, "Substitutes for Leadership," *Working Paper Series*, College of Administrative Science, The Ohio State University, April 1976, p. 18.

the traits and behavior of the leader's superior, the goals of the enterprise, and the intricate configuration of organizational processes and systems pertaining to such matters as job design and requirements, staffing, training, and compensation. Leadership in formal organizations is highly interdependent with personnel management.

This chapter will examine theory and research in the behavioral sciences as related to different leader behaviors and as related to the impact of a number of contingencies in leadership such as subordinate characteristics, the behavior of the leader's leader, and technology. The concept of organizational climate, a concept broader than leadership that relates to the perceptions of organizational members about a broad spectrum of organizational phenomena, including leadership, will also be examined.

LEADERSHIP TERMINOLOGY

Since a number of terms are used extensively in the literature on leadership, it would be well to examine this terminology before analyzing the results of specific research. The terms *laissez-faire, autocratic, authoritarian, bureaucratic, democratic, initiating structure,* and *consideration* are particularly conspicuous in the literature.

LAISSEZ-FAIRE LEADERSHIP

Laissez-faire means, literally, "allow to act." The behavior of the leader in such situations involves little task direction, the allowing of complete group or individual freedom in decision making, and no appraisal or regulation of the performance of subordinates.[3] *Free rein* is sometimes used synonymously with laissez-

faire. In a sense this kind of leadership suggests an absence of leadership.

AUTOCRATIC LEADERSHIP

Autocratic and *authoritarian* are usually synonymous terms implying a high degree of direction from the leader and minimum or no participation in planning and control on the part of subordinates. Authoritarian sometimes has a more precise meaning and refers to scores on the *F-scale* (Fascism Scale), which was an instrument developed by Adorno et al. to measure tendencies in authoritarian personality.[4] The terms *leader-centered* and *directive* are sometimes used synonymously with authoritarian.

BUREAUCRATIC LEADERSHIP

Bureaucratic leadership, as described in the literature, refers to ". . . rule by rules." The leader's behavior is characterized by a high degree of reliance on rules and regulations and by the use of procedures to which both the leaders and subordinates subscribe.[5] Although I will not explore this type of leadership in detail, it implies a strong element of autocratic leadership and initiating structure and will be mentioned again in this context.

DEMOCRATIC LEADERSHIP

As used in the literature of leadership, *democratic* can describe a variety of situations, all the way from subordinates electing their leaders and voting on every matter, including group objectives, to an appointed leader encouraging group discussion only on certain selected mat-

[3] See Ralph White and Ronald Lippitt, "Leader Behavior and Member Reaction in Three 'Social Climates,'" in Dorwin Cartwright and Alvin Zander, eds., *Group Dynamics*, 2nd ed. (Evanston, Ill.: Row, Peterson, and Co., 1960), p. 528.

[4] T. Adorno, E. Frenkel-Brunswik, D. Levinson, and R. Sanford, *The Authoritarian Personality* (New York: Harper & Brothers, 1950), pp. 222–279.
[5] Eugene Emerson Jennings, *The Executive: Autocrat, Bureaucrat, Democrat* (New York: Harper & Row, 1962), pp. 164–165.

ters. One example of usage appears in the research by White and Lippitt, where democratic leadership involves group discussion and decision on policy, technical advice supplied by the leader, free choice of work partners, and "objective" praise and criticism from the leader.[6]

Democratic usually implies a high degree of group participation in decision making and often implies a high degree of support from the leader, but it usually does not imply that the subordinates make decisions about what the goals of the enterprise will be. The terms *employee-centered, equalitarian, consultative,* and *participative* are also often used more or less simultaneously with democratic leadership.

Thus, democratic is a fairly loose term, and actual behavior must be examined to determine what is meant in a particular instance. The *degree* of democracy in a situation can be judged by the number and significance of the decisions made by subordinates.[7]

It is particularly important to note, however, that various forms of democratic leadership tend to involve more extensive within-team interaction than is the case under autocratic styles. The latter places a much higher reliance on downward communications and one-to-one interaction between superiors and subordinates. Figure 7-1 depicts both this one-to-one form of interaction and the type of group interaction characteristic of more democratic organizations.

INITIATING STRUCTURE AND CONSIDERATION

Initiating structure and *consideration* are terms developed through an analysis of factors in statements about behavior of leaders. Two major types of behavior emerged and were given these labels.[8] *Initiating structure* or *structure* is a leader's behavior typified by such acts as assigning tasks, criticizing deficient work, and establishing deadlines and procedures. It implies an emphasis on attaining organizational goals.[9] *Consideration* is a leader's behavior typified by such acts as doing personal favors, being friendly and approachable, obtaining approval of subordinates on major matters, and taking time to listen to subordinates, thus suggesting concern for their needs. These two kinds of behavior are seen as being independent of each other and as occurring in different mixtures in different leaders. A manager might be high or low on both, or low on one and high on the other.[10] Both terms will be used extensively later in this chapter.

Applying these two terms to the other categories of leadership behavior, democratic leadership will include a high degree of consideration and a moderate to high degree of initiating structure. Both autocratic and bureaucratic leadership would be characterized by a high degree of initiating structure and a low degree of consideration. Laissez-faire leadership would be characterized by an almost total absence of both.

These types of leadership styles are obviously rare in their pure form. Depending upon their basic personalities, their attitudes, and the situation, managers will tend to display mixtures or variations of these behaviors. For example, an *autocrat* may be severely dictatorial or may be a *benevolent autocrat,* that is, highly directive but generous about wages, fringe benefits, and

[6] White and Lippitt, "Leader Behavior and Member Reaction," p. 528.

[7] See Robert Tannenbaum and Warren H. Schmidt, "How to Choose a Leadership Pattern," *Harvard Business Review,* 36:98 (March-April 1958); and Tannenbaum and Schmidt, "Retrospective Commentary," *Harvard Business Review,* 51:166–168 (May-June 1973).

[8] J. K. Hemphill, *Situational Factors in Leadership* (Columbus, Ohio: The Ohio State University, Bureau of Educational Research, 1949).

[9] Edwin A. Fleishman and Edwin F. Harris, "Patterns of Leadership Behavior Related to Employee Grievances and Turnover," *Personnel Psychology,* 15:43–44 (Spring 1962).

[10] Fleishman and Harris, "Patterns of Leadership Behavior," pp. 43–44.

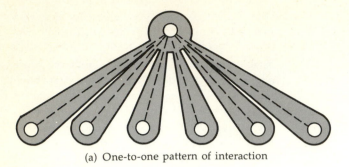

(a) One-to-one pattern of interaction

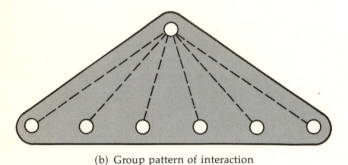

(b) Group pattern of interaction

Figure **7-1**   One-to-one and group patterns of interaction

From Rensis Likert, *New Patterns of Management* (New York: McGraw-Hill Book Company, 1961), p. 107.   Used with permission. Terminology changed slightly.

working conditions.[11] A democratic supervisor may encourage participation in certain matters but be adamant about retaining unilateral decision-making authority in other areas.

THEORY X AND THEORY Y ASSUMPTIONS

A major factor in the leadership behavior of managers and in the overall organizational climate will be the assumptions held by managers at all levels, including the chief executive. The late Douglas McGregor described two sets of assumptions, one called *Theory X* and the other,

Theory Y, which he believed led to quite different kinds of leadership behavior and to quite different personnel practices and policies.

The following are the basic assumptions of Theory X:

1. The average human being has an inherent dislike of work and will avoid it if he can. . . .

2. Because of this human characteristic of disliking work, most people must be coerced, controlled, directed, or threatened with punishment to get them to put forth adequate effort toward the achievement of organizational objectives. . . .

3. The average human being prefers to be directed, wishes to avoid responsibility, has relatively little ambition, wants security above all. . . .[12]

---

[11] See Robert N. McMurry, "The Case for Benevolent Autocracy," *Harvard Business Review,* 36:82–90 (January-February 1958).

[12] Douglas McGregor, *The Human Side of Enterprise* (New York: McGraw-Hill Book Company, 1960), pp. 33–34. For ref-

Theory Y, on the other hand, involves quite a different set of assumptions:

1. The expenditure of physical and mental effort in work is as natural as play or rest. . . .

2. External control and the threat of punishment are not the only means for bringing about effort toward organizational objectives. Man will exercise self-direction and self-control in the service of objectives to which he is committed. . . .

3. Commitment to objectives is a function of the rewards associated with their achievement. . . .

4. The average human being learns, under proper conditions, not only to accept but to seek responsibility. . . .

5. The capacity to exercise a relatively high degree of imagination, ingenuity, and creativity in the solution of organizational problems is widely, not narrowly, distributed in the population. . . .

6. Under the conditions of modern industrial life, the intellectual potentialities of the average human being are only partially utilized. . . .[13]

According to McGregor, Theory X underlies both traditional "principles of management," which have tended to dominate managerial literature, and managerial strategy found in much of industry. Theory Y, on the other hand, is consistent with recent research in behavioral science and shows promise of permitting much more individual growth and development than has been possible under Theory X.[14]

In a posthumous book, McGregor stresses that these two different managerial "cosomologies" (i.e., theories of the universe) are not two ends of a continuum but are *qualitatively* different. Further, he expresses the belief that either X or Y can lead management toward a wide array of strategies, some of which may be called "hard" and some "soft."[15] For example,

he sees Theory X sometimes leading a reactive management toward a "human relations approach" that is too permissive, in the sense that control is reduced without anything put in its place.[16] Theory Y, on the other hand, leads to "clear demands for high performance, clear limits consistently enforced."[17] Thus, while Theory Y obviously places much more confidence in the potentialities of the "average" person, McGregor does not see it as easygoing sentimentality, nor does he see it as creating an easy management situation. Conversely, Theory Y can create a much more challenging and demanding situation for everybody in the organization.

Schein, in a review of McGregor's work several years after McGregor's death, stated that Theory X managers tend to be less flexible in their leadership approach than Theory Y managers and more limited in their diagnostic skills. Schein believes that managers with either orientation need managerial experience and training, but that Theory X people would need ". . . fairly significant growth or development experiences over a period of time . . ." to become Theory Y people.[18]

SYSTEM 1 AND SYSTEM 4, AND THE MANAGERIAL GRID

McGregor's two managerial philosophies generally parallel the philosophies of many contemporary behavioral scientists and their notions about differing leadership patterns and the consequences of these differing patterns. To illustrate, Rensis Likert envisages four "management systems" on a continuum from (1)

---

erence to Maslow's influence on McGregor's thinking, see Ibid., pp. 35–36, 44; and Abraham H. Maslow, *Motivation and Personality*, 2nd ed. (New York: Harper & Row, 1970), p. xii.
[13] Ibid., pp. 47–48.
[14] Ibid., pp. 35, 48–49.
[15] Douglas McGregor, *The Professional Manager* (New York: McGraw-Hill Book Co., 1967), pp. 79–80.

[16] McGregor, *The Human Side of Enterprise*, p. 46.
[17] McGregor, *The Professional Manager*, p. 78.
[18] Edgar H. Schein, "The Hawthorne Group Studies Revisited: A Defense of Theory Y," in Eugene L. Cass and Frederick G. Zimmer, eds., *Man and Work in Society* (New York: Van Nostrand Reinhold Company, 1975), pp. 78–94.

"exploitive authoritative" to (2) "benevolent authoritative," to (3) "consultative," to (4) "participative group." These differing managerial approaches are primarily based on differing attitudes of trust and confidence in subordinates.

For example, Likert's *System 1* features lack of confidence and trust; extensive use of fear, threats, and punishment plus "occasional rewards"; emphasis on downward communications; little interaction between superiors and subordinates; most decisions made at the top of the organization and enforced by orders issued with little or no subordinate participation in setting goals; and controls exercised by the top hierarchy in a policing or punitive manner.

System 4, on the other hand, features a high degree of trust and confidence in subordinates; a system of economic reward based on a high degree of participation; group involvement in setting goals, improving methods, and appraising progress toward goals; much interaction among superiors, individuals, and groups; extensive upward, downward, and lateral communications, which are typically friendly and trusting; widespread decision making integrated by overlapping groups; and extensive exercise of controls at lower levels.[19]

Underlying the leadership philosophy of Likert's System 4 is his *principle of supportive relations*, which is clearly consistent with McGregor's Theory Y:

The leadership and other processes of the organization must be such as to ensure a maximum probability that in all interactions and in all relationships within the organization, each member, in the light of his background, values, desires, and expectations, will view the experience as supportive and one which builds and maintains his sense of personal worth and importance.[20]

Blake and Mouton, as another illustration, see leadership behavior as falling into one of five general categories, depending upon the manager's concern for production versus people. In the *Managerial Grid* (Figure 7-2) the horizontal axis depicts degree of concern for production, while the vertical axis depicts degree of concern for people. The 1.1 style suggests minimal concern for both production and people, while a 9.1 style represents strong emphasis on production and little emphasis on people. A 5.5 style represents a concern balanced between obtaining necessary production and maintaining morale at satisfactory levels. The 9.9 style depicts high concern for both people and production. It should be noted that these categories represent *concern*, not necessarily results. It is implicit in the writings of Blake and Mouton, however, that the 9.9 style is optimal in terms of overall organizational results and the development of people.[21]

As we indicated, the congruencies among the ideas of several contemporary behavioral scientists are quite evident. For example, McGregor, Likert, and Blake and Mouton all implicitly or explicitly emphasize a high concern for people in the context of getting the task of the organization done effectively. These authors, including Herzberg, Bennis, and Argyris, are all interested in creating a developmental environment

[19]Rensis Likert, *The Human Organization: Its Management and Value* (New York: McGraw-Hill Book Company, 1967), pp. 3–10. Likert refers to such dimensions as attitudes, loyalty, etc., as "intervening variables" that reflect the "internal state and health of the organization." "Causal" variables are dimensions such as organizational structure and leadership skills and behavior. Included among "end-result" variables are productivity and company earnings. Ibid., pp. 26–29. While the sequence is generally (1) causal, (2) intervening, and (3) end result, there can be substantial interdependency among such categories of variables. For example, company earnings might influence both morale and the behavior of the leader.

[20]Ibid., p. 47; and Rensis Likert, *New Patterns of Management* (New York: McGraw-Hill Book Company, 1961), p. 103. Willard Gaylin, a psychiatrist, sees supportive relations as an antidote to national pessimism. See Willard Gaylin, "Caring Makes the Difference," *Psychology Today*, 10:34–39 (August 1976).

[21]Robert R. Blake and Jane S. Mouton, *The Managerial Grid* (Houston: Gulf Publishing Company, 1964).

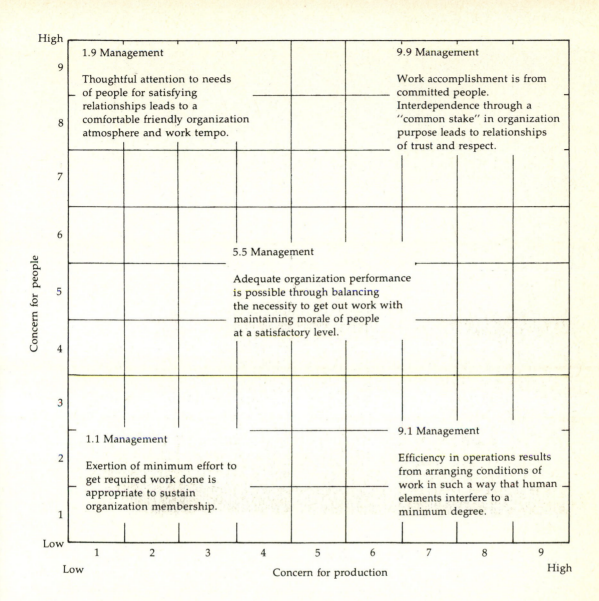

Figure 7-2 The managerial grid

From Robert R. Blake and Jane S. Mouton, "Grid Organization Development," *Personnel Administration*, 30:11 (January-February 1967). Used with permission.

Figure 7-3   Parallel theories about motivation, style of leadership, and organizational climate

		Hierarchically directed ←		→ Participative, self-directed, team interactive
Theories about motivation	Abraham Maslow	Physiological, safety,	Belonging and security needs / esteem needs	Self-actualization and growth needs
	Frederick Herzberg	Dissatisfiers and hygiene factors		Satisfiers and motivating factors
	Chris Argyris	Dependence, submissiveness, frustration		Aspirations toward psychological success
	Douglas McGregor	Theory X cosmology		Theory Y cosmology
Theories about leadership style	Hemphill et al.	Initiating structure		Consideration
	Blake Mouton	Style 9.1 Maximal concern for production, minimal concern for people	Style 5.5 "Middle-of-the-road" concern for both production and people	Style 9.9 Maximal concern for both production and people
Theories about organizational climate	Rensis Likert	System 1 Exploitive authoritative	System 2 Benevolent authoritative / System 3 Consultative	System 4 Participative group
	Warren Bennis	Bureaucratic organization	Principle of supportive relations	Organic-adaptive organization
	Burns and Stalker	Mechanistic systems		Organic systems

in which there is more than the prevailing degree of opportunity for self-actualization and which is more challenging as well as supportive. Argyris, in particular, is concerned with the suppressive environment at the bottom of the formal organization, which he sees as inconsistent with "the needs of individuals aspiring for psychological success. . . ." [22]

In many ways, these behavioral scientists all draw on the Maslow notions of personality growth and self-actualization, and all are concerned with organizations and subunits becoming more open and adaptive to their environments. The latter notions are congruent with organic organizations as depicted by Burns and Stalker and with some of the concepts from systems theory pertaining to open systems as we discussed in earlier chapters. (See Figure 7-3, which depicts some of these parallels in an oversimplified way. The parallels are not exact, nor are the boundaries between theories about motivation, leadership style, and organizational climate. Figure 7-3 is presented only to dramatize some of the common themes.)

RESULTS OF RESEARCH

We now turn to research in behavioral science to discover which patterns of leadership tend to be the most effective. Certain situational variables will also be examined to determine what effect they have on successful leadership.

Before examining the literature, however, it should be pointed out that a critical problem in research on leadership behavior is the selection of performance criteria. Although the subject will not be pursued in detail here, the reader should bear in mind that the criteria of effectiveness or efficiency that are selected will have a major influence on the results of any research

attempting to predict the consequences of different kinds of leadership behavior. [23]

RESULTS OF LAISSEZ-FAIRE LEADERSHIP

Research suggests that, in general, laissez-faire leadership—an absence of leadership—results in chaos, confusion, conflict, and frustration. For example, although we need to be cautious in applying the results to adults, research with boys' clubs by White and Lippit found that laissez-faire leadership resulted in much lower volume and lower quality of work performed than under democratic leadership. Furthermore, there was a good deal of discouragement, frustration, and waste motion. [24] Similar conclusions were reached through observations of leaderless group discussions at the National Training Laboratories (now NTL-Institute for Applied Behavioral Science). [25]

It might be argued that in a scientific laboratory devoted to pure research, for example, leadership logically has a strong element of laissez-faire approach. Even in this situation, however, some leadership relative to appraisal, compensation, and maintenance of appropriate working conditions is essential. A study of research laboratories by Baumgartel found that laissez-faire leadership resulted in less satisfaction than did participatory (democratic) leadership. However, laissez-faire leadership appeared to result in more favorable attitudes than directive (autocratic) leadership. [26]

[22] Chris Argyris, *Integrating the Individual and the Organization* (New York: John Wiley & Sons, Inc., 1964), pp. 37–40.

[23] For a discussion of the criterion problem in such research, see Patricia C. Smith, "Behaviors, Results, and Organizational Effectiveness: The Problem of Criteria," in Marvin D. Dunnette, ed., *Handbook of Industrial and Organizational Psychology* (Chicago: Rand McNally College Publishing Company, 1976), pp. 745–775.
[24] White and Lippitt, "Leader Behavior and Member Reaction," pp. 539–540.
[25] William Foote Whyte, *Leadership and Group Participation* (Ithaca, N.Y.: Cornell University, New York State School of Industrial and Labor Relations), Bulletin 24 (May 1953), pp. 18–26.
[26] Howard Baumgartel, "Leadership Style as a Variable in Research Administration," *Administrative Science Quarterly*, 2:344–360 (December 1957).

RESULTS OF AUTOCRATIC LEADERSHIP

A number of studies have shown that, in general, a high degree of dictatorial behavior on the part of the leader or supervisor has various undesirable consequences. The conclusions of some of these studies will be briefly summarized.

Fleishman and Harris found that the higher the degree of "structure" on the part of production foremen as perceived by subordinates, the greater the number of grievances filed by employees. The relationship was curvilinear, with a very high incidence of grievances associated with structure above a certain point. Similarly, turnover was only slightly related to structure up to a point, but beyond this point turnover increased rapidly with increases in structure.[27] Absenteeism also appeared to be correlated with structure in production groups, although there seemed to be no relationship between absenteeism and structure in nonproduction groups.[28] These results suggest that a certain degree of structure is perceived as necessary by employees, but inordinate structure is met with defensive behavior in the form of grievances and resignation.

It should be pointed out, however, that "structuring" behavior on the part of the supervisor may result in higher efficiency ratings by the supervisor's superior. Supervisors of production foremen [29] and airplane commanders [30] tended to rate structuring behavior highly. Furthermore, there appears to be little or no correlation between (a) how subordinates perceive a supervisor's behavior and (b) how superiors perceive the supervisor in relation to structure.[31]

Likert cites research by Seashore and Georgopoulos that found a marked inverse correlation between pressure felt by employees and their productivity. Furthermore, pressure that was perceived as unreasonable was related to lack of confidence and trust in the supervisor. Conflict between supervisors and their subordinates was also associated with low productivity (Georgopoulos).[32]

In addition, punitive methods of correction appear to have a dampening effect on production. Supervisors of high-producing groups tend to ignore the mistakes or to transform the mistakes of subordinates into educational experiences; on the other hand, less successful supervisors are punitive or critical.[33]

A study of children in experimentally designed democratic and authoritarian clubs found that autocratic leadership resulted in less cooperation among peers and higher submissiveness and apathy than in the democratic organization. Furthermore, autocratic leadership resulted in scapegoating behavior in which group members expressed their frustrations by turning on other individuals within the group.[34]

---

[27] Fleishman and Harris, "Patterns of Leadership Behavior," pp. 48–50.

[28] Edwin A. Fleishman, "A Leader Behavior Description for Industry," in Ralph M. Stogdill and Alvin E. Coons, eds., *Leader Behavior: Its Description and Measurement* (Columbus: The Ohio State University, 1957), Bureau of Business Research, Ohio Studies in Personnel, Research Monograph No. 88, p. 114. For research on the relationship between absenteeism and turnover, see Thomas F. Lyons, "Turnover and Absenteeism: A Review of Relationships and Shared Correlates," *Personnel Psychology*, 25:271–281 (Summer 1972).

[29] Fleishman, "A Leader Behavior Description for Industry," p. 114.

[30] Andrew W. Halpin and B. James Winer, "A Factorial Study of the Leader Behavior Descriptions," in Stogdill and Coons, *Leader Behavior*, pp. 50–51.

[31] Robert O. Besco and C.H. Lawshe, "Foreman Leadership as Perceived by Superiors and Subordinates," *Personnel Psychology*, 12:573–582 (Winter 1959).

[32] Likert, *New Patterns of Management*, pp. 8–9.

[33] Ibid., pp. 11, 12. See also Michael Argyle, Godfrey Gardner, and Frank Cioffi, "Supervising Methods Related to Productivity, Absenteeism, and Labor Turnover," *Human Relations*, 11:38 (1958).

[34] Kurt Lewin, "The Consequences of an Authoritarian and Democratic Leadership," in Alvin W. Gouldner, ed., *Studies in Leadership* (New York: Harper & Brothers, 1950), pp. 409–417.

A similar study, in which leaders using different types of leadership were rotated among boys' groups, found less interest in work and much more expressed dissatisfaction under autocratic leadership than under democratic leadership. In addition, nineteen of twenty boys who made the comparison preferred a democratic leader over an autocratic one.[35] This finding is consistent with the study cited above in which scientists expressed the least satisfaction with directive (autocratic) leadership.[36]

RESULTS OF DEMOCRATIC AND PARTICIPATIVE LEADERSHIP

Behavior patterns usually associated with democratic leadership, that is, a high degree of participation and support, have been found, in general, to be related to certain desirable results. Research suggests that democratic behavior on the part of the leader, in contrast to laissez-faire and authoritarian behavior, results in more positive attitudes toward the leader, a higher degree of acceptance of change, lower absentee rates, and higher production. It should be stressed again, however, that democratic leadership does not preclude a good deal of evaluation and decision making by the leader. What is democratic or autocratic is a matter of degree and must be analyzed in terms of specific behavior.

The classic study by a group of investigators at the Hawthorne Works of the Western Electric Company dramatically demonstrated the powerful effects of participation and recognition on production. Through consulting with the workers and being concerned about their well-being and their hopes and fears, the investigators produced such cooperative attitudes that production went up regardless of the number

and duration of rest pauses and duration of the workday and workweek.[37]

The studies cited by White and Lippitt and by Baumgartel suggest that a democratic approach tends to result in more positive attitudes toward the leader than is the case under both laissez-faire and autocratic leadership. A further report on boys' clubs concluded that, in contrast to autocratic leadership, democratic leadership brought more cooperative behavior, more friendliness, more suggestions, more mutually accepted exchange of objective criticism, and higher production of a higher quality.[38] Similarly, research by Weschler et al. in a research laboratory found job satisfaction of subordinates to be positively correlated with permissiveness on the part of the supervisor.[39] Research by Morse and Reimer found that satisfaction in work increased as participation increased and decreased as participation decreased.[40]

An experimental study by Coch and French at the Harwood Manufacturing Corporation found that employees' participation in planning and implementing changes resulted in sustained or increased productivity. The experiment consisted of introducing changes in production methods and piece rates in four carefully

[35] White and Lippitt, "Leader Behavior and Member Reaction," pp. 543–549.
[36] Baumgartel, "Leadership Style."

[37] F.J. Roethlisberger, *Management and Morale* (Cambridge, Mass.: Harvard University Press, 1946), pp. 9–15. See also F.J. Roethlisberger and William J. Dickson, *Management and the Worker* (Cambridge, Mass.: Harvard University Press, 1939).
[38] Kurt Lewin and Ronald Lippitt, "An Experimental Approach to the Study of Autocracy and Democracy: A Preliminary Note," in A. Paul Hare, Edgar F. Borgatta, and Robert F. Bales, eds., *Small Groups: Studies in Social Interaction* (New York: Alfred A. Knopf, Inc., 1955), pp. 521–523.
[39] Irving R. Weschler, Murray Kahane, and Robert Tannenbaum, *Occupational Psychology*, 26:1–14 (January 1952).
[40] Nancy C. Morse and Everett Reimer, "The Experimental Change of a Major Organizational Variable," *Journal of Abnormal and Social Psychology*, 52:120–129 (January 1956). This study found clerical costs to decrease under both increased and decreased participation, however. The reason seems to be that, in the increased authoritarian situation, higher management simply ordered a cutback in the number of employees.

matched worker groups. One group was permitted no participation in the changes, while a second group participated in the sense that they were permitted to choose representatives who were to receive initial training in the new methods and who were to make suggestions about the changes. All workers in the third and fourth groups participated directly in designing new jobs and making suggestions.

The nonparticipating group had the lowest productivity over a forty-day period, had a high grievance and resignation rate, and showed deliberate signs of restricting production. The represented group had a high relearning rate, was cooperative, and achieved fairly high productivity over the forty days. The high-participation group had the highest relearning rate, had no resignations, showed no hostility, and achieved the highest production rates over the forty-day period.[41]

Consideration—a concept that includes participation—was found by Fleishman and Harris to be inversely correlated with grievances. Above a certain point, however, increased consideration was found not to be associated with reduced grievances. Consideration was also found to be inversely related to turnover, although, again, the turnover rate did not decrease with increased consideration above a certain degree of consideration.[42]

Permitting employees to choose work partners in some situations may also serve to increase satisfactions, reduce turnover, and lower production costs. Interesting research involving carpenters and bricklayers found that, when workers were given their first or second choices of work partners, job satisfaction increased, and turnover, labor costs, and material

costs decreased. In fact, the chief construction engineer reported to his superiors that the procedure resulted in such savings that every twenty-ninth building could be built ". . . entirely free from labor and materials costs."[43]

It should be noted, however, that these people were skilled artisans and that the alternative to the adopted procedure was unpredictability and randomness in assigning partners. Furthermore, they worked in pairs. These conditions are different from those found on a production line of a factory, for example, but might be similar to those of some maintenance groups in industry.

Furthermore, it is not clear whether the research suggests that the resulting increase in job satisfaction produced the lower cost and lowered turnover or whether the increasing job satisfaction and other gains were functions of the same phenomenon. In any event, the results warrant considerable attention. Such sociometric grouping may not be possible in most working situations, but where it is possible, results may be very desirable, provided attitudes move in the direction of accepting managerial goals. It is entirely possible that increased cohesiveness of groups might reduce productivity if the groups did not accept the goals of management.[44]

In a study at the Detroit Edison Company, Mann and Baumgartel found that a number of

---

[41] Lester Coch and John R.P. French, Jr., "Overcoming Resistance to Change," *Human Relations*, 1:512–532 (1948); as reported in Cartwright and Zander, *Group Dynamics*, pp. 319–341.

[42] Fleishman and Harris, "Patterns of Leadership Behavior," pp. 47–53.

[43] Raymond H. Van Zelst, "Validation of a Sociometric Regrouping Procedure," *Supplement to the Journal of Abnormal and Social Psychology*, April 1952, pp. 299–301. A typical tool in sociometric studies is the "sociogram," originally developed by J.L. Moreno, which is a chart with circles representing people and arrows from these people pointing to the people they like best, or dislike the most, etc., depending on the question asked.

[44] There is also some evidence that three-person groups may not work out nearly so well as the two-person teams in the study cited above. One study found that the least active member of a three-member group tended to be isolated. See Theodore M. Mills, "Power Relations in Three Person Groups," *American Sociological Review*, 18:351–357 (August 1953).

conditions that depended upon leadership behavior were related to low absentee rates. Among the conditions associated with good records of attendance were freedom to discuss job problems with the supervisor, group discussions about problems affecting the group, and recognition for good work.[45]

In a geographically decentralized package-delivery organization, Indik et al. found, in general, that high performance was associated with openness in the channels of communication between subordinates and supervisors, with subordinates' satisfaction about the supporting behavior of superiors, and with a relatively high degree of local autonomy. Some exceptions to these conclusions, however, were found in some situations.[46]

A study by Likert and Willits in a life insurance company found that agency managers who were perceived by their subordinates to be "unselfish," "cooperative," "sympathetic," "interested in agents' success," "democratic," "sincere in dealing with agents," and "eager to help" were more likely to be found in the high-producing agencies. Another study found that freedom to set their own pace was associated with high productivity of subordinates, in contrast to situations where freedom was less.[47]

Studies reported by Kahn and Katz suggest that too many restrictions by the supervisor have a dampening effect on productivity. In an insurance company, for example, frequent checking upon subordinates and frequent, detailed work instructions tended to be associated with supervisors of low-production sections. In contrast, supervisors of high-producing sec-

tions were likely to practice a more general, or delegating, kind of supervision.[48]

Finally, an experimental study by Schacter et al. in the General Electric Company points up some additional consequences of highly organized nonsupportive supervision versus a more supportive kind of supervision. This study found that ego-threatening and annoying irritations introduced into the working situation during a transition from one product to another resulted in anger, hostility, and a consequent lowered ability to make the changeover. The experiment consisted of subjecting some experimental groups to threatening and continuous time-study, severe and persistent criticism of their work, and unusual irritations, such as being required to sort out washers from dirty and greasy parts. Workers in other experimental groups were supported and encouraged by flattery, praise, helpfulness, friendliness, and the minimization of irritations. It is interesting that not only did the harassment reduce ability to make the changeover, but the emotional disruption of the harassed group had a greater effect on nonroutine work than on routine activities.[49]

As a concluding comment about democratic or participative leadership, the research we have cited does *not* suggest that participation by itself increases or sustains productivity or facilitates change. Rather, it suggests that *participation in attempts to maintain or increase productivity and efficiency tends to have good results in terms of both morale and productivity.*

Participation is likely to boomerang if used by an arrogant superior to impose a set of conditions upon subordinates. A sincere desire for some outcome, such as obtaining constructive

[45] Floyd Mann and Howard Baumgartel, *Absences and Employee Attitudes in an Electric Power Company* (Ann Arbor: University of Michigan, Survey Research Center, 1952), Human Relations Program, Series 1, Report 2, 24 pp.
[46] Bernard P. Indik, Basil S. Georgopoulos, and Stanley E. Seashore, "Superior-Subordinate Relationships and Performance," *Personnel Psychology*, 14:357–374 (Winter 1961).
[47] Likert, *New Patterns of Management*, pp. 10–11, 20.

[48] Robert L. Kahn and Daniel Katz, "Leadership Practices in Relation to Productivity and Morale," in Cartwright and Zander, *Group Dynamics*, p. 559.
[49] Stanley Schacter, Leon Festinger, Ben Willerman, and Ray Hyman, "Emotional Disruption and Industrial Productivity," *Journal of Applied Psychology*, 45:201–213 (August 1961).

suggestions, clarification, or improved communication must underlie the use of participation if it is to be an effective device. In my opinion, "participation" by subordinates in the face of the superior's lack of belief in the ability of subordinates to make a contribution or a lack of desire to permit genuine participation will soon be perceived as an empty gesture, will be resented, and will be met with defensive behavior.

STRUCTURE AND CONSIDERATION NOT POLAR OPPOSITES

Considerable research verifies that structure of various kinds and/or a production orientation are not the polar opposites of employee-centeredness or consideration. For example, in a study involving employees of Midwest companies manufacturing agricultural equipment, the high-producing groups of employees tended to have supervisors who stressed high production but at the same time were employee-centered. *Employee-centered* meant that the supervisors took a personal interest in the employees, were easily approached by their subordinates, and communicated to them how well they were doing. This research suggests that employee-centered supervision and production-centered supervision are not diametrically opposed to each other, but are two conditions of leadership that can exist at the same time.[50]

A study by Patchen found that work groups had high norms of production (attitudes about production were correlated with actual performance) when the foreman encouraged efficiency and at the same time was effective in "going to bat" for the workers in obtaining rewards. If the foreman did not encourage efficiency, "going to bat" for subordinates had an inverse correlation with the group's norms. Sim-

ilarly, if the foreman encouraged efficiency but did not adequately represent the workers, the group's norms were low.[51] It would seem, therefore, that if high standards of production pay off, the group will set its standards high. On the other hand, if the payoff has no relationship to expectation about efficiency, performance standards will be low. Thus, the supervisor needs to be concerned both about performance standards and about helping subordinates attain their goals.

A similar pattern has emerged in research on initiating structure and consideration. As one example, in Hemphill's study of twenty-two departments in a liberal arts college, departments reputed to be the best administered were found to have chairpersons who were above average on *both* initiating structure and consideration. In other words, heads of well-administered departments were described not only as emphasizing the organization of activities and new methods and procedures for solving group problems, but also as being warm and friendly and concerned with individual and group welfare.[52]

Similarly, in the study by Fleishman and Harris previously cited, grievances and turnover were found to be related to different mixtures of initiating structure and consideration. Although the lowest rates of grievance and turnover were associated with low structure and medium to high consideration, it was found that foremen with high consideration could increase their structuring behavior with only a slight increase in grievances and no increase in turnover.[53] In other words, the fore-

---

[50] Robert L. Kahn, "Productivity and Job Satisfaction," *Personnel Psychology*, 13:275–287 (Autumn 1960).

[51] Martin Patchen, "Supervisory Methods and Group Performance Norms," *Administrative Science Quarterly*, 7:281–284 (December 1962).

[52] John K. Hemphill, "Leader Behavior Associated with the Administrative Reputations of College Departments," in Stogdill and Coons, *Leader Behavior*, pp. 74–85.

[53] Fleishman and Harris, "Patterns of Leadership Behavior," p. 53.

man could concentrate on *both* the needs of subordinates and the goals of the enterprise and, in large measure, succeed in both areas.

In the Halpin and Winer study of military air crews, an index of crews' satisfaction was positively correlated with both structure and consideration. Although consideration correlated directly with the ratings of subordinates, it correlated inversely with the ratings of superiors.[54] A study by Weed, Mitchell, and Moffitt found subordinates to be most satisfied with leaders high in both human relations and task orientation. Leaders high in human relations orientation but low in task orientation were liked next best, and the high task-oriented leaders who were low in human relations orientation were liked the least.[55] In a study by Besco and Lawshe of a cereal-processing plant, superiors' ratings of departmental effectiveness were correlated positively with both consideration and structure as perceived by the superior, but correlated positively only with consideration as it was perceived by subordinates. Structure was not perceived by subordinates as being associated with group effectiveness either one way or the other.[56]

In the study by Fleishman et al. in an equipment-manufacturing company, the workers preferred foremen displaying a high degree of consideration and disliked foremen displaying a high degree of initiating structure. On the other hand, in productional departments, superiors' ratings of foremen's proficiency were correlated inversely with consideration and positively with structure. In the nonproductional or service departments, however, there was a positive correlation between consideration and foremen's proficiency and an inverse correlation with initiating structure. The researchers hypothesized that this reversal between productional and nonproductional units was due to the pressure of time on the foremen.[57]

Thus, it appears that superiors tend to expect a high degree of structure from subordinate managers and may or may not perceive consideration as being related to effective leadership. Conversely, it appears that subordinates almost universally perceive consideration as important to effective leadership, but may or may not approve of structuring behavior. *The supervisor, then, may be caught in the middle between differing expectations and may often be expected to display both kinds of behavior simultaneously.* Fortunately, both logic and research strongly suggest that the two kinds of behavior are not mutually exclusive and that productivity is associated with a medium of above-average degree of both. The research strongly suggests that the effective supervisor excels in perceptively applying a mixture containing a fairly high degree of both kinds of behavior. Either extremely high structure or extremely low consideration, however, is likely to have undesirable consequences.

These conclusions find substantial support in a study by Bowers and Seashore. Research in forty agencies of a leading life insurance company found that leadership behaviors in the form of support for subordinates, goal emphasis, work facilitation, and subordinate interaction facilitation were significantly related to criteria of organizational effectiveness.[58]

[54] Halpin and Winer, "Factorial Study," pp. 50–51.
[55] Stan E. Weed, Terence R. Mitchell, and Weldon Moffitt, "Leadership Style, Subordinate Personality, and Task Type as Predictors of Performance and Satisfaction with Supervision," *Journal of Applied Psychology*, 61:58–66 (February 1976).
[56] Besco and Lawshe, "Foreman Leadership," pp. 573–582.
[57] Edwin A. Fleishman, Edwin F. Harris, and Harold E. Burtt, *Leadership and Supervision in Industry* (Columbus: The Ohio State University, Bureau of Educational Research, 1955), pp. 75–79.
[58] David G. Bowers and Stanley E. Seashore, "Predicting Organizational Effectiveness with a Four-Factor Theory of Leadership," *Administrative Science Quarterly*, 11:250–263 (September 1966).

ADMINISTRATIVE AND TECHNICAL SKILL

Along with emphasizing the importance of both task and "people" kinds of behaviors, the research clearly indicates that effective leadership requires substantial administrative skill and at least some technical skill. Skills in planning and organizing, in particular, are associated with high performance by the group.[59]

For example, the studies by Comrey et al. in a variety of working situations found that subordinates perceived the effective supervisor as doing a good job of planning. Effective supervisors planned jobs before starting them, informed subordinates of their respective duties, planned for necessary materials, and planned for future emergencies and contingencies. Furthermore, they did a better job of organizing in terms of establishing clear lines of authority and avoiding conflicting orders.[60]

A study by Katz et al. about railroad workers found that foremen of high-producing groups mentioned such duties as planning more often than foremen of low-producing groups. Furthermore, workers in high-producing groups see their foremen as effective planners more than do workers in low-producing groups.[61]

In both studies, the effective supervisors clearly communicated to their subordinates who was boss, particularly through the time they spent on such activities as planning and instructing. Less effective leaders spent more time doing work similar to their subordinates, and informal leaders were more likely to arise and act as spokespersons.[62]

There is also evidence that supervisors are more effective when capable of instructing subordinates in how to do the job, and in better work methods, and in solving technical production problems.[63] It is apparent that some minimum level of technical knowledge about subordinates' jobs is essential.

CONTINGENCIES IN EFFECTIVE LEADERSHIP

A number of contingencies that can influence leadership effectiveness have already been alluded to. In particular, I wish to focus on the impact of the relationship between the supervisor (a leader) and the superior (also a leader), the characteristics of subordinates, and the impact of "situational favorableness" and of type of organization. The latter two will be discussed in the context of Fiedler's "Contingency Model of Leadership Effectiveness" and the research of Lorsch and Morse. We will also briefly look at House's "path-goal" theory of leadership.

THE LINKING FUNCTION AND THE SUPERVISOR'S SUPERIOR

If supervisors' traits and behavior have an impact on the performance of their subordinates, it obviously follows that the traits and behavior of the supervisors' superiors have an impact on

---

[59] Floyd Mann hypothesizes that human relations, technical, and administrative competence are needed in different proportions at different levels of the organization and at different points in the history of an organization. See Floyd C. Mann, "Toward an Understanding of the Leadership Role in Formal Organizations," in Robert Dubin et al., *Leadership and Productivity* (San Francisco: Chandler Publishing Company, 1965), pp. 68–103.

[60] A.L. Comrey, J.M. Pfiffner, and W.S. High, *Factors Influencing Organizational Effectiveness* (Los Angeles: University of Southern California, 1954), Final Technical Report, The Office of Naval Research, Contract N6–ONR–23815, p. 54.

[61] Daniel Katz, Nathan Maccoby, Gerald Gurin, and Lucretia G. Floor, *Productivity, Supervision and Morale Among Railroad Workers* (Ann Arbor: Survey Research Center, Institute for Social Research, University of Michigan, 1951), pp. 22–23.

[62] Kahn and Katz, "Leadership Practices in Relation to Productivity and Morale," in Cartwright and Zander, *Group Dynamics*, pp. 555–557; and Comrey, Pfiffner, and High, *Factors Influencing Organizational Effectiveness*, p. 54.

[63] Comrey, Pfiffner, and High, *Factors Influencing Organizational Effectiveness*, pp. 52–55.

the supervisors' performance. The research cited thus far and to be cited later in the chapter, therefore, has implications for any level of the managerial hierarchy.

It should be noted at the outset that the phenomenon of sponsorship can greatly affect the success of a manager in terms of increases in pay or promotions. If, because of some mutual benefit, a manager becomes the protégé of some higher executive, he or she will in all likelihood gain accordingly.[64] There necessarily may not be a correlation between sponsorship and the protégé's effectiveness with subordinates.

Research by Fleishman et al. at the International Harvester Company found that the behavior and attitudes of foremen were greatly influenced by the behavior and attitudes of their superiors. Those foremen working under superiors who created a climate high in consideration in turn scored higher on consideration in terms of both attitudes and behavior than foremen working under managerial climates low in consideration. In addition, the greater the superior's structuring, the greater that of the foreman.[65] Another study found a high degree of structuring on the part of top management carrying over into the attitudes of supervisors about how they should supervise. In contrast, supervisors in a more democratic company believed in imposing less structure on subordinates.[66] A study by Bowers and Seashore in a life insurance company found that there was a strong relationship between managerial leadership behaviors and peer leadership behaviors. To quote their conclusions, ". . . the best pre-

dictor of peer support is managerial support; of peer goal emphasis, managerial interaction facilitation; of peer work facilitation, managerial work facilitation and of peer interaction facilitation, managerial interaction facilitation."[67] Clearly, the behavior of higher management sets the pattern for subordinate leaders and so on down through the organization.

Influence upward and with other groups is also an important leader behavior. Various researchers at the University of Michigan have concluded that supervisors in high-producing groups tend to be effective links with other groups. In particular, the ability of a manager to influence a superior will have an effect on leadership performance. Research by Pelz in a large electric utility company prompted the conclusion that subordinates were more satisfied with supervisors who were influential with their superiors in helping subordinates achieve their goals than with supervisors not so successful in influencing their superiors on behalf of their subordinates.[68] (See Figure 7-4 for a diagram of the linking-pin function.)

Effective liaison with other departments and sections is also important. Likert reports that high-production groups tend to have leaders who are effective links with other organizational groups as well as with the group immediately above.[69] In this sense, then, Likert's diagram in Figure 7-4 should include lateral arrows.

Mann and Dent reported that the supervisor considered by subordinates to be a member and representative of both the working group and management tended to be rated the highest by superiors. The effective supervisor was

[64] For a discussion of sponsorship, see Norman H. Martin and Anselm L. Strauss, "Patterns of Mobility within Industrial Organizations," *The Journal of Business*, 29:106–107 (April 1956).

[65] Edwin A. Fleishman, "Leadership Climate, Human Relations Training, and Supervisory Behavior," *Personnel Psychology*, 6:205–222 (Summer 1953).

[66] Erwin S. Stanton, "Company Policies and Supervisors' Attitudes toward Supervision," *Journal of Applied Psychology*, 44:22–26 (February 1960).

[67] Bowers and Seashore, "Predicting Organizational Effectiveness," p. 257.

[68] Donald C. Pelz, "Leadership within a Hierarchical Organization," *Journal of Social Issues*, 7:47–63 (1951).

[69] Rensis Likert, "How to Raise Productivity Twenty Per Cent," *Nation's Business*, 47:32 (August 1959).

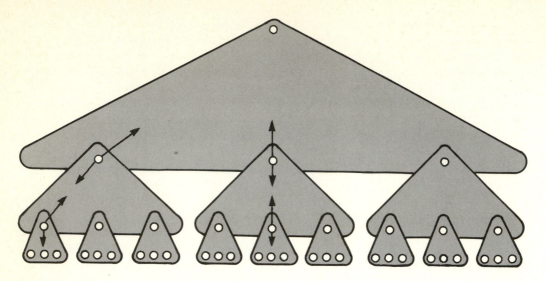

Figure **7-4**   The linking-pin function

From *New Patterns of Management* by Rensis Likert. Copyright © 1961 by McGraw-Hill, Inc. Used with permission of McGraw-Hill Book Company.

seen as integrating the goals of subordinates with enterprising objectives.[70]

In a sense, then, the effective leader is also an effective subordinate. Research shows that those nominated as desired leaders by their peers are also chosen as desired followers. Thus, it appears that the effective leader has attributes that also permit her or him to function well in subordinate relationships with others.[71]

Research by Comrey, Pfiffner, and High into managerial practices in governmental forests, governmental offices, military machine shops, and aircraft production departments found that the supervisors in the more effective groups felt they were given latitude to make the decisions

that they believed they should make and were given adequate authority to do so. Furthermore, they were confident of receiving support from their superiors for their decisions. In addition, supervisors in the better units were perceived by their subordinates to have influence with superiors in obtaining wage increases and other benefits and obtaining support for various decisions.[72]

CHARACTERISTICS OF SUBORDINATES

Chapter 6 discussed research indicating that certain individual and group phenomena have an impact on efficiency and satisfaction. Age, personality adjustment, group values, and group cohesiveness were all shown to have important consequences. Likewise the chapter on executive selection cites research suggesting

[70] Floyd C. Mann and James K. Dent, "The Supervisor: Member of Two Organizational Families," *Harvard Business Review*, 32:103–112 (November-December 1954).
[71] See E.P. Hollander and Wilse B. Webb, "Leadership, Followership, and Friendship: An Analysis of Peer Nominations," in Eleanor E. Maccoby, Theodore M. Newcomb, and Eugene L. Hartley, eds., *Readings in Social Psychology*, 3rd ed. (New York: Holt, Rinehart and Winston, 1958), pp. 489–496.

[72] Comrey, Pfiffner, and High, *Factors Influencing Organizational Effectiveness*, p. 54.

that leaders tend to have higher intelligence than immediate subordinates but that the discrepancy may not be large.[73] This research raises the possibility that too great a discrepancy might create serious problems in understanding and communications between the leaders and subordinates, and also that, if leaders have lower intelligence than one or more of their subordinates, they may find it difficult to maintain their role of leadership.

There is some evidence for the latter possibility. Ghiselli and Lodahl found that when one of a foreman's subordinates was superior to him or her in supervisory ability as measured by a self-descriptive inventory, the foreman was less highly regarded by higher management than if he or she excelled all subordinates. Furthermore, foremen in charge of groups having considerable ability for self-management were rated lower by management than if they were assigned to groups with less ability.[74]

Fleishman et al. have found that, in general, the higher the educational attainment of the work group, the lower the group's grievance rate. The researchers speculated that this phenomenon stemmed from the workers' ability to understand and appreciate the foreman's role and to understand the reason for decisions.[75] The low grievance rate may also be due simply to decisions that are better because they are made in a higher educational group.

Job satisfaction is also related to level of aspiration. In a study of white-collar workers, Morse found that the degree of satisfaction with the job's pay and status was related to level of aspiration, which, in turn, was conditioned partly by expectations derived from their family, education, and friends.[76]

The effectiveness of the supervisor's use of participation seems to be partly determined by the personal characteristics of subordinates. Vroom has found that, in the case of employees with a high need for independence, the greater their psychological (felt) participation in matters pertaining to the job, the more favorable were their attitudes toward the job. On the other hand, in the case of employees with a low need for independence, there was practically no relation between psychological participation and attitude toward the job. In short, personality appeared to be one of the determinants of the relationship between participation and the job's satisfaction. Vroom[77] concludes that studies on participation that ignore the effects of personality tend to underestimate the effects of participation on some people and overestimate the consequences on others.

A study by Haythorn found that the authoritarian tendencies of subordinates, as measured by the F-scale, affected the behavior of the leader and the group, regardless of the leader's personality. For example, observers reported that leaders of authoritarian groups tended to be more aggressive and more autocratic and to strive more for individual prominence than in groups with equalitarian followers. Furthermore, observers reported that the groups with authoritarian followers showed greater dissatisfaction, more conflict among personalities, less motivation toward the group's goal, and less productivity than groups with equalitarian followers.[78] An experimental study by Fodor

[73] Ralph M. Stogdill, "Personal Factors Associated with Leadership: A Survey of the Literature," *The Journal of Psychology*, 25:44–45 (January 1948).

[74] Edwin A. Ghiselli and Thomas M. Lodahl, "The Evaluation of Foremen's Performance in Relation to the Internal Characteristics of Their Work Groups," *Personnel Psychology*, 11:179–187 (Summer 1958).

[75] Fleishman, Harris, and Burtt, *Leadership and Supervision in Industry*, Chapter VI.

[76] Nancy C. Morse, *Satisfactions in the White-Collar Job* (Ann Arbor: Institute for Social Research, University of Michigan, July 1953), pp. 110–112.

[77] Victor H. Vroom, *Some Personality Determinants of the Effects of Participation* (Englewood Cliffs, N.J.: Prentice-Hall, Inc., 1960), pp. 33–35, 61.

[78] William Haythorn, "The Effects of Varying Combinations of Authoritarian and Equalitarian Leaders and Followers," in

found that group stress induced by disparaging remarks by a member of a work crew resulted in more authoritarian behavior on the part of the supervisor.[79]

The level of group dynamics skills among members of a group has long been observed to be an important factor in effective group functioning. Over the years, many trainers in group dynamics workshops have validated the following statement:

Groups may operate with various degrees of diffusion of "leadership" functions among group members or of concentration of such functions in one member or a few members . . . The concept of leadership emphasized here is that of a multilaterally shared responsibility . . .[80]

Some of the group member behaviors observed to be helpful are "information giving," "encouraging," "harmonizing," "gate-keeping," and "reality testing," while some of the dysfunctional behaviors include "attacking," "dominating," and "sympathy seeking."[81]

There is evidence that participation must be "legitimate" in the eyes of the workers if it is to be effective.[82] It may be that subordinates resent participation in matters that they perceive to be the supervisor's problems; further, subordinates undoubtedly resent participation if they see it as being manipulative. In addition, it is likely that discrepancies may vary widely from one setting to another between what supervisors perceive as legitimate and what subordinates perceive as legitimate.

Thus, the supervisor's performance will be partly a function of subordinates' characteristics and behavior. In addition, the supervisor must understand these characteristics and behavior in order to adapt her or his own behavior appropriately.

FIEDLER'S CONTINGENCY MODEL

We have been discussing several important contingencies in effective leadership. Fred Fiedler has devoted more than two decades of research to the contingency theme and has developed a "Contingency Model of Leadership Effectiveness." Basically, the model suggests that group effectiveness is contingent upon the match between leadership style and the extent to which the group situation is favorable to the leader's exercise of influence and control.

Leadership style is measured by asking a respondent to think of all previous coworkers and, using bipolar scales on a questionnaire, to describe a "least preferred coworker" (LPC score). A favorable description (high LPC) of the least preferred coworker is assumed to indicate a relationship-oriented leadership style; an unfavorable description (low LPC) is assumed to indicate a task-oriented style. Situation favorableness is measured along three dimensions: "(a) the degree to which the leader feels accepted by his group . . . ; (b) the degree to which the task is structured; and (c) the degree to which the leader position has power and influence."[83]

Research that has been replicated a number of times tends to indicate that the task-motivated leader performs better in either favorable situations or unfavorable situations but that the relationship-motivated leader performs

Maccoby, Newcomb, and Hartley, *Readings in Social Psychology*, pp. 511–522.

[79] Eugene M. Fodor, "Group Stress, Authoritarian Style of Control and Use of Power," *Journal of Applied Psychology*, 61:313–318 (June 1976).

[80] Kenneth D. Benne and Paul Sheats, "Functional Roles of Group Members," *The Journal of Social Issues*, 4:41–49 (Spring 1948).

[81] Ibid.

[82] John R.P. French, Jr., Joachim Israel, and Dagfinn As, "An Experiment in Participation in a Norwegian Factory," *Human Relations*, 13:3–19 (February 1960).

[83] Fred E. Fiedler, "Personality and Situational Determinants of Leader Behavior," Department of Psychology, University of Washington, *Technical Report 71-18* (June 1971), pp. 4–6.

better in situations that are favorable to an intermediate degree.[84]

While Fiedler draws some tentative conclusions as to the implications of his research for personnel management strategy, in my opinion, the links between LPC scores, relationship orientation and task orientation, and actual leader behaviors are too tenuous, and organizational dynamics are too fluid, for Fiedler's measurement techniques to be translated immediately into personnel practice, e.g., the selection, promotion, or transfer of employees. Fiedler himself states,

While we do not have, at this time, a cookbook or a blueprint which can guide the top manager on how to manage his leadership cadre to the organization's and to his own best advantage, we do have a rudimentary theoretical framework which permits us to predict the effects which various events in the organization's life have on leaders with particular motivational structures.[85]

Further, I am not at all convinced that leadership behavior is fixed. To the contrary, some research indicates that leaders can vary their leadership styles, depending upon the situation.[86] Overall, however, Fiedler has stimulated a great deal of research on leadership, particularly with respect to the contingencies involved.[87]

HARVARD CONTINGENCY STUDIES

A number of studies by Harvard scholars have examined the relationship between organizational structure and leadership style and other variables as they relate to organizational effectiveness. In studies of four manufacturing plants and six research laboratories, Lorsch and Morse found that the more effective plants had more structure and less participation in contrast to the less effective plants. In the laboratories, the situation was reversed, with the more effective laboratories having less structure and more participation than the less effective laboratories. (See Figure 7-5.) Thus, it would appear that leadership style needs to be adjusted to the particular technological and task demands of the organization. It should be kept in mind, however, that these were relative measures; there was some modicum of participation and structure in all the organizations studied. Further, in the manufacturing plants where there was the most participation, subordinates felt they were participating in many matters that were more easily determined top-side.[88] Thus, management needs to be discerning as to which matters are relevant for participation.

PATH-GOAL THEORY OF LEADERSHIP

Robert House and M.G. Evans have articulated a "Path-Goal Theory of Leadership" that draws on expectancy theory (see Chapter 6). Basically, the path-goal approach suggests that the

[84] Fred E. Fiedler, "On the Death and Transfiguration of Leadership Training," Department of Psychology, University of Washington, Technical Report 70-16 (December 1970), p. 5.
[85] Fred E. Fiedler, "New Concepts for the Management of Managers," in Eugene L. Cass and Frederick G. Zimmer, eds., Man and Work in Society (New York: Van Nostrand Reinhold Company, 1975), p. 219.
[86] Robert J. House and Terence R. Mitchell, "Path-Goal Theory of Leadership," Journal of Contemporary Business, 3:83 (Autumn 1971). Porter concludes that Argyris and Vroom are optimistic on this point and Fiedler pessimistic. (Porter, "Introduction," pp. 2–5.)
[87] For a brief review of some of the criticisms of the LPC research, see William G. Scott and Terence R. Mitchell, Organization Theory: A Structural and Behavioral Analysis (Homewood, Ill.: Richard D. Irwin, 1972), pp. 233–234. See also John E. Stinson and Lane Tracy, "Some Disturbing Characteristics of the LPC Score," Personnel Psychology, 27:477–485

(Autumn 1974), and George Graen, James Orris, and Kenneth M. Alvares, "Contingency Model of Leadership Effectiveness: Some Methodological Issues," Journal of Applied Psychology, 55:205–210 (June 1971). One frequent criticism is that this research omits descriptions of actual leader behavior. On the other hand, Mockler sees situational or contingency theory as a unifying thread in management theory. See Robert J. Mockler, "Situational Theory of Management," Harvard Business Review, 49:146–151ff. (May-June 1971).
[88] Jay W. Lorsch and John J. Morse, Organizations and Their Members: A Contingency Approach (New York: Harper & Row, 1974), pp. 74–76.

Figure 7-5   Summary of Lorsch and Morse's findings: type of supervision and degree of structure associated with organizational effectiveness

Type of organization	Degree of structure (Members' perceptions of behavioral conformity and organizational clarity*)	Type of supervision (% of respondents indicating participative**)
Manufacturing Plants		
Effective container plant	More structure (6.16)	Less participation (48)
Effective appliance plant	More structure (6.20)	Less participation (41)
Less effective container plant	Less structure (5.01)	More participation (87)
Less effective appliance plant	Less structure (4.52)	More participation (78)
Laboratories		
Effective communications laboratory	Less structure (4.0)	More participation (74)
Effective medical products laboratory	Less structure (4.18)	More participation (70)
Effective proprietary drug laboratory	Less structure (4.62)	More participation (72)
Less effective communications laboratory	More structure (5.31)	Less participation (52)
Less effective medical products laboratory	More structure (5.38)	Less participation (41)
Less effective drug laboratory	More structure (6.07)	Less participation (50)

*Scores shown are the behavioral conformity and clarity scores combined.
**Scores are based on the percentage of respondents indicating participative type of supervision in contrast to directive, or laissez-faire supervision.

Based on Jay W. Lorsch and John J. Morse, *Organizations and Their Members: A Contingency Approach* (New York: Harper & Row, 1974), pp. 70, 76, 96, 102.

leader's task is to increase the sum of the valences (goal attractiveness) associated with goal attainment and to influence and clarify the effort-performance-reward paths. Supportiveness, for example, increases the rewards available and by linking such rewards to performance the leader can influence the paths chosen for need satisfaction. Further, the leader can assist in making progress easier along these paths through coaching and reducing barriers.[89] This theory is highly congruent with the research cited in this chapter.

ORGANIZATIONAL CLIMATE

Early in the chapter we took the point of view that optimal leadership effectiveness can take

[89] House and Mitchell, "Path-Goal Theory of Leadership," pp. 81–97; and Stogdill, *Handbook of Leadership*, p. 21.

place only in an appropriate organizational climate. Recently, theorists and researchers have begun to refine the concept of organizational climate and to develop scales for the measurement of several variables subsumed under this concept.

Litwin and Stringer define organizational climate as ". . . the perceived, subjective effects of the formal system, the informal 'style' of managers, and other important environmental factors on the attitudes, beliefs, values, and motivation of people who work in a particular organization."[90] Thus, organizational climate is seen by Litwin and Stringer as a set of perceptions and feelings that organizational members have about certain broad aspects of the organization.

Climate is measured by asking organizational members to respond to questionnaire items pertaining to:

1. *Structure* The feeling that employees have about the constraints in the group, how many rules, regulations, procedures there are. . . .

2. *Responsibility* The feeling of being your own boss. . . .

3. *Reward* The feeling of being rewarded for a job well done; emphasizing positive rewards rather than punishment; the perceived fairness of the pay and promotion policies.

4. *Risk* The sense of riskiness and challenge . . . (in contrast to) . . . playing it safe. . . .

5. *Warmth* The feeling of general good fellowship. . . . The emphasis on being well liked; the prevalence of friendly and informal social groups.

6. *Support* The perceived helpfulness of the managers and other employees . . . emphasis on mutual support. . . .

7. *Standards* The perceived importance of implicit and explicit goals and performance standards. . . .

8. *Conflict* The feeling that managers and other workers *want* to hear different opinions; the emphasis placed on getting problems out in the open. . . .

9. *Identity* The feeling that you belong to a company and you are a valuable member of a working team. . . .[91]

In many ways, these item areas parallel Likert's measurement of System 1 through System 4 characteristics, described earlier. Indeed, the "Survey of Organization" questionnaire used by Likert and colleagues includes items referred to as "organizational climate items." These items appear to focus more broadly on the total organization than do the leadership items on the questionnaire. For example, "To what extent does this organization have a real interest in the welfare and happiness of those who work here?" is labeled an organizational climate item, while "To what extent is your supervisor friendly and easy to approach?" is considered a leadership item.[92]

Preliminary experimental research with three simulated business organizations in a university setting found that leadership style created different organizational climates, and, in turn, these climates were associated with significant effects on motivation, performance, and job satisfaction.

The research design and the results were as follows: Each organization had fifteen members

---

[90] George H. Litwin and Robert A. Stringer, *Motivation and Organization Climate* (Boston: Graduate School of Business Administration, Harvard University, 1968), p. 5. See also Renato Tagiuri and George H. Litwin, eds., *Organizational Climate* (Boston: Graduate School of Business Administration, Harvard University, 1968).

[91] Litwin and Stringer, *Motivation and Organizational Climate*, pp. 81–82.

[92] James C. Taylor and David G. Bowers, *Survey of Organizations* (Ann Arbor: Institute for Social Research, The University of Michigan, 1972), pp. 48, 61–74. While some have criticized the organization climate literature on the grounds that measures of climate are really measures of job satisfaction, an analysis of the literature concludes that the concept refers to attributes that can be perceived and that the ". . . responses sought are primarily descriptive rather than evaluative . . ." as in the case of job satisfaction surveys. Don Hellriegel and John W. Slocum, Jr., "Organizational Climate: Measures, Research and Contingencies," *Academy of Management Journal*, 17:225–280 (1974). See also Benjamin Schneider, "Organizational Climates: An Essay," *Personnel Psychology*, 28:447–479 (Winter 1975).

plus a president appointed from the research staff, and with the exception of leadership style, all major variables such as technology, task, and worker characteristics were essentially identical. In essence, the president of the first organization, "British Radar" strongly emphasized structure, assigned roles, relative status, authority of position, punishment for deviation from rules, and communication of a vertical and formal nature. (The reader will note that this is the mechanistic type of organization described in Chapter 5.) The president of the second organization, "Balance Radar," advocated an informal, loose structure and urged group decision making, friendliness, cooperation, teamwork, and group loyalty. An atmosphere of encouragement and help was emphasized, and punishment was not used. Group meetings were inaugurated so that workers could get to know each other better. The president of the third organization, "Blazer Radar," placed strong emphasis on high productivity, participant goal setting and responsibility, reinforcement for creativity and innovation, and rewards in the form of recognition, approval, promotions, and pay raises for excellent performance. An effort was made to create teamwork and pride by emphasizing competition against external standards. Feedback on progress was supplied frequently. Mutual help around "task issues" was encouraged.[93]

Responses to two surveys of most of the items from the organizational climate questionnaire referred to (items pertaining to structure, responsibility, risk, reward, warmth and support, and conflict) showed different leadership patterns to be clearly associated with organizational climate, i.e., the three simulated businesses were significantly different from each other on all of the climate dimensions. For example, the climate of British Radar was seen by organizational members as very structured, of-

fering little chance for individual responsibility, punitive, and nonsupportive. Considerable distance and aloofness between managers and employees was apparent, and considerable interpersonal and group conflict developed in spite of efforts of the president to suppress conflict. Participants in Balance Radar saw the climate of their organization as loosely structured, having norms of democratic decision making and interpersonal and intergroup cooperation, emphasis on friendliness and warmth, and a reward pattern without punishment or criticism. Perceived personal responsibility was high among workers, but fairly low among managers. Blazer Radar was seen as loosely structured, having strong norms of responsibility, personal initiative and risk taking, and having a climate that was both rewarding but critical of poor performance. The climate was generally seen as warm and supportive and with norms of cooperation and teamwork. There was a moderate amount of conflict.[94]

These organizational climate characteristics were, in turn, associated with certain organizational outcomes. In British Radar, for example, the overall performance of the organization was generally low, there was low job satisfaction, and participant attitudes suggested independence, rebelliousness, and minds closed to others' ideas. In Balance Radar, overall productivity was generally low, innovation was moderately high, and job satisfaction was very high. Participant attitudes suggested openness to the ideas of others and mutual dependence. In Blazer Radar, overall productivity was very high, innovation was very high, and job satisfaction was high. Participant attitudes suggested openness to others' ideas and mutual dependence.[95]

While these results must be considered very tentative, they do give credence to a number of

---

[93] Ibid., pp. 98–99.

[94] Ibid., pp. 116–118.
[95] Ibid., pp. 140–141.

conclusions stated earlier, e.g., that productivity and satisfaction are not necessarily correlated, but that warmth and support, participation in goal setting, participation in attempts to increase productivity and efficiency, and recognition and reward for high performance are associated with both high morale and high productivity. It should also be noted that a constellation of leadership behaviors, organizational climate factors, and personnel policies and practices were operating simultaneously to produce these outcomes.

SUMMARY

The research cited in this and other chapters suggests that effective leadership—leadership associated with high employee performance and high employee morale and with the development of human resources rather than their dissipation—results from a complex combination of traits, behaviors, and conditions. Effective leadership is a multidimensional matter, involving attention to a wide variety of factors.

To summarize, the following picture of the effective leader is found to emerge from the research. Although it is an imposing list and perhaps should be considered a picture of the "ideal" leader, who may exist only in theory, the reader will notice that many of these items either overlap or are mutually reinforcing. They are thus more realistic than might appear at the first glance. However, it should be recognized that much of the behavior listed below will depend upon whether the leader's superiors and the broader organization will permit or encourage such behavior or both.

I should note that I am referring to the *formal* leader, that is, the manager or supervisor who has been "officially" assigned to a managerial role. This distinction is important because the group members can effectively assume certain roles of leadership from time to time depending

upon the particular skills needed at the moment and depending upon the skills in group dynamics that the total group has developed.

Although this portrait must be considered tentative and subject to modification by future studies, the picture presented by research appears to be like the following outline.

CHARACTERISTICS

The effective formal leader:

1. Is technically competent enough to instruct and to develop more efficient methods.

2. Has higher basic problem-solving ability than subordinates. (This requirement is probably of less consequence in organizations involving a high degree of colleague authority, that is, a research laboratory.)

3. Is free enough from neurotic tendencies to permit making decisions readily, to get along well with people, and to behave in the pattern pictured below.

4. Is interested in the leadership role and enjoys being a leader.

5. Has a strong drive to get things done.[96]

BEHAVIOR [97]

The effective formal leader, in terms of *attitudes toward subordinates*:

6. Asserts leadership.

7. Has confidence in subordinates and conveys this confidence.

[96] These and other characteristics of effective leaders will be discussed in more detail in Chapter 13.

[97] Many of these items depend partly on conditions existing in the leader's environment. Further, as noted, many depend upon a basic personality orientation that will permit the leader to display such behavior. Given basic aptitude and a supportive management, most individuals can probably develop considerable facility in such behavior through coaching, training, and experience.

8. Is permissive in terms of being approachable and friendly.

9. Is eager to help subordinates to be more effective and works at removing obstacles to achievement.

10. In dealing with subordinates, is emotionally supportive and is careful to avoid ego-threatening behavior.

In terms of *participation:*

11. Permits subordinates to have latitude in the solution of work problems where the subordinate's ingenuity can result in gains and where standardization in method is not imperative.

12. Is cognizant of the need for leadership styles to be somewhat different in different technological settings, e.g., that it is easily possible to overstructure and be too directive in a laboratory setting and to understructure and be too participative in some factory settings.

13. Encourages the participation of subordinates, but only on the basis of a genuine interest in utilizing constructive suggestions and only where subordinates perceive participation as being legitimate.

In terms of *technology and planning:*

14. Utilizes, and encourages subordinates to utilize, the appropriate technology in attaining these goals—e.g., work simplification, appropriate tools, proper layout, etc.

15. Is an effective planner in terms of both short-range and long-range goals and contingencies.

In terms of *performance standards and appraisal:*

16. Works with subordinates in establishing attainable but high performance standards and high goals—which are consistent with the goals of the enterprise.

17. Appraises subordinates as nearly as possible on objective, measurable performance.

In terms of the *linking-pin function:*

18. Is an effective link with higher management and other groups within the enterprise.

19. Is influential with superiors in obtaining increases in pay and other benefits for subordinates, i.e., secures a group payoff for high group performance.[98]

In terms of *rewards and correction:*

20. Uses subordinates' mistakes as an educational opportunity rather than an opportunity for punishment.

21. Gives recognition to good work.

ORGANIZATIONAL CLIMATE

The performance of the effective formal leader is reinforced by:

22. Superiors who subscribe to the above conditions, including an emphasis on both people and production, and who create a climate of *reciprocal influence.*

23. An organizational climate featuring employee perceptions of the following: a reasonable amount of structure, considerable latitude in managing one's own job, rewards and recognition for good work, encouragement for reasonable risk, warmth and support, performance standards, and the acceptability of getting problems and differing opinions out in the open.

24. And finally, as will be discussed in detail in subsequent chapters, an organization where

---

[98] In my opinion, group rewards for high group performance make differential rewards to individuals functional. If there is no group reward (financial or otherwise) for high total performance, individuals find themselves competing for a "package" of rewards that is likely to result in either (a) the group's "pegging" performance to a group-determined level, or (b) lack of cooperation, back-biting, and friction.

there are effective personnel policies and practices, including effective staffing; a fair and equitable compensation program; effective avenues of communication and appeal; effective training and development; and emphasis on fair play and integrity. (This is an extensive list of conditions in itself.)

It should be emphasized, however, that the above list is not a set of rules but instead it is an orientation—a general set of attitudes or a general way of behaving for the total managerial hierarchy. This list also suggests a general set of conditions that must exist if the individual leader is to be effective.

It should also be emphasized that this list cannot be applied exactly and uniformly in all situations because leaders must adapt to very different and very complicated environments. The characteristics and behavior that have been described, however, suggest a good deal of adaptability. Much more research needs to be done on the organizational, technological, and external conditions influencing the degree of effectiveness of differing leadership styles. The research by Woodward cited in an earlier chapter, which found mechanistic and organic systems associated with differing kinds of technology, and the studies by Lorsch and Morse are illustrations of such research.

In conclusion, effective leadership if a function of a complex combination of factors, including factors that are aspects of the broader organization and its environment, the traits and behavior of the leader, and the traits and behavior of the leader's supervisor and subordinates. Finally, if there is one theme that stands out clearly from the research, it is that effective leadership requires the leader to be effective in integrating individual and enterprise goals, with a high concern for the objectives of the enterprise as well as a high concern for human beings.

REVIEW AND DISCUSSION QUESTIONS

1. What are the major organizational variables that can affect the quality of leadership?

2. What are some of the similarities (or differences) between Blake and Mouton's Managerial Grid and the Ohio State concepts of initiating structure and consideration?

3. What are the basic assumptions of Theory X and Theory Y?

4. How could a manager use Likert's "Principle of Supportive Relations" in a situation in which an employee has violated work rules?

5. Which research studies cited in this chapter support Blake and Mouton's emphasis on concern for both production and people?

6. Describe some of the parallels (or differences) between the concepts of self-actualization, Theory Y, System 4, and organic system.

7. What are some of the results of autocratic leadership as indicated by the literature?

8. What are some of the results of laissez-faire leadership?

9. Under what conditions is participative management the most effective?

10. What is meant by the *linking-pin function?*

11. What is the relationship between subordinate characteristics and leadership behavior?

12. What is the relationship between supervisory behavior and absenteeism and turnover?

13. What is the central assertion of Fiedler's "Contingency Model of Leadership Effectiveness"? In terms of personnel practice, what do you see as the practical implications of Fiedler's research?

14. What conclusions do you draw from Lorsch and Morse's contingency studies in factories and laboratories?

15. What is meant by *organizational climate?* How does it differ from *leadership?* Is it a causal or intervening variable?

SUPPLEMENTAL REFERENCES

Abdel-Halim, Ahmed A., and Kendrith M. Rowland, "Some Personality Determinants of the Effects of Participation: A Further Investigation," *Personnel Psychology:* 29:41–55 (Spring 1976).

Argyris, Chris, *Personality and Organization* (New York: Harper & Brothers, 1957).

———, "Some Problems in Conceptualizing Organizational Climate: A Case Study of a Bank," *Administrative Science Quarterly*, 2:501–520 (March 1958).

Bass, Bernard M., Enzo R. Valenzi, Dana L. Farrow, and Robert J. Solomon, "Management Styles Associated with Organizational, Task, Personal, and Interpersonal Contingencies," *Journal of Applied Psychology*, 60:720–729 (December 1975).

Bennis, Warren, *The Unconscious Conspiracy: Why Leaders Can't Lead* (New York: Amacom, 1976).

Bowers, David G., *Systems of Organization: Management of the Human Resource* (Ann Arbor: University of Michigan Press, 1976).

———, and Stanley E. Seashore, "Peer Leadership within Work Groups," *Personnel Administration*, 30:45–50 (September-October 1967).

Chapman, J. Brad, "Comparison of Male and Female Leadership Styles," *Academy of Management Journal*, 18:645–650 (September 1975).

Dubin, Robert, George C. Homans, Floyd C. Mann, and Delbert C. Miller, *Leadership and Productivity: Some Facts of Industrial Life* (San Francisco: Chandler Publishing Company, 1965).

Etzioni, Amatai, "Dual Leadership in Complex Organizations," *American Sociological Review*, 30:688–698 (October 1965).

Fiedler, Fred E., *A Theory of Leadership Effectiveness* (New York: McGraw-Hill Book Company, 1967).

Gellerman, Saul W., "Supervision: Substance and Style," *Harvard Business Review*, 54:89–99 (March-April 1976).

Greene, Charles N., "The Reciprocal Nature of Influence between Leader and Subordinate," *Journal of Applied Psychology*, 60:187–193 (April 1975).

Greiner, Larry E., "What Managers Think of Participative Leadership," *Harvard Business Review*, 51:111–117 (March-April 1973).

Hare, A. Paul, Edgar F. Borgatta, and Robert F. Bales, *Small Groups: Studies in Social Interaction* (New York: Alfred A. Knopf, Inc., 1955).

Hemphill, John K., *Situational Factors in Leadership* (Columbus: The Ohio State University, The Bureau of Educational Research, 1949).

Herold, David M., "Interaction of Subordinate and Leader Characteristics in Moderating the Consideration-Satisfaction Relationship," *Journal of Applied Psychology*, 59:649–651 (October 1974).

Hollander, Edwin P., "Style, Structure, and Setting in Organizational Leadership," *Administrative Science Quarterly*, 16:1–9 (March 1971).

Hunt, J.G., "Breakthrough in Leadership Research," *Personnel Administration*, 30:38–44 (September-October 1967).

Johnston, H. Russell, "A New Conceptualization of Source of Organizational Climate," *Administrative Science Quarterly*, 21:95–103 (March 1976).

Jones, John Paul, "Changing Patterns of Leadership," *Personnel*, 44:8–15 (March-April 1967).

Lassey, William R., ed., *Leadership and Social Change* (Iowa City, Iowa: University Associates Press, 1971).

Likert, Rensis, *The Human Organization* (New York: McGraw-Hill Book Company, 1967).

McGregor, Douglas M., *The Professional Manager* (New York: McGraw-Hill Book Company, 1967).

Myers, M. Scott, "Conditions for Manager Motivation," *Harvard Business Review*, 44:58–71 (January-February 1966).

Patchen, Martin, *Participation, Achievement, and Involvement* (Englewood Cliffs, N.J.: Prentice-Hall, Inc., 1960).

Patten, Thomas H., Jr., *The Foreman: Forgotten Man of Management* (New York: American Management Association, 1968).

Payne, Roy, and Derek S. Pugh, "Organizational Structure and Climate," in Marvin D. Dunnette, ed., *Handbook of Industrial and Organizational Psychology* (Chicago: Rand McNally College Publishing Company, 1976), pp. 1125–1173.

Rice, Robert W., and Martin M. Chemers, "Personality and Situational Determinants of Leader Behavior," *Journal of Applied Psychology*, 60:20–27 (February 1975).

Roethlisberger, F.J., "The Foreman: Master and Victim of Double Talk," *Harvard Business Review*, 43:22–37ff. (September-October 1965).

Rubin, Irwin M., and Max Goldman, "An Open System Model of Leadership Performance," *Organizational Behavior and Human Performance*, 3:143–156 (May 1968).

Schneider, Benjamin, and Robert A. Snyder, "Some Relationships between Job Satisfaction and Organizational Climate," *Journal of Applied Psychology*, 60:318–328 (June 1975).

Schuler, Randall S., "Participation with Supervisor and Subordinate Authoritarianism: A Path-Goal Theory Reconciliation," *Administrative Science Quarterly*, 21:320–325 (June 1976).

Sherif, Muzafer, ed., *Intergroup Relations and Leadership* (New York: John Wiley & Sons, 1962).

Sims, Harry P., Jr., and Andrew D. Szilagyi, "Leader Structure and Subordinate Satisfaction for Two Hospital Administrative Levels: A Path Analysis Approach," *Journal of Applied Psychology*, 60:194–197 (April 1975).

Student, Kurt R., "Supervisory Influence and Work-Group Performance," *Journal of Applied Psychology*, 52:188–194 (June 1968).

Tagiuri, Renato, and George H. Litwin, eds., *Organizational Climate* (Boston: Harvard University, Graduate School of Business Administration, 1968).

Vroom, Victor, *Some Personality Determinants of the Effects of Participation* (Englewood Cliffs, N.J.: Prentice-Hall, Inc., 1960).

Vroom, Victor H., and Floyd C. Mann, "Leader Authoritarianism and Employee Attitudes," *Personnel Psychology*, 13:125–139 (Summer 1960).

Vroom, Victor H., and P.W. Yetton, *Leadership and Decision Making* (Pittsburgh: University of Pittsburgh Press, 1973).

Wofford, J.C., "Managerial Behavior: Situational Factors, and Productivity and Morale," *Administrative Science Quarterly*, 16:10–17 (March 1971).

CHAPTER 8
ORGANIZATIONAL JUSTICE

The purpose of this chapter is to examine a problem that underlies most of personnel management: the determination of *justice, fairness,* or *equity* in the organization. This chapter, then, is about the *process of determining organizational justice* defined as *a complex flow of events that allocates rewards and penalties to organizational members in some relationship to perceptions of fairness or equity*.

Every managerial decision or action rewarding or penalizing individuals or groups has the potential for being labeled fair or unfair. As Roethlisberger states it, "Any person who has achieved a certain rank in the prestige scale regards anything, real or imaginary, which tends to alter his status adversely as something unfair or unjust."[1] Although persuasion and disclosure of reasons for adverse decisions may minimize such perceptions, nevertheless, the possibility of injustice and perceived inequity exists over a wide range of managerial decision areas.

This human tendency to evaluate the fairness of events pervades the organization and is a constant challenge in the utilization of human resources. Thus, the problem of fairness, or justice, is a major one in personnel management and is one with which the personnel manager and every other manager must constantly deal. As Barnard says, "There is no escape from the judicial process in the exercise of executive function."[2]

TOWARD THE MEANING OF JUSTICE

Although we shall use the words *fairness* and *justice* synonymously, it should be pointed out

[1] F.J. Roethlisberger, *Management and Morale* (Cambridge, Mass.: Harvard University Press, 1946), p. 61.

[2] Chester I. Barnard, *The Functions of the Executive* (Cambridge, Mass.: Harvard University Press, 1938), p. 280.

that, in popular usage, the term *justice* is often applied in a context of punishment or penalties, and *fairness* is often applied in a context that relates to the allocation of rewards. Our use of both terms will be in a broader sense and will relate to both rewards and penalties.

Justice, or fairness, has a very elusive meaning.[3] What is just, or fair, has been and will continue to be a matter of dispute in law, philosophy, union-management relations, and in the management of human resources. Nevertheless, if we can sharpen our understanding of this concept we shall have a better grasp of personnel management and some of its most critical problems.

An old edition of *Black's Law Dictionary* defined justice as "the constant and perpetual disposition to render every man his due."[4] What is "every man's due," of course, still remains to be defined.

Roscoe Pound elaborates further as he develops a statement that seems to embody his concept of justice.

Men wish to be free, but they want much besides. Thus we come to an idea of a maximum satisfaction of human wants or expectations. What we have to do in social control, and so in law, is to reconcile and adjust these desires or wants or expectations, so far as we can, so as to secure as much of the totality of them as we can.[5]

Thus, justice has to do with administering to the needs, wants, and expectations of people so that the result is the "greatest good for the greatest number."[6]

The "greatest good for the greatest number" refers to justice in general, or universal justice, which Aristotle (B.C. 384–322) differentiated from "particular justice," or justice more closely related to specific problems.[7] According to Aristotle, particular justice, or the application of justice to specific situations, requires a distinction between *corrective justice* and *distributive justice.*[8] Distributive justice has to do with the allocation of rewards and penalties ". . . according to merit."[9] On the other hand, corrective justice ". . . plays a rectifying part in transactions between man and man."[10] Thus, distributive justice allocates rewards or penalties according to rule, law, or policy; corrective justice makes adjustments if there have been mistakes in decisions about allocations or if there are defects in the rules, laws, or policies. These concepts of distributive and corrective justice are both important in personnel management, as we shall see.

In terms of absolutes, most of us recognize that the process of determining justice must acknowledge the dignity and worth of the human personality and, from the standpoint of society, must seek to make allocations on the basis of the good of all. While bearing in mind some such concept of universal justice, our discussion will focus on the more limited organizational purpose stated in the preceding paragraph. Thus, in the Aristotelian sense, we are focusing on particular justice rather than on universal justice, although, practically speaking, some concept of universal justice cannot be

---

[3] The late Judge Learned Hand likened the jurist's role, a role in which justice determination is central, to ". . . shoveling smoke." See Ernest Havemann, "On a Great Judge's Death: A Moving Memoir," *Life*, August 25, 1961, p. 39.

[4] Henry Campbell Black, *Black's Law Dictionary*, 3rd ed. (St. Paul, Minn.: West Publishing Company, 1933), p. 1050.

[5] Roscoe Pound, *Justice According to Law* (New Haven, Conn.: Yale University Press, 1951), p. 31.

[6] This phrase is usually attributed to Jeremy Bentham (1748–1832), but the concept can also be traced to Beccaria (1738–1794), Priestley (1733–1804), and Francis Hutcheson (1694–1746). Much earlier, Plato (B.C. 427–347), Aristotle's

teacher, expressed a similar concept: ". . . our aim in founding the state was not the disproportionate happiness of any one class, but the greatest happiness of the whole. . . ." See Plato's *The Republic*, Book IV.

[7] Aristotle, *Nicomachean Ethics*, Book V, in Saxe Commins and Robert N. Linscott, eds., *Man and Man: The Social Philosophers* (New York: Random House, 1947), pp. 87–92.

[8] For a discussion of these Aristotelian concepts as they apply to law and society, see Pound, *Justice According to Law*, p. 4.

[9] Aristotle refers to "distributions of honor or money or the other things . . . ," *Nicomachean Ethics*, pp. 92, 93.

[10] Ibid., p. 92.

ignored if defensive behavior is to be minimized and if managers are to maintain some degree of consistency between their business decisions and their philosophical and religious beliefs.

DISTRIBUTIVE JUSTICE

HYPOTHESES AND RESEARCH

Examining Aristotle's writings further, we find that distributive justice involves a *proportional allocation of rewards according to merit*. That is, the total of the available rewards is to be divided into parts and allocated among people on the basis of respective merit.[11] Thus, distributive justice is always relative and involves more than one person. For example, if person A is twice as meritorious as person B, person A should receive twice as many rewards, as follows, assuming a total of three units of rewards available:

$$\frac{2 \text{ rewards } \text{Person A}}{2 \text{ merits } \text{Person A}} : \frac{1 \text{ reward } \text{Person B}}{1 \text{ merit } \text{Person B}}$$

If additional people are involved (as they usually are), distributive justice requires allocation to each in proportion to merit:

$$\frac{\text{reward}_A}{\text{merit}_A} : \frac{\text{reward}_B}{\text{merit}_B} : \frac{\text{reward}_C}{\text{merit}_C}, \text{ etc.}$$

When this condition does not exist, defensive behavior results. As Aristotle stated centuries ago: ". . . but this is the origin of quarrels and complaints—when either equals have and are awarded unequal shares, or unequals equal shares."[12]

In recent years, George Homans has elaborated upon Aristotle's theories. According to Homans, distributive justice requires that an individual's "investments," that is, age, seniority, skill, sex, etc., be in line with the "profits" of the job. Profits are rewards minus costs. Rewards include wages, intrinsic interest in the job, status, autonomy, chance for advancement, etc. Costs are negative aspects of the job, including boredom, responsibility, danger, discomfort, etc.[13] For employees to feel fairly treated, the transactions between the employer and the employee require some proper alignment of workers' investments, job rewards, and job costs, always in relation to the alignment for others.

Thus, according to Homans, distributive justice is found when the ratio of profits (rewards minus costs) to investments of person A are proportional to the ratio of profits to investments of person B. Our interpretation of Homans would be that distributive justice requires the following ratios:

$$\frac{\text{Rewards}_A - \text{Costs}_A}{\text{Investments}_A} : \frac{\text{Rewards}_B - \text{Costs}_B}{\text{Investments}_B}$$

or,

$$\frac{\text{Profits}_A}{\text{Investments}_A} : \frac{\text{Profits}_B}{\text{Investments}_B}$$

Homans then goes on to develop some hypotheses, including the following: "The more to a man's disadvantage the rule of distributive justice fails of realization, the more likely he is to display the emotional behavior we call anger."[14] And also: "Not only do men display

---

[11] Ibid., pp. 90–97.
[12] Ibid., p. 93.
[13] George C. Homans, *Social Behavior: Its Elementary Forms* (New York: Harcourt, Brace & World, Inc., 1961), Chapter 12. It should be noted that Homans believes that distributive justice requires that costs be high if rewards are high. That is, people seem to feel that jobs having high rewards should have high costs, in terms of job demands, responsibility, etc., in addition to the investments brought to the job. (Homans, p. 245.)
[14] Ibid., Chapters 4 and 12.

anger . . . they also learn to do something about it."[15]

Homans cites some research tending to confirm his hypotheses that perceived injustice influences attitudes and behavior in the organizational setting. For example, he cites the Bank Wiring Observation Room Experiment from the Hawthorne Studies as evidence that workers within groups try to keep rewards in line with investments. Further, he cites his own Eastern Utilities Company study as evidence that employees in one job category express considerable dissatisfaction when their rewards are not proportional to worker investments and costs, in contrast to another category of workers. It seems that the rewards of ledger clerks, such as job autonomy, were in a lower ratio of their investments, such as training and seniority, and to their job costs, such as worry about the accuracy of accounts, than the rewards of the cash posters to the latter's investments, costs, and rewards.[16]

As will be discussed in Chapter 19, since modern job evaluation (a method of determining relative job worth) seeks to allocate rewards on the basis of both investments (experience, training, etc.), and costs (hazards, responsibility, etc.), we find it useful to think of distributive justice as requiring the allocation of rewards in proportion to investments plus costs. Thus, our ratio describing distributive justice would be:

$$\frac{Rewards_A}{Investments_A + Costs_A} : \frac{Rewards_B}{Investments_B + Costs_B}$$

We believe this to be a realistic ratio describing what actually happens in job evaluation.[17] In general, people believe that fair treatment requires such a proportion.

One important variable is missing from our proportion if we wish to consider merit rating. With other variables equal, if person A produces more value (more units, more customer good will, and so forth) than person B, the former will feel unfairly treated if the rewards are not proportionately greater. The function of merit rating or an incentive plan is to be more precise in allocating rewards on the basis of value produced.

Of course, job evaluation, which focuses on relative investments and costs, has as its underlying assumption that, in general, those jobs rated high will produce more value than those rated low. (Some exceptions to this rule will be discussed in a moment.) At times, job evaluation specifically recognizes this assumption, especially with a factor such as "potential impact of job on profits." Merit rating serves to refine the decisions made in job evaluation and to assign a more accurate worth to a job and its outcomes by focusing on actual relative value produced.[18] Therefore, distributive justice requires that an additional variable be added to the ratio, as follows:

$$\frac{Rewards_A}{Additional\ Investments_A + Costs_A + value\ produced_A} :$$

$$\frac{Rewards_B}{Additional\ Investments_B + Costs_B + value\ produced_B}$$

[15] Ibid., pp. 232–233.
[16] Ibid., pp. 235–242.
[17] "Pure" job evaluation ignores labor-market conditions and differentials in group bargaining power, although such considerations inevitably creep into job-evaluation decisions.

[18] Hard work per se, in contrast to results, is sometimes perceived as worthy of reward, although most people believe it to be in the interests of justice that value produced be rewarded more amply than effort alone. The free-enterprise system is essentially based on the latter premise. For further discussion of the assumptions underlying merit rating, see Chapter 15.

In situations in which costs, such as discomfort, unpleasantness, danger, etc., are given particularly high weight in job evaluation, job evaluation and merit rating do not necessarily result in jobs being paid in proportion to value produced. Typically, we find under such circumstances that the jobs producing the higher value but the lower wage provide additional rewards, such as status, security, opportunity for advancement, etc. Thus, we need to look at the total reward structure in thinking about justice within the organization, including such matters as fringe benefits, privileges, status, comfort, etc.

In short, our hypothesis is that people feel unfairly treated unless total rewards are proportional to investments plus costs plus additional value produced. Although an oversimplification, we believe it to be essentially true. Some additional complexities will be discussed later.

In his book, *A Theory of Cognitive Dissonance,* Festinger has developed concepts and hypotheses consistent with those of Homans. By *cognitive* Festinger means "knowledge, opinion, or belief . . . ," and by *dissonance* he means "inconsistency." Thus, in his book, Festinger theorizes about perceived inconsistency.

Festinger's two basic hypotheses have to do with the consequences of perceived inconsistency:

1. The existence of dissonance, being psychologically uncomfortable, will motivate the person to try to reduce the dissonance and achieve consonance.

2. When dissonance is present, in addition to trying to reduce it, the person will actively avoid situations and information which would likely increase the dissonance.[19]

Developing a theory of inequity on Festinger's theory of cognitive dissonance, Adams translates Homans' concept of investments into a concept he refers to as "inputs," that is, variables brought by a person to a job. Inputs, to Adams, include such factors as age, education, skill, seniority, social status, and effort expended on the job. Instead of referring to rewards as does Homans, he refers to "outcomes."[20] Presumably, Adams would subtract from outcomes those items that Homans calls "costs," such as danger and discomfort, although he is not explicit about this.

Using the terms *inputs* and *outcomes,* Adams defines inequity as follows: "Inequity exists for Person whenever his perceived job inputs and/or outcomes stand psychologically in an obverse relation to what he perceives are the inputs and/or outcomes of Other."[21] Thus, Adams' definition involves a person's perception of a job's inputs and outcomes relative to the inputs and outcomes of somebody else.

In turn, Adams develops a number of hypotheses about perceived inequity, some of which are in terms of organizational consequences. For example:

. . . Person may increase his inputs if they are low relative to Other's inputs and to his own outcomes. If, for example, Person's effort were low compared to Other's and to his own pay, he could reduce inequity by increasing his effort on the job . . .

. . . Person may decrease his inputs if they are high relative to Other's inputs and to his own outcomes. If Person's effort were high compared to

[19] W. Festinger, *A Theory of Cognitive Dissonance* (Evanston, Ill.: Row, Peterson, 1957). The reader should note that there are a number of exchange theories such as (1) dissonance theory, (2) equity theory, (3) social comparison theory, and (4) exchange theory, all of which tend to emphasize the same idea. See William G. Scott and Terence R. Mitchell, *Organizational Theory* (Homewood, Ill.: Richard D. Irwin, 1972), pp. 80–81. Also see Peter M. Blau, "Exchange Theory," in Oscar

Grusky and George A. Miller, eds., *The Sociology of Organizations: Basic Studies* (New York: The Free Press, 1970), pp. 127–147.

[20] J. Stacy Adams, "Towards an Understanding of Inequity," *Journal of Abnormal and Social Psychology,* 67:422–424 (1963). See also J. Stacy Adams, "Wage Inequities, Productivity, and Work Quality," *Industrial Relations,* 3:9–16 (October 1963); and J. Stacy Adams, "Inequity in Social Exchange," in L. Berkowitz, ed., *Advances in Experimental Social Psychology* (New York: Academic Press, 1965).

[21] Adams, "Toward an Understanding of Inequity," p. 424.

Other's and to his own pay, he might reduce his effort and productivity . . .

. . . Person may "leave the field" when he experiences inequity of any type. This may take the form of quitting his job or obtaining a transfer or reassignment, or of absenteeism.[22]

In citing support for some of his hypotheses on inequity, Adams refers to several studies, including those mentioned by Homans. In addition, he cites a doctoral dissertation by Clark, who found that supermarket bundlers—those who put shoppers' items into bags to be carried out—reduced their output when they were assigned to cashiers who had lower input, such as age and education. Further, the greater the input-reward inequity among stores, the greater were operating costs.[23] (Further research by Adams will be discussed in the chapter on the administration of wages and salaries.)

A number of other studies support Adams' hypotheses. For example, Patchen investigated the relationship in a Canadian oil refinery between absenteeism (attendance is an input) and employees' feelings about fair treatment in promotion and pay (outcomes). He found that workers who felt unfairly treated with respect to promotion had a significantly higher rate of absence than those who felt fairly treated. Further, those who felt unfairly treated as to pay had a higher absence rate than those who felt their pay was fair. He concludes as follows: "When men feel that management is treating them unfairly or neglecting their interests, they feel relieved of the obligation which they, the employees, have assumed."[24] Telly et al., in a study in a large aerospace firm, found perceptions of inequity pertaining to several working conditions and supervision variables correlated

with turnover.[25] Dittrich and Carrell found perceptions of lack of fairness pertaining to work rules and pay to be associated with absenteeism and job dissatisfaction.[26]

COMPLEXITIES OF MEASUREMENT

As will be evident in later chapters, measurements of such variables as rewards, investments, costs, and additional value produced are not easily made. Certain problems immediately arise. For example, what investments and costs should be compensable, and what scale should be used to measure relative differences in these variables? What is the criterion of additional value produced? How are differing degrees of additional value produced to be measured? What is the relative worth of various rewards, such as money, privileges, recognition, etc.? How shall such dissimilar items be totaled and, in turn, allocated? These are problems that must be solved in the administration of justice.

But we must add even another complexity to this problem of distributive justice within the organization—the problem of the difference in

[22] Ibid., pp. 427–429.
[23] Ibid., pp. 431–432.
[24] Martin Patchen, "Absence and Employee Feelings about Fair Treatment," Personnel Psychology, 13:349–360 (Autumn 1960).
[25] Charles S. Telly, Wendell French, and William G. Scott, "The Relationship of Inequity to Turnover among Hourly Workers," Administrative Science Quarterly, 16:164–171 (June 1971).
[26] John Dittrich and Michael R. Carrell, "Dimensions of Organizational Fairness as Predictors of Job Satisfaction, Absence and Turnover," in Robert L. Taylor, Michael J. O'Connell, Robert A. Zawacki, and D.D. Warrick, eds., Academy of Management Proceedings, Proceedings of the 36th Annual Meeting of the Academy of Management, Kansas City, Missouri, August 11–14, 1976, pp. 79–83. For a review of some of the supporting research and suggestions for further research, see Paul S. Goodman and Abraham Friedman, "An Examination of Adams' Theory of Inequity," Administrative Science Quarterly, 16:271–288 (September 1971). For a comparison of equity theory with expectancy theory, see John P. Campbell and Robert D. Pritchard, "Motivation Theory in Industrial and Organizational Psychology," in Marvin D. Dunnette, ed., Handbook of Industrial and Organizational Psychology (Chicago: Rand McNally College Publishing Company, 1976), pp. 109–110.

perception among people and among groups as to what is just or fair. Since perceptions can differ as to (a) which investments are to be considered meritorious or worthwhile, absolutely and relatively, (b) which "costs" should be compensable and in what degree, (c) which job-performance variables produce the most value, and (d) which rewards have the most value, it follows that there can be considerable controversy over the proper allocation of rewards and penalties. The origin of some of these discrepancies will be discussed later with the interaction of needs and rewards.

Since perceptions differ, it follows that systems or procedures must be devised that will help minimize these differences and that will remedy errors once allocations have been made (corrective justice). A discussion of such systems and procedures follows later.

RELATIONSHIP OF JUSTICE TO OTHER PERSONNEL MANAGEMENT PROCESSES

The determination of justice and equity is probably an integral aspect of all the personnel management processes. For example, if performance standards (the task-specialization process) are higher for one person or group than another, but rewards (the compensation process) are the same, the employee or group of whom greater demands are made will feel unfairly treated. Similarly, if work rules (the job-design process) do not apply uniformly to similar kinds of jobs, those subject to the more stringent rules may feel they are treated unjustly. Since the reward process has to do with the allocation of rewards, every event in this particular process is a likely target for the label of either fair or unfair.

In the staffing process, if characteristics unrelated to job performance are used as criteria in selecting new employees or in promotion, such decisions may be looked upon as unfair. Con-

versely, if investments, such as training and experience, are ignored in selection and promotion, rejected candidates are likely to feel unfairly treated. To cite an example from the training and development process, the communication of a performance evaluation that does not permit any discussion of the employee's view of the situation is likely to be perceived as unfair. The collective bargaining process, to a large extent, establishes procedures for solving the problem of differing perceptions of justice.

Various aspects of the leadership process are also intimately related to the question of justice. For example, more frequent attention or recognition to one employee or group than to others may be considered unfair, or reprimanding a subordinate in front of others will be considered unjust since it results in a disproportionate amount of "loss of face." Style in leadership can also be related indirectly to the administration of organizational justice. Managers who are open to suggestions and complaints from individual subordinates and from the total group reporting to them will have much more data for making decisions perceived as fair.

RELATIONSHIP OF JUSTICE TO NEED FULFILLMENT

If rewards are not proportional to investments, costs, and additional value produced, the need for the esteem of others will not be satisfied. The feeling will be that "other people don't care much about me as they should," and this feeling, in turn, may affect self-esteem. If others don't hold us in the proper regard, we may begin to question our own worth.

Rewards that are out of line with investments, costs, and value produced will also prevent fulfillment of the integration or wholeness needs, in that the world will seem inconsistent, things "out of kilter," and the discrepancies hard to understand. Security needs are particularly threatened by unexpected injustices, because the environment becomes unpredictable. Prolonged injustices, if not too severe, may be accepted and tolerated as necessary evils, for a while, but unanticipated injustices are particularly likely to frustrate security needs.

Perceptions of justice or injustice are partly a function of need fulfillment or deprivation. If certain needs are particularly strong in an individual, even slight discrepancies between investments and rewards are likely to be perceived as unjust. For example, if a person has an inordinate need for recognition, any slight extra attention paid to other people might be perceived as being unfair, whereas the same discrepancy may not even be noticed by someone in whom this need is not strong. In short, the degree of perceived injustice will be partly a function of the intensity of need. This is one of the reasons why it is difficult to make administrative decisions that are perceived as just by everyone; people feel differing degrees of need and will perceive a particular action as just or unjust accordingly.

It is interesting to speculate on the effect of discipline on need fulfillment. In the case of the individual who violates a rule and is punished, needs for belonging, the esteem of others, and self-actualization are seriously thwarted, as indicated by the defensive behavior manifested under such circumstances. On the other hand, needs of people in the larger group may be met, since one of the functions of discipline is to keep behavior within predictable and orderly bounds. Without discipline, the security of the group is threatened.

DISTRIBUTIVE JUSTICE: CURRENT PRACTICE AND PROBLEMS

INTERDEPENDENCY OF FACTORS

As in the studies of employee satisfaction and dissatisfaction discussed in Chapter 6, the close interrelation and interdependence of so many of the variables in the working environment complicate the issue of organizational justice. Rewards, penalties, privileges, status symbols, and the like, all interact to produce feelings of justice or injustice. For example, the white-collar worker may not feel unfairly treated if her or his salary is below those of the production and maintenance workers in the plant, provided that there is more opportunity for advancement. An administrative assistant to the president of a company may not feel unfairly treated even though expected to put in longer hours than people at similar pay levels elsewhere in the organization. The value of being close to the center of power, information, and prestige in the organization may partly compensate for the lack of additional monetary rewards. Thus, the whole question involves looking at a number of variables simultaneously. Widely varying events and conditions in every job situation are "carriers of social values" and cannot be looked upon as isolated things or events.[27]

DIFFERING PERCEPTIONS OF FAIRNESS

We have already suggested that perceptions may differ as to what is fair or just. There is some evidence that different socioeconomic groups, at least, have somewhat different perceptions of what is meant by fair treatment on the job. A study by Selznick of male employees found that more than half of the unskilled workers surveyed stated that fair treatment means "equal treatment for all," while only about one-fourth of office supervisors and managers surveyed attributed this meaning of fairness. More than half of the latter group stated

---

[27] See F.J. Roethlisberger and William J. Dickson, *Management and the Worker* (Cambridge, Mass.: Harvard University Press, 1939), p. 374.

Figure **8-1**   Primary meaning of fair treatment by occupational category

	Primary meaning of fair treatment		
Occupational category	Equal treatment for all	Recognition of individual abilities	Total number
Unskilled manual workers	56%	31%	(409)
Skilled manual workers	49	33	(597)
Foremen	44	44	(160)
Clerical personnel	37	50	(102)
Professional and technical personnel	23	58	(477)
Office supervisors and managers	26	58	(202)

Table 1, "Primary Meaning of Fair Treatment, by Occupational Category," in Chapter 5, "Employee Perspectives on Industrial Justice," from LAW, SOCIETY, AND INDUSTRIAL JUSTICE, by Philip Selznick, (c) 1969, Russell Sage Foundation.

that fair treatment means "recognition of individual abilities"[28] (see Figure 8-1). This differing perception carried over into attitudes about layoffs. In this instance 41 percent of unskilled manual workers favored preference for those with seniority in layoffs, while only 23 percent of office supervisors and managers favored the seniority principle in layoffs. Sixty-six percent of union members as a whole, however, favored the seniority principle in layoffs. Overall, 72 percent of the total sample believed that layoffs should be handled according to a set of rules.[29] Thus, different occupational groups had differing perceptions of what is generally meant by fair treatment, had differing perceptions of fairness relative to layoffs, but were in substantial agreement that some set of rules should prevail in case of layoffs.

DISCRIMINATION

One of the most critical problems facing American institutions and the American society is the need to remedy organizational and social injustices stemming from racial prejudice. Black Americans, in particular, have been discriminated against in many ways, such as, for example, being denied full opportunity for employment, housing, and absorption into the broader life of the society. The resulting reductive cycle of (a) lack of cultural opportunity, (b) lack of development of skills and potential, and (c) lack of career opportunity is shown in Figure 8-2. Consequently, the militance of the black community has frequently reached explosive proportions even though the advocates of nonviolence, such as the late Dr. Martin Luther King, Jr., have had great influence.

Considering distributive justice, it is quite clear that many white Americans have perceived race as a negative input (in terms of a characteristic brought to the job) by blacks and other minorities, which has affected the rewards (status, opportunity for advancement, etc.) of the latter. This perception has also frequently affected the capability of minorities to participate in organizational life at the outset. On the other hand, probably the vast majority of Americans, as reflected in federal legis-

[28] Philip Selznick, *Law, Society, and Industrial Justice* (New York: Russell Sage Foundation, 1969), p. 187.
[29] Ibid., pp. 194, 205.

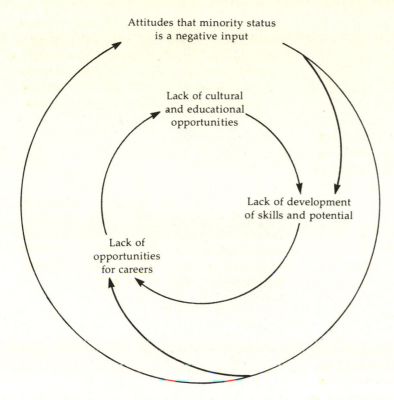

Figure 8-2   The reductive cycle

lation, are convinced that color of skin should be irrelevant in social and organizational justice. But a new problem is arising. While the argument that previous injustices to minorities are relevant "costs" or "investments" and should result in extraordinary opportunities ("outcomes") has many adherents, there are those who argue that such perceptions constitute reverse discrimination, an accusation that is arising with more frequency in the context of affirmative action programs.

NONMONETARY REWARDS

Justice in the allocation of nonmonetary rewards depends upon the skill of managers in administering various rules and policies and the sensitivity of managers in dealing with subordinates. As an example of the latter quality, one supervisor may be careful to give each subordinate considerable recognition and thus contribute to a sense of perceived justice, while another supervisor may show favoritism in giving recognition, with the inevitable result of perceived injustice.

Since many variables in the working environment are carriers of social value, dissimilarities in working conditions, status symbols, or privileges among persons of equal merit will be perceived as unjust. For example, vice presidents who have made similar job investments and are experiencing similar personal costs will expect similar treatment in terms of office space, furniture, secretarial help, parking facilities, etc. Similarly, secretaries in one department with jobs involving investments and costs similar to those of secretarial jobs in another department will expect similar treatment in terms of time off for personal business, and so forth.

Management ordinarily handles the problems of equitable treatment in nonmonetary matters by according similar treatment to large groups of people whose jobs are similar. For example, the privileges and status symbols for the production and maintenance workers may be identical, while a slightly different set of privileges and symbols will apply to the clerical and secretarial staff. Still another set of nonmonetary rewards may apply to supervisory and professional salaried employees below the department-head level, while department heads and officers of the company may be accorded even another set of nonmonetary rewards.[30]

Such differences among major groups of employees tend not to be perceived as unjust unless the discrepancy is obviously out of proportion to the investments and costs of the respective jobs, although unions frequently challenge the assumption underlying such differences. To use an exaggerated illustration, if the production and maintenance workers receive no time off with pay for personal business while the office clerks receive as much as one day per week, the former groups will probably perceive this difference as grossly unfair. The discrepancy becomes immediately apparent if a production employee is married to an office worker!

DISCIPLINE

Almost universally, organizations have work rules that, if violated, can result in various penalties, including discharge. Under collective bargaining agreements, this observation holds true, with management typically retaining the right to administer discipline, although labor contracts usually provide for discharge only for "cause," "just cause," or "proper cause."[31] This provision is usually included in a "management's rights" section of the contract.

The principle of *progressive discipline* (sometimes called "corrective discipline") is widely accepted as a tempering factor in the administration of work rules. In essence, progressive discipline simply means that management responds to a first offense with some minimal action such as an oral warning but to subsequent offenses with more serious penalties such as disciplinary layoff or discharge. A sequence of disciplinary actions might be as follows:

1. Oral warning
2. Written warning stating the consequences of future offenses
3. Disciplinary layoff or demotion
4. Discharge

The wide acceptance of this principle undoubtedly stems in part from arbitrators' decisions, which have frequently examined both the correctability of a situation and the seriousness of an offense vis-à-vis the penalty

---

[30] Some firms, such as Texas Instruments, have moved in the direction of equalizing nonmonetary status symbols between groups. See M. Scott Myers, "Conditions for Manager Motivation," *Harvard Business Review*, 44:66 (January-February 1966).

[31] About 82 percent of all labor contracts provide that discharge can only be for "cause" or "just cause." See Bureau of National Affairs, *Collective Bargaining Negotiations and Contracts*, 40:1 (1971). Some labor contracts include a "statute of limitations" clause, under which, beyond a certain time, past violations are removed from employees' records and/or are no longer considered. Ibid., 40:241 (January 1, 1976). However, it is likely that the employee's entire past record may be permitted as evidence if the union places weight on the employee's character in an arbitration or court hearing. Thus, management might not be wise to remove performance records from employees files unless there is a clear agreement about the matter.

assessed.[32] In terms of equity, it is probable that most workers and managers view discharge as an excessive negative outcome relative to the particular inadequate or negative investment of the employee that precipitated the discipline.

Although it is generally accepted that violations of work rules should result in some form of penalty, direct *rewards* for compliance are seldom considered proper. Compliance with job-performance rules is considered the *quid pro quo* for continued employment. (A small percentage of firms provide some time off with pay as a reward for specified periods of perfect attendance.) The degree of compliance, however, is likely to be indirectly related to rewards, since merit rating may include such factors as "cooperation," "attendance," etc. When compliance with work rules and standards is not up to par, the employee is likely to be rated low on such factors.

There is some evidence that employees and managers alike consider justice better served if a "clinical" approach is used to a certain extent in disciplinary matters. In other words, the feeling is growing that the circumstances of the case, including the environmental factors that may have precipitated the offense, should be considered in meting out discipline. Stessin cites evidence for this trend by noting a drastic decline in the number of clauses in labor contracts providing for specific penalties for various offenses.[33]

Since aggressive defenses in the form of work rules violations may stem from job-induced need deprivation, it seems logical that the working environment should be taken into account in administering discipline. However, until we have a better understanding of the relationship between environmental factors and misconduct, prudence suggests that individual responsibility must be given high emphasis. On the other hand, justice would seem to require giving weight to environmental or extenuating circumstances in disciplinary cases. Indeed, labor arbitrators typically hold that mitigating circumstances should be taken into account in the administration of industrial discipline.[34] (For more discussion on arbitration, see Chapter 25.)

CORRECTIVE JUSTICE: ORGANIZATIONAL DUE PROCESS

Another important aspect of organizational justice relates to the matter of correcting or remedying injustice, an aspect that I call "organizational due process."

The concept of corrective justice largely parallels the legal concept of due process. The latter refers to systematic, orderly procedures, including individuals' rights to controvert and to be heard concerning actions pending against them.[35] Recent nonlegal derivations of this concept that relate to specific types of institutions are academic due process[36] and industrial due process.[37] In both instances, the concepts are consistent with the fundamental aspects of

[32] One of the principles that Selznick sees in contemporary arbitration is that "industrial discipline should be (a) reasonably related to the gravity of the offense, (b) corrective whenever feasible. . . ." Selznick, *Law, Society, and Industrial Justice*, p. 171.

[33] Lawrence Stessin, *Employee Discipline* (Washington, D.C.: The Bureau of National Affairs, 1960), p. 27.

[34] Selznick, *Law, Society, and Industrial Justice*, p. 171. The courtroom judge is usually given latitude in the penalties imposed for crimes, with the law typically establishing the limits of these penalties.

[35] For a definition of *due process of law*, see Henry C. Black, *Black's Law Dictionary*, 4th ed. (St. Paul, Minn.: West Publishing Co., 1957), p. 590. See also Selznick, *Law, Society, and Industrial Justice*, pp. 250–259.

[36] See Louis Joughin, "Academic Due Process," *A.A.U.P. Bulletin*, 50:19–35 (March 1964).

[37] See "Industrial Due Process and Just Cause for Discipline: A Comparative Analysis of the Arbitral and Judicial Decisional Processes," *U.C.L.A. Law Review*, 6:606–677 (July 1959).

due process, that is, the right to object and to be heard without recrimination.

A broader term *organizational due process* might be used for enterprises in general. This concept can be defined, tentatively, as follows: Organizational due process consists of established procedures for handling complaints and grievances, protection against punitive action for using such established procedures, and careful, systematic, and thorough review of the substance of the complaints and grievances.

Components of formalized due-process systems are seen in such devices as grievance procedures under labor contracts and in appeal procedures in military, civil-service, and other organizations. In addition, an analysis of policies and procedures on tenure on the college and university suggests a strong element of organizational due process for the protection and furtherance of academic freedom.

In addition, informal mechanisms for corrective justice should not be overlooked. The degree to which managers are approachable and interested in remedying injustices is undoubtedly a major factor in the corrective justice within any enterprise.

GRIEVANCE PROCEDURES AND ARBITRATION

The most common formalized system for administering corrective justice is the grievance and arbitration procedure of the collective bargaining agreement. The main purpose of the grievance procedure is to provide a means for review and possible modification of the allocation of rewards and penalties. For all practical purposes, what is "just" will be what is agreed upon between the union and the management during the grievance procedure or in the decision handed down by the impartial arbitrator.

Although it is not typical practice, some organizations provide formal appeal for nonunionized employees. A study by Scott found that 91 firms out of 793 (11 percent) responding organizations had a formal appeal program of some kind. An additional 184 firms (22 percent) indicated informal methods of handling complaints of employees.[38] Most of the formal appeal programs were intended for nonexempt employees—those subject to U.S. Fair Labor Standards Act—and the larger the firm, the more likely were formal appeal procedures to be found.[39]

The Glacier Metal Company in England is an example of a firm having a formal appeal procedure pertaining to employees of all ranks. The Company policy states:

Every member of the Company shall have the right to appeal against any executive decision or action of an executive superior which affects him and which he considers to be unfair or unjust; inconsistent with either the provisions or the spirit of agreed or normally accepted policy, or not covered by such policy; or contrary to the best interests of the Company.[40]

Further, the responsibilities of managers when hearing appeals are: "To adopt an encouraging and friendly attitude towards an appealant who might wish to take his case to a higher level."[41] The effective implementation of such policies obviously requires a developmental approach, in contrast to a punitive one, in relationships with subordinates. In addition, effective implementation requires a widespread commitment among the managers to the desirability of such mechanisms of appeal.

[38] William G. Scott, *The Management of Conflict: Appeal Systems in Organizations* (Homewood, Ill.: Richard D. Irwin, Inc., 1965), pp. 56–61.
[39] Ibid., pp. 79–80. For a study that indicates that discharged employees who are reinstated by arbitrators subsequently tend to be satisfactory performers and that management does not tend to set any "traps" for them, see Thomas J. McDermott and Thomas H. Newhams, "Discharge—Reinstatement: What Happens Thereafter," *Industrial and Labor Relations Review*, 24:526–540 (July 1971).
[40] Wilfred Brown, *Exploration in Management* (New York: John Wiley & Sons, Inc., 1960), p. 310.
[41] Ibid., p. 311.

CONTRACT NEGOTIATIONS

In a sense, the process of negotiating a new labor agreement partly serves to correct alleged mistakes in the allocation of rewards and penalties. For example, if the union believes that differentials between job classifications are inequitable or that the job-evaluation system produces inequities, these deficiencies may be remedied through bargaining over the new contract. Likewise, management may succeed in correcting what it believes to be inequities. Although contract negotiations cannot undo specific inequities in the allocation of reward or penalties carried out under a previous contract, negotiations may serve to improve the agreement so that these inequities do not occur in the future.

MANAGERIAL REVIEW

In both unionized and nonunionized organizations, it is common practice for higher management to review planned disciplinary action before it is carried out. Since disciplinary action can result in highly defensive behavior on the part of the person disciplined or can result in widespread feelings of injustice on the part of other employees, top management is usually not disposed to give first-line supervisors unlimited latitude in discipline. In many organizations, however, the supervisor may suspend an employee for flagrant violations of rules pending review of the case.

Disciplinary review boards are sometimes used in business and industrial firms. Such boards usually consist of a committee of three or more managers and, in a small number of companies, include a psychiatrist or psychologist. One of the main functions of such a committee is to correct or amend a disciplinary penalty if it is considered to be unfair or too harsh.

WAGE AND SALARY ADMINISTRATION

If complaints or grievances suggest that jobs have not been evaluated properly, subsequent job evaluation can correct inequities. Periodic review of salaries can also serve to correct inequalities if the total careers of employees are compared. For example, because of time pressures or the competitiveness of the labor market, mistakes can be made in beginning salaries so that they are out of line with the total wage and salary structure, and, unless the annual review considers the total work history, these inequities will be perpetuated. Of course, management should do its best to set initial rates properly so that later correction is not necessary. The explanation, "We hired Bill at a higher rate than you," does not satisfy Joe if he feels that his salary is out of line with Bill's.

THE ROLE OF THE SUPERVISOR

Many complaints of unfair treatment are handled through the informal procedure of the complainant's discussing the problem with a superior. If the superior is a sympathetic listener and sincerely interested in the administration of justice within the organization, inequities can be minimized with little time and cost. On the other hand, if the supervisor is likely to punish people who make complaints, employees quickly learn this tendency, and complaints and grievances are rarely mentioned directly. If there are no alternative, formalized channels for the airing of grievances, defensive behavior will inevitably manifest itself in some other way.

THE CORPORATE OMBUDSMAN

A unique institution in the administration of corrective justice, the ombudsman, has come to the attention of Americans in recent years. The ombudsman is typically an eminent jurist appointed by a legislative body to investigate complaints of citizens against governmental officials and to make reports about findings. Most experience to date with this role has been in Sweden, Denmark, Finland, Norway, and

New Zealand, and has usually been in a government-citizen context.[42]

While a few American organizations, including Xerox Corporation, General Electric, and Boeing Vertol Company, have had some experience with a corporate or institutional ombudsman, little of this experience has been reported in the literature.[43] There have been some suggestions for the use of the ombudsman, however. For example, Silver speaks highly of the potential utility of this role and recommends that a corporate ombudsman investigate grievances and submit a recommendation to both the complaining employee and the manager involved. The matter would go to the president of the institution only when the dispute could not be resolved.[44]

A distinction should be made, however, between governmental and corporate ombudsmen. In the governmental context, as Rowat observes, the ombudsman is appointed by the legislature to investigate complaints against the administrative branch of the government, while this is not the case in the use of the ombudsman appointed internally within an organization. In the latter case, the ombudsman is appointed by the chief executive in circumstances where there is no such separation of powers. Rowat fears that, if this distinction is not made clear, ". . . many American ombudsmen will end up in the vest pockets of chief executives."[45] The degree to which the corporate ombudsman is beholden to management, however, in large part will be determined by the stature of the incumbent and the degree to which management truly wishes to be responsive to complaints and grievances.

[42] Isidore Silver, "The Corporate Ombudsman," *Harvard Business Review*, 45:77–87 (May-June 1967).
[43] Xerox Corporation appointed an ombudsman for managers and salaried employees in 1972. See *Business Week*, May 3, 1976, pp. 114–116.
[44] Silver, "Corporate Ombudsman," pp. 82–83.
[45] .Donald C. Rowat, "The Spread of the Ombudsman Idea," in The American Assembly, *Ombudsman for American Government* (Englewood Cliffs, N.J.: Prentice-Hall, Inc., 1968), p. 35.

IMPACT OF ENVIRONMENT ON DISTRIBUTIVE AND CORRECTIVE JUSTICE

COMMUNITY AND EMPLOYEE ATTITUDES

Prevailing attitudes in the community and in employee groups concerning what is fair will have a major impact on the quality of justice within organizations. A prime factor in the slowness with which nonwhites have been fully integrated into business and industrial firms, for example, has been the prejudice that exists in the broader community and spills over into the attitudes of managers and employees in their work lives. As another example, wages and fringe benefits considered to be fair elsewhere will have an impact on what employees consider fair in their particular organization. Discrepancies cannot be too great or injustice will be perceived. Attitudes about the legitimacy of using appeal procedures will also affect the nature of organizational justice in a given situation.

FEDERAL AND STATE LAWS

Federal and state laws have also had a profound impact on the process of justice within organizations. The Wagner Act, for example, encouraged collective bargaining as a means of enhancing justice in the allocation of rewards and penalties and established certain managerial practices as being unfair. The Taft-Hartley Act further defined public policies toward fairness by outlawing unfair practices on the part of unions, and the Landrum-Griffin Act further modified these policies by regulating the relationship between union members and their officers. Federal wage and hour laws define the public's concept of fairness in relation to minimum wages, child labor, overtime, hours of work, and safety and health. The Equal Pay Act of 1963 is directed toward the prevention of discrimination because of sex. The Civil Rights Law of 1964 forbids discrimination because of race, color, religion, sex, or national origin. The Age Discrimination in Employment Act of 1967 forbids discrimination in hiring, discharge, or wage rates on the basis of age. All such federal laws and their state equivalents and interpretive court decisions serve to define minimum standards of equity in employment.

ACCESS TO GOVERNMENTAL AGENCIES AND THE COURT

Although citizens have access to the courts, judges will rarely become involved in an alleged injustice in an employment relationship unless laws have been violated. Instead, governmental remedies for injustices are likely to be found through the action of administrative agencies in enforcing laws pertaining to minimum wages, child labor, overtime, fair employment, and unfair labor practices. Decisions handed down by such administrative bodies are usually enforced by court action upon proper court review. Appeals of such decisions are also normally handled by the courts.

UNION-MANAGEMENT RELATIONS AND ARBITRATION

Trends in union-management relations have a profound impact on the nature and administration of justice in the organizational setting. The arbitration process, in particular, which I have said is an important instrument in corrective justice, also assists in defining the nature of distributive justice in business and industry. For example, in addition to the principles already cited governing contemporary arbitration, arbitrators have tended to hold that justice requires careful attention to obtaining accurate facts, consideration of previous conduct, fitting the punishment to the crime, and insuring that discipline is consistent over time and among people. Thus, arbitrators obviously assume that justice has ramifications beyond the domain of a particular organization.

Labor contract provisions in general, in addition to those pertaining to grievances and arbi-

tration, often further refine the concept of justice in relationships between organized workers and management. For example, over 65 percent of labor-management agreements require advance warning to the employee or to the union in the case of discharge.[46] Such advance warning gives the union or employee opportunity to appeal, or it gives the employee an opportunity to secure a new job. As another example, almost all the contracts that refer to layoff give some consideration to length of service in retention on the payroll. In the vast majority of contracts, seniority is the determining factor.[47] Justice seems to require that the personal investment represented by length of service be given heavy weight in making decisions about layoffs.

Usually, collective bargaining serves to accommodate differences in perception of distributive and corrective justice, although what is agreed upon as fair may not coincide with the perceptions of outside parties. Nevertheless, what is agreed upon through collective bargaining is a good operational definition of distributive justice, provided the power and bargaining skill of the two parties is about equal.

AUTHORITY AND ACCOUNTABILITY

On the whole, checks and balances in the allocation of rewards and penalties within the organization are necessary to insure a high degree of distributive and corrective justice. Although I believe that the immediate supervisor should have some latitude in meting out monetary rewards and imposing discipline, unilateral authority is obviously not workable. Since, by

[46] U.S. Department of Labor, *Collective Bargaining Provisions*, Bulletin 908, pp. 88–97.
[47] Bureau of National Affairs, *Collective Bargaining Negotiations and Contracts*, 60:61 (1971). For a discussion of seniority as it relates to employee rights, see Philip Selznick and Howard Vollmer, "Rule of Law in Industry: Seniority Rights," *Industrial Relations*, 1:97–116 (May 1962).

definition, justice involves relative rewards and penalties for different people, it is apparent that rewards and penalties must be administered within the framework of established policy and that some individual or group must enforce compliance with policy and concern itself with equitable treatment across subdivisions of the organization. Day-to-day treatment of subordinates, however, including the quality of coaching, recognition, etc., must obviously remain the responsibility of the immediate supervisor, with higher management evaluating the cumulative effectiveness of various supervisors.

Ideally, in the larger organizations, the personnel department will play a major part in the administration of justice through its role in developing policy and in overseeing administration of wages and salaries and other forms of compensation. When reviewing disciplinary cases and requests for privileges, the wise personnel director will keep a record of decisions made for which there is no clear governing policy, in order to insure consistent treatment over time. If the record shows that a trend needs to be corrected, the personnel department will then be in a position to recommend a revised or new policy and to present meaningful reasons for change from past practices.

The corporate personnel director is also in a unique position to interpret perceptions of inequity at any level of the organization. Through diplomatic counseling and intervention, the personnel director can clarify misperceptions or suggest equitable solutions based on a knowledge of the total organization.

CONCLUDING COMMENT

This chapter has presented a number of concepts, hypotheses, and some research relevant to an understanding of fairness and justice in the organizational setting. These ideas will be important in a number of the following chapters, including, in particular, those on staffing, appraisal, and compensation.

The process of determining justice is implicit in a wide range of decisions and actions relative to the administration of human resources. Since perceived injustice results in defensive behavior, which in turn interferes with attaining the goals of the organization, an understanding of the factors in distributive and corrective justice is a major managerial responsibility.

REVIEW AND DISCUSSION QUESTIONS

1. What is the difference between universal and particular justice?

2. What is the difference between distributive justice and corrective justice in the organizational setting?

3. What does Homans mean by *investments? Costs? Rewards?*

4. What does Adams mean by *inputs? Outcomes?*

5. How is leadership style related to the administration of justice in the organization?

6. Analyze perceptions by nonwhites of organizational justice in terms of inputs and outcomes.

7. What is meant by progressive discipline?

8. What factors external to the firm are significant with respect to the determination of organizational justice?

9. What are some of the advantages and disadvantages of formalized mechanisms of corrective justice versus informal mechanisms?

10. What are some of the differences between the role of the governmental ombudsman and the corporate ombudsman?

SUPPLEMENTAL REFERENCES

Aaron, Benjamin, "The Individual's Legal Rights as an Employee," *Monthly Labor Review,* June 1963, pp. 666–673.

American Academy of Political and Social Science, "The Ombudsman or Citizen's Defender," *The Annals of The American Academy of Political and Social Science*, 377 (May 1968).

American Assembly, *Ombudsmen for American Government?* (Englewood Cliffs, N.J.: Prentice Hall, Inc., 1968).

Amis, Lewis R., "Due Process in Disciplinary Procedures," *Labor Law Journal*, 27:94–98 (February 1976).

Blau, Peter M., *Exchange and Power in Social Life* (New York: John Wiley & Sons, Inc., 1964).

Brandt, Richard B., ed., *Social Justice* (Englewood Cliffs, N.J.: Prentice-Hall, Inc., 1964).

Brown, Wilfred, *Exploration in Management* (New York: John Wiley & Sons, Inc., 1960), pp. 250–273.

Dowling, William F., "Conversation with George C. Homans," *Organizational Dynamics*, 4:34–54 (Autumn 1975).

Evan, William M., "Due Process of Law in a Governmental and Industrial Research Organization," *Evolving Concepts in Management*, Proceedings of the 24th Annual Meeting of the Academy of Management, December 1964, pp. 110–115.

———, "Superior-Subordinate Conflict in Research Organizations," *Administrative Science Quarterly*, 10:52–64 (June 1965).

Festinger, L., *A Theory of Cognitive Dissonance* (New York: Harper & Row, 1957).

Goodman, P., and A. Friedman, "An Examination of Adams' Theory of Inequity," *Administrative Science Quarterly*, 16:271–288 (September 1971).

———, "An Examination of the Effect of Wage Inequity on the Hourly Condition," *Organizational Behavior and Human Performance*, 3:340–352 (August 1968).

Gouldner, A.W., "The Norm of Reciprocity: A Preliminary Statement," *American Sociological Review*, 25:168 (April 1960).

Prager, Otto, "Grievance Procedures in the Federal Service," *Monthly Labor Review*, 89:609–612 (June 1966).

Pritchard, Robert D., Marvin D. Dunnette, and Dale O. Jorgenson, "Effects of Perceptions of Equity and Inequity on Worker Performance and Satisfaction," *Journal of Applied Psychology Monograph*, 56:75–94 (February 1972).

Rawls, John, *A Theory of Justice* (Cambridge, Mass.: Harvard University Press, 1971).

Roukis, George S., "Protecting Workers' Civil Rights: Equality in the Workplace," *Labor Law Journal*, 26:3–16 (January 1975).

Scott, William G., "An Issue in Administrative Justice: Managerial Appeal Systems," *Management International*, January 1966, pp. 37–53.

———, *The Management of Conflict: Appeal Systems in Organizations* (Homewood, Ill.: Richard D. Irwin, Inc., 1965), Chapters 1, 4.

Selekman, Benjamin M., *A Moral Philosophy for Management* (New York: McGraw-Hill Book Company, 1959), Chapter 23, "Justice and the New Constitutionalism."

Selznick, Philip, and Howard Vollmer, "Rule of Law in Industry: Seniority Rights," *Industrial Relations*, 1:97–116 (May 1962).

Silver, Isidore, "The Corporate Ombudsman," *Harvard Business Review*, 45:77–87 (May-June 1967).

Tornow, W.W., "The Development and Application of an Input/Outcome Moderator Test on the Perception and Reduction of Inequity," *Organizational Behavior and Human Performance*, 6:614–638 (1971).

Vollmer, Howard M., and Patrick J. McGillivray, "Personnel Offices and the Institutionalization of Employee Rights," *The Pacific Sociological Review*, 3:29–34 (Spring 1960).

Weick, K.E., "The Concept of Equity and The Perception of Pay," *Administrative Science Quarterly*, 11:414–439 (December 1966).

Williams, Whiting, *Mainsprings of Men* (New York: Charles Scribner's Sons, 1925), p. 37.

PART 4
THE TASK-SPECIALIZATION PROCESS

The complex flows of events within each enterprise that determine the nature of each person's job can be called the *task-specialization process*.[1] The division of labor has been called ". . . one of the most fundamental of all social processes. . . ."[2] Although the concept of a task-specialization process is, in a sense, synonymous with the managerial process of organ-izing, it is broader and closely interrelated with some of the most important aspects of personnel management. So much of personnel management is inseparable from, or derived from, this process that it is important to have an understanding of its dynamics if personnel management is to be understood.

In general, the task-specialization process consists of a sequence of events and activities somewhat as follows: (1) the determination of organizational objectives; (2) organizational planning, including organizational and job design based on the tools, machines, and systems technology to be used in achieving enterprise

[1] See Victor A. Thompson, *Modern Organization* (New York: Alfred A. Knopf, Inc., 1961), pp. 25–56.
[2] Everett Cherington Hughes, "The Study of Occupations," in Robert K. Merton, Leonard Brown, and Leonard S. Cottrel, Jr., eds., *Sociology Today* (New York: Basic Books, Inc., 1959), p. 445.

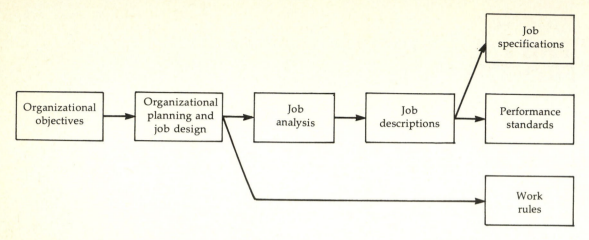

Figure **4-a**   The task-specialization process

objectives; (3) job analysis; (4) the development of implicit or explicit job or position descriptions reflecting the resulting tasks to be performed; (5) the determination of human qualifications required on these jobs (job specifications); (6) the development of performance standards for each job; and (7) the establishment of work rules and conditions. Most of these components tend to stem from the preceding ones, but there is considerable interdependence. The process is roughly diagrammed in Figure 4-a.

Although this process is systematized to a fairly high degree in most enterprises, its essential aspects are implicit in any organization. For example, job descriptions, job specifications, or work rules may not be written down, but much managerial decision and action is based on their implicit existence, even if they exist only in the minds of managers and are thus incomplete and variable.

Chapter 9 will focus on organizational objectives and planning and will examine in some detail the consequences of job design under such topics as "job enrichment." Chapter 10 will begin with a discussion of job analysis and job descriptions, basic tools in personnel management. The chapter will continue with a discussion of job specifications, performance standards, and work rules and conditions. It will also touch on management by objectives, a popular version of the use of performance standards, but a detailed discussion will be deferred until a later chapter. Chapter 10 will also examine the implications of the Occupational Safety and Health Act.

CHAPTER 9
ORGANIZATIONAL OBJECTIVES AND JOB DESIGN

THE DETERMINATION OF ORGANIZATIONAL OBJECTIVES

The determination of organizational objectives is a broad managerial function that necessarily precedes all other organizational activities. It is not uniquely a function of personnel management, but since it has such an effect on the flow of events within personnel management, it is important that the ramifications of its impact be recognized. The total task to be performed by the organization stems from this determination of goals.

Organizational goals are usually multiple, and the goal-establishing process is both dynamic and complex. Although making a profit tends to be a paramount objective in most business and industrial firms, it is typically not the only objective considered in the planning of owners and directors. By itself, this objective has little meaning, since profits are not made in

a vacuum but are achieved through the manufacture of a product or the performance of a service of some kind. Statements of objectives will usually reflect this element. A private power company, for example, might have as its objectives the production of electric power and the performance of high-quality service for customers at a profit. The same organization might have as additional goals the development of the talents and the capacities of its employees, the development of a stable work force, the creation of a company known as a "good place to work," the enhancement of employment and promotion opportunities for minorities, and cooperation with local, state, regional, and federal agencies in effective environmental management.

Although any detailed discussion is beyond the scope of this book, a major problem in the determination of organizational objectives is the perception of some unfulfilled need for products or services that the organization is capable of satisfying. Such perception may be spontaneous, although most such "spontaneity" is based on accumulated knowledge and thought. Determination of objectives is usually based on exhaustive research into need, competition, and feasibility.

Other major problems in the determination of organizational goals are the rapid change and flux in world events, sweeping economic and political changes, and geometrically expanding science and technology. Objectives must change rapidly and appropriately to meet rapidly changing needs for products and services.

RELATIONSHIP BETWEEN ORGANIZATIONAL OBJECTIVES AND OTHER MANAGERIAL PROCESSES

Organizational objectives, to a great extent, determine the nature of all broad managerial processes. Organizational objectives will determine the capital and other monetary resources needed, the types and systems of capital equipment utilized, the kinds of materials used, the kinds of information developed, disseminated, and utilized, and the qualifications and numbers of people employed by the organization.

These broad processes, of course, will have a reciprocal impact on objectives. Entrepreneurs who have accumulated considerable capital in the pursuit of one set of objectives may in turn look for additional objectives as further avenues for putting capital to constructive use. Or, seeing the utility of newly developed machines in manufacturing a product, the directors of an organization may alter objectives to take advantage of the new technology. Such changes in objectives may require rapid reorganization of the enterprise.

Thus, *the determination of organizational objectives will dictate the nature of the resulting components of the specialization process, that is, organi-* *zational planning, job descriptions, job specifications, performance standards, and work rules.* For example, if the objective is to make bricks at a profit, the entire organization and all the jobs in it will reflect this objective. Similarly, if an organization has the objective of assisting in the rehabilitation of people who have been previously hospitalized with serious illnesses, the structure of the organization and the jobs in it will reflect this objective. The types of people recruited and employed, the nature of their training, the system of reward, and opportunities for promotion—all these matters, and others, will be affected by these objectives.

IMPACT OF ENVIRONMENT ON ORGANIZATIONAL OBJECTIVES

National or communal attitudes have a decided impact upon organizational objectives. As discussed in the chapter on the history of personnel management, a growing social consciousness on the part of management has been reflected in attitudes toward employees. Although some managers consider their responsibilities to end with providing jobs, some have a far-reaching sense of social responsibility. For example, the Committee for Economic Development lists some ten major fields in which businesses, in the aggregate, have important responsibilities: economic growth and efficiency, education, employment and training, civil rights and equal opportunity, urban renewal and development, pollution abatement, conservation and recreation, culture and the arts, medical care, and government.[1] Interest in and concern about many of these areas have been stimulated by society's rapidly rising expectations of business, significant recent legislation, and administrative rulings.

[1] Committee for Economic Development, *Social Responsibilities of Business Corporations* (New York: Research and Policy Committee, Committee for Economic Development, June 1971), pp. 36–40.

In particular, federal and state civil rights laws influencing hiring, advancement, and retention practices; antipollution laws pertaining to improving the purity of water and air, such as the Clean Air Act of 1970; and the Federal Occupational Safety and Health Act of 1970 have had a major impact on organizational objectives and will continue to do so in the years ahead. As another example, rulings of the Food and Drug Administration have, in recent years, frequently curtailed the production of some particular food or drug that was found to be unsafe or ineffective. The quality of aircraft and, to a lesser extent, automobiles, is regulated by law, as are the manufacture and sale of many other products. Antitrust laws also affect organizational objectives.

The needs of national defense have also had a major impact on organizations throughout the country, as this nation has witnessed a number of times. Shortages of critical materials may force some organizations to alter their objectives, and requirements of military procurement have the effect of stimulating the development of new objectives in many organizations.

Innovations in technology and science also have a profound effect on organizational goals. Only a few short years ago, the objective of manufacturing high-quality commercial jet transports at a profit would have been unrealistic. Today, such an objective exists, with hundreds of jet aircraft in use throughout the world. The reader can probably think of many examples of inventions or developments, such as television, transistors, new vaccines, etc., that have had a major impact on the objectives of individual organizations.

Such innovations are not necessarily external to the organization. Most manufacturing organizations are constantly seeking to improve present products or to develop new ones. Innovations from research and development can make the current products of an organization obsolete overnight; as a result, the organization must modify its goals and consequently may need to modify the organizational processes stemming from these goals, as well as the design of the organization itself.

Union-management relations also have an important impact on organizational objectives. The necessity to pay higher wages may force some marginal producers out of business or may force organizations to adopt new equipment or systems in order to compete.[2] Products that are only marginally profitable may be dropped as a result of increases in wages and labor costs. Furthermore, union checks on management may have the effect of forcing executives to define or revise organizational subobjectives which relate to people.

Managerial skills and attitudes obviously have an impact on organizational objectives. Imagination and capability can result in the perception of opportunities that organizations with less capable management fail to recognize. The planning and implementing ability of managers will affect the extent to which objectives are met and will, in turn, determine whether those objectives are continued, modified, dropped, or supplemented.

Personal likes and dislikes of the owners or directors of an organization also have an effect on objectives. Some owners of companies may want rapid growth; others may want only moderate growth or no growth. Some owners are simply not interested in certain products or services even though it might be economically feasible to enter competition with those particular goods or services.

Relationships of power among the principals of a firm are a major determinant of organizational objectives. Particularly in the organizing stage of a new firm, the willingness of the various entrepreneurs to manage certain aspects

---

[2] On some occasions when management has been prepared to abandon all its organizational objectives and to liquidate, unions have stepped in with financial help to keep the organization alive.

of the business and their willingness to accept the limitations of certain goals are important factors in determining the goals that finally emerge. In a family business, the period before retirement of the founder may see stagnation or revitalization of organizational purposes, depending upon the wisdom and attitudes of the founder about managerial succession.[3]

The labor market also has an important effect on organizational objectives. For example, if a manufacturer wants to produce a highly complex electronic device requiring the employment of a physicist and a qualified one cannot be obtained, the objective will obviously have to be abandoned. Then, too, large numbers of people available to perform work at a certain level of skill may result in an organization's adopting objectives to take advantage of the particular labor-market conditions. Many organizations tend to look for products that will fit the skills of the people in the communities of which their organization is part. Thus, reappraisal of objectives is a continual process. The more unstable the environment, the more the organization must review its objectives.

AUTHORITY IN DETERMINING ORGANIZATIONAL OBJECTIVES

In general, the determination of organizational objectives is the responsibility of the top management of an organization, particularly the president and the board of directors. In a commercial venture, the owners of capital obviously have the prerogative of determining how their capital will be spent, although they may delegate this authority to hired managers. Other top-management officials, including the personnel director, may be consulted in the development or the modification of objectives. The

personnel department is ordinarily well qualified to speak authoritatively about the availability and current wage levels of various skills or specialities in the labor market.

THE IMPORTANCE OF CLEAR OBJECTIVES

Without clearly defined objectives, activities become confused and erratic. Without objectives, the management of organizational resources cannot be kept in balance, and the management of one process may interfere with the management of another. All organizational processes will suffer, including the process of personnel management. Without objectives, there will be no standards against which to evaluate the performance of individuals or that of the total organization.

Obviously, lack of attention to organizational objectives can be a quick road to organizational disaster. Conversely, systematic attention to refining or revising objectives is the most fundamental of all managerial tasks. The same holds true for the subobjectives that contribute toward overall goals. Thus, all managers at all levels need to be concerned with objectives.

ORGANIZATIONAL PLANNING AND JOB DESIGN

PURPOSE AND DESCRIPTION

Once objectives are determined, the structure of the organization can be planned. The purpose of *organizational planning* is to divide the total task to be performed into manageable and efficient units and to provide for their proper integration. Both differentiation and integration are vital.[4]

---

[3] See Louis B. Barnes and Simon A. Hershon, "Transferring Power in the Family Business," *Harvard Business Review*, 54:106–114 (July-August 1976).

[4] For research that examines differing levels of differentiation and integration in different organizations, see Paul R. Lawrence and Jay W. Lorsch, *Organization and Environment: Managing Differentiation and Integration* (Boston: Graduate

Through organizational planning, the total enterprise is divided into such segments as positions, departments, and divisions. Not only is there a subdivision of work on a horizontal scale, with different tasks across the organization being performed by different people, but there is a subdivision of work on a vertical scale in which higher levels of the organization are responsible for the supervision of more people, the coordination of subgroups, more complex planning, etc. Thus, this subdivision of work occurs at all levels, including boards of directors, and encompasses planning, coordinating, and controlling.

The utilization of technology, including systems technology, is an integral aspect of organizational planning. The technology of industrial engineering, industrial psychology, and mechanical engineering, in particular, plays a major part in organizational planning by commercial organizations. The contributions of engineers in plant layout, work simplification, machine design, and informational and computational systems must be considered an integral part of organizational planning if organizational structure is not to work at cross purposes with the total task to be performed. Thus, organizational planning is interdependent with the technology used. (See also Chapter 5.)

CURRENT PRACTICES AND PROBLEMS

Some authors have stressed the importance of organizing enterprises on the basis of work flow. For example, Chapple and Sayles state: "Because people, not lines on a chart, are the major concern, the elimination of points of stress within the work flow should be the first consideration of organization design." They go on to recommend the identification of segments of work flows, each of which could logically be placed under one supervisor. The higher organizational structure is then constructed.[5]

Thus, although it may be argued that the organization should be designed from the bottom up, most organizations probably experience a constant state of tension because of pressure from top executives to expand or retain their respective spheres of control plus pressures to assign broader responsibility to the most capable employees versus the logic of the organizational technology, including the flow of work. The organizational structure that emerges will be some sort of compromise between the two. Current practice suggests that this paradox has not been resolved in most organizations since, typically, organizational planning departments are separate from industrial engineering or systems groups.

Other questions subsequently emerge in organizational planning. For example, should the organization be subdivided along product lines or along functional lines (such as manufacturing, finance, sales, etc.)? Should the organization be divided into several large divisions or into a large number of smaller units? Should it be divided into shifts (time of day), by geographical location, by type of service offered, by type of customer, or by a combination of these? Should the organization have minimum layers of supervision, and thus a "flat" structure, or should it have a fairly large number of supervisory layers between the rank-and-file employees and the president? These are the kinds of problems with which organizational planning must deal. The answers to these questions will depend partly upon the purposes of the organization. To illustrate, if customer service is a high-priority objective, a company may be subdivided on the basis of the location of customers.

School of Business Administration, Harvard University, 1967).

[5] Eliot D. Chapple and Leonard R. Sayles, *The Measure of Management* (New York: The Macmillan Company, 1961), pp. 40–41.

RELATIONSHIP OF PLANNING TO OTHER PROCESSES

It is clear that planning an organization is reciprocally related to the flows of capital, capital equipment, communications, and materials through an organization. Organizational planning will either facilitate or handicap these flows and their interrelationships.

Planning the technology of an organization is clearly going to have an impact on the various components of the personnel management process. Since, by definition, organizational planning determines the nature and scope of various individual jobs, the components of the specialization process that stem from such planning will be affected. The level of performance required, the qualifications necessary to carry out tasks, and the *skill-mix* in the organization will all be partly a function of organizational planning. In addition, the nature of the task determines its price. Thus, performance standards, work force planning, employment, and the wage and salary structure will be affected. In addition, the "growth" of an employee will to a great extent be a function of the job. Thus, development and training of employees are also affected.

FORCES AFFECTING ORGANIZATIONAL PLANNING AND JOB DESIGN

THE COMPUTER AND OTHER TECHNOLOGICAL DEVELOPMENTS   As indicated in Chapter 5, innovations in technology and science may have a heavy impact on organizational planning and structure. For example, the adoption of high-speed electronic computers can result in the recentralization of authority and control in the headquarters of large organizations.[6] This re-

sult is not inevitable, however, since middle managers may insist on sufficient intellectual content in their jobs to make them challenging, and top management may use information technology to strengthen, rather than weaken, middle-management jobs.[7] In addition, the introduction of such equipment may reduce the number of clerical jobs in a particular department, while at the same time increasing the number of skilled programmers and maintenance people required.

The use of such equipment may thus dramatically change the skill-mix within a department and within a total organization. Mann and Williams, for example, reported the complete reorganization of numerous jobs with the introduction of electronic data-processing equipment into the accounting department of an electric power company. In addition, a number of completely new jobs were created in the process, and a number of people were transferred, demoted, or placed on dead-end jobs when skills did not meet new requirements.[8]

In a study by Whisler of the impact of introducing computers in nineteen insurance companies, it was found that skill changes occurred among clerical and supervisory employees in most of the departments affected. Among those departments where skill changes occurred, 70 percent of clerical jobs required increased skills, but 30 percent required lower skills. In contrast 93 percent of supervisory

---

[6] See Julius Rezler, "Automation: Its Impact on the Organization & Functions of Personnel Management," in *Handbook of Modern Personnel Administration* (New York: McGraw-Hill Book Company, 1972), p. 63-3. See also Floyd C. Mann and

Lawrence K. Williams, "Observations on the Dynamics of a Change to Electronic Data Processing Equipment," *Administrative Science Quarterly*, 5:217–256 (September 1960).

[7] John F. Burlingame, "Information Technology and Decentralization," *Harvard Business Review*, 39:121–126 (November-December 1961). Peter Blau et al., found that the more automated manufacturing becomes, the higher the number of administrative levels. See Peter M. Blau, Cecilia McFalbe, William McKinley, and Phelps Tracy, "Technology and Organization in Manufacturing," *Administrative Science Quarterly*, 21:32 (March 1976).

[8] Mann and Williams, "Observations on the Dynamics of Change," pp. 220–226.

jobs required higher skill levels, while only 7 percent required lower levels of skill.[9]

Other technological developments have caused even more drastic changes in skill-mix across entire industries. The aerospace industry is one illustration. In this industry, the ratio of engineers to production people has increased markedly. While in earlier days managerial, scientific, and technical workers comprised about one-third of the work force of these companies, in recent years such workers comprise two-thirds of the work force, with production workers comprising about one-third.[10]

The rapidly changing needs of government, the aerospace industry, and other technical industries have created in many organizations the necessity for rapid engineering and manufacturing of high-technology products. The widespread use of project management is one result. As described in Chapter 5, a project manager may be assigned responsibility for the overall success of a project, and as a consequence there may be major shifts of authority in the organization, with the project manager assuming large areas of authority and responsibility previously held by managers of functional divisions. In such situations, we find the organization being quickly modified to meet the demands of rapidly changing science and technology.

Similarly, if the organization is constructed by means of detailed study of work or material flows, the resulting structure will be a direct function of such flows. For example, Brewer reported the reorganization of companies in which one executive is appointed to handle such functions as production planning, inventory control, and traffic.[11] Furthermore, changes in machine design by machine manufacturers obviously condition the nature of individual jobs in the organizations that purchase the machines.

AUTOMATION One author sees automation as generally increasing the scope of jobs and as giving operators a broader view of the total process, more technical information, and more interaction with engineers and technicians. This effect is in contrast to what he calls "mass-production systems," for example, the assembly-line systems that have been prevalent in the automobile industry.[12]

The introduction of automation does not always result in job enlargement or in an upgrading of the skill mix, however. As Davis points out, it depends upon what is meant by "automation."[13] One researcher concluded after studying several firms: ". . . there was more evidence that automation had *reduced* the skill requirements of the operating work force, and occasionally of the entire factory force including the maintenance organization."[14]

[9] Thomas L. Whisler, *The Impact of Computers on Organizations* (New York: Praeger Publishers, 1970), pp. 139–141.

[10] *See Business Week*, August 19, 1961, p. 87, and June 22, 1963, pp. 44ff. See also Samuel E. Hill and Frederick Harbison, *Manpower and Innovation in American Industry* (Princeton, N.J.: Industrial Relations Section, Princeton University, 1959), pp. 53–56.

[11] Stanley H. Brewer, *Rhocrematics: A Scientific Approach to the Management of Material Flows* (Seattle: University of Washington, College of Business Administration, Bureau of Business Research, 1960), p. 20.

[12] See Louis E. Davis, "The Effects of Automation on Job Design," *Industrial Relations*, 2:53–71 (October 1962).

[13] Ibid.

[14] James R. Bright, "Does Automation Raise Skill Requirements?" *Harvard Business Review*, 36:4 (July-August 1958). The overall reduction in skill level in the shoe-manufacturing industry due to technological innovations has been described earlier by Warner and Low. Not only did they perceive a reduction of most jobs to a low-skill category, but an almost complete breakdown in the old craftsman-apprentice skill hierarchy. The highly skilled jobs were now found in allied industries, such as the shoe-machine manufacturing industry. See W. Lloyd Warner and J.O. Low, *The Social System of the Modern Factory* (New Haven, Conn.: Yale University Press, 1947), IV, pp. 66–89. There are now 135 shoe-producing occupations in place of the one cordwainer's job of the eighteenth century. See U.S. Department of Labor, *Employment and Training Report of the President*, Employment and Training Administration, 1976, pp. 152–153.

Bright found that the difficulty and complexity of jobs depended on a number of variables, including the degree of automation of the machines used, the reliability of the machines, the number of machines tended per person, and the uniqueness of the equipment.[15] In addition, Walker and Guest have emphasized that the degree of repetitiveness varies a great deal from industry to industry and from job to job.[16]

LABOR RELATIONS   Union-management relations have also had an impact on organizational planning. The union movement has given considerable impetus to centralizing many functions of personnel and labor relations into one department in organizations of medium-to-large size because of the necessity for strong, coordinated efforts in dealing with union demands, and the necessity for processing grievance, arbitration, and National Labor Relations Board cases.

Strongly held craft-union beliefs about the proper scope of certain skilled jobs will affect job design. For example, craft unions typically insist on little or no overlap among the jobs of carpenter, pipefitter, and electrician. Grievances are likely to be filed if workers in one craft believe that workers in another are infringing on their traditional tasks. In addition, in situations where management has negotiated away its right to subcontract maintenance and construction work, organizational planning must take this fact into account.

Unions also have a powerful influence over the introduction of technological changes, and thus on organizational planning and job design. Some unions have traditionally resisted the introduction of labor-saving devices and more efficient methods through insistence upon restrictive clauses in collective-bargaining agreements. Some unions, on the other hand, have just the opposite attitude and have openly favored and fostered introduction of modern machines and more efficient methods. In general, unions are in favor of technological innovations and increased efficiency as the only way to increase the standard of living but are opposed to raising the work load on individual workers. The unions want any resulting dislocation of workers minimized through government- or employer-sponsored unemployment compensation, severance pay, supplemental unemployment benefit programs, and worker retraining. (For a further discussion of union attitudes about technological change, see Chapter 22.)

Events in late 1971 and early 1972 at the Lordstown, Ohio, General Motors automobile assembly plant, one of the most technically sophisticated plants in the world, may be indicative of growing union concern about organizational planning and job design, with particular emphasis upon the impact on younger workers. After a considerable number of jobs had been eliminated on the highly automated assembly line (one hundred Vega cars per hour) and the work distributed to the remaining workers with no change in assembly-line speed, the affected employees, whose average age was twenty-four, began to disrupt production on the grounds that they were being expected to work too fast and too hard to produce quality automobiles. A strike resulted that lasted twenty-two days and idled some ten thousand employees. While job pressure—work "speedup"—and worker concern about quality were reported as factors, job monotony and worker alienation from the decision-making processes—a feeling that they were automatons—were also considered to be important factors in the opinion of both some union officials

---

[15] Bright, "Does Automation Raise Skill Requirements?" pp. 89–96.
[16] Charles R. Walker and Robert H. Guest, *The Man on the Assembly Line* (Cambridge, Mass.: Harvard University Press, 1952), p. 11.

and industrial engineers.[17] Subsequently, the United Auto Workers asked the Chrysler Corporation to begin discussions aimed at developing experiments to "humanize" assembly-line jobs and to increase job satisfaction.[18]

Statements by labor union officials, however, do not suggest that the Lordstown issues were much different from issues in past years, nor that the problems were associated with changed attitudes of young workers. For example, William Winpisinger, General Vice President of the International Association of Machinists and Aerospace Workers, AFL-CIO, stated:

The young workers at Lordstown were reacting against the same kind of grievances, in the same kind of way, as did generations of workers before them. They were rebelling against an obvious speedup. They were protesting safety violations. They were reacting against working conditions that had been unilaterally imposed by a management that was determined to get tough in the name of efficiency.

An almost identical series of incidents took place over much the same issues at Norwood, Ohio, at almost the same time, but very few inferences were drawn about the changing nature of the work force because, in this case, it was older workers who were involved.[19]

The quoted union official also expressed considerable cynicism about contemporary job enrichment efforts and stated flatly: "If you want to enrich the job, enrich the paycheck." He then added that jobs could be enriched by decreasing the number of working hours needed to derive a living wage, by decreasing noise and fumes, and by giving the worker more control over working conditions through such means as advance consultation. And finally, he emphasized the importance of the worker's being able to look forward to doing something better and having some career movement ". . . even if it's only from a job that requires stooping down to one that involves standing erect." The latter was in the context of stressing the value of seniority clauses in labor contracts for providing some mobility.[20] It is quite likely that such issues—e.g., a reduction in working hours and advance consultation on changes in working conditions—will appear with greater frequency in future collective bargaining.

OTHER FACTORS We have already referred to relationships of power and skill among principals of a firm as major determinants of organizational planning. Management's attitudes about centralization versus decentralization will also have a strong influence on organizational planning. Ability to utilize and stimulate technological change will obviously have a major impact. Perceived inefficiencies, overworked executives, bottlenecks in production, and so forth may also be stimulants to reorganization.

The labor supply (both internal and external to the organization) will have an effect on organizational planning. Realistically, organizational and job structure will be a function of the qualifications of the people already in the organization or available in the labor market. For example, it would be pointless to install elaborate equipment or systems with no people to manage them.

[17] Based on Bureau of National Affairs, *Bulletin to Management*, February 3, February 17, March 9, and March 30, 1972. For an article including interviews with some of the workers, see Barbara Garson, "Luddites in Lordstown," *Harpers*, 244:68–73 (June 1972). For a reply by a United Auto Workers official, see "Letters," *Harpers*, 245:8–9 (August 1972). See also *Business Week*, October 7, 1972, p. 27.
[18] Bureau of National Affairs, September 14, 1972, p. 1. After the strike settlement, and after an extensive analysis based on attitude surveys and meetings with supervisors and union officials, management initiated an extensive "communications" program with several components, including plant radio and bulletin board announcements and the use of "communicator-trainers" who were to act as communication "catalysts" or "facilitators." See Hak C. Lee and John J. Grix, "Communication: An Alternative to Job Enrichment," *The Personnel Administrator*, 20:20–23 (October 1975).
[19] William W. Winpisinger, "Job Enrichment: A Union View," *Monthly Labor Review*, 96:54–56 (April 1973).
[20] Ibid., pp. 54–55.

Furthermore, certain functions may be grouped under one executive because of the administrative shortcomings of another, or a special job may be created to utilize the unique skills of one individual. Once on the job, the incumbent will affect the nature and scope of that job. The higher one looks in the organization, the less likely it is that the job will be rigidly designed, and the more likely the scope of the job and level of performance will depend upon the person.

In addition, management attitudes about job enrichment and job enlargement and/or attitudes about employee participation in the design of jobs will have a powerful influence on how jobs are designed. We will next turn our attention to these concepts.

JOB ENRICHMENT AND ENLARGEMENT

Contemporary job enrichment efforts have received considerable impetus from Maslow's need-hierarchy theory and the theories of Herzberg and others that factors pertaining to the job itself such as job challenge, autonomy, and responsibility are powerful motivators (see Chapter 6). Some forms of job enrichment have also received impetus from notions that worker participation in many matters pertaining to work life, including job design, are functional in terms of both productivity and satisfaction (see Myers, below). Other forms, frequently referred to as "sociotechnical systems," have emerged from attempts to develop a better fit between the technology, structure, and social interaction of the work place. The latter experiments were largely done either under the auspices of the Tavistock Institute in England or heavily influenced by the Tavistock experiments. As will be noted, some approaches to job enrichment have featured the creation of semiautonomous work teams; other approaches focus on individual jobs.

THE TEAM APPROACH

A useful frame of reference for thinking about job enrichment and team approaches to job enrichment is provided by M. Scott Myers from his work at Texas Instruments, an organization with extensive experience in participative methods at the rank-and-file level. To Myers, job enrichment is a special form of job enlargement. Job enlargement can be *horizontal, vertical,* or *horizontal plus vertical.* Figure 9-1 gives two examples of each. Horizontal job enlargement can take the form of (a) *a greater variety of tasks on which the employee works,* (b) *an increased number of tasks,* or (c) *job rotation.* Vertical job enlargement, which to Myers is "job enrichment," can take the form of (a) *more planning,* (b) *more controlling,* or (c) *more team participation on the part of employees.* The additional controlling aspect may include self-pacing as well as inspection.[21]

Basically, as shown in Figure 9-2, job enrichment increases the proportion of time spent on the planning and controlling aspects of the job in contrast to the doing aspects. Another important shift is the greatly enlarged team-interaction aspect that is shown in the figure as the shaded area.[22] For example, the radar assemblers in the "vertical" illustration in Figure 9-1 worked with the engineers on methods and design improvements, and the electronic assemblers worked as teams with a team captain to improve the manufacturing process.

Paradoxically, the design of a job may *contract* horizontally while enlarging vertically. For example, stemming from their training in the simplification of work, workers may be encouraged to suggest ways to make jobs simpler

[21] M. Scott Myers, "Every Employee a Manager," *California Management Review,* 10:9–20 (Spring 1968).
[22] For an in-depth discussion of job enrichment, including the impact on the foreman's job, see M. Scott Myers, *Every Employee a Manager* (New York: McGraw-Hill, 1970), pp. 55–95.

Figure **9-1**   Examples of horizontal, vertical, and horizontal plus vertical job enlargement

Horizontal

Assemblers on a transformer assembly line each performed a single operation as the assembly moved by on the conveyor belt. Jobs were enlarged horizontally by setting up work stations to permit each operator to assemble the entire unit. Operations now performed by each operator include cabling, upending, winding, soldering, laminating, and symbolizing.

A similar transformer assembly line provides horizontal job enlargement when assemblers are taught how to perform all operations and are rotated to a different operation each day.

Vertical

Assemblers on a radar assembly line are given information on customer contract commitments in terms of price, quality specifications, delivery schedules, and company data on material and personnel costs, break-even performance, and potential profit margins. Assemblers and engineers work together in methods and design improvements. Assemblers inspect, adjust, and repair their own work, help test completed units, and receive copies of customer inspection reports.

Female electronic assemblers involved in intricate assembling, bonding, soldering, and welding operations are given training in methods improvement and were encouraged to make suggestions for improving manufacturing processes. Natural work groups of five to 25 assemblers each elect a "team captain" for a term of six months. In addition to performing her regular operations, the team captain collects work improvement ideas from members of her team, describes them on a standard form, credits the suggestors, presents the recommendations to their supervisor and superintendent at the end of the week, and gives the team feedback on idea utilization. Though most job operations remain the same, vertical job enlargement is achieved by providing increased opportunity for planning, reorganizing and controlling their work, and earning recognition.

Horizontal Plus Vertical

Jobs are enlarged horizontally in a clad metal rolling mill by qualifying operators to work interchangeably on breakdown rolling, finishing rolling, slitter, pickler, and abrader operations. After giving the operators training in methods improvement and basic metallurgy, jobs are enlarged vertically by involving them with engineering and supervisory personnel in problem-solving, goal-setting sessions for increasing production yields.

Jobs in a large employee insurance section are enlarged horizontally by qualifying insurance clerks to work interchangeably in filing claims, mailing checks, enrolling and orienting new employees, checking premium and enrollment reports, adjusting payroll deductions, and interpreting policies to employees. Vertical enlargement involves clerks in insurance program planning meetings with personnel directors and carrier representatives, authorizes them to sign disbursement requests, permits them to attend a paperwork systems conference, and enables them to recommend equipment replacements and to rearrange their work layout.

From M. Scott Myers, "Every Employee a Manager." Copyright 1968 by the Regents of the University of California. Reprinted from *California Management Review*, vol. XII, no. 3, p. 10 by permission of the Regents.

and more efficient.[23] Thus, reductions in the complexity of the "doing" aspects of jobs can be offset by increased participation in the planning aspects.

The team approach to job enrichment has had some impact on the assembly line of the automobile industry, at least in Europe. Two of the largest automakers in Sweden, Volvo and Saab-Scania, have experimented with team production methods in which a semiautonomous team is responsible for assembling some major

[23] Work simplification was proposed as early as 1937 as a means for employees to participate meaningfully in the design of their jobs, but the techniques typically have been preempted by industrial engineers and supervisors. See Mitchell Fein, "Motivation for Work," in Robert Dubin, ed., *Handbook of Work, Organization and Society* (Chicago: Rand McNally College Publishing Company, 1976), p. 481.

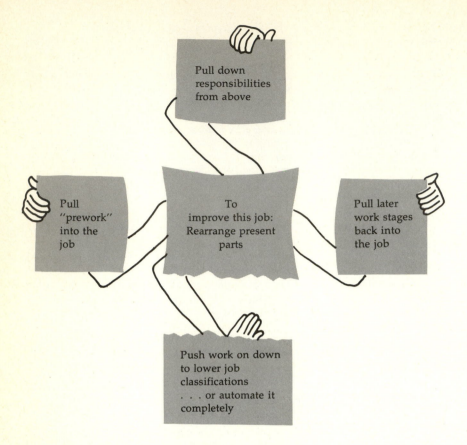

Figure **9-2**   Steps in improving a job

component, including the methods for doing it. Under this structure the average foreman supervises forty to fifty subordinates rather than twenty, although the foreman works with a team leader who is responsible for production scheduling and material handling.[24] Another version involves having the team move along the assembly line performing all the operations.

(A comparable job enrichment experiment has been conducted in Sweden's Scandia Insurance Company.) The Chrysler Corporation is also reported to have conducted some experiments in an attempt to enrich automobile assembly-line jobs, although apparently only a few jobs have been affected.[25]

The "grandparents" of the automobile industry experiments were the early Tavistock studies. One of the earliest, in British coal

[24] A. Mikalachki, "The Effects of Job Design in Turnover, Absenteeism and Health," *Industrial Relations*, 30:377–388 (August 1975).

[25] Bureau of National Affairs, September 14, 1972, p. 1.

mining, involved broadening the scope of jobs and reintroducing a team approach to coal production, supplemented by team pay incentives.[26] Another Tavistock project, in a weaving mill in India, took the same thrust in terms of broadening tasks and creating semiautonomous work groups.[27]

Several job enrichment experiments outside of the automobile industry in the United States that involve team production in contrast to assembly-line production have been widely publicized. These include a project at a General Foods pet food plant and one at a Corning Glass plant producing laboratory hot plates. The common elements have been the creation of work teams responsible for the production of an entire item, including the allocation of work, quality control, and making product improvements. A similar experiment has been conducted at the Rushton Mining Company involving the creation of autonomous work teams of coal miners, with each miner trained to perform every job in the unit. (For results see later in the chapter.)

It is important to note that in some versions of job enrichment, such as the Texas Instruments (TI) approach, employees are involved in the enrichment process itself, not just in the management of jobs already enriched. A particularly good example of this is the use of a "problem-solving goal-setting" approach at TI in which a difficult problem with a customer is presented to a natural work group. Members of the work group analyze the problem, make suggestions for solution, are involved in deciding what changes to make, establish new goals, and implement the changes on the job. Frequently such groups invite specialists such as industrial or manufacturing engineers to assist them. Such a process is obviously an ongoing kind of job enrichment.[28] (The consequences of the TI job enrichment program and of some of the others will be reported later in the chapter.)

THE INDIVIDUAL JOB APPROACH

Most of the job enrichment efforts by Robert Ford and colleagues at AT&T and those conducted in various places by Frederick Herzberg et al., appear to focus largely on the individual job. At AT&T, the basic approach has been to increase both the horizontal and vertical aspects to create a more meaningful work module and to try to automate the more routine aspects or to add those aspects to lower job classifications. (See Figure 9-2.) For example, at the Indianapolis office of the Indiana Bell Telephone Company, where all the directories for the state were compiled, each telephone directory was processed through twenty-one separate steps, such as manuscript verification, keypunch, and keypunch verification. Thirty-three employees were involved. The task fragmentation was reduced by stages through a job enrichment effort to the point where each employee became responsible for one or more directories, performing all the twenty-one production steps. A refinement of this approach to job enrichment, developed at AT&T, is the concept of job "nesting," in which several interrelated jobs are physically grouped together to enhance efficiency and teamwork.[29]

Herzberg and colleagues have taken a similar approach. For example, as part of a series of studies in five British firms, in one experimental study two groups of laboratory technicians were encouraged to write the final reports on each of their experiments and to be

[26]E.L. Trist, G.W. Higgin, H. Murray, and A.B. Pollock, *Organizational Choice* (London: Tavistock Publications, 1965).
[27]A.K. Rice, "Productivity and Social Organization in an Indian Weaving Shed: An Examination of Some Aspects of the Socio-Technical System of an Experimental Automatic Loom Shed," *Human Relations*, 6:297–329 (1953).

[28]See Myers, *Every Employee a Manager*, pp. 81–87.
[29]Robert N. Ford, "Job Enrichment Lessons from AT&T," *Harvard Business Review*, 51:96–106 (January-February 1973).

more involved in planning. They were given time to follow up on some of their own research ideas and were authorized to requisition equipment, materials, and maintenance over their own signatures. Such changes were not made in the control groups. (Results will be reported later in the chapter.) In another experiment, sales representatives were given wide latitude in planning the frequency of their sales calls, were provided with technical service department help "on demand," were authorized to make immediate settlements in the case of customer complaints up to a certain amount, and were given discretionary ranges in which prices could be quoted.[30] Thus, in both job enrichment studies, employees were provided with more complete jobs and were given considerable additional latitude in planning and control.

EFFECT OF JOB DESIGN ON NEED FULFILLMENT

Theoretically, many human needs are affected by organizational planning and job design. The needs for safety and survival are quite clearly affected by machine design and plant layout. Similarly, the needs for affiliation, cooperation, and dominance are frustrated if the narrowness of jobs confines employees to interaction with too few people. To what extent the nature of the job affects the needs for esteem, belonging, and self-actualization is not so clear, however. An analysis of current theory and research produces conflicting conclusions, although the authors concerned with overspecialization seem to be in the majority.

According to Argyris, for example, the more tasks that are specialized, the fewer the abilities that are used, the less self-actualization that takes place, and the more that passivity and dependence are fostered. To illustrate what he

believes has happened to the scope of many jobs, he cites sources suggesting that people of subnormal intelligence have made excellent employees in certain situations.[31]

Other authors have described the impact, as measured by overall satisfaction, of organizational planning on need fulfillment. In a study of the automobile industry, Walker and Guest found that the majority of assembly workers studied disliked the mechanical pacing and the repetitive nature of their jobs, preferring jobs with different and more functions. The authors also found that absenteeism was related to the degree of mass-production characteristics in the jobs.[32] To the extent that absenteeism reflects the lack of need fulfillment, this research suggests that mass-production techniques in the factory tend to reduce the satisfaction of needs.

Kornhauser found similar results. In a study of automobile workers, he found dramatic differences among occupational levels in the way in which employees answered a question about whether the job "gives you a chance to use your abilities." Among young workers, 79 percent in both the skilled and high semiskilled categories answered yes, while 62 percent in ordinary semiskilled and *only 17 percent in repetitive semiskilled jobs* (13 percent in the case of machine-paced work) *answered yes.* Among middle-aged workers, the percentages were 98, 73, 65, and 24 percent for the four occupational levels (19 percent in the case of machine-paced jobs). This would suggest that the lower the level of skill required by the job, the less self-actualization.[33]

---

[30] William J. Paul, Jr., Keith B. Robertson, and Frederick Herzberg, "Job Enrichment Pays Off," *Harvard Business Review*, 47:61–78 (March-April 1969).

[31] Chris Argyris, *Personality and Organization* (New York: Harper & Brothers, 1957), pp. 54–75. See also Chris Argyris, "The Individual and the Organization: An Empirical Test," *Administrative Science Quarterly*, 4:145–167 (September 1959).

[32] Walker and Guest, *Man on the Assembly Line*, pp. 53–64, 121.

[33] Arthur Kornhauser, *Mental Health of the Industrial Worker* (New York: John Wiley & Sons, Inc., 1965), p. 98.

Higher skill levels and less job specialization were generally associated with less "alienation" in a study by Shepard of office and factory workers. Shepard set out to assess the impact on workers of the evolution in technology from nonmechanized production systems (e.g., craftsmen, skilled maintenance workers, secretaries, and clerks) to mechanized production systems (e.g., assemblers in an auto factory, keypunch operators, and sorters), to automated production systems (monitors in a continuous-process industry, and computer operators, programmers, and systems analysts). Among workers, alienation, as measured by five scales (including scales of powerlessness and meaninglessness), was the highest among final assemblers in an auto factory, lower among skilled maintenance workers in the same factory, and even lower among monitors in an oil refinery. Among office workers in insurance companies and a bank, alienation was lowest among computer operators, programmers, and systems analysts. Alienation was higher for the other categories, but no significant differences were found between the nonmechanized and mechanized office jobs. One major implication drawn by the researcher is the need for job enlargement in factories. A second implication is that automation (continuous-process technology) tends to reverse the historical trend toward task specialization and to provide "more freedom, control, meaning, and self-involvement" than has been predicted.[34]

In still another study, which investigated a different set of choices, the researcher found very clear indications that workers preferred "bench work," that is, each person making complete assemblies, over assembly-line work. In this particular instance, a factory had switched from putting together working washing-machine pumps on an assembly line to having individual employees assemble entire pumps. Of sixty-one workers surveyed, forty preferred bench work, and nineteen preferred line work. One did not respond, and another indicated no preference. Preference for line work seemed to be associated with preference for the associated pay system and the pacing of the work. More specifically, the workers tended to dislike the mechanical pacing of the line, being tied to the work and lack of specific association with the quality of the end product. In contrast, they tended to like the social interaction permitted on the assembly line and the use of work simplification applied to assembly-line work. Paradoxically, nearly half of those surveyed approved of both work simplification on the assembly line and enlarging jobs via bench work. Overall, however, the responses quite clearly showed a preference for bench work.[35]

Experience some years ago at Sears, Roebuck Company is consistent with the above reports. According to Worthy,

We have found that when jobs are broken down too finely we are more likely to have both low output and low morale. Conversely, the most sustained efforts are exerted by those groups of employees who perform the more complete sets of tasks (e.g., salesmen, supervisors, master mechanics, etc.) and these likewise exhibit the highest levels of morale and esprit de corps.[36]

[34] Jon M. Shepard, *Automation and Alienation: A Study of Office and Factory Workers* (Cambridge, Mass.: The M.I.T. Press, 1971), pp. 106–128. The author's use of words like *freedom* and *control* suggests that his use of the term *job enlargement* means essentially the same as our use of *job enrichment*. For an account of office employees' reactions to automation, see Einer Hardin, "The Reactions of Employees to Office Automation," *Monthly Labor Review*, 83:925–932 (September 1960).

[35] Eaton H. Conant and Maurice D. Kilbridge, "An Interdisciplinary Analysis of Job Enlargement: Technology, Costs, and Behavioral Implications," *Industrial and Labor Relations Review*, 18:389–391 (April 1965). See also J.F. Biggane and Paul A. Stewart, "Job Enlargement: A Case Study," Bureau of Labor and Management, State University of Iowa, Research Study No. 25, July 1963.

[36] Quoted by Walker and Guest, *Man on the Assembly Line*, p. 58.

Worthy also found that the larger the department, the lower the morale, and that overspecialized departments and functions caused employees to feel that their work was insignificant and uninteresting.[37]

Using the five dimensions of a "job diagnostic survey" (JDS), length of time on the job was found to be a factor mediating between job design and satisfaction. In general, the more that the job included "skill variety," "task identity," "task significance," "autonomy," and "feedback from job" the higher the job satisfaction, but this did not hold for new employees or for those with fifteen or more years on the same job. One of the conclusions that the researcher drew was that: "In situations where task dimensions are to be improved, but the job positions are to remain the same with the same personnel, employees must be assessed for receptiveness . . . especially with regard to job longevity."[38]

Some research and some experience suggest that horizontal job enlargement per se—increasing the number of task elements—is not likely to enhance need fulfillment. In a study involving assembly-line operators in a radio and television-set factory, 202 employees were asked whether they preferred larger or smaller assembly tasks (more or fewer elements) and whether they preferred machine-paced conveyors or operator-paced conveyors. All employees were assumed to have worked under these different conditions. In answer to the first question, about 50 percent preferred smaller assembly tasks, about 36 percent were indifferent, and about 12 percent preferred larger tasks. In answer to the second question, about 84 percent preferred mechanically paced conveyors, about 6 percent had no preference, and about 10 percent preferred operator-paced conveyors. The author concluded as follows: ". . . The employees' answers give little support to the view that the repetitiousness of assembly-line work breeds dissatisfaction and frustration." Further, ". . . the answers constitute a clear-cut refutation of the idea that mechanical pacing is inherently distasteful to most workers."[39] The same researcher reached similar conclusions in another study, in which it was found that incentive pay, group pressures, and the absence of night work had more impact than job repetitiveness.[40]

An attempt to increase job satisfaction through horizontal job enlargement in the form of job rotation backfired in one company. Although the union pressed for, and obtained, a system of job rotation written into the labor contract, the results seemed to be increased hostility permeating the whole plant.[41] Experiments at General Motors in enlarging jobs by

[37] James C. Worthy, "Factors Influencing Employee Morale," *Harvard Business Review*, 28:68–70 (January 1950). Talacchi also found that the larger the organization, the lower the satisfaction of employees. Sergio Talacchi, "Organization Size, Individual Attitudes and Behavior: An Empirical Study," *Administrative Science Quarterly*, 5:398–420 (December 1960). See also Bernard P. Indik and Stanley E. Seashore, "Hidden Costs of Large Size—and How to Avoid Them," *Personnel*, 41:16–25 (March-April 1964).

[38] Ralph Katz, "Career Implications for Job Satisfaction," in Robert L. Taylor, Michael J. O'Connell, Robert A. Zawacki, and D.D. Warrick, eds., *Academy of Management Proceedings*, Proceedings of the 36th Annual Meeting of the Academy of Management, Kansas City, Missouri, August 11–14, 1976, pp. 104–108. For a description of the JDS, see J.R. Hackman and G.R. Oldham, "The Job Diagnostic Survey," Technical Report No. 4, Department of Administrative Science, Yale University, 19-4; and J.R. Hackman and E.E. Lawler III, "Employee Reactions to Job Characteristics," *Journal of Applied Psychology Monograph*, 55:259–286 (June 1971).

[39] M.D. Kilbridge, "Do Workers Prefer Larger Jobs?" *Personnel*, 37:45–48 (September-October 1960).

[40] M.D. Kilbridge, "Turnover, Absence, and Transfer Rates as Indicators of Employee Dissatisfaction with Repetitive Work," *Industrial and Labor Relations Review*, 15:21–32 (October 1961).

[41] Hjalmar Rosen, "Job Enlargement and Its Implications," *The Worker and the New Industrial Environment* (Ann Arbor, Mich.: Monograph prepared by Institute of Labor and Industrial Relations and the Foundation for Research in Human Behavior, University of Michigan, with Wayne State University, 1962), pp. 17–18.

assigning three or four tasks instead of one have not been very successful.[42]

Overall, some general themes are emerging from research on the effects of organizational planning and job scope on the satisfaction of human needs. Job enrichment—not job enlargement per se—appears to offer considerable promise of enhancing morale. The more worker skills are utilized, or the more the worker has control over the planning and pacing of work, or the more the worker can interact meaningfully with others, the higher the morale. Some evidence suggests that the larger the unit in which the worker is employed, the lower the morale; this phenomenon is probably associated with overspecialization. Some research suggests that job enrichment may be less relevant to new and to long-time employees on the same job.

THE EFFECT OF JOB DESIGN ON PRODUCTIVITY AND EFFICIENCY

Job design clearly appears to be a causal factor influencing employee morale, which, in turn, is an intervening or mediating variable relative to organizational end results. Specifically, what is the relationship of job design to such things as costs, turnover, work quality, and the like?

A study at the International Business Machines Corporation (IBM) suggests that a combination of vertical and horizontal job enlargement may have beneficial results. The jobs of several hundred machine operators were broadened to include some tool-sharpening, machine setup, and inspection. The results included higher quality work, a reduction in defective work and scrap, less machine time, lower setup and inspection costs, and a concomitant rise in employee satisfaction.[43]

In the study cited earlier pertaining to the assembly of washing-machine pumps, the switch from an assembly-line operation to bench work where individual employees put together the entire pump brought economic gains as well as better attitudes. Labor costs were reduced, quality was improved, and idle time due to inefficiencies of the production line was eliminated.[44]

The experience of TI with job enrichment also suggests some desirable consequences. Turnover went down and cooperation among production workers improved. In this instance, the planning and controlling aspects were increased partly through training workers in work simplification that they apply to their own jobs—a reduction of the horizontal dimensions. It should be noted that the success of the program seemed to be highly interrelated with other systems, including training and staffing. With respect to the latter, suggestions sometimes came from employees on how their jobs could be eliminated, a development that obviously depended upon the company guaranteeing transfer to other opportunities.[45]

The early Tavistock experiments, cited earlier, had positive results. In the British coal mining project, productivity, safety, and morale all improved significantly, and the results in the Indian project were favorable.[46] The recent coal mining experiment in the United States at the Rushton Mining Company, although running into difficulty from resistance of nonparticipants, resulted in substantially higher productivity, a decrease in lost-time accidents, and greatly enhanced morale.[47]

[42] "The Spreading Lordstown Syndrome," *Business Week*, March 4, 1972, pp. 69–70.

[43] Charles R. Walker, "The Problem of the Repetitive Job," *Harvard Business Review*, 28:54–58 (May 1950).

[44] Conant and Kilbridge, "An Interdisciplinary Analysis of Job Enlargement," pp. 381, 395.

[45] See *Business Week*, April 27, 1968, p. 60; and M. Scott Myers, "Conditions for Manager Motivation," *Harvard Business Review*, 44:69 (January–February 1966).

[46] Trist, et al., *Organizational Choice*, p. 294; and Rice, "Productivity and Social Organization," pp. 297–329.

[47] Ted Mills, "Altering The Social Structure in Coal Mining: A Case Study," *Monthly Labor Review*, 99:3–10 (October 1976).

More recent sociotechnical projects in Scandinavian countries have had mixed to good results. At a Volvo truck plant turnover fell from 50 percent in 1969 to 8 percent in 1973, while turnover in the region declined from 42 percent in 1969 to only 30 percent in 1972. Repair work per truck dropped from 3.5 hours per truck in 1969 to 1.5 hours in 1973. Absenteeism did not significantly change, probably as a result of the social security system, which paid almost full wages for absenteeism of seven days or less.[48] Results at the Södertälje engine assembly plant at Saab-Scania also appear positive. Turnover and absenteeism decreased, while productivity and quality remained high and worker satisfaction increased.[49] However, the reactions of six American workers who participated in the job redesign experiment at the Saab-Scania engine plant were mixed to negative. The Americans liked the leisurely pace of the preassembly line, but thought it was too slow and had too many breakdowns for economical production. They also disliked the rapid pace and pressures in the three-person assembly teams. In addition, they thought the works council and production and development meetings were inefficient and did not focus on results.[50] At the Scandia Insurance Company results were mixed: Productivity did not change significantly, satisfaction went up slightly, and measures of organizational climate improved; but absenteeism also increased somewhat. It is interesting that there was considerable resistance and opposition to the project from middle management at Scandia Insurance.[51]

At the General Foods pet food plant, job enrichment efforts appeared to be associated with 92 percent fewer quality rejects, an absenteeism rate 9 percent below the industry norm, and one of the better turnover and safety records in the company. The conclusion was reached that, "[w]hile new equipment was responsible for some of these results, more than one-half of them derived from the innovative human organization."[52] At the Corning Glass plant where teams of employees assembled complete hot plates, reject rates dropped from 23 percent to 1 percent in the first six months, and absenteeism dropped from 8 to 1 percent while productivity increased.[53] Results at AT&T include such outcomes as reduction in the number of employees needed (from 120 persons to 74 in the Illinois Bell Telephone Company directory compilation unit), higher production, and lower absenteeism (Chesapeake and Potomac Telephone Company).[54]

The studies in British firms cited earlier found mixed but generally favorable results from job enrichment efforts. Experimental and control groups were used in each instance. In a study involving sales representatives, the experimental group increased sales by nearly 19 percent over the previous year, while the control group's sales declined 5 percent. A study of design engineers found that the job satisfaction of two experimental groups increased substantially while satisfaction remained static for

[48] Mikalachki, "Effects of Job Design," pp. 383–384.

[49] Richard B. Peterson, "Swedish Experiments on Job Reform," *Business Horizons*, 19:16 (June 1976). See also Peter Docherty and Bengt Stymne, "Office Worker Participation in Organizational Development: An Experiment in a Swedish Insurance Company," *Organization and Administrative Sciences*, 5:55–71 (Winter 1974/1975).

[50] See Arthur S. Weinberg, "Six American Workers Assess Job Redesign at Saab-Scania," *Monthly Labor Review*, 98:52–53 (September 1975).

[51] Seminar with Ake Magnusson of Stockholm School of Economics, November 14, 1975, Graduate School of Business Administration, University of Washington.

[52] Richard E. Walton, "Innovative Restructuring of Work," in Jerome M. Rosow, ed., *The Worker and the Job* (Englewood Cliffs, N.J.: Prentice-Hall, Inc., 1974), p. 162.

[53] U.S. Department of Labor, "Job Redesign: Some Case Histories," *Manpower*, May 1973, pp. 18–19.

[54] Ford, "Job Enrichment Lessons from AT&T," pp. 96–106.

two control groups. In two other studies, one involving production foremen and the other engineering foremen, a number of improvements occurred in the performance of the foremen in the experimental groups in contrast to the control groups. For example, their selection of subordinates improved, their training became more effective, there was a reduction in repeat disciplinary cases, and there was an increase in consultation with union officials. Job satisfaction increased substantially in the case of the engineering foremen. In the fifth study, experimental groups of technicians substantially improved their performance in the quality of their technical reports in contrast to those produced by control groups.[55]

One well-reported experiment between 1960 and 1965 at Non-Linear Systems, usually referred to as an experiment in participative management, featured elimination of the assembly line and the creation of small groups of workers headed by a supervisor. Each group was assigned to build entire instruments and had wide latitude in devising its own methods. Although early reports indicated substantial success in terms of employee morale, a reduction in capital tied up in work-in-process, and considerable reduction in customer complaints,[56] the company experienced sharp drops in sales in 1963 and 1965, and the experiment was essentially abandoned.[57]

After examining a number of accounts of the project and of the difficulties experienced by the company, as well as talking with one of the consultants involved, it appears to me that the

company paid insufficient attention to rapidly changing customer needs, the size of its inventories, and the need to undergo drastic employee layoffs when sales took a sharp down turn. Further, in retrospect, it appears that top management morale was sharply lowered as a result of essentially immobilizing the vice presidents by turning them into consultants.[58] In general, it seems that lack of top management responsiveness to the external environment may have been the flaw, not job enrichment or worker participation.

One of the difficulties in interpreting the research on job enrichment, however, is that variables in addition to those examined were usually involved. In the IBM study, for example, since wages were raised because of the job enrichment and since a level of supervision between foremen and workers was eliminated (the jobs of set-up workers and inspectors), it is difficult to assess the impact of job enrichment alone. It is quite clear, however, that this constellation of events had an overall desirable result. Similarly, the effect of employment practices is not obvious in the studies by Kilbridge. It might be that good selection practices resulted in a high degree of satisfaction with repetitiveness.

Another matter that is not clear is the impact of employee participation in the enrichment process itself. Who concludes that there is a problem, and who attempts to solve that problem through redesigning jobs? These are important issues. In the TI illustrations cited earlier, it would appear that the workers whose jobs were affected were frequently involved in early aspects of problem diagnosis and in deciding what changes to make in job design, with good results in terms of morale and efficiency. (This participative approach is highly

[55] Paul, Robertson, and Herzberg "Job Enrichment Pays Off," pp. 61–78.

[56] Arthur H. Kuriloff, *Reality in Management* (New York: McGraw-Hill Book Company, 1966), pp. 41–45. See also Abraham H. Maslow, *Eupsychian Management: A Journal* (Homewood, Ill.: Richard D. Irwin, Inc., 1965).

[57] Erwin L. Malone, "The Non-Linear Systems Experiment in Participative Management," *The Journal of Business*, 48:52–64 (January 1975).

[58] See Ibid., pp. 52–64; and "Where Being Nice to Workers Didn't Work," *Business Week*, January 20, 1973, pp. 98–100.

congruent with notions about the nature of effective systems, as described in Chapter 4.)

On the other hand, the researchers who conducted the successful job enrichment experiments in the British firms were not entirely sold on the efficacy of participation of employees in the job enrichment process itself. They state somewhat pessimistically, "It seems that employees themselves are not in a good position to test out the validity of the boundaries of their jobs."[59] This conclusion was based on experiences other than the experimental studies, however. Their experimental research was not aimed at shedding any light on this issue, and the research design dictated that the job incumbents would not participate in the job changes.

Another variable that is frequently not analyzed in job enrichment studies is compensation. Equity theory would suggest that as job scope and responsibility increase, and as productivity and effectiveness increase, compensation should increase. Indeed, Ford's conclusions from the AT&T experiments are that

Trouble can be expected, of course, if the economics of increases in productivity are not shared equitably . . . An employee who takes the entire responsibility for preparing a whole telephone directory . . . ought to be paid more, although a new clerical rating must be established. Job enrichment is not in lieu of cash; good jobs and good maintenance are two sides of the same coin.[60]

Writing about the General Foods plant, Walton reaches a similar conclusion. He states,

. . . there is growing interest in some additional mechanism for sharing the fruits of increased productivity. Although a productivity or profit bonus may not have been necessary to induce very high performance, I believe that some such scheme will become necessary in order to preserve a sense of equity.[61]

RESPONSIBILITY FOR ORGANIZATIONAL PLANNING AND JOB DESIGN

In most enterprises, major restructuring of the organization is the responsibility of the chief executive and immediate subordinates, including the personnel director. In large organizations, the personnel department is more and more frequently assigned a major role in the planning of such restructuring. In a study of 249 large companies, mostly in manufacturing, which is "generally recognized to be the cutting edge of change," 205 (82 percent) had assigned organizational planning to the personnel department.[62]

Industrial-engineering departments, which typically are involved in such matters as plant layout, time-and-motion study, and methods improvement, are most often found reporting to the manufacturing director.[63] Engineers working for a department of industrial engineering or for the manufacturing department, along with their superiors, will have the most to say about the introduction of changes in systems, machines, and equipment.

Organizational planning units and industrial engineering departments are usually separate. The former seem to work from the top down, and the latter from the bottom up (and both

---

[59] Paul, Robertson, and Herzberg, "Job Enrichment Pays Off," p. 75. For additional variables to examine in job enrichment efforts, see Noel M. Tichy, "When Does Work Restructuring Work? Organizational Innovations at Volvo and GM," *Organizational Dynamics*, 5:63–80 (Summer 1976).

[60] Ford, "Job Enrichment Lessons from AT&T," p. 106.

[61] Richard E. Walton, "From Hawthorne to Topeka and Kalmar," in Eugene L. Cass and Frederick G. Zimmer, eds., *Man and Work in Society* (New York: Van Nostrand Reinhold Company, 1975), p. 127. For a critique of job enrichment practices and research, see Fein, "Motivation for Work," in Dubin, *Handbook of Work, Organization, and Society*, pp. 465–530.

[62] National Industrial Conference Board, "Personnel Administration: Changing Scope and Organization," *Studies in Personnel Policy*, No. 203, 1966, p. 24.

[63] National Industrial Conference Board, "Industrial Engineering—Organization and Practices," *Studies on Business Policy*, No. 78, 1956, p. 4.

frequently ignore the perceptions of nonsupervisory employees). To what degree their activities concide or work at cross-purposes when these functions meet in the middle would make an interesting study.

On the other hand, personnel departments are expected more and more to have broad knowledge about the motivational climate of the total organization and are gradually having some impact on the design of jobs at the production level. In general, industrial engineers have traditionally focused on making additional refinements in the specialization of tasks, and the activities of personnel departments—job evaluation, collective bargaining, employment, etc.—have traditionally been directly influenced by the activities of the industrial engineers. But recently some personnel departments have been raising questions about the optimum level of task specialization and urging managers to experiment with various forms of job enrichment. Perhaps the behavioral sciences will become the common meeting ground of industrial engineers, personnel specialists, and line managers. In any event, it is quite likely that personnel departments of the future will become more involved in making recommendations about the design of work.

Implicit in the above is the suggestion that the specialists in human resources administration and the specialists in technology cooperate extensively in the design of work. Perhaps both industrial engineers and behavioral scientists should be assigned to organizational planning units. Some firms, including TRW Systems, have successfully teamed industrial engineers with behavioral scientists. Other firms that have also experimented in this direction are Procter & Gamble, Texas Instruments, Eastman Kodak, and Maytag.[64]

In addition, since organizational planning has such an impact on the effectiveness with which human resources can be utilized, the chief executive of any organization would be wise to follow the practices of large manufacturing firms and include the personnel director in overall organizational planning activities. The personnel department should also make recommendations on personnel policies when proposed organizational changes require transfer, layoff, or upgrading of employees at any level, and it should help the communication of proposed changes to employees. In addition, the personnel department should enforce agreed-upon rules for the transfer and displacement of people. All too often, however, the personnel department is called upon after the planning has been done to help minimize the disruption resulting from the inauguration of changes.[65] As Davis says, ". . . all production technologies, whether designed or selected, include social system choices."[66]

These recommendations, of course, imply high competence on the part of the personnel staff. Effective assistance by the personnel department in optimizing the use of human resources and in minimizing undesirable aspects of organizational change depends in large part upon the qualifications of the personnel director and staff. People in personnel must obviously be well versed in the areas of human needs, motivations, and the causes of defensive behavior if they are going to be of much help in organizational planning and in the design of jobs.

[64] Sharon L. Lieder and John H. Zenger, "Industrial Engineers and Behavioral Scientists: A Team Approach to Improving Productivity," *Personnel*, 44:68–75 (July-August 1967).

[65] The consequences of lack of planning and after-the-fact participation of the personnel department with regard to the psychological and social factors in the introduction of new technology are described in Floyd C. Mann and L. Richard Hoffman, *Automation and the Worker: A Study of Social Change in Power Plants* (New York: Henry Holt and Company, 1960), Chapter 7.

[66] Louis E. Davis and James C. Taylor, "Technology, Organization, and Job Structure," in Dubin, *Handbook of Work, Organization, and Society*, p. 381.

SUMMARY

Task specialization is a fundamental organizational process, which comprises, sequentially, the determination of organizational objectives, organizational planning, and job design. Many forces, including changes in technology, union-management relations, labor market conditions, and relationships in power and skill among executives, have a major impact on this process.

The impact of automation on the design of jobs and organizations appears to depend on the particular situation. It is associated with such variables as the design of particular machines, the number of machines tended per operator, and the uniqueness of the equipment. Automation frequently creates jobs with more autonomy and meaning than assembly-line jobs and, in turn, frequently has a positive impact on morale.

Job enlargement can be horizontal, vertical, or a combination of horizontal and vertical. Jobs can be enlarged in one dimension and constricted in another. Vertical job enlargement is called "job enrichment." Job enrichment programs have received impetus from the theories of Maslow, Herzberg, and others, from theory and research about the efficacy of participation, and from early sociotechnical systems research at Tavistock.

Results of studies about attitudes of workers toward repetitive work are conflicting. A major difficulty in such research is that many factors, including the reward system, impinge on worker attitudes and productivity, and the impact of such factors on job design is difficult to isolate.

What little reporting has been done on the consequences of job enlargement suggests that vertical job enlargement, or vertical plus horizontal job enlargement—i.e., job enrichment—produces desirable economic and morale consequences but that horizontal job enlargement, alone, does not. Skill level is positively associated with job satisfaction. Size of organization appears to be negatively associated with employees' feelings about job satisfaction and rewards.

A change in the system of task specialization through job enlargement or enrichment typically requires changes in other systems, such as training and selection. In general, it would appear that job enrichment has a number of desirable outcomes and that optimal results are associated with employee participation in the job enrichment process itself along with the provision of training programs designed to assist employees in both the enrichment process and with new aspects of their jobs.

A major deficiency in many of the research studies is lack of detail about a number of variables that may play a significant moderating role. For example, changes and/or expectations about the reward system, the degree of worker participation in the job enrichment process itself, and the degree of support and involvement of top and middle managers and the labor union, may be crucial variables in job enrichment programs.

The chief executive and immediate subordinates are responsible for making major structural changes, and personnel departments increasingly are assigned a major role in such planning. Industrial engineering groups typically focus on the structuring of tasks at the bottom of the organization, which raises interesting questions about the congruency of these efforts for change vis-à-vis those initiated at the top. Collaboration on job design among job incumbents, personnel people, industrial engineers, behavioral scientists, and line managers is needed. Increased competency in the behavioral sciences by personnel departments will result in the personnel departments having a greater impact on both organizational planning and job design.

APPENDIX: FREDERICK TAYLOR ON JOB ENLARGEMENT

The following is from Congressional hearings held in 1912, *Hearings Before Special Committee of the House of Representatives to Investigate the Taylor and Other Systems of Shop Management Under Authority of House Resolution 90:* [67]

The Chairman.   If the workman has to obey instructions implicitly as to how the work should be done, would he not thereby simply become an automaton, and would not that ultimately reduce the skill and value of the workman?

Mr. Taylor.   Mr. Chairman, I want to give an illustration in answer to that question, because I think my answer can be made very much clearer through an illustration than through a single sentence.

The workmen—those men who come under scientific management—are trained and taught just as the very finest mechanic in the world trains and teaches his pupils or apprentices. Now, I think you will agree with me as to who this finest and highest-class mechanic in the world is. So far as I know there will be no question about him, for we will all agree that the highest-class mechanic in the world is the modern surgeon. He is the man who combines the greatest manual dexterity and skill with the largest amount of intellectual attainment of any trade that I know of—the modern surgeon.

Now, the modern surgeon applied the principles of scientific management to his profession and to the training of the younger surgeons long before I was born—long before the principles of scientific management were ever dreamed of in the ordinary mechanical arts. Let us see how this man trains the young men who

come under him. I do not believe that anyone would have an idea that the modern surgeon would say to young doctors who come into the hospital or who come under him to learn the trade of surgeon—I do not think the surgeon would say anything of this kind: "Now, boys, what I want, of all things, is your initiative; what I want, of all things, is your individuality and your personal inventiveness."

I do not think anyone for an instant would dream that a surgeon would say to his young men, for instance, "Now, young men, when we are amputating a leg, for instance, and we come down to the bone, we older surgeons are in the habit of using a saw, and for that purpose we take this particular saw that I am holding before you. We hold it in just this way and we use it in just that way. But, young men, what we want, of all things, is your initiative. Don't be hampered by any of the prejudices of the older surgeons. What we want is your initiative, your individuality. If you prefer a hatchet or an ax to cut off the bone, why chop away, chop away!" Would this be what the modern surgeon would tell his apprentices? Not on your life! But he says, "Now, young men, we want your initiative; yes. But we want your initiative, your inventive faculty to work upward and not downward, and until you have learned how to use the best implements that have been developed in the surgical art during the past hundred years and which are the evolution of the minds of trained men all over the world; until you have learned how to use every instrument that has been developed through years of evolution and which is now recognized as the best of its kind in the surgical art, we won't allow you to use an iota of ingenuity, an iota of initiative. First learn to use the instruments which have been shown by experience to be the best in the surgical art and to use them in the exact way which we will show you, and then when you have risen up to the highest

[67] From Frederick Winslow Taylor, *Scientific Management* (New York: Harper & Brothers, 1947), pp. 196–199. Used with permission.

knowledge in the surgical art, then invent, but, for God's sake, invent upward, not downward. Do not reinvent implements and methods abandoned many years ago.''

REVIEW AND DISCUSSION QUESTIONS

1. What factors influence the determination of organizational objectives? What are some contemporary events that are making an impact on organizational objectives?

2. What is the difference between job enlargement and job enrichment?

3. Describe some of the differences between these versions of job enrichment: (a) M. Scott Myers, (b) Robert Ford, and (c) sociotechnical systems (Tavistock).

4. According to the research, which forms of job enlargement appear to have the most beneficial results in terms of efficiency or morale or both?

5. What conclusions can be reached about the desired role of job incumbents in the job enrichment process itself?

6. What is the impact of the computer on skill-mix?

7. What factors determine whether automation results in job narrowing or job enlargement? What are the morale implications?

8. What factors might have a bearing on whether or not repetitive work is desirable from the employees' standpoint?

9. What is the relationship between skill level and job satisfaction?

10. What might be an appropriate role for a personnel department in job design?

SUPPLEMENTAL REFERENCES

Adam, John, Jr., "Put Profit in Its Place," *Harvard Business Review*, 51:150–154ff. (March-April 1973).

Anderson, John W., "The Impact of Technology on Job Enrichment," *Personnel*, 47:29–37 (September-October 1970).

Barrett, Jon H., *Individual Goals and Organizational Objectives* (Ann Arbor: Crusk Institute for Social Research, University of Michigan, 1970).

Borwick, Irving, "Team Improvement Laboratory," *Personnel Journal*, 48:18–24 (January 1969).

Davis, Louis E., "The Design of Jobs," *Industrial Relations*, 6:21–45 (October 1966).

———, and J.L. Taylor, eds., *Design of Jobs: Selected Readings* (Harmondsworth, Middlesex: Penguin Books, 1972).

———, and Ernest S. Valfer, "Studies in Supervisory Job Design," *Human Relations*, 19:339–352 (November 1966).

Donaldson, Lex, "Job Enlargement: A Multidimensional Process," *Human Relations*, 28:593–610 (September 1975).

Ford, Robert N., "Job Enrichment Lessons from AT&T," *Harvard Business Review*, 51:95–106 (January-February 1973).

Gallagher, William E., Jr., and Hillel J. Einhorn, "Motivation Theory and Job Design," *Journal of Business*, 49:358–373 (July 1976).

Gooding, Justin, *The Job Revolution* (New York: Walker and Company, 1972).

Graen, George, "Role-Making Processes within Complex Organizations," in Marvin D. Dunnette, ed., *Handbook of Industrial and Organizational Psychology* (Chicago: Rand McNally College Publishing Company, 1976), pp. 1201–1245.

Hackman, J. Richard, "Is Job Enrichment Just a Fad?" *Harvard Business Review*, 53:129–138 (September-October 1975).

———, "On the Coming Demise of Job Enrichment," in Eugene L. Cass and Frederick G. Zimmer, eds., *Man and Work in Society* (New York: Van Nostrand Reinhold Company, 1975), pp. 97–115.

————, and Edward E. Lawler III, "Employee Reactions to Job Characteristics," *Journal of Applied Psychology* Monographs, 55:259–286 (June 1971).

————, and Greg R. Oldham, "Development of the Job Diagnostic Survey," *Journal of Applied Psychology*, 60:159–170 (April 1975).

Imberman, A.A., "Assembly Line Workers Humbug Job Enrichment," *The Personnel Administrator*, 18:29–31ff. (March-April 1973).

Jenkins, David, *Job Power: Blue and White Collar Democracy* (London: William Heinemann, Ltd., 1974).

Kahn, Robert L., "The Work-Module—A Tonic for Lunch Pail Lassitude," *Psychology Today*, February 1973, pp. 35–39ff.

Lawrence, Paul R., and Jay W. Lorsch, *Organization and Environment: Managing Differentiation and Integration* (Homewood, Ill.: Richard D. Irwin, 1969).

McColough, C. Peter, "The Corporation and Its Obligations," *Harvard Business Review*, 53:127–138 (May-June 1975).

Maher, John R., ed., *New Perspectives in Job Enrichment* (New York: Van Nostrand Reinhold Company, 1971).

Mann, Floyd C., "Psychological and Organizational Impacts," in John T. Dunlop, ed., *Automation and Technological Change* (Englewood Cliffs, N.J.: Prentice-Hall, Inc., 1962), pp. 43–65.

Mead, Margaret, ed., *Cultural Patterns and Technical Change* (New York: The New American Library of World Literature, Inc., 1955), p. 48.

Miller, Eric J., "Socio-Technical Systems in Weaving, 1953–1970: A Follow-up Study," *Human Relations*, 28:349–386 (May 1975).

Myers, M. Scott, "Overcoming Union Opposition to Job Enrichment," *Harvard Business Review*, 49:37–49 (May-June 1971).

National Commission on Productivity, *First Annual Report of the National Commission on Productivity* (Washington, D.C.: U.S. Government Printing Office, 1972).

Perrow, Charles, "The Analysis of Goals in Complex Organizations," *American Sociological Review*, 26:854–866 (December 1961).

Reif, William E., and Fred Luthans, "Does Job Enrichment Really Pay Off?" *California Management Review*, 15:30–37 (Fall 1972).

Reif, William E., and Ronald C. Tinnell, "A Diagnostic Approach to Job Enrichment," *MSU Business Topics*, 21:29–37 (Autumn 1973).

Rothberg, Herman J., "Job Redesign for Older Workers: Case Studies," *Monthly Labor Review*, 90:47–51 (January 1967).

Rush, M.F., *Job Design for Motivation* (New York: The Conference Board, 1971).

Sales, S.M., "Organizational Role as a Risk Factor in Coronary Disease," *Administrative Science Quarterly*, 14:325–326 (September 1969).

Schein, Edgar H., *Organizational Psychology*, 2nd ed. (Englewood Cliffs, N.J.: Prentice-Hall, Inc. 1970), pp. 35–37. (On the Tavistock Institute coal mining studies.)

Schwab, Donald P., and L.L. Cummings, "A Theoretical Analysis of the Impact of Task Scope on Employee Performance," *The Academy of Management Review*, 1:23–35 (April 1976).

Shils, Edward B., *Automation and Industrial Relations* (New York: Holt, Rinehart and Winston, 1963).

Silberman, Charles E., *The Myths of Automation* (New York: Harper & Row, Publishers, Inc., 1966).

Silverman, William, "The Economic and Social Effects of Automation in an Organization," *The American Behavioral Scientist*, 9:3–8 (June 1966).

Sirota, David, and Alan D. Wolfson, "Job Enrichment: What Are the Obstacles?" *Personnel*, 49:8–17 (May-June 1972).

Stieglitz, Harold, "Organization Planning," *National Industrial Conference Board*, 1962.

Thompson, James D., and William J. McEwen, "Organizational Goals and Environment," in Amitai Etzioni, ed., *Complex Organizations: A*

Sociological Reader (New York: Holt, Rinehart & Winston, 1961), pp. 177–186.

Trist, E.L., and K.W. Bamforth, "Some Social and Psychological Consequences of the Long-wall Method of Coal-Getting," *Human Relations*, 4:3–38, No. 1 (1951).

Trist, E.L., G.W. Higgin, H. Murray, and A.B. Pollock, *Organizational Choice* (London: Tavistock Publications, 1963).

Turner, A.N., and Paul R. Lawrence, *Industrial Jobs and the Worker* (Boston: Graduate School of Business Administration, Harvard University, 1965).

Umstot, Dennis D., Cecil H. Bell, Jr., and Terence R. Mitchell, "Effects of Job Enrichment and Task Goals on Satisfaction and Productivity: Implications for Job Design," *Journal of Applied Psychology*, 61:379–394 (August 1976).

Walters, Roy W., *Job Enrichment for Results: Strategies for Successful Implementation* (Reading, Mass.: Addison-Wesley, 1975).

Walton, Richard E., "How to Counter Alienation in the Plant," *Harvard Business Review*, 50:70–81 (November-December 1972).

Weinberg, Arthur S., "Industrial Democracy in the Netherlands, *Monthly Labor Review*, 99:48–49 (July 1976).

Whitsett, David A., "Where Are Your Unenriched Jobs?" *Harvard Business Review*, 53:75–80 (January-February 1975).

CHAPTER 10
JOB ANALYSIS AND DESCRIPTIONS, PERFORMANCE STANDARDS, AND WORK RULES AND CONDITIONS

Although organizational objectives and organizational planning to a great extent determine the duties, scope, and level of the individual jobs in the enterprise, jobs are also partly designed through the development of job descriptions, job specifications, performance standards, and work rules and conditions. Not only do these devices and circumstances tend to condition the nature of individual jobs, but also they make explicit the behavior and characteristics required of workers. They are important aspects of the task-specialization process and components of other vital personnel processes, as we shall see later.

JOB ANALYSIS AND JOB DESCRIPTIONS
DEFINITION AND PURPOSE

Job descriptions, or *position descriptions,* typically are one- or two-page summaries of the basic tasks performed on a job, and constitute part of the role expectations relative to that job. Role expectations are the attitudes and beliefs that people who interact with the job incumbent have about what the incumbent should and should not do.[1] Job descriptions usually have a label called a "job title." (See Figure 10-1 for an example of a job description with appended job specifications, called, in this case, "job requirements.")

The factual basis for a job description can vary from a mental image in the employer's mind to an elaborate investigation and analysis of the job by means of observations, interviews, questionnaires, or critical incidents

---

[1] For a discussion of role expectations, see Robert Kahn, Donald M. Wolfe, Robert P. Quinn, and J. Diedrick Snoeck, *Organizational Stress: Studies in Role Conflict and Ambiguity* (New York: John Wiley & Sons, 1964), pp. 14–15.

```
                              JOB DESCRIPTION

Job Title        RESEARCH ASSISTANT       Branch
Job Number       3135-I                   Division      ECONOMIC RESEARCH
Salary Grade     9                        Department
Date                                      Section

                                JOB DUTIES

Compiles     industrial and economic data by: obtaining current and comparative
             statistics relative to trends in production, commerce, employment, etc.,
             from newspapers, periodicals, publications of government agencies, trade
             associations, and other standard sources; maintaining a set of statisti-
             cal records for the department concerning industries and areas of the re-
             gion; selecting and classifying for the department library pertinent ar-
             ticles from the above-mentioned sources; digesting suitable material on
             national and regional economic developments; plotting acquired statis-
             tics and developing informative graphs, tables, and charts; preparing
             special statistical and other reports.

             Also computes department's own seasonally adjusted employment data se-
             ries. Furnishes various industrial and economic data to bank and other
             officials.

Prepares     the Weekly Business Briefs by gathering and assembling data and writing
             original copy to provide a digest of regional and national business news
             for the Bank's staff, officers, and customers. Uses own judgment in
             selecting articles of significance.  Submits material for final ap-
             proval.

             Also researches and prepares section for the Summary of Regional Indus-
             tries. Researches and prepares local business section for the Metropoli-
             tan Real Estate Research Report.  Prepares statistical data for charts
             and tables in the quarterly and annual issues of the Summary.  Prepares
             statistical data and writes a section on local home price trends for the
             Metropolitan Real Estate Research Report.  Prepares special reports on
             various subjects as requested.

             Assists in maintaining research library; assists Economist in developing
             new statistical series and ideas for charts; assists other staff members
             with miscellaneous functions.

             The Research Assistant, under general supervision, is engaged primarily
     in the acquiring of pertinent, factual data relative to varied industries, their
     trends and any other significant details. In large part this material provides the
     basis for analysis, opinions, and recommendations by the Economist, although some of
     the analysis is included in the duties of the Research Assistant.

     Form 171 Pers. KI
```

Figure 10-1 Job description from a large bank

JOB REQUIREMENTS

Education	A broad knowledge of a technical workfield applicable to duties such as economics and business theory, and an understanding of statistical methods and the application and analysis thereof. Equivalent to college degree in Economics or Business Administration.
Experience	Job requires practical experience in statistical methods and analysis and a period to acquire a knowledge of various information sources. Time — six months to a year.
Resourcefulness	Job requires judgment and initiative in determining sources of information and judgment in selection of significant data and application of statistical formulas to develop informative results. Under general supervision.
Responsibility	Considerable care is required as most errors are difficult to locate. Reports and publications are distributed beyond the bank and relied upon as being correct and indicative of trends. Work must be prepared promptly, and deadlines met.
Contacts	Routine staff contacts plus frequent public contacts by phone and occasionally in person requesting or furnishing information. Courtesy and tact are required.
Supervision	Does not supervise.
Mental Effort	Requires considerable care and attention due to the concentration required for the selection, development, and analysis of economic information.
Physical Effort	Medium office position. Job requires frequent use of calculator and adding machine. Also requires frequent referral to department library and occasional trips to public library and other outside offices for information.
Job Conditions	Average office conditions.

Figure **10-1**   Continued

Used with permission.

(worker behaviors that characterize either very good or very poor performance).[2] Such a sys-

[2]The use of critical incidents has been developed by Flanagan and others and has evolved into what are called "behaviorally anchored rating scales." These scales, whose main use seems to have been in performance appraisal (see Chapter 15), and secondarily in the development of test cri-teria, have not had much applicability to date in job analysis leading to job descriptions, job specifications, and job evaluation. Theoretically, however, the information generated in the development of these scales for classes of jobs could be useful for these purposes as well as in training. For a description of a procedure for developing behaviorally anchored rating scales, see Donald Schwab, Herbert G. Heneman III, and Thomas A. DeCottiis, "Behaviorally Anchored Rating Scales: A Review of the Literature," *Personnel Psychology*, 28:549–562 (Winter 1975).

tematic investigation, called "job analysis," is the basis for the job description shown in Figure 10-1. The categories of information obtained in job analysis might include what activities are performed, and how, when, and why; the machines, tools, or equipment used; what interactions with others are required; the physical and social working conditions; and the training, skills, and abilities required on the job.[3] Careful job analysis is becoming increasingly important in order to demonstrate the job-relatedness of job specifications and information obtained from the application blank, interview, and tests.

Job descriptions have several important uses, one of which stems from their development. From my experience, preliminary drafts can be used as a basis for productive group discussion, particularly if the process starts at the executive level. Thus, if the top managers jointly discuss each others' responsibilities, overlap or confusion can be discovered, questions can be raised about the major thrust of each position, and problems of structure can be identified. When these problems have been resolved, each manager can then work with subordinates in reviewing and discussing their job descriptions, and so on. A further benefit of this approach is that executives and subordinates normally feel committed to supporting a defined structure that they have helped to create. In this way, the job description becomes a vehicle for both organizational change and improvement.

A second use of job descriptions is in the development of job specifications, i.e., a summary of the worker's qualifications needed on the job. These specifications, in turn, are useful in planning recruitment, in recruiting, and in hiring people with appropriate skills.

Thirdly, the job description itself is useful in work force planning and recruiting. Planners can plan more intelligently if they know the basic duties of the job as well as the qualifications required of the worker, and recruiters can be more effective in recruiting if they are able to describe jobs to applicants.

Job descriptions can also be used to orient new employees toward basic responsibilities and duties. Job descriptions may not include all the detailed responsibilities of the job, however, so that the employee and supervisor should have a clear understanding of the duties not covered in this document. Furthermore, job descriptions do not include policies and procedures to be followed, and they may not include many of the nuances of the job, which may vary with the incumbent. Job descriptions thus have significant limitations in orientation and training.[4]

Job descriptions are also the basic documents used in developing performance standards. *Performance standards*, which we shall discuss briefly here and then in more detail in Chapter 15 under the topic of "Management by Objectives," essentially supplement or expand job descriptions and set forth in quantitative and qualitative terms the goals to be achieved during a certain period of time.

Finally, job descriptions can be used for job evaluation, a wage and salary administration technique. *Job evaluation* is the process of determining the relative worth of jobs within an organization, and job descriptions, if written with this objective in mind, can provide the basic information for making these decisions.

Some companies have more than one job description for each job. A lengthy detailed version may be used in training and in job evaluation, while a shorter version may be used in the planning and hiring of the work force.

[3] See Ernest J. McCormick, "Job and Task Analysis," in Marvin D. Dunnette, ed., *Handbook of Industrial and Organizational Psychology* (Chicago: Rand McNally College Publishing Company, 1976), pp. 652–654.

[4] See Douglas McGregor, *The Human Side of Enterprise* (New York: McGraw-Hill Book Company, 1960), pp. 79–82, for a discussion of these and other limitations of job descriptions.

CURRENT PRACTICES AND PROBLEMS

Probably a vast majority of companies have job analysis programs and use written job descriptions as tools in personnel management. One study found over 75 percent of firms performing job analyses,[5] and, presumably, all these analyses resulted in a document that could be called a job description. These job descriptions were used for wage and salary administration (job evaluation), for writing job specifications, for recruitment and placement, for labor relations, for work force utilization (planning, organizing, and avoiding job overlap), and for placement. Approximately one-fourth of the firms used this job information in hiring the handicapped, and somewhat less than half use the information in the development of performance standards.[6]

It should always be remembered that these job descriptions are not perfect reflections of jobs. As stated by Kerr and Fisher, "the object of a job description is to differentiate the job from other jobs and to set its outer limits."[7] Furthermore, research has indicated that executives, at least, tend to carry their work patterns with them into new jobs, thus drastically modifying the jobs to which they are assigned. This tendency is probably less marked at lower levels of the organization. Obviously, care must be exercised in writing job descriptions to make them as accurate as possible, and the job description should be reviewed and discussed after the new incumbent has held the job for a while, because jobs tend to be dynamic and their descriptions quickly become out of date.

It is also important that both supervisors and subordinates understand the uses of job descriptions, so that appropriate information is recorded. Further, the relevant parties should agree that the description is a fair reflection of the job. Otherwise, job evaluation and performance review may also be considered unfair.

The way job descriptions are used can reflect both leadership style and the type of organization. As I stated in Chapter 5, one frequent characteristic of a mechanistic organization is a high emphasis on writing job descriptions implying that jobs are semipermanently structured. On the other hand, job descriptions that are the product of frequent team decisions about how best to accomplish team objectives can be symptomatic of an organic organization and a participative leadership style. In either situation, it is important that job descriptions, like any other managerial device, reflect a dynamic organization and neither straitjacket performance nor dampen creativity and ingenuity.

Opinions vary on how to write job descriptions. One school of thought would have them written in detail and in terms of work flow. Using the example of a superintendent's job description, Chapple and Sayles state:

Ignoring any technical know-how required, anyone could step into the job and know what he will receive, from whom, what he should do with it, and where it should go. In addition, he will know what day of the week a particular report comes in and, if tight schedules of time are necessary, even the approximate hour.[8]

(To me, this is much more detail than is usually desirable; such detail might go into an operations manual.)

Another approach would be to write job descriptions in terms of goals or results to be achieved—in other words, as performance standards. (The use of performance standards—a popular version is called "management by objectives"—will be discussed later in the chapter.) The most prevalent school of thought

---

[5] Jean J. Jones, Jr., and Thomas A. DeCottiis, "Job Analysis: National Survey Findings," *Personnel Journal*, 48:805 (October 1969).

[6] Ibid., p. 806.

[7] Clark Kerr and Lloyd H. Fisher, "Effect of Environment and Administration on Job Evaluation," *Harvard Business Review*, 28:93 (May 1950).

[8] Eliot D. Chapple and Leonard R. Sayles, *The Measure of Management* (New York: The Macmillan Co., 1961), p. 50.

suggests that job descriptions be written in terms of duties and responsibilities, i.e., in terms of functions to be performed. Thus, job descriptions themselves frequently reflect the emphasis of a major purpose. In the first example training appears to be a major purpose for the job descriptions; in the second example goals or end results are emphasized; while the third example is designed to insure that certain activities are carried out.

ACCOUNTABILITY FOR JOB ANALYSIS AND JOB DESCRIPTIONS

The personnel department in medium-sized and larger firms typically performs the job analysis function and coordinates the writing of job descriptions. The subunits most frequently mentioned as being responsible for job analysis are "Wage and Salary" and "General Personnel." This tendency undoubtedly reflects the widespread use of job analysis and job descriptions for both job evaluation and recruitment and placement purposes.[9] The actual writing may be done by personnel department representatives, job incumbents, or supervisors. In any event, if the job description is to be used for recruiting and salary administration, it is necessary that both the personnel department (or president or management committee in smaller firms) and the department concerned agree upon the description. Typically, the chief executive of the organization will hold the personnel department accountable for coordinating the development and maintenance of job descriptions. Managers throughout the organization are held accountable for cooperating in this program and for supplying accurate information. Thus, the personnel director and other top managers are held jointly accountable for

[9] Jones and DeCottiis, "Job Analysis," p. 807.

the development and maintenance of job descriptions.

VALIDITY OF JOB DESCRIPTIONS

A job description is valid to the extent that it accurately reflects job content. The importance of job description validity becomes clear when the influence of job descriptions on employment and evaluation practices is taken into consideration. These two functions are likely to be performed away from the job scene and possibly by people not immediately familiar with the details of the various jobs. If the job description is inaccurate and misleading, job specifications will be inaccurate and candidates without proper qualifications may be referred to department heads, or jobs may be ranked improperly in terms of worth to the organization. Inaccurate job descriptions can also reduce the effectiveness of training, and can result in the development of unrealistic standards of performance. These problems demonstrate the importance of periodic, systematic information gathering, careful writing of descriptions, and checks of accuracy with job incumbents and supervisors.

JOB SPECIFICATIONS

DEFINITION AND PURPOSE

Another useful device is the *job specification*, which translates the job description into terms of human qualifications required for successful performance of the job. Specifications are often appended to the job description. (See the section on "Job Requirements" in Figure 10-1.) They are intended to serve as a guide in hiring and to be used in job evaluation. In hiring, they are presumed to be a partial guide to the characteristics sought in the application blank, the tests, the interviews, and the checking of references.

CURRENT PRACTICES AND PROBLEMS WITH JOB SPECIFICATIONS

Specifications are typically determined by discussion among various managerial people of what qualifications seem to be appropriate and reasonable for the particular job in question. Past experience is the usual guide.

Results of predictive studies, however, may have an important bearing on the writing of specifications. For example, if it has been found that ability to type 90 words per minute and take shorthand at 120 words per minute is essential for success on a certain secretarial job, these requirements may very well be written into the job specification.

Since job specifications evolve from organizational planning and job descriptions, they are subject to most of the same influences. On the other hand, certain cultural influences, not obvious until the actual hiring process, have an illogical or irrational impact on job specifications. I am referring to prejudice about race, age, and sex, in particular. These societal influences are, in turn, modified by the governmental legislation and administrative orders that they have precipitated.

VALIDITY OF JOB SPECIFICATIONS

An underlying assumption of job specifications is that the qualities listed, if characteristic of the person selected, will lead to success on the job and perhaps to jobs higher in the organization. The validity of this assumption can be tested through research on the extent to which different degrees of the characteristics listed are predictive of performance.

In recent years, many organizations, Congress, and federal and state governmental agencies have been concerned that, in many instances, job specifications are either unrealistically high or not relevant to the job. If job specifica-tions are too stringent, the result is that high-talented labor is hired but is underutilized. Or, people who could perform the work effectively are prohibited from employment. This is a particularly sensitive issue as it relates to minority groups, women, and disadvantaged persons.

A Supreme Court decision has had an extensive impact on job specifications. Based on the Civil Rights Act of 1964 (see Chapter 11) and rulings by the Equal Employment Opportunity Commission, the U.S. Supreme Court ruled in the *Griggs* v. *Duke Power Company* case that the employer unlawfully discriminated against blacks by requiring a high school education or the passing of an intelligence test as conditions of employment or advancement into certain jobs. The thrust of the Court's argument was that these specifications were not significantly related to job performance. The Court went on to say:

The facts of this case demonstrate the inadequacy of broad and general testing devices as well as the infirmity of using diplomas or degrees as fixed measures of capability. History is filled with examples of men and women who rendered highly effective performances without the conventional badges of accomplishment in terms of certificates, diplomas, or degrees. Diplomas and tests are useful servants, but Congress had mandated the common-sense proposition that they are not to become masters of reality.[10]

In some instances, making the job specifications conform with the job description will solve some of these problems. For example, many jobs do not require a high school diploma or a college degree, and those specifications can be removed. In those cases where the specification is realistic in terms of the demands of the job, the job can perhaps be restructured—usually several jobs simultaneously—to permit

[10] U.S. Supreme Court, *Willis S. Griggs et al.* v. *Duke Power Company*, March 8, 1971. See also George R. Wendt, "Should Courts Write Your Job Descriptions?" *Personnel Journal*, 55:442–445ff. (September 1976).

hiring people with lower skills. A number of situations can influence organizations to go the latter route—a shortage of skills on the labor market, a desire to provide employment for disadvantaged persons, and/or a combination of skill shortages and rapidly rising costs. The use of nurses' aides to take over some nursing activities in hospitals and the use of paramedics to handle the more routine aspects of medical practice are illustrations. However, the emergence of such new job categories requires special training programs.[11]

The so-called hard-core unemployed, however, constitute a massive social problem that cannot be solved by simply revising job specifications and hiring standards downward. If present specifications are valid, this problem requires that management assess its objectives and determine to what extent it wishes to assume the burden of solution. Partial solutions lie in major effort to provide training opportunities (see the chapter on skill training) and in job restructuring. The employment of handicapped persons and the mentally retarded are also problems requiring simultaneous attention to several organizational dimensions, including organizational objectives, job structure, job specification, and training.

Thus, several questions should be periodically asked about specifications, especially if they lack *face validity* (obvious or surface validity), which may be defined as the quality of appearing sensible on the face of things.[12] In the first place, are people being hired who are overly qualified or who have the wrong skills? Do these factors result in their becoming dissatisfied with the job? Are skills and talents, therefore, wasted? Is the quality of the work force too low? Do current specifications really serve any purpose? Do current specifications keep out individuals who could make an important contribution to the organization? Attitudes and assumptions of management on current specifications should be periodically examined in order to avoid the mistakes implied in these questions.

To the extent job specifications are nonexistent or invalid, hiring practices are that much less likely to serve the needs of the organization. Improper placement, high training costs, excess wastage of materials, dissatisfaction, low productivity, high turnover, and inefficient use of skills and talents are all possible consequences of poor administration of job specifications. Thus, valid job specifications are basic to sound personnel management.

ACCOUNTABILITY FOR JOB SPECIFICATIONS

As an outgrowth of job descriptions, job specifications are typically developed with the cooperation of the personnel department and various supervisors throughout the organization. The personnel department coordinates the writing of job descriptions and job specifications and secures agreement on the qualifications desired.

Because of the supervisor's knowledge of the job, the personnel director will give a great deal of weight to the suggestions of a supervisor concerning needed qualifications, but the personnel director will want to make certain that specifications are realistic, fair, and designed to assist the organization in attaining its goals. Furthermore, the personnel department must exert control over specifications to the extent that hiring practices comply with federal and state laws and governmental rulings.

---

[11] For a discussion of trends in the employment of "allied health personnel," see U.S. Department of Labor, *Manpower Report of the President* (Washington, D.C.: U.S. Government Printing Office, March 1972), pp. 135–138.

[12] Referring to testing, Thorndike defines *face validity* as ". . . that quality in a test which makes it appear sensible for the use to which it is being put. . . ." Thorndike's definition also applies to such personnel devices as job specifications, application-blank items, and interview questions. See Robert L. Thorndike, *Personnel Selection* (New York: John Wiley & Sons, 1949), p. 4.

PERFORMANCE STANDARDS

DEFINITION AND PURPOSE

Performance standards are major aspects of job design in that they make employee role expectations more explicit in terms of quantitative or qualitative performance levels to be achieved. Management's purpose in using performance standards is to establish the subgoals to be achieved by individuals, yardsticks against which actual performance can be measured. Other purposes may be to encourage more self-direction in the development of personal goals congruent with overall organizational objectives and to enhance creativity and job commitment.

The contemporary concepts of *management by objectives*, and the less-used term *results management*, are synonymous with the idea of performance standards. The words *targets* and *goals* are also used frequently in this context. While job descriptions essentially set forth *what* is to be done on a job—i.e., what functions or tasks are to be performed—performance standards describe *how much* or *how well* the job is to be performed. Performance standards may be in the form of job descriptions expanded to include a statement of job goals for a particular year or for some other time interval, or they can be separate statements supplemental to job descriptions. Advocates of performance standards recommend that they be written in quantitative terms whenever possible, but in actual practice some job aspects are difficult to reduce to quantitative terms, and qualitative statements must be made.

CURRENT PRACTICES AND PROBLEMS WITH PERFORMANCE STANDARDS

Although the development of performance standards for managerial and white-collar positions is relatively new, their use is growing rapidly.[13]

[13] See Glenn H. Varney, "Performance Appraisal—Inside and Out," *The Personnel Administrator*, 17:15–17 (November-December 1972).

Since the development of scientific management and time studies around the turn of the century, however, performance standards for production jobs have been fairly common. Most such standards are written in terms of the number of units to be produced in a certain period of time. Typically, such performance standards on wage jobs are connected with incentive systems under which bonuses are paid for production above and beyond a standard production rate. (Incentive systems will be discussed in more detail in a separate chapter on that subject.)

Many organizations have implied performance standards, that is, they may not be spelled out in connection with job descriptions. For example, if the president of a company has established a goal for the sales department of an increase in sales of industrial chemicals by 10 percent during the next year, this goal really becomes a performance standard for the sales manager even though the statement may not be in writing. Similarly, targets with respect to safety, reduction in scrap, increases in new accounts, building of new plants, etc., are all performance standards implicit in the jobs affected. The advantage of writing out performance standards for each job, however, is that each person knows specifically what is expected of his or her performance in terms of targets or goals. Performance standards, as management by objectives implies, must be related to organizational objectives; indeed, the top executives of organizations should work out their standards or targets in conjunction with the president after standards have been determined with the board of directors. In short, the development of standards should be based on overall objectives and should spread from the top down throughout the entire organization. This is a slow, tedious process, but many organizations that have developed performance standards believe the results well worth the time and effort involved.

As I will discuss in Chapter 15, the greatest pitfall in developing performance standards is that they may tend to ignore the personal commitment of subordinates. If performance standards are imposed upon members of the organization in an autocratic and dictatorial manner, the whole process is likely to be resisted. On the other hand, according to the experience of some authors, if subordinates participate in setting their own standards, they are likely to set them high and to be committed to achieving them.

Union-management relationships may also have an important bearing on the establishment of standards for unionized jobs. In some situations, unions have cooperated with management to establish standards based on time-and-motion studies. In Scanlon Plan companies, union and management cooperate in establishing standards of production, and employees share in the financial results of production gains that exceed the established standards. (See Chapter 21 for a description of the Scanlon Plan.) In other situations, unions have resisted the development of any standards. The early days of the scientific management movement were characterized by such union resistance.[14] In the absence of an incentive system of some kind, unions have traditionally resisted any managerial attempts to increase production beyond what is considered "a fair day's work." Chapter 15 will discuss performance standards in more detail under the topic "Management by Objectives."

ZERO-DEFECTS PROGRAMS: A SPECIALIZED FORM OF PERFORMANCE STANDARDS

In recent years, extraordinary demands for reliable products in the armed services and the aerospace, jet aircraft, and defense industries have given rise to special programs for reducing errors in workmanship. These programs are specialized kinds of performance-standard programs that have had various names, including "PRIDE," "Target-Zero," and "Zero-Defects." The latter has been used with the most frequency.

Such "Zero-Defects" programs are essentially efforts designed to encourage the commitment of employees to high quality standards and to "do it right the first time." The first such program was started at the Martin Marietta Company in 1961 and by the end of the decade had spread to some one thousand major American companies. These programs have been particularly popular in the aerospace and defense industries and have been used in such organizations as Litton, Boeing, Douglas Aircraft, General Electric, North American, Curtiss-Wright, Westinghouse Electric, and the U.S. Air Force. Although these programs typically feature some razzle-dazzle in the form of rallies, speeches, parties, etc., they rely on the basic assumption that most people want to do quality work provided they are given the proper support and recognition. The recognition given is typically in the form of plaques, certificates, letters, or news items. By making thoroughly visible management's expectations that work is to be accurate and by inviting, encouraging, and giving recognition to suggestions for eliminating errors, a number of companies have reported major savings through reduction in scrap and rework and through increased reliability of products.[15] Some undesirable side effects of these programs have been reported, however, including resentment by employees who thought there was an implication they

---

[14]See William Gomberg, *A Trade Union Analysis of Time Study*, 2nd ed. (New York: Prentice-Hall, Inc., 1955), Chapter 1.

[15]Based on Lloyd A. Swanson and Darrel Corbin, "Employee Motivation Programs: A Change in Philosophy?" *Personnel Journal*, 48:895–898 (November 1969); American Management Association, "Zero Defects: Doing It Right the First Time," *Management Bulletin*, No. 71 (1965).

were not already doing their best.[16] I also wonder about the impact of some companies encouraging employees to sign pledge cards, and the implicit coercion that may be present. In addition, the programs seem to be more relevant to jobs in production than in research and development or engineering.[17]

WORK RULES AND WORKING CONDITIONS

DEFINITION AND PURPOSE

Work rules are minimum standards or boundaries of conduct or performance that apply to groups of people. Although they do not reflect a specialization of behavior to the extent that job design and performance standards do, they do establish behavioral patterns unique to a particular enterprise and often to a particular segment of that enterprise. They may also be considered an integral part of each job, because, in a sense, they are adjuncts to job descriptions and performance standards. They are seldom, if ever, included in these documents, because work rules tend to apply uniformly to large segments of the total work force and are usually spelled out in employee handbooks and policy manuals. By *working conditions* is meant the state of the working environment with respect to health, safety, comfort, and aesthetics. I will deal only briefly with these topics because of limited space, but particular attention will be paid to the Occupational Safety and Health Act.

Some examples of work rules are those pertaining to starting and stopping work, total hours worked, rest periods, insubordination, fighting or drinking on the job, smoking in hazardous areas, reporting of injuries, and time keeping. One purpose of such rules is to in-

sure reasonable predictability of behavior so that the organization can function without undue disturbance and so that the total task of the organization can be done. Another purpose of many work rules is to protect employees—rules about wearing radiation monitoring badges in an atomic energy power plant, for example.

Work rules, then, serve as control devices, since management uses them as standards against which to apply sanctions in order to insure a reasonable level of conformity. Violations of rules usually result in punishments or penalties, although a few companies will give positive rewards for above-average compliance with rules pertaining to such matters as tardiness and absenteeism.

CURRENT PRACTICE AND PROBLEMS

VIOLATION OF WORK RULES A wide variety of work-rule violations can lead to disciplinary action in business and industrial firms. For example, the following partial list illustrates the types of offenses that may lead to disciplinary action:

Absence without permission
Dishonesty, deception, or fraud
Drunkenness or possession of liquor on the job
Deliberate damage of material or property
Fighting or dangerous "horseplay" on the job
Gambling
Use of drugs
Stealing
Failure to meet work standards
Falsifying records
Smoking in prohibited areas
Abusive, threatening, or profane language
Insubordination
Repeated tardiness
Carrying concealed weapons
Immoral conduct
Sleeping on duty
Failure to comply with safety rules.[18]

---

[16]Gerald V. Barrett and Patrick A. Cabe, "Zero Defects Programs: Their Effects at Different Job Levels," *Personnel*, 44:40–46 (November-December 1967).
[17]Ibid., p. 42.

[18]See Lawrence Stessin, *Employee Discipline* (Washington, D.C.: The Bureau of National Affairs, 1960), pp. 25–26.

Not all these offenses may be considered serious enough for discharge on the first offense, although most are likely to involve discharge for repeated offenses. Offenses frequently considered serious enough to warrant immediate discharge are dishonesty, insubordination, intoxication, and deliberate damage to material or property.[19] Specific offenses such as these are often mentioned in labor contracts. Lesser penalties for violations of some of the less serious infractions include oral or written warnings, demotion, transfer, or disciplinary layoff. (See Chapter 8 for a discussion of progressive discipline.)

Some work rules are violated with enough frequency in many organizations to require formalized security programs. "Periodic" or "often" thievery by employees was reported in almost half of the organizations surveyed in one study. Vandalism was reported as occurring relatively frequently in about one-fourth of the organizations; and drug abuse was reported as occurring "periodically" in about one-seventh of responding firms.[20] While this prevalence of work rules violations is clearly a major problem in modern organizations, in the aggregate only a very small proportion of the work force is involved. However, such incidents may have a dampening impact on trust and morale levels throughout an organization as well as having an adverse economic impact.

THE WORKDAY AND THE WORKWEEK Work rules have changed a good deal over the years. For example, the workday in the Philadelphia Navy Yard prior to 1835 was sunrise to sunset, with time off for breakfast and other meals. This meant an extremely long working day during the summer months, although actual work time dropped to slightly below eight hours for a short period in December and early January.

Actual work hours for late June 1835 totaled eleven hours and fifty-four minutes, not including time off for meals. In 1836, the workday was reduced to ten hours all year round.[21] One hundred and forty years later, in 1976, the typical workday in the United States was eight hours and the typical workweek forty hours. In large part, this pattern was set in 1938 when the Fair Labor Standards Act established forty hours as the standard for workers employed by firms in interstate commerce.[22]

THE COMPRESSED WORKWEEK Currently, the concept of a *four-day, forty-hour workweek* is reversing the trend toward a shorter workday in a number of instances. This concept is being tried or considered by a number of firms in the United States and elsewhere. Although the practice cannot be considered widespread, the advent of the four-day, forty-hour week may be as significant as the appearance of a few five-day workweeks in firms about 1929.[23] One report states that some 700 to 1,000 American firms have some form of a four-day week for at least part of the work year and/or for part of the work force.[24] The General Accounting Office reported a substantially higher figure and es-

[19] Ibid., p. 24.
[20] "ASPA-BNA Survey: Industrial Security," Bureau of National Affairs, No. 1153, March 16, 1972.
[21] O.L. Harvey, "The 10 Hour Day in the Philadelphia Navy Yard: 1835–36," *Monthly Labor Review*, 85:258–260 (March 1962).
[22] Although the working time of women employees was regulated and limited in forty states, Puerto Rico, and Washington, D.C., until the early 1970s [see Russell Greenman and Eric J. Schmertz, *Personnel Administration and the Law* (Washington, D.C.: The Bureau of National Affairs, 1972), p. 66], most such laws have been declared invalid or ruled in conflict with the Civil Rights Act. See Bureau of National Affairs, *Labor Relations Reporter, State Laws*, 4, SLL 1:11–13.
[23] The authors of a new book on the four-day workweek found history repeating itself in the sense that they discovered themselves saying some of the same things that were said in a 1929 National Industrial Conference Board book, *The Five-Day Week in Manufacturing Industries*. See Riva Poor, ed., *4 Days, 40 Hours* (Cambridge, Mass.: Bursk and Poor Publishing, 1970), p. 18.
[24] Douglas L. Fleuter, *The Workweek Revolution: A Guide to the Changing Workweek* (Reading, Mass.: Addison-Wesley Publishing Company, 1975), p. 12.

timated that one million workers in some three thousand private firms in the United States were under a four-day week.[25] Another report based on a random sample of American Management Association members found that 5 percent (43 out of 811 firms) had a four-day week plan in operation, but about 18 percent (142 firms) were planning or evaluating a four-day week. About 12 percent of reporting firms discontinued such a program after a trial.[26] A 1974 survey of 185 Canadian companies found approximately 50 percent had adopted some form of compressed workweek.[27]

A four-day workweek does not mean that the plant or company operates only four days, but that the individual employee's work commitment is for only four days, and typically for ten hours per day. However, the total number of hours worked per employee varies under different programs from as low as thirty-two to as high as forty-eight. Furthermore, not all employees in such organizations are on a four-day schedule. Frequent starting points for such programs are in units such as data-processing departments or hospital nursing staffs.[28]

Some of the desirable consequences of the four-day week as reported by using companies are increased morale, reduced absenteeism, enhanced recruiting, improvements in traffic flow, and increased productivity. Disadvantages as reported by using companies included difficulty in scheduling working mothers for ten-hour shifts, less effective service to customers, and worker fatigue.[29] Other difficulties include

the Walsh-Healy Act requirement of overtime payments beyond eight hours in one day for work on government contracts, federal and state laws requiring overtime beyond eight hours for nonsupervisory employees, and various state laws limiting the length of the working day for women.[30]

Typically, the four-day week has been initiated by management, usually in nonunionized organizations. However, in a number of instances unions have concurred with management in experiments with the shorter week and occasionally have taken the initiative in the matter.[31] In general, the union movement has advocated a reduction in total working hours as well as working days, and the retention of current wage levels as desirable goals. That is, a four-day, forty-hour workweek per se is not seen as particularly advantageous; a four-day, thirty-two-hour workweek with forty hours of pay is seen as desirable.

One example of union initiative is the United Auto Workers' (UAW) desire to experiment with the four-day week in one or more Chrysler plants. Management, however, saw too many obstacles to success, and the first talks on the subject were ended. Some of the problems as seen by Chrysler were difficulties in scheduling a three-shift operation, the Walsh-Healy requirement for overtime pay for work beyond eight hours in one day, union demands for overtime pay for Friday work, and a need to

[25] Monthly Labor Review, 98:85 (January 1975).
[26] Kenneth E. Wheeler, Richard Gurman, and Dale Tarnowieski, The Four-Day Week (New York: American Management Association, 1972), pp. 1–3.
[27] Gary M. Stewart and Arthur Guthrie, "Alternative Workweek Schedules: Which One Fits Your Operation?" Supervisory Management, 21:2–3 (June 1976).
[28] Wheeler, Gurman, and Tarnowieski, The Four-Day Week, p. 10.
[29] Ibid., pp. 13–15; and Fleuter, Workweek Revolution, pp. 13–15. See also James L. Steele and Riva Poor, "Work and

Leisure: The Reactions of People at 4-Day Firms," in Poor, 4 Days, 40 Hours, pp. 105–122; and Kenneth E. Wheeler, "Small Business Eyes the Four-Day Workweek," Harvard Business Review, 48:142–147 (May-June 1970). For results in sixteen organizations, see U.S. Department of Labor, "The Revised Workweek: Results of a Pilot Study of 16 Firms," Bulletin 1846, 31 pp., 1975.
[30] The Civil Service Commission reported that it planned to seek legislation to remove obstacles to compressed and flexible work schedules. Monthly Labor Review, 98:85 (January 1975).
[31] Wheeler, Gurman, and Tarnowieski, The Four-Day Week, pp. 7–9.

enlarge storage facilities and to modify receiving docks.[32]   Later, an experimental program was tried at the Chrysler parts depot at Tappan, New York, but employees voted to discontinue the project after about three months.   Workers liked the program during the summer, but became disenchanted when their children returned to school in the fall and three-day weekend trips were no longer feasible.   Other problems included complaints by workers who commuted long distances that they had too little time with their families on the long ten-hour days.[33]

Generally worker reactions to the four-day, forty-hour week have been favorable.   Hodge and Tellier found a sample of 223 respondents from twelve companies generally more satisfied with their jobs as a result of the four-day week.[34]   Fleuter cites a number of situations where employees appear to favor the change.[35] Ivancevich conducted a study involving two divisions of a manufacturing company, with one division serving as the experimental group and the other as a control group.   All participants in the study were members of the United Steelworkers of America.   Data were collected one month before the experimental group was converted to a forty-hour week and three months and twelve months afterwards.   A small, but significant improvement in job satisfaction occurred in the experimental group during the

thirteen-month period.   There was some improvement on measures of anxiety and an increase in supervisory ratings of employee production, team member effectiveness, and overall performance.   No differences occurred between the two groups in terms of unexcused absences.[36]   Goodale and Aagard found about 70 percent of employees surveyed were enthusiastic about a four-day, thirty-eight-hour workweek introduced in the accounting division of a large multinational corporation.   The day off each week for each employee was rotated so that every fifth week an employee had a four-day weekend.   Some difficulties were reported, however.   Sixty-two percent of the respondents found their work more tiring, and nearly half reported problems with work-related interpersonal contact and scheduling.[37]

Currently, *flextime* (sometimes called the "flexible hours workweek," "flexitime," "variable working hours," or *Gleitzeit* or "gliding time") is also receiving considerable attention. Basically, under such plans employees can manage their own starting and quitting times within certain guidelines.   For example, at the Messerschmitt-Bolkow-Blohm Company in Germany, a firm employing mostly white-collar technicians, employees may arrive any time between 7:00 and 8:00 A.M. and leave between 4:00 and 6:00 P.M.   (For an illustration of a flextime schedule, see Figure 10-2).   All employees, including executives, clock in; any extra work up to ten hours in any one month can be credited to the employee's work schedule for the next month; if the employee works less than a normal work load, the time can be made up the following month.   The company reports that the plan has resulted in improved morale, de-

[32]*Monthly Labor Review*, 95:78 (March 1972).

[33]*Monthly Labor Review*, 97:72–78 (December 1974).   A shorter work year became an objective in 1976 with the UAW at the Ford Motor Company striking over demands for additional days off per year; up to seven additional days were agreed to in the settlement.   Some employers are concerned that these demands may translate into specific demands for a four-day, thirty-two-hour week in the near future. *Business Week*, September 27, 1976, pp. 28–29.

[34]B.J. Hodge and Richard D. Tellier, "Employee Reactions to the Four-Day Week," *California Management Review*, 18:25–30 (Fall 1975).   See also Thomas A. Mahoney, Jerry M. Newman, and Peter J. Frost, "Worker's Perceptions of the Four-Day Week," *California Management Review*, 18:31–35 (Fall 1975).

[35]Fleuter, *Workweek Revolution*, pp. 15–19.

[36]John M. Ivancevich, "Effects of the Shorter Workweek on Selected Satisfaction and Performance Measures," *Journal of Applied Psychology*, 59:717–721 (December 1974).

[37]James G. Goodale and A.K. Aagard, "Factors Relating to Varying Reactions to the 4-Day Workweek," *Journal of Applied Psychology*, 60:33–38 (February 1975).

Figure **10-2**   Example of a flextime schedule

7:00 A.M.	9:00 A.M.	11:30 A.M.	1:30 P.M.	4:00 P.M.	6:00 P.M.
Flexible	Core period	Flexible lunch time (30 minutes)	Core period	Flexible	

creased turnover and absenteeism, improved recruiting, and an improved traffic situation.[38]

Generally favorable results have been reported by both European and American organizations. According to Fleuter, 5,000 firms in Europe have adopted some version of flextime, and in England, Parliament has authorized its use for Britain's half-million civil servants. While applications in the United States have been less widespread, more and more American companies are adopting the approach. Very few, if any, of these programs appear to have been terminated.[39] The few research studies that have been conducted to date report generally positive results in terms of job satisfaction and either no change or an increase in job performance.[40]

Some of the immediate *advantages* to flextime appear to be as follows:

∘ Employees and work teams can manage their own schedules within limits and adjust to particular life styles.

∘ Stress, stemming from concern about tardiness beyond one's control, is reduced.

∘ Peak traffic times can be avoided, and less time is spent commuting. If most organizations adopted flextime, traffic congestion would tend to be dispersed.

∘ Personal matters such as dentist or doctor appointments can be attended to more readily. Deceptive use of sick leave diminishes.

∘ Tardiness almost disappears.

Some of the immediate *disadvantages* appear to be:

∘ Lack of availability of employees during the flexible work periods at the beginning and end of the workday. This can adversely affect both customers and fellow employees.

∘ Increased need to communicate within and between units as to time availability and to insure coverage of vital functions, such as staffing switchboards, etc.

∘ Compliance with wage and hour laws and laws pertaining to lunch and rest breaks restricts flexibility, e.g., in the case of government contracts, the Walsh-Healy Act requires overtime payments to nonexempt employees working more than eight hours in any one day.

∘ Time reporting becomes more burdensome because employees may vary their hours and carry over hours.[41]

Variations in such plans as seen in other European firms include allowing working women

[38] "Choose Your Own Office Hours," *International Management*, June 1970, pp. 34–35. Fleuter reported in 1975 that Messerschmitt used time cards filled out at the end of each ten-hour accounting period. Fleuter, *Workweek Revolution*, p. 85.

[39] Fleuter, *Workweek Revolution*, pp. 73–102.

[40] See, for example, Robert A. Zawacki and Jason S. Johnson, "Alternative Workweek Schedules: One Company's Experience with Flextime," *Supervisory Management*, 21:15–19 (June 1976); and Robert T. Golembiewski, Rick Hilles, and Munro S. Kagno, "A Longitudinal Study of Flexi-Time Effects: Some Consequences of an OD Structural Intervention," *Journal of Applied Behavioral Science*, 10:503–532, No. 4 (October 1974).

[41] Based on Fleuter, *Workweek Revolution*, pp. 77–84; and Golembiewski, Hilles, and Kagno, "Longitudinal Studies of Flexi-Time," pp. 510–511.

to set their own schedules or, if part-time, to choose between morning or afternoon work.[42] Considerable flexibility in scheduling the work of part-time employees, however, has been common in the United States and Europe for many years.

Paradoxically, as in the Messerschmitt illustration, the flexible hours workweek may be revitalizing the use of the time clock, a practice that has declined markedly in recent years. While employees who gain a flexible work schedule may not find the time clock onerous, those employees who traditionally have had a somewhat flexible workweek and have not been punching a time clock—for example, managers and scientists—may view the extension of such flexibility to the total work force and a return to the time clock as restrictive and as removing some of the status differentials that they had previously enjoyed.[43] An "honor system" of reporting time on a card or sheet, as practiced in some companies, may be less objectionable.

PERMANENT PART-TIME WORK   Increasingly, organizations are revising their work rules and employment practices in order to utilize permanent part-time employees. A large proportion of these workers are women who want to be employed significantly less than full time in order to take care of children or to pursue other responsibilities or interests. Some firms report low turnover, ease in recruitment, and high productivity as advantages in utilizing this category of employee.[44] Congruent with such use is the concept of the shared-job, in which a job is split into two four-hour segments and shared, for example, by two homemakers.[45]

OCCUPATIONAL SAFETY AND HEALTH ACT OF 1970

The Occupational Safety and Health Act of 1970 (OSHA) is having a significant impact on work rules, job design, and the overall working environment. It is reflective of a growing national concern about the quality of life in organizations. Under the Act, Congress authorized the secretary of labor to establish mandatory safety and health standards in businesses engaged in interstate commerce. Both employers and employees are expected to assume responsibilities under the Act.

Sec. 5 (a) Each employer—

1. shall furnish to each of his employees employment and a place of employment which are free from recognized hazards that are causing or are likely to cause death or serious physical harm to his employees;

2. shall comply with occupational safety and health standards promulgated under this Act.

Sec. 5 (b) Each employee shall comply with occupational safety and health standards and all rules, regulations, and orders issued pursuant to this Act which are applicable to his own actions and conduct.

Civil penalties to employers up to $10,000 per violation for willful and repeated violations can be assessed. Willful violations resulting in the death of an employee can produce a six-month jail sentence for a first offense, in addition to fines. Penalties can be appealed to an Occupational Safety and Health Review Commission and from there to a U.S. Court of Appeals.[46]

[42]"Choose Your Own Office Hours," *International Management*, p. 34.
[43]For a discussion of a number of such considerations, see John R.M. Gordon and Alvar O. Elbing, Jr., "The Flexible Hours' Work Week—European Trend is Growing," *The Business Quarterly*, 36:66–72 (Winter 1971).
[44]See, for example, "Permanent Part-Time Jobs Thrive at Massachusetts Mutual," *World of Work Report*, 5:9 (July 1976).
[45]Richard J. Schonberger, "Private Lives Versus Job Demands," *Human Resource Management*, 14:30 (Summer 1975).
[46]Occupational Health and Safety Act of 1970; and U.S. Department of Labor, "The Williams-Steiger Occupational Safety and Health Act of 1970: A Handy Reference Guide" (1971). In 1976 a U.S. Court of Appeals upheld an OSHA finding that an employer was liable even though a violation

Penalties for noncompliance by employees were not included in the Act.

One of the intents of the Act is to encourage the respective states to "assume the fullest responsibility for the administration and enforcement of their occupational safety and health laws . . ." (Sec. 2.). States that establish standards and enforcement practices at least as effective as federal standards are provided grants for the administration and enforcement of their programs. The Act also created a National Institute for Occupational Safety and Health within the Department of Health, Education and Welfare.

The following list issued by the Occupational Safety and Health Administration represents the twenty-four areas where standards are most frequently violated. This list provides some insight into the impact that the Act is having on work rules and job design:

Walking-working surfaces—general
Machines—general requirements
Grounding, electrical
Welding, cutting, and brazing
Overhead and gantry cranes
Abrasive wheel machinery
Outlets, switches, junction boxes
Spray finishing
Portable wood ladders
Means of egress—general requirements
Flexible cords and cables
Respiratory protection
Woodworking machinery
Mechanical power transmission
Sanitation
Guarding wall and floor openings
Flammable and combustible liquids
Hand and portable power tools
Powered industrial trucks
Handling materials—general
Electrical—general

Fixed ladders
Personal protective equipment [47]

For example, portable ladders must be used at a pitch such that the horizontal distance of the foot of the ladder is about one-fourth the length of the ladder; respirators, hard hats, goggles, and/or hearing protectors are required on many industrial jobs; and asbestos materials must be mixed in closed containers. [48]

One indication of the widespread impact of the Act came during the first fiscal year after it became effective. Of the 29,505 establishments that were inspected, only about 25 percent were found to be in compliance with federal regulations. After penalties were assessed, a total of 1,033 appeals were made to the Review Commission during the twelve months following receipt of the first appeal. The number of Commission judges was increased from 29 to 85 during the second year of the Act and the number of inspectors was increased from some 500 to 900. [49]

Subsequently, employers, labor unions, and the federal government have experienced considerable difficulty with OSHA. Employer complaints about "nitpicking" inspections and unreasonable standards have been widespread. Organized labor has complained about "endless delay" in the establishment of safety and health standards. [50] From the government's perspective, insufficient appropriations for inspections and enforcement, and a U.S. district court ruling in 1976 that OSHA inspectors may not enter a work place without the owner's consent unless a search warrant has been obtained, have handicapped administration of the law.

[47] *Industrial Relations News*, September 9, 1972, p. 4.
[48] See various publications of the U.S. Department of Labor, including *Occupational Safety and Health, Compliance Operations Manual*, and *Safety Standards*.
[49] *Occupational Safety and Health Review*, September 1972, pp. 1–8.
[50] *Occupational Safety and Health Review*, June 1975, p. 3.

might be attributable to the actions of an experienced employee acting contrary to specific company safety instructions. *Occupational Safety and Health Review*, June 1976, pp. 5–6.

The latter was appealed to the Supreme Court by the U.S. Department of Labor.[51]

RELATIONSHIP OF WORK RULES TO VARIOUS MANAGERIAL PROCESSES

One can easily visualize the consequences to an organization if stealing, falsification of records, erratic work schedules, unsafe practices, and unlimited socializing are condoned. Unless minimum standards of conduct are enforced, the flows of vital organizational resources will be disrupted. Work rules are an inherent necessity in organizational life.

From a process-systems standpoint, work rules assist in channeling the processes of the enterprise in the direction of the enterprise's goals. As in the case of personnel policies, they are predetermined decisions that a certain course of action will be required once certain contingencies arise. Thus, they become integral parts of the systems designed to facilitate all broad operational processes.

On the other hand, work rules can create too much structure and can adversely affect morale and superior-subordinate relationships. As I discussed in Chapter 7, work rules and their administration have an effect on whether leadership is perceived by subordinates as punitive or supportive and on whether the organization is perceived as appropriately structured or excessively structured.

EFFECT OF WORK RULES AND WORKING CONDITIONS ON NEED FULFILLMENT

Work rules can affect a wide range of human needs. For example, needs for affiliation and cooperation can be either frustrated or sup-

ported by work rules dealing with socializing on the job. Rules that limit job scope, whether management or union imposed, can serve to frustrate needs for self-actualization. Work rules that permit substantial employee discretion, e.g., such as under flextime, can enhance expression of needs for autonomy, independence, and self-actualization. If work rules are arbitrary and unreasonable, they may impede an employee's desire to understand the work environment and to express needs for autonomy; thus, there is a necessity for reasonable rules and clear explanations. The cynical comment, "There's no reason for it—it's just policy," frequently has its basis in fact rather than fiction.

Further, reasonable and stable work rules help to fulfill the needs for security, order, predictability, and the avoidance of physical harm for members of an organization. (For some of the realities of physical harm, see Figure 10-3 for statistics on the frequency and severity of accident rates. During 1974, one out of every ten employees in the private sector suffered job-related injury or illness,[52] and the total cost of work accidents in the United States was $15.3 billion.[53]) Since most people understand that these needs will not be satisfied in a chaotic environment, they are willing to accept a minimum number of rules. People in military organizations, for example, will accept a high degree of control when it is related to survival in combat and to unit security. Mine workers understand the need for strict rules about the firing of explosives. People in a manufacturing plant will ordinarily understand the interdependency of their jobs and accept fairly rigorous rules pertaining to starting and stopping

---

[51] *Occupational Safety and Health Review*, March 1976, p. 7.

[52] *Monthly Labor Review*, 99:2 (January 1976).

[53] National Safety Council, *Accident Facts 1975 Edition* (Chicago: National Safety Council, 1975), p. 24.

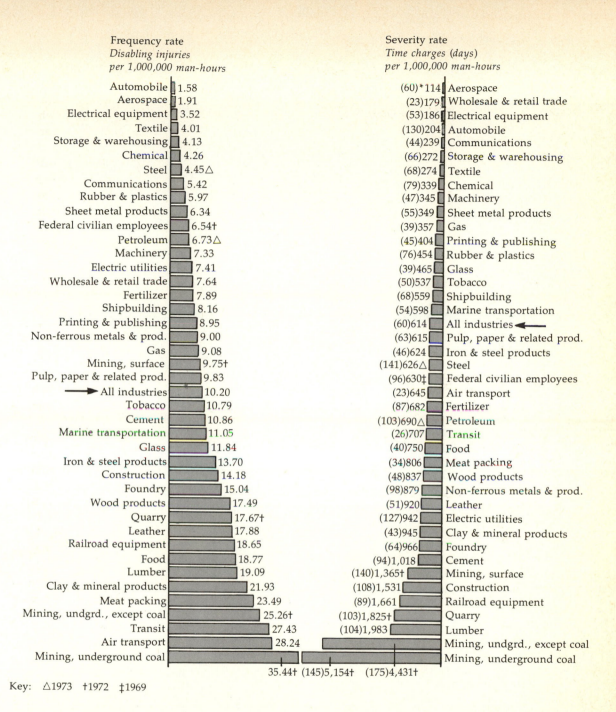

Frequency rate
*Disabling injuries
per 1,000,000 man-hours*

Severity rate
*Time charges (days)
per 1,000,000 man-hours*

Frequency rate		Severity rate	
Automobile	1.58	(60)*114 Aerospace	
Aerospace	1.91	(23)179 Wholesale & retail trade	
Electrical equipment	3.52	(53)186 Electrical equipment	
Textile	4.01	(130)204 Automobile	
Storage & warehousing	4.13	(44)239 Communications	
Chemical	4.26	(66)272 Storage & warehousing	
Steel	4.45△	(68)274 Textile	
Communications	5.42	(79)339 Chemical	
Rubber & plastics	5.97	(47)345 Machinery	
Sheet metal products	6.34	(55)349 Sheet metal products	
Federal civilian employees	6.54†	(39)357 Gas	
Petroleum	6.73△	(45)404 Printing & publishing	
Machinery	7.33	(76)454 Rubber & plastics	
Electric utilities	7.41	(39)465 Glass	
Wholesale & retail trade	7.64	(50)537 Tobacco	
Fertilizer	7.89	(68)559 Shipbuilding	
Shipbuilding	8.16	(54)598 Marine transportation	
Printing & publishing	8.95	(60)614 All industries ◄	
Non-ferrous metals & prod.	9.00	(63)615 Pulp, paper & related prod.	
Gas	9.08	(46)624 Iron & steel products	
Mining, surface	9.75†	(141)626△ Steel	
Pulp, paper & related prod.	9.83	(96)630‡ Federal civilian employees	
All industries ►	10.20	(23)645 Air transport	
Tobacco	10.79	(87)682 Fertilizer	
Cement	10.86	(103)690△ Petroleum	
Marine transportation	11.05	(26)707 Transit	
Glass	11.84	(40)750 Food	
Iron & steel products	13.70	(34)806 Meat packing	
Construction	14.18	(48)837 Wood products	
Foundry	15.04	(98)879 Non-ferrous metals & prod.	
Wood products	17.49	(51)920 Leather	
Quarry	17.67†	(127)942 Electric utilities	
Leather	17.88	(43)945 Clay & mineral products	
Railroad equipment	18.65	(64)966 Foundry	
Food	18.77	(94)1,018 Cement	
Lumber	19.09	(140)1,365† Mining, surface	
Clay & mineral products	21.93	(108)1,531 Construction	
Meat packing	23.49	(89)1,661 Railroad equipment	
Mining, undgrd., except coal	25.26†	(103)1,825† Quarry	
Transit	27.43	(104)1,983 Lumber	
Air transport	28.24	Mining, undgrd., except coal	
Mining, underground coal	35.44†	(145)5,154† (175)4,431† Mining, underground coal	

Key: △1973   †1972   ‡1969

Figure 10-3   Accident frequency and severity rates, by industry, 1974

*Figures in parentheses show average days charged per case. Rates compiled in accordance with the American Standard Method of Recording and Measuring Work Injury Experience, ANSI Standard Z16.1–1967 (R 1973).

Source: *Accident Facts 1975 Edition* (Chicago: National Safety Council, 1975), p. 26.

work. On the other hand, scientists in a laboratory are not likely to accept stringent controls pertaining to working hours.

If rules are irrelevant or unreasonably strict, people have a way of circumventing them. For example, two paid rest periods per day—each ten to fifteen minutes in length—are provided for both plant and office workers in a high percentage of companies. On the other hand, executives in half of the firms that have no authorized rest periods stated that employees took breaks anyway.[54] Other research has also shown that employees tend to take breaks whether they are permitted or not.[55] Thus, the informal organization will have a powerful impact on whether actual behavior corresponds to stated work rules.

AUTHORITY AND ACCOUNTABILITY

When enterprises are small, the development of rules for working is the concern of the entrepreneur as chief executive and the immediate subordinates. As firms become larger and more complex, specialized duties in personnel tend to be assigned to one manager who may be expected to suggest revisions of work rules in top management and to participate extensively in collective bargaining. Once these work rules are endorsed by top management or are negotiated into a labor agreement, all managers are responsible for their enforcement. Typically, the personnel executive will offer advice in the administration of work rules and will monitor procedures used in the disciplining of employees who have committed violations. In serious disciplinary cases, approval of the per-

[54]*Personnel Management: Policies and Practice* (Englewood Cliffs, N.J.: Prentice-Hall, Inc., 1961), Par. 7026.
[55]See Joseph Tiffin and Ernest J. McCormick, *Industrial Psychology,* 4th ed. (Englewood Cliffs, N.J.: Prentice-Hall, Inc., 1958), p. 459.

sonnel department is customarily considered a necessary control before final decisions are made. However, the initiation of disciplinary action is almost universally the prerogative of the immediate supervisor.

SUMMARY

The process of task specialization—a flow of events that culminates in dividing the total work of the enterprise into manageable segments and in establishing requirements for the performance of employees—includes several important components. Two broad managerial functions—the determination of organizational objectives and organizational planning, including job design—are critical components of this process.

Job analyses and job descriptions have a number of purposes. They are used for development of job specifications, for recruiting and training, for salary administration, and as basic documents for performance standards. Job specifications and work rules need to be frequently reassessed with respect to whether they are relevant and whether they are sufficiently rigorous or too stringent in the light of changing job requirements.

Work rules are inescapable in organizational life, but rules that are too strict or confining may lead to subterfuge and resentment, while rules that are lax may impede the work of the enterprise. Work rules that tend to protect jobs, e.g., lines of demarcation between crafts, may serve to provide job security in the short run but may have serious consequences in terms of organizational effectiveness and survival over the long pull.

The Occupational Health and Safety Act is having a major impact on job design and work rules. It is reflective of a growing national concern about the quality of life in organizations.

Although use is not yet widespread in the United States, substantial interest is currently being shown in the compressed workweek—particularly the four-day, forty-hour week—and in the flexible hours workweek (flextime). The latter has been adopted extensively in Europe with generally favorable results. The use of permanent part-time employees also appears to be growing. There are many contingencies affecting the applicability of these practices in specific circumstances.

Participative group methods in developing job descriptions, performance standards, and work rules show considerable promise for increasing overall group performance and enhancing job satisfaction. However, if these documents are imposed by higher management without proper efforts to tap the creativity and energy of individuals and groups in the organization, they can be sterile instruments at best, reductive and restrictive at worst. *How* the task specialization process is managed, then, is an extremely important matter.

REVIEW AND DISCUSSION QUESTIONS

1. Define: (a) job analysis, (b) job description, (c) job specification, (d) job evaluation.

2. What are the implications of the *Griggs* v. *Duke Power Company* case?

3. What are the uses for job descriptions? Describe how they might be used as (a) constraints on performance, and (b) mechanisms for organizational change and improvement.

4. What are some of the questions that need to be asked in reviewing the validity of job specifications?

5. What is the difference between the concept of performance standards and management by objectives?

6. What are some of the contingencies that management would want to examine before establishing a four-day, forty-hour week?

7. What appear to be the advantages and disadvantages of flextime?

8. What is the basic thrust of the Occupational Safety and Health Act of 1970, and what impact is it having on job design?

9. What is the current status of state laws pertaining to work hours for women?

10. What work rules would you probably want established in your organization if you were the owner-president of an electronics firm with one hundred employees, and how would you go about establishing those rules?

SUPPLEMENTAL REFERENCES

"Absenteeism and Lateness: How Much Is Too Much?" (Englewood Cliffs, N.J.: Prentice-Hall, Inc., 1974) (pamphlet, 30 pp.).

American Society for Personnel Administration, *Safety Fundamentals for the Personnel Administrator,* 1974 (pamphlet, 18 pp.).

Ashford, Nicholas A., "Worker Health and Safety: An Area of Conflicts," *Monthly Labor Review,* 98:3–11 (September 1975).

Barnako, Frank R., Alexander J. Reis, and Michael Wood, "An Assessment of Three Years of OSHA," in James L. Stern and Barbara D. Dennis, eds., *Proceedings of the Twenty-Seventh Annual Winter Meeting,* Industrial Relations Research Association, 1975, pp. 31–51.

Cathy, P.J., "Is Zero Defects Still Alive and Well?" *Iron Age,* 207:50–51 (February 25, 1971).

Cummings, Paul W., "Handling the Alcoholic Employee," *Training and Development Journal,* 29:42–44 (February 1975).

Davis, Herbert J., Richard O. Blalack, and K. Mark Weaver, "A Quantitative Decision-Making Guide to Four-Day Workweek Conversion,"

The Personnel Administrator, 21:45–50 (February 1976).

Dobelis, M.C., "The Three-Day Week—Offshoot of an EDP Operation," *Personnel*, 49:24–33 (January-February 1972).

Drucker, Peter F., *The Practice of Management* (New York: Harper & Brothers, 1954).

Elbing, Alvar O., Herman Gadon, and John R.M. Gordon, "Flexible Working Hours: It's About Time," *Harvard Business Review*, 52:18–20 (January-February 1974).

Greenberg, Leon, *A Practical Guide to Productivity Measurement* (Washington, D.C.: Bureau of National Affairs, 1973).

"How Technicon Helped Trap a Spy," *Business Week*, May 10, 1976, pp. 53–54.

Jones, Ronald E., "Alcoholism and the Workplace," *Manpower*, February 1975, pp. 3–8.

Loveland, John P., and Jack L. Mendleson, "Employee Responsibility: A Key Goal for Personnel Managers," *Human Resource Management*, 13:32–36 (Spring 1974).

McGregor, Douglas, *The Human Side of Enterprise* (New York: McGraw-Hill Book Company, 1960), Chapter 6.

McLean, Alan, *Mental Health and Work Organizations* (Chicago: Rand McNally & Company, 1970).

Magoon, Warren, and Larry Schnicker, "Flexible Hours at State Street Bank of Boston: A Case Study," *The Personnel Administrator*, 21:34–37 (October 1976).

Maier, Norman R.F., *Psychology in Industrial Organizations*, 4th ed. (Boston: Houghton Mifflin Company, 1973), Chapter 17.

Martin, Virginia H., *Hours of Work When Workers Can Choose* (Washington, D.C.: Business and Professional Women's Foundation, 1975) (booklet).

Miner, John B., and J. Frank Brewer, "The Management of Ineffective Performance," in Marvin D. Dunnette, ed., *Handbook of Industrial and Or-ganizational Psychology* (Chicago: Rand McNally College Publishing Company, 1976), pp. 995–1029.

Myers, M. Scott, "Restrictive Systems," in *Every Employee a Manager* (New York: McGraw-Hill Book Company, 1970), pp. 52–53.

Nord, Walter, "Improving Attendance through Rewards," *Personnel Administration*, 33:37–41 (November-December 1960).

Owen, John D., "Workweeks and Leisure: An Analysis of Trends, 1948–75," *Monthly Labor Review*, 99:3–7 (August 1976).

Pasquale, Anthony M., "Working at Home—A New Fringe Benefit?" *Personnel*, 49:56–59 (May-June 1972).

Perkel, George, "A Labor View of the Occupational Safety and Health Act," *Labor Law Journal*, 23:511–517 (August 1972).

Peterson, Donald J., "OSHA Compliance Training: Its Impact on Your Company," *The Personnel Administrator*, 21:33–35 (May 1976).

Poor, Riva, ed., *4 Days, 40 Hours* (Cambridge, Mass.: Bursk and Poor Publishing, 1970).

Prien, Erich P., and W.W. Ronan, "Job Analysis: A Review of Research Findings," *Personnel Psychology*, 24:371–396 (Autumn 1971).

Rosen, Benson, and Thomas H. Jerdee, "Factors Influencing Disciplinary Judgments," *Journal of Applied Psychology*, 59:327–331 (June 1974).

Silberman, Laurence H., "The Occupational Safety and Health Act: Major Policy Issues," *Labor Law Journal*, 23:504–510 (August 1972).

Sirota, David, and Alan D. Wolfson, "Work Measurement and Worker Morale," *Business Horizons*, 15:43–48 (August 1972).

Stender, John H., "An OSHA Perspective and Prospective," *Labor Law Journal*, 26:71–78 (February 1975).

U.S. Chamber of Commerce, *Analysis of Workmen's Compensation Laws* (Washington, D.C.: U.S. Chamber of Commerce, 1971).

U.S. Department of Labor, *Occupational Safety and Health*.

————, Occupational Safety and Health Administration, *All About OSHA* (pamphlet, 18 pp.).

Wade, Michael, *Flexible Working Hours in Practice* (Epping, Essex: Gower Press, 1973).

Walters, Kenneth, "Employee Freedom of Speech," *Industrial Relations*, 15:26–43 (February 1976).

————, "Your Employees' Right To Blow the Whistle," *Harvard Business Review*, 53:26–34ff. (July-August 1975).

Widdop, F.R., "Why Performance Standards Don't Work," *Personnel*, 47:14–20 (March-April 1970).

5

PART 5
THE STAFFING PROCESS

11. **Human Resources Planning and Recruitment**

12. **The Employee-Selection Process**

13. **Effective Managers: Their Characteristics and Selection**

14. **Induction, Transfers, Promotions, Demotions, and Separations**

The staffing process is a flow of events that results in the continuous assignment of human resources to all organizational positions at all levels. This process includes the following subprocesses: human resources planning, authorization for staffing, developing sources of applicants, evaluation of applicants, employment decisions and offers, induction and orientation, transfers, demotions, promotions, and separations. (See Figure 5-a.) In a sense, this process is the flow of human resources into, within, and out of the enterprise.

A number of devices and subsystems are commonly used in the systems designed to manage the staffing process. These devices and subsystems include tables and charts, application blanks, interviews, tests, reference checks, physical examinations, performance reviews, and exit interviews.

Chapter 11 will be devoted to a discussion and analysis of human resources planning, authorization for staffing, and developing sources of applicants. Chapter 12 will focus on the evaluation of applicants including the use of

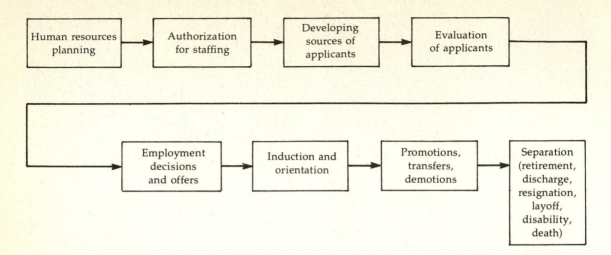

Figure **5-a**   The staffing process

application blanks, interviews, tests, physical examinations, and reference checks. Decisions and offers to employ will also be discussed in Chapter 12. Chapter 13 will focus on the char-acteristics and selection of managers. Chapter 14 will examine induction, orientation, trans-fers, demotions, promotions, and separations.

CHAPTER 11
HUMAN RESOURCES PLANNING AND RECRUITMENT

HUMAN RESOURCES PLANNING

An integral part of effectively managing the staffing process is the subprocess of human resources planning. This subprocess includes an analysis of the levels of skill in the organization (frequently called a "skills inventory"); an analysis of current and expected vacancies due to retirements, discharges, transfers, promotions, sick leaves, leaves of absence, or other reasons; and an analysis of current and expected expansions or curtailments in departments. Plans are then made for internal shifts or cutbacks in human resources, for training and development of present employees, for advertising job openings, and/or for recruiting and hiring new people. Human resources planning must also be responsive to rapidly changing forces in society, including technological innovations, labor market conditions, and governmental legislation, rulings, and court decisions.

Thus, human resources planning is a comprehensive, ongoing process. Broadly conceived, as Patten states it, human resources planning ". . . is the process by which a firm insures that it has the right number of people, and the right kind of people, in the right places, at the right time, doing things for which they are economically most useful."[1] This means that human resources planning is a broader process than making projections, but it does include this activity.[2]

[1] Thomas H. Patten, Jr., *Manpower Planning and the Development of Human Resources* (New York: John Wiley & Sons, 1971), p. 14.
[2] See Felician F. Foltman, *Manpower Information for Effective Management, Part 2: Skills Inventories and Manpower Planning* (Ithaca: Cornell University, New York State School of Industrial and Labor Relations, 1973), pp. 18–20.

199

CURRENT PRACTICES AND PROBLEMS

In organizations of any complexity, human resources planning must be systematic to insure continuous and proper staffing. In large organizations, planning should be continual on both a unit and a total organizational basis, with a central planning group assembling the overall information. Often, however, such planning takes place on an emergency basis when needed skills are in short supply.

Many problems emerge if human resources planning is haphazard or neglected. For example, planning should take into account staff reductions in all parts of the organization and should be tied into any system of transfer in effect. It would be obvious mismanagement to lay off people in one part of the enterprise when their critical skills were needed in another. Similarly, it would be unwise to prevent the requested transfer of an employee to a job requiring higher skill provided that the employee were qualified and a replacement could be found. Although members of units, if qualified, may be given priority for promotion within their particular unit, decisions on promotions should include an analysis of what is best from the point of view of the total enterprise.

Human resources planning should also take into account budgetary allocations for staffing, and, reciprocally, budgets must reflect a realistic appraisal of human resource requirements. If the people in accounting and finance work directly with the various departments when developing staffing budgets, they may unfortunately bypass the accumulated knowledge of the personnel department. It is important that the personnel department and the accounting and finance departments work closely together in planning, and that their planning be based on realistic marketing, income, and cost projections. (See Figure 11-1 for a suggested system for human resources planning that takes into

account a number of such critical variables. Figure 11-2 depicts the sequence of events from plant to corporate level in a large organization.)

Obviously, hiring should not occur at a faster rate than the overall budget permits. There may be points in an organization's history when the organization cannot afford certain skills because of limited financial resources. Planned expenditures for wages and salaries must be balanced against plans for adding or buying new machinery, increasing inventories, etc. If continual and high-quality planning is to take place, necessary data must be systematically collected, processed, and interpreted. Electronic data processing (EDP) can be particularly helpful in large organizations where plans must be made involving many thousands of employees with different skills and pay grades.[3] In smaller organizations, lists of names or numbers, or both, broken down by different categories may suffice. In either case, charts and tables are helpful in visualizing trends.[4]

A necessary prerequisite for collecting data is the intelligent planning of the questions to be answered by the data. The questions to be answered will determine the devices and systems to be used. For example, questions such as "What jobs in our plants require a chemical engineering degree?" "How many newly graduated chemical engineers will we need each year for the next five years?" and "How many people in each salary grade are at, below, or above

---

[3] For more detailed information about the utility of EDP systems in human resources planning, information material, and record keeping, see Felician F. Foltman, *Manpower Information for Effective Management, Part 1: Collecting and Managing Employee Information* (Ithaca: Cornell University, New York State School of Industrial and Labor Relations, Key Issues No. 14, 1973); Carlton W. Dukes, "EDP Personnel File Searching: A Variable Parameter Approach," *Personnel*, 49:20–26 (July-August 1972); and Wesley R. Liebtag, "How an EDP Personnel System Works for Corporate Growth," *Personnel*, 47:15–21 (July-August 1970).

[4] For a description of useful devices in collecting data and visualizing trends, see Patten, *Manpower Planning and the Development of Human Resources*.

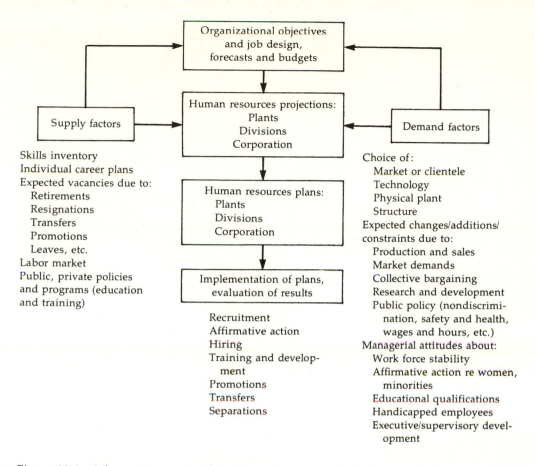

Figure 11-1 A human resources planning system

Partially based on Felician F. Foltman: *Manpower Information for Effective Management, Part 2: Skills Inventories and Manpower Planning* (Ithaca: Cornell University, New York State School of Industrial and Labor Relations, 1973) Key Issues, No. 14, p. 27.

the midpoint of the grade?" will begin to construct the data system.

RELATIONSHIPS TO OTHER ORGANIZATIONAL PROCESSES

To be meaningful, human resources planning must be based on personal specifications that, in turn, stem from the design of jobs. Thus, human resources planning is directly related to the flow of events I have called the task-specialization process.

There is also a reciprocal relationship between human resources planning and the task-specialization process; planning may reveal shortages or surpluses in skills, a condition that might influence organizational objectives and organizational structure. Furthermore, human resources planning must be integrated with overall organizational plans pertaining to sales and production, the purchase and use of equipment, research and engineering, the financial situation of the organization, and the planning of physical facilities.

Figure 11-2   Flow chart of a human resources planning system in a complex organization

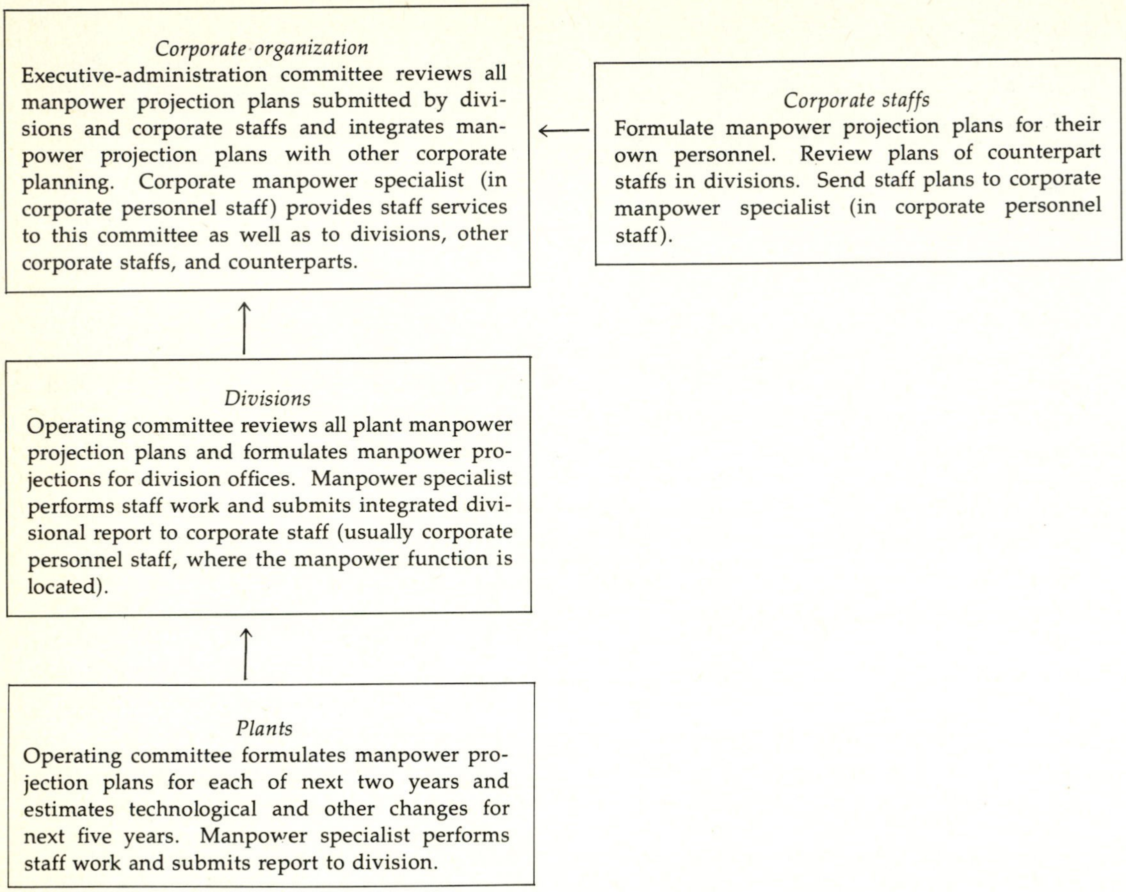

Corporate organization
Executive-administration committee reviews all manpower projection plans submitted by divisions and corporate staffs and integrates manpower projection plans with other corporate planning. Corporate manpower specialist (in corporate personnel staff) provides staff services to this committee as well as to divisions, other corporate staffs, and counterparts.

Corporate staffs
Formulate manpower projection plans for their own personnel. Review plans of counterpart staffs in divisions. Send staff plans to corporate manpower specialist (in corporate personnel staff).

Divisions
Operating committee reviews all plant manpower projection plans and formulates manpower projections for division offices. Manpower specialist performs staff work and submits integrated divisional report to corporate staff (usually corporate personnel staff, where the manpower function is located).

Plants
Operating committee formulates manpower projection plans for each of next two years and estimates technological and other changes for next five years. Manpower specialist performs staff work and submits report to division.

From Thomas H. Patten, Jr., *Manpower Planning and the Development of Human Resources* (New York: John Wiley & Sons, 1971), p. 62. Used with permission.

Similarly, human resources planning may point up needs in training and development, and conversely, the quality of training and development going on in the organization will affect the quality of the work force, a fact that must be noted in human resources plans. This demonstrates the desirability of close coordination between training specialists and those involved in human resources planning. (In some

organizations, the training director may be the specialist in human resources planning.)

The collective-bargaining process and human resources planning are also highly interrelated. Any labor agreement will typically have provisions regulating transfers, demotions, discharges, layoffs, bidding on job openings, and the contracting of maintenance and construction work. For example, 88 percent of all labor contracts require that seniority be a factor in layoff procedures and 81 percent of all contracts provide for recall in reverse order of layoff.[5] Such contract provisions must be considered in human resources planning.

In addition, the rules in the labor contract concerning transfer affect which jobs are to be filled from the outside. If the union contract requires the posting of a job in order to give union members an opportunity to apply for it, the net effect may be that higher-skilled jobs usually will be filled from within and that new employees will be hired into the lower classifications.

Work stoppages resulting from a breakdown in the collective-bargaining process are special situations requiring planning for such matters as the proper shutdown of equipment, protection of plant equipment and property, and perhaps operation with nonstriking employees. However, the potential crisis nature of such aspects of collective bargaining always creates the possibility that there may be lack of adequate planning relative to the nonunionized components of the work force. It is vital that human resources planning encompass all positions at all levels in the organization.

RELATIONSHIP TO EXTERNAL ENVIRONMENT

Along with internal aspects of the organization, the external labor market is particularly significant in human resources planning. Except for skills developed within the organization, every enterprise is dependent upon the quality and quantity of human resources external to it. Thus, the quality of training and education in the broader society is of great consequence to each organization.

Changing demands for various skills and educational backgrounds within the labor market have a direct bearing on the staffing process. Innovations in technology and science, in particular, tend to have a dramatic and rapid impact on skill and talent needs. The speedy obsolescence of products, equipment, or work methods can create shortages or surpluses of skills in a relatively short time. Shortages of certain skills may suggest the need to develop specialized internal training programs, to restructure jobs or objectives, or to encourage educational institutions to expand programs in certain skills. As a general illustration of such a problem, projections indicate that the need for professional and technical employees will increase much more than the need for sales employees through the mid-1980s. (See Figure 11-3.) Of course, there are wide variations among specialities within these broad categories. For example, there was a much larger demand for computer programmers than for accountants during the early 1970s.

Changes in general economic conditions and/or cutbacks in federal expenditures can also have an abrupt and extensive effect on human resources availability. For example, in the early 1970s a continued decline in the level of economic activity and cutbacks in governmental expenditures in space and defense programs produced massive layoffs of engineers and scientists in the aerospace industry and in government-financed research programs. Unemployment among engineers almost tripled over a one-year period.[6]

Attitudes and legislation in the nation and community with respect to race, national origin, religion, age, sex, and handicaps also have an important bearing on human resources planning and the entire staffing process. For example, in many organizations over the years,

---

[5] Bureau of National Affairs, *Collective Bargaining Negotiations and Contracts*, 75:2–4 (December 1970). See also Winston L. Tillery, "Layoff and Recall Provisions in Major Agreements," *Monthly Labor Review*, 94:41–46 (July 1971).

[6] U.S. Department of Labor, *Manpower Report of the President* (April 1971), p. 18.

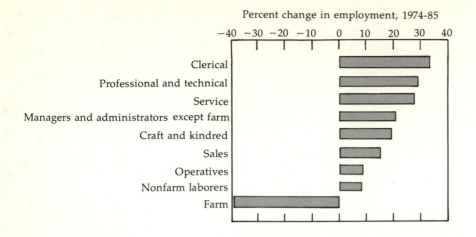

Figure **11-3**   Employment growth to vary widely among occupations through the mid-1980s

From U.S. Department of Labor, *Occupational Outlook Handbook, 1976–1977 Edition,* Bulletin 1875, 1976, p. 17.

attitudes of managers or employees, or both, have tended to prohibit or suppress the employment of people of certain races or religions in certain jobs—supervisory and office jobs, in particular—with members of minority groups being relegated to unskilled laboring or production and maintenance jobs. While these situations are being corrected, much remains to be accomplished. To illustrate, Figure 11-4 shows that blacks and other minorities attained a much larger share of white-collar and skilled jobs between 1950 and 1975, but were a long way from reaching their proportion of the labor force (about 11 percent) in some job categories, such as managerial and sales occupations.

THE IMPACT OF FEDERAL LEGISLATION AND RULINGS

Growing sentiment against discrimination on the basis of race, color, religion, sex, or national origin culminated in the Civil Rights Act of 1964, and sentiment against discrimination on

the basis of sex resulted in the Equal Pay Act of 1963. Sentiment against discrimination on the basis of age resulted in the Age Discrimination in Employment Act of 1967. All these areas are covered by a combination of Executive Orders 11246 and 11141, which prohibit discrimination by contractors and subcontractors doing business with the federal government. The Vocational Rehabilitation Act of 1973 also prohibits such contractors from discriminating against the handicapped.

THE CIVIL RIGHTS ACT AND THE EQUAL PAY ACT

Title VII of the Civil Rights Act of 1964, as amended in 1968 and 1972, is aimed at eliminating discrimination in employment on the basis of race, color, religion, sex, or national origin in industries affecting interstate commerce, and in state and local government employment and in educational institutions. Key persons or organizations concerned are (a) employers, an employer being defined as ''. . . a person

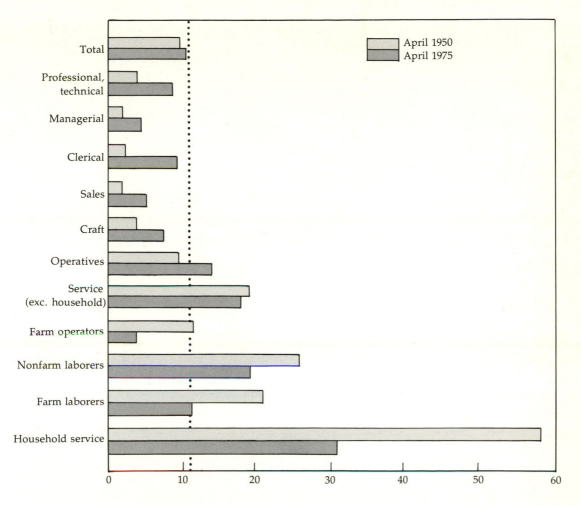

Figure 11-4   Percent of jobs held by blacks and other minority groups

Note: Dotted vertical line shows the percent of blacks and other minority group members in the labor force in 1950 and 1975.

U.S. Department of Labor, *Employment and Training Report of the President,* Employment and Training Administration, 1976, p. 153.

engaged in an industry affecting commerce who has fifteen or more employees for each working day in each of twenty or more calendar weeks in the current or preceding calendar year . . . ," (b) employment agencies, and (c) labor organizations.

The most significant aspects of the law read as follows:

Sec. 703.

(a) It shall be unlawful employment practice for an employer—

(1) to fail or refuse to hire or to discharge any individual, or otherwise to discriminate against any individual with respect to his compensation, terms, conditions, or privileges of employment, because of such individual's race, color, religion, sex, or national origin; or

(2) to limit, segregate, or classify his employees or applicants for employment in any way which would deprive or tend to deprive any individual of employment opportunities or otherwise adversely affect his status as an employee, because of such individual's race, color, religion, sex, or national origin.

(b) It shall be an unlawful employment practice for an employment agency to fail or refuse to refer for employment, or otherwise to discriminate against, any individual because of his race, color, religion, sex, or national origin, or to classify or refer for employment any individual on the basis of his race, color, religion, sex, or national origin.

(c) It shall be an unlawful employment practice for a labor organization—

(1) to exclude or to expel from its membership, or otherwise to discriminate against, any individual because of his race, color, religion, sex, or national origin;

(2) to limit, segregate, or classify its membership or applicants for membership or to classify or fail or refuse to refer for employment any individual in any way which would deprive or tend to deprive any individual of employment opportunities, or would limit such employment opportunities or otherwise adversely affect his status as an employee or as an applicant for employment, because of such individual's race, color, religion, sex, or national origin; or

(3) to cause or attempt to cause an employer to discriminate against an individual in violation of this section.

(d) It shall be an unlawful employment practice for any employer, labor organization, or joint labor-management committee controlling apprenticeship or other training or retraining, including on-the-job training programs to discriminate against any individual because of his race, color, religion, sex, or national origin in admission to, or employment in, any program established to provide apprenticeship or other training.

Sec. 704.

(b) It shall be an unlawful employment practice for an employer, labor organization, employment agency, or joint labor management committee controlling apprenticeship or other training or retraining, including

on-the-job training programs to print or cause to be printed or published any notice or advertisement relating to employment by such an employer or membership in or any classification or referral for employment by such a labor organization, or relating to any classification or referral for employment by such an employment agency, or relating to admission to, or employment in, any program established to provide apprenticeship or other training by such a joint labor-management committee indicating any preference, limitation, specification, or discrimination, based on race, color, religion, sex, or national origin. . . .[7]

Exceptions to the law may be made, however, where religion, sex, or national origin is a "bona-fide occupational qualification," but not on the basis of race or color. Further, organizations are not required to give preferential treatment because of race, color, or the other dimensions listed above in the event of any imbalance existing with respect to total numbers or percentages of such persons in any community, state, section, or other area.

An Equal Employment Opportunity Commission (EEOC) composed of five members was created by the Civil Rights Act of 1964 to hear and investigate charges of discrimination and to attempt to resolve problems "by informal methods of conference, conciliation, and persuasion." While the original act relied on court action by the aggrieved party if these informal methods did not solve the problem, amendments to the law in March 1972 permit the EEOC to go directly into the federal court itself to seek orders to enforce its decisions.

In cases occurring in states or cities having laws on fair employment practice, appropriate agencies are given a period of time in which to process charges before the Commission acts further. The Commission defers to such agencies in forty-seven of the fifty states. The exceptions are three states in the Deep South.[8]

---

[7] Title VII, Equal Employment Opportunity, Civil Rights Act of 1964, as amended March 24, 1972.
[8] Bureau of National Affairs, *Labor Relations Reporter, Fair Employment Practices Manual*, 451:7, 15–18 (March 1976).

Penalties for violations of the act vary. They include the court's enjoining the accused from engaging in the unlawful practice, reinstatement or hiring of employees with or without back pay, and the payment of reasonable attorney's fees.[9]

The impact of the Civil Rights Act and the Equal Pay Act can readily be seen in court awards and in out-of-court settlements. In the case of *Hodgson* v. *Wheaton Glass*, a U.S. district court required the company to pay more than $900,000 in back wages, plus interest, to some two thousand employees.[10] In another case, AT&T agreed to pay $15 million in back wages to women and minority employees whose pay had been held arbitrarily low because of discrimination practices.[11] In the two years after the agreement, AT&T increased the number of women in second-level management positions and above by 46 percent, the number of women in craft jobs by 119 percent, the number of blacks in second-level management and above by 82 percent, and the number of males in clerical and operator jobs by 147 percent.[12]

Other widely publicized cases have been the steel industry agreement involving about $32 million in back pay,[13] the Bank of America agreement involving a payment of $3,750,000,[14] and a consent settlement with Merrill, Lynch, Pierce, Fenner & Smith involving $1.9 million in back pay to women and minority employees. The latter settlement also included an agreement to spend $1.3 million to recruit Spanish-Americans, blacks, and women for broker positions over five years. One hundred women sales assistants were to be offered promotion to account executives.[15]

Initially, the ban of discrimination on the basis of sex was referred to as a "sleeper" in the Act. However, although most of the Congressional debate centered on racial discrimination and the provision about sex was introduced by opponents in an attempt to defeat the bill, alleged discrimination based on sex now constitutes a high percentage of the cases filed with the EEOC. Many of the recent cases culminating in consent settlements, including some of the ones cited earlier, have involved discrimination against women in hiring, pay, and promotion. Consequently, many traditional employment practices are being altered dramatically.

Among the traditional practices that are changing is the customary usage of job and personnel management terminology. For example, due to women's pressure groups and to avoid implications of discrimination in employment, the following are among many other changes in the *Dictionary of Occupational Titles* (DOT), U.S. Department of Labor, 1976. *Airplane stewardess* has been changed to *airplane flight attendant, bat boy* has been changed to *bat keeper, surveying axman* to *surveying brush clearer, brewmaster* to *brewing director, bus boy* to *dining room attendant, fisherman* to *fisher, foreman* to *supervisor, governess* to *child mentor, new car salesman* to *new car associate,* and *salesman* to *salesperson.*

It is not just the federal government and women who are overturning traditions. Some discrimination complaints are being filed by men. For example, the Supreme Court declined to reverse a circuit court of appeals ruling that an airline's refusal to hire a male flight attendant was in violation of the Civil Rights

[9] Title VII, Civil Rights Act of 1964, Sections 706–707.

[10] Bureau of National Affairs, *Bulletin to Management,* July 13, 1972, p. 2.

[11] *Time,* January 29, 1973, p. 77.

[12] Ruth G. Shaeffer, *Nondiscrimination in Employment, 1973–1975* (New York: The Conference Board, Report No. 677, 1975), p. 6.

[13] *Fair Employment Digest,* March 1976, p. 6; and *Monthly Labor Review,* 97:69–80 (June 1974).

[14] *Monthly Labor Review,* 97:87–88 (August 1974).

[15] *Business Week,* June 21, 1976, p. 38. The EEOC itself was faced in 1974 with a class action suit charging discrimination against 600,000 Filipino-Americans because of lack of identification of Filipino-Americans in EEOC forms and reports. *Monthly Labor Review,* 97:88 (August 1974).

Act.[16] Since then an increasing number of men have been employed as flight attendants. And as the AT&T consent settlement indicates, males are being hired as telephone operators with increasing frequency.[17]

Most of the traditions being overturned, however, involve women seeking roles traditionally filled by men. As one illustration, after a female clerk with a telephone company was turned down for a switchman's (switchperson's?) job because of a weight-lifting requirement, a court of appeals ordered that she be given the assignment and $30,000 in back wages.[18] As another example, a woman employed by Consolidated Edison donned a hard hat and work boots and started on an excavation job using a ninety-pound jackhammer.[19] Women are being employed as blacksmiths, truck drivers, locomotive engineers, hog buyers, baseball umpires, airplane pilots, and zoo keepers.[20] Further, laws in three of the seven states having protective laws for women pertaining to weight lifting were declared invalid as of 1975.[21]

Traditions are also being upset by executive orders from the executive branch of the federal government. For example, in the mid-1970s women were admitted for the first time to the Naval and Air Force Reserve Officers Training Corps and to the military academies at West Point, Annapolis, and Colorado Springs. Women have also been assigned to sea duty in the Navy, and to naval flight training, although prohibited from combat duty. In addition, the Women's Army Corps was disbanded and its members integrated into the Army.

The potential magnitude of the sex-discrimination problem is reflected in Figure 11-5, which shows changes in the occupational distribution of women between 1962 and 1974. Traditionally, the proportion of women relative to the total employed work force has been low among craft workers and in the managerial ranks, but very high in private household and clerical occupations. In the professional category, however, in both 1962 and 1974 women were represented slightly higher proportionately than their membership in the total work force.[22]

Many assumptions and stereotypes about working women need to be examined carefully. For example, the notion that most women are just working for pin money has been refuted by a University of Michigan study that found that one-third of working women surveyed were the *sole* wage earners in their households. The same study found that most women were just as concerned about opportunities for self-actualization and promotion as were men.[23] The latter conclusion is consistent with the study reported in Chapter 6, which found that females were more dissatisfied than males with their jobs.

Affirmative action plans required of federal contractors and subcontractors under Executive Order 11246 are also having a major influence on human resources planning and on recruit-

[16] American Society for Personnel Administration, *Fair Employment Digest*, December 1971, p. 3.
[17] *The Wall Street Journal*, June 6, 1972, p. 1.
[18] *Seattle Times*, February 21, 1972, p. A-7.
[19] *The Wall Street Journal*, February 22, 1972, p. 1.
[20] *Business Week* states that "(t)he most sought-after employee in the U.S. today is a black, Spanish-surnamed female engineer." *Business Week*, January 27, 1975, p. 94. About one thousand women flew military aircraft in noncombat assignments during World War II, yet some thirty years passed before the first women pilots appeared on the commercial airlines scene. Los Angeles *Times*, November 19, 1976, Part 1-A, pp. 6–7.
[21] Bureau of National Affairs, *Labor Relations Reporter, State Laws*, 4, SLL 1:11–13.

[22] Stuart H. Garfinkle, "Occupations of Women and Black Workers, 1962–74," *Monthly Labor Review*, 98:25–29 (November 1975). Between 1900 and 1970, the percent of women in professional and technical jobs increased from 25 to 40 percent, in managerial jobs from 4 to 17 percent, and in clerical jobs from 24 to 74 percent. U.S. Department of Labor, *Employment and Training Report of the President*, pp. 151–152.
[23] "Women in Work—Facts and Fictions," *Newsletter*, Institute for Social Research, The University of Michigan, Autumn 1972, pp. 4–5. One out of eight families was headed by a woman in 1975. See Beverly J. McEaddy, "Women Who Head Families: A Socio-economic Analysis," *Monthly Labor Review*, 99:3 (June 1976).

Figure **11-5** Occupational distribution of employed women, 1962 and 1974 (numbers in thousands)

Occupational group	Employed women		Change, 1962–74		Women as a percent of all employed	
	1962	1974	Number	Percent	1962	1974
All employed	23,029	33,417	10,388	45.1	33.9	38.9
Professional	2,890	4,992	2,102	72.7	35.9	40.5
Managerial	1,138	1,650	512	45.0	15.3	18.5
Sales	1,715	2,265	550	32.1	39.2	41.8
Clerical	6,918	11,676	4,758	68.8	68.8	77.6
Craft workers	232	511	279	120.2	2.5	4.5
Operatives	3,392	4,331	939	27.7	25.9	31.1
Nonfarm laborers	94	354	260	276.6	2.6	8.1
Farmers and farm managers	132	98	−34	−25.8	5.1	6.0
Farm laborers	730	385	−345	−47.3	32.0	27.4
Service workers, except private household	3,457	5,955	2,498	72.2	53.5	58.7
Private household	2,330	1,201	−1,129	−48.5	97.3	97.8

NOTE: Data for 1962 are not strictly comparable with 1974 figures because of definitional changes in occupational categories and because 14- and 15-year-olds are included in 1962 and excluded from 1974 data.

From: Stuart H. Garfinkle, "Occupations of Women and Black Workers, 1962–74," *Monthly Labor Review*, 98:27 (November 1975).

ment and hiring practices. Basically, under the executive order, contractors are required to develop and administer an affirmative action plan with timetables that will raise the level of minority and female employment in their firms. Typically, the goal is to raise the percentage of minority employment to a level comparable to the percentage of minority workers in the local work force.[24]

Forty-two states now have laws forbidding employment discrimination for reasons of race, religion, or sex.[25] These laws are designed to protect qualified people against unrealistic job specifications. Thus, both federal and state legislation have a decided impact on the staffing process.

THE OLDER WORKER AND THE AGE DISCRIMINATION IN EMPLOYMENT ACT

Myths also exist about the older worker. One is that the older worker is less productive. Schwab and Heneman, in a research study involving a random sample of semiskilled assemblers in a factory, found this to be untrue.

[24] Commerce Clearing House, *1973 Guidebook to Fair Employment Practices*, Report 19, October 19, 1972, pp. 67–75. For a description of a flow model for planning hiring and promotions under an affirmative action program, see Neil C. Churchill and John K. Shank, "Affirmative Action and Guilt-Edged Goals," *Harvard Business Review*, 54:111–116 (March-April 1976).

[25] Bureau of National Affairs, *Labor Relations Reporter*, Fair Employment Practices Manual, 451:21–26 (August 1975).

In their sample, productivity increased with age.[26] Other myths hold that the older worker is more costly to the firm in terms of absenteeism, illness, insurance, pensions, workmen's compensation, etc. None of these may be true in a given firm and only a careful analysis of personnel policies in the individual company will reveal the costs of employing older versus younger workers. For example, if a pension plan is based on years of service, age may have little bearing on costs. On the other hand, if pensions are based solely on age and the same amount is paid to retirees at age sixty-five regardless of length of service, it would cost a company more to hire the older worker.

The Age Discrimination in Employment Act of 1967, which went into effect June 12, 1968, was designed to protect workers against arbitrary age discrimination in hiring, retention, compensation, and other conditions of employment. This Act applies to anyone subject to Title VII of the Civil Rights Act of 1964 and is enforced by the secretary of labor.

The Age Discrimination in Employment Act is specifically designed to protect individuals at least forty years of age but less than sixty-five. However, organizations may discriminate against those younger than forty and against those sixty-five and older; in short, employers may give the forty-to-sixty-five group preference in employment. Further, covered organizations may apply age criteria where age is a bona fide occupational qualification, although this exemption is interpreted narrowly by the secretary of labor. In addition, employers may

observe the terms of bona fide seniority, retirement, pension, insurance, or other benefit plans and may discharge or discipline older workers providing such action does not circumvent the Act. For example, the provisions of a retirement plan are no excuse to refrain from hiring an individual, but an employer is not required to place the individual under the plan if a certain age bracket has been excluded.[27]

Suits and awards involving discrimination based on age are increasing. For example, the Department of Labor found 1,836 employers to have conducted illegal "help wanted" advertising in 1973. In addition, some 1,031 workers were awarded a total of $1,866,226 because of lost working time or other consequences of age discrimination.[28] As another example, in the Friendly Ice Cream Corporation case affecting 380 restaurants in eleven states, the firm agreed to establish an affirmative hiring program for older workers and to pay $40,000 in lost wages to applicants after the Department of Labor alleged the company had discriminated against older applicants for its management trainee program.[29]

THE HANDICAPPED WORKER AND THE VOCATIONAL REHABILITATION ACT

Discrimination against physically handicapped persons is also now prohibited by federal law in the case of government contracts in excess of $2,500. The Vocational Rehabilitation Act of 1973 requires affirmative action "to employ and advance in employment qualified handicapped

[26] Donald P. Schwab and Herbert G. Heneman III, "Effects of Age and Experience on Productivity," in Robert L. Taylor, Michael J. O'Connell, Robert A. Zawacki, and D.D. Warrick, eds., *Academy of Management Proceedings,* Proceedings of the 36th Annual Meeting of the Academy of Management, Kansas City, Missouri, August 11–14, 1976, pp. 281–283. For an additional discussion of some of the erroneous beliefs about hiring the older worker, see William H. Wandel, "Hiring Older Workers: The Pension and Insurance Barriers," *The Management Review,* 45:275–276 (April 1956).

[27] Age Discrimination in Employment Act of 1967. See also Prentice-Hall, "The New Age Discrimination Law," *Personnel Management—Communications,* Report Bulletin 25, June 4, 1968.

[28] *Fair Employment Digest,* March 1974, p. 7; and *Action,* American Society for Personnel Administration, 10:10 (February 1974).

[29] George S. Roukis, "Protecting Workers' Civil Rights: Equality in the Workplace," *Labor Law Journal,* 26:11 (January 1975).

individuals. . . ."[30] Generally, personnel managers and first-line supervisors favor hiring such workers, according to one study. Handicapped workers were not observed to have lower production rates or higher turnover, absenteeism, or accident rates than workers in general.[31] The survey, however, did point up some very real difficulties in such employment. The hiring of the handicapped requires very careful study by individual organizations of their particular job requirements and advanced planning to place such workers in appropriate jobs. If thought is given to the problem only when handicapped applicants appear, in all likelihood such applicants will not be hired because of prejudices or overly stringent job specifications.

OTHER FORCES AFFECTING HUMAN RESOURCES PLANNING

Attitudes about other kinds of qualifications will also have an impact on human resources planning. For example, managers may insist that applicants for technical sales positions have engineering degrees even though an objective set of specifications for the job would not suggest such a need. Or they may insist upon graduates in the upper ranks of their classes when, realistically, such a requirement may be unnecessary for the jobs to be filled.

Managerial attitudes toward responsibilities for maintaining a stabilized work force will also be a factor in human resources planning. Managers and planners may be given directives to attempt to smooth out the peaks and valleys in

company employment levels. Such attempts, of course, will be affected by the degree of diversification in products, by the requirements of customers, and by cash flow realities. Successful efforts by a firm to minimize wide fluctuations in its labor force may be rewarded by such gains as enhanced community relations, reduced recruiting and training costs, and reduced unemployment compensation rates.

AUTHORITY AND ACCOUNTABILITY IN HUMAN RESOURCES PLANNING

Since the personnel department is at the center of an information network on labor-market conditions, skill-mix of various departments, and departmental wage and salary structures, it would seem logical that the major burden of coordinating staffing requirements falls upon that department. One study found human resources planning to be a function assigned to the personnel department in 96 percent of 249 firms surveyed, all of which employed 1,000 or more people.[32] In general, the larger the company, the more likely that such planning was assigned to the personnel department. Since the various departments must cooperate in developing the basic data, however, the chief executive would be wise to hold the personnel director and department heads jointly accountable in this vital undertaking. A top-level human resources planning and development committee involving the personnel director and several line managers can be an extremely useful mechanism for sharing information, for planning, and for gaining joint commitment on programs.[33]

As shown in Figure 11-2, within relatively

---

[30] Sec. 503(d), Vocational Rehabilitation Act of 1973.
[31] Vera M. Schletzer, Rene V. Dawes, George W. England, and Lloyd H. Lofquist, *Attitudinal Barriers to Employment* (Minneapolis: Industrial Relations Center, University of Minnesota, 1961), Minnesota Studies in Vocational Rehabilitation, XI, pp. 1–4. For a discussion of hiring the mentally retarded, see Bernard Rosenberg, "A New Source of Manpower: The Mentally Retarded," *Personnel Administration*, 30:15–18 (November-December 1967).

[32] Allan R. Janger, *Personnel Administration: Changing Scope and Organization* (New York: National Industrial Conference Board, 1966), p. 25.
[33] For a discussion of top-management committees in human resources planning, see Patten, *Manpower Planning and the Development of Human Resources*, pp. 211–219.

large organizations human resources planning must take place at a divisional, plant, and/or departmental level. In manufacturing, for example, production schedules may require constant reallocation of people to different assignments almost on an hourly basis. Therefore, internal departmental planning is a necessity. However, when planning involves other departments and the outside labor market, it must be conducted by a central agency. Thus, the personnel department must develop information by soliciting projected future needs from departments and relating these data to probable rates of transfer and turnover and to possible surpluses of employees. Such data must be checked against information being developed by any industrial-engineering groups undertaking work-simplification or efficiency programs or planning changes in equipment or work flow that could affect staffing needs (see Figure 11-1).

Planning for promotions is a special aspect of human resources planning. Typically, the identification of future openings to be filled by promotions occurs at both a departmental level and at an overall organizational level; and since such planning will have consequences for employee training and development, the training people should be involved.

Usually, the personnel department is involved in any planning of work force cuts, but it does not make such decisions unilaterally. The authority to make work force cuts is likely to be held by the president or jointly by the president and top operating officials. In addition, provisions in the labor contract about layoff and termination will restrict unilateral action.

AUTHORIZATION FOR STAFFING

Authorization for staffing is usually expedited through the use of employee requisitions. (See Figure 11-6.) Requisitions serve to notify the people responsible for recruitment (either from outside the firm or from internal transfer or promotion) that employees with certain skills are needed at certain times and that the appropriate person has authorized all such additions to the staff.

Requisitions often serve to control labor costs because the executive responsible for approving or disapproving them will have the power to expand, shrink, or maintain the number of employees in the total organization or in subunits. Since requisitions typically state range of salary and specifications for the position, the power to approve is also the power to control the structure of salaries and the levels of skills within the organization. This authority may be invested in one executive or in two or more on a joint approval basis. If the organization is attempting to reduce costs and to increase efficiency in staffing methods, such authority may reside in a position such as vice president for administration. Typically, however, the executive in whose unit the vacancy exists and the personnel director will jointly approve requisitions. The personnel department will be vitally concerned because of the role of the department in work force planning, transfers, promotions, and administration of wages and salaries. Control may be supplemented through the use of agreed-upon employment and skill levels and through the establishment of quotas with which middle-level managers are expected to comply.

The system of requisitions should be carefully planned to avoid unnecessary bottlenecks and authorizations. Since requisitions are useful controls in wage and salary administration, in allocating expenditures for labor, and in maintaining a proper skill-mix, and since they provide necessary information for human resources planning, they may be reviewed by several managers before any staffing actually takes place.

University of Washington
Personnel Request

To: Department of personnel services   Date:_____

For staff positions

Instructions: Complete this form for permanent and temporary staff vacancies. Submit white, blue and yellow
copies, retain the pink. The blue copy, with approved classification and salary range, will be returned to your office for permanent record.

Department	Budget no.	Requested by	Bldg. & room no.	Phone ext.

Title of position	Date needed	Working hours	Person replaced

Budget class_____   Position number_____   No. of employees needed_____
New position_____   Replacement_____
Full time_____   Part time_____ %
Permanent_____   Temporary_____
                                         (Service period)   Department head

(This box to be completed by personnel services department)

Classification of position	Department	Salary range	Date received	Date needed	Approved by personnel services department

Desired qualifications and description of position:

Referrals:

Name	Date	Remarks	Name	Date	Remarks

Name of new employee_____ Date filled_____ Hiring salary_____

Figure **11-6**   Example of an employee requisition

Used with permission.

DEVELOPING SOURCES OF APPLICANTS
DESCRIPTION AND PURPOSE

Developing sources of applicants may include advertising; job posting (advertising the job within the organization—see Chapter 14); listing needs with private, academic, or public placement agencies; campus and field recruiting; invitations to applicants to visit the employer's premises; and maintaining files on applicants. The purpose of this subprocess is to interest a sufficient number of qualified people in employment with the organization.

CURRENT PRACTICES AND PROBLEMS

Developing sources of applicants requires considerable coordination with human resources planning. The labor market must be analyzed to ascertain where specific skills may be located, and decisions need to be made on which schools, colleges, and cities should be contacted or visited, where advertising should be placed, and who should do the recruiting.

Advertising in newspapers and trade and professional journals is one method of developing sources of applicants. Such publications may have a local, regional, national, or even international readership. A glance at any metropolitan newspaper will show that a very high proportion of organizations use this method of securing applicants. Many organization advertise in minority media to enhance affirmative action programs.

Another source of applicants is the commercial employment agency. According to a nationwide survey, 21 percent of job-seekers used private employment agencies as one method of securing employment.[34] Fees vary from a fraction of the new employee's monthly salary to more than one month's pay. During periods of

shortages in certain skills, competition may result in the company's paying the agency a fee for a successful referral. In the case of executive recruiting, fees are often paid to consulting firms for seeking talent even if the right person cannot be located.

Another source of applicants is the state employment service, which assists in placing people in jobs on a statewide as well as a national basis. Seventy-six percent of firms surveyed used this source.[35] These state services are partially supported by federal funds administered by the U.S. Employment Service under the Wagner-Peyser Act of 1933. In some respects, the USES, private- and public-school placement services, and private commercial employment agencies compete with each other, since each may be vying with the others for clientele. Placement services in schools, of course, usually assist their own students and alumni on an exclusive basis.

It has become common practice for thousands of U.S. firms, particularly larger ones, to recruit on a nationwide scale. Such recruiting is intensely competitive and includes both campus recruiting and field (off-campus) recruiting. Thus, not only are graduating seniors recruited, but also managerial, technical-professional, or other specialized talent is obtained through systematic "raids" on other companies.

Recruiting at secondary schools, colleges, and universities is usually preceded by communications between the seeking organization and the campus placement office in order to arrange a recruiting date and schedule. The placement office in turn publicizes the visit of the recruiting organization and attempts to have interested students available for inter-

[34] U.S. Department of Labor, "Job Seeking Methods used by American Workers," *Bulletin 1886*, 1975, p. 4.

[35] Bureau of National Affairs, *Bulletin to Management*, March 23, 1972, p. 1. In 1971, President Nixon issued Executive Order No. 11598 requiring all federal agencies and most federal contractors and subcontractors to list with appropriate state employment services all job openings paying less than $18,000 per year.

views, although the company may advertise in student or local newspapers as well. Typically, high schools, business and trade schools, and colleges and universities have either placement offices or one or more people responsible for maintaining a liaison in placement work between the school and the business and industrial community.

Field recruiting is usually preceded by advertising in appropriate local newspapers, and applicants are subsequently interviewed at local hotels or at the offices of the state employment service. Firms with branch offices may use those offices for recruiting. In addition, professional associations will often run placement services for their members, and may have a special room at a national convention for the purpose of bringing employers and job seekers together. Much recruiting of public-school administrators and of faculty members in colleges and universities is conducted in this manner. Some industrial recruiting also takes place at military separation centers.

Frequently, out-of-town applicants who satisfactorily pass an initial campus or field screening are invited to visit the employer's place of work at the employer's expense for further interviews. This procedure permits additional representatives of the employing organization to interview candidates, and permits candidates to obtain more information for making career decisions. While plant visits are more likely to occur in the case of managerial and technical applicants, plant tours are sometimes used by companies to interest local applicants of various skill categories, including operative or maintenance workers. One manufacturing company uses the following interesting procedure.

At the new Eaton plants, the hiring process is a meaningful, two-way exchange, which replaces the structured interview and the more common "get-me-twelve-warm-bodies-by-Tuesday" factory-hiring syndrome. Applicants and their spouses are invited in small groups to an after-dinner "coffee" where the plant's products, processes, and philosophy are discussed. Both factory and office employees take the group on a plant and office tour and encourage the applicant to spend additional time in departments that seem most attractive to him. Personnel people ask the newcomer to express his job preferences within his general skill level for initial placement or for later transfer if there is no opening in the department he selects. The people conducting the tour introduce the applicant to people he may be working for and with. With this open review of the job, the job seeker ends up knowing more about the company and its people than they do about him. This process extends to a drill press operator or a file clerk the concern and dignity that industry usually extends only to its applicants for managerial posts.[36]

An interesting aspect of nationwide field recruiting of professional-technical employees is that many job offers are made by the recruiters without the applicant visiting company premises. Consequently, only one interview may occur; the new employee's supervisor may never meet the person until the first day of work; and the applicant may rely to a great extent on the "company image" projected by the recruiter and the available literature. This procedure requires top-notch interviewing skills on the part of the field recruiter and effective advertising and public relations in recruiting.

A government survey involving some ten million workers found that, from the job seeker's perspective, the most frequent methods by which jobs were obtained were, in rank order: direct application to an employer, asking friends or relatives for information, and answering newspaper ads.[37] In the case of scientific, professional, and technical employees, from the standpoint of the employer, the most productive sources are advertising, on-campus recruiting, and employment agencies in that order, although on-campus recruiting is considered less costly than securing applicants

[36] Donald N. Scobel, "Doing Away with the Factory Blues," *Harvard Business Review*, 53:136 (November-December 1975).
[37] U.S. Department of Labor, "Job Seeking Methods," pp. 1–10.

through agencies.[38] The most effective recruiting sources for minority employees, according to a sample of 160 personnel executives, are community agencies, present minority employees, educational institutions, advertising, and employment agencies, in that order.[39]

Of course, advertising and recruiting practices must not violate federal and state laws against discrimination. For example, it is unlawful for job notices or advertisements to contain such clauses as "college student," "recent college graduate," "age 25–35," "young," "age 40–50," "age 50," "age over 65," "boy," or "girl." It is also illegal for newspapers to run ads under "male wanted" or "female wanted" column heads. However, advertising may state a preference for college graduates, or some minimum age which is less than 40, providing the employer can justify such requirements as bona fide occupational qualifications. If not, such advertising can be held as discriminating.[40]

The use of temporary help obtained from firms specializing in "renting out" employees is also a common, and growing, practice. Although the first such firms concentrated on providing temporary secretarial and office employees, blue-collar, technical, and scientific help have also become available through such sources. Paradoxically, some temporary help suppliers are beginning to furnish employees who constitute an essentially "permanent" staff. For example, Manpower, Incorporated, supplies employees who run service stations.[41]

RELATIONSHIP TO OTHER ORGANIZATIONAL PROCESSES

Various managerial processes affect the development of sources of applicants. For example, a favorable public image will facilitate the flow of applicants, while poor public relations will obviously handicap a recruiting program. Thus, marketing, advertising, and public relations have an impact on the staffing process. We have already discussed how technological changes and other forces affect human resources planning and thus recruiting.

Unsatisfactory results in recruiting may bring about changes in the firm's compensation practices. Premium wages may be paid to applicants whose particular specialties are in short supply or for jobs that are particularly undesirable. Such raising of beginning salaries has widespread implications throughout the organization (to be discussed further in Chapter 19).

The overall quality of the human relationships in an organization will have a major effect on securing qualified applicants. One comprehensive survey found that almost 20 percent of job seekers secured employment by asking friends or relatives about jobs where they worked.[42] Poor employee relations or poor union-management relations will reduce both the quality and quantity of people referred.

A self-inflicted handicap to recruiting exists under many local civil service systems. To me, the practice of restricting employment to residents of a particular jurisdiction seems highly dysfunctional in terms of employing the most qualified people for particular jobs. This practice is reported in one out of every four local jurisdictions.[43]

[38] Bureau of National Affairs, "Solving the Shortage of Specialized Personnel," *Survey No. 62*, September 1961, p. 1.
[39] Bureau of National Affairs, "Equal Employment Opportunity: Programs and Results," *Personnel Policies Forum: Survey No. 112*, March 1976, p. 3.
[40] Based on Commerce Clearing House, *1975 Guidebook to Fair Employment Practices*, p. 19. Greyhound Lines was able to convince the U.S. Court of Appeals, Seventh Circuit (Chicago), that a maximum age of forty was a bona fide occupational qualification. See Shaeffer, *Nondiscrimination in Employment*, p. 36.
[41] *Business Week*, August 23, 1976, p. 41.

[42] U.S. Department of Labor, "Job Seeking Methods," p. 7.
[43] Winston W. Crouch, ed., *Local Government Personnel Administration* (Washington, D.C.: International City Management Association, 1976), p. 84.

IMPACT OF ENVIRONMENT

As we indicated previously, state and federal legislation and community and national attitudes about race, religion, national origin, age, sex, or handicap status will affect specifications, human resource planning, and thus recruiting. Attitudes held by applicants concerning the desirability of certain work will also affect recruitment. As I have already suggested, vast changes in science and technology have resulted in special staffing needs and consequent recruiting problems.

State licensing laws will have a direct impact on the availability of applicants with certain skills. Depending upon the state, licenses may be required to practice as a plumber, electrician, stationary engineer, fire-fighter, barber, beautician, and the like. The practice of certain professions—medicine, dentistry, and law, for example—requires licensing. Such licensing, while having as its main purpose the protection of the public, also serves to restrict entrance into a craft or profession. Unions and professional associations are typically given considerable voice in the administration of these licensing laws.[44]

In certain industries, such as the construction, garment, and maritime industries, unions have traditionally been very active in matters of employment. Presumably outlawed by the closed-shop provisions of the Taft-Hartley Act, union hiring halls persisted in these industries, largely because of convenience to employers.[45] Amendments to the Act in 1959 essentially legalized the union hiring hall in the building and construction industry.[46] Technically, unions in

this industry cannot discriminate against non-union applicants, but practically, legitimate requirements, such as length of experience in a trade, probably result in the referral of union members. In the case of many craft unions, the union may also directly affect the staffing process by negotiating agreements on apprenticeship wage rates and on ratios of apprentices to journeymen. Such agreements tend to control entrance into the trade.

AUTHORITY AND ACCOUNTABILITY

The personnel department is usually held accountable for developing adequate sources of applicants. Contacts with newspapers, agencies, and schools are typically coordinated by that department. In the event that other departments attempt to recruit without central coordination, duplication of effort and inefficiencies are bound to occur. Furthermore, unless one central office maintains files on applicants, such information will not be available to the total organization when needed.

It is common, however, for the managers and employees throughout the firm to make recommendations to the personnel department that certain individuals be considered for employment. The personnel department usually welcomes this assistance, unless pressure is applied to hire people lacking proper qualifications. In addition, personnel officers typically call on other departments for help in recruiting. For example, a manufacturing executive may be requested to visit his or her alma mater to recruit new graduates. Such a trip must be coordinated centrally in order to insure that recruiting needs for the entire organization are properly considered.

Although the degree of detail in the budgets of personnel departments will vary from firm to firm, once a recruiting and advertising budget is approved by the chief executive or the chief financial officer, the personnel director will

[44] See Gordon F. Bloom and Herbert R. Northrup, *Economics of Labor Relations*, 6th ed. (Homewood, Ill.: Richard D. Irwin, 1969), pp. 179–180.

[45] Under a closed-shop provision of a labor-management contract, only members of the union may be hired. In contrast, a union-shop provision requires the new employee to join the union within a certain period of time.

[46] Labor Management Relations Act, 1947, as amended by Public Law 86-257, 1959.

usually administer the expenditure of these funds. The personnel director will, of course, be held accountable for the results of these expenditures.

UTILITY OF SYSTEMS

There is obviously no one best system for developing sources of applicants. The procedures used will vary with the many factors discussed above. It is equally obvious, however, that contacts, advertising, and recruiting must be carefully planned. This planning must be long-range, since contacts with schools, colleges, universities, and other organizations must be developed over a period of years. In this regard, the personal qualifications of the personnel staff and recruiters will be as important as the systems or procedures used.

SUMMARY

For human resources planning to be useful, the personnel department must work in cooperation with all parts of the enterprise to develop a continuous flow of pertinent data. Human resources planning is as vital to the enterprise as planning the procurement and utilization of finances, material, capital equipment, and market resources. Without proper planning, some skills may be in short supply while the supply of others may be in excess. Without the right people in the right jobs at the right time, any of the vital management processes can become so inefficient as to threaten the existence of the organization.

While effective management of organizations under any circumstances requires effective human resources planning, compliance with federal and state laws about hiring, promotion, and retention now makes careful and comprehensive human resources planning even more

indispensible. The Civil Rights Act, the Equal Pay Act, the Age Discrimination in Employment Act, the Vocational Rehabilitation Act, executive orders, and numerous EEOC and court rulings have upgraded an important function into a vital one.

The development of continuous sources of qualified people consistent with human resources plans is both an external and internal matter, and requires effective approaches to recruitment, employee development, transfer, and promotion. Recruitment should be viewed as an aspect of the broad staffing process and carefully linked to the dynamic process of effective internal utilization and development of human resources.

APPENDIX: E.L. THORNDIKE ON SEX DISCRIMINATION

The following strikingly up-to-date statement is from a 1915 book by a famous psychologist of that day.

The individual differences within one sex so enormously outweigh the differences between the sexes in these intellectual and semi-intellectual traits that for practical purposes the sex differences may be disregarded. So far as ability goes, there could hardly be a stupider way to get two groups, than to take the two sexes. As is well-known, the experiments of the past generation in educating women have shown their equal competence in schoolwork of elementary, secondary, and collegiate grade. The present generation's experience is showing the same fact for professional education and business service. The psychologist's measurements lead to the conclusion that this equality of achievement comes from an equality of natural gifts, not from an overstraining of the lesser talents of women.[47]

[47] E.L. Thorndike, *Educational Psychology* (New York: Briefer Course, Teachers College, 1915). Cited in *Professional Psychology*, 5:263 (August 1974).

REVIEW AND DISCUSSION QUESTIONS

1. What internal and external factors need to be considered in human resources planning?

2. What is the difference between human resources planning and making human resources projections?

3. What is the relationship of the respective states to the Civil Rights Act?

4. What are the central responsibilities of the EEOC?

5. How does the Age Discrimination in Employment Act of 1967 relate to retirement plans?

6. What are some of the current consequences of the Civil Rights Act as it pertains to discrimination based on sex?

7. If you were a personnel director, what would you be prohibited from doing in recruiting new employees?

8. If you were a personnel director, how would you go about analyzing the usefulness of various sources of applicants?

9. If you have ever been interviewed by campus recruiters, what were some of the more effective (and less effective) practices you have experienced?

SUPPLEMENTAL REFERENCES

American Assembly, "Women and the American Economy," *Report of the Forty-Ninth American Assembly*, October 30-November 2, 1975.

Alfred, Theodore M., "Checkers or Choice in Manpower Management," *Harvard Business Review*, 45:157–169 (January-February 1967).

Bassett, Glenn A., "Manpower Forecasting and Planning: Problems and Solutions," *Personnel*, 47:8–16 (September-October 1970).

Bergmann, Barbara R., and William R. Krause, "Evaluating and Forecasting Progress in Racial Integration of Employment," *Industrial and Labor Relations Review*, 25:399–409 (April 1972).

Bjorklund, Robert L., David A. Gray, and Max S. Wortman, Jr., "Project Step-up: A Systems Approach to Upgrading Laid-off Disadvantaged Workers," *Proceedings of the Twenty-Third Annual Winter Meeting*, Industrial Relations Research Association Series, December 28–29, 1970, pp. 286–295.

Blitz, Rudolph C., "Women in the Professions, 1870–1970," *Monthly Labor Review*, 97:34–39 (May 1974).

Block, Herman D., "Some Economic Effects of Discrimination in Employment," *The American Journal of Economics and Sociology*, 25:11–24 (January 1966).

Boulding, Kenneth E., "Role Prejudice as an Economic Problem," *Monthly Labor Review*, 97:40 (August 1974).

Bowman, Worthy, and Stephen A. Greyser, "Are Women Executives People?" *Harvard Business Review*, 43:14ff. (July-August 1965).

Bright, William E., "How One Company Manages its Human Resources," *Harvard Business Review*, 54:81–93 (January-February 1976).

Brown, William, III, "The Equal Employment Opportunity Act of 1972—The Light at the Top of the Stairs," *Personnel Administration*, 35:4–7ff. (June 1972).

Burack, Elmer H., *Strategies for Manpower Planning and Programming* (Morristown, N.J.: General Learning Corporation, 1972).

Carroll, Stephen J., "Relationship of Various College Graduate Characteristics to Recruiting Decisions," *Journal of Applied Psychology*, 50:421–423 (October 1966).

Charnes, A., W.W. Cooper, R.J. Niehaus, and D. Sholtz, "A Systems Approach to Manpower Management and Planning," *The Journal of Navy Civilian Manpower Management*, 4:1–11 (Winter 1970).

Cruz, Daisy, "Affirmative Action at Work," *Personnel Journal*, 55:226–227ff. (May 1976).

Curd, Edith F., "The Changing Role of Women in The Business World," *Personnel Administration*, 35:29–31 (June 1972).

Eckley, Robert S., "Company Action to Stabilize Employment," *Harvard Business Review*, 44:51–61 (July-August 1966).

Fischer, Frank E., "Manpower Management," in Joseph J. Famularo, ed., *Handbook of Modern Personnel Administration* (New York: McGraw-Hill Book Company, 1972), Chapter 9.

Ford, David L., Jr., "Perspective: Minorities in Organizations," *Paper No. 501*, Krannert Graduate School of Industrial Administration, Purdue University, March 1975.

Geisler, Edwin B., "Manpower Planning: An Emerging Staff Function," American Management Association, *AMA Management Bulletin*, 1967.

Ginzberg, Eli, *The Development of Human Resources* (New York: McGraw-Hill Book Company, 1966).

Haire, Mason, "Approach to an Integrated Personnel Policy," *Industrial Relations*, 7:107–117 (February 1968).

Hayghe, Howard, "Families and The Rise of Working Wives—An Overview," *Monthly Labor Review*, 99:12–19 (May 1976).

Hedges, Janice N., and Stephen E. Bemis, "Sex Stereotyping: Its Decline in Skilled Trades," *Monthly Labor Review*, 97:14–21 (May 1974).

Heneman, Herbert, and George Seltzer, *Manpower Planning and Forecasting in the Firm: An Exploratory Probe* (Minneapolis: University of Minnesota, Industrial Relations Center, March 1968).

Hilaael, Timothy M., "A Three Step Plan for Implementing an Affirmative Action Program," *The Personnel Administrator*, 21:35–39 (July 1976).

Hopper, Kenneth, "The Growing Use of College Graduates as Foremen," *Management of Personnel Quarterly*, 6:2–12 (Summer 1967).

Ingraham, Albert P., and Carl F. Lutz, "Managing Positions—The Key to Effective Organization, Compensation, and Productivity," *Human Resource Management*, 13:12–21 (Summer 1974).

Johnson, Lawrence A., *Employing the Hard-Core Unemployed* (New York: American Management Association, 1969), AMA Research Study 98.

Milkovich, G., A.J. Annoni, and T.A. Mahoney, "The Use of the Delphi Procedures in Manpower Forecasting," *Working Paper 71-07*, Industrial Relations Center, University of Minnesota, 1971.

Municipal Manpower Commission, *Governmental Manpower for Tomorrow's Cities* (New York: McGraw-Hill Book Company, 1962).

Munts, Raymond, and David C. Rice, "Women Workers: Protection or Equality?" *Industrial and Labor Relations Review*, 24:3–13 (October 1970).

Perham, John C., "The Corporate Switch to Inside Recruiting," *Dun's Review*, 107:64–65 (May 1976).

Reid, Graham L., "Job Search and The Effectiveness of Job-Finding Methods," *Industrial and Labor Relations Review*, 25:479–495 (July 1972).

Rosen, Benson, and Thomas H. Jerdee, "The Nature of Job-Related Age Stereotypes," *Journal of Applied Psychology*, 61:180–183 (April 1976).

Rowland, Kendrith, and Michael Sovereign, "Markov-Chain Analysis of Internal Manpower Supply," *Industrial Relations*, 9:88–99 (October 1969).

Sand, Robert H., "Back Pay Liability Under Title VII," in James L. Stern and Barbara D. Dennis, eds., *Proceedings of the Twenty-Seventh Annual Winter Meeting*, Industrial Relations Research Association Series, 1975, pp. 225–230.

Sue, Stanley, Derald W. Sue, and David W. Sue, "Asian Americans as a Minority Group," *American Psychologist*, 30:906–910 (September 1975).

Terry, Robert W., *For Whites Only* (Grand Rapids, Mich.: William B. Eerdmans Publishing Company, 1970).

Torrey, Jane W., "The Consequences of Equal Opportunity for Women," *Journal of Contemporary Business*, 5:13–27 (Winter 1976).

U.S. Department of Labor, "A Manpower Profile of the Spanish Speaking," *Manpower Report of the President*, 1973, pp. 87–89.

———, *Occupational Licensing and the Supply of Nonprofessional Manpower*, Manpower Research Monograph No. 11 (Washington, D.C.: U.S. Department of Labor, Manpower Administration, 1969).

———, "Special Problems of Women Workers," *Manpower Report of the President*, 1975, pp. 72–74.

Vetter, Eric W., *Manpower Planning for High Talent Personnel* (Ann Arbor: The University of Michigan, Bureau of Industrial Relations, Graduate School of Business Administration, 1967).

Waldman, Elizabeth, and Beverly J. McEaddy, "Where Women Work—An Analysis by Industry and Occupation," *Monthly Labor Review*, 97:3–13 (May 1974).

Wallenstein, Gerd D., "Fundamentals of Technical Manpower Planning," American Management Association, *Management Bulletin 78*, 1966.

Wells, Theodora, "The Covert Power of Gender in Organizations," *Journal of Contemporary Business*, 2:53–68 (Summer 1973).

Wickstrom, Walter S., *Manpower Planning: Evolving Systems* (New York: Conference Board, 1971).

Wilensky, Harold L., "Women's Work," *Industrial Relations*, 7:235–248 (May 1968).

CHAPTER 12
THE EMPLOYEE-SELECTION PROCESS

The process of selecting employees is an important subprocess of the broader staffing process. Systems designed for the management of this subprocess almost universally include application blanks and interviews. In addition to these devices, tests, reference checks, and physical examinations are often used. (See Figure 12-1.)

THE APPLICATION BLANK
PURPOSE

The purpose of the *application blank* is to secure desired information from an applicant in a form convenient for evaluating the applicant's qualifications. It also serves as a convenient device for circulating information about the applicant to appropriate members of management and as a useful device for storing information for later reference.[1] (See Figure 12-2 for an example of an application blank.)

Different forms may be used for different kinds of jobs. A company may use one form in the case of applicants for salaried positions and a different form in the case of those applying for hourly-paid jobs in production or maintenance. In addition, some organizations may use a short form for preliminary screening or in the event of no immediate vacancies and a longer form when the applicant is being considered for a specific vacancy. The short form is easier to file and requires less time to complete but still provides enough information for preliminary screening.

---

[1] Résumés (background summaries) contain similar information, but the format is the applicant's design, rather than the organization's. Résumés are used by job-seekers in initiating contact with employers and are often requested by companies in their recruiting advertisements.

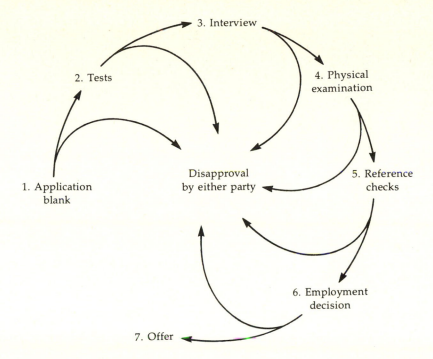

Figure **12-1** Typical devices and events in the employment-decision process

Although this chapter focuses on selection of employees, the term *employment decision* is used in this illustration, since both parties are making a decision in the process.

CURRENT PRACTICES AND PROBLEMS

Application forms vary somewhat from organization to organization, but are almost universally used.[2] Although their usefulness in evaluating applicants has seldom been questioned, recent federal and state equal employment rulings have challenged the job-relatedness of many items, and organizations are finding it necessary to take a hard look at the application blank.

For example, court rulings and administrative guidelines under the Civil Rights Act, the Age Discrimination in Employment Act, the Equal Pay Act, and various state laws have drastically modified the kinds of pre-employment questions that can be asked through such devices as the application blank, required résumés, and the interivew. Many state laws now either prohibit or curtail questions pertaining to race, color, religion, national origin,[3] age, marital status, handicaps, or convictions. Questions about a spouse, child care arrangements, military discharge, membership in organizations, pregnancy, or whether the applicant owns or rents a home are generally prohibited or circumscribed. (See Figure 12-3 for excerpts from

[2] One estimate is that one billion application blanks and résumés are prepared and screened each year in the United States. Edward L. Levine and Abram Flory III, "Evaluation of Job Applications—A Conceptual Framework," *Public Personnel Management*, 4:378 (November-December 1975).

[3] Alien status is not the same thing as national origin according to the U.S. Supreme Court. *Espinoza* v. *Farah Mfg. Co.*, 414 U.S. 86 (1973).

the employment regulations of the Washington State Human Rights Commission.) Although not specifically outlawed by federal legislation, such questions are looked upon "with extreme disfavor" by the Equal Employment Opportunity Commission (EEOC) and the Department of Labor.[4] The requirement that a photograph accompany an application may also be considered evidence of discrimination. Such inquiries do not violate federal law if the factors inquired about are a necessary qualification for a particular job or if the information is necessary in order to comply with rules laid down by governmental agencies. However, if complaints occur, the burden of justification rests with the employer.[5] For example, although requesting age is not in itself prohibited, the Department of Labor states that ". . . employment application forms which request such information . . . will be closely scrutinized . . . ," and the application blank should contain a statement like the one on the bottom of the first page of the application blank shown in Figure 12-2.[6]

RELIABILITY OF APPLICATION BLANK DATA

In general, a test or survey is reliable if it repeatedly produces consistent results. The reliability of responses on an application blank can be measured by the consistency of information supplied by applicants with information obtained from previous employers. One study involving applicants for jobs as nurses' aides found "substantial disagreement" between these two kinds of data. For example, there was disagreement in 57 percent of the cases as to duration of previous employment and dis-

agreement in 25 percent of the cases as to the reason for leaving. In those instances where salary data could be compared, applicants overstated their previous salaries in 72 percent of the cases.[7] While we cannot generalize from these results to other employment situations, this study does demonstrate the importance of crosschecking the various kinds of data that are supplied by applicants during the employment process.

When requesting that the applicant report certain information on an application blank, management is making an implicit assumption that this information will be useful in predicting success or lack of success on the job in question. In general, it would appear that the application blank has considerable "face validity" (obvious correctness or correctness on the surface) in that relevant past performance is probably a good predictor of future performance. It would be reasonable to assume, however, that the majority of firms in the United States have not performed statistical studies to discover to what extent the various items on the application blank do indeed predict success.

The typical procedure in determining the validity of an application blank is to try to discover a correlation between application-blank responses and the success of applicants on their jobs. Such a study would require that individual items on the application blank be reduced to a dichotomized or quantitative score in relation to a *criterion*—a measure of success or performance of some kind. It may be determined

---

[4] Based on policy statements issued by the Equal Employment Opportunity Commission, January 4, 1966, and May 27, 1968.
[5] Bureau of National Affairs, *Labor Policy and Practice, Fair Employment Practices*, 421:408. For a checklist of what preemployment information can and cannot be solicited, see Robert L. Minter, "Human Rights Laws and Pre-Employment Inquiries," *Personnel Journal*, 51:431–433 (June 1972).
[6] Bureau of National Affairs, *Labor Relations Reporter, Fair Employment Practices Manual*, 401:5078.

[7] Irwin L. Goldstein, "The Application Bank: How Honest are the Responses?" *Journal of Applied Psychology*, 55:491–492 (October 1971). Candid responses may not be wise in all instances, particularly with respect to psychiatric treatment. Since employers have widely diverse attitudes about counseling and psychotherapy, the chairperson of the committees on confidentiality of the American Psychiatric Association and the American Psychoanalytic Association suggests that "when an employment form seeks information on treatment for emotional problems, applicants are well advised to interpret that to mean major psychiatric treatment." *Business Week*, August 23, 1976, p. 73.

Application for employment
Hourly

Boise Cascade Corporation

"An Equal Opportunity Employer"

Date _____

Name _____ _____ _____ Soc. Sec. No. _____
(Last)   (First)   (Middle)

Address _____ , _____ , _____ , _____
(Street)   (City)   (State)   (Zip)

Phone _____ *Date of Birth _____

Who referred you to Boise Cascade Corporation?
( ) Private Placement Agency   ( ) College Placement Service   ( ) Walk-in
( ) Reply to Advertisement   ( ) State Employment Office   ( ) Personal Contact

EDUCATION

Highest Grade Completed: 1 2 3 4 5 6 7 8 9 10 11 12   College   1 2 3 4

Special Training _____

Special Skills (Including machinery operation) _____

PREVIOUS WORK EXPERIENCE — List below, beginning with most recent

Employer	From	To	Type of Work	Beginning Rate	Ending Rate	Reason for Leaving
1. a. Name						
b. Address and Phone Number						
2. a. Name						
b. Address and Phone Number						
3. a. Name						
b. Address and Phone Number						

SERVICE RECORD

Branch of Military Service — U.S. _____

National Guard? _____ Date obligation ends _____

Type of discharge and date _____

1010 Rev. 4-74

*The Age Discrimination in Employment Act prohibits discrimination on the basis of age with respect to individuals who are at least 40 but less than 65 years of age.

If you are presently working, may we contact your employer? _____

Any previous work injuries? _____

Relatives in Company employ _____

Notify in case of emergency _____ , _____ , _____
(Name)   (Address)   (Phone No.)

Have you worked for Boise Cascade Corporation before? _____ If yes, where? _____

Dates worked _____ Reason for leaving _____

To determine my qualifications for employment, I authorize Boise Cascade Corporation to conduct an investigation of my application. I understand that any false or misleading information furnished by me on this application form or in connection with my application for employment may result in rejection of the application, or if employed by Boise Cascade Corporation, in the termination of employment.

Signature _____

DO NOT WRITE BELOW THIS LINE

This section to be completed by Boise Cascade Corporation only after applicant is hired. Information is to be used only for completing records and not for hiring purposes.

Sex: Male _____ Female _____   Race: _____   Marital Status: Single _____ Married _____

Date to Start Employment _____ Shift _____

Classification _____ Department _____

Starting Rate of Pay _____

INTERVIEWER'S COMMENTS
Date _____

COMPANY COMMENTS ON TERMINATION
Date _____

Figure 12-2 Example of an application blank

Used with permission of Boise Cascade Corporation.

Figure **12-3** Fair and unfair pre-employment inquiries, excerpts from the employment regulations of the Washington State Human Rights Commission

Subject	Fair pre-employment inquiries	Unfair pre-employment inquiries
a. Age	Inquiries as to birth date and proof of true age are permitted. . . .	Any inquiry which implies a preference for persons under 40 years of age.
b. Arrests (See also Convictions)	None. (Law enforcement agencies are exempt from this rule. . . .)	All inquiries relating to arrests.
c. Citizenship	Whether applicant is prevented from lawfully becoming employed in this country because of visa or immigration status. Whether applicant can provide proof of citizenship, visa, or alien registration number after being hired.	Whether applicant is citizen. Requirement before hiring that applicant present birth certificate, naturalization or baptismal record. Any inquiry into citizenship which would tend to divulge applicant's lineage, ancestry, national origin, descent, or birthplace.
d. Convictions (See also Arrests)	Inquiries concerning specified convictions which relate reasonably to fitness to perform the particular job(s) being applied for, *Provided* that such inquiries be limited to convictions for which the date of conviction or prison release, whichever is more recent, is within 7 years of the date of the job application. . . .	Any inquiry which does not meet the requirement for fair pre-employment inquiries.
e. Family	Whether applicant can meet specified work schedules or has activities, commitments or responsibilities that may prevent him or her from meeting work attendance requirements.	Specific inquiries concerning spouse, spouse's employment or salary, children, child care arrangements, or dependents.
f. Handicap	Whether applicant has certain specified sensory, mental or physical handicaps which relate reasonably to fitness to perform the particular job. Whether applicant has any handicaps or health problems which may effect work performance or which the employer should take into account in determining job placement.	Over-general inquiries (e.g. "Do you have any handicaps?") which would tend to divulge handicaps or health conditions which do not relate reasonably to fitness to perform the job.
g. Height and weight	Inquiries as to ability to perform actual job requirements. Being of a certain height or weight will not be considered to be a job requirement unless the employer can show that no employee with the ineligible height or weight could do the work.	Any inquiry which is not based on actual job requirements.
h. Marital status (See also Name and Family)	None.	( ) Mr. ( ) Miss ( ) Mrs. ( ) Ms. Whether the applicant is married, single, divorced, separated, engaged, widowed, etc.

226

Figure **12-3**   Fair and unfair pre-employment inquiries, excerpts from the employment regulations of the Washington State Human Rights Commission (*cont.*)

Subject	Fair pre-employment inquiries	Unfair pre-employment inquiries
i. Military	Inquiries concerning education, training, or work experience in the armed forces of the United States.	Type or condition of military discharge. Applicant's experience in other than U.S. armed forces. Request for discharge papers.
j. Name	Whether applicant has worked for this company or a competitor under a different name and, if so, what name. Name under which applicant is known to references if different from present name.	Inquiry into original name where it has been changed by court order or marriage. Inquiries about a name which would divulge marital status, lineage, ancestry, national origin or descent.
k. National origin	Inquiries into applicant's ability to read, write and speak foreign languages, when such inquiries are based on job requirements.	Inquiries into applicant's lineage, ancestry, national origin, descent, birthplace, or mother tongue. National origin of applicant's parents or spouse.
l. Organizations	Inquiry into organization memberships, excluding any organization the name or character of which indicates the race, color, creed, sex, marital status, religion, or national origin or ancestry of its members.	Requirement that applicant list all organizations, clubs, societies, and lodges to which he or she belongs.
m. Photographs	May be requested *after* hiring for identification purposes.	Request that applicant submit a photograph, mandatorily or optionally, at any time before hiring.
n. Pregnancy (See also Handicap)	Inquiries as to a duration of stay on job or anticipated absences which are made to males and females alike.	All questions as to pregnancy, and medical history concerning pregnancy and related matters.
o. Race or color	None.	Any inquiry concerning race or color of skin, hair, eyes, etc.
p. Relatives	Names of applicant's relatives already employed by this company or by any competitor.	Names and addresses of any relative other than those listed as proper.
q. Religion or creed	None.	Inquiries concerning applicant's religious denomination, religious affiliations, church, parish, pastor, or religious holidays observed.
r. Residence	Inquiries about address to the extent needed to facilitate contacting the applicant.	Names or relationship of persons with whom applicant resides. Whether applicant owns or rents own home.
s. Sex	None.	Any inquiry.

Employment Regulations, Washington State Human Rights Commission, II, November 1975, pp. 4–6.

that some items predict success better than others, and in making subsequent decisions on the selection of employees, these items may be given more statistical weight. Thus, the term *weighted application blank* has come into use. Research of this kind can significantly improve the effectiveness of the selective process.

The pay-off from such research tends to be greater when there are relatively large numbers of applicants for similar types of jobs held by a fairly large number of people in a company. For example, if an organization employs several thousand secretaries, or even several hundred, research on the extent to which certain items on the application blank predict secretarial success would seem not only feasible but profitable. (For a more detailed discussion of validity see the sections on "Validity" later in the chapter.)

A number of studies have been made over the past several decades to determine the validity of application blanks and to improve them. One of the earliest studies examined the predictability of success in sales from various items on the application blank.[8] Other studies have examined the validity of the application blank in predicting success in various office, hospital, military, and unskilled jobs, and in predicting turnover.[9] Still other studies have examined the usefulness of background data in predicting success in technical-professional, supervisory,

or military jobs.[10] Overall, scored autobiographical data forms have been good predictors of various criteria.[11]

CONCLUSIONS ABOUT THE APPLICATION BLANK

Sufficient research has been done to indicate that studies on the validity of the application blank by individual firms can result in improved data gathering and more effective selection of employees. However, it should be pointed out that while some of the studies cited above examine the general usefulness of background data in predicting job success, some of this information has been obtained from interviews and questionnaires as well as from the application blank. Indeed, the biodata (short for biographical data) obtained from a weighted application blank that is filled out by the applicant could be identical to the biodata obtained in a patterned interview (see later discussion) in which the form is filled out by the interviewer. Therefore, research within the organization might profitably focus on the broad question of what background data predicts job success, thus focusing on the interview, the résumé, the application blank, and the reference check. Research needs to be conducted on all of these devices to avoid redundancy and enhance their validities.

[8] H.S. Canagy and C.S. Yoakum, *Selection and Training of Salesmen* (New York: McGraw-Hill Book Company, 1925), p. 194. For a more recent study see Gilmore J. Spencer, "The Application Form Revisited," *Personnel*, 36:20–30 (September-October 1959).

[9] See Stanley R. Novack, "Developing an Effective Application Blank," *Personnel Journal*, 49:419–423 (May 1970); W.K. Kirchner and M.D. Dunnette, "Applying the Weighted Application Blank in a Variety of Office Jobs," *Journal of Applied Psychology*, 41:206–208 (August 1957); Edwin A. Fleishman and Joseph Berninger, "One Way to Reduce Office Turnover," *Personnel*, 37:63–69 (May-June 1960); and Richard D. Scott and Richard W. Johnson, "Use of the Weighted Application Blank in Selecting Unskilled Employees," *Journal of Applied Psychology*, 51:393–395 (October 1967).

[10] See Robert V. Penfield, "Identifying Effective Supervisors," *Personnel Journal*, 50:209–212ff. (March 1971); William D. Buel, Lewis E. Albright, and J.R. Glennon, "A Note on the Generality and Cross-Validity of Personal History for Identifying Creative Research Scientists," *Journal of Applied Psychology*, 50:217–219 (June 1966); Melany E. Baehr and Glenn B. Williams, "Prediction of Sales Success from Factorially Determined Dimensions of Personal Background Data," *Journal of Applied Psychology*, 52:98–103 (April 1968); and Barukh Nevo, "Using Biographical Information to Predict Success of Men and Women in the Army," *Journal of Applied Psychology*, 61:106–108 (February 1976).

[11] See William A. Owens, "Background Data," in Marvin D. Dunnette, ed., *Handbook of Industrial and Organizational Psychology* (Chicago: Rand McNally College Publishing Company, 1976), p. 617.

THE INTERVIEW

PURPOSE

The *interview*, which years ago was called a "conversation with a purpose,"[12] is used almost universally in the staffing process. Some years ago it was estimated that about 150 million employment interviews took place each year in the United States,[13] and the figure is probably double that now. Sixty-four percent of 2,500 firms in one study reported the interview to be their most important selection device.[14]

As in the case of the application blank, the assumption underlying the interview is that data can be obtained that will be useful in predicting success on the job. While obtaining such data is at least a central purpose, most interviews have multiple purposes. For example, part of the interview may be devoted to giving the applicant information and to "selling" the firm and the job. In many instances the selling aspects of recruiting take the form of fairly elaborate and thorough orientation seminars, tours, and interviews at the company's plants or offices. Many firms will spend perhaps half of the interview giving the applicant information and the other half receiving information from the applicant. In this sense, the interview extends the process of developing sources of applicants.

The selling aspects must be realistic, of course, if subsequent disillusionment and turnover are not to occur. Some organizations have used what are called "realistic job previews" (RJPs) to portray both the positive aspects of the job and the frustrations and problems that can be anticipated.[15]

Other purposes of the interview might be screening for further referral, advising applicants about alternatives in employment, and furthering public relations. Objectives of the group interview might be to assess interpersonal skills and to see who displays the most effective leadership behaviors.

AUTHORITY AND ACCOUNTABILITY

In one study, 84 percent of the responding firms maintained centralized employment departments where preliminary screening of hourly workers or nonexempt salaried candidates was conducted. Generally, the employment office screened both hourly and salaried applicants.[16]

In most organizations, the immediate superior interviews candidates who have been referred by the personnel department. It would be desirable for higher management to hold all such interviewers accountable for proficiency in interviewing. The personnel department is often given the assignment of training supervisors in interviewing skills.

IMPACT OF ENVIRONMENT

The three environmental factors that have probably had the most effect on interviewing are (a) commonly shared attitudes about the treatment of people, (b) scientific developments in clinical and counseling psychology and in the use of patterned interviews, and (c) state and federal administration and court rulings in the area of

---

[12] Walter Van Dyke Bingham and Bruce V. Moore, *How To Interview*, 3rd rev. ed. (New York: Harper & Brothers, 1941), p. 1.

[13] Roger M. Bellows and M. Frances Estep, *Employment Psychology: The Interview* (New York: Holt, Rinehart and Company, 1957), p. 5.

[14] "Employee Testing and Selection Procedures—Where are They Headed?" P-H/ASPA Survey, Reprinted from Prentice-Hall *Personnel Management: Policies and Practices*, 1975, pp. 651–653.

[15] Douglas T. Hall and Francine S. Hall, "What's New in Career Management," *Organizational Dynamics*, 5:18–19 (Summer 1976).

[16] National Industrial Conference Board, "Personnel Practices in Factory and Office: Manufacturing," *Studies in Personnel Policy*, No. 194, 1964, p. 11.

civil rights legislation. In the first place, people usually share the belief that others should be treated with courtesy and tact. This attitude is reflected in most interviewing situations, including preliminary screening at employment offices. However, if the assumption is made that a stressful situation can reveal characteristics important for predicting success, interviewers may abandon courtesy for practices bordering on psychological cruelty. The validity of this assumption will be discussed later.

Developments in psychology and in interviewing techniques have had a major impact on interviewing practices. Training in nondirective counseling and skilled listening, in particular, has probably raised the quality of interviewing a great deal in the last thirty years.

Just as court decisions and administrative rulings have affected the application blank, they have also limited the kinds of questions that may be asked in an interview. As stated earlier, a wide variety of questions are off limits in all aspects of the selection process. EEOC Guidelines state:

Selection techniques other than tests . . . may be improperly used so as to have the effect of discriminating against minority groups. Such techniques include, but are not restricted to, unscored or casual interviews and unscored application forms. Where there are data suggesting employment discrimination, the person may be called upon to present evidence concerning the validity of his unscored procedures.[17]

The basic rule seems to be that if discrimination is alleged, the employer must be able to demonstrate statistically that there has been no unequal impact of the procedure on different groups, e.g., between minorities and non-minorities.

Thus, in one case the EEOC held that a black applicant for a mechanic's job was discriminated against when he was told he could not be hired because of his "police record." The applicant, an experienced mechanic, had been fined $26 for gambling. The EEOC reasoned that while 11 percent of the population is black, 70 percent of arrests for gambling involve blacks, and therefore, hiring policies based on gambling arrests records are discriminatory.[18] In another case, *EEOC* v. *Detroit Edison*, a federal court of appeals upheld a lower court decision that the company's interviewing procedures were unlawful. It was found that Detroit Edison's interviewers, who were white, had no structured format for interviewing applicants and that their interviews placed heavy reliance on subjective judgment. Since the company's employment practices had an adverse impact on the hiring of blacks, the practices were found to be unlawful.[19]

EFFECT ON NEED FULFILLMENT

It seems self-evident that interviewers should take into account the needs of the person being interviewed. This would include the needs for security, belonging, esteem, wholeness, and self-actualization. Orderly proceedings, cordiality, and the avoidance of unnecessary ego-damaging events are ingredients found in the best interviews. An applicant who is kept waiting unduly, treated coldly, insulted, or given no information is likely to display some kind of behavior inimical to a successful interview. The ill-will resulting from an unsatisfactory interview could seriously affect relations with employees or the community. The consequence of the interview, such as acceptance or rejection of the applicant, will obviously have important ramifications in need fulfillment.

[17] EEOC Guidelines, Sec. 1607.13.

[18] *Newsletter*, Greater Seattle Chapter of Pacific Northwest Personnel Management Association—American Society for Personnel Administration, March 8, 1972.

[19] Robert D. Gatewood and James Ledvinko, "Selection Interviewing and EEO: Mandate for Objectivity," *The Personnel Administrator*, 21:15–18 (May 1976).

TYPES OF INTERVIEWS BY NUMBER OF PARTICIPANTS

An applicant may be interviewed by one or a series of individuals, or by a panel or board, all of whom are present at one time; or the applicant may be involved in a series of different types of interviews. Some organizations make use of a group interview in which several applicants and one or more interviewers or observers are present. Usually this type of interview takes the form of applicants' interacting with each other instead of with interviewers, while observers make ratings of performance. This is called the "leaderless group discussion," or the "group oral performance test."[20]

One study found that a very small percentage of firms used either the group oral interview or the panel interview. It would appear that the vast majority of firms use a series of single interviews, with typical practice in the case of rank-and-file plant and office employees consisting of a screening interview conducted by the personnel department followed by an interview with the immediate supervisor. However, in the case of sales personnel and engineering applicants, this study found that the median number of interviews was three, while in the case of applicants for supervisory and executive jobs the median number of interviews was four. Findings in these last two instances suggest the participation of more people than the personnel department interviewer and the immediate supervisor.[21]

TYPES OF INTERVIEWS BY TECHNIQUE

Interviews may be highly structured as in the so-called *patterned* interview, or may be quite unstructured as in a *nondirective* type of interview. In the patterned interview, the interviewer probes certain selected aspects of the applicant's background and follows a specific, detailed checklist of items. In the nondirective type of interview, the essential technique is to allow the interview to reflect the feelings expressed by the applicant. The interviewer follows the lead of the person being interviewed—a type of interview that is an outgrowth of an approach found very useful in psychotherapy and that has been developed by Carl Rogers and others.[22]

Probably no employment interview uses the purely nondirective approach. In the pure nondirective interview, the interviewer focuses entirely on the feelings expressed by the person being interviewed and seldom, if ever, asks questions or gives information. In the employment interview, the interviewer may use the nondirective approach for certain periods of time. For example, the interviewer may ask a question such as, "How did you get along with your boss on your last job?" and then respond for a period of time by simply reflecting feeling.

In the *situational* or *problem* type of interview, a problem or project to be solved or completed is presented to the applicant or to a group of applicants. The group oral performance test is an example of this type of interview. The objective is to see how well individuals perform on the particular task or in the particular situation. The assumption underlying such a technique is that the behavior displayed in the solution of the problem is related to potential success on the job.

So-called *stress* interviews are deliberate attempts to create pressure to see how well a candidate will perform under stress. The Office of Strategic Services in World War II used stress situations a great deal in an attempt to predict

---

[20] For a discussion of the latter device, see Jayson B. Strode, "The Group Oral Performance Test," *Personnel Journal*, 50:486–487 (June 1971); and Harvey O. Blum, "New Techniques for Use with Multiple Oral Committees, *Public Personnel Review*, 27:192–194 (July 1966).

[21] Milton M. Mandell, *The Employment Interview* (New York: American Management Association, 1961), pp. 39–41.

[22] See Carl Rogers, *Counseling and Psychotherapy* (Boston: Houghton Mifflin Company, 1942).

how well candidates would perform behind enemy lines under situations of extreme stress.[23] The outcome of the OSS experiments was inconclusive.

PROBLEMS IN INTERVIEWING

One common mistake in interviewing is the tendency on the part of the interviewer to stereotype people, i.e., to have predetermined notions about broad categories of people. For example, if the interviewer has the notion that "farmers are stupid," an applicant from a farm might be treated accordingly. Stereotyping is obviously a major aspect in racial and sex discrimination.[24]

The *halo effect* is a phenomenon that has been written about a great deal. If the interviewer likes the applicant, the tendency might be to rate the applicant too high on many characteristics. On the other hand, if the interviewer dislikes someone, the tendency might be to rate that person low on all or most characteristics. Thus, to be objective in decision making, the interviewer must be careful to correct irrational feelings of either a negative or positive kind. Hostility or nervousness on the part of the applicant may be minimized if the interviewer makes an effort to establish rapport and ease at the outset of the interview.

Another problem in interviewing is the phrasing of questions. "Leading" questions can produce unreliable data. For example, the question, "You would like to work in a manufacturing firm, wouldn't you?" is likely to produce the answer, "Yes." Thus, very little information has been obtained about the applicant's real feelings and attitudes toward working for a manufacturing firm. The structure of the question suggested the answer the interviewer wanted to elicit.

Different types of interviews have certain inherent deficiencies or are susceptible to certain kinds of problems. For example, although the patterned interview insures thoroughness, it may cut down on the spontaneity of the interview and may reduce the possibility of following, or listening to, important matters mentioned by the person being interviewed. Without some use of the nondirective approach, it may be difficult to gain much information about the applicant's emotional adjustment to various matters. However, these disadvantages of the patterned interview can be overcome by thorough training of the interviewer.[25]

In the panel or board interview during which an applicant is interviewed by a number of interviewers, questions may be asked according to some prearranged order, or may be asked in random order as they arise spontaneously. The chief disadvantage of this type of interview is that it may put the applicant under considerable stress, and this may not be a valid procedure. Furthermore, panel members sometimes attempt to impress each other or to give expression to mutual hostilities at the expense of the applicant. An applicant caught in the crossfire of an internal organizational feud may be treated quite unfairly.

RELIABILITY

The reliability of a given *interviewer* in using various techniques in interviewing is determined by the consistency with which a particu-

[23] The OSS Assessment Staff, *Assessment of Men* (New York: Rinehart and Company, 1948). For a description of similar experiments in England, see Henry Harris, *The Group Approach to Leadership-Testing* (London: Routledge & Kegan Paul Ltd., 1949).

[24] For an article that discusses unconscious discrimination in interviews, see Jay T. Rusmore, "Tests, Interviews & Fair Employment." *Personnel Administration*, 31:50–55 (March–April 1968).

[25] See Robert N. McMurry, "Validating the Patterned Interview," *Personnel*, 23:263–272 (January 1947).

lar style or procedure is applied. The reliability of an *interviewing technique* is the extent to which the *technique* applied by different interviewers produces the same results when the same person is interviewed. If an interviewer has wide fluctuations in mood that result in liking people one day and disliking everybody the next, the reliability of the interviews is going to be very low. Then, too, if a number of people interview a certain candidate and their reactions to the person are quite different from one another, their techniques of interviewing might be considered unreliable.

There has been some research on the reliability of the interview. Research studies conducted during and after World War I concluded that the interview was relatively useless in the selection process. McMurry summarized this early research and concluded that nothing was proven either way, because the interviewers were probably not trained in analyzing the interview material, job specifications were lacking in two of the three experiments, none of the interviewers had an organized plan, none was necessarily intellectually qualified, and there was no check in interviewers' objectivity. On the other hand, McMurry concluded from his experiments in validity that the patterned interview can have high reliability.[26] Similar results have been reported by Schwab and Heneman[27] and by Carlson et al.[28]

Research in the U.S. Coast Guard also has demonstrated that interviews may be very reliable—the interviewers may agree in their conclusions—when conducted by ". . . well-trained interviewers working under carefully defined conditions. . . ."[29] Comparable findings are reported by Carlson et al.[30] Research on the leaderless group discussion has found high agreement among raters and high consistency in results when tests were repeated. This statement was particularly true when the raters used checklists to record characteristics of behavior.[31]

The reliability of the *interviewee* is still another issue. A study of a sample of physically handicapped people in the Minneapolis–St. Paul metropolitan area found work-history data obtained in the interview to be highly unreliable. Although memory was a factor, distortions by those interviewed were generally in a more socially desirable direction.[32] Of course, it should be noted that this was a unique sample of applicants.

VALIDITY

The validity of the employment interview is judged by the extent to which the type of interview or the kind of interviewer behaviors predict some criterion such as job acceptance by the applicant or later success or failure on the job. There has been little research on the interview's validity, an unfortunate situation in view of the almost universal use of the interview in the staffing process.

[26] Ibid., pp. 263–265, 272.
[27] D.P. Schwab and H.G. Heneman, "Relationship between Interview Structure and Inter-interviewer Reliability in an Employment Situation," *Journal of Applied Psychology*, 53:214–217 (1969).
[28] R.E. Carlson, D.P. Schwab, and H.G. Heneman, "Agreement among Selection Interview Styles," *Journal of Applied Psychology*, 5:8–17 (June 1970).
[29] Sidney Newman, Joseph Bobbitt, and Dale Cameron, "The Reliability of the Interview Method in an Officer Candidate Evaluation Program," *The American Psychologist*, 1:109 (April 1946).
[30] R.E. Carlson, P.W. Thayer, E.C. Mayfield, and D.A. Peterson, "Improvements in the Selection Interview," *Personnel Journal*, 50:268–275 (1971).
[31] Bernard M. Bass, "The Leaderless Group Discussion," *Psychological Bulletin*, 51:465–492 (September 1954). This article presents a history of this selection technique and a review of the research literature on its applicability, reliability, and validity.
[32] David J. Weiss, Rene V. Dawes, George W. England, and Lloyd H. Lofquist, *Validity of Work Histories Obtained by Interview* (Minneapolis: Industrial Relations Center, University of Minnesota, 1961), Minnesota Studies in Vocational Rehabilitation, XII, pp. 1–6.

What research has been undertaken suggests that the patterned interview results in the highest validities. McMurry reports correlation coefficients of .43 and .61 in two studies that compared ratings from patterned interviews with length of service. Another study, in which evaluations based on patterned interviews were related to supervisors' ratings, resulted in a correlation of .61.[33] Still another study found that ratings based on a standardized form could be correlated with overall ratings of supervisors. Scores on validity ranged from .48 to .99.[34] Ghiselli found a correlation of .51 between ratings made after a one-hour structured interview and survival in a stock brokerage firm.[35]

McMurry explains why the patterned interview employed with other devices is likely to improve the judgment of the interviewers:

. . . First, the interviewer works from definite job specifications; he knows what qualities each job requires. Second, he has a plan; he knows what questions to ask. Third, he has been trained in the techniques of conducting an interview, i.e., he knows how to put the candidate at ease, how to make him talk, and how to extract pertinent information. Fourth, prior to the interview, he has checked with outside sources (previous employers, schools, etc.) and already knows a great deal about the applicant. Fifth, he has a series of clinical concepts, e.g., that of emotional immaturity—which provide him with a yardstick for interpreting and evaluating the information obtained from the candidate. Sixth, the interviewer himself has been carefully selected to assure that he has adequate intelligence and is emotionally well-adjusted. [36]

Although McMurry's step four may not be practical, since reference checking is time consuming and the interviewer may prefer to postpone this step until the applicant passes the interview, nevertheless it highlights an important concept. *The more carefully clues about an applicant are checked against other information, the higher the validity of the selection procedure is likely to be.*

Research to date suggests that the stress interview has few data to support it. The OSS experiments cited earlier found that reactions to unusually stressful situations were not predictive of later performance. On the other hand, results of the leaderless group discussion have been found to correlate with leadership performance in other situations.[37]

Although the group oral examination and leaderless group discussions seem to have considerable validity in terms of predicting supervisory success, research suggests that they have about equal validity with the individual interview, the panel interview, and role-playing situations. Furthermore, when different devices are added in sequence, they contribute little to increased validity.[38] The selection of a "best" technique, therefore, may boil down to a question of economics. For example, it will cost less for one person to observe and evaluate four candidates in a group situation during the space of an hour than to interview four people

---

[33] See McMurry, "Validating the Patterned Interview," pp. 263–272. As noted earlier, the patterned interview seems to result in the highest reliability, which is an important factor in validity.

[34] K.A. Yonge, "The Value of the Interview: An Orientation and a Pilot Study," *The Journal of Applied Psychology*, 40:25–31 (February 1956). See also May H. Palacios, Lawrence A. Newberry, and Richard R. Bootzin, "Predictive Value of the Interview," *Journal of Applied Psychology*, 50:67–72 (February 1966).

[35] Edwin E. Ghiselli, "The Validity of a Personal Interview," *Personnel Psychology*, 19:389–394 (Winter 1966). See also Robert E. Carlson, Paul W. Thayer, Eugene C. Mayfield, and Donald A. Paterson, "Improvements in the Selection Interview," *Personnel Journal*, 50:268–275ff. (April 1971).

[36] McMurry, "Validating the Patterned Interview," pp. 266–267.

[37] Bass, "Leaderless Group Discussion," p. 488. Behavior measured in the leaderless group discussion tends to be of the initiating structure type rather than of the consideration type. (See Chapter 7.) See also Milton Mandell, "Validation of Group Oral Performance Test," *Personnel Psychology*, 3:179–185 (Summer 1950).

[38] Robert Glazer, Paul A. Schwarz, and John C. Flanagan, "The Contribution of Interview and Situational Performance Procedures to the Selection of Supervisory Personnel," *Journal of Applied Psychology*, 42:67–73 (April 1958).

on an individual basis for one hour each. (For more on the group oral performance test in the context of assessment centers, see Chapter 13.)

While most validity studies have focused on the type of interview by number of participants or by the general technique used as related to some subsequent measure of job performance, a few studies have inquired into the more specific behaviors of the interviewer as related to the impact on the person being interviewed. Schmitt and Cole, for example, found that students interviewed for permanent or summer jobs were more likely to accept a job offer if the interviewer was warm and thoughtful.[39]

CONCLUSIONS ABOUT THE INTERVIEW

The interview is almost universally used as a device for both parties to obtain information in making employment decisions. Since the employment interview has such significance in the staffing process and thus in all managerial processes, it would seem advisable for individual firms to conduct both extensive training and research with the objective of improving the validity of interviewing practices. At present, the patterned interview appears to have the most promise for the highest validities. Research, such as that conducted by Schmitt and Cole, which examines the interview as an interpersonal process, shows considerable promise for adding to our knowledge about effective interviewing.

PSYCHOLOGICAL TESTING

DEFINITION AND PURPOSE

Psychological tests are devices used by many organizations in the staffing process. In gen-

eral, tests constitute a sample of behavior from which inferences are drawn as to future behavior or performance. Although there is considerable overlapping, psychological tests can be conveniently grouped into five categories: personality, interest, aptitude (potential ability), achievement (or knowledge), and mental ability (or intelligence). Thus, our term "psychological testing" implies testing of all types—not just personality tests.

When used in employment, tests are usually administered after the application blank has been examined and a preliminary interview has been conducted. Many applicants are rejected for a variety of reasons before tests are even administered.

Tests are used in business and industry for three primary purposes: (a) the selection and placement of new employees—the most extensive business use, (b) appraising employees for promotional potential, and (c) counseling employees. Tests are also sometimes used in selecting employees for training programs and in evaluating candidates for transfer. If properly used, psychological tests can make contributions to each of these purposes.

CURRENT PRACTICES AND PROBLEMS

The use of testing appears to have diminished somewhat in recent years as a result of the Civil Rights Act and the enforcement of EEOC guidelines on testing. A few years ago, a study of firms of 250 employees or more reported that 77 percent had testing programs of some sort. Among these, a very high percent were using clerical and mechanical ability or aptitude tests, and almost three-fourths were using intelligence tests. More than one-third were using personality tests.[40] A more recent study, involving 2,500 firms of all sizes, found that 64

[39] Neal Schmitt and Bryan W. Cole, "Applicant Decisions in the Employment Interview," *Journal of Applied Psychology*, 61:184–192 (April 1976). See also C.P. Alderfer and C.G. McCord, "Personal and Situational Factors in the Recruitment Interview," *Journal of Applied Psychology*, 54:377–385 (August 1970).

[40] National Industrial Conference Board, *Studies in Personnel Policy*, pp. 14–15.

percent were using tests; 49 percent were using them for hiring purposes, and 24 percent were using them for promotion decisions. (Some firms used tests for both purposes.) In most prevalent usage were clerical achievement and work sample tests for clerical jobs, and mechanical knowledge and work knowledge tests for skilled hourly jobs at the entry level.[41] Assuming that this study used the term *general aptitude tests* to include intelligence tests, the data suggest a drastic decline in the use of intelligence and personality tests. Since personality tests have had the lowest reliabilities and validities over the years, their drastic decline is not surprising. But the apparent rapid decline (perhaps temporary) of intelligence testing is surprising since intelligence test scores have had relatively high predictive utility in a fairly wide range of jobs over the years.[42]

In general, there are a number of problems that emerge in the use of psychological tests. Foremost among these are the problems of validity and reliability, which I will discuss later. Another problem has to do with the qualifications of those using tests. Ordinarily, the administration of tests does not require as high a degree of qualification as does the interpretation. However, all testing should be properly supervised, and some tests, such as projective tests, should be administered only by qualified

psychologists. In general, interpretation of tests calls for a much higher level of professional skill, and a sizable number of tests should be interpreted only by qualified psychologists. Personality tests, in particular, are subject to misuse in the hands of the layperson.

Another problem is that a properly validated test or weighted application blank may deteriorate as a selective instrument with misuse. If managers do not use the test in the way it was designed to be used, it can become worthless as a selective device.

Certain costs involved in the use of tests should be considered. As a general rule, the tests themselves are not expensive, but equipment, space, and the salaries of those administering and interpreting tests are costs of consequence. If tests are administered to employees during regular working hours, time away from the job must be considered a cost item. The process of validating tests, now almost mandatory under EEOC guidelines, also tends to be expensive.[43] These costs must be evaluated in terms of possible savings to be gained as a result of improving the selection process.

Applicants' or employees' acceptance is another problem. If testing is going to repel qualified applicants or disrupt an entire work force, it is probably not worth the trouble. Acceptance of testing can usually be gained but, increasingly, job relevancy is a factor in the minds of applicants as well as government officials.

Then, too, ethical problems can arise in the use of tests. Safeguards must be maintained so that unauthorized persons do not have access to test results. If promises are made during research that test results will not be used to anyone's disadvantage, this agreement must be

---

[41] "Employee Testing and Selection Procedures—Where Are They Headed?" *Personnel Management: Policies and Practices,* p. 658.

[42] This may be explained partly by the fact that an intelligence test figured in the U.S. Supreme Court *Griggs* v. *Duke Power Company* case (discussed later in this chapter). For a review of the validity of personality tests, see Robert M. Guion and Richard F. Gottier, "Validity of Personality Measures in Personnel Selection," *Personnel Psychology,* 18:135–164 (Summer 1965). For a discussion of intelligence tests, see Alexander Wesman, "Intelligent Testing," *American Psychologist,* 23:267–274 (April 1968). For a summary of the validity of different kinds of tests, see E.E. Ghiselli, *The Validity of Occupational Aptitude Tests* (New York: John Wiley & Sons, 1966); and Edwin E. Ghiselli, "The Validity of Aptitude Tests in Personnel Selection," *Personnel Psychology,* 20:461–477 (Winter 1973).

[43] Twenty-eight percent of firms in one survey spent more than $5,000 per type of job studied. "Employment Testing and Selection Procedures," *Personnel Management: Policies and Practices,* p. 676.

meticulously kept. Furthermore, the results of certain kinds of tests—personality tests, in particular—should not be given to managers untrained in their use because of the dangers of misinterpretation.

There is also the major problem that results of a test may become substituted for managerial judgment. This problem is not restricted to psychological testing. It is a problem in the use of any personnel device. Results of tests should be only one factor in staffing decisions.[44]

VALIDITY

Probably the most common deficiency found in industrial testing programs is lack of knowledge about the validity of the tests. Far too often assumptions are made about what the tests are doing, but there is no attempt to verify the assumptions. Sometimes tests are used that have been validated in other situations; but, unless the organization using the test is confident that its situation is very similar, no one may be sure what the test is measuring. Even if the situations appear very similar, there may be some doubt.[45]

From a statistical standpoint, *validity* is the extent to which a test predicts a criterion. As Horst states it, ". . . statistical validity refers to the correlation between a predictor and a criterion measure."[46] The criterion is a measure of some degree of success in performance, that is, the criterion is what you are trying to predict. Ordinarily, in industrial testing, validity means the extent to which a test will predict some criterion of job success, although such criteria as attendance or safety records are sometimes used. *The most common mistake, then, is use of a test without knowledge of how accurately the test predicts job performance.*

Selecting a criterion is a big problem in itself. In other words, what is meant by success, if success is what we want to predict? A number of complexities are immediately encountered. For example, if we want to decide on a criterion of success for a salesperson, should we use gross sales per year, number of new customers per year, or net profit on the items that were sold? If we use gross sales per year, should we also take into account type and size of territory, previous sales effort, the kind of customers located in this area, etc? If we use success ratings by supervisors as a criterion of success, are the ratings of the various supervisors objective and free from personal biases? Does one supervisor rate subordinates high and another rate subordinates low? How reliable are the ratings of an individual supervisor? Do raters evaluating the same people know them equally well? How valid is the criterion, that is, to what degree is it related to contributing to the goals of the enterprise? Are we trying to predict success on the immediate job, or are we trying to predict long-range success at higher levels of responsibility? All these are problems in determining an appropriate criterion of success. *Determining an appropriate criterion is probably the most difficult problem in testing; it is probably the step most often not done at all; and, ideally, it is one of the first things that should be done.*[47]

---

[44] For a further discussion of problems in industrial testing, see William C. Byham and Stephen Temlock, "Operational Validity—A New Concept in Personnel Testing," *Personnel Journal*, 51:639–647ff. (September 1972).

[45] It should be emphasized that the validity problem also plagues the use of other personnel devices, such as the application blank and the interview. Furthermore, it should be emphasized that *high scores* are not necessarily related to success in some kinds of jobs. The problem in a validity study is to find out what kind of a score—high, medium, or low—is related to successful performance. For a description of a test validation procedure, see Raymond W. Kulhovy, "Personnel Testing: Validating Selection Instruments," *Personnel*, 48:20–24 (September-October 1971).

[46] Paul Horst, "The Logic of Personnel Selection and Classification," in Robert M. Gagne, ed., *Psychological Principles*

---

in System Development (New York: Holt, Rinehart and Winston, 1962), p. 258.

[47] For an extensive discussion of the criterion problem, see Patricia C. Smith, "Behavior, Results, and Organizational Ef-

Once scores on the criterion are obtained, statistical validation requires the computation of the correlation between scores on tests and scores on the criterion. The correlation coefficient becomes the measure of validity. Once this coefficient is computed, statements about the probability of success, given different test scores, can be calculated. For statistical stability, such research should involve at least fifty people in similar jobs, people for whom both test scores and criterion scores are available.[48]

Among other approaches to validation is the identification of "job component validity," more commonly called "synthetic validity." This procedure involves identifying the major components of jobs through job analysis, determining what human qualities are required to perform these components, and then selecting tests that have previously been shown to be predictive of performance in these components. Batteries of tests are then assembled for various jobs consistent with their respective job components.[49] This technique is useful when there is a need to validate tests for jobs with small sample sizes.

It should be noted that the Supreme Court, in *Albermarle Paper Company et al.* v. *Joseph P. Moody*, confirmed the EEOC's interpretation that performance ratings, frequently used as criteria in prediction studies, fell within the category of "tests." The clear implication is that such criteria must be carefully defined and must be justifiable in terms of behaviors required by the job.[50] It should also be noted in the *Washington* v. *Davis* case, the Supreme Court held that success in a training program that was job related could be used as a criterion for validating employment tests.[51]

A CLINICAL-STATISTICAL APPROACH

In addition to statistical validation, there is also "clinical" or "judgmental" validation. In clinical validation, the psychologist uses an individual's score on tests in conjunction with as many other data about the person as can be reasonably obtained, and draws upon his or her experience to determine what certain test scores tend to mean in terms of behavior on the job. In the absence of statistical validation, clinical validation is much better than no validation at all. Even with clinical validation, however, wisdom suggests keeping track of one's "batting average" so as to check assumptions about what tests are really predicting. In the absence of strong reasons prohibiting it, statistical validation should always be undertaken.[52]

fectiveness: The Problem of Criteria," in Dunnette, ed., *Handbook,* pp. 745–775.

[48] For space reasons, this discussion will not go into the details of different criteria-related validation procedures. For predictive, concurrent, and classificatory methods of validation, see *Principles for the Validation and Use of Personnel Selection Procedures*, Division of Industrial-Organizational Psychology, American Psychological Association, 1975 (pamphlet, 19 pp.) This publication includes a glossary of terms. See also Marvin D. Dunnette, "The Strategies and the Statistics of Validation," *Personnel Selection and Placement* (Belmont, Calif.: Wadsworth, 1966), pp. 113–159; and Robert M. Guion, "Recruiting, Selection, and Job Placement," in Dunnette, ed., *Handbook,* pp. 777–828.

[49] See Ernest J. McCormick and Angelo S. DeNisi, "An Alternate Approach to Test Validation," *The Personnel Administrator,* 21:56–59 (January 1976). For other essays on validation procedures, see Arthur I. Siegel and Brian A. Bergman, "A Job Learning Approach to Performance Predicting," *Personnel Psychology,* 28:325–339, No. 3 (Autumn 1975); Craig Eric Schneier, "Content Validity: The Necessity of a Behavioral Job Description," *The Personnel Administrator,* 21:38–44 (February 1976); and Sidney Gael, Donald L. Grant, and Richard J. Ritchie, "Employment Test Validation for Minority and Nonminority Telephone Operators," *Journal of Applied Psychology,* 60:411–419 (August 1975).

[50] Mark Lifter, "Validation Requirements Clarified by Supreme Court," *The Industrial-Organizational Psychologist,* 13:24–25 (February 1976).

[51] For details of the case, see Washington Newsletter, *American Society for Personnel Administration,* December 10, 1975, pp. 1–4.

[52] The relative accuracy of statistical versus clinical validation has been discussed by Paul Meehl, *Clinical Versus Statistical Prediction* (Minneapolis: University of Minnesota Press, 1954). While Meehl finds that statistical prediction appears to be the most accurate, and concludes by saying ". . . always the actuary will have the final word" (p. 138), Korman

From my experience, a viable approach to using tests for selection involves a combination of statistical and clinical validation. Since no tests will have perfect statistical validity, the more data that can be used to confirm or reject clues obtained from testing, the better. In my opinion, data from tests should always be used in conjunction with information from the interview, the application blank or résumé, and the reference check. Through such crosschecking, the highest validities are likely to be obtained.

RELIABILITY

Closely related to the problem of validity is that of reliability. *Reliability* is the extent to which test results are consistent. In developing tests there have been three traditional ways of determining some indication of reliability: (1) the *repeat* or *test-retest* method (giving the test again); (2) the *alternate-form* method (giving a second form of the test to see if similar results are obtained); and (3) the *split-half* method (dividing the test into two parts). In each method, a correlation coefficient is computed to determine the degree of consistency.

An important factor affecting reliability is the degree to which responses on tests can be faked by the person taking the test. Although this is unreliability on the part of the test-taker, it presents a test-reliability problem. "Fakability" is probably increasing as people become more familiar with tests through direct experience or through articles and books.

If a test is unreliable—if it measures inconsistently—validity is bound to be low. If the accuracy of the test score cannot be relied upon, the statistics that relate test scores to the criterion cannot be relied upon. Most publishers of tests present statistics as to test reliability; validity statistics, however, are less readily available.

IMPACT OF ENVIRONMENT

CRITICISM AND NAIVETÉ Popular and professional literature that either condemns or praises psychological testing has a significant impact on both the general public and company executives responsible for determining whether tests will be used. Probably in no other area of personnel management has there been so much controversy. It is interesting to note that less is known about the validity of the interview than is known about test validity, yet the latter has been subjected to far more criticism.

In recent years, critics of psychological testing have been particularly active in scholarly journals and the popular press, as well as in the hearing room or courtroom. But criticism of psychological testing is not new, since it has been a controversial subject for nearly seventy years.[53] A good deal of the recent criticism focuses on the use of personality tests. While some of the criticisms have merit, such as those that question the use of tests with dubious reliability and validity, some criticisms are fallacious. For example, the argument has been advanced that attempting to predict human behavior is immoral because it violates the personal destiny of a person. This argument fails to hold up, because every selection decision, whether made by a business person in hiring or promoting or by a voter at the ballot box, assumes that the candidate selected will perform better than someone else. There is little question, however, that tests are often misused and

---

finds that "judgmental prediction" may be as useful as actuarial prediction. See Abraham K. Korman, "The Prediction of Managerial Performance: A Review," *Personnel Psychology*, 21:295–322 (1968). See also Jack Sawyer, "Measurement and Prediction, Clinical and Statistical," *Psychology Bulletin*, 66:178–200 (September 1966).

[53] For example, a 1911 article by C.S. Myers in the *British Medical Journal* was entitled "The Pitfalls of 'Mental' Tests." See also a critical review of Hugo Munsterberg's book, *Psychology and Industrial Efficiency*, in a 1919 book by Roy Kelly, *Hiring the Worker* (New York: The Engineering Magazine, 1919), pp. 234–235. In his review, Kelly was very critical of Munsterberg's claims as to the utility of psychological testing.

that managers can be too gullible and overenthusiastic about them.[54]

Thus, sensational criticism and administrative and court rulings, on the one hand, and gullibility and overenthusiasm, on the other, have had an impact on the use of tests by organizations. The first has sometimes resulted in a complete rejection of tests, the second, in over reliance or improper use.

CIVIL RIGHTS LAWS AND COURT DECISIONS   As indicated above, the civil rights movement has also had a major impact on testing programs. *Myart* v. *Motorola*, involing alleged discrimination against a black in Chicago on the basis of a brief intelligence test,[55] served to dramatize the concern of civil rights leaders that testing procedures might be discriminating unfairly against minorities. As a partial consequence, Congress included a statement in the Civil Rights Act prohibiting discrimination through testing, but specifically affirming the rights of employers to use tests:

. . . nor shall it be unlawful employment practice for an employer to give and to act upon the results of any professionally developed ability test provided that such test, its administration or action upon the results is not designed, intended or used to discriminate because of race, color, religion, sex or national origin. . . .[56]

Subsequently, both the Equal Employment Opportunity Commission and the Office of Federal Contract Compliance (OFCC) issued guidelines on testing. These guidelines go into considerable detail and focus particularly on validation standards, including those pertaining to minority group inclusion in validation samples, type of criteria used, and test utility. (See Figure 12-4 for excerpts from EEOC guidelines on testing.[57])

Although a great deal of litigation has occurred to probe the full meaning of the testing provisions of the Civil Rights Act and the EEOC and OFCC guidelines, a decision by the U.S. Supreme Court in the *Griggs* v. *Duke Power Company* case has served to clarify some of the issues. In this case, the Court held that the employer discriminated against blacks by requiring a high school education or the passing of a standardized intelligence test as a condition of employment or transfer because

. . . (a) neither standard is shown to be significantly related to successful job performance, (b) both requirements operate to disqualify Negroes at a substantially higher rate than white applicants, and (c) the jobs in question formerly had been filled only by white employees as part of a longstanding practice of giving preference to whites.[58]

Of additional significance are the following statements in the *Griggs* v. *Duke* court decision:

Congress did not intend by Title VII, however, to guarantee a job to every person regardless of qualifications. In short, the Act does not command that any person be hired simply because he was formerly the subject of discrimination, or because he is a member of a minority group. Discriminatory preference for any group, minority or majority, is precisely and only what Congress has proscribed. What is required by Congress is the removal of artificial, arbitrary, and unnecessary barriers to employment when the barriers operate invidiously to discriminate on the

[54]Stagner has described the naiveté of some personnel directors about testing. Ross Stagner, "The Gullibility of Personnel Managers," *Personnel Psychology*, 11:347–352 (Autumn 1958).

[55]See Howard C. Lockwood, "Testing Minority Applicants for Employment," *Personnel Journal*, 44:356–360ff. (July-August 1965).

[56]Title VII, Civil Rights Act of 1964, Section 703 (h). Age discrimination through testing is also of concern to the wage-hour administrator. Interpretative statements (860:14) refer to the "test-sophistication" of younger people, and indicate that when tests are used as the sole or controlling factor, their use as it impacts the age factor will be carefully scrutinized." Bureau of National Affairs, *Labor Relations Reporter, Fair Employment Practices Manual*, 401:5077.

[57]A draft of a new "Uniform Selection Guidelines," developed by the Equal Employment Opportunity Coordinating Council composed of representatives from five federal agencies, was published for comment in 1976.

[58]U.S. Supreme Court, *Willie S. Griggs et al.* v. *Duke Power Company*, March 8, 1971.

Figure **12-4**   Excerpts from Equal Employment Opportunity Commission Guidelines on Employee Selection Procedures

---

§ *1607.2   "Test" defined.*

For the purpose of the guidelines in this part, the term "test" is defined as any paper-and-pencil or performance measure used as a basis for any employment decision. The guidelines in this part apply, for example, to ability tests which are designed to measure eligibility for hire, transfer, promotion, membership, training, referral or retention. This definition includes, but is not restricted to, measures of general intelligence, mental ability and learning ability; specific intellectual abilities; mechanical, clerical and other aptitudes; dexterity and coordination; knowledge and proficiency; occupational and other interests; and attitudes, personality or temperament. The term "test" includes all formal, scored, quantified or standardized techniques of assessing job suitability including, in addition to the above, specific qualifying or disqualifying personal history or background requirements, specific educational or work history requirements, scored interviews, biographical information blanks, interviewers' rating scales, scored application forms, etc.

§ *1607.3   Discrimination defined.*

The use of any test which adversely affects hiring, promotion, transfer or any other employment or membership opportunity of classes protected by Title VII constitutes discrimination unless: (a) the test has been validated and evidences a high degree of utility as hereinafter described, and (b) the person giving or acting upon the results of the particular test can demonstrate that alternative suitable hiring, transfer or promotion procedures are unavailable for his use.

§ *1607.4   Evidence of validity.*

(a) Each person using tests to select from among candidates for a position or for membership shall have available for inspection evidence that the tests are being used in a manner which does not violate § 1607.3. Such evidence shall be examined for indications of possible discrimination, such as instances of higher rejection rates for minority candidates than nonminority candidates. Furthermore, where technically feasible, a test should be validated for each minority group with which it is used; that is, any differential rejection rates that may exist, based on a test, must be relevant to performance of the jobs in question.

(b) The term "technically feasible" as used in these guidelines means having or obtaining a sufficient number of minority individuals to achieve findings of statistical and practical significance, the opportunity to obtain unbiased job performance criteria, etc. It is the responsibility of the person claiming absence of technical feasibility to positively demonstrate evidence of this absence. . . .

§ *1607.5   Minimum standards for validation.*

(a) For the purpose of satisfying the requirements of this part, empirical evidence in support of a test's validity must be based on studies employing generally accepted procedures for determining criterion-related validity, such as those described in "Standards for Educational and Psychological Tests and Manuals" published by American Psychological Association, 1200 17th Street NW., Washington, D.C. 20036. Evidence of content or construct validity, as defined in that publication, may also be appropriate where criterion-related validity is not feasible. However, evidence for content or construct validity should be accompanied by sufficient information from job analyses to demonstrate the relevance of the content (in the case of job knowledge or proficiency tests) or the construct (in the case of trait measures). Evidence of content validity alone may be acceptable for well-developed tests that consist of suitable samples of the essential knowledge, skills or behaviors composing the job in question. The types of knowledge, skills or behaviors contemplated here do not include those which can be acquired in a brief orientation to the job. . . .

(1) Where a validity study is conducted in which tests are administered to applicants, with criterion data collected later, the sample of subjects must be representative of the normal or typical candidate group for the job or jobs in question. This further assumes that the applicant sample is representative of the minority population available for the job or jobs in question in the local labor market. Where a validity study is conducted in which tests are administered to present employees, the sample must be representative of the minority groups currently included in the applicant population. If it is not technically feasible to include minority employees in validation studies conducted on the present work force, the conduct of a validation study without minority

Figure 12-4 Excerpts from Equal Employment Opportunity Commission Guidelines on Employee Selection Procedures (*cont.*)

candidates does not relieve any person of his subsequent obligation for validation when inclusion of minority candidates becomes technically feasible.

(2) Tests must be administered and scored under controlled and standardized conditions, with proper safeguards to protect the security of test scores and to insure that scores do not enter into any judgments of employee adequacy that are to be used as criterion measures. Copies of tests and test manuals, including instructions for administration, scoring, and interpretations of test results, that are privately developed and/or are not available through normal commercial channels must be included as a part of the validation evidence.

(3) The work behaviors or other criteria of employee adequacy which the test is intended to predict or identify must be fully described; and, additionally, in the case of rating techniques, the appraisal form(s) and instructions to the rater(s) must be included as a part of the validation evidence. Such criteria may include measures other than actual work proficiency, such as training time, supervisory ratings, regularity of attendance and tenure. Whatever criteria are used they must represent major or critical work behaviors as revealed by careful job analyses.

(4) In view of the possibility of bias inherent in subjective evaluations, supervisory rating techniques should be carefully developed, and the ratings should be closely examined for evidence of bias. In addition, minorities might obtain unfairly low performance criterion scores for reasons other than supervisors' prejudice, as, when, as new employees, they have had less opportunity to learn job skills. The general point is that all criteria need to be examined to insure freedom from factors which would unfairly depress the scores of minority groups.

(5) Differential validity. Data must be generated and results separately reported for minority and non-minority groups whenever technically feasible. . . .

(c) In assessing the utility of a test the following considerations will be applicable:

(1) The relationship between the test and at least one relevant criterion must be statistically significant. This ordinarily means that the relationship should be sufficiently high as to have a probability of no more than 1 to 20 to have occurred by chance. However, the use of a single test as the sole selection device will be scrutinized closely when that test is valid against only one component of job performance.

(2) In addition to statistical significance, the relationship between the test and criterion should have practical significance. The magnitude of the relationship needed for practical significance or usefulness is affected by several factors, including:

(i) The larger the proportion of applicants who are hired for or placed on the job, the higher the relationship needs to be in order to be practically useful. Conversely, a relatively low relationship may prove useful when proportionately few job vacancies are available;

(ii) The larger the proportion of applicants who become satisfactory employees when not selected on the basis of the test, the higher the relationship needs to be between the test and a criterion of job success for the test to be practically useful. Conversely, a relatively low relationship may prove useful when proportionately few applicants turn out to be satisfactory;

(iii) The smaller the economic and human risks involved in hiring an unqualified applicant relative to the risks entailed in rejecting a qualified applicant, the greater the relationship needs to be in order to be practically useful. Conversely, a relatively low relationship may prove useful when the former risks are relatively high. . . .

§ *1607.8 Assumption of validity.*

(a) Under no circumstances will the general reputation of a test, its author or its publisher, or casual reports of test utility be accepted in lieu of evidence of validity. . . .

From *U.S. Equal Employment Opportunity Commission Guidelines,* August 1970.

basis of racial or other impermissible classification. . . .

If an employment practice which operates to exclude Negroes cannot be shown to be related to job performance, the practice is prohibited. . . .

Nothing in the Act precludes the use of testing or measuring procedures; obviously they are useful. What Congress has forbidden is giving these devices and mechanisms controlling force unless they are demonstrably a reasonable measure of job performance. Congress has not commanded that the less qualified be preferred over the better qualified simply because of minority origins. Far from disparaging job qualifications as such, Congress has made such qualifications the controlling factor, so that race, religion, nationality, and sex become irrelevant. What Congress has commanded is that any tests used must measure the person for the job and not the person in the abstract. . . .[59]

Therefore, it is important that the employer be able to show (1) that the selection device does not exclude a disproportionate percentage of a particular protected group, or (2) that, if it does exclude a disproportionate percentage of the protected group, the selection device is reasonably necessary to the efficient and orderly operation of the enterprise.[60]

Two test validation questions, then, emerge: Does the test predict successful or unsuccessful job performance and to what degree? Is the test a better predictor of performance for one ethnic group than another? Contradictory results have emerged with respect to this second question. One study suggests that tests (a) may not be equally predictive of success for different ethnic groups and (b) that an ethnic group may score lower on a battery of tests but perform equally well on the job. The researchers who arrived at these conclusions studied the test scores and the job performance of 1,208 subjects, including 795 white, 88 Spanish-speaking, and 325 black workers, in six job situations. As a result, one

of their recommendations is that organizations either validate tests separately for different ethnic groups or that test scores be adjusted to correct for differentials in validities.[61] As one author puts it, *"Unfair discrimination exists when persons with equal probabilities of success on the job have unequal probabilities of being hired for the job."* [62]

In general, however, research tends not to support the notion of differential validities between groups.[63] For example, a study conducted jointly by the Educational Testing Service and the U.S. Civil Service Commission, found that carefully selected tests predicted job performance fairly for both minority and majority groups. This study was conducted over a six-year period to ". . . explore the oft-expressed belief that tests are biased against minority groups. . . . Six years later, we found that belief was wrong, if you define bias as meaning the scores are unrealistically low in relation to performance on the job." [64] Basically, the study compared scores on job-related

[59]Ibid.

[60]See Mary T. Matthies, "The Developing Law of Equal Employment Opportunity," *Journal of Contemporary Business*, 5:29–46 (Winter 1976).

[61]"Employment Tests and Ethnic Discrimination," *Employment Service Review*, 4:22–23 (October 1967). For similar conclusions, see Edward Ruda and Lewis E. Albright, "Racial Differences on Selection Instruments Related to Subsequent Job Performance," *Personnel Psychology*, 21:30–41 (Spring 1968).

[62]Robert M. Guion, "Employment Tests and Discriminatory Hiring," *Industrial Relations*, 5:26 (February 1966).

[63]Cameron Fincher, "Differential Validity and Test Bias," *Personnel Psychology*, 28:481–500 (Winter 1975). For a survey of the literature that concluded that research has not conclusively demonstrated that test scores have different validites among subcultures, see Merle E. Ace, "Psychological Testing: Unfair Discrimination?" *Industrial Relations*, 10:301–315 (October 1971). See also Virginia R. Boehm, "Negro-White Differences in Validity of Employment and Training Selection Procedures," *Journal of Applied Psychology*, 56:33–39 (February 1972).

[64]Quote from Dr. Joel T. Campbell, director of the project, in "Tests Win a Vote of Confidence," *Manpower*, December 1972, p. 11. For the original study, see Lois A. Crooks, ed., *An Investigation of Sources of Bias in the Prediction of Job Performance: A Six-Year Study*, Proceedings of Invitational Conference, The Barclay Hotel, New York, New York, June 22, 1972 (Princeton, N.J.: Educational Testing Service, 1972).

tests and subsequent job performance as measured by supervisory ratings, a job knowledge test, and a work sample. Included in the sample were 1,409 federal employees, including 423 blacks and 174 Spanish-speaking Americans. Three jobs were included in the study: medical technician, cartographic technician, and inventory management specialist. Job incumbents across the ethnic groups were performing essentially the same kind of work, and were similar in education, training, experience, and age. The results showed that the tests were predictive of job success and that they predicted about equally as well for the different ethnic groups. While the minority groups, on the average, performed less well on the tests, some minority members scored substantially above the average for the sample as a whole, and some minority members scored substantially below the average for minority members.[65]

The latter findings may serve to identify the problem associated with the first question we raised. The tests may, indeed, be predicting job success, and the test results, in turn, may be reflecting differences in educational and cultural backgrounds. In short, certain educational and cultural attributes may be associated with job success. In such instances, as one author puts it, ". . . it is not the tests that are unfair, it is society."[66] As a short-range, partial solution, the organization may wish to establish remedial training programs, which can make an important social contribution and, in many instances, be profitable as well.

LABOR-MANAGEMENT RELATIONS   Psychological tests are also a controversial matter in labor-management relations and collective bargaining. Labor unions are beginning to question the validity of testing practices and filing grievances in this connection, taking cases to arbitration, and, in some instances, winning their cases. In at least one instance, a strike was precipitated because of alleged misuses of tests.[67] In 1968 the AFL-CIO suggested to its member unions that they bargain to have testing prohibited. If this failed, unions were urged to bargain for a number of controls, including proper validation procedures.[68]

As examples of arbitration cases focusing on tests, an arbitrator handed down a decision stating that the tests used by the management of a steel company to measure employees' ability to perform the work of jobs that were open were not appropriate to the jobs in question.[69] In another case, involving a hardware company, an arbitrator ruled that a test was invalid and that it could not be used "to predict job performance with reasonable accuracy."[70] In still another case an arbitrator held that, when challenged through the grievance procedure, management was obliged to disclose the method of administering tests and to demonstrate the validity of tests used in making promotions.[71]

TECHNOLOGY AND SCIENCE   Technology and science have had a major impact on testing in two ways. In the first place, the development of statistical procedures for use in designing and validating tests are scientific innovations. Secondly, the development of high-speed com-

[65] Ibid., pp. 11–12.
[66] Richard S. Barrett, "Gray Areas in Black and White Testing," *Harvard Business Review*, 46:92–95 (January-February 1968).
[67] George Hagglund, "Psychological Tests and Grievance Arbitration," in Bureau of National Affairs, *Collective Bargaining Negotiating and Contracts*, 1, 17:281, February 4, 1971.
[68] William C. Byham and Morton E. Spitzer, "Personnel Testing: The Law and Its Implications," *Personnel*, 48:8–19 (October 1971).
[69] Bureau of National Affairs, *Bulletin to Management*, March 3, 1960, p. 1.
[70] *Summary of Labor Arbitration Awards*, American Arbitration Report No. 9, December 15, 1959, p. 1.
[71] Bureau of National Affairs, *Labor Arbitration Reports*, 33LA 713. See also John H. Metzler, "Testing Under Labor Contracts and Law," *Personnel*, 43:40–44 (July-August 1966).

puters has made it possible to solve very complex problems in prediction and classification.

LABOR MARKET The labor market and an organization's success in developing sources of applicants will partly determine the feasibility of any testing program. If, for example, there are only 80 applicants and 230 job openings, it may be necessary to employ almost all the applicants, and there would be little point in testing applicants. On the other hand, if there are 50 applicants and 1 job opening, testing might assist in making the decision. A test with a much lower validity coefficient can be used in the latter case rather than in a situation where only a few applicants are to be rejected. If only a small percentage of applicants is to be rejected, the tests must be able to do an excellent job in predicting success or failure.[72] (See the EEOC Guidelines in Figure 12-4.)

EFFECT ON NEED FULFILLMENT

Applicants for new positions, transfers, or promotions are likely to be curious about any tests to which they are subjected; more and more applicants are concerned about the appropriateness of the tests they are required to take. These needs for knowledge and understanding will be frustrated if no explanation or description of testing purposes is given to the applicant. Although scores on tests may be only one of a number of factors used in staffing decisions, the probable weight of the test scores is likely to loom extremely high in the eyes of the applicant. For these reasons, careful explanation of the pertinence and use of tests is highly

desirable from the point of view of relations with the public and employees.

AUTHORITY AND ACCOUNTABILITY

Ordinarily, tests are administered by the personnel department, and any research on the validity of the instruments used will be conducted or coordinated by that office. One of the obvious implications of the Civil Rights Act and federal and state guidelines on testing is that the staff of the personnel department must either develop considerable competency in testing and test validation or employ outside experts—probably qualified psychologists and/or psychometricians—to assist in these processes. Regardless of how the testing activities are assigned, central control of testing is of paramount importance if misuse of tests is to be avoided. Serious mistakes are bound to occur in any testing program if every supervisor feels qualified to administer and interpret psychological tests. It should be noted that numerous court decisions have ruled that tests must be applied fairly to all candidates.[73]

Cut-off points used in selection should be based on careful research. Although the personnel department may be justified in establishing such cut-offs, mutual discussion of minimum standards between the personnel staff and department heads is recommended. Joint decision making in employment is the usual practice, and results of tests are typically used as only one of a number of variables considered in staffing decisions.

A unique authority situation exists under many civil service systems. After an "examination announcement" is made, candidates who pass a preliminary screening on the basis of credentials (such as a high school diploma) are tested, and the top three, five, or however

[72] Lee J. Cronbach and Goldine C. Gleser, *Psychological Tests and Personnel Decisions*, 2nd ed. (Urbana: University of Illinois Press, 1965); and Ervin W. Curtis and Edward F. Alf, "Validity, Predictive Efficiency, and Practical Significance of Selection Tests," *Journal of Applied Psychology*, 53:327–337 (August 1969).

[73] Bonnie Sandman and Faith Urban, "Employment Testing and the Law," *Labor Law Journal*, 27:52 (January 1976).

many predetermined by a referral rule, are entered on a register. The supervisor then chooses among those on the list. This so-called rule of three (or five, etc.) procedure has tended to thwart the entrance of minority group members into civil service employment and increasingly has come under challenge.[74] As a result, civil service rules in some jurisdictions are being liberalized.[75] Implicit in this is that city, county, state, and federal civil service commissions have wide authority in establishing personnel rules and procedures.

CONCLUSIONS ABOUT TESTING

Testing can improve managerial decision making in the staffing process, but the users must be aware of the many technical, administrative, ethical, and legal problems involved. In any testing program, there is no substitute for joint planning and cooperation between the well-informed executive and the trained psychologist. Typically, the personnel department will be held accountable for the proper administration of the testing program, which has obvious implications for the qualifications of the members of that department. Results of tests must not be used as substitutes for managerial decision making but should be used as tools in making decisions in conjunction with other data obtained about applicants.

In particular, testing can make its most useful contribution in the context of a comprehensive clinical-statistical approach to selection by (1) careful development of a theory about successful performance on specific jobs based on evi-

dence from research, (2) use of background, interview, test, and reference-checking data to develop a composite picture of a candidate, with clues from one source always crosschecked against clues from another source, (3) prediction about performance on the job in question, and (4) continual refinement of theory through statistical validation studies, further research evidence, and the careful evaluation of past experience. Through this approach, coupled with upgrading the qualifications of people interpreting tests, employee selection can be significantly improved.

PHYSICAL EXAMINATIONS

The physical examination is another device (or subsystem) typically found as a component in the staffing system of business and industrial enterprises. In one study, 71 percent of the responding firms reported pre-employment physical examinations in the case of both blue-collar and white-collar employees, and another 14 percent reported using them in the case of blue-collar employees only.[76]

These examinations conducted by a physician can have a number of purposes. One objective would be to screen out applicants who might be expensive liabilities because of excessive absenteeism due to illness or injury. Another purpose would be to prevent injury or damage to the health of employees by placing them in appropriate job situations. Although medical specialists prefer to emphasize placement rather than selection as the purpose of physical examinations, it is clear that physical examinations are partly used by many firms for screening purposes. However, research has usually not identified the purposes of the examinations among different firms, and it is difficult to assess the trends precisely. It appears, how-

[74] Philip Ash and Leonard P. Kroeker, "Personnel Selection, Classification, and Placement," in Mark R. Rosenzweig and Lyman W. Porter, eds., *Annual Review of Psychology*, 1975, 26, pp. 489–490.
[75] N. Joseph Cayer, *Public Personnel Administration in the United States* (New York: St. Martin's Press, 1975), pp. 77–78. See also Jean J. Couturier, "The Quiet Revolution in Public Personnel Laws," *Public Personnel Management*, 5:150–167 (May-June 1976).
[76] National Industrial Conference Board, p. 116.

6

5548

ever, that labor-market shortages in World War II encouraged the use of physical examinations for placement, and that this practice has grown steadily.[77]

The degree to which a company is liable for subsequent injuries to an already handicapped individual varies from state to state, and the development of employment policies must be considered in light of these laws. In general, provisions for a second-injury fund in state laws limit a second employer's liability in the event of a subsequent job-incurred injury and restrict liability to injuries or diseases resulting from the present job.[78]

Although not often mentioned in the literature, one purpose of physical examinations at the time of employment is to have a record of the physical condition of the applicant in order to prevent employees' filing workers' compensation claims for preexisting injuries.

Proponents of the preplacement physical examination argue that many applicants—including handicapped people—are ably suited for many kinds of jobs if a positive approach is taken to their placement. Furthermore, it is argued that because of technological innovations physical strength is becoming less important in job situations and that many other attributes are becoming more important. In addition, industries have found that the preemployment physical examination does not guarantee that accident rates or workmen's compensation claims will be lowered.[79]

REFERENCE CHECKS

Reference checking consists of verifying information provided by an applicant, or obtaining additional information, by communicating with previous employers or others who have known the applicant. Reference checks are usually made by telephone, less frequently by mail, and occasionally in person.

One survey indicated that more than half of 2,500 reporting firms checked with candidates' previous employers concerning job performance.[80] This is a marked decline from a previous study completed eleven years earlier that indicated that more than 90 percent of employers checked references,[81] but it still indicates widespread usage. Undoubtedly, this decline is due to civil rights legislation and EEOC guidelines that have instilled considerable caution in employers.

The opinions of previous supervisors, to the degree they are candid, can be especially useful in rounding out a picture of potential performance on a particular job. Here again, the assumption is made that the data are useful in predicting successful performance. There is considerable face validity in this assumption, since previous performance is usually a fair predictor of future performance. Telephone conversations are particularly useful. Through such conversations specific questions pertinent to the job may be asked.

On the other hand, requesting information by letter may be much less satisfactory. In the absence of very detailed questions, the person answering a letter is likely to give the applicant the benefit of the doubt to such an extent that

[77] See Albert Q. Maisel, ed., *The Health of People Who Work* (New York: The National Health Council, 1960), pp. 95–98.
[78] See *State Workmen's Compensation Laws: A Comparison of Major Provisions with Recommended Standards* (Washington, D.C.: U.S. Department of Labor, Bureau of Labor Standards, December, 1961), Bulletin No. 212, Revised, p. 22; and National Commission on State Workmen's Compensation Laws, *The Report of the National Commission on State Workmen's Compensation Laws*, Washington, D.C., 1972.
[79] Maisel, *Health of People Who Work*, p. 95. The preplacement approach does not necessarily exclude the selection approach. No one would argue that an applicant who cannot safely perform the work should be employed. In this sense,

these terms may not accurately convey the purpose of the examination. Perhaps most are "employment-placement" examinations.
[80] "Employee Testing and Selection Procedures, *Personnel Management: Policies and Practices*, p. 264.
[81] National Industrial Conference Board, *Studies in Personnel Policy*, p. 12.

such letters tend to be of little help. The person reading the letter may tend to look for what the letter does not say. In short, such a procedure is probably highly unreliable. Family friends, in particular, are likely to be charitable toward the applicant and therefore unreliable in this sense.

Commercial credit-rating organizations are also sometimes used. For a fee, the credit-rating organization—which collects information broader than the extent to which bills have been paid—will submit a report that may include information on character, general reputation, use of alcohol or drugs, civic and community activities, etc. However, such reports are now governed by the Fair Credit Reporting Act passed by Congress in 1970, and users need to be aware that the applicant is entitled to full disclosure from the reporting agency.[82] In addition, the applicant must be notified in writing that such information is being sought.[83] In organizations doing classified work for the government, security necessitates thorough checks by federal agents before new employees are granted access to classified information.

As implied above, reference checking in any form, including the use of credit-rating firms, is coming under increasing scrutiny by the EEOC, the courts, and Congress; employers and respondents need to be meticulous about the job-relatedness of the information sought and furnished. For example, in one case, the EEOC ruled that unlawful discrimination had occurred when a black employee was discharged after an unfavorable performance report—which turned out to be false—had come in from a previous employer.[84] In another case, when the employer could not show job relevance, the EEOC ruled that a refusal to hire a minority applicant, partly because of an unfavorable credit report, was unlawful.[85] In a court case, a man with an M.B.A. degree was awarded $56,000 after a prospective employer declined to hire him after, among other statements, an ex-employer had said he was a "character."[86] The latter kind of case is resulting in both seekers and suppliers of information becoming more cautious. Some firms, when a prospective employer is checking references, will verify only the dates and nature of employment and the last salary of the candidate.[87]

EMPLOYMENT DECISIONS AND OFFERS

DEFINITION AND PURPOSE

After candidates have been recruited and screened, decisions must be made on who will be offered employment and on the terms of such employment. Offers are then made. Although this decision making is an important and difficult step, the degree of effectiveness of the steps leading up to this point will make decision making that much easier.

CURRENT PRACTICE AND PROBLEMS

Typical practice is for the personnel department to make screening decisions, thus having a veto in hiring, and for the department head to give final approval. If the personnel department sends only recommended candidates, there is real joint decision making in employment. If initial screening is only cursory, the real decision making rests with the department head.

[82] M.L. Howell, "Complying With the Fair Credit Reporting Act," *The Personnel Administrator*, 17:10–12 (January-February, 1972).

[83] Commerce Clearing House, *Employment Practices Guide*, 1193, August 3, 1972.

[84] "Employee Testing and Selection Procedures, *Personnel Management: Policies and Practices*, p. 654.

[85] Ibid.

[86] *PAIR Potpourri*, American Society for Personnel Administration, March 1976, p. 7.

[87] Lawrence A. Wangler, "Employee Reference Request Revisited," *The Personnel Administrator*, 20:60–62 (November 1975).

In my opinion, joint decision making is the most effective.

THE JOB OFFER

Offers of employment can be made by either the department head or the personnel department, but it is clear that the personnel department must give prior approval to the initial hiring rate and pay grade in order to maintain the internal consistency of the wage and salary structure. For this reason, and because of the personnel department's heavy role in the staffing process, offers of employment are frequently made by the personnel department.

There is, of course, the possibility in each situation that the applicant will reject the employment offer. One survey indicated that the average firm queried had 43 percent of its job offers to engineers accepted and 58 percent of its offers for general business positions accepted.[88] Organizations having acceptance rates significantly lower than current averages in their industries would be wise to assess the reasons for lack of success in attracting desired applicants. A good source of data for making this assessment, of course, is the rejecting applicant.

RELATIONSHIP TO OTHER PROCESSES

Offers of employment must obviously be related to the plans developed in human resources planning. In other words, the skills obtained and the date of reporting to work should coincide with the plans that have been made. The employment of people without prior planning usually creates serious disturbances within an organization. (Such hiring can occur for various reasons, including an executive's desire to do a favor for someone.) Almost invariably, promotion, leadership, reward, communications, and other processes are disrupted. Overhiring, of course, can seriously affect the financial management process.

The rejection of an applicant who might be qualified for a position other than the one under consideration is similarly short-sighted. A broad *differential placement* perspective on the part of the employer is desirable, particularly in periods when some skills are in short supply.[89]

As suggested earlier, any offer of employment must be related to the present structure of wages and salaries. If a wage or salary is too low, it may result in the candidate's declining the job. If the offer is low and the candidate accepts, the consequence may be a disgruntled employee when what other people with comparable experience and backgrounds and in similar jobs are paid is learned. If the offer is too high, problems with present employees may be created. In an attempt to pacify present employees, salaries might be raised, an expedient that may produce a "chain reaction" resulting in spiraling and, consequently, greatly increased labor costs. Solutions to these problems are typically imperfect; compromises are usually sought that will produce the least friction and still keep labor costs under control.

Thus, employment offers and beginning salaries are directly related to, and have an impact on, the processes of compensation and justice-determination in an enterprise. In the case of employment into a bargaining unit, collective bargaining will have predetermined the hiring rate or range, and initial hiring rates will be reviewed through the grievance process.

IMPACT OF ENVIRONMENT

The quality and quantity of human resources available on the labor market will also have a

---

[88] National Industrial Conference Board, *Management Record*, 22:13 (January 1960).

[89] For a discussion of a differential placement system, see Sidney A. Fine, "What's Wrong with the Hiring System?" *Organizational Dynamics*, 4:55–67 (Autumn 1975).

decided impact on offers of employment. Shortages of certain skills may force an organization to lower standards; surpluses may result in higher selectivity. Managerial attitudes toward appearance, age, sex, race, and so forth, will also affect decisions in employment offers. Only through constant attention to the matter of validity can undesirable bias be eliminated.

EFFECT ON NEED FULFILLMENT

Acceptance or rejection is bound to have some impact on the need fulfillment of applicants. When applicants are turned down, the procedure should result in as little "loss of face" as possible for the applicant. Under some circumstances, a frank explanation that qualifications were not as high as those presented by another candidate is acceptable to the rejected candidate. When the reasons might be highly ego-threatening, however, such as in the case of personality deficiencies, the explanation, if given at all, must be in general terms. Brief counseling will sometimes be very helpful to a rejected candidate, and the gain in public relations as well as the beneficial results to society may be worth the cost involved. Here again, however, a firm must remain aware of its main objectives, which will usually prohibit extensive counseling because of time pressures.

UTILITY OF SYSTEMS

Orderly procedures for reaching agreements on employment offers, including the initial hiring rate, must be worked out. Lack of systematizing may result in some preliminary step being overlooked, such as reference checking or a check against the structure of wages. Lack of orderly procedures may also result in time delays that can result in the loss of a desired applicant. Systematization, then, is essential for making sound decisions on employment.

CONCLUSIONS ABOUT EMPLOYMENT DECISIONS AND OFFERS

Although decisions on employment and offers of employment are critical phases in the staffing process, the quality of such decisions to a great extent will be a function of the quality of administration of preceding components of this process. Not only will serious organizational disruptions occur if employment decisions and offers are not based on careful manpower planning, recruitment, and applicant evaluation, but the ability of the enterprise to achieve its objectives may be seriously impaired. Employment decisions and offers must be based on careful short- and long-range planning and on valid recruitment and devices for selection if the enterprise is to be successful in attaining its goals.

REVIEW AND DISCUSSION QUESTIONS

1. What impact are civil rights legislation, EEOC rulings, and court decisions having on (a) the application blank, (b) the interview, and (c) testing practices?

2. How would you go about validating an application blank?

3. How would you measure the reliability of interviews? How does reliability relate to validity?

4. What are some of the common mistakes made in interviewing?

5. What kind of interview appears to have the highest validity?

6. What is meant by a *criterion?*

7. Discuss the criticism of testing, made by one writer, that attempting to predict future behavior is immoral.

8. What are the central issues in testing applicants from minority groups?

9. What is meant by a *clinical-statistical approach* to the use of tests?

10. What are some of the reasons given for a pre-employment physical exam?

11. What would be the ingredients of a reliable reference-checking program?

SUPPLEMENTAL REFERENCES

Alderfer, Clayton P., and Charles G. McCord, "Personal and Situational Factors in the Recruitment Interview," *Journal of Applied Psychology*, 54:377–385 (August 1970).

American Society for Personnel Administration, "Test Justification and Title VII," *The Personnel Administrator*, 21:46–51 (January 1976).

Ash, Philip, "Discrimination in Hiring and Placement," *Personnel* 48:8–17 (November-December 1967).

Austin, David, "Is the Interview an Analog?" *The Personnel Administrator*, 17:13–15 (January-February 1972).

Barrett, Gerald V., and Byron Svetlik, "Validity of the Job—Concept Interview in an Industrial Setting," *Journal of Applied Psychology*, 51:233–235 (June 1967).

Bigoness, William J., "Effect of Applicant's Sex, Race, and Performance on Employers' Performance Ratings: Some Additional Findings," *Journal of Applied Psychology*, 61:80–84 (February 1976).

Carlson, Robert E., and Eugene C. Mayfield, "Evaluating Interview and Employment Application Data," *Personnel Psychology*, 20:441–460 (Winter 1967).

Cascio, Wayne F., "Accuracy of Verifiable Biographical Information Blank Responses," *Journal of Applied Psychology*, 60:767–769 (December 1975).

Cohen, Stephen L., and Kerry A. Bunker, "Subtle Effects of Sex Role Stereotypes on Recruiters' Hiring Decisions," *Journal of Applied Psychology*, 60:566–572 (October 1975).

Commission on Tests, *Report of Commission on Tests: I. Righting the Balance* (New York: College Entrance Examination Board, 1970).

Cronbach, Lee J., *Essentials of Psychological Testing*, 3rd ed. (New York: Harper & Brothers, 1970).

———, "Five Decades of Public Controversy Over Mental Testing," *American Psychologist*, 30:1–14 (January 1975).

Dipboye, Robert L., Howard L. Fromkin, and Kent Wiback, "Relative Importance of Applicant Sex, Attractiveness, and Scholastic Standing in Evaluation of Job Applicant Résumés," *Journal of Applied Psychology*, 60:39–43 (February 1975).

Drake, John D., *Interviewing for Managers: Sizing up People* (New York: American Management Association, 1972).

Dunnette, Marvin D., *Personnel Selection and Placement* (Belmont, Calif.: Wadsworth Publishing Company, 1966).

England, George W., *Development and Use of Weighted Application Blanks* (Dubuque, Iowa: Wm. C. Brown Co., 1961).

Fear, Richard A., *The Evaluation Interview* (New York: McGraw-Hill Book Company, 1958).

Ghiselli, Edwin E., *The Validity of Occupational Aptitude Tests* (New York: John Wiley & Sons, Inc., 1966).

Goldberg, Lewis R., "Simple Models or Simple Processes? Some Research on Clinical Judgments," *American Psychologist*, 23:483–496 (July 1968).

Grant, Donald L., and Douglas W. Bray, "Validation of Employment Tests for Telephone Company Installation and Repair Occupations," *Journal of Applied Psychology*, 54:7–14 (February 1970).

"Guidelines for Assessing Sex Bias and Sex Fairness in Career Interest Inventories," National Institute of Education, 1975.

Gunn, Bruce, "The Polygraph and Personnel," *Personnel Administration*, 33:32–36 (May-June 1970).

Hakel, Milton D., and Marvin D. Dunnette, *Checklists for Describing Job Applicants*

Minneapolis: Industrial Relations Center, University of Minnesota), March 1970.

Hakel, Milton D., and Allen J. Schuh, "Job Applicant Attributes Judged Important across Seven Diverse Occupations," *Personnel Psychology*, 24:45–52 (1971).

Heneman, Herbert G., III, and Donald P. Schwab, "Interviewer Differences in Similarity Bias," in Robert L. Taylor, Michael J. O'Connell, Robert A. Zawacki, and D.D. Warrick, ed., *Academy of Management Proceedings*, Proceedings of the 36th Annual Meeting of the Academy of Management, Kansas City, Missouri, August 11–14, 1976, pp. 273–275.

Heneman, Herbert G., III, Donald P. Schwab, Dennis L. Huett, and John J. Ford, "Interviewer Validity as a Function of Interview Structure, Biographical Data, and Interviewee Order," *Journal of Applied Psychology*, 60:748–753 (December 1975).

Himler, Leonard E., "Interviewing: Guides from a Psychologist," *Management of Personnel Quarterly*, 4:32–38 (Winter 1966).

Horst, Paul, "A Technique for the Development of a Differential Prediction Battery," *Psychological Monographs*, 68 (1954).

Jablin, Frederick, "The Selection Interview: Contingency Theory and Beyond," *Human Resource Management*, 14:2–9 (Spring 1975).

King, Martin Luther, Jr., "The Role of the Behavioral Scientist in the Civil Rights Movement," *American Psychologist*, 23:180–186 (March 1968).

Kirkwood, John H., "To Test or Not To Test?" *Personnel*, 44:18–26 (November-December 1967).

Koenig, Peter, "They Just Changed the Rules on How to Get Ahead," *Psychology Today*, 8:87–103 (June 1974).

Landy, Frank J., "The Validity of the Interview in Police Officer Selection," *Journal of Applied Psychology*, 61:193–198 (April 1976).

Levy, Martin R., and Hayward M. Fox, "Psychological Testing Is Alive and Well," *Professional Psychology*, 6:420–424 (November 1975).

Lipsett, Laurence, "Selecting Personnel without Tests," *Personnel Journal*, 51:648–654 (September 1972).

Lopez, Felix F., Jr., *Personnel Interviewing: Theory and Practice* (New York: McGraw-Hill Book Company, 1965).

Mandel, Jerry E., and Ellis R. Hays, "Behavioral Objectives," *The Personnel Administrator*, 15:21–22 (September-October 1970).

Miner, John B., "Psychological Testing and Fair Employment Practices: A Testing Program that Does Not Discriminate," *Personnel Psychology*, 27:49–62 (Spring 1974).

Nash, Allan N., and Stephen J. Carroll, Jr., "A Hard Look at The Reference Check," *Business Horizons*, 13:43–49 (October 1970).

Robertson, Wyndham, "The Ten Highest Ranking Women in Big Business," *Fortune*, April 1973, pp. 81–89.

Schmitt, Neal, "Social and Situational Determinants of Interview Decisions: Implications for the Employment Interview," *Personnel Psychology*, 29:79–101 (Spring 1976).

Scobel, Donald N., "Doing Away with Factory Blues," *Harvard Business Review*, 53:132–142 (November-December 1975).

Sonneman, Ulrich, and John P. Kernan, "Handwriting Analysis—A Valid Selection Tool? *Personnel*, 39:8–14 (November-December 1962).

Sparks, Charles P., "Validity of Psychological Tests," *Personnel Psychology*, 23:39–46 (Spring 1970).

Steinkamp, Stanley W., "Some Characteristics of Effective Interviews," *Journal of Applied Psychology*, 50:487–492 (December 1966).

Tatsuoka, Maurice M., *What Is Job Relevance?* (Champaign, Ill.: Institute for Personality and Ability Testing, 1973) (pamphlet, 16 pp.).

Tyler, Leona E., *Tests and Measurements* (Englewood Cliffs, N.J.: Prentice-Hall, Inc., 1963).

Wisner, Roscoe W., "The Kirkland Case—Its Implications for Personnel Selection," *Public Personnel Management*, 4:263–267 (July-August 1975).

CHAPTER 13
EFFECTIVE MANAGERS: THEIR CHARACTERISTICS AND SELECTION

The selection of effective supervisors and managers is a vital aspect of the system of personnel selection in an organization. While training and development are important ingredients in the subsequent performance of managers, the initial decisions on hiring and promotions are extremely critical ones.

Although, as discussed in Chapter 7, many situational factors are significant in effective managerial behavior, the manager's own characteristics and traits are also highly important for success. Research indicates quite clearly that success is much more likely if the manager has certain characteristics and has had certain experiences.[1] Although the presence of these success-contributing traits does not guarantee success, significant deficiencies will almost surely guarantee failure in top managerial jobs. For example, it is obvious that someone who has chronic and serious difficulties in getting along with other people or who is lazy and apathetic will not make a successful manager.

It is logical to assume that in order to succeed in a top executive job certain capabilities in coping with one's environment and "surviving" during a long process of selection are necessary. This selective process, to a certain extent, starts with endowments at birth, particularly the endownment of intelligence. Other traits subsequently develop and modify each other as the person proceeds through many experiences in life toward maturity and adulthood.[2]

---

[1] Paradoxically, it has become popular in recent years to downgrade the importance of traits in discussing leadership and to focus on behavioral and situational variables. In my opinion, all three approaches to the study of leadership are essential. For concurrence with this point of view, see Ralph M. Stogdill, *Handbook of Leadership* (New York: The Free Press, 1974), pp. 81–82.

[2] For a description of executive selection in terms of such a process of development, see Edwin R. Henry, "Some Points of View about Research on Executive Selection," in Renato

253

This chapter will discuss those traits, characteristics, and experiences that research has shown to be associated with the supervisory and/or managerial role and success. The chapter will then move on to some current practices in the selection of supervisors, in particular the assessment center concept. Finally, the chapter will examine some problems and challenges relative to the selection and utilization of minority and women managers.

THE CRITERION PROBLEM

In the previous chapter, difficulties in selecting adequate criteria of success were discussed with reference to psychological testing. Researchers attempting to predict executive success have met similar problems. A number of different criteria have been proposed or used, including actual occupancy of a high-level position, ratings by superiors or peers, salary, rapidity of advancement, and combinations of such measures. Other measures that have been used or suggested are a company's growth, subordinates' ratings, and various measures of efficiency or inefficiency, such as work stoppages, turnover, and absenteeism among the executive's subordinates.[3]

The use of almost any criterion has certain inherent problems. For example, ratings by an executive's superiors may be inherently biased because the superiors' prejudices about religion, sex, and color may have affected selection for executive ranks. That is, factors other than ability or performance may be major variables in selection. The widespread phenomenon of sponsorship—the tendency for executives to bring loyal protégés into top management with them—and internal power politics are also seen as detracting from the usefulness of rank by itself as an adequate criterion of success.[4]

Another possible criterion—salary—has some of the same deficiencies as rank and presents additional problems because of differences in salary levels among companies, industries, functions within companies, and because of its usual correlation with length of service. Furthermore, salary may not necessarily be related to measures of organizational effectiveness, such as profit. In addition, the demands of an executive position may change over time, and the characteristics needed today may not suffice a year from now. Likewise, executive positions with similar titles may vary greatly in terms of actual job content. Finally, traditional methods of measuring managerial effectiveness may be inadequate, since an executive may *appear* to be running a highly efficient unit although in reality the person is depleting its human resources.[5] Thus, the problem of a criterion in executive selection has no easy or perfect solution.

In spite of these difficulties in developing adequate criteria of success, the various criteria, such as rank and ratings of performance, are

Taguiri, ed., *Research Needs in Executive Selection* (Boston: Harvard Graduate School of Business Administration, 1961), pp. 2–3.
[3] For a survey of the literature on the criterion problem relative to executive success prediction, see Thomas W. Harrell, *Managers' Performance and Personality* (Cincinnati: South-Western Publishing Co., 1961), pp. 18–34; and Charles L. Hulin, "The Measurement of Executive Success," *Journal of Applied Psychology*, 46:303–306 (October 1962). See also Patricia C. Smith, "Behavior, Results, and Organizational Effectiveness: The Problem of Criteria," in Marvin D. Dunnette, ed., *Handbook of Industrial and Organizational Psychology* (Chicago: Rand McNally College Publishing Company, 1976), pp. 745–775.

[4] Stanley Stark, "Research Criteria of Executive Success," *The Journal of Business*, 32:1–14 (January 1959). These variables, of course, are powerful situational factors related to attaining high positions. They may have little to do with achieving the goals of the enterprise, however. For a further discussion of sponsorship, see Eugene E. Jennings, *The Mobile Manager* (Ann Arbor: Graduate School of Business Administration, University of Michigan, 1967).
[5] See Rensis Likert, *The Human Organization: Its Management and Value* (New York: McGraw-Hill Book Company, 1967), Chapter 9.

reasonable enough for meaningful research to be conducted and for considerable credence to be given the results. If the criterion and the predictive variables have face validity, tentative conclusions and hypotheses based on imperfect research are better than none at all. In order for top management to improve its "batting average" in executive and managerial selection, management must develop some plausible theory about the characteristics of successful executives.

A COMMENT ABOUT CHARACTER

Before we examine some of the research on executive and managerial characteristics, a comment should be made about character. Such traits as honesty and dependability are not likely to differentiate executives from the general population, or the more successful executives from the less successful, since these traits are found in the majority of persons. The absence of such characteristics, however, is highly correlated with failure in most, if not all, managerial and professional occupations. Therefore, it is important to attempt to identify such shortcomings when selecting and promoting employees. Especially in the top managerial ranks, shortcomings like dishonesty can be enormously costly.

Such traits are not dealt with in the research that follows. Nevertheless, the indispensable qualities of integrity, honesty, and dependability constitute the *minimum* characteristics necessary for managerial success. It is obvious that organizations cannot afford embezzlement, thievery, and forgery or even the lesser consequences of distortion, malicious gossip, and erratic attendance and performance.

A WORD OF CAUTION

A word of caution is also in order. The following analysis of research in the behavioral sciences and the conclusions drawn from the analysis should not be automatically applied in a program of selection. From my experience, test data, in particular, should be carefully crosschecked with the employment history and other information about a candidate's background and with very carefully conducted interviews. Furthermore, the uniqueness of each situation and the validity of a particular instrument in predicting success in that situation should always be of serious concern.

It should be remembered, also, that deficiencies in one area of ability or temperament may be offset by extraordinary capabilities in other areas. For example, strong drive, persistence, and thoroughness may offset some slowness in problem solving. Exceptional intelligence may compensate for deficiencies in personality, and so forth.

DIFFERENCES BETWEEN MANAGERS AND OTHER GROUPS

When compared with the general population and with various other groups, managers have been shown to be, on the average, strikingly different in certain ways. Research on leadership in school or college tends to add plausibility to the results of business studies.

INTELLIGENCE

The clearest and most consistent finding in the research is that the average executive has significantly higher intelligence than the average person. For example, one study of 33 top executives found that the executives scored higher than 96 percent of the general population of industrial and business workers on the Wonderlic Personnel Test (Form A), an intelligence test.[6]

[6] Robert M. Wald and Roy A. Doty, "The Top Executive—A Firsthand Profile," *Harvard Business Review*, 32:52 (July-August 1954).

Another study of 250 executives found that the "typical executive" scored between the 95th and 97th percentiles on the Thurstone Primary Mental Ability Test.[7] Norms published in the manual for the Thurstone Test of Mental Alertness indicate that the average score of a sample of 60 executives was equivalent to the 89th percentile when compared with a sample of retail-sales supervisors, and above the 90th percentile when compared with retail-sales personnel, stockclerks, clerical workers, or clerical applicants.[8] That is, only about 10 percent of these groups scored as high as the average executive.

Intelligence, as measured by the Wesman Personnel Classification Test, was found to differentiate female executives from a matched group of females who were in similar organizations but were not executives. In addition to higher intelligence, the executive group scored higher on self-esteem and the need for power dimensions.[9]

Studies of leadership among children, teenagers, and groups at college lend strong support to these findings from the business situation. In an exhaustive survey of the literature, Stogdill found twenty-eight studies that showed that, on the average, the level of intelligence of the child- or student-leader exceeded the average level in her or his group. Only five studies were found that showed no difference in intelligence, no studies were found that showed lower intelligence.[10] Thus, a relatively

high degree of intelligence has been found to characterize leaders in general, regardless of the type of organization. These conclusions have been drawn by researchers in a wide variety of companies and situations.[11]

PERSONALITY

Certain characteristics as measured by personality tests tend to differentiate executives from the general population. Although the evidence is not as clear as with intelligence, some general and plausible conclusions may be drawn about the average executive.

We should again stress the likelihood that personality, although relatively stable, may not be as stable as intelligence, and that personalities may change over time and with the situation. In addition, as mentioned above, most personality tests can be faked to some extent by intelligent and socially perceptive people. Thus, these tests may be more reliable in research, where the subject has nothing to lose, than in selection.

Huttner et al. found their sample of executives to have better mental health than the average person as measured by the Minnesota Multiphasic Personality Inventory (MMPI) and the Bernreuter Personality Inventory. For ex-

[7]L. Huttner, S. Levy, E. Rosen, and M. Stopol, "Further Light on the Executive Personality," *Personnel*, 36:42–43 (March-April 1959).

[8]L.L. Thurstone and Thelma Gwinn Thurstone, *Examiner Manual for the Thurstone Test of Mental Alertness* (Chicago: Science Research Associates, 1952), pp. 8–11.

[9]Robert F. Morrison and Marian Luise Sebald, "Personal Characteristics Differentiating Female Executive from Female Non-executive Personnel," *Journal of Applied Psychology*, 59:656–659 (October 1974).

[10]Ralph M. Stogdill, "Personal Factors Associated with Leadership: A Survey of the Literature," *The Journal of Psychology*, 25:44–45 (January 1948). Stodgill cites several studies that

suggest that extreme differences in intelligence between potential leaders and followers act to prevent the individuals with extraordinary intelligence from assuming leadership because of wide differences in vocabulary, interests, and goals. This suggestion emphasizes one of the important functions of first-line and middle-management supervisors: to interpret the chief executive to the rank-and-file workers and vice versa.

[11]Similar conclusions are reported by Edward N. Hay & Associates in their newsletter *Men and Management*, May 1961; by James C. Worthy, "Planned Executive Development: The Experience of Sears, Roebuck and Co.," in *Practical Methods of Management Development* (New York: American Management Association, 1951), Personnel Series No. 137, pp. 16–17; and by Charles D. Flory and J. Elliot Janney, "Psychological Services to Business Leaders," *Journal of Consulting Psychology*, 10:115–119 (May-June 1946).

ample, they tended to be confident, optimistic, and capable of tolerating a good deal of frustration. The tests further indicated a strong need for position, status, and authority, and a tendency to be strongly competitive. The tests also indicated a strong orientation toward other people, an outgoing personality, and a desire to be liked and accepted, as well as a tendency to be tactful and considerate of others. Furthermore, these executives had the ability to evaluate different courses of action and to push toward making a decision.[12]

Guilford found that a sample of 208 executives of a large chain grocery company exceeded a sample of 143 first-line supervisors on several dimensions of three Guilford-Martin personality tests. The executives were found to be more sociable, free from depression and inferiority feelings, emotionally stable, happy-go-lucky, socially bold, self-confident, calm and composed, objective, agreeable, and cooperative.[13]

A major finding of a study by Henry, who used the Thematic Apperception Test and other personality tests and interviews, was that successful executives have drives toward high achievement and high mobility. That is, it was found that they have strong desires to get things done and to assume additional responsibility and that they have a strong need to obtain the financial and social rewards of accomplishment. Furthermore, Henry found successful executives to be active and aggres-

sive, but their motivation was channeled into striving for prestige and status—not in the direction of hostility toward other people.[14] These findings are generally consistent with McClelland's research on entrepreneurial business managers (see Chapter 6).

Wald and Doty, using the Adams-Lepley Personnel Audit, found their sample of executives to be above the 90th percentile on "measure of firmness"—positiveness and decisiveness. They were able to evaluate the facts, sort out the relevant ones, and reach a conclusion relatively easily and quickly. In addition, they scored above the 80th percentile on "frankness," which the researchers interpreted as indicating directness, sincerity, and honesty, but with an appropriate amount of tact, diplomacy, and skill in human relations.[15] These researchers, however, found their sample to be only average in self-confidence and emotional stability, with these traits less pronounced than suggested by the research of Huttner et al., and Henry's study.[16]

A study by Richardson and Hanawalt using the Bernreuter Personality Inventory is generally consistent with the above findings. Managers having fifteen or more persons under their supervision were found to be less neurotic and more self-confident than nonsupervisors. Similar results were obtained in comparing what the authors called "office-holders" with non-office-holders. Office-holders were people who had held, since the age of twenty-one, at

[12] Huttner, Levy, Rosen, and Stopol, "Further Light on Executive Personality," p. 43. The reader should be cautioned that studies such as the one by Huttner et al. report differences in terms of words attempting to describe *scores on tests*—not differences in terms of observable behavior. For example, if it is concluded that a test suggests that a person is "highly aggressive," the assumption is being made that the way a person answered certain questions on the test is consistent with how he or she actually behaves. This kind of assumption is the most questionable in relation to paper and pencil personality tests, where some faking is possible.

[13] Joan S. Guilford, "Temperament Traits of Executives and Supervisors Measured by the Guilford Personality Inventories," *Journal of Applied Psychology*, 36:228–233 (August 1952).

[14] William E. Henry, "The Psychodynamics of the Executive Role," in W. Lloyd Warner and Norman H. Martin, *Industrial Man* (New York: Harper & Brothers, 1959), pp. 24–34. Presumably this study was of 437 executives; see Burleigh B. Gardner, "What Makes Successful and Unsuccessful Executives?" *Advanced Management*, 13:116–125 (September 1968).

[15] Wald and Doty, "Top Executive—A Firsthand Profile," pp. 51–52.

[16] Stogdill found thirty-three studies that included a dimension of "emotional balance and control" of which eight showed zero or negative correlations with leadership success. Stogdill, *Handbook of Leadership*, pp. 75–79.

least two important chairmanships or presidencies in business, civic, professional, religious, or other organizations.[17]

Studies of leadership in situations during childhood or at school are generally in accord with these findings. In his summary of the literature, Stogdill found that research generally indicated that the average leader exceeded the average in her or his group in initiative, persistence, self-confidence, desire to excel, and sociability. The evidence with regard to dominance and emotional control was not so clear.[18]

It is interesting to note that Wald and Doty's study of executives found a history of leadership going back into the school years.[19] Relating this conclusion to Stogdill's findings, it would appear that there are some personal attributes of leaders that tend to persist over the years. These are probably in the areas of persistence, initiative, and desire to excel.

Experiments with a self-descriptive inventory are also of interest. Using a checklist of forced-choice adjectives, Ghiselli has found that people at different occupational levels describe themselves differently. Using a scoring procedure involving weights, top-management and professional people were found to have a higher average score than middle-management personnel, who, in turn, scored higher than foremen, and so on.[20] In particular, a scale of initiative derived from this self-inventory differentiated occupational levels in the direction suggested by the research cited above. In other words, the higher the rank within the organization, the higher the self-description in terms of initiative.[21]

INTERESTS

Harrell cites data indicating that a group of executives had significantly broader interests than a group of nonexecutives. In a sample of fifty-two executives, 94 percent scored above a T-score of 40 (B plus or A) on three or more of the occupational-group sales of the Strong Vocational Interest Blank while only 15 percent of a nonexecutive group had similar scores.[22]

The standardization of the Strong Vocational Interest Blank, follow-up research, and logic suggest that, in general, interest in managerial kinds of occupations is a prerequisite to continued membership in management. The Strong test was designed on the basis of demonstrated differences in interests among people in different occupations, including various managerial and nonmanagerial occupations.[23]

Using the Kuder Preference Record, Wald and Doty found top-level executives scored above or near the 80th percentile on the persuasive and literary scales. In addition, the group scored above the 60th percentile on the computational scale. This finding suggests that

---

[17]Helen M. Richardson and Nelson G. Hanawalt, "Leadership as Related to the Bernreuter Personality Measures: III. Leadership among Adult Men in Vocational and Social Activities," *Journal of Applied Psychology*, 28:308–317 (August 1944). Such studies do not show the extent, if any, to which personalities change when people assume managerial jobs.
[18]Stogdill, "Personal Factors," p. 63.
[19]Wald and Doty, "Top Executive—A Firsthand Profile," p. 48.
[20]Edwin E. Ghiselli, "Occupational Level Measured through Self-Perception," *Personnel Psychology*, 9:169–176 (Summer 1956). A second study found the most striking differences to appear when top and middle management were grouped together and contrasted with first-line supervisors and rank-and-file workers as a group. See Edwin E. Ghiselli, "Traits Differentiating Management Personnel," *Personnel Psychology*, 12:535–544 (Winter 1959).

[21]Edwin E. Ghiselli, "Correlates of Initiative," *Personnel Psychology*, 9:311–320 (Autumn 1956). Research suggests that it is difficult to fake responses on this scale. See Edwin E. Ghiselli, "A Scale for the Measurement of Initiative," *Personnel Psychology*, 8:157–164 (Summer 1955). The question must be raised, however, as to what degree the fact of occupying a certain job level influences self-perception. The same question can be asked about the impact of job level on personality.
[22]Harrell, *Managers' Performance and Personality*, p. 91.
[23]See Edward K. Strong, Jr., *Vocational Interests of Men and Women* (Stanford, Calif.: Stanford University Press, 1943), Chapters 3, 7.

executives like dealing with people, words, and numerical calculations.

KNOWLEDGE AND OTHER BACKGROUND VARIABLES

Research on the background of executives shows that the executive group greatly exceeds the average population in terms of educational attainment. In a study of the chief executive officers (CEOs) of the 500 largest industrial corporations and 300 top executives in some 50 other large corporations, *Fortune* found these executives, on the average, to be highly educated. Twenty-eight percent had graduated from college and another 18 percent had done some postgraduate study. An additional 24 percent had master's degrees, and still another 16 percent had attained a doctorate. Overall, 95 percent of the top executive group had some education beyond high school, and 86 percent had achieved at least a college degree.[24] This is in contrast to the median number of years of schooling for white employed males, 12.3, as shown by 1970 Census data.[25] The only group in the Census report comparable in terms of education to the *Fortune* executive group was the "self-employed" category, with a median of 18 years' schooling, i.e., the equivalent of a master's degree.[26]

It is obvious that experience and knowledge are also important factors in differentiating executives from the general population. In the *Fortune* study of 800 top executives, only two

were under age forty, about 13 percent were between forty and fifty, and the remaining 85 percent were fifty years of age or older.

The importance of knowledge per se is also demonstrated by experiments in leadership summarized by Stogdill. The results of these studies strongly suggest that specialized knowledge and knowing how to get things done are essential attributes of leaders.[27]

OVERLAP BETWEEN OCCUPATIONAL LEVELS

The previous conclusions notwithstanding, although there are some clear differences *on the average* between executives and the general population, and among some widely dispersed occupational levels, the overlap between occupational groups and the variability within occupational groups on such dimensions as intelligence are cause for considerable modesty among managerial and professional groups. Research conducted during World War II demonstrates this point. An analysis by Stewart of the Army General Classification Test (AGCT) scores of 81,553 World War II Army enlisted men, when grouped according to their 227 civilian occupations, found a definite hierarchy of mean scores. However, there was considerable overlapping of scores between groups, and in particular, there were wide ranges of scores in the occupations toward the lower end of the continuum. The fairly narrow range of scores in the "upper-level" occupations (in the sense of test scores) was due largely to an absence of low AGCT scores. The wide dispersion in scores within the lower-level occupations included many low scores, but there were an impressive number of higher-scoring persons whose scores overlapped somewhere in the

[24] Charles G. Burek, "A Group Profile of the *Fortune* 500 Chief Executive," *Fortune*, May 1976, pp. 173–177ff. More than half majored in either business or economics, and more than one-fourth studied business in a graduate school. Only one woman—Katherine Graham of *The Washington Post*—and no blacks appeared among the executives studied.

[25] U.S. Bureau of the Census, *Educational Attainment*, 1970 Census of Population, U.S. Department of Commerce, March 1973, pp. 213, 217, 221.

[26] Ibid.

[27] Stogdill, "Personal Factors Associated with Leadership," p. 47.

Figure **13-1**   Mean and median GCT standard scores, standard deviations and range of scores of 18,782 AAF white enlisted men by civilian occupations

Occupation	N	M	Median	Standard deviation	Range
Accountant	172	128.1	128.1	11.7	94–157
Lawyer	94	127.6	126.8	10.9	96–157
Engineer	39	126.6	125.8	11.7	100–151
Public relations man	42	126.0	125.5	11.4	100–149
Auditor	62	125.9	125.5	11.2	98–151
Chemist	21	124.8	124.5	13.8	102–153
Reporter	45	124.5	125.7	11.7	100–157
Chief Clerk	165	124.2	124.5	11.7	88–153
Teacher	256	122.8	123.7	12.8	76–155
Draftsman	153	122.0	121.7	12.8	74–155
Stenographer	147	121.0	121.4	12.5	66–151
Pharmacist	58	120.5	124.0	15.2	76–149
Tabulating machine operator	140	120.1	119.8	13.3	80–151
Bookkeeper	272	120.0	119.7	13.1	70–157
Manager, sales	42	119.0	120.7	11.5	90–137
Purchasing agent	98	118.7	119.2	12.9	82–153
Manager, production	34	118.1	117.0	16.0	82–153
Photographer	95	117.6	119.8	13.9	66–147
Clerk, general	496	117.5	117.9	13.0	68–155
Clerk-typist	468	116.8	117.3	12.0	80–147
Manager, miscellaneous	235	116.0	117.5	14.8	60–151
Installer-repairman, tel & tel	96	115.8	116.8	13.1	76–149
Cashier	111	115.8	116.8	11.9	80–145
Instrument repairman	47	115.5	115.8	11.9	82–141
Radio repairman	267	115.3	116.5	14.5	56–151
Printer, job pressman, lithographic pressman	132	115.1	116.7	14.3	60–149
Salesman	494	115.1	116.2	15.7	60–153
Artist	48	114.9	115.4	11.2	82–139
Manager, retail store	420	114.0	116.2	15.7	52–151
Laboratory assistant	128	113.4	114.0	14.6	76–147
Tool maker	60	112.5	111.6	12.5	76–143
Inspector	358	112.3	113.1	15.7	54–147
Stock clerk	490	111.8	113.0	16.3	54–151
Receiving and shipping clerk	486	111.3	113.4	16.4	58–155
Musician	157	110.9	112.8	15.9	56–147
Machinist	456	110.1	110.8	16.1	38–153
Foreman	298	109.8	111.4	16.7	60–151
Watchmaker	56	109.8	113.0	14.7	68–147

Figure **13-1**   Mean and median GCT standard scores, standard deviations and range of scores of 18,782 AAF white enlisted men by civilian occupations (*cont.*)

Occupation	N	M	Median	Standard deviation	Range
Airplane mechanic	235	109.3	110.5	14.9	66–147
Sales clerk	492	109.2	110.4	16.3	42–149
Electrician	289	109.0	110.6	15.2	64–149
Lathe operator	172	108.5	109.4	15.5	64–147
Receiving & shipping checker	281	107.6	108.9	15.8	52–151
Sheet metal worker	498	107.5	108.1	15.3	62–153
Lineman, power and tel & tel	77	107.1	108.8	15.5	70–133
Assembler	498	106.3	106.6	14.6	48–145
Mechanic	421	106.3	108.3	16.0	60–155
Machine operator	486	104.8	105.7	17.1	42–151
Auto serviceman	539	104.2	105.9	16.7	30–141
Riveter	239	104.1	105.3	15.1	50–141
Cabinetmaker	48	103.5	104.7	15.9	66–127
Upholsterer	59	103.3	105.8	14.5	68–131
Butcher	259	102.9	104.8	17.1	42–147
Plumber	128	102.7	104.8	16.0	56–139
Bartender	98	102.2	105.0	16.6	56–137
Carpenter, construction	451	102.1	104.1	19.5	42–147
Pipe fitter	72	101.9	105.2	18.0	56–139
Welder	493	101.8	103.6	16.1	48–147
Auto mechanic	466	101.3	101.8	17.0	48–151
Molder	79	101.1	105.5	20.2	48–137
Chauffeur	194	100.8	103.0	18.4	46–143
Tractor driver	354	99.5	101.6	19.1	42–147
Painter, general	440	98.3	100.1	18.7	38–147
Crane hoist operator	99	97.9	99.1	16.6	58–147
Cook and baker	436	97.2	99.5	20.8	20–147
Weaver	56	97.0	97.3	17.7	50–135
Truck driver	817	96.2	97.8	19.7	16–149
Laborer	856	95.8	97.7	20.1	26–145
Barber	103	95.3	98.1	20.5	42–141
Lumberjack	59	94.7	96.5	19.8	46–137
Farmer	700	92.7	93.4	21.8	24–147
Farmhand	817	91.4	94.0	20.7	24–141
Miner	156	90.6	92.0	20.1	42–139
Teamster	77	87.7	89.0	19.6	46–145

From Thomas W. Harrell and Margaret S. Harrell, "Army General Classification Test Scores For Civilian Occupations," *Educational and Psychological Measurement*, 5:231–232 (Autumn 1945).

lower 25 or 50 percent of the range of scores in the higher occupations.[28]

In a similar analysis of AGCT scores of 18,782 Army Air Forces Air Services Command enlisted men, other studies found a definite ranking of occupations by mean scores, but the overlap between occupations adjacent to each other was considerable. *Almost all the occupational groups represented included some people who attained scores above the mean score of every one of the occupational groups.* (See Figure 13-1.) Significant statistical differences appeared only between occupations substantially removed from each other on the scale.[29]

Thus, while lower scores on a test of general intelligence such as the AGCT might be indicative of a serious competitive disadvantage within one of the higher-scoring occupations, one cannot assume that a given individual within a lower-scoring occupation does not possess the intelligence to be or to have been successfully engaged in one or more of the higher-scoring occupations, given different circumstances or given a different configuration of characteristics, including interests and drive. Nor can one assume that a given individual does not have the capability of successfully interacting with members of higher-scoring occupational groups. These conclusions and the research cited give credence to McGregor's Theory Y assumption that "the capacity to exercise a relatively high degree of imagination, ingenuity, and creativity in the solution of organizational problems is widely, not narrowly, distributed in the population."[30] One obvious implication is that it is vitally important to organizations and society that this talent be identified so that it can emerge and be properly utilized.

DIFFERENCES BETWEEN SUCCESSFUL AND UNSUCCESSFUL MANAGERS

Since the managerial group tends to be a very select group in terms of intelligence and the other factors described earlier, it is to be expected that differences between the more and the less successful will not be as readily identified as differences between the total group and the general population. Nevertheless, research does shed some light on the differences between successful and unsuccessful managers.

Using increase in salary over a fixed period as a criterion, Huttner et al. found that the higher-paid executives, in contrast to the lower-salaried executives, were higher in intelligence, had more drive and enthusiasm, were less anxious, and were more optimistic.[31]

Mahoney et al., using a ranking of overall effectiveness as a criterion of success, found that the "more effective" managers, in contrast to "less effective" managers, were more intelligent, aggressive, self-reliant, and persuasive. Furthermore, they had more education and had been more active in hobbies and sports as young people.[32]

---

[28] Naomi Stewart, "AGCT Scores of Army Personnel Grouped by Occupations," *Occupations*, 26:5–41 (October 1947).

[29] Thomas W. Harrell and Margaret S. Harrell, "Army General Classification Test Scores for Civilian Occupations," *Educational and Psychological Measurement*, 5:229–239 (Autumn 1945); and John O. Crites, *Vocational Psychology* (New York: McGraw-Hill Book Company, 1969), pp. 69–72.

[30] Douglas McGregor, *The Human Side of Enterprise* (New York: McGraw-Hill Book Company, 1960), p. 48.

[31] Huttner et al., "Further Light on Executive Personality," pp. 46–47. For an experimental study that demonstrated the importance of leader intelligence in small group effectiveness, see Edgar F. Borgatta, Arthur S. Couch, and Robert F. Bales, "Some Findings Relevant to the Great Man Theory of Leadership," in A. Paul Hare, Edgar F. Borgatta, and Robert F. Bales, eds., *Small Groups: Studies in Social Interaction* (New York: Alfred A. Knopf, 1955), pp. 568–574.

[32] Thomas A. Mahoney, Thomas H. Jerdee, and Allan N. Nash, *The Identification of Management Potential—A Research Approach to Management Development* (Dubuque, Iowa: Wm. C. Brown Company, 1961), pp. 22–23, 39–41. For another report of the same study, see Thomas A. Mahoney, Thomas A. Jerdee, and Allan N. Nash, "Predicting Managerial Effectiveness," *Personnel Psychology*, 13:147–163 (Summer 1960).

Using ratings by supervisors and peers as criteria, Hicks and Stone concluded, with the use of a codified Rorschach test (Structured-Objective) and the Guilford-Zimmerman Aptitude Survey, that the more successful managers had a high degree of emotional strength, did not plan and organize their activities to the extent of less successful managers, viewed things broadly and theoretically, and avoided too much attention to detail.[33]

Guilford found certain dimensions in personality as measured by Guilford-Martin's inventories of personality to be correlated with ratings of "job performance" made by a training staff. Although the coefficients of validity were low, the dimensions of sociability, absence of inferiority feelings, and cooperativess correlated with the criteria of success.[34]

In comparing thirty-one different variables with ratings of success, Wagner found that extent of education was the best predictor of executive success. A "preference for familiar and stable situations" as shown by the Kuder Preference Record, Personal, showed a significant *inverse* correlation. Wagner's sample consisted of 150 executives, aged thirty-five years or under.[35]

College grade-average has been shown to be related to success in the Bell Telephone System. In a study of about 17,000 graduates of accredited colleges, it was found that there was a distinct relationship between rank in one's graduating class and salary. The criterion was annual salary in comparison to the salaries of those who had the same length of service in the company. It was found, for example, that 45 percent of those graduating in the top third of their classes were in the top third in terms of salary when compared with those of the same length of service. Fifty-one percent of those graduating in the top tenth of their class were in the top third of salaries. By contrast, only 26 percent of those graduating in the bottom third of their college class attained the top third of salaries.[36]

The quality of the college from which a person graduated was also found to be moderately related to success in salary. After ranking colleges "above average," "average," and "below average" in terms of admission requirements and academic standards, it was found that coming from an "above average" college was somewhat predictive of success in terms of salary. For example, 55 percent of those graduating in the top third of their classes from above-average colleges achieved the top third of salaries, while 42 percent of the top third from the average colleges attained the top third of salaries.[37] Although this factor was not as strong as scholastic success, it is clear that quality of a college was somewhat related to salary in this study.

Leadership in college extracurricular activities was also found to be related to size of salary. By categorizing the people on the basis of "substantial," "some," and "none" relative to extracurricular activities—"none" designated both those who participated but did not achieve leadership and those who did not par-

[33] John A. Hicks and Joice B. Stone, "The Identification of Traits Related to Managerial Success," *Journal of Applied Psychology*, 46:428–432 (December 1962).
[34] Guilford, "Temperament Traits."
[35] Edwin E. Wagner, "Predicting Success for Young Executives from Objective Test Scores and Personal Data," *Personnel Psychology*, 13:181–186 (Summer 1960).

[36] *College Achievement and Progress in Management*, Personnel Research Section, American Telephone and Telegraph Company, March 1962, pp. 1–3. In general, being in the lowest salary third represented a failure to reach the middle-management level. The study does not tell us, however, to what degree success in specialized technical fields was also being measured. If the Bell System has a "parallel ladder" concept in salary administration (see Chapter 25) the study may be partly predicting salary success in specialized fields as well as in management.
[37] Ibid., pp. 3–5.

ticipate at all—it was found that "substantial" extracurricular achievement tended to support progress in salary. For example, 67 percent of the persons from the top third of their classes who were from above-average colleges and who had substantial achievement on campus attained the top-third group of salaries. In addition, substantial extracurricular achievement tended to compensate for differences in schools. Thus, assuming the same scholastic rank, those from below-average schools who had substantial achievement on campus were apparently about as successful as those from above-average schools who had no campus activities. On the other hand, achievement on campus did not compensate completely for lack of scholastic attainment, and failure to become a leader on campus did not necessarily predict failure in a career. Scholastic achievement clearly appeared to be the strongest predictor of success in this study.[38]

Although not a study of measured differences, a survey by Gaudet and Carli of opinions of executives on why subordinate executives had failed found that executives gave the following reasons the most weight, in this order: lack of breadth of knowledge, inability to delegate, inability to analyze and evaluate, lack of personnel and administrative knowledge, inability to judge people, and inability to cooperate.[39] A combination of intelligence, personality, and knowledge seems to have been operating, which is consistent with the findings of studies reported thus far.

DIFFERENCES BETWEEN SUCCESSFUL AND UNSUCCESSFUL MANAGERS WITHIN VARIOUS SPECIALTIES

There has been some research on the differences between successful and unsuccessful managers within various fields. What little research has been done is generally consistent with the research cited up to this point.

ENGINEERING AND R&D EXECUTIVES

Huttner et al. found the more successful executive in research and development (R&D) and in engineering to be better informed, both professionally and in a business sense, to be less prone to depression and anxiety, and to have interests more nearly like those of business managers than less effective R&D executives. The criterion of success was increase in salary over a certain period.[40]

SALES EXECUTIVES

Using rankings by higher management as a criterion, Dunnette and Kirchner investigated the differences between higher- and lower-ranking sales managers. The more effective sales managers were found to be more intelligent, to have broader interests, to be more dominant, more self-confident, more extroverted, and less dependent than the less effective managers. The intelligence tests used were the Wechsler Adult Intelligence Scale and the Miller Analogies Test. The Strong Vocational Interest Blank was used to assess patterns of interest, and the Edwards Personal Preference Schedule and the California Psychological Inventory were used to obtain measures of personality.[41]

[38]Ibid., pp. 5–7. See also *A Study of Factors in College Achievement as Related to Progress in Management,* Personnel Research Section, American Telephone and Telegraph Company, March 1962. The latter report goes into more detail than the one cited above. It is also of interest that degree of self-support and college major were not found to be related to salary success. Ibid., pp. 7–8.
[39]Frederick J. Gaudet and A. Ralph Carli, "Why Executives Fail," *Personnel Psychology,* 10:7–21 (Spring 1957).
[40]Huttner et al., "Further Light on Executive Personality," p. 47.
[41]Marvin D. Dunnette and Wayne K. Kirchner, "Validation of Psychological Tests in Industry," *Personnel Administration,* 21:20–27 (May-June 1958).

Huttner et al. found successful sales executives in contrast to the less successful, to be more intelligent, better in communicating both orally and in writing, able to read faster, more outgoing, and more dominant. Successful executives were also found to have fewer anxieties and to be more emotionally stable.[42]

ADMINISTRATIVE AND ACCOUNTING EXECUTIVES

Huttner et al. found that the more effective administrative and accounting executives had higher intelligence, better verbal facility, and competencies outside of their specialties. These executives were also more optimistic, less introverted, and more sociable than the less effective executives.[43]

PRODUCTION EXECUTIVES

Stockford reports a study in which supervisors of production were ranked and designated as superior, good, fair, or poor. On the average, the superior and good supervisors had higher intelligence, more previous experience in related work, and more advanced technical training. In addition, the superior and good groups were inclined to participate in outside activities of a group nature, while those in the fair and poor groups were inclined to pursue individual activities in their off hours.[44]

Using a criterion based on rankings of overall effectiveness, Huttner and Stene found that intelligence as measured by the Wonderlic Personnel Test and the Primary Mental Abilities Test differentiated between "good" and "poor" supervisors. In other words, the "good" group averaged higher intelligence. In addition, the Supervisory Aptitudes Test differentiated between the two groups. This was a test designed to assess the orientation of the supervisors toward "people" versus "things." Presumably, the higher the orientation toward "people" in the test results, the better.[45]

PEER AND SUPERIOR RATINGS AS PREDICTORS OF SUPERVISORY EFFECTIVENESS

Peer ratings have been shown to have some utility in predicting subsequent supervisory success. Most studies involving peer ratings have been done in military organizations, but a few have been conducted in industrial firms. (Examples of each will be cited.) One study found that ratings by fellow West Point cadets were highly correlated with success as an officer during the first eighteen months after commission.[46] Another study, this one of Naval aviation cadets, found that "buddy ratings" on leadership significantly predicted whether the cadet would pass the total flight-training program.[47] A study involving ROTC cadets found peer nominations for promotion to be in high agreement with nominations by superiors.[48] Peer ratings of Army colonels have been found

[42] Huttner et al., "Further Light on Executive Personality," p. 47.
[43] Ibid., p. 47.
[44] Lee Stockford, "A Controlled Testing Program Pays Off," in M. Joseph Dooher and Elizabeth Marting, eds., Selection of Management Personnel (New York: American Management Association, 1957), I, pp. 138–144.
[45] Ludwig Huttner and D. Miriam Stene, "Foreman Selection in Light of a Theory of Supervision," Personnel Psychology, 11:403–409 (Autumn 1958). Huttner, Levy, Rosen and Stopol ("Further Light on Executive Personality," p. 47) did not find significant differences between the more and less effective production executives in their sample.
[46] Donald E. Baier, "Selection and Evaluation of West Point Cadets," The American Psychologist, 2:325–326 (August 1947).
[47] E.P. Hollander, "Buddy Ratings: Military Research and Industrial Implications," Personnel Psychology, 7:388 (Autumn 1954).
[48] Gene S. Booker and Ronald W. Miller, "A Closer Look at Peer Ratings," Personnel, 43:42–47 (February 1966).

to be highly correlated with subsequent promotion to brigadier general. The ratings were not used in the selection process.[49]

Another experiment, this one in industry at the Ansul Chemical Company, used peer ratings among rank-and-file workers to assist in making promotions to foreman. Management was reported to be highly pleased with the performance of those selected.[50] Another study found that ratings by peers made in a middle-management training program were predictive of subsequent promotion into senior executive positions. The ratings were kept confidential and had not been used in promotional decisions.[51] Still another study, cited earlier, found that peer ratings of insurance agents in three insurance companies were predictive of later managerial success.[52] Finally, managers attending a month-long management development program rated each other on thirteen characteristics. The ratings, which were not used in promotion, were found to be highly associated with promotions over the next two years. Ratings by the training staff were also predictive, but less so than the peer ratings.[53]

As suggested by the last study cited, ratings by superiors and faculty members appear to have some utility in the prediction of subsequent leadership behavior, but they appear to be less accurate predictors than peer ratings. Korman reviewed the literature and found seven studies involving superior ratings conducted in Marine, Army, and Navy settings and two studies involving ratings by Stanford faculty members and subsequent success of Stanford M.B.A.s. Prediction correlations were positive, but overall they were lower than those found in peer-rating studies.[54]

THE ASSESSMENT CENTER CONCEPT

After summarizing the research of studies predicting managerial performance, Korman has concluded that "judgmental" or clinical prediction has considerable utility in managerial selection and that it may be superior to actuarial prediction. Judgmental prediction involves experts' making judgments after reviewing a variety of data on candidates, e.g., work history, intelligence test scores, interview impressions, etc. This is in contrast to psychometric or actuarial prediction that ". . . involves the assessing of individuals or an instrument(s), assigning scores as a result of the assessment, and relating these scores in a statistical manner to scores on a criterion measure." He goes on to explain why clinical prediction may be working well. He suggests that it is because the people doing the predicting change the meaning of the criterion to include ". . . the general level of adequacy with which the person will be able to function in a complex, demanding environment. . . ."[55] (These statements are congruent with the conclusions reached in Chapter 12 concerning the "clinical-statistical" approach.)

The *assessment center* concept appears to be a practical approach to managerial selection, which draws on previous research results about the characteristics of successful supervisors and managers but features clinical or judgmental selection based on multiple dimensions. A growing number of organizations are having success

[49]R.G. Downey, F.F. Medland, and L.G. Yates, "Evaluation of a Peer Rating System for Predicting Subsequent Promotion of Senior Military Officers," *Journal of Applied Psychology*, 61:206–209 (April 1976).

[50]"Foremen by Popular Acclaim," *Business Week*, March 26, 1965, p. 171.

[51]Harry E. Roadman, "An Industrial Use of Peer Ratings," *Journal of Applied Psychology*, 48:211–214 (August 1964).

[52]Eugene C. Mayfield, "Peer Nominations—A Neglected Selection Tool," *Personnel*, 48:37–43 (July-August 1971).

[53]Allen I. Kraut, "Prediction of Managerial Success by Peer and Training-Staff Ratings," *Journal of Applied Psychology*, 60:14–19 (February 1975).

[54]Abraham K. Korman, "The Prediction of Managerial Performance: A Review," *Personnel Psychology*, 21:295–322 (1968).

[55]Ibid., pp. 296, 316.

with assessment centers in identifying promotion potential among rank-and-file employees or first-level supervisors. Huck and Bray report the use of assessment centers in ". . . hundreds of businesses, government agencies, and educational institutions . . ." including the United States, Canada, Japan, Australia, Brazil, and elsewhere.[56] Among the organizations in the United States using assessment centers are AT&T, Sears, IBM, Sohio, the IRS, and Universal Oil Products.[57]

A type of assessment center appears to have been used first by Professor Henry Murray in the 1930s. It typically includes " . . . a standardized program that employs a variety of objective, projective, and situational tests, as well as interviews and sociometric measures; and a committee of assessors . . . to arrive at certain kinds of conclusions about the assessees."[58] Military applications in World War II were seen in the OSS Assessment Program, the British War Officer Selection Boards, and the German Officers Program.[59]

Probably the best-known industrial program originated with AT&T in 1956 and has been in operation in a number of the Bell System companies since then. The typical assessment center processes a dozen candidates per week, with each group of candidates spending $2\frac{1}{2}$ to 3 days in the center. The staff spends the remainder of the week writing comprehensive reports, discussing results, and making ratings.

Line managers nominate candidates for the center or candidates may nominate themselves.

The devices used in assessment centers are extensive interviews; tests of mental ability, skill in reasoning, and knowledge of current affairs; the leaderless group discussion; presentations by each member of the group; and simulation exercises. One such exercise is the "in-basket" exercise (see Chapter 17 on management development). Other devices used sometimes are a business game in which teams of six candidates "run" a toy company, the exercise called the "Irate Customer Phone Call" (used at J.C. Penney), and mock interviews. Staff members attend these exercises.[60]

Research suggests that assessment centers can increase the proportion of successful to unsuccessful supervisors and higher managers. One longitudinal study, during which line managers did not receive the results of assessments for use in advancing candidates, found that, of those young, first-level supervisors predicted to reach middle management within ten years, 78 percent had reached this level within eight years. Of those assessed as not having potential for advancement, 95 percent had not progressed beyond their first-level assignments.[61] Other studies have shown that the quality of supervision is increasing because of assessment-center assistance in selection.[62]

[56] James R. Huck and Douglas W. Bray, "Management Assessment Center Evaluations and Subsequent Performance of White and Black Females," *Personnel Psychology*, 29:13 (Spring 1976).

[57] Robert B. Finkle, "Managerial Assessment Centers," in Dunnette, ed., *Handbook of Industrial and Organizational Psychology*, pp. 861–888.

[58] D.L. Hardesty and W.S. Jones, "Characteristics of Judged High Potential Management Personnnel—The Operations of an Individual Assessment Center," *Personnel Psychology*, 21:85 (Spring 1968). For a description of Murray's procedures, see H.A. Murray, *Explorations in Personality* (New York: Oxford University Press, 1938).

[59] Ibid., pp. 85–86.

[60] Ann Howard, "An Assessment of Assessment Centers," *Academy of Management Journal*, 17:115–134 (March 1974); Richard J. Campbell and Douglas W. Brown, "Assessment Centers: An Aid in Management Selection," *Personnel Administration*, 30:6–13 (March-April 1967); Walter S. Wickstrom, "Assessing Managerial Talent," *The Conference Board Record*, 4:39–44 (March 1967); John H. McConnell, "The Assessment Center in The Smaller Company," *Personnel* 46:40–46 (March-April, 1969).

[61] Wickstrom, "Assessing Managerial Talent," pp. 39–44. For another validity study, see Herbert B. Wollowick and W.J. McNamara, "Relationship of the Components of an Assessment Center to Management Success," *Journal of Applied Psychology*, 53:348–352 (October 1969).

[62] See Douglas W. Bray and Richard J. Campbell, "Selection of Salesmen by Means of an Assessment Center," *Journal of Applied Psychology*, 52:36–41 (February 1968).

The assessment center also shows high promise for identifying management potential among women and minority group employees. For example, a study at the Michigan Bell Telephone Company found ratings of the assessment center performance of both white and black females who were then promoted to supervisory positions to be predictive of subsequent behavioral ratings made by their superiors. In terms of overall ratings, 76 percent of those rated high at the assessment center were rated "better than satisfactory" in their supervisory jobs, while only 18 percent of those who had been rated low were considered "better than satisfactory" in their jobs. In terms of potential for advancement, 66 percent of those with high assessment ratings were subsequently considered "better than satisfactory," while only 14 percent of those with low ratings at the assessment center were subsequently identified as having "better than satisfactory" potential for advancement. Criterion contamination did not appear to be a factor in the study.[63]

Another study found performance of women at the assessment center to be strongly related to subsequent promotions into the managerial ranks and later advancement. The dimensions found most strongly relating to subsequent managerial level were the same as those predicting promotion: "organizing and planning," "decision making," and leadership."[64]

In addition to the identification of talent per se, the increased involvement of women and minority group employees in assessment programs would clearly signal management's intentions to enhance the upward mobility of these groups. The assessment center also shows considerable promise for the identification of lower-level managerial people who are promotable to higher positions. In such cases, the assessment center can be a vehicle for upward mobility across department or division lines.[65]

MINORITY MANAGERS

Although research focusing on minority and women managers is increasing, a large majority of the research studies cited in this chapter pertains to white males. This is a reflection of the small numbers of minorities and women represented in the executive ranks in the United States. However, many forces, including civil rights legislation and awakening public and organizational concern, are rapidly changing this situation. Increasingly, minorities and women will be included in managerial and executive positions. Recent estimates are that minorities—blacks, American Indians, Asian-Americans, those of Spanish heritage, and other ethnic groups—account for only 4.8 percent of the persons employed in managerial or executive occupations. (See Chapter 11, Figure 11-4.)[66] Many of these minority executives must deal with a number of serious obstacles in their careers. These obstacles can be of a psychological, organization-climate, or personnel-policy nature.

[63] Huck and Bray, "Management Assessment Center Evaluations," pp. 13–30.
[64] Joseph L. Moses and Virginia R. Boehm, "Relationship of Assessment-Center Performance to Management Progress of Women," *Journal of Applied Psychology*, 60:327–529 (August 1975). These researchers report that initially women were assessed in all-women groups within the Bell System but that by the latter part of the 1960s, women were assessed in integrated groups with men.
[65] For further discussion, see Douglas W. Bray, "The Assessment Center: Opportunities for Women," *Personnel*, 48:30–34 (September-October 1971); and Allen I. Kraut, "A Hard Look at Management Assessment Centers and Their Future," *Personnel Journal*, 51:317–326 (May 1972).
[66] See also David L. Ford and Lucian B. Gatewood, "Organizational Responses to Minority Group Managers: Less than Satisfactory," Krannert Graduate School of Industrial Administration, Purdue University, Paper No. 503, March 1975, p. 3; Ernest Holsendolph, "Black Executives in a Nearly All-White World," *Fortune*, 86:140–144ff (September 1972); and "A Manpower Profile of the Spanish Speaking," U.S. Department of Labor, *Manpower Report of the President, 1973*, p. 99.

For example, blacks may be torn between their ties to the black community and the necessity to conform to the culture of the organization. This frequently includes substantial amounts of what Stuart Taylor, a black psychologist at the Harvard Business School, calls "micro-aggressive offenses from whites. . . ."[67] A study using the Allport, Vernon, Lindsey "Study of Values" tends to confirm this dilemma. This study found black executives to score significantly higher than white executives on the social and religious scales, but there were no significant differences between the economic and political values of the two groups. These findings were interpreted to mean that blacks tend to have stronger social and religious concerns stemming from their experiences as part of an oppressed subculture within a white culture.[68]

Another situation faced by black executives is that they are frequently assigned to positions outside of the central aspects of corporation life. In some firms they are placed in jobs where they deal mostly with other blacks. For example, they may be assigned to community relations, urban affairs, black employee recruitment, or to marketing jobs having to do with black markets. Not only do such assignments place black executives out of the mainstream of corporate life, but they frequently give them the feeling that they have been hired mainly for their visibility and to enhance public or government relations. Another major obstacle is that blacks frequently feel they are under pressure to be "superblacks" in order to be accepted on a par with white executives.[69]

Although largely produced by past discriminatory practices, the expectations and attitudes of minority members may be having a dampening effect on their own morale and initiative, thus compounding the problem. For example, one study of black managers found a majority to be very pessimistic about advancement to the top executive ranks, and about 60 percent felt that they did not have equal business opportunities with whites.[70] Another study of the attitudes of workers about promotion found that, although about the same proportion of white and black workers never expected to be promoted, 16 percent of the blacks not expecting promotion attributed their expectations to discrimination. Only 5 percent of the whites not expecting promotion attributed their expectations to discrimination.[71]

In the main, these are obstacles that white executives can do much about. White managers need to confront their own attitudes and to create organizational climates and policies that do not create unfair burdens and obstacles to minority managers.

WOMEN EXECUTIVES

The Civil Rights Act, the Equal Pay in Employment Act, and other forces are having a far-reaching impact relative to the emergence of women in the ranks of managers and executives. However, there are a number of constraints that are operating.

As shown in Figure 11-5, women constitute less than one-fifth of the managerial group in the United States, although they comprise approximately two-fifths of the employed population. In 1962 women were 15.3 percent of the managerial group; in 1974 they comprised 18.5

[67]Stuart W. Taylor, "Action-Oriented Research: An Application of Organizational Behavior Methodology to Black American Executives." Address to the Academy of Management, Minneapolis, Minnesota, August 1972. Unpublished draft, p. 10.
[68]Ibid., pp. 5–7.
[69]This paragraph is based largely on Holsendolph, "Black Executives," pp. 140–144ff.

[70]"Blacks See Little Room at the Top," Business Week, January 6, 1973, pp. 19–20.
[71]U.S. Department of Labor, "Worker Attitudes toward Promotion," Manpower Report of the President, 1974, pp. 124–125.

percent. Estimates are that women total 15 percent of entry management jobs (a big jump over the previous decade), 5 percent of middle management, and 1 percent of top management.[72]

Pressure by the EEOC and consent settlements like the Merrill Lynch agreement to promote one hundred women sales assistants to account executives (see Chapter 11) and the settlement with AT&T pertaining to managers will undoubtedly accelerate the process of women's entering the managerial ranks. In the AT&T settlement, the company agreed to pay $7 million in back pay to 7,000 management employees, more than half of whom were women being paid less than white males in similar jobs. In another major settlement, the Bank of America agreed to increase the proportion of women officers from 31 to 40 percent by the end of 1978.[73]

A large part of the reason for the disproportionate representation of women within the managerial and executive ranks lies deeply inbedded in the culture and finds expression in a number of assumptions that male executives make about women. According to one study based on a survey of the attitudes of some 2,000 executives—half men and half women—most objections to taking affirmative action relative to increasing the proportion of women executives take one or more of the following forms:

Women's exclusion from the ranks of management is self-imposed.

Opportunities for women are equal when they have what it takes.

Women as women are not qualified for management positions.

Women—whether or not they are qualified—should stay home to nurture and guide the youth of today for the world of tomorrow.[74]

Another essay contributes some additional assumptions made by males about women managers:

Women will get married and leave. . . .

Women will not work while they have young children. . . .

Women are uncomfortable in a man's world and make men uncomfortable when they intrude on it. . . .

Women are not dependable—they are too emotional and are likely to fall apart in a crisis. . . .

Women managers are not transferable when their husbands have equal or better jobs. . . .[75]

According to Orth and Jacobs, some of these assumptions ". . . are the product of a limited experience with an older generation of career-oriented women. Others are based on misinformation, on old wives' (and old husbands') tales, or on unhappy experiences. Some few have a real basis in fact, and these are as much concern to women as to men. . . ."[76] By and large, many of these assumptions are being challenged and/or refuted by a number of studies and essays that are emerging. For example, in a study of fifty-two male and fifty-three female retail sales managers in a large midwestern retail organization, participants indicated their preferences for a variety of work outcomes such as responsibility, prestige, pay, promotion, self-fulfillment, etc. No significant pattern of male-female differences was found.[77]

[72]"Up the Ladder, Finally," *Business Week*, November 24, 1975, p. 58.

[73]*Monthly Labor Review*, 97:87–88 (August 1974).

[74]Gardd W. Bowman, N. Beatrice Worthy, and Stephen A. Greyser, "Are Women Executives People?" *Harvard Business Review*, 43:168 (July-August 1965). For an essay that examines some of the stereotypes of women and the consequences, see Jane W. Torrey, "A Psychologist's Look at Women," *Journal of Contemporary Business*, 2:25–40 (Summer 1973).

[75]Charles D. Orth, III, and Frederic Jacobs, "Women in Management: Pattern for Change," *Harvard Business Review*, 49:141–142 (July-August 1971).

[76]Ibid., p. 141.

[77]Arthur P. Brief and Richard L. Oliver, "Male-Female Differences in Work Attitudes among Retail Sales Managers," *Journal of Applied Psychology*, 61:526–528 (August 1976). For other studies and essays on women executives, see Lawrence C. Hackamack and Alan B. Solid, "The Woman Executive," *Business Horizons*, 15:89–93 (April 1972); and Virginia E. Schein, "Fair Employment of Women through Personnel Research," *Personnel Journal*, 51:330–335 (May 1972).

Some of the handicaps to women relative to entering the executive ranks may stem from the traditional division of labor in the home. One study found that when a wife undertakes paid employment, her husband's contribution to household work tends to remain unchanged. Total workloads for women increased an average of thirteen hours per week, while the total workloads for their husbands actually decreased an average of one and one-half hours.[78] These circumstances would be particularly stressful if the women were in executive or high-level staff roles in contrast to nonsupervisory positions.

Loving and Wells provide some practical guidelines for organizations wishing to take immediate action in increasing the number of women managers. The same philosophy could also apply to the selection and utilization of minority managers. The organization should:

◦ Provide a climate of success. Prepare the way, avoid tokenism; get good people, do awareness training, promote from within.

◦ Make sponsorship a requirement, and evaluate supervisors and managers on it.

◦ Make affirmative action an "in" project so tensions are at a minimum.

◦ Recruit the best possible women and give them the same accoutrements and help as you would any man in the same role.

◦ Engender a climate of social approval of women managers along with the requirement to work together.

◦ Provide supplementary training in tasks and skills not traditionally experienced by women.[79]

Such approaches can make a significant contribution to increasing the proportion of women supervisors and executives within the managerial hierarchy. Finally, as in the case of increasing the numbers of minority members in the executive ranks, the more that male executives are willing to examine their own attitudes toward women in management and to modify their own behaviors, the faster the transition will occur.

SUMMARY

An analysis of the research (most of which has been done on white males) strongly suggests that, on the average, executives differ in the degree to which they possess several characteristics. Research shows that executives are more intelligent and better educated than nonexecutives, have strong drives and motivations in the direction of managerial activities, are active and aggressive, have an absence of neurotic traits that would impair their ability to relate to other people or to make decisions, can force their way to a decision in spite of the complexities of the situation, have histories of leadership in high school or college, have stronger and broader interests in managerial and related fields, and have experience and knowledge relevant to the executive role. What little research has been done on the characteristics of female executives suggests that these conclusions hold true for both males and females. Although all these characteristics may not be found in all executives, and some, or most, may be found in many nonexecutives, and although occasional research presents contradictory evidence, the overwhelming preponderance of data from research paints this composite picture.

[78]U.S. Department of Labor, "Special Problems of Women Workers," *Manpower Report of the President, 1975,* p. 73.
[79]Rosalind Loving and Theodora Wells, *Breakthrough: Women in Management* (New York: Van Nostrand Reinhold Company, 1972), pp. 172–173. See also M. Jane Kay, "A Positive Approach to Women in Management," *Personnel Journal,* 51:38–41 (January 1972); and Dennis P. Slevin, "What Companies are Doing about Women's Job Equality," *Personnel,* 48:8–18 (July-August 1971).

Studies of leadership in situations of childhood and school strongly support these conclusions. Furthermore, studies contrasting successful with unsuccessful executives in both general managerial positions and in specialized functional fields show that the stronger the common traits, the more likely the executive will be considered successful. In addition, scholastic attainment seems to be correlated with managerial success.

Studies of the characteristics of people in different occupational groups—based on intelligence tests—indicate that although there is a definite hierarchy of jobs in terms of mean scores, the variability within and among occupations is great. It would seem that a prudent assumption for all supervisors and managers would be that within any occupational group there are likely to be persons with considerable unused talent, in short, a Theory Y assumption.

Research on managerial and executive selection indicates that global judgments made after examining a number of dimensions (clinical predictions) are as accurate or more accurate than statistical predictions using scores alone (actuarial prediction.) This conclusion is supportive of the assessment center concept. Peer ratings, also involving global judgments, have been shown to have considerable utility in predicting supervisory success.

Assessment centers, involving up to three days of interviews, tests, and group tasks, have been used in a growing number of large organizations. Results indicate that the procedures used have considerable utility in selecting qualified managers, including women and minority members.

Organizations are under increasing pressure from the federal government and interest groups to rapidly increase the proportion of women and minorities within the managerial group. However, minority members and women face strong deterrents to entrance into and progress within these ranks. While the mythologies surrounding women and minority executives are abating, tailor-made, participative, affirmative-action programs are needed for rapid progress. Affirmative-action efforts that are based on merit can only enhance the overall productivity and effectiveness of organizations and society.

While Chapter 7 approached the subject of effective leadership from the standpoint of what actual behavior tends to be associated with managerial success and the effect that situational variables have on this success, this chapter has shown that certain traits and experiences are powerful determinants of both entrance into and success in managerial and executive jobs. In summary, traits and experiences, leadership style, and situational variables are all important dimensions in successful versus unsuccessful executive behavior. Improved managerial performance in an organization then must focus simultaneously on three areas: managerial selection, skills in leadership, and the total organizational environment.

REVIEW AND DISCUSSION QUESTIONS

1. How important is drive to achieving success as a manager? What is meant by *drive?*

2. In the terminology of Chapter 8, "Organizational Justice," what are the "costs" in the executive's job?

3. What are some of the problems in establishing criteria for predicting managerial success?

4. Which tests are likely to be the most and least reliable in selecting managers?

5. What does research suggest about the intelligence dimension of different occupational groups? What action implications do you draw from this?

6. What techniques are used in assessment centers, and how valid is the overall concept?

7. Which of the variables mentioned in this chapter can be modified by the individual, if given the opportunity, and how?

8. What does the research show about the validity of peer ratings for selecting supervisors/managers? Under what circumstances do you believe this to be a workable technique?

9. In your judgment, which of the assumptions listed in this chapter about women managers are partially true, and what data do you have to support your conclusions?

10. If asked by a corporation, what steps would you recommend to increase the proportion of minority members within the executive ranks?

11. What is the difference between statistical and judgmental prediction?

SUPPLEMENTAL REFERENCES

Bartol, Kathryn M., and D. Anthony Butterfield, "Sex Effects in Evaluating Leaders," *Journal of Applied Psychology*, 61:446–454 (August 1976).

Bass, Bernard M., "How to Succeed in Business According to Business Students and Managers," *Journal of Applied Psychology*, 52:254–262 (June 1968).

Bassett, Glenn A., "Strategies of Executive Selection," *Personnel*, 43:8–15 (September-October 1966).

Bennis, Warren, "Leadership: A Beleaguered Species?" *Organizational Dynamics*, 5:3–16 (Summer 1976).

Bray, Douglas W., "The Assessment Center: Opportunities for Women," *Personnel*, 48:30–40 (September-October 1971).

Braybrooke, David, "The Mystery of Executive Success Reexamined," *Administrative Science Quarterly*, 8:533–560 (March 1964).

Brightman, Harvey J., and Thomas F. Urban, "PSMO: A Problem Solving Managerial Orientation Test Battery," *The Personnel Administrator*, 20:56–59 (November 1975).

Buchanan, Estill H., "Women in Management," *Personnel Administration*, 32:21–26 (September-October 1969).

Bursk, Edward C., and Timothy B. Blodgett, eds., *Developing Executive Leaders* (Cambridge, Mass.: Harvard University Press, 1971).

Byham, W.C., "Assessment Centers for Spotting Future Managers," *Harvard Business Review*, 48:150–160 (July-August 1970).

Cameron, Juan, "Black America: Still Waiting for Full Membership," *Fortune*, April 1975, pp. 162–172.

Campbell, John P., Marvin D. Dunnette, Edward E. Lawler III, and Karl E. Weick, Jr., *Managerial Behavior, Performance, and Effectiveness* (New York: McGraw-Hill Book Company, 1970).

Crowley, Joan, "Facts and Fictions about Working Women Explored . . . ," *Newsletter*, Institute for Social Research, The University of Michigan (Autumn 1972), pp. 4–5.

Csoka, Louis S., "A Relationship between Leader Intelligence and Leader Rated Effectiveness," *Journal of Applied Psychology*, 59:43–47 (February 1974).

Curd, Edith F., "The Changing Role of Women in the Business World," *Personnel Administration*, 35:29–31 (June 1972).

Dailey, C.A., *Assessment of Lives* (San Francisco: Jossey-Bass, 1971).

Drucker, Peter F., *The Effective Executive* (New York: Harper & Row, 1967).

Dunnette, Marvin D., *Personnel Selection and Placement* (Belmont, Calif.: Wadsworth Publishing Company, 1966).

England, George W., *The Manager and His Values: An International Perspective from the United States, Japan, Korea, India, and Australia* (Cambridge, Mass.: Ballinger Publishing Company, 1975).

Finkle, Robert B., and William S. Jones, *Assessing Corporate Talent: A Key to Managerial Manpower Planning* (New York: John Wiley & Sons, 1970).

Ghiselli, Edwin E., "Managerial Talent," *American Psychologist,* 18:631–642 (October 1963).

Gordon, Francine E., and Myra Strober, *Bringing Women into Management* (New York: McGraw-Hill Book Company, 1975).

Guion, Robert M., *Personnel Testing* (New York: McGraw-Hill Book Company, 1965), Ch. 15.

Hackamack, Lawrence C., and Alan B. Solid, "The Woman Executive," *Business Horizons,* 15:89–93 (April 1972).

Hardesty, D.L., and W.S. Jones, "Characteristics of Judged High Potential Management Personnel—The Operations of an Industrial Assessment Center," *Personnel Psychology,* 21:85–98 (Spring 1968).

Harrell, Thomas W., *Managers' Performance and Personality* (Cincinnati: South-Western Publishing Company, 1961).

Hedges, J.N., and J. Barnett, "Working Women and the Division of Household Tasks," *Monthly Labor Review,* 95:9–14 (April 1972).

Helfrich, Margaret L., *The Social Role of the Executive's Wife* (Columbus, Ohio: Bureau of Business Research Monograph No. 123, College of Commerce and Administration, 1965).

Heneman, Herbert G., III, "Comparisons of Self- and Superior Ratings of Managerial Performance," *Journal of Applied Psychology,* 59:638–642 (October 1974).

"A 'Hire Blacks' Drive Backfires," *Business Week,* April 29, 1972, p. 23.

Hitschmann, Edward, *Great Men: Psychoanalytic Studies* (New York: International University Press, 1956).

Howard, Cecil D., "Why U.S. Executives Fail Abroad," *Human Resource Management,* 11:32–36 (Spring 1972).

Huck, James R., "Assessment Centers: A Review of the External and Internal Validities," *Personnel Psychology,* 26:191–212 (Summer 1973).

Hulin, Charles L., "The Measurement of Executive Success," *Journal of Applied Psychology,* 46:303–306 (October 1962).

Hund, James M., *Black Entrepreneurship* (Belmont, Calif.: Wadsworth Publishing Company, 1970).

Jaco, Daniel E., and George L. Wilber, "Asian Americans in the Labor Market," *Monthly Labor Review,* 98:33–38 (July 1975).

Jennings, Eugene Emerson, *Executive Success* (New York: Appleton-Century-Crofts, 1967).

———, *The Mobile Manager* (Ann Arbor: Graduate School of Business Administration, University of Michigan, 1967).

Johnson, Richard Tanner, "Management Styles of Three U.S. Presidents," *Stanford Alumni Bulletin,* 42:2–5ff. (Fall 1973).

Jones, Edward H., *Blacks in Business* (New York: Grosset & Dunlap, 1971).

Katz, Robert L., "Skills of an Effective Administrator," *Harvard Business Review,* 33:33–42 (January-February 1955).

Katzell, R.A., R.S. Barrett, D.H. Vann, and J.M. Hogan, "Organizational Correlates of Executive Roles," *Journal of Applied Psychology,* 52:22–28 (February 1968).

Koff, Louis Ann, and Joseph H. Handlon, "Women in Management: Keys to Success or Failure," *The Personnel Administrator,* 20:24–28 (April 1975).

Kraut, Allen I., "New Frontiers for Assessment Centers," *Personnel,* 53:30–38 (July-August 1976).

Kuriloff, Arthur H., "Identifying Leadership Potential for Management," *Personnel Administration,* 30:3–5ff. (November-December 1967).

Leavitt, Harold J., "Beyond the Analytic Manager, Part I," *California Management Review,* 17:5–12 (Spring 1975).

———, "Beyond the Analytic Manager, Part II," *California Management Review,* 17:11–21 (Summer 1975).

Levinson, Harry, *The Exceptional Executive: A*

Psychological Conception (Cambridge, Mass.: Harvard University Press, 1968).

Loving, Rosalind, and Theodora Wells, *Breakthrough* (New York: Van Nostrand Reinhold, 1973).

McClelland, David C., and David H. Burnham, "Power Is the Great Motivator," *Harvard Business Review,* 54:100–110 (March-April 1976).

McConnell, John J., "An Assessment Center Program for Multi-Organizational Use," *Training and Development Journal,* 26:6–14 (March 1972).

McCune, Shirley, "Discrimination of Women as Viewed by Female ASTD Members," *Training and Development Journal,* 24:24–26 (November 1970).

MacKinnon, Donald W., *An Overview of Assessment Centers,* Center for Creative Leadership, Technical Report No. 1, May 1975.

Miner, John B., "The Real Crunch in Managerial Manpower," *Harvard Business Review,* 51:146–158 (November-December 1973).

Mitchel, James O., "Assessment Center Validity: A Longitudinal Study," *Journal of Applied Psychology,* 60:573–579 (October 1975).

"One Hundred Top Corporate Women," *Business Week,* June 21, 1976, pp. 56–68.

Paisos, John, and Miriam Ringo, "A New Dimension in Executive Recruiting," *California Management Review,* 14:20–23 (Spring 1972).

Parker, Warrington S., Jr., "Black-White Differences in Leader Behavior Related to Subordinates' Reactions," *Journal of Applied Psychology,* 61:140–147 (April 1976).

Patton, Arch, "Executive Motivation: How It Is Changing," *Management Review,* 57:4–20 (July 1968).

Peery, Newman S., Jr., and Y.K. Shetty, "An Empirical Study of Executive Transferability and Organizational Performance," in Robert L. Taylor, Michael J. O'Connell, Robert A. Zawacki, and D.D. Warrick, eds., *Academy of Management Proceedings,* Proceedings of the 36th Annual Meeting of the Academy of Management, Kansas City, Missouri, August 11–14, 1976, pp. 145–149.

Purcell, Theodore, "Case of the Borderline Black," *Harvard Business Review,* 49:128–133ff. (November-December 1971).

Roberts, Edward B., "How To Succeed in a New Technology Enterprise," *Technology Review,* 73:22–27 (December 1970).

Schreier, James W., "Is the Female Entrepreneur Different?" *MBA,* 10:40–43 (March 1976).

Schwartz, Eleanor Brantley, "Entrepreneurship: A New Female Frontier," *Journal of Contemporary Business,* 5:47–76 (Winter 1976).

Seder, John, and Berkeley G. Burrell, *Getting It Together: Black Businessmen in America* (New York: Harcourt Brace Jovanovich, 1971).

Sellery, Robert A., Jr., "How to Hire an Executive," *Business Horizons,* 19:26–32 (April 1976).

Shaeffer, Ruth G., *Staffing Systems: Managerial and Professional Jobs* (New York: The Conference Board, 1972).

Slevin, Dennis P., "The Assessment Center: Breakthrough in Management Appraisal and Development," *Personnel Journal,* 51:255–261 (April 1972).

Steiner, Jerome, "What Price Success?" *Harvard Business Review,* 50:69–74 (March-April 1972).

Stogdill, Ralph M., *Handbook of Leadership* (New York: The Free Press, 1974).

Tagiuri, Renato, ed., *Research Needs in Executive Selection* (Boston: Division of Research, Graduate School of Business Administration, Harvard University, 1961).

Thompson, David W., "Some Criteria for Selecting Managers," *Personnel Administration,* 31:32–37 (January-February 1968).

Unterman, Israel, "Minority-Group Managers: What's Wrong with Opportunities in Business?" *Personnel,* 48:22–27 (March-April 1971).

Walker, E. Jerry, " 'Til Business Us Do Part?"

Harvard Business Review, 54:94–101 (January-February 1976).

Ward, Lewis, "The Ethnics of Executive Selection," *Harvard Business Review,* 43:6ff. (March-April 1965).

Wells, Theodora, "The Covert Power of Gender in Organizations," *Journal of Contemporary Business,* 2:53–68 (Summer 1973).

"Why Executives Say 'I Quit,' " *Personnel Administration,* 17:24–28 (July-August 1972).

Wickert, Frederic R., and Dalton E. McFarland, eds., *Measuring Executive Effectiveness* (New York: Appleton-Century-Crofts, 1967).

The Woman MBA, P.O. Box 6209, Boston, Mass. 02209.

Woods, Marion M., "What Does It Take for a Woman To Make It in Management?" *Personnel Journal,* 54:39–41ff. (January 1975).

Worbois, G.M., "Validation of Externally Developed Assessment Procedures for Identification of Supervisory Potential," *Personnel Psychology,* 28:77–91 (Spring 1975).

Zaleznik, Abraham, and Manfred F.R. Kets de Vries, *Power and the Corporate Mind* (Boston: Houghton Mifflin Company, 1975).

CHAPTER 14
INDUCTION, TRANSFERS, PROMOTIONS, DEMOTIONS, AND SEPARATIONS

INDUCTION AND ORIENTATION

DESCRIPTION AND PURPOSE

The main purposes of induction and orientation, sometimes called the "joining-up process," are to help the new employee and the organization become acquainted with each other and to assist the new employee in making a productive beginning. Included in this process may be financial assistance for travel and moving expenses, the filling out of payroll and other forms, an explanation of the company's policies and practices, introductions to new colleagues, orientation to the job, and many other events that serve to integrate the new employee into the enterprise.

CURRENT PRACTICE AND PROBLEMS

Professional or managerial employees recruited from outside a metropolitan area are likely to be given financial assistance in relocating. The employer may pay family moving and traveling expenses as well as assist the new employee in locating a home for rent or purchase. Such assistance is not so likely to be extended to production, maintenance, or office employees even though they may come from another area.

On the day the new employee reports to work and on subsequent days, some form of induction and orientation process occurs, whether systematic or haphazard. The more thorough induction and orientation procedures include introductions to coworkers and supervisors, a tour of the facilities, and information about (a) the daily routine, (b) employee benefits and services, (c) personnel policies and practices, (d) safety rules and programs, (e) company organization and operations, (f) company products or services, and (g) company history and business policy. Formal programs of orientation may be spaced over periods of time varying from a half-hour to several months. Information may be given through interviews, group meetings, handbooks, films, tours, or other devices, or combinations of these. Checklists are often used to insure thoroughness of induction and orientation. Many programs include follow-up interviews at the end of three or six months' employment to determine how well the new employee is getting along.

Problems that may emerge in induction-orientation programs are varied. Some programs are haphazard and obviously ineffective. Others are so comprehensive that they overwhelm the new employee and/or are excessively costly. One problem involves securing the cooperation of first-line supervisors who may be reluctant to release the new employee for orientation sessions. Another potential problem is the possibility of overenthusiastically "selling" the company's policies and practices. This could result in resentment by the new employee later on.

IMPACT OF ENVIRONMENT

Certain environmental factors are important in orientation and induction. For example, laws pertaining to hours of work and overtime, along with the company's rules stemming from these laws, should be explained to new employees in order to avoid infractions. As an illustration, in the case of governmental contracts under the surveillance of the Walsh-Healy Act, new nonexempt employees should be informed that they are not to work beyond eight hours in one day unless overtime is scheduled by the supervisor. Otherwise the company may be held for overtime payments.

New technology presenting unique hazards should, of course, be carefully explained as part of the employee's orientation. In the case of a worker hired into a collective-bargaining unit, the union-management agreement with respect to the checkoff of dues and union membership

should be explained as well as the role of union stewards and officers.

The number of people being hired is likely to affect programs of induction and orientation. Large companies hiring large numbers of new employees will probably have fairly elaborate programs, including large group meetings. Smaller companies may give more individual attention to each new employee.

EFFECT ON NEED FULFILLMENT

Needs for security, belonging, esteem, and knowledge are met through proper induction and orientation. Haphazard procedures, casual greetings, and lack of information can precipitate anxiety, discouragement, disillusionment, or defensive behavior, including quitting. The fact that resignations occur with the greatest frequency in the first few months of employment suggests the importance of proper induction and orientation as well as proper recruitment and selection.

A successful induction should include a deliberate effort to reduce the anxiety of the new employee. Through systematic interviewing, a department manager at Texas Instruments discovered the following about new employees:

Their first days on the job were anxious and disturbing ones.

"New employee initiation" practices by peers intensified anxiety.

Anxiety interfered with the training process.

Turnover of newly hired employees was caused primarily by anxiety.

The new operators were reluctant to discuss problems with their supervisors.

Their supervisors had been unsuccessful in translating motivation theory into practice.[1]

[1] Earl R. Gomersall and M. Scott Myers, "Breakthrough in On-the-Job Training," *Harvard Business Review*, 44:62–72 (July-August 1966).

Further interviews with supervisors and middle managers uncovered additional information about supervisors:

They experienced as much anxiety as new assemblers.

They felt inadequate with seasoned, competent subordinates.

They cut off downward communication to conceal ignorance.

Supervisory defensiveness discouraged upward communication.

Motivation principles learned in the classroom were not being implemented on the assembly line.[2]

As a result, an experiment was devised to see whether a different method of induction and orientation would minimize some of these problems. A control group, after participating in the usual two-hour orientation seminar, was then sent to the supervisor for job instructions and finally to the work station. An experimental group of new employees attended the usual two-hour orientation seminar, but it was sent for the rest of the day to a special "anxiety-reduction seminar," which focused on information about the job environment and supervisors and which permitted extensive opportunity for questions and answers. The new employees in the experimental group were given statistics indicating the high probability of their success, were told what to expect in the way of hazing and rumors from older employees, were urged to take the initiative in asking supervisors questions, and were given information about the personality and practices of their new supervisors.

The outcome clearly suggested that reduced anxiety and other by-products of the experimental program had good results. By the end of four weeks, the experimental group was performing significantly better than the control

[2] Ibid., pp. 64–65.

group in assembling, welding, and inspection and also in attendance.[3]

Another major factor in successful induction is preparing the organization for the new employee. Such methods as explaining to co-workers the role to be filled by the newcomer, dispelling irrational fears of present employees, and holding colleagues responsible for assisting the new employee tend to make the first days and weeks easier and more productive for everyone concerned.

One innovative and successful attempt to manage the assimilation process combined a number of these features into a long-range program involving superiors, peers, and new employees. In this instance, a task force made a careful analysis of the assimilation process based on questionnaires to new employees and to the next two levels of management above the new employee. The analysis uncovered a number of deficiencies that needed correcting. For an example, the task force found that supervisors frequently lacked the necessary skills to help bring new employees aboard, the nature of the first assignment frequently interfered with assimilation, there was usually very little feedback about early performance, and there were many confusions and concerns about such matters as the reward system, transfer policies, career development, and how decisions were made. As a result, a number of corrective devices were initiated, including a three-day supervisory training program attended by the supervisor about one month before the new employee was to arrive and the establishment of a procedure whereby the new employee's progress would be followed for six months. Another feature, a one-day workshop involving

[3] Ibid., pp. 66–68. For interview results describing the anxieties and mistrusts of the first few days on the job, see Theodore V. Purcell, S.J. Rodgers, and Irene W. Rodgers, "Young Black Workers Speak Their Minds," *California Management Review*, 14:45–51 (Summer 1972).

a facilitator and supervisors and their new employees, was designed to encourage feedback and to iron out confusions and misunderstandings. The overall results of this program, as compared to previous methods of assimilation, included substantially enhanced productivity, much higher job satisfaction among the new employees, and substantial annual savings stemming from improved performance.[4]

UTILITY AND VALIDITY OF INDUCTION AND ORIENTATION SYSTEMS

Along with the two studies cited above, what little research has been done suggests that formalized induction and orientation programs tend to be superior to unplanned activities in a number of ways. For example, in terms of subsequent employee effectiveness, one study found formal sessions designed to introduce employees to the job were significantly superior to "sink or swim" methods or relying on supervisors or peers to carry out the orientation process.[5] Another study concluded that a systematic, company-supervised program for previously hard-core unemployed persons was superior to either quasitherapeutic sessions conducted by outsiders or to unsystematic, casual methods. In particular, this study concluded that orientation programs for the hard-core unemployed required some structure and considerable focus on work-related matters. The study also concluded that orientation sessions should be conducted by management people who were knowledgeable about company practices and policies and who could mediate problems between the new employees and their supervisors. They further found that

the managers conducting the orientation sessions could use part of the periods for counseling problem employees. Such orientation appeared to have salutary effects on both absenteeism and turnover rates.[6]

In general, it appears essential that induction and orientation procedures be well planned and thorough and that those conducting the programs address specific problems faced by the new employees. No one system will be best in all circumstances, but it is clear that participation and genuine human concern, warmth, and interest are vital ingredients. Interviews with new employees and supervisors can assist in assessing the induction and orientation needs of different categories of employees and in planning improvements in the program.

It is also clear that neglect in the area of induction and orientation may lead to employee turnover, confusion, and wasted time. Further, at least two of the studies cited above suggest that a climate in which both supervisors and new employees can deal openly with their anxieties and problems will have positive results. Such approaches depart substantially from traditional practices and permit a higher degree of participation by new employees.

AUTHORITY AND ACCOUNTABILITY

Central coordination by the personnel department is essential for orderly and effective induction and orientation. Supervisors, however, have major roles in this process and must be held accountable by higher management for

---

[4] John P. Cotter, "Managing the Joining-Up Process," *Personnel*, 49:46–56 (July-August 1972).

[5] Martin J. Gannon and Frank T. Paine, "Sources of Referral, Job Orientation, and Employee Effectiveness," Address to the Academy of Management, Minneapolis, Minnesota, August 1972.

[6] Hjalmar Rosen and John Turner, "Effectiveness of Two Orientation Approaches in Hard-Core Unemployed Turnover and Absenteeism," *Journal of Applied Psychology*, 55:296–301 (August 1971). These authors stress the importance of a long-range approach to modifying habit patterns among the hard-core unemployed, particularly with respect to the time constraints inherent in organized effort. For a discussion of the use of a "buddy system" in assimilating disadvantaged persons into the organization, see Patricia Marshall, "A Buddy Is Everywhere," *Manpower*, 4:33–37 (August 1972).

the proper orientation of new employees to the immediate job and to the job environment. Thus, the chief executive should hold the personnel department and all managers jointly accountable for the effective induction and orientation of new employees.[7]

TRANSFERS, DEMOTIONS, AND PROMOTIONS

DESCRIPTION AND PURPOSE

Transfers may be from one job to another, one unit to another, or one shift to another, and they may involve a new geographical location. They may be initiated by the organization or by the employee with the approval of the organization. Transfers have a number of purposes, such as moving employees to positions with a higher priority in terms of organizational objectives, filling department vacancies with employees from overstaffed departments, or placing employees in positions more appropriate to their interests or abilities.

Demotions are a particular type of transfer involving a cut in pay, status, privilege, or opportunity. They may result from organizational staff reductions, disciplinary penalties, or the inability of an employee to perform adequately in a particular job. In the latter case, the purpose of a demotion is to remedy a previous mistake in staffing. In many instances, however, mutually satisfactory demotions occur because of health problems or changing interests.

A promotion is a type of transfer involving reassignment of an employee to a position having higher pay, increased responsibilities, more

privileges, increased benefits, greater potential, or all these advantages. The purpose of a promotion is to staff a vacancy that, in general, is worth more to the organization than the incumbent's present position.

What constitutes a transfer, promotion, or demotion, of course, depends upon one's point of view. Sometimes promotions are offered to people who consider them demotions or a step backward in their careers.

CURRENT PRACTICES AND PROBLEMS

Lateral transfers, either at the employee's request or at the request of the organization, are far more common in business and industrial organizations than demotions. Demotions occur quite infrequently, and many managers would prefer to discharge employees rather than to face the problems resulting from demotion. In either case careful thought, planning, and concern for the employee should precede such moves.

Most organizations have policies and procedures governing transfers, and these policies and procedures have been developed as a result of three particular problem situations: (a) the problem of the marginal employee whom the department head does not want; (b) the problem of transferring an employee into a position that is appropriate to other qualifications, and (c) the problem of relating present salary to a different salary structure of another unit. As to the first problem, many firms have found that, without definite rules about transfers, marginal employees will be transferred from one department to another in a kind of organizational game of musical chairs. Many firms will try to avoid transferring a worker who presents a problem, and company rules will call for a solution on the present job. Of course, transfers often remedy a problem, but careful evaluation is necessary to make certain that the

[7] For an essay that describes the ingredients of a thorough orientation program, see Robert W. Hollmann, "Let's Not Forget about New Employee Orientation," *Personnel Journal*, 55:244–247ff. (May 1976). For an essay that focuses on a group that is frequently overlooked in orientation, see Ted L. Kromer, "New Employee Orientation for Managers," *Personnel Journal*, 51:434–438 (June 1972).

move is also in the interests of the total organization.[8]

As to the second problem, careful appraisal of an employee should precede any transfer to make certain that the person's qualifications suit the new job. It is illogical and inefficient to select new employees carefully for specific jobs and then to transfer them later with little or no planning. Thirdly, wage-and-salary considerations cannot be ignored. It is obviously not financially sound or fair to other employees to transfer a $1,200-a-month employee into a $600-a-month job and to continue paying the $1,200, unless careful planning suggests that the move and salary are in the long-range interests of the organization.

Transfers or promotions from one city to another present additional problems. Employees so transferred at company request are typically assisted with moving expenses. One survey indicated that, in almost 99 percent of firms surveyed, top management and supervisory employees were thus assisted, while in almost 70 percent of the firms, production or operations employees were helped with moving expenses. In the case of employee-requested transfers, the percentages dropped off to 26 percent and 18 percent, respectively.[9] In addition, other assistance is sometimes given, including help in the sale of homes.

The impact of an involuntary move from one location to another on employees (usually male executives, but increasingly women executives will be affected) and their families is coming under increasing scrutiny. According to one source, the reason for the relocation of more than half of the 40 million people who move

each year in the United States is company transfers. Further, about 68 percent of American executives in the twenty-five-to-forty age group move at least once every three years, approximately 23 percent move every two years, and some 18 percent move each year. The impact appears to be the greatest on families with school-age children. Wives of male executives, in particular, seem to carry the heaviest burden with regard to adjusting to the new community. Their concerns and anxieties are often transmitted to the children, and the family's discontent is soon felt by the husband. Other consequences of frequent moves may be a lack of personal commitment and involvement in the community where the family is temporarily living and a drastic limiting of employment opportunities for spouses who wish to be employed.[10]

For these reasons, plus a desire to reduce the economic costs associated with relocating, many corporations are examining their policies and practices regarding transfers. Some of the larger firms are making transfers optional with the employee; others are carefully assessing the degree to which a proposed transfer represents a developmental or promotional opportunity in the eyes of the employee.[11]

One problem with any promotion is that the organization must continue to live amicably with the people by-passed, a case that is different from that of an applicant rejected in the hiring process. Ideally, therefore, promotional policies and procedures must be reasonably ac-

[8] For an article that advocates carefully planned trading of marginal employees between organizational subunits, see Norman R.F. Maier, "How To Get Rid of an Unwanted Employee," *Personnel Administration*, 28:25–27 (November-December 1965).

[9] National Industrial Conference Board, "Company Payment of Employees' Moving Expenses," *Studies in Personnel Policy*, No. 154, 1956, p. 11.

[10] See Lionel Tiger, "Is This Trip Necessary? The Heavy Human Costs of Moving Executives Around," *Fortune*, September 1974, pp. 139–141ff.

[11] Ibid., p. 114. As one would expect, the higher the education, the more the mobility. Among men with five years or more of college, 15.6 percent can be expected to move between states in a year's time (13.5 percent in the case of women); while only 5.2 percent of men and women with a high school education can be expected to move within the same period of time. U.S. Department of Labor, *Manpower Report of the President, 1974*, p. 84.

ceptable to the unsuccessful candidates. The confidence of employees in the fairness and thoroughness of selective procedures will minimize the defensive behavior likely to be produced in the by-passed candidate.

Another problem arises in deciding whether to promote from within or to employ someone from the outside. Probably a high percentage of organizations make it a policy to promote from within whenever possible, but most organizations are aware that under special circumstances outside people must be sought and hired. There are also instances where organizations may be forced to fill supervisory or executive jobs from the outside because employees with inadequate potential for promotion have been hired in the past.

In unionized situations, the union-management agreement will govern promotion, transfer, and demotion procedures. Almost all labor contracts (99 percent) covering single employers and 75 percent of industry or area agreements provide for seniority systems. The most common applications are to promotions, transfers, layoff, and recall.[12] In these contracts, the relative importance given to seniority and ability will determine who is promoted. Management tends to argue for the importance of ability; unions tend to emphasize seniority. A compromise is typically made through the use of a formula, such as promoting the employee with the greatest seniority if ability and experience are equal. If one candidate is "head and shoulders" above another in terms of ability, many contracts permit promotion on this basis regardless of seniority. However, practices vary a great deal from firm to firm.

As discussed in Chapter 12, the Civil Rights Act has had a major impact on testing practices and appears to have reduced some kinds of

testing. The use of tests in evaluating candidates for promotion, however, has remained at about the same level over recent years. Although test usage has been discontinued in many firms because of concern about EEOC rulings, this decline has been at least partly offset by an increase in the number of organizations using assessment centers (see Chapter 13) that include testing as part of the overall procedure. Although not strictly comparable, a 1975 study reported 24 percent of some 2,500 firms using tests for promotion,[13] while a study two decades earlier reported 22 percent using tests for this purpose.[14] Practices vary widely by industry and job level, however. For example, in the more recent study, 24 percent of public utilities used tests in evaluating skilled workers for promotions within the hourly ranks, while only 10 percent of retail stores used tests for the same purpose. In the case of testing for promotion to managerial jobs, the usage was reversed, with 6 percent of the public utilities and 19 percent of the retail stores using tests.[15]

A number of other devices are in current use to facilitate promotions, e.g., job ladders and job posting. *Job ladders* (or "promotion ladders") are charts that illustrate possible progression from one job to another, including both horizontal and upward movement. (See the career progression model in Figure 14-1.) Detailed versions might include the salary for each job and the experience and training required. Job ladders can assist employees in visualizing potential advancement within the organization and in planning the sequence of training and work experience necessary to reach career objectives. The charting of job ladders can also

[12]U.S. Department of Labor, "Administration of Seniority," *Major Collective Bargaining Agreements,* Bulletin 1425–14, 1972, pp. 1–2.

[13]"Employee Testing and Selection Procedures—Where Are They Headed?" P-H/ASPA Survey, *Personnel Management: Policies and Practices,* Prentice-Hall, 1975, pp. 658–664.
[14]National Industrial Conference Board, "Personnel Practices in Factory and Office," *Studies in Personnel Policy,* No. 145, 1954, pp. 12, 69.
[15]"Employee Testing and Selection Procedures," p. 656.

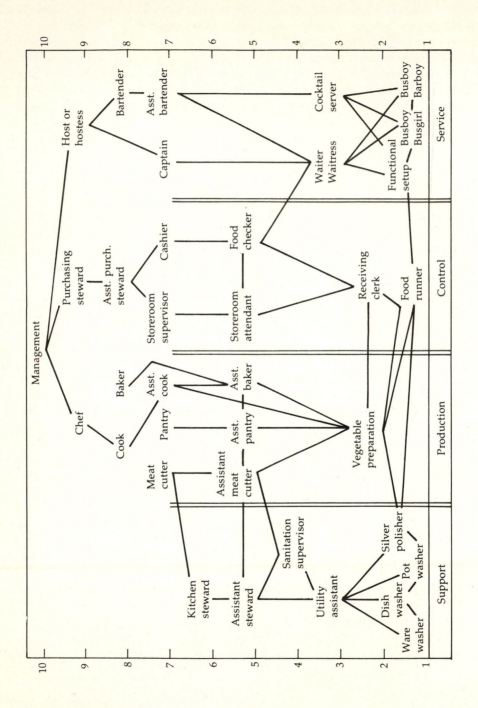

Figure **14-1** Functionally integrated career progression model for a foodservice facility

From William P. Fisher and Paul Gaurnier, *Career Ladders in the Food Service Industry* (Chicago: National Restaurant Association, 1971), p. 25.

assist management in examining existing progression patterns in order to eliminate dead-end jobs, in developing training programs, and in advising.[16]

Job posting is a device also used by a number of organizations to facilitate promotions and transfers. Under a job posting system, job openings are usually announced by bulletin board displays and the distribution of bulletins that list the abilities, experience, and/or seniority required. Employees may then apply or "bid" for these openings. Job posting and bidding procedures are included in some labor contracts, and in some organizations job posting is used for almost all jobs. Increasingly, job posting is being required under court orders to insure that minorities are notified of the more desirable jobs. For example, in the *Myers* v. *Gilman Paper Company* case, the court found that the failure of the company to notify blacks of openings in essentially all-white departments was a violation of the Civil Rights Act.[17]

Civil rights legislation and court decisions are having a clear impact on promotion practices. As cited in Chapter 10, in the *Griggs* v. *Duke Power Company* case, the U.S. Supreme Court ruled that an employer unlawfully discriminated against blacks by requiring a high school education or the passing of a general intelligence test as a condition of advancement to higher job classification on the grounds that these qualifications were not significantly related to successful job performance.[18] As another example, a federal judge found Northwest Airlines guilty of discriminating against female flight attendants in contrast to male pursers

in hiring, pay, promotions, and working conditions.[19]

EFFECT ON NEED FULFILLMENT

Transfers may affect a number of needs, including those for security, belonging, esteem, understanding, and self-actualization. Unexpected or unexplained transfers can obviously affect the needs for security, belonging, and understanding, and if the transfer appears to be arbitrary or unreasonable, the need for integration, or wholeness, can be affected.

Demotions, in particular, will have a serious impact on need fulfillment. Needs for esteem and belonging will be particularly frustrated. Consequently, some form of defensive behavior will probably result, including complaining, emotional turmoil, apathy or depression, inefficiency, and/or resignation. This is why, as mentioned earlier, many managers would prefer to discharge rather than to demote an employee. Because severe defensive behavior may undermine the morale of a work group, a disciplinary demotion may not be a wise course. However, demotion due to a reduction in staff is much more acceptable to affected employees.

To a large extent, the impact of demotions will be a function of the particular culture of the organization. In one large corporation, the researcher found that the possibility of demotion was generally accepted among executives. The reasons were partly that it was frequently unclear as to whether executive moves should be labeled transfers, demotions, or promotions, and promotions sometimes occurred after demotions. A majority of the managers and executives participating in the study accepted such

[16]For further discussion, see Elaine F. Gruenfeld, *Promotion: Practices, Policies, and Affirmative Action,* Key Issues Series— No. 17 (Ithaca, N.Y.: New York School of Industrial and Labor Relations, Cornell University, 1975), pp. 24–28.
[17]Mary T. Matthies, "The Developing Law of Equal Opportunity," *Journal of Contemporary Business,* 5:37 (Winter 1976).
[18]Commerce Clearing House, *Employment Practices Guide,* 1241, August 3, 1972.

[19]The judge ruled also that the company could not require periodic weight checks for only the female attendants, nor require them to wear contact lenses while the pursers could wear eyeglasses. *Seattle Times,* November 13, 1973, p. A19; and *Monthly Labor Review,* 97:74 (June 1974).

a "zig-zag" pattern of instability as part of the values held by the organization.[20] In many instances people prefer demotions to layoffs, or choose demotions in order to stay in or be transferred to a particular geographical area.

There are some data to suggest that demotions can be managed more effectively in an organization that has been involved in an "organization development" program. (See Chapter 26.) In one study, group methods were used by outside resource consultants to assist demoted sales managers in working through their emotional states and in formulating action plans with their new supervisors relative to problems that would confront the demoted persons in their new assignments. Based on before and after scores from a psychological test, emotional states of anxiety, depression, and hostility all decreased significantly, and none of the demotees who participated resigned. Thus, the effort assisted both the demotees and the company, the latter retaining valuable human resources.[21]

Promotion, of course, is likely to have satisfactory effects on the promoted individual's needs for esteem, belonging, and security. A promotion usually will also give opportunity for greater self-actualization through more varied or challenging assignments. Unfortunately, many such opportunities are missed, with obvious economic and human consequences. Instead of development and promotion occurring internally, an excessive number of positions in the United States are filled from external sources. According to the president of an executive recruiting firm, ". . . at least half of the executives recruited outside of corporations could, instead, have been found and promoted from within."[22]

In some instances, fear of failure or fear of being unable to carry out the responsibilities of a new job may result in the person's declining a promotion or discouraging overtures about the possibility. A 1972–1973 University of Michigan study found almost 45 percent of workers surveyed did not want a promotion with their present employer, either because of present satisfaction, some unfavorable aspect of the higher-level job, or because they planned to leave or believed they lacked the proper qualifications.[23]

Sometimes the promoted individual will request a return to a previous job. To manage situations in which a promotion does not work out, some companies have a policy of considering the first three or six months of any new job a probationary period, at the end of which either the employee or the organization may request a return to the former job. This kind of policy is more applicable to promotions to nonsupervisory jobs involving higher technical skill or to first-level supervisory positions than to higher management positions. In the latter case, a return to a previous job could disrupt at least two superior-subordinate teams if the original vacancy has been filled.

The concept of a *fallback position* is sometimes used in the case of an unsuccessful promotion

[20]Fred H. Goldner, "Demotion in Industrial Management," *American Sociological Review*, 30:714–724 (October 1965).

[21]Robert T. Golembiewski et al., "Toward Building New Work Relationships: An Action Design for a Critical Intervention," *Journal of Applied Behavioral Science*, 8:135–148 (March-April 1972).

[22]Thomas M. Meade, "Executive Promotions: Does Familiarity Breed Oversight?" *Personnel*, 49:45–48 (September-October 1972). A survey of over 300 presidential appointments made during 1969 showed that approximately one-fourth involved executives brought in from outside the company. See Wayne A. Dressel, "Coping with Executive Mobility," *Business Horizons*, 12:53–58 (August 1970). A *Fortune* survey found that the chief executives of the largest 100 firms had worked for an average of 1.8 companies, while the CEOs of the firms ranking from 401 to 500th in size had worked for an average of 2.8 companies. Charles G. Burck, "A Group Profile of the *Fortune* 500 Chief Executive," *Fortune*, May 1976, p. 177.

[23]*Manpower Report of the President*, pp. 124–125.

of a manager. Under this concept, one or more positions that have equal status and pay to the person's original job are identified ahead of time. As stated by Hall and Hall, establishing a fallback position ". . . lets everyone know that (1) there is some risk in the promotion or transfer, (2) the company is willing to accept some of the responsibility for it, and (3) moving into the fallback position does not constitute failure."[24] Some of the firms that have used this concept are Continental Can, Procter & Gamble, Lehman Brothers, and the Heublein organization.[25]

AUTHORITY AND ACCOUNTABILITY

Since the personnel department has an overall view of the work force situation, that department is typically given the authority to coordinate transfers, to review plans for demotions, and to monitor compliance with company policy on promotions. Unless the company's policies and orderly procedures are followed in these matters, other enterprisewide processes may be seriously affected. For example, since most promotions involve pay increases, central control is necessary to insure consistency with the companywide program for wages and salaries. Although the personnel department will monitor rules and policies regarding transfers, demotions, and promotions, managers who must initiate these moves and whose concurrence must be obtained will also exercise a good deal of authority over these aspects of the staffing process. In the case of a labor contract, the collective bargaining agreement will spell out the rules and procedures to be followed with respect to employees in the bargaining unit.

[24]Douglas T. Hall and Francine S. Hall, "What's New in Career Management," *Organizational Dynamics*, 5:23–24 (Summer 1976).
[25]Ibid.

RELIABILITY AND VALIDITY

Since devices such as interviews, psychological tests, and job histories are often used in evaluating candidates for promotion, and occasionally for transfer or demotion, the reliability and validity of these devices when used for such purposes is just as important as when used for initial employment. Thus much of our discussion in Chapter 12 is relevant here. (Chapter 15 contains a supplemental discussion of the reliability and validity of various appraisal devices.)

In addition, the validity of policies and practices relative to moving people horizontally or vertically within the enterprise should be questions for research or, at least, questions for examination through careful thought and discussion. For example, it may be assumed that the frequent transfer of operatives in a factory does not hamper production; the opposite may be true.

CONCLUSIONS ABOUT TRANSFERS, DEMOTIONS, AND PROMOTIONS

The shifting of human resources within an organization is as important as the recruitment and selection of people from the outside. The same careful planning and systematic procedures should be utilized. Inadequate attention to internal staffing can create all kinds of problems in internal morale and productivity and, in turn, can seriously impair the ability of the organization to attain its objectives.

Promotion of the right people into key managerial jobs is a particularly important matter. Since, by definition, promotions mean the advancement of some people and not others, the promotional process must provide that successful candidates are sufficiently acceptable to other employees in order to insure that the effective administration of organizational processes is not disrupted. Remedying a mistake in promotion is a very difficult matter and involves either demotion or discharge. Both can be very disrupting to the organization, particularly when positions of extensive power are affected. In general, since decisions on promotion ultimately determine who will make the key decisions within the enterprise, the quality of the management of all resources in the organization is at stake.

SEPARATIONS: RESIGNATION, LAYOFF, DISCHARGE, RETIREMENT

RESIGNATION

Resignations should be analyzed in terms of their significance for the enterprise. Although some resignations may permit an organization to correct a mistake in staffing or to bring "new blood" into the affected unit, excessive turnover can be costly. In addition, investment in recruiting, selection, and training may be lost as well as the human resource potential now unavailable to the enterprise.[26]

Many companies systematically analyze rate of turnover—usually calculated as the ratio of separations to total work force for some period—and attempt to maintain it within healthful proportions. This analysis is sometimes made of departments, of divisions, or of classes of employees in order to identify problem areas.[27]

"Exit interviews" are widely used to obtain data for analyzing causes of turnover. They are usually conducted by a representative of the personnel department, where the terminating employee comes to pick up the last paycheck.

These interviews serve additional purposes, such as making certain that company property has been checked in and that the employee understands the disposition of various benefit programs. Postemployment surveys are sometimes made on the assumption that the data obtained are more valid than those obtained during the exit interview. Indeed, research indicates that the exit interview tends to be deficient in identifying the terminating employee's dissatisfaction and conflict with management in contrast to subsequent questionnaires or interviews by an outside consultant.[28] In either case, supervisors are likely to be defensive about the criticism of their performance that may emerge in such interviews, and personnel departments will need to use the data in a developmental, nonpunitive way if supervisors are to learn from the experience.[29] The other side of the coin is that turnover may be a compliment to the developmental skills of the supervisor, with the employee leaving to assume greater challenges elsewhere. Ideally, a supervisor will request feedback information from exit interviews.

LAYOFFS AND WORKSHARING

Layoffs involve temporary of indefinite removal from the payroll of people with surplus skills. The purpose of the layoff is to reduce the financial burden on the organization in the event that human resources cannot be utilized effectively.

Notwithstanding many instances of layoffs of white-collar employees, hourly paid production

---

[26]One estimate of the cost of turnover of managers and professionals is $40,000 per person. See Hall and Hall, "What's New in Career Management," p. 18.

[27]The *Monthly Labor Review* reports turnover rates by major industry groups and breaks down the statistics into accession rates (total), accession rates (new hires), separations (total), separations (quits), and separations (layoffs).

[28]John R. Hinrichs, "Measurement of Reasons for Resignation of Professionals: Questionnaire versus Company and Consultant Exit Interviews," *Journal of Applied Psychology*, 60:530–532 (August 1975).

[29]For a study that suggests supervisors can be quite defensive about critical comments emerging from exit interviews, see John H. Kilweir, "A New Look at the Exit Interview," *Personnel Journal*, 45:371 (June 1966).

workers are typically the first to be affected by production cutbacks. In the unionized organization, the labor contract governs the order of layoff and the method of recall. Seniority (usually plantwide but sometimes departmental) is usually the controlling factor. Furthermore, the contract typically defines *layoff* and establishes the maximum period during which a laid-off employee has recall and other rights.[30] "Bumping" provisions usually permit employees with more seniority to move down in classification and to replace more junior workers in a layoff situation.

Worksharing provisions are found in almost 25 percent of collective bargaining agreements as an alternative to layoffs. The most common form of worksharing is a reduction in hours worked by the employees under the agreement in order to spread the work. Another form, division of work, involves dividing the work equally among employees, and is usually found in situations involving piecework or incentive systems. Still another kind of worksharing, rotation of employment, provides for short periods of layoff to be rotated equally among all employees.[31]

Accrued vacation pay, supplemental unemployment benefits (SUB), and continued health and life insurance, if provided by the layoff provisions of the labor contract, will be of some assistance to the employee affected by a layoff. Provisions for supplemental unemployment benefits, designed to extend or enlarge the unemployment benefit payments under the state law, are found in a higher percentage of labor contracts each year. Although severance pay, usually a lump-sum payment at the time of permanent separation, is more common in the case of nonunionized salaried employees than in the case of unionized production and maintenance workers, about 39 percent of union contracts provide for severance pay, and about 25 percent of contracts containing layoff provisions provide for financial payment to the affected employee if advance notice of layoff is not given.[32]

The long-established practice of layoffs based on seniority ("last hired, first fired") has come squarely into conflict with EEOC requirements of some firms that they increase the numbers of minority and women employees on the work force. Court rulings in this matter have been contradictory. In one case involving the Jersey Central Power and Light Company, a court of appeals ruled that a conciliation agreement to establish an affirmative action program to hire more women and blacks was not inconsistent with the collective bargaining agreement that provided for layoffs in reverse order of seniority. But in the *Watkins* v. *United Steelworkers* case, a federal district court ordered the employer to apply seniority to white and black workers separately and to allocate future layoffs between white and black workers in proportion to their representation on the work force at the time of the layoffs.[33]

The concept of *inverse* seniority in layoffs is gaining some adherents as a way out of the dilemma between the principle of reverse seniority in layoffs, on the one hand, and affirmative action, on the other. Under the concept of inverse seniority, the most senior workers are

[30] For an extensive discussion, see Winston L. Tillery, "Layoff and Recall Provisions in Major Agreements," *Monthly Labor Review*, 94:41–46 (July 1971).

[31] U.S. Department of Labor, "Layoff, Recall, and Worksharing Procedures," *Major Collective Bargaining Agreements*, Bulletin 1425–13, 1972, p. 3.

[32] Bureau of National Affairs, "Basic Patterns in Union Contracts," *Collective Bargaining Negotiations and Contracts*, Vol. 2, May 10, 1975, p. 53:1; and Tillery, "Layoff and Recall Provisions," p. 42.

[33] William R. Walter and Anthony J. Obadal, "Layoffs: The Judicial View," *The Personnel Administrator*, 20:13–16 (May 1975). In a far-reaching decision that will affect layoffs, job assignments, promotion consideration, and other matters, the U.S. Supreme Court ruled that retroactive seniority should commonly be awarded to plaintiffs whose job applications had been rejected in violation of the Civil Rights Act. Craig E. Polhemus, "Significant Decisions in Labor Cases," *Monthly Labor Review*, 99:51 (June 1976).

given the first opportunity to elect temporary layoff, and are provided with unemployment compensation plus supplemental unemployment benefits (SUB). The success of inverse seniority plans depends upon the SUB program in existence and state employment authorities' concurring in the legality of unemployment compensation payments.[34]

Bitterness, anger, shock, and/or disappointment are some of the emotions that are commonly experienced by those affected by a layoff. (See, for example, Figure 14-2.) In some instances, layoffs affect relatively small groups of people; sometimes, when a large corporation runs into serious problems, large numbers are laid off; and in some cases, an entire plant on which a local economy largely depends is shut down. In the latter two instances, a ripple or multiplier effect occurs in the community or region, affecting employment in many organizations and creating adverse local economic conditions.

Because of the human and economic consequences of large-scale layoffs, many contemporary organizations are going to considerable lengths to avoid laying off employees in precipitous and inhumane ways. For example, when the American Oil Company decided that it was necessary to close its El Dorado, Arkansas, refinery, employees were notified nine months in advance and hiring in the company's other facilities was frozen so that every effort could be made to relocate employees at other company sites. All employees were given a choice of transferring at company expense, or assistance in locating jobs elsewhere in the community, or early retirement. While there was some initial shock, even though a shutdown had been rumored for years, by and large most employees

and the community were appreciative of the way the company handled the situation.[35]

Outplacement programs to assist the affected worker in locating a new position, such as conducted by the American Oil Company, are becoming more prevalent in the case of employees who are laid off or terminated for whatever reason. Such programs typically include such components as:

1. Information to affected employees concerning planned action, including termination payments, and/or extension of benefits and outplacement services.

2. Announcements to other employers and to employment agencies concerning the availability of qualified employees.

3. Newspaper ads urging employers to contact the firm faced with the separations.

4. Development of résumés for each affected employee to be sent to potential employers.

5. Counseling with affected employees concerning job seeking methods and progress.[36]

Some firms that have enjoyed continuous growth have adopted a policy of retraining workers whose skills are no longer needed, in contrast to using layoffs. IBM, for example, has not laid off employees for economic reasons during a thirty-five-year period, but

---

[34]See R.T. Lund, D.C. Bumstead, and S. Friedman, "Inverse Seniority: Timely Answer to the Layoff Dilemma?" *Harvard Business Review*, 53:65–72 (September-October 1975).

[35]*The Wall Street Journal*, February 28, 1972, p. 1. For a description of the socially responsible effort to relocate those laid off from the Kennedy Space Center, see John A. Babec and John W. Lee, "The Cooperative Placement Center: Corporate Action to Assist Terminated Employees," *Personnel Journal*, 49:819–823 (October 1970). For interviews that highlight the physical and mental health consequences on terminated employees when a plant closes down, see Alfred Slote, *Termination: The Closing at Baker Plant* (Indianapolis: The Bobbs-Merrill Company, 1969).

[36]For a description of a comprehensive outplacement program, see Stanley R. Kase, "Your Employees: Outplaced—Not Out of Work," *The Personnel Administrator*, 21:49–52 (May 1976). See also George Lehner, "How to Manage the Victims of a Cutback," *Innovation*, May 1971, pp. 42–47.

(Paid advertisement)

Why don't they re-cycle engineers and technicians?

Because when you mass produce them, they are cheap enough to throw away and use new ones . . .

Engineers and technicians just don't last forever like the lawyers, doctors, dentists, etc. that you are going to school with.

As a bargaining agent for thousands of engineers and technicians in this country, SPEEA urges all engineers and technicians to consider the extreme overpopulation in this field. Maybe you should be considering a more permanent career opportunity — the risk is high, pay is low, and rewards are few — when they are done with you, you are just out in the cold.

Seattle Professional Engineering Employees Association

Univerity of Washington *Daily* Tuesday, October 19, 1971

Figure **14-2** An example of reactions to layoffs in Seattle, Washington

Used with permission.

has retrained and relocated them through an extensive corporate education program.[37]

DISCHARGE

Discharges involve separating employees from the payroll for violation of company rules or for inadequate performance. Union members and officials often label the discharge "capital punishment." Since discharge is a traumatic experience for everyone concerned, most managers are extremely reluctant to undertake such action. Fortunately, timely warnings and a developmental approach by supervisors in correcting problems can salvage a high proportion of

[37]*Business Week*, November 10, 1975, p. 110.

marginal cases. (See the discussions of progressive discipline in Chapter 8 and performance review in Chapter 15.) Further, many business organizations require each discharge case to be reviewed by higher authority before finalization. Federal civil service regulations, as well as most state and local civil service regulations, require all dismissals to be reviewed.[38]

Increasingly, the discharge of employees is being affected by the Civil Rights Act, the Age Discrimination in Employment Act, EEOC rulings, and court decisions. For example, in one case, 160 older employees of all ranks ranging up to the executive group at Standard Oil of California were terminated during a reduction in force; they complained that they were being separated to make way for younger replacements. The U.S. Department of Labor sued, and the consequence was an agreement that Standard Oil of California would reinstate the older workers and pay them $2 million.[39] In another case, female cabin attendants in the airline industry originally discharged after becoming pregnant were rehired as a result of court action.[40]

The discharge of employees is not uncommon, however, and management jealously guards the prerogative to discharge as an indispensable tool in maintaining standards of performance. Although labor-contract provisions and arbitration rulings tend to require discharge for "just cause," and the Civil Rights Act and the Age Discrimination in Employment Act are bringing discharge practices under increasing scrutiny, the principle of the right to discharge is well established in the United States.

RETIREMENT

The majority of employees in firms of above the smallest size are retired with the guarantee of some kind of pension in addition to government social security payments. One study, made some years ago, which excluded pension plans based on the profitability of the firm, found 69 percent of responding firms with pension plans for both white-collar and blue-collar employees, while 4 percent had plans for blue-collar employees only, and 5 percent had plans for white-collar employees only.[41] The proportion of firms with pension plans is undoubtedly higher now.

Typically, the age at which most employees may retire and receive full pension benefits is sixty-five, although some firms provide optional earlier retirement. Under EEOC guidelines, employers are now prohibited from establishing different retirement ages based on sex or from providing different benefits for the sexes.[42]

Actual age of retirement is frequently different from the normal retirement age stated in company manuals, with *some* employees working beyond age sixty-five in 79 percent of a sample encompassing 542 companies. The majority of firms generally have some mandatory retirement age, however, even though employees are permitted to work beyond the normal retirement age. The larger the firm, the more likely that the normal retirement age of sixty-five is a mandatory retirement age as well.[43]

[38]Robert W. Fisher, "When Workers Are Discharged—An Overview," *Monthly Labor Review*, 96:8 (June 1973).
[39]Bureau of National Affairs, *Bulletin to Management*, June 19, 1975, p. 5.
[40]*Seattle Times*, September 19, 1972, p. A-7.

[41]National Industrial Conference Board, "Personnel Practices in Factory and Office: Manufacturing," *Studies in Personnel Policy*, No. 194, 1964, p. 124.
[42]Equal Employment Opportunity Commission, *Guidelines on Discrimination Because of Sex*, as amended April 4, 1972.
[43]National Industrial Conference Board, pp. 15–18. When companies make a distinction between hourly paid and salaried workers in retirement policies or practices, salaried em-

One study, in a sample of 201 companies representing a cross section of industry and geography, found that a surprising 47 percent retirees had retired at an age earlier than that specified by the company as the normal retirement age. More than 75 percent of these early retirees had retired voluntarily.[44]

The whole notion of compulsory retirement is a controversial subject with persuasive arguments on both sides. Some argue that people differ greatly at age sixty-five in terms of mental alertness, health, interests, and drive and that retirement plans should be flexible. Others maintain that the only fair way to handle retirement is to set a maximum age and require everyone to comply with it. They reason further that, even if there were "objective" ways of measuring differences in capability among older employees, the hard feelings this practice would engender make such a plan highly undesirable. The concept of early retirement of executives at age sixty is also a controversial one, with many advocates on both sides of the issue.[45]

Mandatory retirement cases are also reaching the courts under the Age Discrimination in Employment Act. For example, a federal district court judge ruled that the city of Little Rock, Arkansas, violated the Act by compelling two firefighters to retire at age sixty-two. The court found no evidence that the employees would be more of a risk to the public and to their co-workers if they were to be retained until age sixty-five and that the city's apprehensions could be alleviated by giving older employees regular physical examinations.[46] Generally, the Department of Labor holds that mandatory retirements before age sixty-five are illegal unless the retirement requirement is (a) contained in a bona fide pension or retirement plan, (b) not optional under the plan, and (c) necessary for the economic survival of the plan. Plans that give employers the option of selecting employees for early retirement are suspect.[47]

As the statistics cited earlier suggest, there are alternatives to a single, fixed age for retirement. One fairly common practice establishes a "normal" retirement age at sixty-five and a mandatory retirement at some other age, such as sixty-eight. Other alternatives include (a) setting no fixed date but requiring an annual review of health and performance, (b) inviting selected retirees to return as consultants, (c) permitting retirees to apply for part-time or seasonal work, or (d) permitting "gradual retirement" (see below). It should also be noted that early retirement is sometimes used as a managerial device to remedy a staffing mistake. Voluntary early retirement also frequently occurs, as indicated by the study cited earlier.

A high percentage of firms have introduced a number of practices to help the older employee prepare for retirement. In one study, more than three-fourths of companies had some form of preretirement planning program.[48] Activities like preretirement seminars to discuss retirement problems and opportunities, individual and group counseling, and newsletters or

---

ployees are much less likely to be allowed to work beyond age sixty-five than hourly workers. Ibid., pp. 16–17.

[44] U. Vincent Manion, "Retiring Early?" *Personnel Administrator*, 17:18–21 (September-October 1972).

[45] For example, see the arguments advanced in "The Growing Trend to Early Retirement," *Business Week*, October 7, 1972, pp. 74–78; also, see Clarence B. Randall, "The Myth of Retirement," *Dun's Review and Modern Industry*, 76:34–36 (December 1960).

[46] Bureau of National Affairs, "Summary of Developments," *Labor Relations Reporter*, June 28, 1976, pp. 1–2. Yet the U.S. Supreme Court ruled that the Massachusetts law requiring retirement of state police officers at age fifty did not violate the equal protection clause of the 14th Amendment to the Constitution. Bureau of National Affairs, *Labor Relations Reporter*, Special Supplement, June 26, 1976, 12 FEP Cases 1569–1573.

[47] Bureau of National Affairs, *Bulletin to Management*, June 19, 1975, p. 5.

[48] "New Directions in Employee Pre-Retirement Planning Programs," *P-H/ASPA Survey*, Prentice-Hall, 1976, p. 15.

magazines written especially for those of preretirement age are frequently included in such programs.[49] In addition, some companies make an effort to have retirees remain identified with the company by inviting them to social events, having special days for retirees to visit the company, retaining the names of retired employees on mailing lists for the company's newspaper or magazine, and sponsoring retired-employees' clubs. A small minority of firms permit gradual retirement, involving a gradual reduction of the workweek or providing for progressively longer annual paid vacations or leaves without pay.

Paradoxically, although motivational theory suggests that very effective performers express high satisfaction with the intrinsic aspects of the job—challenge, responsibility, sense of achievement, for example—these same employees may have the most difficult adjustment to make upon retirement. One study of male managers between the ages of sixty and sixty-five found that the "job-oriented" managers—those expressing satisfaction with achievement, recognition, advancement, and so forth—had less favorable attitudes about retirement than did the "context-related" managers—those expressing satisfaction with such aspects of the job as salary, interpersonal relations, and working conditions.[50] This suggests that while a continuation of social relationships will be important to some retirees, others will need in-

trinsically challenging and meaningful tasks to occupy their energies after retirement. Preretirement seminars, the gradual retirement concept, and consulting opportunities would seem to have particular promise for the latter group.

SOME SUMMARY COMMENTS, PART 5

The staffing process consists of a complex flow of events that include human resources planning, authorization for staffing, developing sources of applicants, evaluation of applicants, employment decisions and offers, induction and orientation, transfers, demotions, promotions, and separations. This flow of events is directed toward keeping organizational positions filled with qualified people so that organizational objectives can be achieved.

It is obvious that effective recruitment and selection of human resources and their subsequent reassignment are as vital to the health of an organization as the effective procurement and allocation of capital, capital equipment, and materials and as the location and development of markets. None of these activities can exist without the others. It is equally obvious that the quality of those who manage the other broad managerial processes depends to a large extent upon the quality of the staffing process. Inefficient use of capital, equipment, and materials, high turnover of personnel, and organizational turmoil can easily result from poor administration of this process.

Effective staffing must be based on both short-range and long-range plans. Provisions must be made not only for the successful completion of current tasks, but also for the adequate staffing of new tasks as they evolve and for the adequate replacement of key personnel as they leave the organization. A shortage of managerial talent or technical skills can result in a serious time lag in competitive ability while

[49] For a description of a company preretirement planning course, see Chester T. O'Connell, "Long-Service and Retiring Employees," in Joseph J. Famularo, *Handbook of Modern Personnel Administration* (New York: McGraw-Hill Book Company, 1972), Chapter 71. For a discussion of some of the important issues and data that preretirement discussion groups can profitably address, see Manfred Tatzmann, "How to Prevent Retirement Shock," *Personnel Administrator*, 17:45–48 (September-October 1972). Other organizations, such as churches, universities, unions, and libraries also sponsor preretirement programs.

[50] Shoukry D. Saleh and Jay L. Otis, "Sources of Job Satisfaction and Their Effects on Attitudes toward Retirement," *Journal of Industrial Psychology*, 1:101–106 (December 1965).

the required resources are being recruited or upgraded. For long-range success, the staffing process must be based on a long-range viewpoint.

Given the crucial role of devices such as job specifications, application blanks, interviews and tests in staffing decisions, it is essential that each enterprise carefully study the validity of these devices in the context of organizational objectives, civil rights legislation, Equal Employment Opportunity Commission rulings, and court decisions. The concept of job-relatedness has become increasingly important. A combination of statistical and clinical validation has been recommended as a way of increasing the validity of devices used in staffing and thus the validity of staffing decisions.

The identification of managerial talent is also a critical aspect of the staffing process. Traits, behaviors, and the environmental context all appear to be significant in successful management performance. The promotion of women and minorities into managerial positions is now an urgent matter for many organizations under contemporary EEOC and court rulings. Assessment centers are being used more extensively for the identification of management talent and have proved useful in affirmative action.

Involuntary moves of managers are coming under increasing scrutiny by critics and by companies. Fallback positions are sometimes used in promotion situations.

Analyzing rates of resignation and reasons for terminations can assist in identifying possible areas of mismanagement. Group induction and orientation methods that help the new employee understand the new assignment, deal with anxieties, and understand the culture of the organization show promise of reducing turnover and enhancing performance.

Job ladders can be useful in planning careers and developing training programs. Job posting is required under some labor contracts and is being used increasingly as a vehicle for communicating opportunities to employees and/or complying with EEOC ratings.

Traditional seniority rights and affirmative action programs are in direct conflict in many layoff situations, and court decisions are beginning to probe the dilemma. Inverse seniority provisions have been negotiated in some labor management agreements as a partial solution. Outplacement programs, in the case of layoff situations, have been successfully used by many firms.

The right to discharge nonproductive employees is essential in maintaining standards of performance, but the discharge of an employee must be for just cause and only after judicious review. Although controversy exists over whether a company should have a uniform, fixed, and mandatory retirement age, most managers agree that preretirement orientation programs and postretirement relationships with retired employees are highly desirable. Assisting preretirees in finding avenues for significant expression of self-actualization needs after retirement presents a major challenge. The EEOC, the Department of Labor, and the courts are increasingly involved in cases pertaining to both discharge and retirement.

REVIEW AND DISCUSSION QUESTIONS

1. What are some of the problems faced by the new employee? How can they be minimized?

2. What is meant by job posting? What would be the pros and cons of posting all vacancies in an organization?

3. Discuss demotions in the light of Maslow's need hierarchy, and, more specifically, discuss the procedures used in the Golembiewski study vis-á-vis Maslow's ideas.

4. What do you think the role of the personnel department should be in (a) orientation, (b) transfers, (c) promotions, (d) demotions, and (e) discharges?

5. How might exit interviews be most constructively used?

6. Discuss retirement in the light of Maslow's need hierarchy.

7. What procedures do you think should be followed in the shutdown of one plant in a multiplant company?

8. Discuss the functional and dysfunctional aspects of geographical transfer of managers.

9. What is the difference between reverse seniority and inverse seniority in layoffs?

10.   What is meant by a fallback position?

11. What do EEOC guidelines and court decisions under civil rights legislation say about what a company can or cannot do with respect to (a) promotions, (b) layoffs, (c) discharge, and (d) retirement?

SUPPLEMENTAL REFERENCES

Brackett, Jean, "Retired Couples Budget Updated to Autumn 1971," *Monthly Labor Review*, 95:35–36 (July 1972).

Burren, James E., Robert N. Butler, Samuel W. Greenhouse, Louis Sekeloff, and Marian R. Yarrow, *Human Aging: A Biological and Behavioral Study* (Washington, D.C.: U.S. Department of Health, Education, and Welfare, 1963).

Couch, Peter D., and Earl F. Lundgren, "Making Voluntary Retirement Programs Work," *Personnel Journal*, 42:135–138 (March 1963).

Domm, Donald R., and James E. Stafford, "Assimilating Blacks into the Organization," *California Management Review*, 15:46–51 (Fall 1972).

Dunnette, Marvin D., Richard D. Arvey, and Paul A. Banes, "Why Do They Leave?" *Personnel*, 50:25–39 (May-June 1973).

Ferguson, Lawrence L., "Better Management of Manager's Careers," *Harvard Business Review*, 44:139–152 (March-April 1966).

Finkle, Robert B., and William S. Jones, *Assessing Corporate Talent* (New York: Wiley-Interscience, 1970).

Hahn, Marilyn L., "Equal Rights for Women in Career Development," *Personnel*, 47:55–59 (July-August 1970).

Helfgott, Roy B., "Easing the Impact of Technological Change on Employees: A Conspectus of United States Experience," *International Labor Review*, 91:503–520 (June 1965).

Hopkins, Mary E., and Marcia A. Wood, "Who Wants to Retire?" *The Personnel Administrator*, 21:38–41 (October 1976).

Jennings, Ken, "When a Quit Is Not a Quit," *Personnel Journal*, 50:927–932 (December 1971).

Kleemeier, Robert W., ed., *Aging and Leisure* (New York: Oxford University Press, 1961).

LaLiff, James M., "The Exit Interview: Antiquated or Underrated?" *The Personnel Administrator*, 21:55–60 (May 1976).

Lipsky, David B., "Interplant Transfer and Terminated Workers: A Case Study," *Industrial and Labor Relations Review*, 23:191–206 (January 1970).

Little, Royal, "Don't Let Your Brain Lie Down," *Fortune*, 84:164–167ff. (November 1971).

Marriott, Dave, "A Sociologist Looks at Induction," *Personnel Review*, 3:4–9 (Winter 1974).

Miller, G.A., and L.W. Wagner, "Adult Socialization, Organizational Structure and Role Orientation," *Administrative Science Quarterly*, 16:151–163 (June 1971).

More, Douglas M., "Demotion," *Social Problems*, 9:213–221 (Winter 1962).

Purcell, Theodore V., S.J. Rodgers, and Irene W. Rodgers, "Young Black Workers Speak Their Minds," *California Management Review*, 14:45–51 (Summer 1972).

"The Push for Pension Reform," *Business Week*, March 17, 1973, pp. 46–58.

Schein, E.H., "Organizational Socialization and the Profession of Management," *Industrial Management Review*, 9:1–16 (Winter 1968).

Shepard, David I., "Relationship of Job Satisfaction to Situational and Personal Characteristics of Terminating Employees," *Personal Journal*, 46:567–571 (October 1967).

Speigelman, Paul J., "Bona Fide Seniority Systems and Relief from 'Last Hired, First Fired' Layoffs under Title VII," *Employee Relations Law Journal*, 2:141–154 (Autumn 1976).

Sukov, Marvin, "Creative Retirement," *Geriatrics*, 26:83–87 (July 1971).

Tyson, Robert C., "Let's Keep Our Dual Retirement System," *Harvard Business Review*, 46:2–4ff. (March-April 1968).

U.S. Department of Labor, "Seniority in Promotion and Transfer Provisions," *Major Collective Bargaining Agreements*, Bulletin 1425-11, March 1970.

Van Maanen, John, "Breaking In: Socialization to Work," in Robert Dubin, ed., *Handbook of Work, Organization, and Society* (Chicago: Rand McNally College Publishing Company, 1976), pp. 67–130.

Westcott, Robert F., "How To Fire an Executive," *Business Horizons*, 19:33–36 (April 1976).

6

PART 6
THE APPRAISAL AND TRAINING AND DEVELOPMENT PROCESSES

Part 6 will examine two major personnel processes—performance appraisal and training and development. These processes are so highly interdependent in today's business organizations that it seems logical to put them together in the same section. Part 6 will also include a chapter on the management and development of a particularly highly trained segment of the work force—engineers, scientists, and other professionals.

PERFORMANCE APPRAISAL

The term *appraisal,* as used in this section, means *evaluation* of the performance of employees. The communication and the impact of appraisals are so interdependent with the appraisal that I will deal also with these subjects.

Broadly speaking, appraisal is a continual process in the majority of enterprises in the sense that it is occurring most of the time. The

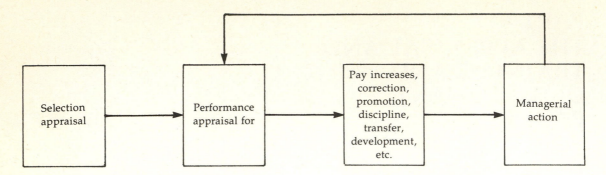

Figure **6-a**   The appraisal process

concept *appraisal process* emphasizes the pervasiveness and universality of evaluating performance and provides a convenient context for discussing this phenomenon. Obviously, appraisal can also be discussed in connection with each of the various personnel management processes we have identified, including staffing, compensation, training, and development. For convenience and emphasis, however, appraisal is analyzed separately in this section.

Evaluation of employees' performance or potential occurs for a number of reasons, including the development of data for decisions on selection, correction, training, and development, increases in pay, promotions, transfers, discipline, and the like. The purpose of appraisal, then, is to provide data about past, present, and expected performance so that appropriate decisions can be made.

Although appraisals tend to be taking place somewhere within the organization at any moment in time, systematic or formalized appraisals of an individual employee are likely to occur at intervals throughout that person's history of employment. Thus, Jane Smith is appraised when she is considered for employment, during the first few days on the job for the purpose of correction, at the end of six months and each six months thereafter for the purpose of salary review, at the end of one year

and each subsequent year for the purpose of an *appraisal* or *coaching interview*, at the end of three years for the purpose of evaluating her for promotion, and so forth. In a sense, then, as shown in Figure 6-a, the appraisal procedure as it applies to an individual employee is cyclical in that it tends to be repeated again and again.

It should be recognized, however, that, in addition to systematic or formalized appraisal, informal and nonsystematic appraisal tends to occur constantly within a going enterprise. People are always evaluating each other either at a conscious or subconscious level. Even in the unlikely situation where a supervisor pays little or no attention to a subordinate, evaluation is really going on, since the continuation of wages must assume at least some minimum level of performance. Thus, the problem is not one of deciding whether to engage in the appraisal process but rather one of deciding upon the frequency of appraisal, upon the devices and systems to be used, and how to make appraisal constructive. Another issue is how unilateral versus collaborative the appraisal is to be.

It should be recognized that subordinates are constantly appraising each other and their superiors, although such appraisals are seldom formalized. Some discussion of appraisal by peers and evaluation of superiors by subordinates occurs in the chapter that follows, although the chapter's primary focus will be on systematic or formalized appraisals of subordinates by superiors.

As in other areas of personnel management, we encounter semantic problems. In addition to the word *appraisal,* the terms *merit rating* and *performance review* are often used to denote the evaluation of employees. I use these terms interchangeably.

TRAINING AND DEVELOPMENT

The *training and development process* is a complex combination of many subprocesses concerned with increasing the capabilities of individuals and groups in contributing to the attainment of organizational goals. Included in the highly complex flows of events are the determination of training and developmental needs, induction and orientation (previously discussed as an aspect of the staffing process), skill training, the appraisal interview (to be discussed in Chapter 15), employee counseling, and programs for the development of all employees, including managers and professionals. Also included are self-initiated developmental activities during off hours, such as attendance at high school, college, and university; reading; and participation in community activities.

Implicit also are the demands, challenges, and experiences of the job itself, which, if they lead to personal growth, may be considered part of the organizational training and development process. The way the individual responds, or is motivated to respond, to these demands and challenges is as much an aspect of training and development as formal seminars or programs of appraisal. My discussion, however, will emphasize the more formalized activities that are consciously planned to result in increased individual, group, or organizational effectiveness.

A process highly related to training and development is *organization development,* which will be treated separately in Part 9. During the past few years, the managers of many organizations, both in the United States and abroad, have been trying to create organizations largely corresponding to the "organic systems" described in Chapter 5. These efforts at change tend to focus on work teams learning how to manage group processes and their relationships with other units more effectively. In such organizations, then, we may refer to a broad *organizational training and developmental process.* (See Figure 6-b.)

Although there is no standardized usage of the terms *skill training* and *development,* the former is ordinarily used to mean vocational training of an immediate or relatively narrow application. Examples of skill training are learning how to wire a tabulating machine, read blueprints, interpret radar signals on a radar screen, and take shorthand. *Management and employee development* connotes future or general applicability and suggests heavier emphasis on concepts, theory, and intellectual and emotional growth. Examples are seminars in such areas as organization theory, management of operations, business and its environment, and the human aspects of administration. A private conference between superior and subordinate that summarizes performance to date and makes plans for the subordinate's future growth might also be called "development." Thus, the terms *training* and *development* are not mutually exclusive, but they do suggest a difference in emphasis or level of abstraction.

Chapter 16 will emphasize skill training— formalized vocational training in the classroom or on the job. It will also include a discussion of certain problems relevant to both skill training and general developmental programs, such as determining the need for such programs. Chapter 17 will focus primarily on educational and developmental programs with broader or more general purposes, such as changing attitudes or increased capacity to carry out future

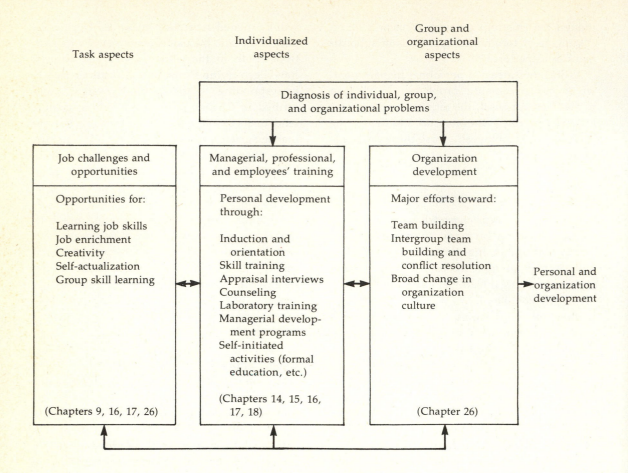

Figure **6-b**   The organizational training and development process

managerial assignments. Organization development will be discussed in Chapter 26.

THE MANAGEMENT AND DEVELOPMENT OF THE ENGINEER, SCIENTIST, AND PROFESSIONAL

The final chapter of Part 6 will focus on engineers, scientists, and other professionals. Science and technology are changing our organizations, our communities, and our world so rapidly that it seems important to focus not only on the phenomenon of change itself but on the people who, along with others, are key instruments in such change. Along with the managerial and executive group, scientists, engineers, and other professionals in some ways constitute a special "problem" in personnel management or challenge of major importance to our institutions and society. Chapter 18 will discuss why these people constitute a unique challenge and some of the special problems associated with their management and development.

CHAPTER 15
PERFORMANCE APPRAISAL AND MANAGEMENT BY OBJECTIVES

This chapter will focus on different kinds of appraisal systems and will discuss management by objectives.

Because the *way* in which such systems are used may have more of an impact than the details of any particular appraisal device, I will also deal with the communication of appraisals and the context in which they occur. Probably no other area of management is so fraught with anxiety on the part of both supervisors and subordinates and has so much potential for either positive or negative consequences in terms of morale, motivation, and development. We will begin with a discussion of merit rating, then move on to a discussion of appraisal interviews and coaching, followed by a further look at management by objectives and its effect on personnel management.

MERIT RATING

A large majority of industrial organizations use systematic performance appraisal procedures for both nonsupervisory and managerial employees. Nonindustrial organizations, including branches of the military services, government, hospitals, and universities, also make extensive use of such plans.

One study of 150 firms reported that 84 percent had some form of appraisal system for office employees; 54 percent used appraisal systems for production employees. Of those firms having appraisal systems, 81 percent used a standard rating form in the case of office employees; 76 percent used a standard form for production workers. About half of the systems required a written statement about the employee's performance; more than one-fourth used some kind of checklist. A small proportion of firms used some other method, such as ranking. Five percent used "other methods" that, presumably, included the use of some form of performance standards or management by objectives (MBO), i.e., some formalized system of superior-subordinate goal setting.[1]

Another study, based largely on manufacturing companies (about 1,000 firms) reported about the same proportion of responding firms—more than 80 percent—had some form of appraisal system. But in sharp contrast to the study just cited, approximately 20 percent of the firms used some form of trait rating, while over 75 percent reported the use of some form of MBO or performance standard system.[2]

In still another study, a questionnaire was sent to the top personnel/industrial relations executives in the "Fortune 500" list of largest industrial firms. Out of 403 responses, 181 (45 percent) said that MBO was being utilized in at least part of the company. A second questionnaire was sent to those companies that had indicated use of MBO, giving a more detailed description of MBO and additional questions. Eleven companies were frank to say they did not use MBO as defined; and 50 of the original respondents failed to respond the second time. The data, along with comments from respondents, were interpreted by the researchers to mean that the number of users of MBO was substantially less than first reported.[3] (To see how many of these MBO efforts were considered successful, see "Validity of MBO" at the end of this chapter.)

Formal appraisal programs for managers are also found in a high proportion of organizations. One study found about 75 percent of 139 responding firms had some form of formalized appraisal system, usually pertaining to all levels of management. The most common techniques used were the essay evaluation (52 percent of companies with appraisal programs), and rating scales (45 percent). More than one technique was in use in some companies, e.g., both rating scales and an essay evaluation might be used. Although it was not clear to what extent formalized MBO programs were being used, 77 percent of the firms using formal appraisal systems reported that achievement of goals was a major factor in appraisals.[4]

Surveys typically indicate more use of formal performance appraisal procedures for midlevel managers, supervisors, and nonexempt white-collar employees than for blue-collar workers. The lesser incidence with blue-collar workers undoubtedly reflects the widespread practice of paying production and maintenance workers straight hourly rates or using rate ranges through which they progress based on length of service (see Figure 21-2, Chapter 21).

The most common interval between formal ratings as indicated in these studies was one year. This held true for office, production, and managerial employees. The second most frequent interval was six months.[5]

The most common uses of appraisals in the studies cited above were for determining wage or salary increases, and for making promotion decisions. Other uses were goal setting, determining training and management development needs, human resources planning, and validat-

[1] Bureau of National Affairs, "Employee Performance: Evaluation and Control," Personnel Policies Forum Survey, No. 108, February 1975, pp. 2–4.

[2] Glenn H. Varney, "Performance Appraisal—Inside and Out," The Personnel Administrator, 17:17 (November–December 1972). Another study could be interpreted as finding 26 out of 46 (57 percent) large firms having some form of MBO program. See Robert A. Zawacki and Robert L. Taylor, "A View of Performance Appraisal from Organizations Using It," Personnel Journal, 55:290–292ff. (June 1976).

[3] Fred E. Schuster and Alva F. Kindall, "Management by Objectives: Where We Stand—A Survey of the Fortune 500," Human Resource Management, 13:8–11 (Spring 1974).

[4] Bureau of National Affairs, "Management Performance: Appraisal Programs," Personnel Policies Forum, Survey No. 104, January 1974, pp. 1–3.

[5] Bureau of National Affairs, "Employee Performance," p. 2.

ing selection and promotion procedures. While in a high proportion of firms appraisal results were discussed with the employee, most firms did not report feedback and discussion as a primary purpose of the appraisal.[6]

Many different kinds of formal merit-rating systems are in use. Mahler cites some twenty different major variables that can differentiate these systems, including the general method, method of installation, frequency of rating, who does the rating, the number of raters, extent of training given raters, the traits rated, the use of scores, the purpose of the ratings, and so forth.[7] I would add the following: whether the rating system is part of a comprehensive MBO effort (ratings still need to be made even if there is an MBO program), how much open dialogue occurs between the rater and ratee about the appraisal, and the extent of union involvement. Any or all of these variables constitute dimensions that can make an appraisal system in one organization quite different from an appraisal system in another organization.

TRADITIONAL MERIT-RATING DEVICES

There are numerous devices used in traditional merit rating. The *graphic rating-scale method*, also called the "chart method," is the most frequently used.[8] With this method the rater places a check mark on a form next to the word or phrase describing the degree of merit for each of several different traits, such as "quality of work," "quantity of work," "cooperation,"

and so forth. Degrees of merit might run from "inadequate" to "superior," "below average" to "above average," and the like. (See Figure 15-1.)

A major problem with graphic rating scales is that words like *superior*, *average*, and the like mean different things to different people. The traits themselves—loyalty, production, and cooperation, for example—also are subject to different interpretations. These problems can be minimized by training raters or by using descriptive statements to explain the various degrees on each scale of traits.

Another device in traditional merit rating is the *rank-order method*, in which a supervisor ranks all employees from best to poorest in one or more traits. If groups differ in size, statistical corrections need to be made to compare the relative standing of individuals in one group with that of individuals in another group.[9] Another difficulty with ranking methods such as the rank-order method or the paired-comparison method (see below) is that the distance in performance between two people tends to be obscured.

Another rating technique is the *forced-distribution method*, in which the individuals rated are distributed along one or more scales and fixed percentages of employees are assigned to the best and worst ends of the scale and to the middle bracket. This method is similar to the teaching technique of "grading on the curve."

Another device is the *paired-comparison method* in which, for each trait to be considered, every subordinate is compared with every other subordinate. When the number of favorable choices is tallied for each individual, the method then reveals itself to be a detailed-ranking method. The only difference between this method and straight ranking is that in the

[6] Bureau of National Affairs, "Management Performance Appraisal Programs," pp. 1–7; and "Employee Performance," pp. 1–10.

[7] Walter R. Mahler, "Let's Get More Scientific in Rating Employees," in M. Joseph Dooher and Vivienne Marquis, eds., *Rating Employee and Supervisory Performance* (New York: American Management Association, 1950), pp. 53–54.

[8] See Richard V. Miller, "Merit Rating in Industry: A Survey of Current Practices and Problems," *ILR Research*, 5:14 (Fall 1959); and Joseph Tiffin, "6 Merit Rating Systems," *Personnel Journal*, 37:288 (January 1959).

[9] See Joseph Tiffin, "Merit Rating: Its Validity and Techniques," in Dooher and Marquis, *Rating Employee and Supervisory Performance*, p. 17.

Performance appraisal — Salaried employees–non-exempt

Name | Position
Division | Department
Date | Date of last review

Instructions

Evaluate the employee on the job *now being performed*. Circle the dot in the space above the horizontal line which most nearly expressed your over-all judgment on each quality. The care and accuracy with which this appraisal is made will determine its value to you, to the employee and to the organization.

Consider the employee's performance since the last appraisal and show by a check (√) whether he/she has gone back, remained stationary or gone ahead in each of the qualities listed to the left.

Quality	(best)				(worst)	Has improved	Little or no change	Has gone back	Comments
Knowledge of work: Consider knowledge of the job gained through experience; general education; specialized training.	Well informed on all phases of work.	Knowledge thorough enough to perform without assistance.	Adequate grasp of essentials. Some assistance.	Requires considerable assistance.	Inadequate knowledge.				Comments
Quantity of work: Consider the volume of work produced under normal conditions. Disregard errors.	Rapid worker. Usually big producer.	Turns out good volume.	Average.	Volume below average.	Very slow worker.				Comments
Quality of work: Consider neatness, accuracy and dependability of results regardless of volume.	Exceptionally accurate, practically no mistakes.	Acceptable, usually neat, occasional errors or rejections.	Seldom necessary to check work.	Often unacceptable, frequent errors or rejections.	Too many errors or rejections.				Comments
Ability to learn new duties: Consider the speed with which he masters new routine and grasps explanations. Consider also ability to retain this knowledge.	Exceptionally fast to learn and adjust to changed conditions.	Learns rapidly. Retains instructions.	Average instruction required.	Requires a great deal of instruction.	Very slow to absorb. Poor memory.				Comments
Initiative: Consider the tendency to contribute, develop and/or carry out new ideas or methods.	Initiative resulting in frequent saving in time and money.	Very resourceful.	Shows initiative occasionally.	Rarely shows any initiative.	Needs constant prodding.				Comments
Cooperation: Consider manner of handling business relationships.	Goes out of the way to cooperate.	Gets along well with associates.	Acceptable.	Shows reluctance to cooperate.	Very poor cooperation.				Comments
Judgment and common sense: Does employee think intelligently and make decisions logically?	Thinks quickly, logically. Outstanding.	Judgment usually logical.	Fairly reliable.	Inclined to be illogical.	Poor. Unreliable.				Comments

Figure 15-1 Example of performance appraisal form

Used with permission.

(Back)

Instructions: Based on the appraisal you have made on the reverse side please answer the following questions in your own words.

Do you see any need for improvement on the previous performance factors? ☐ Yes ☐ No (If "yes" please explain)

Is employee well suited for type of work he/she is now doing? ☐ Yes ☐ No (If "no" indicate type of work for which he/she is suited)

What contribution has employee made to company, department or division beyond normal requirements of position?

What would be your overall evaluation of employee? (Place check (√) above horizontal line)

Excellent	Good	Satisfactory	Fair	Poor

Any difference of opinion between the immediate supervisor and the reviewing supervisor should be reconciled if possible. If not possible, the points of difference should be noted in this space.

Reviewed by _____ | Date _____

Questions to be answered after discussion of appraisal with employee

What was the attitude of the employee toward the discussion of the appraisal?

If improvement is indicated what suggestions have you made?

Remarks or any further comments you may have for improvement.

Completed by _____ | Date _____

This appraisal was discussed with employee on: _____ | Date _____

Figure 15-1   Continued

paired-comparison method only two individuals are considered at one time, which presumably makes choice easier and more accurate. One difficulty, however, is that the number of comparisons increases geometrically as the size of the group to be rated increases. The number of comparisons will be $N(N-1)/2$, where N is the number of people to be rated.[10]

The *critical-incident technique* involves keeping a record of unusually good or undesirable incidents occurring in an employee's work and provides a factual record for subsequent discussions and decision making.[11] One drawback in this method is the possibility that the supervisor may accumulate a number of "bad" incidents, unload them on subordinates at six-month or one-year intervals, and neglect to discuss them at the time of occurrence, when discussion would be the most meaningful. (See also behaviorally anchored rating scales, later in the chapter.)

The *forced-choice rating method* features a series of descriptive statements in sets of four, with the rater choosing the most descriptive and least descriptive statements from each set. This method appears to minimize both the problem of the halo effect and the problem of different interpretation of the meaning of points on trait-scales.[12] The halo effect, as discussed in Chapter 12, is the tendency for the rater to rate a person high on every trait if the person is outstanding in one particularly desirable characteristic and to rate the person low on all traits if there is some particularly conspicuous undesirable characteristic.[13]

PROBLEMS WITH MERIT RATING

In addition to the problems of reliability and validity, which will be discussed later, a number of problems in appraising performance are particularly important. Assuming the performance of groups to be relatively equal, one problem is the tendency of some supervisors to rate their people high and other supervisors to rate their particular subordinates low. One study of thirty department heads found that four of them rated their subordinates so severely that all were rated below the poorest ratings made by the two most lenient department heads.[14] Other studies have found some appraisers to be "high differentiators," i.e., allocating subordinate ratings across most of or all the range of scales, and some to be "low differentiators," i.e., using a limited range of the scale in differentiating subordinates.[15] This kind of problem can be partly solved through training, forced distributions, or statistical corrections.

It is, however, possible for one group to be superior to others, although, realistically, the kind of discrepancies described are not too likely. Because of such causes as differences in

[10]For a description of these and other methods, see Winston Oberg, "Make Performance Appraisal Relevant," *Harvard Business Review*, 50:61–67 (January-February 1972); Norman R.F. Maier, *Psychology in Industrial Organizations*, 4th ed., (Boston: Houghton Mifflin Company, 1973), pp. 183–193; and Andrew R. Baggaley, "A Scheme for Classifying Rating Methods," *Personnel Psychology*, 27:139–144 (1974).

[11]See John C. Flanagan and Robert K. Burns, "The Employee Performance Record: A New Appraisal and Development Tool," *Harvard Business Review*, 33:95–102 (September-October 1955). A later version that has been suggested provides the rater with a *specimen checklist* that assists the rater in recalling incidents. See Barry M. Cohen, "A New Look at Performance Appraisal: The Specimen Check List," *Human Resources Management*, 11:18–22 (Spring 1972).

[12]See Reign Bittner, "Developing an Employee Merit Rating Procedure," *Personnel Psychology*, 1:430–32 (Winter 1948).

[13]Research shows that the presence of noncompliant workers, i.e., those who resist orders, results in increased rewards and higher ratings for compliant workers. Ronald J. Grey and David Kiphis, "Untangling the Performance Appraisal Dilemma: The Influence of Perceived Organizational Context on Evaluative Processes," *Journal of Applied Psychology*, 61:329–335 (June 1976).

[14]Lee Stockford and H.W. Bissell, "Factors Involved in Establishing a Merit-Rating Scale," *Personnel*, 26:97 (September 1949).

[15]Abraham Pizam, "Social Differentiation—A New Psychological Barrier to Performance Appraisal," *Public Personnel Management*, 4:244–247 (July-August 1975).

standards in original selection or differences in leadership or motivation, one group may be quite superior to another. These differences must be taken into account if employees are to feel fairly treated. Assessing such possible differences between groups is particularly difficult. As in the case of comparisons within groups, the more objective the data management can obtain about between-group differences, the better these assessments will be.

Another problem is that any use of numerical scores can be misleading unless appropriate statistics and good judgment are applied. For example, when "above average" is assigned ten points on a "quality of work" scale, and "above average" is assigned five points on a "cooperation" scale, it is commonly assumed that quality of work is being given more weight than cooperation. The fact is that the *distribution* of scores on these traits is a major determiner of the weighting. To illustrate: If all employees are rated above average on "quality of work," this trait will not distinguish one employee from the other and will not affect relative ranking on a total score. On the other hand, if employees are distributed widely on the "cooperation" scale, the latter is the scale that actually has more weight.

Another problem has to do with the relevance of the traits rated. Obviously, there is no validity in rating traits that have no relationship to the job in question. Other problems include the halo effect and the obtaining of information on the actual performance of the ratee. Ratings made when little is known about actual performance are going to be that much less valid. Thus, there is the need for systematic attention to obtaining relevant data about jobs and employees' performance on those jobs.

Other problems, which can occur in the use of any personnel system or device, are (a) the tendency of some managers to rely too heavily on the system or device rather than exercising appropriate judgment, and (b) the distortions that can occur if the rules of administration require a particular course of action for a particular rating. Taking automatic action on the basis of a rating without regard to its meaning or without regard to other important variables makes appraisal a monster rather than a useful tool. The Federal Civil Service discovered this effect soon after the Classification Act of 1923 required dismissal if a civil servant's rating fell below "good" on a scale of excellent, very good, good, fair, and unsatisfactory. As a consequence, it was rare for any agency to rate anyone below "good."[16] Some of the deficiencies of the law were remedied in the Performance Rating Act of 1950, but ratings still resulted in automatic consequences. Since the law required a minimum of three levels—"outstanding," "satisfactory," and "unsatisfactory"—and required that *all* aspects of an employee's performance must be "outstanding" in order to receive an outstanding ranking and that discharge was mandatory in the case of an "unsatisfactory" ranking, 99 percent of the employees were rated "satisfactory."[17]

PEER AND SUBORDINATE RATINGS

Although most rating systems involve superiors rating subordinates, and most people probably prefer this arrangement,[18] *peer ratings*—ratings by those of equal rank—and *subordinate ratings*—ratings by those of inferior rank—have

[16] Felix A. Nigro, *Public Personnel Administration* (New York: Henry Holt and Company, 1959), p. 307.

[17] Ibid., pp. 295, 309–310. For a discussion of some of the competitive and political problems associated with performance appraisal, see Alan L. Patz, "Performance Appraisal: Useful But Still Resisted," *Harvard Business Review*, 53:74–80 (May-June 1975).

[18] There is some evidence for this observation. In one study, 78 percent of a group of 1,800 army officers said "no" when asked if they would prefer to be rated by officers of equal rank, 77 percent said "no" when asked if they would prefer to be rated by officers of lower rank. Bittner, "Developing an Industrial Merit Rating Procedure," p. 409.

been used with effectiveness in a few situations. The greatest use of the peer-rating technique seems to have occurred in research about military organizations, although there has been some actual use of such ratings in assigning people to military combat teams, in selecting supervisors in industry, and in assisting supervisors to improve their performance. Ratings of supervisors by their subordinates have been used in industry to assist managers in improving their own performance. Students' ratings are also used in universities to assist professors in improving lectures and course content.

To give an example of the use of peer ratings, among rank-and-file workers at the Ansul Chemical Company peer ratings have been used to assist in making decisions about promotions to the position of foreman.[19] Peer ratings have also been used in the life insurance industry to assist in making decisions about promotions to managerial jobs.[20] Peer ratings, along with ratings by superiors and subordinates, have been used in a refinery of the Gulf Oil Corporation as a tool in improving supervisory performance.[21] Subordinates' ratings of superiors have been used by the Esso Research and Engineering Company with the objective of improving supervisory performance.[22]

Probably a major problem in the use of peer or subordinate ratings is the potential danger that the ratings may be made on the basis of performance that is useful to the rater but not necessarily to the enterprise. For example, in

Chapter 7 I cited some evidence that subordinates prefer a different pattern of behavior from supervisors than is expected by the supervisors' superiors. Thus, management must be cautious in interpreting the results of peer and subordinate ratings and must not abdicate decision making to subordinates.

Thought must also be given to the purposes of peer and subordinate ratings. Distortion of "true" judgments are probably least likely to occur when such ratings are made for purposes of research. On the other hand, these distortions are probably greatest when such ratings are used for decisions on pay increases and/or promotions, since such decisions can have an effect on the rater. To illustrate, a person might rate a peer lower than warranted if one thought a higher rating might reduce one's own pay increase. However, there is some evidence that peers may not distort peer ratings, at least when rating colleagues for possible promotion. In a study made in three insurance companies, agents were told that the results of peer ratings might ". . . be used administratively as one part of the overall process of assistant manager selection . . ." yet the results were predictive of future managerial success in all three companies.[23] (See additional research under the topic of "Peer and Superior Ratings" in Chapter 13.)

GROUP OR COMMITTEE APPRAISAL

Although the person who typically performs the appraisal is the immediate supervisor, the next most frequent structure involves the superior plus the next higher level of supervision. Although most such ratings are made independently, whether involving one or more superiors, ratings are sometimes made by a group or committee. This procedure has been supported on the grounds that several people who know

[19]"Foremen by Popular Acclaim," *Business Week*, March 26, 1965, p. 171.
[20]Eugene C. Mayfield, "Peer Nominations—A Neglected Selection Tool," *Personnel*, 48:37–43 (July-August 1971). A related technique is sociometric choice that can have similar applications. See Chapter 7 for a study by Van Zelst.
[21]Rexford Hersey, "As Others See Us," *Personnel*, 39:8–16 (July-August 1962).
[22]P.W. Maloney and J.R. Hinrichs, "A New Tool for Supervisory Self-Development," *Personnel*, 36:46–53 (July-August 1959).

[23]Mayfield, "Peer Nominations," p. 40.

the subject of the rating can provide more data than just the supervisor alone.[24] Actual knowledge of performance is as important in such a procedure as in independent ratings, however. Without objective data to make appraisals, a committee may simply be pooling their collective ignorance.

EFFECT ON NEED FULFILLMENT

Whenever appraisals are used for discipline, pay increases, promotion, discharge, or layoff, they are likely to be regarded with apprehension by the less productive members of the organization, by those who chronically underestimate themselves, or by those who feel that appraisals will be arbitrary or unjust. In order to dispel the qualms of the latter two groups, managerial practice over the long run should be designed to demonstrate the lack of basis for such fears. In the case of marginal employees, a problem-solving approach to improving performance will be a much better motivator than reliance on criticism and fear.

In most unionized organizations, union members have reduced their feelings of insecurity about layoff based on merit rating by insisting upon a length-of-service criterion instead. Seniority is looked upon as much surer protection for one's job and wages.

In general, unless employees understand the criteria against which their performance is appraised, their needs for knowledge, understanding, and fair treatment will not be met. Further, the more appraisals are used as developmental rather than constraining devices, the more the need for self-actualization will be satisfied.

A particularly serious problem with rating techniques such as the rank-order, forced-distribution, and paired-comparison methods is that they create a kind of "zero-sum" climate in the organization. In this atmosphere, as described by Thompson and Dalton, both managers and subordinates feel trapped in a world in which half of the people are "below average," and if one person rises to the "above average" category it is at the expense of someone whose ranking must fall. Thus, the net result is always zero. Thompson and Dalton believe, and I agree, that such zero-sum approaches frequently lead to ". . . widespread discouragement, cynicism, and alienation." The authors suggest that ways out of this dilemma are to focus on a goal or results approach, to use many kinds of feedback, and to avoid ranking kinds of comparisons.[25] (See further discussion of merit rating as it relates to compensation in Chapter 19.)

IMPACT OF ENVIRONMENT

Union-management relations usually have a direct bearing on appraising the performance of unionized employees. Almost universally, seniority plays a part in governing the order of layoff and recall, but approximately 44 percent of labor contracts provide for some consideration of ability or other factors. Seniority also is a major factor in about 93 percent of labor contracts, but typically other factors, such as skill and merit, are considered.[26] These labor-management agreements, then, require some

[24] Virgil K. Rowland, "The Mechanics of Group Appraisal," *Personnel,* 34:36–43 (May-June 1958). See also Richard S. Elster, Gerald L. Musgrave, and William H. Githens, "Employee Development Using Group Appraisal," *The Journal of Navy Civilian Manpower Management,* 9:1–5ff. (Fall 1975).

[25] Paul H. Thompson and Gene W. Dalton, "Performance Appraisal: Managers Beware," *Harvard Business Review,* 48:149–157 (January-February 1970).

[26] U.S. Department of Labor, "Layoff, Recall, and Worksharing Procedures," *Major Collective Bargaining Agreements,* Bulletin 1425–13, 1972, pp. 1–32; and "Seniority in Promotion and Transfer Provisions," Bulletin 1425–11, March 1970, pp. 1–7.

form of merit rating if dimensions other than seniority are to come into play.

In general, management tends to favor merit as a basis for pay increases, transfers, promotions, and layoffs. On the other hand, unions tend to favor seniority as a basis, and the result is usually some kind of compromise. The more that seniority is emphasized, of course, the less important any system of appraisal becomes and a perusal of the seniority roster becomes the basic system for making decisions relative to staffing and reward.

The opinion of one former labor-union official suggests that unions prefer wage-incentive plans involving standards of performance to merit rating, such as the graphic-rating scale, on the assumption that, if rewards should be based on anything, they should be based on output. Unions look particularly askance at merit-rating items like "loyalty."[27]

Practices vary with respect to union surveillance of any merit-rating system in use. Some unions will agree with management that merit rating is a managerial prerogative and will avoid any involvement except through the grievance procedure. Other unions will insist upon bargaining about the details of merit-rating plans, a right that has been upheld by the National Labor Relations Board.[28] Since wage provisions in labor contracts tend to emphasize a straight rate for jobs once the proficiency has been achieved, disputes over merit rating tend to focus on the speed with which the job rate is achieved or on the relative weight to be given merit in promotions.

The use of performance appraisals for unionized employees is also indirectly affected by federal labor law and administrative rulings. The Taft-Hartley Act provides a minimum

period of thirty days after employment in the bargaining unit, during which the employer may terminate a new employee for any reason other than union activity. During this period, decisions relative to discharge or retention may be based solely on merit rating.

In addition, systematic and periodic merit ratings may be used by management to demonstrate to the National Labor Relations Board that disciplinary action is not based upon union activity, or to an arbitrator that some penalty is not capricious. In either situation, however, the appraisal of performance is less subject to challenge if there are both established standards and records of actual performance.

AUTHORITY AND ACCOUNTABILITY

The basic responsibility for the appraisal must reside with the immediate supervisors of those being appraised, since they are in the most advantageous position to assess performance. The personnel department, however, can play an important role in the design and implementation of appraisal systems to be used for purposes of pay increases, promotions, and the like, and in training managers in the use of such systems. This department is also the logical group to conduct research on the equity of appraisals throughout departments and on the reliability and validity of whatever systems are established.

UTILITY OF SYSTEMATIZATION

Appraisal for the purpose of day-to-day coaching by superiors does not require a high degree of organizationwide systematization, although organizationwide supervisory training in leadership and coaching is usually helpful. On specific jobs, of course, some degree of systematization will be essential in order to detect undesirable trends in performance. For example, systematic observation, encouragement

[27] William Gomberg, "On Merit Rating," *Management Record*, 8:201 (June 1946).
[28] See Harold W. Davey, *Contemporary Collective Bargaining*, 2nd ed. (Englewood Cliffs, N.J.: Prentice-Hall, Inc., 1959), p. 263.

of questions from subordinates, and examination of production records can provide information on which the supervisor exercises judgment about when to attempt to correct behavior or to make changes in the environment.

A higher degree of systematization is desirable, however, when decisions must be made about pay increases, promotions, transfers, and what to communicate in periodic appraisal interviews. There are three reasons for this: (1) such appraisals assume a review of performance across a span of time and should reflect more than recent impressions; (2) managerial action based on the appraisals can produce serious defensive behavior if this action is not perceived as fair; and (3) criteria for use in evaluating performance must stem from those who establish the goals of the enterprise. To make the last point in another way, systematization is necessary for insuring that performance is evaluated in terms of its contribution to the enterprise's goals. Systematization may be overdone, however. In particular, if appraisal systems appear coercive and do not permit inputs from either the supervisors who are expected to use the systems or from subordinates being rated, the systems will be correspondingly deprived of a substantial amount of relevance.

RELIABILITY

One measure of the reliability of performance appraisal is the consistency with which a supervisor rates a subordinate in successive ratings, assuming no change in the subordinate's performance nor in the appraisal form. Another measure is the consistency with which two or more supervisors rate performance when they have comparable information. Such research on the reliability of ratings has been rare. One study at the Lockheed Aircraft Corporation discovered that *supervisors' ratings based on graphic-rating scales went up significantly when the*

supervisors found out they were to discuss ratings with subordinates. There was a time lapse of ten days between the first and second ratings, and the change in ratings varied a good deal from supervisor to supervisor.[29] This phenomenon raises the interesting question of whether ratings that are to be discussed with subordinates are more or less reliable than results that are not to be divulged. In any event, the supervisors in this study rated people differently with the change in the situation.

The same study also found that explanations on the various scales increased reliability. For example, lengthy descriptive phrases on the rating scales such as "seldom needs help; has good knowledge of his job and related work; is well-informed" increased reliability over scales using terms like "above average" or "excellent."[30]

Although the reliability of graphic-rating scales can be improved by using descriptive statements, ranking methods seem to be the most reliable. In particular, a forced-distribution method that rates employees on only two characteristics, job performance and promotability, seems to be the most reliable. Factor analysis has shown that, because of the halo effect, other traits are highly correlated with these two factors, and rating systems might just as well be simplified to two or three basic factors.[31] One study, for example, found that three traits, "amount of work," "quality of work," and "interpersonal relations," would be just as predictive of an overall rating as a seven-trait scale.[32] However, obtaining acceptance by employees of a two- or three-factor rating system might be a problem.

[29] Stockford and Bissell, "Factors Involved in Merit-Rating," pp. 94–116.
[30] Ibid.
[31] Joseph Tiffin, in Dooher and Marquis, *Rating Employee and Supervisory Performance*, pp. 17–19.
[32] Theodore J. Carron, "Simplification of Employee Appraisal Programs," *Journal of Industrial Psychology*, No. 4, 3:81–90 (1965).

Peer ratings have been found to be high in reliability in a study of officer candidates at a United States Navy school. Peer nomination scores at the end of the third week of training correlated .90 with scores made at the end of the sixth week.[33]

Training of raters in the use of rating devices probably increases the consistency with which employees are rated by two or more raters as well as the consistency with which a given rater uses a rating device. Thus, training sessions in the use of appraisal devices before their use and periodically thereafter may be useful.

VALIDITY

The validity of any performance-appraisal system is judged by the extent to which ratings reflect real differences in the degree to which those being rated are contributing to the goals of the enterprise. As we have indicated, logic suggests that the more the supervisor uses data on actual performance in ratings, the more valid the ratings become. Thus, conclusions based on a comparison of actual performance with standards of performance should be the most valid. Conclusions based on graphic scales, such as "initiative" or "health," would seem to have less face validity. Furthermore, since reliability is an essential ingredient of validity, an instrument that has high reliability and high face validity would seem to have high overall validity.

Although not a great deal of research has been done on the validity of merit rating, some useful studies have appeared in recent years. Most seem to have been done in military situations. The difficulty with this kind of research is illustrated by the following study. One au-

thor, after summarizing the results of several Army and industrial studies, concluded that there was no appreciable difference between the validity of the forced-choice scales and the more conventional rating devices.[34] The typical criteria against which the scales were compared to check validity were ratings by peer or traditional ratings by supervisors, a procedure that is, of course, questionable, since comparisons were being made between one instrument of unknown validity against other devices of equally unknown validity. The results of these studies appear to be measures of reliability—consistency among raters—rather than validity, a conclusion with which the author summarizing the studies seems to agree.[35] Knowledge of the reliability of a device, however, is a good start toward understanding its validity.

Research suggests that ratings conducted by more effective supervisors are more valid than those made by less effective supervisors. One study found that the better supervisors tended to discriminate more among subordinates and tended to rate independent and aggressive action highly, while the less effective supervisors were more lenient, showed less spread among rated subjects, and preferred behavior that did not "rock the boat.[36] Thus, it appears that the more effective supervisors tended to reward behavior that was related to attaining the enterprise's goals, while the less effective super-

[33] E.P. Hollander, "The Reliability of Peer Nominations under Various Conditions of Administration," *Journal of Applied Psychology*, 41:85–90 (April 1957).

[34] Lee W. Cozan, "Forced Choice: Better than Other Rating Methods?" *Personnel*, 36:80–83 (May-June 1959). For one of the original studies, see E. Donald Sisson,"Forced Choice—the New Army Rating," *Personnel Psychology*, 1:365–381 (Autumn 1948).

[35] Ibid., p. 83. Thus, the problem is to determine the validity of ratings when ratings themselves are the most frequently used criteria of successful performance. When we are dealing with the question of merit-rating validity, we are dealing with the criterion problem as discussed in Chapter 13.

[36] Wayne K. Kirchner and Donald J. Reisberg, "Differences between Better and Less-Effective Supervisors in Appraisal of Subordinates," *Personnel Psychology*, 15:295–302 (Autumn 1962).

visors tended to reward behavior that would support the status quo.

Another study found a very low relationship between scores on rating scales and measurable output. In the same study, equally qualified supervisors agreed with each other more when descriptive phrases, rather than subjective phrases, were used on rating scales, although agreement was not high in either case. Assuming that agreement is a measure of validity, different traits also had differing degrees of validity. The trait "quality of work" produced much more agreement than the item on which there was least agreement, "cooperation."[37] Thus, research suggests that the use of variables relating to performance has the greatest reliability, a suggestion that, since such variables also have the highest face validity, implies that the more appraisals are based on actual performance, the higher is their validity.

VALIDITY OF RATINGS BY SUBORDINATES

Ratings of supervisors by subordinates have also been tried with apparent success. In the experiment at the Esso Research and Engineering Company cited earlier, subordinates' evaluations of superiors brought a number of desirable results. These ratings were made at all levels up to, but not including, the vice-presidential level and were made available only to the person being rated. An opinion survey of both rated subjects and raters found that 60 percent of both superiors and subordinates agreed that productivity had been favorably affected, 88 percent of the superiors reported that they had tried to change their behavior as a result, 25 percent of the subordinates reported lasting changes in superiors, and 75 percent of the superiors wanted a follow-up rating.[38]

The experiment at Gulf Oil, cited earlier, which involved ratings by both peers and subordinates, resulted in favorable reports from both participants and superiors. Among the participants, 77 percent felt their colleagues had improved; about 84 percent were seen by their superiors as having improved significantly; and 100 percent of the participants believed the program had helped them personally to improve.[39] (For discussion of the validity of peer ratings, see Chapter 13.)

BEHAVIORALLY ANCHORED RATING SCALES

An outgrowth of the critical incident technique is the development of what are called "behaviorally anchored rating scales," which show some promise for minimizing some of the problems found in traditional rating devices. These scales reduce the amount of judgment or subjectivity required of the rater, and as Schwab and Heneman state it, "[t]he evaluator is cast more in the role of an observer and less in the role of a judge."[40] Their job-relatedness can also be more readily demonstrated, thus making them less vulnerable to charges of contributing to discriminatory practices.

Basically, five steps are used in the development of scales:

1. Persons knowledgeable about the job describe specific examples of effective and ineffective performance.

2. Those developing the scales cluster the incidents into five to ten performance dimensions.

3. A second group of participants who know the jobs reallocate the critical incidents to the

---

[37]Stockford and Bissell, "Factors Involved in Merit-Rating." Again, if agreement is a measure of reliability, such reliability is a necessary prerequisite to validity.

[38]Maloney and Hinrichs, "New Tool for Supervisory Self-Development."

[39]Hersey, "As Others See Us," p. 15.

[40]Donald P. Schwab, Herbert G. Heneman III, and Thomas A. DeCotiis, "Behaviorally Anchored Rating Scales: A Review of the Literature," *Personnel Psychology*, 28:550 (Winter 1975).

Figure **15-2**   Example of one dimension* from a behaviorally anchored rating scale

Extremely good performance	7	This checker would organize the order when checking it out by placing all soft goods like bread, cake, etc. to one side of counter; all meats, produce, frozen foods, to the other side, thereby leaving the center of the counter for can foods, boxed goods, etc.
Good performance	6	
		When checking, this checker would separate strawberries, bananas, cookies, cakes, and breads, etc.
Slightly good performance	5	You can expect this checker to grab more than one item at a time from the cart to the counter.
Neither poor nor good performance	4	After bagging the order and customer is still writing a check, you can expect this checker to proceed to the next order if it is a small order.
Slightly poor performance	3	This checker may be expected to put wet merchandise on the top of the counter.
		This checker can be expected to lay milk and by-product cartons on their sides on the counter top.
Poor performance	2	
		This checker can be expected to damage fragile merchandise like soft goods, eggs, and light bulbs on the counter top.
Extremely poor performance	1	

*Dimension: organizational ability of checkstand work

From Lawrence Fogli, Charles Hulin, and Milton R. Blood, "Development of First-Level Behavioral Job Criteria," *Journal of Applied Psychology*, 55:7 (February 1971). Copyright 1971 by the American Psychological Association. Reprinted by permission.

dimensions. Those incidents about which there is little agreement are dropped out.

4. The second group of participants is asked to rate on a seven- to nine-point scale the behavior represented by the incidents in terms of how effectively the incidents represent performance on the performance dimension. (Again, the incidents with the widest variability are dropped out.)

5. A final instrument is developed by using scales for each dimension, each of which has incidents assigned along the scale depending upon their ratings in Step 4.[41] (Figure 15-2 shows an example of a dimension and a number of selected incidents from research in a grocery chain.)

[41] Schwab, Heneman, and DeCotiis, "Behaviorally Anchored Rating Scales," pp. 549–551.

The main advantage of this procedure over less rigorously developed graphic-rating scales appears to be the development of scales and terminology that are clear, more meaningful and more job related, thus presumably increasing both reliability and validity.[42] However, research on such dimensions as leniency effects, the independence of the dimensions, and reliability has produced mixed results. Schwab et al. conclude that research on behaviorally anchored rating scales needs to recognize that regardless of the instrument, evaluation scores "... are potentially a function of the evaluatee (both performance relevant and irrelevant), the evaluator, and the evaluation context, such as the intended purposes of the assessment procedure."[43]

In addition, the costs of the procedure and the degree of its applicability need to be assessed. It would appear that gathering incidents and using panels of experts would be very time consuming and costly and that the procedure might not be practical unless it were used in instances of a fairly large number of almost identical jobs.

THE APPRAISAL INTERVIEW

DESCRIPTION AND PURPOSE

Traditionally, the appraisal interview has been a verbal communication of the results of employee appraisal to the employee concerned, a communication that may or may not involve active participation by both appraiser and appraisee. The appraisal interview may have one or more purposes, including those of encouraging present behavior, changing behavior, warning, or providing information. (For a discussion of on-the-job coaching, a less formalized discussion between superior and subordinate that occurs as problems arise, see Chapter 17.) One study of 150 firms found that in 97 percent of all firms using an appraisal procedure for office and production employees, the evaluation was discussed with the employee.[44] Another study of 139 firms found that in 91 percent of the firms using formalized appraisal procedures for managers, the results were discussed with the managers.[45] According to a study conducted by GE, at least 70 percent of exempt employees in eighty out of ninety of the company's components had appraisal interviews during a one-year period.[46]

Although most authors believe that such interviews are worthwhile, a number have raised serious questions about the underlying assumptions and results of appraisal interviews. One problem is created by multiple objectives. According to Maier, some objectives are so incompatible that they canot be achieved in the same interview. For example, he suggests that telling employees where they stand is incompatible with motivating them to develop on their present jobs. Maier believes that the first objective requires an informative and persuasive kind of interview and that it tends to result in considerable defensive behavior on the part of the subordinate. The second objective, "developing" the employee, requires encouraging the subordinate in self-appraisal and performance and then discussing possible solutions to the problems raised, that is, a problem-solving approach.[47] As we shall see later, research has substantiated Maier's views.

[42] Ibid., pp. 551–552, 560.

[43] Ibid., p. 560. See also Walter C. Borman and Marvin D. Dunnette, "Behavior-Based versus Trait-Oriented Performance Ratings: An Empirical Study," *Journal of Applied Psychology*, 60:561–565 (October 1975).

[44] Bureau of National Affairs, "Employee Performance: Evaluation and Control," p. 6.

[45] Bureau of National Affairs, "Management Performance Appraisal Programs," p. 1.

[46] E. Kay, J.R.P. French, Jr., and H.H. Meyer, *A Study of the Performance Appraisal Interview* (New York: Management Development and Employee Relations Services, General Electric Company), March 1962, p. 1.

[47] Norman R.F. Maier. "Three Types of Appraisal Interview," *Personnel*, 34:27–38 (March-April 1958).

IMPACT OF ENVIRONMENT

The environmental variables that probably most affect the appraisal interview are managerial attitudes, quality of leadership, and changes in competition and technology requiring different levels of performance. For example, if management believes in "telling people how they stand," the approach will differ from that used by a management believing in the type of problem-solving approach discussed by Maier. In addition, if the president of a company favors systematic appraisal interviewing, such interviews are much more likely to be conducted than if the president is indifferent to the matter.

The overall quality of leadership in the enterprise is indirectly, but significantly, related to the communication of appraisals. Effective leadership will attempt to remove obstacles to achievement. When no such effort has been made, the performance of a subordinate may be appraised as inadequate and communicated as such, when in reality it is higher management that has failed to create an environment conducive to success.

Changes in competition and technology, of course, may require levels of performance from employees above their current performance and, consequently, will affect the content of appraisal interviews. If every effort has been made to assist subordinates in adapting to these new demands but without success, reorganization of the job, demotion, transfer, or discharge may have to be the consequence. Obviously, such actions must be communicated.

EFFECT ON NEED FULFILLMENT

A number of authors have stressed the belief that defensive behavior is an all-too-common product of appraisal interviews.[48] Research findings, however, provide conflicting evidence. One study found that employees believed annual appraisals were a good thing in that they insured a discussion of performance.[49] On the other hand, another study reported that only 5 percent of the employees surveyed found that the guidance and correction received from performance review was "very helpful," 21 percent found the interview of "some help," 35 percent found the interview of "little help," and 39 percent found the interview of "no use at all."[50]

One interpretation of these conflicting results is that employees liked the idea of appraisals because they need periodic reassurance, but the actual interviews were so superficial as to be essentially meaningless. McGregor reports a study indicating that this may be what happens.[51] According to another interpretation, the interviews in the different situations had different objectives and involved different methods.

Research at GE demonstrates that criticism by supervisors in the appraisal interview leads to defensive behavior by subordinates, but more participation by subordinates in planning goals improves the supervisor-subordinate relationship.[52] These results of research at GE are what theory would lead one to expect. If the

[48] See Maier, *The Appraisal Interview;* Douglas MacGregor, "An Uneasy Look at Performance Appraisal," *Harvard Business Review,* 35:89–94 (May-June 1957); and Philip R. Kelly, "Reappraisal of Appraisals," *Harvard Business Review,* 36:59–68 (May-June 1958).
[49] Robert H. Finn, "Is Your Appraisal Program Really Necessary?" *Personnel,* 37:16–25 (January-February 1960).
[50] Mortimer R. Feinberg, "Performance Review . . . Threat or Promise?" *Supervisory Management,* 6:2–12 (May 1961).
[51] McGregor, "Uneasy Look at Performance Appraisal," p. 90.
[52] Kay, French, and Meyer, *Study of Performance Appraisal,* pp. 17–27. Another study found that participation in the appraisal interview was correlated with satisfaction. Martin M. Greller, "Subordinate Participation and Reactions to the Appraisal Interview," *Journal of Applied Psychology,* 60:544–549 (October 1975).

appraisal interview is perceived to further the attainment of such goals as higher pay, promotion, recognition, or greater acceptance, it will enhance the fulfillment of such needs as security, belonging, esteem, and self-actualization. On the other hand, if the appraisal interview is regarded as punishment or rejection, defensive behavior will result.

An interesting aspect of appraisal interviewing is that many supervisors are reluctant to conduct them,[53] particularly in the case of marginal employees as opposed to the best performers or to those clearly performing below standards. Apparently, such interviews threaten the supervisor's need for esteem from subordinates. Perhaps supervisors also fear the defensive behavior that is likely to result, and thus the supervisor's need for orderliness and predictability (security) is threatened. Attempts on the part of the supervisor to improve the performance of marginal employees may be particularly frustrating, and the supervisor may feel that communicating appraisals is a futile procedure.

In terms of need fulfillment, most people probably want the traditional appraisal interview to produce one of the first two of the following results, in descending order of desirability:

1. Reassurance that they are doing well, with considerable discussion and helpful suggestions on how to be even more successful—satisfaction of needs for security, belonging, esteem, and self-actualization

2. Reassurance that they are doing well—satisfaction of needs for security, belonging, and esteem

In the absence of these they would prefer:

3. No communication at all—avoidance of any ego-threatening events—but continuing signals that things are all right, such as periodic pay increases, and so forth

Least desirable of all to employees is:

4. Considerable criticism or indication that things are not going well—people do not want this; defensive behavior is highly probable

In my opinion, the method appearing to have the most promise of need fulfillment for most people involves joint superior-subordinate establishment of goals and objectives, mutual review of a subordinate's accomplishments, but not limited to those related to formal goal setting, and mutual discussion of how to minimize or remove obstacles to achievement. Throughout such a procedure, a high degree of subordinate initiative is permitted and there is a minimum of "telling" by the superior.[54] (See the discussion of MBO later.)

AUTHORITY AND ACCOUNTABILITY

The supervisor scheduling the appraisal interview will have the essential authority over the conduct of that interview. Although the personnel department may conduct training sessions in appraisal interviewing, or top management may urge a particular procedure, the conduct of this private interview must be the responsibility of the supervisor.

Higher management may dictate that appraisal interviews be held, of course, and certain controls may be initiated to insure compliance. For example, top management may require that a performance-appraisal form be

[53] See Finn, "Is Appraisal Program Really Necessary," p. 17; and McGregor, "Uneasy Look at Performance Appraisal," pp. 89, 90.

[54] For further discussion of the needs of both superior and subordinate relative to the appraisal interview, see Harry Levinson, "A Psychologist Looks at Executive Development," Harvard Business Review, 40:69–75 (September-October 1962).

submitted showing signatures of both subordinate and superior and attesting that a discussion took place. (In my opinion, however, the requirement of a subordinate's signature attesting to *agreement* with the assessment is frequently coercive.) In addition, the personnel department may monitor compliance through a top-management directive to analyze reports on appraisals in order to assess training and development needs. Where appraisals are used for decisions on promotion, transfer, or layoff of unionized employees, the personnel department is likely to act as a central point of control. In general, however, each manager must be held accountable for the effective development of subordinates, while the personnel department should be held accountable for consultation that will assist managers in this important function.

UTILITY OF SYSTEMS

Since human interaction is involved, the use of appraisal interviews in an organization is not subject to a great deal of systematizing. The overall program can be constructed to require that superiors rate their subordinates with the use of a particular form and that they discuss results with them, but the conduct of the interview cannot be prescribed so as to insure uniformity—properly so, since any effective interview must be conditioned by the particular personalities of the participants and cannot be run purely by technique. Each supervisor, in turn, may use different methods of structuring the appraisal interview, all the way from a lecture to the opposite extreme of requiring subordinates to evaluate themselves and present plans for improvement.

Any appraisal-interview program that seems to be highly systematized and that features a high degree of direction from supervisors is bound to be much less systematic than appearances indicate. Formally organized interviews

permitting little expression of feeling by the subordinate will later result in defensive behavior that manifests itself in many subtle ways. Superiors themselves may tend to sabotage such programs by avoiding direct statements about quality of performance. As an example of this phenomenon, McGregor discusses an apparently well-organized and formally constructed program of appraisal in which about two-thirds of the employees stated that they had not been told "where" they stood, although about four-fifths had signed statements indicating they had been through the appraisal interview.[55] Furthermore, any coaching occurring as problems arise cannot be systematized in the sense of an externally imposed regimen. Managers may attend conferences on the subject of coaching, but in the final analysis they are obviously on their own in day-to-day dealings with subordinates.

On the other hand, unless a general structure or system is designed that has top-executive support, periodic appraisal interviews are not likely to take place.[56] Most authors are in agreement on this point; most disagreement in the literature is over the philosophy and general approach to be used in appraisal interviews.

VALIDITY

The validity of the appraisal interview depends upon the extent to which the interview contributes to the attainment or organizational goals. Although many responsible people have expressed considerable faith in the usefulness of appraisal interviews, significant numbers have expressed the opinion that certain kinds of appraisal interview do more harm than good. Very little research has been done on these questions.

[55] McGregor, "Uneasy Look at Performance Appraisal," pp. 89, 90.
[56] See Harold Mayfield, "In Defense of Performance Appraisal," *Harvard Business Review*, 38:83 (March-April 1960).

If employees' opinions are any guide, the study quoted earlier suggests that the majority of employees find appraisal interviews of at least some, even though small, use in correcting performance.[57] A study at General Motors (GM) found the attitudes of participants generally favorable toward performance-appraisal programs, although some criticisms were expressed.[58] Still another study of forty-nine managers and specialists found that 43 percent reported taking specific constructive action to improve performance after the appraisal interview. The more skilled the superior in handling the interview, the more likely the constructive action.[59]

Another study—an analysis of stories written about pictures dramatizing appraisal interviews—reports that the pictures projected considerable anxiety about the interviews. In general, the less anxious the interviewee, the more likely that she or he had plans to improve. The study also reports the opinion that emphasis on weak points by the person conducting the interview was unlikely to produce change, whereas emphasis on strong points or the exchange of ideas was very likely to result in plans for improvement.[60]

The study at GE cited earlier is one of the most thorough and informative to date. According to this study, the more the criticism and resulting defensive behavior in the appraisal interview, the less the evidence of improvement in performance twelve to fourteen weeks later.[61]

MANAGEMENT BY OBJECTIVES

A management by objectives (MBO) program is a specialized form of the use of performance standards (see Chapter 10) although, in a broader sense, it can be a pervasive management system. Because MBO has received so much publicity and attention since Drucker articulated the process in 1954,[62] and because its thrust is so different from systems that rely largely on traditional merit-rating and appraisal interview procedures, I wish to examine it in some detail here.

Typically, management by objectives is a *system that features a periodic agreement between a superior and a subordinate on the subordinate's objectives for a particular period and a periodic review of how well the subordinate achieved those objectives.* An attempt is usually made to write objectives in quantitative terms, although some authors argue that some objectives or targets can (or should) be stated in qualitative terms. Further, the broader process includes a focus on overall organizational goals to which the objectives of the different units, managers, and employees relate. In some organizations, the process focuses largely on the managerial, supervisory, and professional levels; in some instances, the process is extended to all employees.

Some of the terminology of MBO should be discussed first. There is no universal agreement on terms like *goals, objectives, targets,* etc. However, *goals* are usually considered to be broad and long range, e.g.: "To increase profits by 25 percent over the next four years," or "To increase the number of patients served in suburban clinics by 300 percent within ten years." Statements of *objectives* are usually considered to be narrower and more short-range, e.g.: "To

[57] Feinberg, "Performance Review . . . Threat or Promise?"
[58] Richard E. Clingenspeel, "How Employees Feel about Performance Appraisal," *Personnel,* 39:70–77 (May-June 1962).
[59] Herbert H. Meyer and William B. Walker, "A Study of Factors Relating to the Effectiveness of a Performance Appraisal Program," *Personnel Psychology,* 14:291–298 (Autumn 1961).
[60] Kenneth E. Richards, "Some New Insights into Performance Appraisal," *Personnel,* 37:28–38 (July-August 1960).
[61] Kay, French, and Meyer, *Study of Performance Appraisal Interview,* pp. 1–27; and Herbert H. Meyer, Emanuel Kay, and John R.P. French, Jr., "Split Roles in Performance Appraisal," *Harvard Business Review,* 43:123–129 (January-February 1965).

[62] Peter F. Drucker, *The Practice of Management* (New York: Harper & Row, 1954).

increase the number of monthly contacts of potential customers of high-quality, high-profit product lines by 100 percent by the end of two years"; or "To expand patient services by building and operating a clinic in Forest Park within five years." *Targets* are usually even more specific, e.g.: "To analyze product line profitability and make recommendations to the Executive Committee for revising product lines by June 15"; "To have monthly meetings with all sales staff to review progress"; or "To have architect drawings approved by the Building Committee and Executive Committee by December 2." As long as users are aware that there is a descending level of abstraction and there is agreement on terminology within the particular organization, the semantics issue is not too important to the establishment of an MBO program.

The reader will note that all the cited statements have a quantitative aspect. The statement, "To have monthly meetings . . . ," however, would be considered a qualitative statement by some authors, and they would recommend it be translated into some measurable intended outcomes of the meetings. A statement "To increase cooperation between the sales and manufacturing departments" would be considered clearly qualitative and therefore inadequate.[63]

Some authors make distinctions between types of goals or objectives. For example, Odiorne recommends that each manager develop the following kinds of goals: goals for routine duties, problem-solving goals, creative goals, and personal goals.[64]

SOME DIFFICULTIES WITH MBO [65]

In their better forms, I see MBO programs as systems of joint target setting and performance review designed to intensify the focus on objectives and to increase the frequency of problem-solving discussions between supervisors and subordinates and, ideally, within work teams. In their worst forms, however, MBO programs can be unilateral, autocratic mechanisms designed to force compliance with a superior's directives. Some MBO efforts would be more honest if the top manager simply stated: "I want more control, and this is how I'm going to get it." Additional control may be desirable, but control flying under the banner of participation usually has unfortunate consequences.

My estimate is that many MBO programs are imposed by line managers and/or personnel departments without much joint diagnosis to test the immediate relevancy of a formal program and/or the readiness of employees for such a program. Successful efforts usually require up to three years or more before they become pervasive aspects of managing the organization, as well as a great deal of patience and hard work. Further, my guess is that most MBO programs do not use a team approach and that they do not provide for sufficient acknowledgement of interdependency between jobs. (In an in-depth study of one organization, researchers found that 22 percent of the managers believed their MBO effort was interfering with teamwork.)[66] In addition, the thrust of MBO is to focus on end results, but *how* one gets there is equally important, in my judgment.

MBO efforts tend to focus on what Likert calls

[63] See Anthony P. Raia, *Managing by Objectives* (Glenview, Ill.: Scott, Foresman and Company, 1974), pp. 25–26.
[64] George S. Odiorne, *Management by Objectives* (New York: Pitman Publishing Corporation, 1965); George S. Odiorne, "Evaluating the Personnel Program," in Joseph J. Famularo, ed., *Handbook of Modern Personnel Administration* (New York: McGraw-Hill Book Company, 1972), pp. 8–1 through 8–7.

[65] The first part of this discussion is based partly on Wendell French and Cecil Bell, *Organization Development: Behavioral Science Interventions for Organization Improvement* (Englewood Cliffs, N.J.: Prentice-Hall, Inc., 1973), pp. 167–168.
[66] See Walter R. Nord and Douglas E. Durand, *Organizational Dynamics*, 4:13 (Autumn 1975).

"end-result variables" such as productivity level, product quality, scrap loss, profits, etc., but "causal variables" such as leadership style, level of support and training, employee selection, etc., are also extremely important.[67] It seems apparent that if an MBO program does not focus on both, there can be a gradual, or even rapid, erosion of human resources. In short, an MBO program needs to focus on both means and ends.

Levinson also sees a number of difficulties with MBO programs. For example, he sees most MBO efforts as not giving adequate weight to large areas of potential discretion in a manager's job, e.g., spontaneous or creative activities or responses to an immediate challenge or problem. Further, he sees MBO as focusing too much on the individual job, not adequately recognizing the interdependency of jobs, and not enhancing teamwork. Levinson also believes that ". . . a man's most powerful driving force is comprised of his needs, wishes, and personal aspirations, combined with a compelling wish to look good in his own eyes for meeting those deeply held personal goals . . ." and that an MBO effort must, therefore, pay a great deal of attention to personal goals if it is to be successful in the long run.[68]

MBO programs need to include ingredients somewhat like the following in order to be developmental in contrast to dictatorial or punitive. I call this "Collaborative Management by Objectives":

1. Real subordinate participation in setting goals. Many goal-setting procedures are basically unilateral and autocratic.

2. A team approach to reviewing targets and achievements, and problem-solving dialogues between team members and superiors and subordinates. These ingredients recognize the interdependency of roles, and call for a much more collaborative mode of interaction among team members than typically exists in organizations.

3. Continuously helping relationships within teams and in superior-subordinate relationships. This suggests, of course, that the reward system recognizes joint efforts and mutual assistance.

4. Attention to personal and career goals in a real effort to make these complimentary to organizational goals.

COLLABORATIVE MANAGEMENT BY OBJECTIVES

An MBO effort that included these ingredients might look something like the procedure described as follows and diagrammed in Figure 15-3. (Such a program would be congruent with the organization development efforts described in Chapter 26.)

Basically the essential process is one of overlapping work units interacting with "higher" and "lower" units on overall organizational goals and objectives, unit goals and objectives, and individuals interacting with peers and superiors on role definition and individual goals and objectives.

Phase I: Diagnosis of Organizational Problems. A collaborative organizational diagnosis, by discussion or questionnaires involving a cross-section of organization members, suggests the usefulness of a CMBO effort in solving *identified problems.* It appears . . . that MBO, as frequently practiced, is a solution in search of a problem. For a variety of reasons, including the existence of a strong goal emphasis under some other name, overwork of many key people in the organization, or problems requiring other solutions, MBO may not be timely or appropriate.

---

[67] See Rensis Likert, *The Human Organization* (New York: McGraw-Hill Book Company, 1967).

[68] Harry Levinson, "Management by Whose Objectives?" *Harvard Business Review,* 48:128–129 (July-August 1970). White and Barnes propose that appraisal interviews should focus on *relationships* rather than the performance of subordinates. See B. Frank White and Louis B. Barnes, "Power Net-

works in the Appraisal Process," *Harvard Business Review,* 49:101–109 (May-June 1971).

Phase II: Information and Dialogue. Workshops on the basic purposes and techniques of CMBO are held with top management personnel, followed by workshops at the middle- and lower-management levels. These workshops can be conducted by qualified members of the personnel or training departments, by line managers trained in the approach, or if the organization prefers, by a qualified consultant. Having top-level managers conduct the workshops with middle and lower managers may speed up the process of shifting toward the more supportive climate necessary for CMBO.

Phase III: Diagnosis of Organizational Readiness. This diagnosis, based upon interviews and group meetings, must indicate an interest in and a willingness to use the process on the part of several organizational units, especially those at the top of the organization. Ideally, a number of overlapping units should express a desire to implement CMBO; for example, in addition to the president of a manufacturing firm and . . . immediate subordinates expressing interest, the manufacturing director and . . . immediate subordinates may want to be involved, and two of these subordinate managers may wish to start the process with their subordinate teams, and so forth. Favorable interest in CMBO from a few units randomly scattered throughout the organization would probably be inadequate to create enough interaction and momentum to give the approach a fair try. A good deal of diagnosis of organizational readiness will have already occurred in the information-and-dialogue phase. Similarly, diagnosis of organizational readiness may reveal the need for supplemental CMBO workshops for some units or for suspending the CMBO effort.

Phase IV: Goal Setting—Overall Organization Level. Overall organization goals and specific objectives to be achieved within a given time period are defined in team meetings among top executives, largely on the basis of consensus. It is important that this phase be an interactive process with middle and lower levels of the organization; inputs about organization goals and objectives from subordinate managerial and supervisory levels must be obtained during (or before) this phase.

Phase V: Goal Setting—Unit Level. Unit goals and objectives essential to achieving overall organization goals and objectives are defined in team situations, largely by consensus. Again, this is an interactive process between higher units and their respective subordinate units.

Phase VI: Goal Setting—Individual Level. This phase begins with individual managers developing their specific objectives in terms of results to be achieved and appropriate time periods. Personal career and development goals are part of this "package." If desired, the manager's superior may simultaneously develop a list of objectives for the subordinate. The superior and subordinate discuss, modify, and tentatively agree on the subordinate's objectives. These discussions are followed by group meetings in which team members discuss each other's objectives, making suggestions for modification, and agree upon each manager's final list of objectives.

Phase VI assumes that there is agreement on the major responsibilities and parameters of the team members' roles. If major responsibilities need to be reviewed or redefined, the following sequence is used as the preliminary stage of phase VI: (1) individual team members list their major responsibilities; (2) individual team members meet with their superior to discuss, modify, and tentatively agree upon their major responsibilities; and (3) team members discuss and work toward consensus on their major responsibilities in group meetings.

Phase VII: Performance Review. On a continuing basis, either the subordinate or the superior initiates discussion whenever progress toward objectives should be reviewed; matters of team concern are discussed in regularly scheduled team meetings. Particularly relevant at this stage are occasions when internal or external factors suggest the need for revision in the original set of goals and objectives; if appropriate, these revisions should be made in collaborative team meetings.

At the end of the agreed-upon time period, each manager prepares a report on the extent to which his objectives have been achieved and discusses this report in a preliminary meeting with his superior. These reports then are presented by each individual in a group meeting, with the discussion including an analysis of the forces helping and hindering attainment of objectives. This review process occurs at all levels (organization, unit, and individual) and ordinarily would start at the lower levels as a convenient way to collate information.

Phase VIII: Rediagnosis. Diagnosis needs to reoccur, but at this phase it is the CMBO process itself that needs examining, as well as the readiness of additional units to use CMBO. Is the CMBO process helping? hindering? in what way? What is the pro-

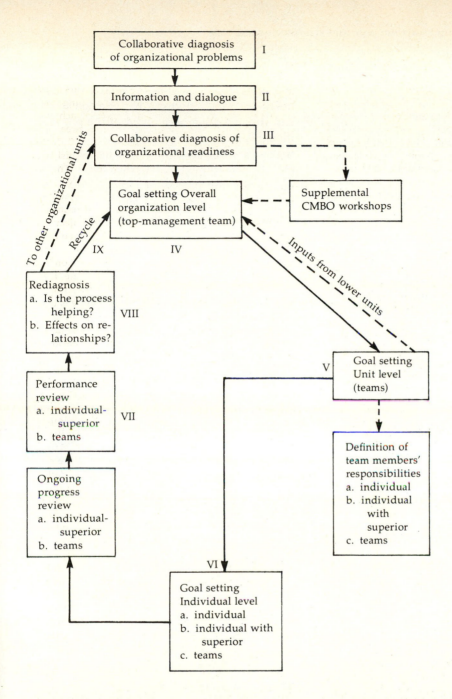

Figure **15-3** A strategy for implementing collaborative management by objectives

From Wendell L. French and Robert W. Hollman, "Management by Objectives: The Team Approach," © 1975 by the Regents of the University of California. Reprinted from *California Management Review*, Vol. XVII, No. 3, pp. 18–19, by permission of the Regents.

cess doing to the relationships between superiors and subordinates and within teams? Something has gone awry if goal setting and performance review are perfunctory or avoided, if the process seems unattached to the basic processes of getting the work of the organization done, or if relationships are becoming strained. On the other hand, if superiors and subordinates and teams find that the process is challenging and stretches and develops their capabilities, and if they feel good about it, the CMBO process is probably on the right track toward increased organizational effectiveness. Ideally such diagnosis should be ongoing as the CMBO process evolves.

Phase IX: Recycle. Assuming that rediagnosis has resulted in the decision to continue the CMBO effort, the cycle of phases IV through VIII is repeated, probably once a year at the overall organization level. Ongoing individual and team progress reviews may result in modification of unit- or individual-level goals more often than once a year. Through periodic problem sensing and rediagnosis, the details of the process will undoubtedly meet the needs of teams and individuals.[69] [The nine-phase strategy for implementing CMBO is presented in Figure 15-3.]

SOME CONTINGENCIES

Collaborative Management by Objectives (CMBO) is not likely to be an easy process for many organizations. Initial successes depend on a strong desire on the part of the top-management team to cooperate with and help each other. In addition, the process requires some modicum of skill in interpersonal relations and group dynamics. Training in these skills can accompany the CMBO effort, or if an OD effort is under way, such skills will be emerging as part of this broader process. Proper timing in the introduction of CMBO is also very important. CMBO is by no means a managerial panacea; it should be introduced only when diagnosis suggests its applicability

and usefulness as well as organizational readiness. A CMBO effort can be time consuming, and strong resistance can occur if the process is thoughtlessly superimposed at the wrong time—for example, during a period when people are preoccupied and harried with the annual budgeting process or faced with a major external threat to the organization. It is equally important to recognize that the utility of diagnosing organizational readiness is contingent upon the adequacy of information presented to managers in the CMBO workshops (phase II).

Successful expansion of the process to lower levels of the organization requires commitment to and skills in participative management, as well as a willingness and ability to diagnose the impact of the goal-setting and review processes on organization members and organizational functioning. Such a diagnosis of how things are going might result, for instance, in temporarily postponing phase VI. Successful completion of phases I through V and the appropriate team aspects of phases VII through IX might in itself be a major achievement and a move forward in organizational effectiveness. Developing effective group dynamics takes time, and an organization should proceed with caution in this area. A major shift to a collaborative mode cannot be made overnight.

VALIDITY OF MBO

TRADITIONAL FORMS Research has consistently demonstrated that goal setting improves performance whether in laboratory or organizational settings, or whether at the managerial or non-supervisory levels. This seems to hold true whether the goals are assigned by superiors or whether they are established in a participative manner.[70] These research results reinforce the

[69] Wendell L. French and Robert W. Hollman, "Management by Objectives: The Team Approach," © 1975 by the Regents of the University of California. Reprinted from *California Management Review*, Vol. XVII, No. 3, pp. 18–19, by permission of the Regents.

[70] See Donald J. Campbell and Daniel R. Ilgen, "Additive Effects of Task Difficulty and Goal Setting on Subsequent Task Performance," *Journal of Applied Psychology*, 61:319–324 (June 1976); and Gary P. Latham and Gary A. Yukl, "A Review of the Research on the Application of Goal Setting in Organiza-

high face validity of MBO programs. However, the assumption should not be made that goal setting occurs only in formalized programs like MBO. Goal and objective setting are significant activities in most organizations.

The issues, then, include such matters as whether participative goal setting or assigned goal setting is best, how much systematization is desirable, whether a team or a one-on-one form is best, and what kind of organizational climate is necessary for effective applications of different forms of MBO. Research and theory provide some information for resolving these issues.

On balance, research tends to point to the superiority of participation in goal setting over assigned goal setting. Latham and Yukl reviewed the research and found some studies that supported participatory methods but found others in which the results were mixed. Some of the dimensions of situations in which participation was not superior included (a) employees who usually worked with little participation, or (b) managers who had low self-assurance. One study of managers found no correlation between perceived participation and goal effort and performance ratings in the case of managers with a high need for achievement.[71] One of the researches reviewed was a study of logging crews in which it was found that participative goal setting for educationally disadvantaged crews was superior to assigned goal setting.[72]

Of two studies published after the Latham and Yukl review, one concluded that participation in goal setting had advantages over as-

signed goal setting, and the other was inconclusive. Arvey et al. found that participation by scientists and engineers in goal setting was related to job satisfaction.[73] A study by Latham and Yukl found that the performance of typists under both assigned and participatory methods of goal setting improved, but that there was no significant difference between the two methods. Job satisfaction declined slightly under both methods.[74]

Thus, research results clearly indicate that goal setting enhances performance, and the research tips in the direction of participative methods usually being more advantageous than unilateral approaches. However, formalized goal setting in an MBO context is another matter. In the study cited earlier of the *Fortune* 500 companies, only 2 percent (10 companies) said they had highly successful applications of MBO, and 18 percent (88 companies) reported "moderately successful" applications. Reading between the lines, the researchers were inclined to place the number of successful applications at something less than 10 percent. Comments like, "Our major problem . . . has been forcing managers to take the time . . ." and "The number one man . . . has never endorsed the program . . ." were interpreted by the researchers as indications of fairly widespread misapplications of the concept. The researchers concluded, ". . . that the potential of MBO is great. The implementation is difficult . . ." and ". . . that successful application of MBO requires a sizable commitment of time and effort throughout the organization."[75]

tions," *Academy of Management Journal*, 18:824–845 (December 1975).

[71] Latham and Yukl, "A Review of the Research," pp. 838–840.

[72] Gary P. Latham and Gary A. Yukl, "Assigned Versus Participative Goal Setting with Educated and Uneducated Woods Workers," *Journal of Applied Psychology*, 60:299–302 (June 1975).

[73] Richard D. Arvey, H. Dudley Dewhirst, and John C. Boling, "Relationships between Goal Clarity, Participation in Goal Setting, and Personality Characteristics on Job Satisfaction in a Scientific Organization," *Journal of Applied Psychology*, 61:103–105 (February 1976).

[74] Gary P. Latham and Gary A. Yukl, "Effects of Assigned and Participative Goal Setting on Performance and Job Satisfaction," *Journal of Applied Psychology*, 61:166–171 (April 1976).

[75] Schuster and Kindall, "Management by Objectives," pp. 8–11.

Such comments may provide clues as to why some MBO efforts succeed and others fail. It is quite likely that inadequate attention is given to a wide variety of dimensions that can affect the success of a formalized goal-setting effort. Matters like diagnosis of the prevailing organizational climate and the extent to which goal setting is already occurring, the involvement and commitment of the top managers, training of employees in the goal-setting procedures, the degree of participation used and the extent of managers' and employees' experience in participation—any or all such variables could be operating. That is why I believe that an effective MBO effort cannot be *installed;* it needs to emerge slowly and carefully as part of the broader process of managing the culture of the organization.

COLLABORATIVE MANAGEMENT BY OBJECTIVES
There has been little experimentation with the collaborative form of MBO I have described. Some research, however, suggests that such an approach can be viable in organizations that want to become more participative and supportive along with having a more extensive focus on goals and objectives. For example, in the research at GE cited earlier, it was found that criticism by the superior tended to produce defensiveness and impaired performance, that goal setting and mutual goal setting between superior and subordinate were associated with improved performance, and that coaching needed to be a day-to-day activity. The study further concluded that discussions about salary should be separate from sessions on "work-planning and review" (WPR).[76] Another study found managers' perceptions of the supportiveness of the organizational climate and their

attitudes toward MBO to be significantly related.[77]

In another study, a system of formal appraisal with three objectives—(a) improvement of work, (b) action on salaries, and (c) storage of information for administrative purposes—was found not to be meeting its goals. Subsequently, a program of management by objectives, designed specifically to meet the first objective only, was inaugurated for part of the organization, while the earlier appraisal system was continued in the remaining units. The new program featured periodic, problem-solving sessions between managers and subordinates. According to questionnaires before and after the introduction of the new program, subordinates reported taking action on 70 percent of the suggestions made by their superiors in the case of the new program, while they acted upon only 40 percent of the suggestions made by superiors in the context of the traditional program. As an important by-product, subordinates under the new program found their supervisors to be much more helpful in planning future development.[78]

While a team approach was not used in these studies, at least one experiment did involve a team approach. Likert cites a study in a sales organization in which sales managers held group meetings at regular intervals to set goals, discuss procedures, and identify results to be achieved before the next group meeting.[79] During these meetings, which the supervisor chaired, a constructive, problem-solving approach was stressed, and the superior encouraged high performance and provided technical

[76] Kay, French, and Meyer, *Study of Performance Appraisal,* pp. 1–27; and Meyer, Kay, and French, "Split Roles in Performance Appraisal," pp. 123–129.

[77] Robert W. Hollmann, "A Study of the Relationships between Organizational Climate and Managerial Assessment of Management by Objectives" (unpublished Ph.D. dissertation, University of Washington, 1973).
[78] Edgar F. Huse, "Performance Appraisal—A New Look," *Personnel Administration,* 30:3–5ff. (March-April 1967).
[79] Likert, *The Human Organization,* pp. 55–59.

advice when necessary. The results of the study showed that sales personnel using group meetings had more positive attitudes toward their jobs and sold more on the average than those not using group meetings. According to Likert:

Appreciably poorer results are achieved whenever the manager, himself, analyzes each man's performance and results and sets goals for him. Such man-to-man interactions in the meetings, dominated by the manager, do not create group loyalty and have far less favorable impact upon the salesmen's motivation than do group interaction and decision meetings. Moreover, in the man-to-man interaction little use is made of the sales knowledge and skills of the group.[80]

PERFORMANCE APPRAISAL AND EQUAL EMPLOYMENT OPPORTUNITY

Increasingly, the courts are applying the Equal Protection clause of the 14th Amendment and the EEOC Guidelines on Employee Selection Procedures (see Chapter 12) to appraisals, whether used for test validation criteria, promotion, transfer, or layoff. While, as two authors state it, "[f]or years the courts obviously considered performance rating systems as serving an accepted and legitimate function within the overall personnel management system . . . ,"[81] in recent times they have become increasingly critical of the procedures used.

It has been evident since the 1970 EEOC Guidelines were issued that ratings used as criteria for validating tests must be job related. As stated in the Guidelines:

The work behaviors or other criteria of employee adequacy which the test is intended to predict or identify must be fully described; and, additionally, in the case of rating techniques, the appraisal form(s) and instructions to the rater(s) must be included as a part of the validation evidence. Such criteria may include measures other than actual work proficiency, such as training time, supervisory ratings, regularity of attendance and tenure. Whatever criteria are used they must represent major or critical work behaviors as revealed by careful job analyses.[82]

Subsequently, in the *Albermarle Paper Company v. Moody* case (see Chapter 12), the U.S. Supreme Court confirmed the EEOC's interpretation that ratings were "tests" and criticized the paper company's test validation procedures in which ratings were used as criteria. The rating procedures were found to be too vague and subject to each supervisor's own interpretation. Furthermore, the Court stated that

. . . there is no way of knowing precisely what criteria of job performance the supervisors were considering, whether each supervisor was considering the same criteria—or whether, indeed, any of the supervisors actually applied a focused and stable body of criteria of any kind.[83]

Less evident at the outset, but increasingly clear, is the emergence of court decisions applying EEOC Guidelines and the 14th Amendment to the Constitution to rating procedures used for purposes other than test validation, such as promotion or layoff. For example, courts have found the following to be discriminatory: regular service ratings in a police department relative to promotion (14th Amendment), an efficiency rating system used for promotion in a municipal fire department (14th Amendment), lack of a well-defined rating system for use in selecting foremen in a company (Civil Rights Act), and using subjective performance rating for determining personnel layoffs (Civil Rights

---

[80] Ibid., p. 57. For a description of goal setting at TI, see M. Scott Myers, "Conditions for Manager Motivation," *Harvard Business Review*, 44:67–68 (January-February 1966).

[81] William H. Holley and Hubert S. Field, "Performance Appraisal and the Law," *Labor Law Journal*, 26:426 (July 1975).

[82] U.S. Equal Employment Opportunity Commission Guidelines, August 1970, 1607.5(3).

[83] As quoted in Robert I. Lazer, "The Discrimination Danger in Performance Appraisal," *The Conference Board Record*, March 1976, p. 61.

Act). In the foreman selection case, the court ordered the company to make several corrections, including providing foremen with written instructions setting forth objective criteria and specific qualifications necessary for transfer or promotion. In the last case, the court ordered the company to suspend performance ratings, because the evaluators were not all in a position to observe performance on a daily basis, and the appraisals were not administered and scored under standardized and controlled conditions.[84]

SUMMARY

Performance appraisal assists managers in making decisions about differential treatment to be accorded individual employees in training, coaching, pay, promotion, transfer, discipline, and other matters. Presumably this differential treatment is designed to enhance the attainment of organizational goals.

If the appraisal lacks validity in the sense of being unrelated to organizational purposes, the resulting differential treatment is likely to be dysfunctional in many ways. On the other hand, if the appraisal is based on measures of an employee's contribution to organizational goals, rewards can be made to encourage congruence between behavior and goals, or corrective action can be taken in an attempt to align behavior more closely with the objectives of the enterprise. However, overcontrol can be a serious problem, and rating methods that involve employee-ranking or forced distribution techniques tend to create a "zero-sum" climate that can foster cynicism and discouragement.

Research suggests that traditional merit-rating devices can be reduced to just a few traits, for example, "amount of work," "quality

of work," and "interpersonal relationships." A few traits appear to be just as predictive of a final rating as a larger number. Research further suggests that descriptions of traits to be rated and of ranking methods serve to increase reliability.

Behaviorally anchored rating scales have the advantage of demonstrable job-relatedness, but research has not demonstrated clear superiority in terms of reliability and the avoidance of bias. These scales also appear expensive to develop.

Although supervisors' ratings of subordinates are used most frequently, there have been some reports that ratings by peers and ratings of superiors by subordinates have some usefulness. Ratings by peers, in particular, show promise of being useful in promotional decisions (see Chapter 13), and ratings by subordinates may have some usefulness in managerial development, provided that the ratings are used solely by the person being rated.

MBO programs have high face validity and have considerable support from experimental research in goal setting. The research consistently shows that goal setting improves performance. Participative methods in goal setting probably are advantageous in most situations, although some of the research on this point has been inconclusive.

Although the value of goal setting is supported by experimental research, only a small percent of personnel executives whose firms use formal superior-subordinate goal-setting programs, i.e., MBO, believe the programs to be highly successful. MBO efforts can differ along many dimensions, and it is likely that inadequate attention is being paid to such aspects as initial diagnosis, the prevailing and desired organizational climate, and top-management commitment.

The use of management by objectives, or target setting, does not eliminate the need for the more traditional kind of rating. Some traditional form of merit rating must still be used to

---

[84]Holley and Field, "Performance Appraisal and the Law," pp. 423–430.

make comparisons among employees for purposes of merit increases or promotions. To say it in another way, conclusions still must be drawn about the implications of the discrepancies or congruencies between goals and achievement.

The Civil Rights Act, the 14th Amendment to the Constitution, and EEOC Guidelines on testing are increasingly being used to challenge the validity of appraisal systems as used for promotion, transfer, and layoff, as well as for test validation. (Salary administration decisions based on ratings are another area vulnerable to challenge.) Job-relatedness, detailed instructions for raters, familiarity with the employees' day-to-day performance, and standardized methods of administration are necessary ingredients if appraisal systems are not to be found discriminatory.

In general, theory and research suggest that appraisal interviews occurring in the following context will have the greatest usefulness:

1. Top management supports a system of target setting and coaching—work planning and review, or collaborative management by objectives, as we have described it, including managerial and supervisory training in the WPR or CMBO system.

2. Goals and objectives are periodically set by means of a real give-and-take discussion with subordinates and, ideally, are supplemented by peer review in a team setting.

3. Superiors do all they can to remove obstacles to achievement and to provide appropriate rewards for different degrees of performance.

4. Significant incidents involving excellent performance are recognized as they occur, and incidents involving below-standard performance are discussed as they happen, utilizing a coaching or problem-solving approach.

5. The superior and subordinate both periodically and independently evaluate the subordinate's performance, with subsequent discussion emphasizing the subordinate's participation and self-evaluation.

6. In this periodic appraisal interview, superior and subordinate discuss how obstacles in the environment can be overcome to enhance attainment of goals.

7. Team discussions and problem solving relative to goal attainment also occur.

8. Personal goals and aspirations are considered a legitimate and important area for dialogue at the subordinate's initiative.

9. A supportive and developmental climate throughout the organization is fostered.

Not only is such a procedure likely to result in a high degree of attainment of the enterprise's goals, but it is likely to result in a high degree of attainment of the personal needs and goals of the individuals involved.

Since the concept of appraisal tends to be universally accepted in organizations, the choice is not whether to appraise. The choices lie in (a) the set of basic assumptions about human behavior that will be followed in designing the system, (b) how participative and collaborative the system will be, (c) what type of an organization (e.g., mechanistic or organic) top management wishes to create, (d) what purposes will be emphasized in the system, and (e) how goal- and measurement-oriented the system will be.

REVIEW AND DISCUSSION QUESTIONS

1. Differentiate between (a) graphic rating scale, (b) forced distribution method, (c) paired-comparison method, (d) forced-choice rating method, and (e) management by objectives.

2. For what purposes are appraisals used? Which of these purposes are the most significant in your judgment, and why?

3. What procedures of appraisal produce the greatest reliability?

4. What are some of the advantages and disadvantages of ratings by peers?

5. What are some of the problems in measuring the validity of various appraising devices?

6. How might appraisals and their communication be different in a Theory X environment in contrast to a Theory Y environment?

7. If a company did not have systematized procedures of appraisal, in what ways would appraisals be carried out?

8. What are behaviorally anchored rating scales? What are their advantages and disadvantages?

9. In what ways has equal employment opportunity legislation and rulings affected performance appraisals?

10. What should be the responsibilities of the personnel department with respect to the appraising process?

11. What were the conclusions of the GE research study on appraisal?

12. What are some of the dimensions that might differentiate one version of MBO from another?

13. How does traditional MBO differ from collaborative MBO as described in the chapter?

14. How would you go about diagnosing whether an MBO program might be useful to an organization?

SUPPLEMENTAL REFERENCES

Baird, Lloyd S., "Feedback: A Determinant of the Relationship between Performance and Satisfaction," in Robert L. Taylor, Michael J. O'Connell, Robert A. Zawacki, and D.D. Warrick, eds., *Academy of Management Proceedings,* Proceedings of the 36th Annual Meeting of the Academy of Management, Kansas City, Missouri, August 11–14, 1976, pp. 70–73.

Barrett, Richard S., *Performance Rating* (Chicago: Science Research Associates, Inc., 1966).

Beck, Arthur C., Jr., and Ellis D. Hillman, eds., *A Practical Approach to Organization Development through MBO: Selected Readings* (Reading, Mass.: Addison-Wesley, 1972).

Beer, Michael, and Robert A. Ruh, "Employee Growth through Performance Management," *Harvard Business Review,* 54:59–66 (July-August 1976).

Blood, Milton R., "Spin-Offs from Behavioral Expectation Scale Procedures," *Journal of Applied Psychology,* 59:513–515 (August 1974).

Blumberg, Herbert H., Clinton B. De Soto, and James L. Kuethe, "Evaluation of Rating Scale Formats," *Personnel Psychology,* 19:243–259 (Autumn 1966).

Borman, Walter C., "The Rating of Individuals in Organizations: An Alternate Approach," *Organizational Behavior and Human Performance,* 12:105–124 (1974).

Brady, Rodney H., "MBO Goes to Work in the Public Sector," *Harvard Business Review,* 51:65–74 (March-April 1973).

Burke, Ronald J., "Characteristics of Effective Performance Appraisal Interviews," *Training and Development Journal,* 24:9–12 (March 1970).

————, "Why Performance Appraisal Systems Fail," *Personnel Administration,* 35:32–40 (June 1972).

Carroll, Stephen J., Jr., and Henry L. Tosi, "Goal Characteristics and Personality Factors in a Management by Objectives Program," *Administrative Science Quarterly,* 15:295–305 (September 1970).

Carvalho, Gerard F., "Installing Management by Objectives: A New Perspective in Organization Change," *Human Resource Management,* 11:23–30 (Spring 1972).

Colby, John D., and Ronald L. Wallace, "Performance Appraisal: Help or Hindrance to Employee Productivity?" *The Personnel Administrator,* 20:37–39 (October 1975).

Flanagan, John C., "The Critical Incident Technique," *Psychological Bulletin*, 51:327–358 (July 1954).

Gruenfeld, Leopold W., and Peter Weissenberg, "Supervisory Characteristics and Attitudes toward Performance Appraisal," *Personnel Psychology*, 19:143–151 (Summer 1966).

Hollmann, Robert W., "Applying MBO Research to Practice," *Human Resources Management* (in press).

Howell, Robert A., "Managing by Objectives— A Three-Stage System," *Business Horizons*, 13:41–45 (February 1970).

Hughes, Charles L., "Why Goal Oriented Performance Reviews Succeed and Fail," *Personnel Journal*, 45:335–341 (June 1966).

Ivancevich, John J., "Changes in Performance in a Management by Objectives Program," *Administrative Science Quarterly*, 19:563–573 (December 1974).

———, "A Longitudinal Assessment of Management by Objectives," *Administrative Science Quarterly*, 17:126–138 (March 1972).

Kavanagh, Michael J., Arthur C. MacKinney, and Leroy Wolins, "Issues in Managerial Performance: Multitrait and Multimethod Analyses of Ratings," *Psychological Bulletin*, 75:34–49 (1971).

Kay, Emanuel, Herbert H. Meyer, and John R.P. French, Jr., "Effects of Threat in a Performance Appraisal Interview," *Journal of Applied Psychology*, 49:311–317 (October 1965).

Kellogg, Marion S., *What to Do About Performance Appraisal* (New York: American Management Association, Inc., 1965).

Kerr, Stephen, "Some Modifications in MBO as in OD Strategy," in Vance Mitchell, Richard Barth, Frances Mitchell, eds., *The Academy of Management Proceedings*, Proceedings of the 32nd Annual Meeting of the Academy of Management, August 13–16, 1972, pp. 39–42.

Kim, Jay S., and W. Clay Hamner, "Effect of Performance Feedback and Goal Setting on Productivity and Satisfaction in an Organizational Setting," *Journal of Applied Psychology*, 61:48–57 (February 1976).

Kirchhoff, Bruce A., "A Diagnostic Tool for Management by Objectives," *Personnel Psychology*, 28:351–364 (August 1975).

———, "MBO: Understanding What the Experts Are Saying," *MSU Business Topics*, 22:17–22 (Summer 1974).

Klimoski, Richard J., and Manuel London, "Role of the Rater in Performance Appraisal," *Journal of Applied Psychology*, 59:445–451 (August 1974).

Lawler, Edward E., III, "The Multitrait-Multirater Approach to Measuring Managerial Job Performance," *Journal of Applied Psychology*, 51:369–381 (October 1967).

Levinson, Harry, "Appraisal of What Performance?" *Harvard Business Review*, 54:30–36ff. (July-August 1976).

———, "Management by Objectives: A Critique," *Training and Development Journal*, 26:3–8 (April 1972).

Liberman, Aaron, R. Amidon, P. Retish, B. Arbeit, and E. Williams, "Personnel Evaluation—A Proposal for Employment Standards," *Public Personnel Management*, 4:248–258 (July-August 1975).

Mahler, Walter R., "Improving Coaching Skills," *Personnel Administration*, 27:28–33 (January-February 1964).

———, *Twenty Years of Merit Rating* (New York: The Psychological Corporation, 1946).

Millard, Cheedle W., Fred Luthans, and Robert L. Ottemann, "A New Breakthrough for Performance Appraisal," *Business Horizons*, 19:66–73 (August 1976).

Morrisey, George L., *Management by Objectives and Results* (Reading, Mass.: Addison-Wesley, 1970).

Oberg, Winston, "Make Performance Appraisal Relevant," *Harvard Business Review*, 50:61–67 (January-February 1972).

Patten, Thomas H., Jr., "OD, MBO, and the R/P System," *Personnel Administration*, 35:14–23 (March-April 1972).

Paul, Robert J., "Employee Performance Appraisal: Some Empirical Findings," *Personnel Journal*, 47:109–113 (February 1968).

Prather, Richard, "Training: Key to Realistic Performance Appraisal," *Training and Development Journal*, 24:4–7 (December 1970).

Purcell, Theodore V., "How GE Measures Managers in Fair Employment," *Harvard Business Review*, 52:99–104 (November-December 1974).

Raia, Anthony P., *Managing by Objectives* (Glenview, Ill.: Scott, Foresman and Company, 1974).

Reeser, Clayton, "Executive Performance Appraisal—The View from the Top," *Personnel Journal*, 54:42–46ff. (January 1975).

Ross, Paul F., "Reference Groups in Man-to-Man Job Performance Ratings," *Personnel Psychology*, 19:115–142 (Summer 1966).

Schuster, Fred E., "Management by Objectives—What and Why?" *Personnel Administration*, 17:18–21 (November-December 1972).

Sokolik, Stanley L., "Guidelines in the Search for Effective Appraisal," *Personnel Journal*, 46:660–668 (November 1967).

Strauss, George, "Management by Objectives: A Critical View," *Training and Development Journal*, 26:10–15 (April 1972).

Taylor, Robert L., and William D. Wilsted, "Capturing Judgment Policies in Performance Rating," *Industrial Relations*, 15:216–224 (May 1976).

Tosi, Henry, John Hunter, Rod Chesser, Jim R. Tarter, and Stephen Carroll, "How Real Are Changes Induced by Management by Objectives," *Administrative Science Quarterly*, 21:276–306 (June 1976).

Tosi, Henry L., John R. Rizzo, and Stephen J. Carroll, "Setting Goals in Management by Objectives," *California Management Review*, 12:70–78 (Summer 1970).

Wallace, William H., "Performance Appraisal of Nonself Directed Personnel," *Personnel Journal*, 50:521–527 (July 1971).

Werther, L.B., Jr., and H. Weihrich, "Refining MBO through Negotiations," *MSU Business Topics*, 23:53–59 (Summer 1975).

Whisler, Thomas L., and Shirley F. Harper, eds., *Performance Appraisal, Research and Practice* (New York: Holt, Rinehart and Winston, Inc., 1962).

Wickstrom, Walter S., *Managing by and with Objectives*, Studies in Personnel Policy No. 212 (New York: National Industrial Conference Board, 1968).

Wortman, Max S., Jr., and Haakon L. Andreasen, "Appraisal Interviews," *The Personnel Administrator*, 13:1–7 (January-February 1968).

Zander, Alvin F., *Performance Appraisals* (Ann Arbor: Foundation for Research on Human Behavior, 1963).

CHAPTER 16
TRAINING AND RETRAINING IN SKILLS

DESCRIPTION AND PURPOSES

The purpose of training and retraining in skills is to bring the competencies of individuals up to desired standards for present or potential assignments. In a more general sense, the purpose of skill training is to provide the basic skills and knowledge required in carrying out various specialized parts of the overall task of the enterprise.

One example of skill training is a one-month course in drafting after employment and before placement on a permanent job. Other examples are the step-by-step training given an employee by a supervisor during the first few days on the job, courses given experienced technicians and professionals to acquaint them with the intricacies of operating new electronic equipment, or courses in decision making and critical-path analysis for managers. Apprenticeship is an example of a longer, more extensive kind of skill training, although programs of apprenticeship may include general courses as well.

CURRENT PRACTICES AND PROBLEMS

TRAINING IS BIG BUSINESS

The annual expenditure during recent years for training and development programs in the business and industry of this country has been estimated to exceed $25 billion. Included in these costs are training department expenditures, costs of induction and orientation, and training costs resulting from transfers and technological changes.[1] Most studies indicate that

[1]George S. Odiorne, "Training for Profit," *Journal of the American Society of Training Directors*, 15:8 (July 1961); Theodore W. Schultz, *Investment in Human Capital* (New York: The Free Press, 1971), Chapter 5; and Jacob Mincer, "On-the-Job Training: Costs, Returns, and Some Implications," in B.F.

Figure **16-1**   Rank order of frequency of use of eighteen training techniques, by type of firm

	Type of firm			
	Manufacturing[a]		Nonmanufacturing[b]	
Training technique	Rank order	Mean value[c]	Rank order	Mean value[c]
1. Job instruction training	1	3.9	1	4.0
2. Conference or discussion	2	3.5	2	3.4
3. Apprentice training	3	3.1	6.5	2.5
4. Job rotation	4	2.8	3	2.8
5. Coaching	5	2.6	6.5	2.5
6. Lecture	6	2.4	5	2.6
7. Special study	7	2.3	4	2.7
8. Case study	8	2.1	10	2.2
9. Films	9	2.0	8.5	2.4
10. Programmed instruction	10	1.9	8.5	2.4
11. Internships and assistantships	11	1.8	11	2.0
12. Simulation	12	1.7	12	1.9
13. Programmed group exercises	13.5	1.6	16.5	1.3
14. Role playing	13.5	1.6	13	1.6
15. Laboratory training	15	1.5	16.5	1.3
16. Television	16	1.4	14.5	1.4
17. Vestibule training	17	1.2	14.5	1.4
18. Junior board	18	1.1	18	1.1

[a] Consists of 63 firms.
[b] Consists of 14 transportation, 13 finance, 10 retail, and 12 "other" firms.
[c] Computed from the following values: 5= Always; 4= Usually; 3= Average; 2= Seldom; 1= Never.

From Stuart B. Utgood and Rene V. Dawes, "The Most Frequently-Used Training Techniques," *Training and Development Journal*, 24:41 (February 1970). Reproduced by special permission from the February 1970 *Training and Development Journal.* Copyright 1970 by the American Society for Training and Development, Inc.

a high percentage of firms, particularly the larger ones, have formal training programs.

The training techniques used most frequently in manufacturing firms, according to a study conducted in the Minneapolis–St. Paul area, appear to be job instruction training, conference or discussion, apprenticeship training, job rotation, coaching, and lecture, in that order. The use of cases, films, and programmed instruction appeared at about the middle of the list, while the use of junior boards (a special advisory board of younger members of the organization) and vestibule training (skill training after employment but before job assignment) were practically nonexistent.[2] (See Figure 16–1.) Man-

---

Kiker, ed., *Investment in Human Capital* (Columbia, S.C.: University of South Carolina Press, 1971), pp. 279–323.

[2] Stuart B. Utgaard and Rene V. Dawes, "The Most Frequently-Used Training Techniques," *Training and Development Journal,* 24:40–43 (February 1970).

uals also are widely used in teaching the operation of a vast array of equipment; they are typically published by the equipment manufacturer.

It should be noted that apprentice training, internships, and assistantships are much broader concepts than most of the others. Apprenticeship programs are typically four years in length, and they include both classroom instruction and on-the-job training. Internships, or assistantships, are used at the managerial or professional level, and may be a year or more in length. Further, some training activities might include several of these techniques. Human relations training for supervisors, for example, might include role playing, lectures, case study, films, and discussion. Some of these techniques or approaches—job instruction training (JIT), apprenticeship training, and programmed instruction—will be discussed later. Laboratory training and group exercises will be discussed in Chapter 17.[3]

THE JIT SYSTEM

A widely used system of job training is the Job Instruction Training (JIT) system originally developed by the War Manpower Commission during World War II. During the war, this system was taught to large numbers of supervisors who, in turn, used the procedure in training their subordinates.[4] Figure 16-2 shows the essential steps of the JIT system as presented on pocket cards for supervisors. The reader will

note that the procedure includes determination of training needs, cognizance of the needs of the trainee, feedback from the trainee, frequent appraisal, and correction.

APPRENTICESHIP TRAINING

Apprenticeship programs are the chief means of entry into approximately four hundred skilled trades in the United States.[5] This training involves the novice in classroom learning of theory and auxiliary skills as well as extensive skill practice on the job under the tutoring of experienced workers. The typical apprenticeship program is four years in length, although this varies from one to six years, depending upon the complexity of the craft. Most programs are conducted under a cooperative relationship between unions, employers, and vocational schools.[6] A few apprenticeship programs, however, have emerged in the nonunion sector of the construction industry.[7]

Research suggests that formal apprenticeship programs are more successful than other methods of teaching craft skills. In a study in the construction industry, apprenticeship graduates were found to have greater employment stability than informally trained persons, to be represented in larger proportions in supervisory positions, and to advance more rapidly into supervisory jobs.[8]

PROGRAMMED INSTRUCTION

A device that has been used extensively in skill training as well as in general education is the *teaching machine*. Teaching machines feature materials organized in sequential frames of a

[3] See also John P. Campbell, Marvin D. Dunnette, E.E. Lawler, and K.W. Weick, "Training and Development: Methods and Techniques," in *Managerial Behavior, Performance, and Effectiveness* (New York: McGraw-Hill Book Company, 1970), pp. 233–252.
[4] The JIT program was one of several subprograms within a broad Training Within Industry (TWI) program of the War Manpower Commission. Other programs within the TWI program were Job Relations Training (JRT) and Job Methods Training (JMT). See Office of Industrial Resources, International Cooperation Administration, *Job Relations Training Manual*, rev., Technical Bulletin No. 3.

[5] U.S. Department of Labor, *Employment and Training Report of the President, 1976*, p. 129.
[6] *Employment and Training Report of the President*, p. 128.
[7] Ibid., p. 74.
[8] Robert W. Glover, "Breadth of Training in Apprenticeship," *Monthly Labor Review*, 98:46–47 (May 1975).

Figure **16-2** How to instruct

Practical methods to guide you in instructing a new man on a job, or a present worker on a new job or a new skill

FIRST, here's what *you must* do to *get ready* to teach a job:
1. Decide what the learner must be taught in order to do the job efficiently, safely, economically and intelligently.
2. Have the right tools, equipment, supplies and material ready.
3. Have the work place properly arranged, just as the worker will be expected to keep it.

THEN, you should *instruct* the learner by the following *four basic steps:*

STEP I—PREPARATION (of the learner)
1. Put the learner at *ease*.
2. Find out what he already knows about the job.
3. Get him interested and desirous of learning the job.

STEP II—PRESENTATION (of the operations and knowledge)
1. *Tell, Show, Illustrate,* and *Question* in order to put over the new knowledge and operations.
2. Instruct slowly, clearly, completely and patiently, one point at a time.
3. Check, question and repeat.
4. Make sure the learner really knows.

STEP III—PERFORMANCE TRY-OUT
1. Test learner by having him perform the job.
2. Ask questions beginning with *why, how, when* or *where.*
3. Observe performance, correct errors, and repeat instructions if necessary.
4. Continue until you *know he knows.*

STEP IV—FOLLOW-UP
1. Put him "on his own."
2. Check frequently to be sure he follows instructions.
3. Taper off extra supervision and close follow-up until he is qualified to work with normal supervision.

REMEMBER—If the learner hasn't learned, the teacher hasn't taught.

From War Manpower Commission, The Training Within Industry Report (Washington, D.C.: Bureau of Training, Training Within Industry Service, War Manpower Commission, 1945), p. 195.

film or paper strip. This method of organization is significantly different from traditional textbooks in that the learner is not allowed to proceed from point to point until the necessary information has been grasped. The principles are applicable to textbooks, however, and some programmed textbooks and training manuals have appeared.

The principles of the teaching machine have been known for more than fifty years. In 1924 S.L. Pressey exhibited a teaching machine at the American Psychological Association meet-ings; in 1926 he published an article on the subject; and in subsequent years he continued to explore the effectiveness of teaching machines. In recent years, one of the foremost experimenters has been B.F. Skinner. In addition, N.A. Crowder is well known for his innovations in programming.[9]

[9] For theories on the development and use of teaching machines, see Stanely L. Levine and Leonard C. Silvern, "The Evolution and Revolution of the Teaching Machine," *Journal of the American Society of Training Directors,* 14:4–16 (December 1960). For a procedure to evaluate programmed in-

The learning principles underlying the use of the teaching machine and other forms of programmed instruction include: (1) immediate reinforcement of correct responses, (2) direction to the source of correct material when mistakes are made, (3) practice with the skill or knowledge, and (4) allowing the trainee to proceed at his or her own pace. More specifically, the essential features of programmed instruction are as follows: (a) a piece of information is presented to the trainee; (b) the trainee is then asked questions about the material; (c) if the answer selected from several possible choices is correct, the trainee is immediately informed and allowed to proceed; (d) if the answer is incorrect, the trainee is so informed, usually with reasons, and is instructed to reread the material and make another choice. The trainee cannot proceed until the material is mastered. In addition, a certain amount of review is presented as the trainee proceeds, so that retention of the material is enhanced. Furthermore, the trainee's errors are recorded by the machine, so that the supervisors of such training programs can keep track of efficiency in the learning and can spot any deliberate attempts to guess at answers.[10]

Computer assisted instruction is an extension of the techniques of programmed instruction. Basically, instead of interacting with teaching machine programs, the learner interacts with material programmed into the computer.

Both programmed instruction and computer assisted instruction are seen as costly and limited to certain kinds of training objectives. According to Hinrichs, programmed instruction ". . . is costly, appropriate to . . . training objectives where control is clear and objectives readily identifiable, and because of its low social involvement probably of limited use where one of the training objectives is the facilitation of social interaction."[11] Computer assisted instruction is seen as being comparable to programmed instruction in terms of learned performance and achievement, but it may have some advantages in terms of time saved.[12]

MAJOR PROBLEMS IN THE TRAINING AND DEVELOPMENT PROCESS

In any attempt to determine the most effective administration of the training and development process in a particular firm, certain problems immediately emerge. Some of these problems are: (a) How can training needs be determined, and how can a training need be distinguished from an organizational need that can be satisfied in some other way? (b) How can people be motivated to increase their capabilities? (c) What are the relative utilities of various training methods and devices? (d) How can it be determined to what extent the objectives of the training program have been achieved? These problems will be discussed in this chapter and to some extent in the chapter that follows.

DETERMINING THE NEED FOR TRAINING

In American industry there are a number of widely varied methods of identifying problems to be solved through systematic training. As

struction, see Gabriel M. Della-Piana, "A Technique for Evaluating the Efficiency of Programmed Instruction," *Training and Development Journal*, 24:40–41 (January 1970).

[10] For further discussions of programmed instruction, see Theodore B. Dolmatch, Elizabeth Marting, Robert E. Finley, eds., *Revolution in Training: Programmed Instruction in Industry* (New York: American Management Association, 1962); B.F. Skinner, "The Theory behind Teaching Machines," *Journal of the American Society of Training Directors*, 15:27–29 (July 1961); Marion McClintock et al., "Orienting the New Employee with Programmed Instruction," *Training and Development Journal*, 21:18–22 (May 1967); and Harry E. Cather, "Programmed Instruction in the Aerospace Industry," *Training and Development Journal*, 20:29–32 (October 1967).

[11] John R. Hinrichs, "Personnel Training," in Marvin D. Dunnette, ed., *Handbook of Industrial and Organizational Psychology* (Chicago: Rand McNally College Publishing Company, 1976), pp. 850–851.

[12] Ibid., p. 851.

Patten has observed, however, probably ". . . hunches and the crystal ball have . . . been the most widely used ways of determining educational and training needs. . . ."[13] For example, training officials in 150 firms indicated that the method they most frequently used in determining training needs was some kind of request from top management.[14] Presumably perception, judgment, expressed needs of first-level and middle managers, or a desire to follow the practices of other firms were the determining factors in these requests. Other methods used with considerable frequency were informal observations, conversations with supervisors, and group discussions and conferences. Used with less frequency were analyses of various reports (such as cost, turnover, grievances, and suggestions), formal training advisory committees, employee questionnaires, and merit or performance rating. In total, some sixteen different techniques were reported in use.[15]

In addition the use of job ladders for counseling employees (see Chapter 14) has considerable promise in identifying training needs. Job specifications are also basic documents that can be used in planning training. Thus, organizations have several sources of information that assist in determining training needs, with supervisors typically playing a major role in the generating and forwarding of training-needs data.

Lack of skills available in the local labor market is unquestionably a major factor in the establishment of many formal training programs. The employment office and the human resources planners simply find that job specifications cannot be met. As a result, night school or vocational programs may be established in cooperation with public school officials; apprenticeship programs may be started; or people may be hired and placed in training classes before being assigned to job responsibilities. In many large industries, these kinds of programs are the most substantial and expensive parts of the training effort.

Thus, the determination of training needs in American industry ranges from subjective beliefs about the value of training and education to systematic identification of problems requiring solutions. The latter seems the wisest course in order to ensure that training contributes to the goals of the enterprise. Experimental proof of the extent to which training actually does contribute to the attainment of organizational objectives is an extremely complicated problem in measurement, as we shall see later. By and large, this means that managers must rely on judgment rather than experimental evidence.[16]

THE PROBLEM OF MOTIVATION

A great deal has been written about the theory of learning and training. Although this theory will not be reported in detail here, it is consistent with the discussion of needs and motivation in Chapter 6 and with the following theoretical discussion of motivation as it relates to training.[17]

---

[13] Thomas H. Patten, Jr., *Manpower Planning and the Development of Human Resources* (New York: John Wiley & Sons, 1971), p. 119.

[14] Walter R. Mahler and Willys H. Monroe, *How Industry Determines the Need for and Effectiveness of Training,* Personnel Research Branch, Department of the Army, March 1952, PRB Technical Research Report 929, pp. 24–28.

[15] Finnegan lists some twenty ways in which training needs get transmitted to the training manager. See John Finnegan, *Industrial Training Management* (London: Business Books Limited, 1970).

[16] For a logical sequence in determining training needs and planning training programs, see Gale E. Newell, "How to Plan a Training Program," *Personnel Journal,* 55:220–225 (May 1976). For a review of the state of the art in training-needs analysis, see Michael L. Moore and Philip Dutton, "Training Needs Analysis: Review and Critique," Michigan State University, *Working Paper,* 1976.

[17] For a discussion of learning theory, see Norman R.F. Maier, *Psychology in Industrial Organizations,* 4th ed. (Boston: Houghton Mifflin Company, 1973), Chapter 12.

The dynamics of motivating people through training and development programs may be described in the following manner: In order to change behavior in the direction of greater contribution to the attainment of organizational goals, the individual must perceive the new, expected behavior as serving to fulfill needs, or at least as not leading to deprivation of fulfillment. If the motivational structure of the firm emphasizes punishment for noncompliance, behavior is likely to be at the minimum level tolerated by the organization. The reason for this effect is that avoidance of punishment, by itself, does little or nothing to satisfy the needs for self-esteem or self-actualization. As a matter of fact, if the environment provides little satisfaction, these needs will require that the individual fight the organization, either openly or tacitly.

Thus, supplying goals that fulfill needs and are within reasonable reach of employees is very important in providing motivation as it relates to training and development. In other words, the environment must be conducive to changes in behavior.

For these reasons, if programs of training or development are imposed upon people and are interpreted as punishment for deficiencies, there will be little enthusiasm and probably little effective learning. Similarly, if training programs are imposed upon an individual who is overworked or under a great deal of stress, the training is likely to interfere with effective performance and effective learning. Furthermore, if what is learned by an employee is contrary to the behavioral patterns of immediate or higher superiors, the work environment will not tolerate expression of what has been learned. In short, we suggest that, to be effective, training and development must be perceived as leading to the attainment of need-satisfying goals as well as to the avoidance of ego-damaging events. In addition, it must take place in an environment that is not so stressful as to prohibit effective learning and that permits expression of new behavior patterns.

PROBLEMS IN DETERMINING VALIDITY

A review of the literature cited by Mahler and Monroe indicates that most research on the validity of training has inquired into the difference between before-training performance and after-training performance, with few studies comparing the effectiveness of different devices relative to their costs. Apparently, very little research has been done on the comparative usefulness of various training devices, procedures, and systems. The one conclusion that seems warranted is that systematic training is better than unsystematic training.[18]

As in gauging the validity of tests, the major problem in research on the value of training is finding adequate criteria for measuring degrees of performance. Measures of productivity probably reflect actual job performance most accurately, with performance ratings a second best. Another criterion, which is often used but which may not be sufficiently objective, is the judgment of "experts"—usually top management. Other criteria that might be used are scores on examinations, changes in attitude, or the opinions of trainees. Such measures, however, leave unanswered the question of their relationship to actual performance in the attainment of organizational goals.

Most of the studies in the literature conclude that a particular training program has had beneficial results. Mahler and Monroe mention studies that have concluded that training has

[18] See Mahler and Monroe, "How Industry Determines Need for Training," pp. 9–14, 68–93. See also Ralph F. Catalanello and Donald L. Kirkpatrick, "Evaluating Training Programs—the State of Art," *Training and Development Journal*, 22:2–9 (May 1968). For a study of the relative effectiveness of teaching machines versus the conventional lecture-discussion method, see J.L. Hughes, "Industrial Applications of Teaching Machines," *Journal of the American Society of Training Directors*, 15:30–41 (July 1961).

resulted in savings on materials, increased output, fewer accidents, reduced time in reaching production standards, and reduced turnover and absenteeism. These studies represented various degrees of sophistication in research, and most did not involve control groups.[19] The use of control groups is strongly recommended by Belasco and Trice, who also recommended ". . . a simple unpretested two-group design as the most efficient and valid evaluation mechanism."[20]

IMPACT OF ENVIRONMENT

The Smith-Hughes Act of 1917, as amended by the George-Elsey Act of 1934 and the George-Deen Act of 1936, has had a major impact on the training programs of business and industry. These laws provide for matching state and local funds to finance vocational education. Using these funds, local school districts work with business and industrial firms in setting up a wide variety of courses in vocational education, courses that may be directed at pre-employment skills or at upgrading or updating skills of employees already on the payroll.

The Department of Labor also gives assistance in apprenticeship training programs through the Apprentice Training Service. The Apprentice Training Service assists in establishing or improving apprenticeship programs and other training programs. It also helps with problems in labor relations emerging from such programs. In addition, the Fair

Labor Standards Act and the Walsh-Healy Act have an impact on job training through requirements pertaining to the wages of trainees, to the kinds of training that may be done on an off-hours basis, and to the kinds of training that must involve paid time.

Technology and science have had a drastic effect on both the kind and amount of job training required in individual firms through their impact on the task-specialization process. The rapidity with which modern technological innovations change the nature of jobs continually creates a major training and retraining problem in many industries. Consequently, a number of large firms long have had major retraining programs, including the Ford Motor Company, General Mills, GM, IBM, and Xerox Corporation. IBM, for example, as part of its long-range policy to use retraining programs to avoid layoffs from recessions or technological changes, selected people from all over the corporation to be retrained as programmers.[21]

In recent years, the U.S. Congress has responded to the problem of obsolescence in the skills of employees by enacting various kinds of legislation, particularly the Manpower Development and Training Act of 1962 (MDTA), and the Comprehensive Employment and Training Act of 1973 (CETA). The 1962 legislation established a broad program for assisting unemployed or underemployed workers in obtaining employment through the development of new or increased skills. Its intent was to train those whose jobs had disappeared through technological advances or changes in demand for consumer or industrial products. Funds were provided for both school and on-the-job training of certain kinds with priority going to the training

[19]Mahler and Monroe, "How Industry Determines Need for Training," pp. 9–20, 94–119. For studies that featured rigorous research methodology, see pp. 109–122 of the same book.

[20]James A. Belasco and Harrison M. Trice, *The Assessment of Change in Training and Therapy* (New York: McGraw-Hill Book Company, 1969), Chapter 4, p. 156. See also Stephen D. Anderson, "Applied Methods for Evaluating Training," *Proceedings of the Twenty-Third Annual Winter Meeting*, Industrial Relations Research Association Series, December 1970, pp. 232–239.

[21]Walter Burdick, "A Look at Corporate and Personal Philosophy," *The Personnel Administrator*, 21:21–26 (July 1976). For research on the retraining of workers made technologically obsolete, see Ned A. Rosen, Lawrence K. Williams, and F.F. Foltman, "Motivational Constraints in an Industrial Retraining Program," *Personnel Psychology*, 18:65–79 (Spring 1965).

of skills in short supply. In addition, provision was made for modest subsistence and travel allowances as well as a counseling and training program for youths aged sixteen through twenty-one.[22] Amendments to MDTA emphasized training of chronically unemployed and disadvantaged persons.[23] The 1973 legislation (CETA) continued the emphasis on providing job training and employment opportunities for economically disadvantaged, unemployed, and underemployed persons. A major difference between the 1962 and the 1973 legislation is that, under CETA, "block grants" are provided to local and state sponsors operating human resource programs instead of the previous practice of allocating funds for narrow categories of projects.[24]

Partially as an outgrowth of experience under the MDTA, the federal government inaugurated a JOBS Program in 1968 aimed at supporting the efforts of private industry in training and employing the hard-core unemployed. Spearheaded by leading business executives organized in the National Alliance of Businessmen (NAB), programs were started to train and employ the hard-core unemployed in addition to providing summer jobs.[25] By 1974, NAB had accomplished the hiring and placement of 2 million adults in the private sector, including veterans and ex-offenders as well as the disadvan-

taged. In addition, NAB had provided over a million summer jobs for poverty-level youths.[26]

In general, efforts to employ and train the disadvantaged appear to be reasonably successful. A survey of 313 firms participating in the National Alliance of Businessmen–JOBS program found that the retention rate of disadvantaged persons was "normal or better" in 52 percent of the firms and that the productivity of these employees was normal or better in 68 percent of the firms. Disciplinary records were normal or better in 71 percent of the organizations, and punctuality was normal or better in 51 percent. However, attendance was poorer than normal in 56 percent of the companies, and training costs were higher than normal in 62 percent. Further, *all* the firms reported that the time/cost of supervisory support was more than normal.[27] The latter finding is consistent with the findings of a number of research studies that indicate that the factor most associated with the work effectiveness of the previously hard-core unemployed person is *the degree of supportiveness of the organizational climate* in which the new employee is immersed.[28] Thus, various kinds of additional support appear to be a very critical factor in the success of such programs.

Union-management relations also have an impact on job training through the mutual interest of employers and unions in apprenticeship programs and wage rates for trainees. The retraining of workers slated for layoff has also become a bargainable issue. Contracts between Armour and Company and the Amalgamated Meatcutters and Butcher Workmen

---

[22] See Robert C. Goodwin, "The Labor Force Adjustment of Workers Affected by Technological Change," *Manpower Implications of Automation*, U.S. Department of Labor, December 1964, pp. 68–69. See also "A Critique of Cost-Benefit Analysis of Training," *Monthly Labor Review*, 90:45–51 (September 1967).
[23] See U.S. Department of Labor, *Manpower Report of the President*, March 1972, p. 8.
[24] See *The Comprehensive Employment and Training Act of 1973*, Public Law 93–203; and U.S. Department of Labor, "The Comprehensive Employment and Training Act of 1973: Questions and Answers," 1974 (pamphlet, 10 pp.).
[25] U.S. Department of Labor, *Manpower Report of the President*, April 1968, p. 201. Some MDTA funds were utilized for training and educational programs for minority entrepreneurs. See U.S. Department of Labor, *Manpower Report of the President*, 1974, p. 179.

[26] "The NAB: Taking Stock after 7 Years," *Manpower*, 6:22–26 (December 1974).
[27] Allen R. Janger, *Employing the Disadvantaged: A Company Perspective* (New York: The Conference Board, 1972), p. 60.
[28] See Frank Friedlander and Stuart Greenberg, "Effect of Job Attitudes, Training, and Organization Climate on Performance of the Hard-Core Unemployed," *Journal of Applied Psychology*, 55:287–295 (August 1971).

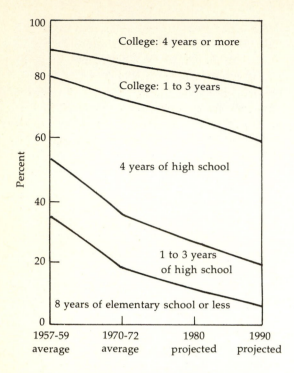

Figure **16-3** Educational attainment of the civilian labor force 25-years-old and over, 1957–1959 average, 1970–1972 average, and projected 1980 and 1990

From *Monthly Labor Review,* 96:106 (November 1973).

Union and between Armour and the United Packinghouse Workers established pilot experiments in an attempt to retrain employees for new jobs[29]; a similar arrangement was agreed to between R.H. Macy and the Retail, Wholesale and Department Store Union.[30] Although early reports on the results of such programs were somewhat discouraging,[31] such joint

union-management concern about retraining those whose skills have been made obsolete by technological change seems to be the trend.

Finally, internal training programs need to adjust to the changing educational levels of the work force. For example, as shown in Figure 16–3 the proportion of the work force with one or more years of college is expected to grow from about 27 percent of the civilian labor force in 1972 to 40 percent in 1990.[32]

RELATIONSHIP TO OTHER PROCESSES

Training is related to numerous other organizational processes. It was noted earlier that the orientation of new employees can be considered both training and part of the staffing process. Further, the skill training needed in an organization will depend partly on the nature of the tasks, determined through the task-specialization process. For example, if a job is created that involves the operation of a small vehicle and the delivery of messages and supplies to various points in a manufacturing plant, such information as how to start and operate the machine and inplant traffic rules will be required before anyone can carry out the minimum requirements of the job. (What appears to be a simple job is rife with the possibilities of making safety, task, and human relations mistakes.) In addition, the amount of training required for the job will depend on the staffing process. In other words, if a person is employed who has the necessary skills and aptitudes to operate such a vehicle and has had previous experience, training may be very brief.

Apprenticeship training programs are largely an outgrowth of the collective-bargaining process. Although such programs are of benefit both to the employer and to the union, unions,

[29]*Business Week,* April 15, 1961, pp. 135–136. See also "Progress Report of Armour's Tripartite Automation Committee," *Monthly Labor Review,* 84:851–857 (August 1961). For subsequent contrast settlements, see *Wage Chronology: Armour and Co. 1941–67,* Bulletin No. 1481, Bureau of Labor Statistics, U.S. Department of Labor, 1966.
[30]*Business Week,* April 29, 1961, p. 81.
[31]See *Fortune,* July 1961, pp. 241–242ff., and *Business Week,* April 15, 1961, pp. 135–136.

[32]Denis F. Johnston, "Education of Workers: Projections to 1990," *Monthly Labor Review,* 96:104–113 (November 1973).

in particular, have pressed for broadly conceived apprenticeship training to enhance the long-range job opportunities of workers. Employers, more cost-conscious, have frequently been prone to train more narrowly or to hire already trained workers when not pressed by the unions to establish broader programs.[33]

Training is also related to the process of compensation. If the internal consistency of a firm's wage and salary structure will be seriously upset by paying wages high enough to recruit people with certain skills, it might be more advantageous for the firm to do its own training and thus retain integrity in the structure of its rewards. Furthermore, in a broad sense, training is inseparable from the process of leadership in that training is inherent in most supervisory positions. Thus, training is closely interrelated with other organizational processes.

AUTHORITY AND ACCOUNTABILITY

Supervisors and managers, in my judgment, are the key to effective training-needs analysis. The personnel department (or the training unit within that department) must assume leadership for developing a comprehensive plan for determining training needs, but supervisors must play a major role in forwarding data that have real meaning to them and to their subordinates for the establishment of training programs. The way for the training unit to avoid collecting great masses of useless data is to involve supervisors in this way. As to actually doing the training, the typical training department appears to be less active in skill training than in general kinds of training and development, such as training in human relations, principles of supervision, and safety. Answers to a questionnaire that asked training directors about the programs furnished by the training department indicated that programs of immediate relevance to initial jobs were infrequently furnished. Only 20 percent of the respondents were involved in apprenticeship training, for example, and only 3 percent in machine-shop training.[34] However, there may be wide variations among industries.

Presumably, almost all personnel departments are involved in procedures of induction and orientation, but surprisingly few training departments are thus involved. In the study already cited, only 24 percent of the training directors responding reported that their departments were involved in the orientation function.[35]

Apparently, supervisors carry on the largest part of skill training. This observation is confirmed by a study in which supervisors almost universally felt that training at the immediate work place was their responsibility and that the training staff gave them little assistance in this activity.[36] One survey has concluded that, in general, the quality of training in a large proportion of firms is not high, partly because the training department is not expected to give much help to supervisors in improving the training of subordinates.[37]

---

[33] Robert W. Glover, "Apprenticeship in America: An Assessment," *Proceedings of the Twenty-Seventh Annual Winter Meeting,* San Francisco, 1974, Industrial Relations Research Association, 1975, pp. 64–65.

[34] Harry S. Belman and John E. Bliek, "The Nature of Current Training Function Activities," *Journal of the American Society of Training Directors,* 15:31–34 (February 1961).
[35] Ibid.
[36] Helen Baker and Robert R. France, *Centralization and Decentralization in Industrial Relations* (Princeton, N.J.: Industrial Relations Section, Department of Economics and Sociology, Princeton University, 1954), pp. 102, 103. For further discussion of responsibility for training, see Donald L. Kirkpatrick, "Whose Responsibility Is Training?" *Training and Development Journal,* 21:22–25 (March 1967).
[37] See Walter R. Mahler, "A Critical Look at Training in American Industry," *Journal of the American Society of Training Directors,* 16:5–6 (December 1962).

SUMMARY

Lack of attention to skill training can be disastrous to the enterprise in terms of cost and inefficiencies. Extreme examples make this conclusion obvious. Thus, no one would dream of allowing an untrained individual to pilot a jet airliner, nor would it be reasonable to expect productivity from an untrained person assigned to operate a bulldozer, a lathe, or a drillpress.[38] Managerial experience plus evidence from the literature lead to the conclusion that systematic job training can make a significant contribution to the achievement of organizational objectives, provided good judgment is exercised about diminishing returns.

Effective skill training depends upon (a) careful identification of training needs by supervisors and managers, in cooperation with the personnel or training department; (b) systematic training procedures; (c) adequate attention to meeting the needs of trainees; (d) evaluation of the results of training; and, (e) modification of training programs based on such evaluation. Specialized training units can make a major contribution in helping line managers with all five aspects of training. Both training new employees and updating skills of experienced employees are important. Such training is very likely to reduce costs and inefficiencies immediately as well as in the long run, and it can avoid obsolescence of the organization's human resources. To an increasing extent, the acceleration of technological change is making effective training in organizations a vital aspect of organizational success through its impact on the task-specialization process.

---

[38] Mann and Hoffman stress the economic importance of thorough training from their studies of new power plants. See Floyd C. Mann and L. Richard Hoffman, *Automation and the Worker* (New York: Holt, Rinehart and Winston, 1960), pp. 205–207.

REVIEW AND DISCUSSION QUESTIONS

1. If you were a personnel director, what procedures would you want to establish for determining training needs?

2. What are the essential steps in the JIT method of instruction?

3. What are the essential features of programmed learning?

4. What are some of the problems in determining the validity of various training devices and programs?

5. In what ways has federal legislation affected training?

6. In what ways has collective bargaining influenced training programs?

7. How does training relate to other organizational processes?

8. What are some of the costs associated with training the hard-core unemployed person?

9. Discuss the changing educational levels of the labor force. What are the implications for training?

SUPPLEMENTAL REFERENCES

Barbash, Jack, "Union Interests in Apprenticeship and Other Training Forms," *The Journal of Human Resources*, 3:63–85 (Winter 1968).

Belasco, James A., and Harrison M. Trice, *The Assessment of Change in Training and Therapy* (New York: McGraw-Hill Book Company, 1969).

Bienvenu, Bernard J., *New Priorities in Training* (New York: American Management Association, 1969).

Brennan, Peter J., "Realizing Apprenticeship's Potential," *Manpower*, 6:2–7 (September 1974).

Dvorin, Robert S., "Evaluation of Training," in Joseph H. Famularo, ed., *Handbook of Modern*

Personnel Administration (New York: McGraw-Hill Book Company, 1972), Chapter 26.

Foltman, F.F., "An Assessment of Apprenticeship," *Monthly Labor Review*, 87:28–35 (January 1964).

French, Elliott, "Manpower Development and Training Act's On-The-Job (OJT) Provisions," *Training Directors Journal*, 17:3–5 (May 1963).

Furst, Hans, "The Economics of Training and Development," *Training and Development Journal*, 24:30–33 (October 1970).

Gassler, Lee S., "How Companies Are Helping the Undereducated Worker," *Personnel*, 44:47–55 (July-August 1967).

McGehee, William, and Paul W. Thayer, *Training in Business and Industry* (New York: John Wiley & Sons, Inc., 1961).

Marshall, Roy, and Vernon M. Briggs, Jr., "Negro Participation in Apprenticeship Programs," *The Journal of Human Resources*, 2:51–69 (Winter 1967).

Minter, Robert L., "Mismanagement of Training Programs," *Training and Development Journal*, 26:2–5 (July 1972).

National Training Laboratories, *Human Forces in Teaching and Learning* (Washington: National Training Laboratories, National Education Association, 1961).

Odiorne, George S., *Training by Objectives: An Economic Approach to Management Training* (New York: The Macmillan Company, 1970).

Otto, Calvin P., and Rollin O. Glasser, *The Management of Training* (Reading, Mass.: Addison-Wesley Publishing Company, 1970).

Prieve, E. Arthur, and Dorothy A. Wentorf, "Training Objectives—Philosophy or Practice," *Personnel Journal*, 49:235–240 (March 1970).

Schmidt, Warren H., "How to Evaluate a Company's Training Efforts," *California Management Review*, 12:49–56 (Spring 1970).

Seymour, W. Douglas, "Retraining for Technical Change," *Personnel Management*, 48:191–195 (December 1966).

Smith, Wendell I., and J. William Moore, eds., *Programmed Learning: Theory and Research* (Princeton, N.J.: D. Van Nostrand Company, Inc., 1962).

Tracey, William R., *Evaluating Training and Development Systems* (New York: American Management Association, 1968).

———, *Managing Training and Development Systems* (New York: Amacom, 1974).

Warren, Malcolm W., *Training for Results* (Reading, Mass.: Addison-Wesley Publishing Company, 1969).

Wolfbein, Seymour L., *Manpower Policy: Perspectives and Prospects* (Philadelphia: School of Business Administration, Temple University, 1973).

CHAPTER 17
MANAGEMENT AND EMPLOYEE DEVELOPMENT

This chapter will discuss five important topics: (1) on-the-job coaching, (2) management- and employee-development programs (3) laboratory training, (4) employee-counseling, career-planning, and transactional analysis, and (5) other developmental opportunities. Along with skill training and appraisal interviews, these topics are directly related to the broad training and developmental process.

ON-THE-JOB COACHING AND JOB EXPECTATIONS

Before the more formalized methods of management and employee development are discussed, the importance of on-the-job coaching needs to be stressed. By coaching, I mean the informal advice giving, correcting, suggesting, and encouraging provided by the superior.

Numerous research studies cited throughout this book suggest that the day-to-day interactions between a superior and subordinates have a powerful impact on the performance and development of employees. They further suggest that a supportive, problem-solving climate tends to be superior for learning and development in contrast to dictatorial or punitive modes. This holds true for both ongoing interactions and for the more formalized appraisal interviews growing out of merit-rating or MBO programs. The development activities described later can be very significant in the career growth of managers and other employees, but they are not substitutes for on-the-job coaching of high quality.

Further, there is preliminary evidence that the extent of challenge on the first year of a management job is associated with level of performance, job success, and salary in later years.

Berlew and Hall studied sixty-two managers in the Bell System who had been hired out of college as management trainees, and on whom data were available over a time span of several years. The researchers found that the higher the company's expectations of the person on the first management job in terms of eighteen different factors (technical competence, group membership skills, etc.), the more likely the person was to be successful later. While the results could have a different explanation if the company had assigned the most capable young management trainees to the most challenging assignments, the data suggested that the trainees had been assigned randomly.[1] The implications are that careful attention by organizations to the level of challenge presented to new managers is likely to have very beneficial results in subsequent years.

MANAGEMENT AND EMPLOYEE DEVELOPMENT PROGRAMS

DESCRIPTION AND PURPOSES

Management and *employee development programs* are those types of organization-sponsored programs aimed at educating supervisory and/or nonsupervisory employees above and beyond the immediate technical requirements of jobs. Courses in human relations, decision making, and the executive's role are examples of courses that might be included.

One study of objectives in management-development programs found that more than 75 percent of the 167 United States firms replying to a questionnaire stated that their main objective was "to improve the performance of all managers on their present jobs." The next most frequently stated objective (34 percent of

the firms) was "to prepare selected managers for possible future promotions."[2]

Broadly speaking, the purpose of most, if not all, employee and management development programs is to increase the organization's present and future capability in attaining its goals. Implicit in the objectives of many programs is the avoidance of managerial and employees' obsolescence, a constant danger in a highly competitive, changing business and industrial world.

Based on responses from more than 2,000 firms, one study found 43 percent of the organizations had well-defined in-house management development programs, 66 percent regularly sent managers to professional management training organizations for courses, 39 percent regularly sent managers to college or university executive and management development courses, and 79 percent had tuition refund programs for managers.[3]

Formalized management trainee programs specifically designed to groom candidates for managerial positions are also widespread. According to one survey, about two-fifths of responding firms (and a majority of the larger firms) had programs to prepare trainees for positions in middle management.[4] Another study indicated that approximately half of the college graduates recruited to work for the 240 responding firms were given a period of special training—typically seven to twelve months—before being assigned to a specific job.[5]

[2]Walter S. Wickstrom, "Why Companies Develop Their Managers," *Management Record*, 23:6–8 (November 1961).

[3]Robert F. Pearse, *Manager to Manager: What Managers Think of Management Development*, AMA Survey Report (New York: American Management Association, 1974), p. 18.

[4]Bureau of National Affairs, "Management Trainee Programs," *Personnel Policies Forum*, Survey No. 72 (December 1963), p. 1.

[5]National Industrial Conference Board, "Employment of the College Graduate," *Studies in Personnel Policy*, No. 152, 1956, p. 33. For brief descriptions of the programs in thirty-six universities (by no means a complete listing), see "What the

[1]David E. Berlew and Douglas T. Hall, "The Socialization of Managers: Effects of Expectations on Peformance," *Administrative Science Quarterly*, 11:207–223 (1966).

The rapid growth of seminars in management offered by universities since World War II and their wide acceptance and encouragement by business and industry provide further evidence of the widespread belief in the management development concept. In a recent thirteen-year period, university executive programs multiplied from four to more than forty.[6]

In addition to in-plant and college-campus seminars, many one-day to two-week courses are conducted off company property at hotels, resorts, and elsewhere. These seminars may have one or more sponsors, including the company, consultants, schools, or universities, and nonprofit business research or educational organizations such as the American Management Association, the Conference Board, NTL Institute for Applied Behavioral Sciences (formerly National Training Laboratories), or professional societies. Many firms make a practice of sending selected managers to such seminars, and occasionally nonsupervisory employees are sent to special courses, although this latter practice is relatively infrequent. For example, secretaries of executives are sometimes sent to special seminars, and skilled mechanics are often sent to special schools to learn the theory essential to the maintenance of new equipment. A notable innovation has been the establishment by a number of large corporations of their own management-development "colleges," to which executives from company operations throughout the country are sent. A number of companies have also established programs for executives that feature liberal arts seminars.

The techniques used in general developmental programs are quite varied. Lectures, reading assignments, films, demonstrations, cases, role playing, managerial games, discus-sion, closed-circuit television, long-distance telephone interviews, and recordings are all examples of techniques or devices used. A survey made several years ago indicated that the conference or discussion method, study of cases, and lectures, in that order, were the most popular techniques in in-plant supervisory-training programs, with role playing used in only a small number of situations.[7]

The subjects offered by general development programs are also widely varied, although programs tend to have certain courses in common. For example, the typical university advanced management seminar will include some coverage of the human aspects of administration, of accounting and finance, and of the economic and social environment surrounding business. In-plant supervisory-training programs generally offer courses in human relations, techniques of supervision, and communications. In addition, the company's policies and organizational structure are explained during the course of the training program. Courses in work simplification for both supervisors and nonsupervisory employees are quite frequent.[8]

Managerial games are also gaining in popularity. Many feature decision making relative to the simulated operations of a company over a span of time. Decisions are often scored with electronic data-processing equipment. One type of business game is the "in-basket exercise" in which the trainee makes decisions based on the memos and messages brought to

---

Colleges Offer," *Business Management*, 33:50–56 (October 1967).

[6] Robert J. House, ed., *Management Development* (Ann Arbor: Bureau of Industrial Relations, Graduate School of Business Administration, University of Michigan, 1967), p. 9.

[7] Bureau of National Affairs, "Supervisory Development, Part I," *Personnel Policies Forum*, Survey No. 31 (July 1955), p. 3. For a description of a number of training devices, see Malcolm W. Warren, *Training for Results* (Reading, Mass.: Addison-Wesley Publishing Company, 1969), pp. 71–87. For a description of the "Incident Process," a variation of the case method, see Paul Pigors and Faith Pigors, *Case Method in Human Relations: The Incident Process* (New York: McGraw-Hill Book Company, 1961).

[8] For a description of the context in which work simplification courses are conducted at Texas Instruments, see M. Scott Myers, "Conditions for Manager Motivation," *Harvard Business Review*, 44:69 (January-February 1966).

the in-basket during the day. The task of the trainee is to do the best job he or she can in handling the problems presented.[9] (See also Chapter 13 under the topic of "Assessment Centers.")

An interesting combination of work on actual company problems and seminars has been developed at Vickers Incorporated and Northern Natural Gas. Executives are asked to investigate company problems outside their own area of responsibility and then meet some months later to discuss and defend their reports. The objectives of these programs are to increase teamwork among executives, to increase potentiality for advancement, and to solve a company's real problems.[10] Another interesting experiment involves a *manager's letter program* in which subordinate managers, after several training sessions, write letters setting forth their future plans, their effort to solve current problems, and any suggestions they wish to transmit to higher management.[11]

CURRENT PROBLEMS

A number of questions emerge in the administration of management and employee development seminars in addition to the problems discussed in the previous chapter. For example, is a particular program a passing fad, or does it have real relevance to the problems of organizations? Should programs be compulsory? Who should participate? Is attendance at an executive development program a signal that a manager is being groomed for promotion? Is this resented by colleagues?

Probably nowhere else in management are there so many fads in technique as in management development programs. Currently, managerial games and laboratory training (to be discussed later) are very popular, while a few years ago brainstorming was particularly prevalent.[12] I am not suggesting that these innovations in technique lack usefulness nor that they are necessarily transient, but I am suggesting that management should be thoughtful about adopting just any training and developmental technique in vogue. Furthermore, management should avoid regarding any single technique as a panacea. Some experimentation with new techniques probably is healthy; on the other hand, major investments in training programs without careful assessment of their relevance to solving present or potential problems in an enterprise may be an economic waste.

The question of who participates is likely to depend on the attitudes of top management. In general, although most management development programs are declared to be voluntary, strong enthusiasm on the part of top management will probably be interpreted so as to make participation mandatory. Compulsory attendance at programs usually results in less learning than voluntary attendance. Coercion on the part of management should be avoided. This is particularly true with respect to laboratory (T-Group) training. Under ideal conditions, management development programs will be perceived as being highly relevant to personal growth and advancement in a career, and the problem should become one of meeting demand rather than pressuring people to attend.

[9] For a description of the "in-basket exercise," see Lewis B. Ward, "The Use of Business Problems," *Management Record,* 22:30–33 (June 1960). For a description of a variety of management development techniques, see Allen A. Zoll, III, *Dynamic Management Education* (Seattle: Management Education Associates, 1966).

[10] See "New Technique Yields Triple Dividends," *Nation's Business,* 50:40–42 (August 1964). Top management was reported to be pleased with the results. This approach to management development has considerable face validity.

[11] Frances B. Torbert, "Experiments with a Manager's Letter Program," *Personnel,* 41:30–39 (January-February 1964).

[12] Marvin D. Dunnette, John Campbell, and Kay Jaastad, "The Effect of Group Participation on Brainstorming Effectiveness for Two Industrial Samples," *Journal of Applied Psychology,* 47:30–37 (February 1963).

Whenever managers are selected for special managerial- or executive-training programs, the interpretation of such action by colleagues or by the people themselves may create problems. Special training may be perceived as grooming of possible successors. However, such interpretation is not as likely to develop if all managers have an equal opportunity to participate in developmental programs. In general, this problem has not been considered serious with regard to university seminars.[13] It has probably been more important when college recruits enter special management-training courses, but in this case, the resentment of present employees has often been minimized by the provision of programs for which they may apply.

IMPACT OF VARIOUS ENVIRONMENTAL VARIABLES

Attitudes of union leaders can have an effect on developmental programs, such as courses for aspirants to supervisory jobs. Depending upon the situation, union attitudes have varied from enthusiasm to opposition, but either approval or disinterest have apparently been prevalent. The most favorable attitudes seem to have been engendered when union officials have participated as discussion leaders or when management has actively sought the support of the union. On the whole, unions are very much in favor of education; their interest is demonstrated by their support of public education and their own training and developmental programs, which are growing in scope and size.

[13] Kenneth R. Andrews, "Is Management Training Effective? II. Measurement, Objectives, and Policy," *Harvard Business Review*, 35:70 (March-April 1957). The person singled out to attend a university seminar is probably already generally acknowledged as a "comer" by colleagues. One study found the most frequently used selection criteria for such seminars were either a recently awarded promotion or a pending promotion. See S.G. Huneryager, "What 60 Companies Think about Back-to-College Programs," *Personnel Journal*, 38:215–219 (November 1959).

Union-sponsored developmental programs for stewards and other union officers can, however, constitute a problem to the uninformed supervisor or manager. The old adage, "Knowledge is power," is relevant in the organizational context, and the supervisors who lag behind their subordinates in education may find themselves losing their effectiveness as leaders.

Union members sometimes refer to human-relations training programs for supervisors as "charm schools," although the impact of such comments is probably not great. The comments might reflect resentment, envy, or good-natured banter, depending upon the philosophy underlying the course and upon any resulting changes in the supervisor's behavior.

A high degree of specialization in many managerial and professional jobs probably gives impetus to a good deal of general managerial development. That is, the necessity of having managers who can deal not only with their specialties but who can also manage complex organizations tends to stimulate interest in broad training for such areas as administration, human relations, organization theory, or specialties other than their own. As will be discussed later, however, top management's support for managerial development is one thing; creating an environment in which what is learned can be put into practice is another.

EFFECT ON NEED FULFILLMENT

Opportunities for general training and development give expression to needs for self-actualization and understanding. As the previous chapter indicated, however, if courses are perceived as punishment, needs will not be met. Conversely, if attendance at a management development seminar is perceived as a reward for superior performance, such programs will have considerable intrinsic value in enhancing the self-esteem of participants. Moreover, from my observation, participation in supervisory-training classes seems to fulfill some important needs for belonging as well as provide recognition and attention from higher management.

There are some research data to support these assertions. In a study of training effects in a large firm in the Northeast, researchers found the following unanticipated consequences:

Principally, participation in the training provided the supervisors with an opportunity to share problems with other similarly situated individuals. Even if the supervisor disagreed with the opinions of the others, he generally felt relieved to know that he was not the only one lacking confidence about the "right thing to do." Many supervisors discovered that others shared their own feelings of frustration and aloneness. The therapeutic value of the training sessions is best illustrated by the persistent requests for the formation of a "Supervisors Anonymous" where supervisors could meet periodically and discuss mutual problems.

In addition, the training served to indicate that the organization cared about its supervisors and their problems. Attendance at the sessions, formal memos, reminder telephone calls, and graduation certificates all were visible symbols of their importance. The supervisors developed a feeling of inclusion which served to increase their identification with the organization.[14]

The researchers concluded that "these ceremonial effects, which have been largely overlooked in the past, may be the most important functions of training. The actual content of the training may be of only secondary importance."[15]

AUTHORITY AND ACCOUNTABILITY

Typically, the role of the people in the personnel department in a general training and developmental program includes assistance in determining training needs, recommendation of programs, development of seminars and teaching aids, scheduling of classes, follow-up on the effectiveness of programs, and occasionally acting as lecturers or conference-leaders for such classes. The last case is very likely to occur when a training department is a separate subunit of the personnel department.

The determination of who will attend in-plant seminars is made by the immediate supervisors involved or by higher management. In some instances, suggestions from top management on who should attend will have the impact of an order, or top-management enthusiasm may be interpreted as a signal that anyone nominated had better be enthusiastic. Managers at various levels are not likely to resist outwardly what they think top management expects them to do. Thus "voluntary" programs may not be so voluntary.

The personnel department may serve as a central source of information about available outside seminars and will sometimes work with universities or other organizations in developing courses and seminars to which company people can be sent. The personnel department may also develop specific plans and budgets for sending managers to outside seminars, but the final determination of who will attend, as in the case of in-plant seminars, is likely to be made by the immediate superiors of the managers involved. However, if the personnel director is considered a key person in any top-management committee concerned with the overall planning of managerial development, or if the personnel director participates in selecting managers for promotion, she or he is also likely to participate in selecting people to attend advanced management seminars.

UTILITY OF SYSTEMS

The opinions of training directors lend some insight into the relative utility of various training devices or techniques. In a study involving 117 training directors from the 200 firms in the

[14]James A. Belasco and Harrison M. Trice, *The Assessment of Change in Training and Therapy* (New York: McGraw-Hill Book Company, 1969), pp. 147–148.
[15]Ibid., p. 148.

United States having the largest number of employees, opinions were solicited as to the relative effectiveness of different training methods in accomplishing six different objectives.[16] The training methods were case study, conference method, lecture, business games, movie films, programmed instruction, role playing, sensitivity training, and television lecture. The training directors were asked to evaluate each training method separately relative to each objective, and to use the following scale of effectiveness: "highly effective (5), quite effective (4), moderately effective (3), limited effectiveness (2), and not effective (1)."[17] The results are shown in Figure 17-1.

One of the major conclusions drawn from the study was that training directors clearly perceive that some training methods are more relevant to attaining certain objectives than are other methods. For example, sensitivity training was seen as most effective in changing attitudes and developing interpersonal skills, but ineffective in contributing to knowledge acquisition. Conversely, programmed instruction was seen as the most effective method for knowledge acquisition, but as having limited effectiveness in changing attitudes and developing interpersonal skills.[18] Thus, the relevance of a particular method to attaining a particular organizational goal needs to be considered, and reliance on "canned" programs to have a ubiquitous good effect may be a mistake.

A number of authors and industrial managers are concerned about "packaged" training programs. The danger is that such programs will not fit particular needs of the organization and will not contribute to its objectives. As Lyndall Urwick once stated, "One of the greatest dangers threatening the spread of healthy plans of management development in American business is that men will mistake the systems and techniques for the thing itself. . . ."[19]

Therefore, orderly, systematic procedures for determining training needs, presenting material, and assessing results are very important. Of particular importance is systematic attention to the advice of participants and their superiors.

VALIDITY

There is considerable evidence in the literature that participants in the various developmental programs have found them of considerable value. For example, one study of the reactions of participants in university seminars on managerial development found 82 percent of the respondents with favorable reactions to the programs in which they participated.[20]

Another study, which surveyed presidents of 106 leading United States corporations, found these top executives overwhelmingly in favor of management development programs. The presidents were not only in favor of such programs but were expecting to spend more money for this purpose in the future. On the other hand, they expressed a desire for managerial development to be more job related, for more development of subordinates by their immediate superiors, and for fewer lectures and

[16]Stephen J. Carroll, Jr., Frank T. Paine, and John J. Ivancevich, "The Relative Effectiveness of Training Methods—Expert Opinion and Research," *Personnel Psychology*, 25:495–509 (Autumn 1972).

[17]Ibid., p. 496. For an essay that supplements some of the descriptions of training and development techniques in this chapter and Chapter 16, see John P. Campbell, Marvin D. Dunnette, E.E. Lawler, and K.E. Weick, "Training and Development: Methods and Techniques," in *Managerial Behavior, Performance, and Effectiveness* (New York: McGraw-Hill Book Company, 1970), pp. 233–252.

[18]Ibid., pp. 499–506.

[19]Lyndall F. Urwick, *Management Education in American Business, Management Education for Itself and its Employees*, Part I (New York: American Management Association, 1954), p. 30.

[20]Kenneth R. Andrews, "Reaction to University Development Programs," *Harvard Business Review*, 39:119–121 (May-June 1961). See also Kenneth R. Andrews, *The Effectiveness of University Management Development Programs* (Boston: Division of Research, Graduate School of Business Administration, Harvard University, 1966), p. 73.

Figure 17-1 Ratings of training directors on effectiveness of alternative training methods for various training objectives

Training method	Knowledge acquisition		Changing attitudes		Problem-solving skills		Interpersonal skills		Participant acceptance		Knowledge retention	
	Mean	Mean rank	Mean	Mean rank	Mean	Mean rank	Mean	Mean rank	Mean	Mean rank	Mean	Mean rank
Case study	3.56^b	2	3.43^d	4	3.69^b	1	3.02^d	4	3.80^d	2	3.48^e	2
Conference (discussion) method	3.33^d	3	3.54^d	3	3.26^e	4	3.21^d	3	4.16^a	1	3.32^f	5
Lecture (with questions)	2.53	9	2.20	8	2.00	9	1.90	8	2.74	8	2.49	8
Business games	3.00	6	2.73^f	5	3.58^b	2	2.50^e	5	3.78^d	3	3.26^f	6
Movie films	3.16^g	4	2.50^f	6	2.24^g	7	2.19^g	6	3.44^g	5	2.67^h	7
Programmed instruction	4.03^a	1	2.22^h	7	2.56^f	6	2.11^g	7	3.28^g	7	3.74^a	1
Role playing	2.93	7	3.56^d	2	3.27^e	3	3.68^b	2	3.56^e	4	3.37^f	4
Sensitivity training (t group)	2.77	8	3.96^a	1	2.98^e	5	3.95^b	1	3.33^g	6	3.44^f	3
Television lecture	3.10^g	5	1.99	9	2.01	8	1.81	9	2.74	9	2.47	9

[a] More effective than methods ranked 2 to 9 for this objective at .01 level of significance.
[b] More effective than methods ranked 3 to 9 for this objective at .01 level of significance.
[c] More effective than methods ranked 4 to 9 for this objective at .01 level of significance.
[d] More effective than methods ranked 5 to 9 for this objective at .01 level of significance.
[e] More effective than methods ranked 6 to 9 for this objective at .01 level of significance.
[f] More effective than methods ranked 7 to 9 for this objective at .01 level of significance.
[g] More effective than methods ranked 8 to 9 for this objective at .01 level of significance.
[h] More effective than method ranked 9 for this objective at .01 level of significance.

From Stephen J. Carroll, Jr., Frank T. Paine, and John J. Ivancevich, "The Relative Effectiveness of Training Methods—Expert Opinion and Research," *Personnel Psychology*, 25:495–509 (Autumn 1972), p. 498.

"canned" programs. The study also reported that many presidents indicated that management development programs had definitely improved performance of the participants.[21]

What little social-science research has been done on the effectiveness of supervisory or management development training has generally been inconclusive or negative. One study found foremen with human-relations training to be less considerate of their subordinates than untrained foremen. Another study involving foremen and the impact of human-relations training indicated no statistically significant differences between "before" and "after" behavior on the job, as evidenced by workers' descriptions. These findings were evident even though the foremen participating in the human-relations courses had shown in examinations that they had increased their knowledge of human-relations principles.

Although the two studies did not find that training in human relations had positive effects on supervisory behavior, they demonstrated that there were wide differences in the impact of the training on the foremen and that *the attitudes of the foremen's superiors best predicted the foremen's behavior after training*. In short, the environment had much to do with the ability of the foremen to put the training into practice. The conclusion was that future research should examine personal and situational variables as they interact with the effects of training and development.[22]

An earlier study reached similar conclusions. It held that the relative ineffectiveness of human relations training programs for foremen resulted partly from deficiencies in the working relationships between the foremen and their immediate superiors and from the methods used in the training conferences. It concluded that two major ingredients were needed to assist the foremen: (1) an environment encouraging growth and development, including informal coaching by superiors, and (2) training conferences that focused on the specific needs and problems of the foremen. Instead, training sessions had focused on "abstract theories" and "rules of behavior."[23] These conclusions emphasize that the more training and development is based on actual need, and the more the environment permits expression of newly learned skills and insights, the more effective training and development is likely to be.

Because of the many variables involved, any attempt to scientifically determine the validity of general training and developmental programs is probably not going to be very satisfactory. As we move from semiskilled jobs to executive positions and from task training to general development, the complexity of evaluation increases rapidly. In training workers to perform semiskilled jobs, measures of performance are much more readily identified than in the case of executive positions.

At the present time, the validity of general training and developmental programs are probably best measured by the considered opinions of participants and their superiors on the degree to which such programs have met specific training and developmental objectives. To a great extent, a good deal of training and development must no doubt be taken on faith, as is the case with education in general.

[21] Does Management Training Pay Off?" *Dun's Review and Modern Industry*, 74:41–43 (November 1959).

[22] Floyd C. Mann, "Studying and Creating Change: A Means to Understanding Social Organization," in Conrad M. Arensberg et al. eds., *Research in Industrial Human Relations* (New York: Harper & Brothers, 1957), pp. 153–157. See also Robert J. House, "Leadership Training: Some Dysfunctional Consequences," *Administrative Science Quarterly*, 12:556–571 (March 1968). For a study showing positive results in terms of job performance, see Herbert H. Hand and John W. Slocum, Jr., "A Longitudinal Study of the Effects of a Human Relations Training Program on Managerial Effectiveness," *Journal of Applied Psychology*, 56:412–417 (October 1972).

[23] A. Zaleznik, *Foreman Training in a Growing Enterprise* (Boston: Graduate School of Business Administration, Harvard University, 1951), pp. 205–214.

Any personnel or training director who sets out to prove the dollar-and-cents worth of general training and development is likely to be disappointed, which is not to say that efforts to validate developmental programs should be abandoned. These efforts should continue, but intermediate criteria, such as opinions of managers, need to supplement statements of profit. The trouble with the latter type of criterion is that too many variables are involved to isolate the effect of training and development.[24]

CONCLUSIONS ABOUT GENERAL DEVELOPMENT AND TRAINING

Top executives in most American corporations, as well as participants, appear to have confidence in the usefulness of management development programs and give a great deal of support to them. Most managers subscribe to the belief that, whenever a job's present or potential responsibilities require knowledge, insights, and understanding above and beyond those held presently by the employee, relevant education and training become useful, if not imperative. It is important, however, that training and developmental programs be tailored to the needs of the individuals and organizations involved.

LABORATORY TRAINING

It is difficult to write about laboratory training, T-groups, and sensitivity training, because the terms are often used interchangeably, while at the same time actual practice under these labels varies considerably. However, it is generally accepted that the terms *laboratory training* or *laboratory education* refer broadly to experience-based learning workshops and that the concept is broader than the term T-group. *T-groups*, usually synonymous with sensitivity training, are a specialized form of laboratory training but are frequently major components in laboratory training workshops.[25] (See Figure 17–2.)

T-groups usually involve small groups of approximately twelve participants meeting under the guidance of a "trainer" and are largely unstructured in the sense that there is a very minimum kind of agenda and a minimum of formal leadership. The discussions are essentially unguided except for a strong implicit focus on the affective domain (feelings) and the mutual impact of the participants.[26]

HISTORY

Laboratory training began around 1946 largely through a growing recognition by Leland Bradford, Ronald Lippitt, Kenneth Benne, and others that training in human relations that focused on the feelings and concerns of the participants was frequently a much more powerful and viable educational device than the lecture method. Some of the theoretical constructs and insights from which these pioneers in laboratory training drew stemmed from earlier research by Kurt Lewin, Ronald Lippitt, and Ralph White. By 1949 the term *T-group*, a

[24] Profits are typically considered along with such criteria as cost savings, improved ability to handle people, and extent of innovations. See Bureau of National Affairs, "Executive Development, *Personnel Policies Forum*, Survey No. 81 (September 1967), pp. 15–19. For a discussion of some of the complexities in evaluating general training and development programs, see John R. Rizzo, "The Evaluation of Management Development," in House, *Management Development*, pp. 79–96; and John R. Hinrichs, "Personnel Training," in Marvin D. Dunnette, ed., *Handbook of Industrial and Organizational Psychology* (Chicago: Rand McNally College Publishing Company, 1976), pp. 829–860.

[25] This paragraph is largely based on Wendell French, Cecil Bell, and Robert Zawacki, *Organization Development: Theory, Practice, and Research* (Dallas: Business Publications, Inc., in press), Part IV.
[26] See Edgar H. Schein and Warren G. Bennis, *Personal and Organizational Change through Group Methods: The Laboratory Approach* (New York: John Wiley & Sons, 1965); and Robert Tannenbaum, Irving R. Weschler, and Fred Massarik, *Leadership and Organization: A Behavioral Science Approach* (New York: McGraw-Hill Book Company, 1961), pp. 119–140.

Figure 17-2   Example of an NTL "management work conference" schedule

Time	Sunday	Monday	Tuesday	Wednesday	Thursday	Friday	Saturday
8:00	Breakfast						
9:00–10:15		T-group	T-group	Intergroup exercise	T-group	T-group	T-group
10:15–10:45	Coffee						
10:45–11:15		General session	General session	Intergroup exercise	General session	General session	General session and adjournment
11:15–12:15		T-group	T-group	General session	N-group*	T-group	
12:15–2:00	Lunch						
2:00–4:00	Registration	Free Time					
4:00–5:45	4:00–5:30 General session	Case exercises	N-group	Free time	T-group	N-group	
5:45–6:30	5:30–7:00 Reception	Refreshments					
6:30–8:00	7:00–8:30 Dinner	Dinner					
8:00–10:00 or later	Micro-lab	Case exercises	N-group	T-group	N-group	N-group	

*Note: "N-group" refers to "new group," i.e., groups different from the original T-group assignment.

shortened label for "Basic Skill Training Group," had emerged, and both terms were used to identify the programs evolving in the newly formed National Training Laboratories (now NTL-Institute for Applied Behavioral Science).[27]

Laboratory training programs have proliferated widely, and many organizations, including colleges and universities, offer or sponsor laboratory training experiences. Actually, a number of diverse forms of laboratory training have emerged, several of which include a strong T-group emphasis but that have additional objectives. "Personal growth" and "group process" laboratories, to be mentioned briefly later, are examples.[28]

OBJECTIVES

Ordinarily, sessions in laboratory training have certain objectives in common. The following

[27] From Leland P. Bradford, "Biography of an Institution," *The Journal of Applied Behavioral Science*, 3:127–143, No. 2 (1967). See also Kenneth D. Benne, Leland P. Bradford, Jack R. Gibb, and Ronald Lippitt, *The Laboratory Method of Changing and Learning: Theory and Application* (Palo Alto, Calif.: Science and Behavior Books, Inc., 1975).

[28] For some history of various off-shoots of laboratory training, e.g., Esalen, see Kurt W. Back, *Beyond Words: The Story of Sensitivity Training and the Encounter Movement* (New York: Russell Sage Foundation, 1972).

list by two internationally known behavioral scientists is probably highly consistent with the objectives of most programs.

Self
1. Increased *awareness* of own feelings and reactions and of own impact on others.

2. Increased *awareness* of feelings and reactions of others and of their impact on self.

3. Increased *awareness* of dynamics of group action.

4. *Changed attitudes* toward self, others, and groups; i.e., more respect for, tolerance of, and faith in self, others, and groups.

5. Increased *interpersonal competence,* i.e., skill in handling interpersonal and group relationships toward more productive and satisfying relationships.

Role
6. Increased *awareness* of own organizational role, organizational dynamics, dynamics of larger social systems, and dynamics of the process of change in self, small groups, and organizations.

7. *Changed attitudes* toward own role, role of others, and organizational relationships, i.e., more respect for, and willingness to deal with, others with whom one is interdependent, greater willingness to achieve collaborative relationships with others based on mutual trust.

8. Increased *interpersonal competence* in handling relationships of own organizational role with superiors, peers, and subordinates.

Organization
9. Increased *awareness of changed attitudes* toward, and increased *interpersonal competence* about specific organizational problems existing in groups or units which are interdependent.
10. *Organizational improvement* through the training of relationships or groups rather than isolated individuals.[29]

SELECTION OF PARTICIPANTS

Over the years, experimentation with different laboratory designs have led to diverse criteria for the selection of laboratory participants. Probably a majority of NTL-IABS laboratories in human relations are "stranger groups," i.e., involving participants who come from different organizations and who are not likely to have met earlier. As indicated by the preceding objectives 9 and 10, however, the incidence of special labs designed to increase the effectiveness of persons working together appears to be growing. Thus terms like *cousin labs*—labs involving people from the same organization but not the same subunit—and *family labs* or *team-building* sessions—labs involving a manager and all subordinates—are becoming familiar. (Team building, a central aspect of OD efforts, should not automatically be equated with T-groups, however. See Chapter 26.) Participants in labs designed for organizational members not belonging to the same unit may be selected from the same rank—*horizontal slice*—or from heterogeneous ranks—*diagonal slice.* Further, NTL-IABS has encouraged at least two members from the same organization to attend NTL Management Work Conferences and Key Executive Conferences in order to maximize the impact of the learning in the situation back home.

In general, experienced trainers recommend that persons with severe emotional illness or involved in psychotherapy should not participate in laboratory training unless the programs are designed specifically for group therapy. Designers of programs make the assumptions, as Argyris states them, that T-group participants should have

1. A relatively strong ego not overwhelmed by internal conflicts.

2. Defense sufficiently low to allow the individual to hear what others say to him. . . .

3. The ability to communicate thoughts and feelings with minimal distortion. . . .[30]

---

[29]Schein and Bennis, *Personal and Organizational Change,* p. 37.

[30]Chris Argyris, "T-Groups for Organizational Effectiveness," *Harvard Business Review,* 42:60–74 (March-April 1964).

As a result of such screening, the incidence of breakdown during sensitivity training is substantially less than that reported for organizations in general.[31] A review of the research on the dangers of T-groups concluded that they ". . . may be less stressful than university examinations. . . ."[32]

On the other hand, since the line between emotional health and illness is very blurred, most NTL-trained staff members are equipped to diagnose severe problems and refer individuals to psychiatrists and clinical psychologists when the need occurs. Further, most are equipped to give adequate support and protection to participants with low ability to assimilate and learn from feedback. In addition, group members in T-groups generally have a considerable ability to sense when a member is having difficulty and to provide needed emotional support.

DURATION OF LABS

The duration of laboratory training programs varies widely. Microlabs, designed to give people a brief experience with sensitivity training, may last only one hour. Some labs are designed for a long weekend. As a rule, NTL labs in basic human relations last two weeks, and participants are expected to meet mornings, afternoons, and evenings with some time off for recreation. NTL labs for middle managers and executives typically run for one week.

(Attendance at stranger labs for key managers is sometimes a supplemental part of an organization development effort.) (See Chapter 26.)

CONTENT AND TRAINER'S ROLE

Sensitivity-training sessions usually start with the trainer making a few comments about his or her role—the trainer is there to be helpful, that the group will have control of the agenda, that the trainer will deliberately avoid a role of leadership but might become involved as both a leader and a member from time to time, and so forth. The following is an example of what the trainer might say.

This group will meet for many hours and will serve as a kind of laboratory where each individual can increase his understanding of the forces which influence individual behavior and the performance of groups and organizations. The data for learning will be our own behavior, feelings, and reactions. We begin with no definite structure or organization, no agreed-upon procedures, and no specific agenda. It will be up to us to fill the vacuum created by the lack of these familiar elements and to study our group as we evolve. My role will be to help the group to learn from its own experience, but not to act as a traditional chairman nor to suggest how we should organize, what our procedure should be, or exactly what our agenda will include. With these few comments, I think we are ready to begin in whatever way you feel will be most helpful.[33]

The trainer then lapses into silence. The group's discomfort precipitates a dialogue that, with skilled assistance from the trainer, is typically an intense but generally highly rewarding experience for its members. What goes on in the group becomes the data for the learning experience.

Interventions by the trainer will vary greatly, depending upon the lab's purpose and the participants' state of learning. A common intervention, however, is that of encouraging people

---

[31] Based on discussions with NTL staff members. One estimate is that the incidence of "serious stress and mental disturbance" during laboratory training is "less than one per cent of participants and in almost all cases occurs in persons with a history of prior disturbance." Charles Seashore, "What Is Sensitivity Training," *NTL Institute News and Reports,* 2:2 (April 1968).

[32] Gary L. Cooper, "How Psychologically Dangerous are T-Groups and Encounter Groups?" *Human Relations,* 28:249–260 (April 1975). See also Dianna Hartley, Howard B. Roback, and Stephen I. Abramowitz, "Deterioration Effects in Encounter Groups," *American Psychologist,* 31:247–255 (March 1976).

[33] Charles Seashore, "What Is Sensitivity Training," p. 1.

to focus on, and own up to, their own feelings about what is going on in the group rather than to make judgments about others. In this way, the participants begin to have more insight into their own feelings and to understand how their behavior affects others.

Although T-group work tends to be the focal point in human relations laboratories, laboratory training typically includes sessions in theory followed by discussion and sometimes exercises such as role playing or diagnostic questionnaires.[34]

(An example of the schedule of one NTL "Management Work Conference" involving approximately forty-eight participants and four T-groups is shown in Figure 17-2.) Group process labs will tend to put greater emphasis on group dynamics in contrast to interpersonal dynamics, and personal growth labs may incorporate music, art, and exercises in sensory awareness as part of the workshop experience.[35] (See the chapter on organization development for

some of the differences between various forms of laboratory training and team building.)

VALIDITY

The validity of sensitivity training has been argued a good deal in the last few years. Proponents believe that sensitivity training makes people more effective in their interpersonal relationships, that it can help in diagnosing human-relations problems, and that is a maturing experience. Critics say that the outcomes may have little relevance to the requirements of particular enterprises; that resulting changes in personality may actually handicap some managers in their present jobs and their future careers; and that the personality's defense mechanisms may be removed without being replaced by growth in personality. On the other hand, substantial efforts are currently being made to relate laboratory training to the going problems of organizations, and, as indicated earlier, there is little evidence that such training under the direction of qualified trainers has any destructive consequences in the case of reasonably healthy people.[36] Another concern is that some sensitivity training may be conducted by people who do not possess the insights or skills to maximize constructive learning by participants. The latter concern, of course, can be met by assessing carefully the qualifications of people involved in such training.[37]

House has carefully reviewed the literature on the impact of T-group training, and he has concluded that the research shows mixed results. In particular, he considers inconclusive the research on changes reflected in inventories of personality. However, his conclusions about

[34] For a description of what goes on in T-groups, see Schein and Bennis, *Personal and Organizational Change*, pp. 10–27; Leland P. Bradford, Jack R. Gibb, and Kenneth D. Benne, eds., *T-Group Theory and Laboratory Method* (New York: John Wiley & Sons, 1964), pp. 55–67; Dorothy S. Whitaker, "A Case Study of a T-Group," in Galvin Whitaker, ed., *T-Group Training: Group Dynamics in Management Education* (Oxford: Basil Blackwell, 1965), A.T.M. Occasional Papers, pp. 14–22; and Irving Weschler and Jerome Reisel, *Inside a Sensitivity Training Group* (Los Angeles: University of California, Institute of Industrial Relations, 1959), Monograph No. 4. For use of scored exercises or questionnaires ("instrumented training") see Robert R. Blake and Jane S. Mouton, "The Instrumented Training Laboratory," in Irving R. Weschler and Edgar H. Schein, eds., *Five Issues in Training* (Washington, D.C.: National Training Laboratories, 1962), pp. 61–76; and W. Warner Burke and Harvey A. Hornstein, "Conceptual vs. Experimental Management Training," *Training and Development Journal* 21:12–17 (December 1967).

[35] For a further discussion of different forms of laboratory education, including encounter groups and Tavistock conferences, see Clayton P. Alderfer, "Understanding Laboratory Education: An Overview," *Monthly Labor Review*, 93:18–27 (December 1970). For additional information on the Tavistock method, see K.G. Van Auken, Jr., "A Further View on Laboratory Education," *Monthly Labor Review*, 94:63–65 (March 1971).

[36] See Henry L. Tosi, Jr., "Development Methods," in House, *Management Development*, pp. 68–71.

[37] For a discussion of the qualification problem and other issues, see Martin Lakin, "Some Ethical Issues in Sensitivity Training," *American Psychologist*, October 1969, pp. 923–928.

studies that examine the behavior of participants upon returning to the job are generally more positive.[38] House cites six studies, all of which used control groups and concludes:

All six studies revealed what appear to be important positive effects of T-Group training. Two of the studies report negative effects as well . . . all of the evidence is based on observations of the behavior of the participants in the actual job situations. No reliance is placed on participant response; rather, evidence is collected from those having frequent contact with the participant in his normal work activities.[39]

Campbell and Dunnette, on the other hand, point out that the usefulness of such training in terms of job *performance* has yet to be demonstrated, although they concede the research shows that T-group training produces changes in *behavior,* at least as reported by associates of the trainees. They urge that research be directed toward "forging the link between training-induced changes in behavior and changes in job-performance effectiveness."[40] In summary, they state:

. . . the assumption that T-Group training has positive utility for organizations must necessarily rest on shaky ground. It has been neither confirmed nor disconfirmed. The authors wish to emphasize . . . that utility for the organization is not necessarily the same as utility for the individual.[41]

Pearse found 15 percent of top managers in a large sample of firms having had sensitivity training or T-group experience. Twenty percent of those who had such training said that it had made a "major" contribution to their interpersonal effectiveness, and 47 percent said that it had made a "moderate" contribution. Thirty-three percent said the experience had made a "minimal" or "no particular" contribution to their effectiveness.[42]

At least two reasons may account for the inconclusiveness of research concerned with the impact of T-group training on job performance. One reason is simply that little research has been done on this question. The other reason centers on cultural isolation. To oversimplify, a major part of what one learns in laboratory training is how to work more effectively with others in groups, *particularly with others who have developed comparable skills.* Unfortunately, most participants return from T-group experiences to environments that include colleagues and superiors who have not shared the same affective (emotional, feeling) learning experiences, who are not familiar with the terminology and underlying theory, and who may have anxieties, usually unwarranted, about what might happen to them in a T-group situation.

This cultural distance, which can result from laboratory training, is one of the reasons why many behavioral scientists are currently encouraging more than one person from the same organization to undergo T-group training. This assumes that the organization is ready for such training and that such training is reasonably compatible with the present or emerging culture of the total system. Thus, along with the research cited earlier on the effectiveness of human relations training for supervisors, theory and research emphasize the importance of congruency between the organizational environment and the particular kind of training or development activities.

EMPLOYEE COUNSELING, CAREER PLANNING, AND TRANSACTIONAL ANALYSIS

COUNSELING

Although formal counseling programs aimed at assisting employees with emotional problems

---

[38]Robert J. House, "T-Group Education and Leadership Effectiveness: A Review of the Empiric Literature and a Critical Evaluation," *Personnel Psychology*, 20:1–32 (Spring 1967).

[39]Ibid., pp. 18–19.

[40]John P. Campbell and Marvin D. Dunnette, "Effectiveness of T-Group Experiences in Managerial Training and Development," *Psychological Bulletin*, 70:73–104 (August 1968).

[41]Ibid., p. 101.

[42]Pearse, "What Managers Think of Management Development," pp. 32–33.

may be considered an aspect of health maintenance, such counseling may also be considered an integral part of the process of developing the employees. Certainly any insight, knowledge, or emotional maturity gained through counseling that increases the employees' ability to perform constructive work is part of the broad process of the employee's development.

One study found personnel departments in 95 percent of 166 responding companies providing some sort of counseling or advisory service for employees, and employees were actively encouraged to avail themselves of such services in 83 percent of the responding firms. The items most frequently checked as subjects for counseling and arranged by order of frequency were: absenteeism, grievances, retirement, health problems, career development, accidents, finances, family problems, and alcoholism. Only about 10 percent of the responding firms in the above study employed full-time specialists to assist in counseling.[43]

Although most firms may not be able to afford full-time counseling psychologists, every enterprise should certainly be prepared to refer seriously disturbed employees to outside specialized agencies. The personnel and medical departments, in particular, should have knowledge about such agencies and should be skilled in such referrals. When counseling psychologists are used, however, counseling services should probably be limited to short-run and relatively minor problems.

Ideally, every supervisor should have some knowledge of effective listening or nondirective counseling in order to give "emotional first-aid."[44] Not only can such interviewing assist in the general mental health of the employee in the enterprise, but it can also further the very immediate and important objectives of improved communications and better understanding between superior and subordinate.

CAREER PLANNING

"Life and career planning" workshops have been utilized by many individuals as a developmental experience independent of their organizational affiliation. Some firms, however, have made such workshops available to employees, usually as an outgrowth of an OD program (see Chapter 26). Life and career planning workshops may be designed to last from a few hours to two or three days and usually involve, under the direction of a qualified trainer, a series of exercises of which the following assignment may be typical:

Prepare a life inventory of important "happenings" for you, including the following:

a. Any peak experiences you have had.

b. Things which you do well.

c. Things which you do poorly.

d. Things you would like to stop doing.

e. Things you would like to learn to do well.

f. Peak experiences you would like to have.

g. Values (e.g., power, money, etc.) you want to achieve.

h. Things you would like to start doing now.

Discuss in subgroups.[45]

Participants are usually strangers or people who do not have reporting relationships, and small group discussions are used extensively.

[43] "Practices in Employee Counseling," *Industrial Relations News, Special Report*, April 1963, pp. 1–4.

[44] This term has been used by Harry Levinson. See "Practices in Employee Counseling," p. 3.

[45] From Wendell L. French and Cecil H. Bell, Jr., *Organization Development: Behavioral Science Interventions for Organization Improvement* (Englewood Cliffs, N.J.: Prentice-Hall, Inc., 1973), pp. 144–145. Herbert Shepard is generally credited as being the originator of such exercises. See also Gordon L. Lippitt, "Developing Life Plans," *Training and Development Journal*, May 1970, pp. 2–7.

TRANSACTIONAL ANALYSIS

Transactional analysis (TA)[46] has become a conspicuous topic for workshops and publications in the last few years, and it warrants attention here. Essentially, TA can be viewed as a diagnostic tool for assessing the nature of the many transactions, including "games," that occur between people. The purpose of TA training is to provide perspective and insight so that one can modify one's own dysfunctional behaviors and/or respond more effectively to the behavior of others.

As described by Eric Berne, the psychiatrist who did much of the early development of the concepts, the approach is based on the idea that each person has a repertoire of behavior associated with a system of three "ego states," the parent, adult, and child. In particular, "crossed transactions" are likely to be dysfunctional, as when an employer gives an "adult" directive to an employee but the "child" in the employee responds as though dealing with a "parent." "Games" are essentially "ulterior transactions" in which two or more ego states come into play simultaneously.[47]

The main use for TA in business and industrial settings appears to be to help employees be more sensitive to the nature of their interactions with others—customers, for example—and to be aware of alternative behaviors they have at their disposal in order to minimize or solve human relations problems.[48] Successful applications would appear to be associated with avoiding treating TA as a panacea, with avoiding playing games with the terminology (which was designed to identify and minimize game

playing), and with a widely shared commitment by employees at all levels to improve the quality of their interpersonal transactions.

The use of such devices as TA or life/career planning workshops must be carefully assessed as to their organizational relevance in each instance. In short, their use, like other training devices, should be based on careful training needs analysis. Further, potential users should be alert to any emerging research on their validity. My impression is that there has been very little research on either life/career planning or transactional analysis.

OTHER DEVELOPMENTAL OPPORTUNITIES

In any large metropolitan area, universities, colleges, vocational schools, lectures, libraries, and many other resources in the community are available to the general public. The variety of opportunities tends to be less in smaller communities, but most cities and towns in modern America offer a number of valuable educational resources available to their adults. Many of these educational activities have an important bearing on job performance and career opportunities. The enrollment of millions of adults in evening programs reflects the importance that these people ascribe to education in both their careers and personal lives.

Many corporations support such educational programs with full or partial refunds of tuition to their employees. One study showed that 65 percent of 426 firms with 250 employees or more had programs of tuitional refunds for nonexempt employees. Typical practice was to refund from 50 to 100 percent of the tuition upon successful completion of the course, provided the particular course had been previously approved as consistent with the tuition-program policies.[49] Very few firms, however,

[46]This discussion is based largely on French, Bell, and Zawacki, *Organization Development: Theory, Practice, and Research*, Part IV.

[47]See Eric Berne, *Games People Play: The Psychology of Human Relationships* (New York: Grove Press, Inc., 1964), Chap. 1, 2.

[48]Harold M.F. Rush and Phyllis S. McGrath, "Transactional Analysis Moves into Corporate Training," *The Conference Board Record*, 10:38–44 (July 1973).

[49]National Industrial Conference Board, "Personnel Practices in Factory and Office: Manufacturing," *Studies in Personnel Policy*, No. 194, 1964, pp. 59–60.

appear to have studied the extent to which such programs have benefited their organizations. One researcher found that only 7 percent of firms with tuition-aid programs had studied their impact.[50]

Many companies also encourage participation in community service programs, professional societies, and public speaking as important activities for self-development, and are increasingly encouraging their employees to participate in politics. The underlying assumptions are that good government requires the help of responsible citizens, that participation in government or politics increases the capabilities of the employee, that the company gains good will through employees active in important affairs of the community, and that business and industry indirectly gain by having people in office with a "business point of view."[51]

Interference with the job's activities is considered a minor problem when companies encourage employees to participate in politics.[52] It would seem desirable, however, that the company articulate, and adhere to, a nonpartisan policy toward employees' political activity and hold employees accountable for proper performance on the job. Some executives allow subordinates to take as much time off as necessary to fulfill their community obligations, with the stipulation that their job functions must be performed according to proper standards.

Sabbatical leaves of up to a year for managers are not widespread but their use appears to be growing. These leaves are used for various purposes, depending upon company policy. In some instances, they are used for participation in advanced education programs, for social welfare projects, or in an exchange capacity as between government and industry or between industries. As one example, Xerox Corporation has initiated a series of sabbaticals permitting employees to take a year's leave of absence with full pay to pursue self-selected projects of a social welfare nature.[53] As another example, most of the staff of the National Alliance of Businessmen, which assists the hard-core unemployed to find and keep jobs (see Chapter 16), are on loan from business and industry. In still another case, the Los Angeles law firm of Munger, Tolles, Hills, and Rickershauser provides leaves with pay for partners after seven years of service.[54]

Finally, how the individual responds to the demands, challenges, and opportunities of life in general will have an important impact on self-development, which in turn will partially determine what kind of person he or she is on the job. As managers have long recognized, the employee is a "whole" person, and experiences off the job affect performance on the job, and vice versa.

SUMMARY

The organizational training and developmental process is a complex flow of events aimed at increasing the individual's capability for contributing to the attainment of enterprise goals.

[50]Raymond L. Hilgert, "Tuition-Aid Programs," *Training and Development Journal*, 21:24–34 (February 1967).

[51]See Opinion Research Corporation, "What Happens When Company Employees Get into Politics," *The Public Opinion Index for Industry*, July 1960, pp. 5–7.

[52]Ibid., p. 5.

[53]*Behavioral Sciences Newsletter*, American Institutes for Research in the Behavioral Sciences, October 1, 1971, p. 1.

[54]"Executive Sabbaticals," *U.S. News & World Report*, January 20, 1975, pp. 74–75. See also Thomas H. Patten, Jr., *Manpower Planning and the Development of Human Resources* (New York: John Wiley & Sons, Inc., 1971), pp. 467–469; and Eli Goldston, "Executive Sabbaticals: About to Take Off?" *Harvard Business Review*, 51:57–68 (September-October 1973). Former Secretary of Labor Willard Wirtz proposed a "National Leave of Absence Program" within a "Technological Displacement Act" that would provide every member of the work force with ". . . a two-year leave of absence at whatever point he or she wants to take it during his or her working career . . . at 75 to 100 percent of the individual's current earning rate." Seymour L. Wolfbein, ed., *Manpower Policy: Perspectives and Prospects* (Philadelphia: School of Business Administration, Temple University, 1973), p. 21.

Included in this flow of events, and discussed thus far, are determination of training and developmental needs, employee orientation, skill training, appraisal interviews and coaching, management and employee development programs, and employee counseling. In addition to educational opportunities away from the job, a wide variety of events within the organization, including the demands and challenges of the job itself, have major potential for the development of human resources.

Whether planned or unplanned, training and development occur within the organization. For optimum validity of this process, systematic attention must be given to determining training and developmental needs, to assessing the value of different training and developmental methods, to creating an environment conducive to intellectual and emotional growth, and to applying what is learned. To stress the last point, it is extremely important that training and development, if they are to be optimally useful, must take place in an environment that encourages and supports application of new knowledge and insights. Thus, effective training and development efforts require attention to the organizational climate in which they occur.

REVIEW AND DISCUSSION QUESTIONS

1. If you were the training director of a company, how would you determine the management development needs of the organization?

2. What are some of the problems in evaluating the effectiveness of management development programs? What are some of the criteria an organization might use?

3. What similarities and differences are there among role playing, in-basket exercises, and the case method of instruction?

4. What are some of the potential problems surrounding management development programs, and how can these problems be minimized?

5. What are some of the potential benefits of an employee counseling program? Pitfalls?

6. What is the difference between laboratory training and sensitivity training?

7. What are the objectives of sensitivity training as contrasted with transactional analysis (TA)?

8. Discuss the potential desirable and undesirable consequences of sabbaticals for (a) professionals and executives, and (b) all employees.

SUPPLEMENTAL REFERENCES

Argyris, Chris, "Do Personal Growth Laboratories Represent an Alternative Culture?" *The Journal of Applied Behavioral Science*, 8:7–28 (January-February 1972).

————, "On the Future of Laboratory Education," *The Journal of Applied Behavioral Science*, 3:153–183, No. 2 (1967).

Back, Kurt W., *Beyond Words: The Story of Sensitivity Training and the Encounter Movement* (New York: Russell Sage Foundation, 1972).

————, "Sensitivity Training: Questions and Quest," *Personnel Administration*, 34:22–26 (January-February 1971).

Bare, Carole E., and Rie R. Mitchell, "Experimental Evaluation of Sensitivity Training," *The Journal of Applied Behavioral Science*, 8:263–276 (May-June 1972).

Bass, Bernard M., and James A. Vaughn, *The Psychology of Learning for Managers* (New York: American Foundation for Management Research, 1965).

Beckhard, Richard, "The Appropriate Use of T-Groups in Organizations," in Galvin Whitaker, *T-Group Training: Group Dynamics in Management Education* (Oxford: Basil Blackwell, 1965), A.T.N. Occasional Papers, No. 2.

Belasco, James A., and Harrison M. Trice, *The Assessment of Change in Training and Therapy* (New York: McGraw-Hill Book Company, 1969).

Bowen, Donald D., and Raghu Nath, "Transactions in Management," *California Management Review*, 18:73–85 (Winter 1975).

Campbell, John P., and Marvin D. Dunnette, "Effectiveness of T-Group Experimenting in Managerial Training and Development," *Psychological Bulletin*, 70:73–104 (August 1968).

Cone, Paul R., and Richard N. McKinley, "Management Development Can Be More Effective," *California Management Review*, 14:13–19 (Spring 1972).

Cross, Joseph L., "Return on Personal Assets," *Personnel Journal*, 46:502–507 (September 1967).

Desatnick, Robert L., *A Concise Guide to Management Development* (New York: American Management Association, 1970).

Dunnette, Marvin D., and John P. Campbell, "Laboratory Education: Impact on People and Organizations," *Industrial Relations*, 8:1–27 (October 1968).

Dyer, William G., "Forms of Interpersonal Feedback," *Training and Development Journal*, 26:8–12 (July 1972).

————, *The Sensitive Manipulator: The Change Agent Who Builds with Others* (Provo, Utah: Brigham Young University Press, 1972).

Dubin, Samuel S., Everett Alderman, and H. LeRoy Marlow, *Managerial and Supervisory Educational Needs of Business and Industry in Pennsylvania* (University Park: The Pennsylvania State University, 1967).

Eddy, William B., "From Training to Organization Change," *Personnel*, 34:37–43 (January-February 1971).

Ferguson, Lawrence L., "Better Management of Managers' Careers," *Harvard Business Review*, 44:139–152 (March-April 1966).

Fiedler, Fred, "The Effects of Leadership Training and Experience: A Contingency Model Interpretation," *Administrative Science Quarterly*, 17:453–470 (December 1972).

Finnigan, J., *Industrial Training Management* (London: Business Books Limited, 1970).

Hall, Douglas T., and Francine S. Hall, "What's New in Career Management," *Organizational Dynamics*, 5:17–33 (Summer 1976).

Hall, Jay, "The Use of Instruments in Laboratory Training," *Training and Development Journal*, 24:48–55 (May 1970).

Harrison, Roger, "Research on Human Relations Training: Design and Interpretation," *Journal of Applied Behavioral Science*, 7:71–85 (January-February 1971).

Jongeward, Dorothy, *Everybody Wins: Transactional Analysis Applied to Organizations* (Reading, Mass.: Addison-Wesley Publishing Company, 1973).

Kolb, David A., "Management and the Learning Process," *California Management Review*, 18:21–31 (Spring 1976).

Korman, Abraham, and Robert Tanofsky, "Organizational Counseling: A Research-Based Approach," *Personnel Journal*, 54:25–26ff. (January 1975).

Krumboltz, John D., *Revolution in Counseling: Implications of Behavioral Science* (Boston: Houghton Mifflin Company, 1966).

Levinson, Harry, et al., *Men, Management, and Mental Health* (Cambridge, Mass.: Harvard University Press, 1962).

Lippitt, Gordon L., and Leslie E. This, "Leaders for Laboratory Training," *Training and Development Journal*, 21:2–13 (March 1967).

Livingston, J. Sterling, "Myth of the Well-Educated Manager," *Harvard Business Review*, 49:79–89 (January-February 1971).

Lundberg, Craig C., "Planning the Executive Development Program," *California Management Review*, 15:10–15 (Fall 1972).

Mann, Edward K., "Sensitivity Training: Should We Use It?" *Training and Development Journal*, 24:44–48 (March 1970).

Markwell, D.S., and T.J. Roberts, *Organization of Management Development Programmes* (London: Gower Press Limited, 1969).

Miner, John B., *Introduction to Industrial Clinical Psychology* (New York: McGraw-Hill Book Company, 1966).

Moment, David, "Career Development: A Future-Oriented Historical Approach for Research and Action," *Personnel Administration*, 30:6–11 (July-August 1967).

Odiorne, George S., "The Trouble with Sensitivity Training," *Training and Development Journal*, 17:9–20 (October 1963).

Patten, Thomas H., Jr., "Organizational Processes and the Development of Managers: Some Hypotheses," *Human Organization*, 26:242–255 (Winter 1967).

Pearse, Robert F., *Manager to Manager: What Managers Think of Management Development*, AMA Survey Reports (New York: American Management Association, 1974), 52 pp.

Peterfreund, Stanley, "Education in Industry—Today and in the Future," *Training and Development Journal*, 30:30–40 (May 1976).

Plattner, John W., and Lowell W. Herron, "Simulation: Its Uses in Employee Selection and Training," *AMA Management Bulletin No. 20* (New York: American Management Association, Inc., Personnel Division, 1962).

Porter, Elias H., *Manpower Development: The Systems Training Concept* (New York: Harper & Row, Publishers, 1964).

Powell, Reed M., and John E. Stinson, "The Worth of Laboratory Training," *Business Horizons*, 14:87–95 (August 1971).

Tasca, Anthony J., "Management Development: A Need or a Luxury?" *Training and Development Journal*, 29:16–22 (March 1975).

Tills, Marvin, "Current Activities in Management Training," *Training and Development Journal*, 22:42–47 (June 1968).

Walter, Gordon, "Effects of Videotape Training Inputs on Group Performance," *Journal of Applied Psychology*, 60:308–312 (June 1975).

Wilkerson, C. David, "A Results-Oriented Development Plan," *The Conference Board Record*, 3:40–45 (March 1966).

Wilson, John E., Robert B. Morton, and Donald P. Muller, "The Trend in Laboratory Education for Managers—Organization Training or Sensitivity?" *Training and Development Journal*, 26:18–25 (June 1972).

Zenger, John H., "A Comparison of Human Development with Psychological Development in T-Groups," *Training and Development Journal*, 24:16–20 (July 1970).

CHAPTER 18
ENGINEERS, SCIENTISTS, AND OTHER PROFESSIONALS: THEIR MANAGEMENT AND DEVELOPMENT

While this chapter will focus primarily on the management and development of scientists and engineers, it also has implications for the management of a broader range of professionals employed by business, industry, and other institutions. Such professionals include economists, nurses, psychologists, physicians, accountants, lawyers, and many others.[1]

There are at least four reasons why it is important to examine the topic of managing scientists, engineers, and other professionals. In the first place, intensified competition in business and rapidly changing worldwide political events are placing greater demands for technological and managerial innovations upon firms in business and industry. Thus, firms in Ohio and California must develop products in order to compete for markets not only with firms in Illinois, New York, Oregon, and Hawaii, but also with companies in West Germany, India, Japan, Norway, Argentina, and the Philippines. And increasingly, Communist-bloc countries are part of the global, competitive trading scene. Furthermore, technological innovation is basic to assisting other countries in their development.

A second reason stems from rapidly changing technology. Rapid changes create obsolescence in human resources as well as in equipment and products. The engineer and scientist, and others in science-related professions, are particularly vulnerable. How to counteract this

---

[1] For convenience, the Department of Labor's definition of a professional will be used: ". . . any employee whose primary duty consists of the performance of work requiring knowledge of an advanced type in a field of science or learning customarily acquired by a prolonged course of specialized intellectual instruction and study. . . ." *Code of Federal Regulations*, Office of the Federal Register, *Title 29—Labor*, January 1, 1968, p. 104.

accelerating obsolescence is a serious organizational and social problem.

Third, the subject is important because the composition of the work force of many firms and in the country as a whole is shifting toward a higher and higher ratio of professionals to other employees. While the growth in employment of engineers and scientists slowed to a halt in 1970, projections through the mid-1980s suggest that employment requirements for these groups, as well as for other technical and professional groups, will increase by nearly 30 percent. In contrast, employment requirements for the labor force as a whole will grow by only about 20 percent over the same period.[2]

A fourth reason for focusing on the management of the scientist, engineer, and other professionals stems from the problems presented by the unique nature of technical-professional jobs. In comparison with other types of jobs, responsibilities and standards of performance relating to engineering and scientific positions are less readily established, performance is less readily measured, relative job worth not so easily determined, and a rationale for promotion not so easily developed. These and other complexities of technical-professional positions mean that personnel devices, systems, and policies used elsewhere within a given organization may not be entirely applicable to the management of this group.

To develop further the discussion of some of these problems requires an examination of the degree to which scientists and engineers differ from other employees and an examination of certain other problems in the management of these specialists. Implications for staffing, appraisals, compensation, and other aspects of personnel management will then be discussed.

CHARACTERISTICS OF ENGINEERS AND SCIENTISTS

In discussing the characteristics of engineers and scientists, it is important at the outset to emphasize the obvious: Any differences between engineers and scientists and the rest of the work force are differences only in degree and only in certain dimensions. It seems reasonable to assume that their basic needs and drives are the same as those of other employees. However, they do differ in some important ways and these differences create special organizational problems.

INTELLIGENCE AND EDUCATION

In the first place, the engineer-scientist clearly surpasses the average industrial employee in educational background and problem-solving ability. Although some engineers and scientists do not have college degrees, most do, and generally their educational attainment greatly exceeds that of the average person. According to the 1970 census, the median number of years of school completed in the case of "professional, technical and kindred workers" was 16.5.[3] Furthermore, while the typical college graduate scores significantly higher on intelligence tests than the average member of the general population, scientists and engineers tend to attain even higher intelligence-test scores on the average than the overall college population.[4]

PERSONALITY

There is also evidence that the personalities of engineers and scientists tend to differ to a cer-

[2] U.S. Department of Labor, *Occupational Outlook Handbook,* 1976–77 Edition, Bulletin 1875, 1976, p. 17; and U.S. Department of Labor, *Manpower Report of the President,* March 1972, pp. 110–113.

[3] U.S. Bureau of the Census, *Educational Attainment,* 1970 Census of Population, U.S. Department of Commerce, March 1973, p. 213.
[4] Dael Wolfe, *America's Resources of Specialized Talent* (New York: Harper & Brothers, 1954), pp. 142–149, 197–204.

tain extent and in certain ways. Research shows, for example, that when engineers are compared with nonengineers, the former often have higher drives toward achievement and a preference for dealing with objects and processes rather than with people. Although they tend to be somewhat reticent socially in their younger years, their social confidence and competence grow with increased maturity and experience. The characteristic that stands out most clearly is their tendency to be much more interested and involved in their work than most other people.[5]

VALUE ORIENTATION

All categories of employees may hold values that can come into conflict with organizational goals, but researchers are in general agreement that scientists and engineers tend to have a unique set of values that, at times, can be seriously at odds with the immediate goals of the enterprise. This is probably more true with respect to "basic" or "pure" researchers in business and industry than it is with individuals in applied sciences.[6] In other words, the research chemist engaged in basic research in the laboratory may have values that seem to differ much more from those of top management than do the values of the chemical engineer performing trouble-shooting work in the manufacturing plant.

Representing the extreme end of a range of attitudes, the research scientist is perceived as identifying with the pursuit of truth and knowledge for its own sake. This identification may be contrasted to the business executive's concern with sales, production, practical results, and getting things done through people.[7] Furthermore, scientists often consider the judgments of their colleagues in science more valid and important than the opinions of the managerial hierarchy and may resist direction and control from nonscientist managers. Thus, the notion of "colleague authority" clashes with the traditional concept of executive authority.[8] In addition, since the scientific community tends to be her or his reference group, the scientist may not have a strong identification with the company and may be more career-oriented than company-oriented.[9]

The scientist, then, may be more of a "cosmopolitan" than a "local" as defined by Gouldner. *Cosmopolitans* are those who have low loyalties to their employing organizations, who are highly committed to a set of specialized skills, and who are oriented toward an outer reference group.[10]

The engineer, on the other hand, may be more of a "local" in the sense of Gouldner's

[5] Carroll E. Izard, "Personality Characteristics of Engineers as Measured by the Edwards Personal Preference Schedule," *Journal of Applied Psychology*, 44:332–335 (October 1960). See also Herbert E. Krugman and Harold A. Edgerton, "Profile of a Scientist-Manager," *Personnel*, 36:38–39 (September-October 1959); and Lee E. Danielson, *Characteristics of Engineers and Scientists* (Ann Arbor: The University of Michigan, Bureau of Industrial Relations, 1960), p. 12.

[6] There is some research evidence for this assumption. See Louis B. Barnes, *Organizational Systems and Engineering Groups* (Boston: Harvard University Division of Research, Graduate School of Business Administration, 1960), p. 24; and David G. Moore and Richard Renck, "The Professional Employee in Industry," *The Journal of Business*, 28:62 (January 1955).

[7] See Barnes, *Organizational Systems and Engineering Groups*, pp. 20–21; and Stephen B. Miles, Jr., and Thomas E. Vail, "Thinking Ahead: Dual Management," *Harvard Business Review*, 38:27, 30ff. (January-February 1960).

[8] Simon Marcson, *The Scientist in American Industry* (New York: Harper & Brothers, 1960), pp. 121–144. A relatively high degree of colleague authority is likely to be found in the university setting.

[9] See Moore and Renck, "Professional Employee in Industry," p. 62.

[10] Alvin W. Gouldner, "Cosmopolitans and Locals: Toward an Analysis of Latent Social Roles," *Administrative Science Quarterly*, 2:290 (December 1957). See also Mark Abrahamson, "The Integration of Industrial Scientists," *Administrative Science Quarterly*, 9:208–218 (September 1964); and Peter P. Gil and Warren G. Bennis, "Science and Management: Two Cultures?" *The Journal of Applied Behavioral Science*, 4:75–108, No. 1 (1968).

definition. *Locals* have high loyalty to their employing organizations, a low commitment to specialized skills, and orientation toward reference groups within the organization.[11] Research tends to confirm this picture, at least with respect to internal loyalties and reference groups. Studies indicate that engineers are strongly oriented toward achieving organization goals, and most aspire to move into the managerial hierarchy.[12]

The research scientist, on the other hand, places quite a different value on administrative work. Scientists tend to believe that research should offer status and financial advancement at least equal to the opportunities in administration, up to perhaps the vice-presidential level. On the other hand, administrators may believe that the highest rewards should go to those with managerial responsibilities.[13] A rationalization that can easily be provided for the scientist's attitude is the belief of scientists and engineers that they are mainly responsible for our high standard of living.[14]

These differences in value orientation probably give rise, in part, to certain other perceptions that scientists hold about themselves and management. For example, in distinct contrast to themselves, scientists see managers as measuring results in dollars, having little depth of knowledge, striving for power over people, oversimplifying problems, manipulating people for their own purposes, and concerned with short-range matters.[15]

This orientation of the typical scientist toward values and goals is not necessarily permanent, however, nor does it necessarily apply to all scientists. Research by Marcson has found that the orientation of scientists tends to shift as their careers develop (a) from basic research to applied research, or (b) from research to administration. According to Marcson, although the career development of the majority of scientists falls into the first category, some scientists develop aspirations in the direction of administration but for different reasons. They begin to realize that they are not in situations of "colleague authority" but are employees within an administrative hierarchy, and they begin to seek rewards through the administrative route. Others begin to reach the ceiling on prestige and financial compensation from scientific research and view administration as a way of pushing through this ceiling. Still others find they can no longer compete in research and move into administration for this reason.[16]

---

[11] Gouldner, "Cosmopolitans and Locals."

[12] Richard Ritti, "Work Goals of Scientists and Engineers," *Industrial Relations*, 7:118–131 (February 1968).

[13] For a further discussion of these value conflicts, see William Kornhauser, *Scientists in Industry* (Berkeley: University of California Press; Institute of Industrial Relations, 1962), pp. 12–15. See also Herbert A. Shepard, "Nine Dilemmas in Industrial Research," *Administrative Science Quarterly*, 1:295–309 (December 1956); and Marcson, *Scientist in American Society*, pp. 145–151. The resistance of many scientists to the assumption of administrative responsibilities can be explained by this value orientation. In my opinion, such resistance often stems, not from a particularly low opinion of administrative jobs, but from a realization that moving over to the administrative ladder might preclude the possibility of competing successfully for recognition from the scientific community. This possibility is hard to give up, once the scientist has headed in this direction.

[14] Of 622 technical-professionals employed by industry, 82 percent held this belief. Opinion Research Corporation, *The Conflict Between the Scientific Mind and the Management Mind* (Princeton, N.J.: Opinion Research Corporation), September, 1959 Research Report of the Public Opinion Index for Industry, p. 9 (pamphlet).

[15] Ibid., p. 13.

[16] Marcson, *Scientist in American Society*, pp. 51–71. Attitudes about research are also related to supervisory rank. The more the scientist is engaged in administration the more importance is attached to administration as a personal goal and the less importance is attached to research as a personal goal. See Clovis Shepard and Paula Brown, "Status, Prestige, and Esteem in a Research Organization," *Administrative Science Quarterly*, 1:348–353 (December 1956). This conclusion, of course, does not tell us whether this attitude would take a particular scientist into administration or whether attitudes change with responsibilities. Probably both are true.

IMPLICATIONS FOR JOB DESIGN

WHAT SCIENTIST-ENGINEERS WANT FROM THEIR JOBS Their educational, value-orientation, and other characteristics lead scientists and engineers to want certain things from their jobs. One study, for example, in which engineers and scientists were interviewed about the criteria they used in evaluating an institution as an employer or potential employer, found that scientists and engineers want (not in any particular rank order):

1. Freedom to publish and discuss work with other scientists and engineers

2. Association with, and intellectual stimulation from, high-caliber colleagues

3. A technically trained management, including research directors with national reputations

4. Freedom in choosing problems

5. An organization with a reputation for scientific advancement

6. Adequate facilities, resources, and assistance from technicians

7. Opportunity for advancement in salary and status along either (a) the administrative route or (b) the research route

8. Competitive salaries

9. Job security

10. A community providing schools, colleges, libraries, other cultural opportunities, and good transportation

11. Treatment as individuals, as important entities

12. Opportunity to continue formal education while employed [17]

When the effects of age relative to a number of these variables is examined, research suggests that job security becomes more important beyond age fifty for engineers and scientists. Need of self-fulfillment and autonomy and increased involvement on the job seemed to be of relatively less concern for this group than in earlier career periods. [18]

Another study, which tabulated the reasons cited by scientists for remaining on their present jobs during a specified period found that "worthwhile and stimulating work," "personal reasons," a "variety of problems" for research, and "good salary" were the four most frequently mentioned reasons, in that order. "Freedom and independence," "good employer," and "good staff and superiors" were mentioned next in order of frequency. Scientists who had left their jobs during the same period chose new jobs for the following reasons, in order of frequency: "salary increase or best salary offered," "work in scientist's field of specialization," "interesting activity," "personal reasons," "to study," "good prospects for promotion," and "new or broader experience." Reasons cited for leaving jobs, in order of frequency, were "inadequate salary or better offer elsewhere," "war-connected reasons," "to study," "insufficient opportunity for advancement or better opportunity offered," "personal reasons," "desire for new or broader experience," and "insecurity." [19]

In another study, engineers and scientists who had left governmental jobs were asked to specify those conditions that made other positions more desirable. Eighty percent listed the opportunity to do important and interesting

[17] Douglas Williams, "Attracting Topflight Scientists and Engineers," Personnel, 34:79–81 (May-June 1958). See also Danielson, Characteristics of Engineers and Scientists, p. 80.

[18] Douglas T. Hall and Roger Mansfield, "Relationships of Age and Seniority with Career Variables of Engineers and Scientists," Journal of Applied Psychology, 60:201–210 (April 1975).
[19] Theresa R. Shapiro, "What Scientists Look for in Their Jobs," The Scientific Monthly, 76:337–339 (June 1953).

work in an environment of freedom and individual responsibility. Sixty percent listed inadequate compensation and opportunity for advancement.[20]

The reader will note that, in many ways, what the engineer-scientist wants from a job is quite similar to what most employees want, namely, an interesting and challenging job, fair supervision, equitable pay, and opportunity for increased earnings and recognition (see Chapter 6). The essential differences, however, are in the *specifics* that are required to satisfy these needs. For example, the organic chemist may want a series of challenging assignments in synthesizing new compounds, while the machinist may want to tackle a new series of challenging problems in machining parts to specifications. Further, while the machinist may want recognition from the supervisor and work associates, the scientist often wants recognition from the broader scientific community, and the engineer wants recognition from top management.

WHAT SCIENTIST-ENGINEERS COMPLAIN ABOUT
Surveys of attitudes in past years have tended to show chronic frustration and general dissatisfaction among engineers and scientists. According to the surveys, these professionals had only slightly more favorable attitudes about their jobs than factory production workers, and attitudes about the same as routine office workers. They were definitely more dissatisfied than skilled workers, sales clerks, foremen, and other managers.[21] However, a more recent study found that people in the professional, technical, and managerial categories, when surveyed as a group, had substantially higher job satisfaction than persons employed in clerical and sales, service, and machine trades jobs, and slightly higher than employees in structural work occupations.[22] (See also Figure 6-6 in Chapter 6.) It is difficult to assess whether this reflects a change in the satisfactions of technical-professional employees or whether the attitudes of this group are obscured by combining them with other professionals and with managers. (Given the research cited later, including that by Dalton and Thompson on rating and compensation practices, my guess is that the satisfaction of engineers and scientists would be lower than in the case of managers.)

In any event, the earlier research points to some specific areas of dissatisfaction to which top management and personnel people need to be alert; some examples follow. In one study, interviews were held with 622 technical-professionals from six leading companies representing the aircraft, drug, electrical equipment, petroleum, and rubber industries. Of this group 80 percent felt that experienced scientists and engineers were underpaid compared with other groups, 72 percent felt that management misused engineering and scientific talent, and 71 percent felt that companies forced engineers and scientists to overspecialize.[23] Another study found that scientists believed their tasks were beneath their capabilities 35 percent of the time and were highly critical of the common practice of having large numbers of scientists working together in one room. More than half of these respondents reported working in

---

[20] Clark D. Ahlberg and John C. Honey, *Attitudes of Scientists and Engineers about Their Government Employment* (Syracuse, N.Y.: Syracuse University, 1950), I, p. 37, as cited in Shapiro, "What Scientists Look for in Jobs," p. 340.

[21] Moore and Renck, "Professional Employee in Industry," p. 60. See also Opinion Research Corporation, *The Conflict Between the Scientific Mind and the Management Mind*, p. 4.

[22] Neal Q. Herrick, "Who's Unhappy at Work and Why?" *Manpower*, January 1972, pp. 2–7.

[23] Opinion Research Corporation, *The Conflict Between the Scientific Mind and the Management Mind*, p. 5. In regard to salaries, one author estimates that it takes 17½ years after graduation from high school for the scientist or engineer to catch up with cumulative earnings of the worker who starts industrial employment right after graduation from high school. See Robert M. Page, "Motivations of Scientists and Engineers," *Personnel Administration*, 21:32 (September-October 1958).

rooms with 13 or more other people.[24] Other studies show professional and technical workers putting in long hours, with only 18 percent of these employees getting paid overtime.[25]

Surveys usually find that scientists and engineers are highly critical of management, engineers even more so than natural scientists. Engineers were more critical about management than 85 percent of all groups surveyed in one series of studies. However, those research teams that had been unusually successful in developing new products were less critical of management and had much higher morale.[26] In general, the kinds of complaints mentioned above are noted consistently by studies in both industry and government.

ADDITIONAL PROBLEMS IN MANAGING THE TECHNICAL-PROFESSIONAL EMPLOYEE

In addition to the problems enumerated thus far, managers are likely to encounter other complexities in the management of scientists and engineers. A set of problems arises when the scientist or engineer is transferred from one project to another as the person's skills are needed. Some of these transfers may be between departments and may involve working not only for different supervisors, but for different top executives as well. If the professional is working for more than one department in the interim between salary reviews, how can the person be assured that his or her contributions will receive proper recognition and re-

ward? What happens to the professional's motivation if a transfer occurs before a project is completely finished? What happens to the motivation and attitudes of the nurse who is transferred from one clinic to another without being consulted? Who is concerned with the person's long-range development and advancement? As discussed in Chapter 5, these uncertainties may create serious problems for professional-technical people.

Another problem concerns team effort. If a team of scientists is assigned to a project, how is the contribution of each to be evaluated? This difficulty is particularly great when contributions take the form of ideas and recommendations expressed verbally. Further, how can communications among people from diverse specialties be enhanced?

Other problems emerge in the case of scientific research projects requiring months or even years of intense concentration and perseverance. How is performance to be evaluated if the results of experiments to date are all negative? How is the motivation of the scientist to be sustained if the frequency of reward and recognition is low? What happens to the mental health of the independent researcher whose needs for belonging, affiliation, and recognition go unfulfilled during extended periods?

A particularly important problem is created in companies' salary administration programs by the competition for scientific, engineering, or other professional talent. As competition forces starting salaries up, the salaries for beginning scientists or engineers or other professionals such as accountants, may become chronically inflated relative to those of other entrants into the labor market from other fields, or relative to those who entered the labor market in earlier years. These distortions in compensation programs lead to resentment among employees with longer service who have not received proportional increases and among new graduates from other fields.

---

[24] Irving Hirsch, William Milwitt, and William J. Oakes, "Increasing the Productivity of Scientists," *Harvard Business Review*, 36:67, 70 (March-April 1958). One study found turnover to be relatively low among engineers who did not mind routine detail, but higher among those of more imagination and those with more interest in people. J.B. Boyd, "Interests of Engineers Related to Turnover, Selection, and Management," *Journal of Applied Psychology*, 45:143–149 (June 1961).
[25] Diane N. Westcott, "Trends in Overtime Hours and Pay, 1969–74," *Monthly Labor Review*, 98:50 (February 1975).
[26] Moore and Renck, "Professional Employee in Industry," pp. 59:62.

Another problem, which relates to salary administration, appraisal, and motivation—and probably also to mental health—is the human obsolescence suggested by the declining performance rankings of technical-professional employees after they reach their middle thirties. In a study of 2,500 design and development engineers from six organizations, Dalton and Thompson found that performance rankings of these technical people, on the average, rose until their early thirties, dropped slightly in the late thirties, *and then fell steadily until retirement.* Average pay increases followed the same pattern. Further, the complexity of tasks assigned to the engineers peaked in their late twenties and dropped from then on.[27]

As suggested by the research, at least some of this obsolescence is due to management practices, and some may simply be consciously or unconsciously assumed by managers to minimize certain problems. As one example, Dalton and Thompson cite the discouraging and immobilizing rating practices—usually below- or above-average rankings that are communicated—that tend to create a kind of self-fulfilling prophecy. An engineer rated below average may, in Dalton and Thompson's words, "develop a stubborn 'what the heck' attitude; then comes a lower rating, lower self-confidence, and still a lower rating, and so on." As another example, realizing that the younger engineers are usually highly mobile, management frequently tries to retain them with substantial salary increases, promotions, and exciting job assignments; however, this process adversely affects the older engineers. Sometimes the high performance rankings are given to justify these rewards, rather than the other way around.[28]

Although industrial practice and social science research have not found perfect solutions to these and other problems mentioned in this chapter, the discussion that follows, and some of the concepts discussed in the next two chapters, may suggest partial solutions.

IMPLICATIONS FOR PERSONNEL ADMINISTRATION

JOB DESIGN

Assuming that scientific and engineering skills are in relatively short supply and that professional-technicals are paid mainly for their technical output, it would seem to be good management to exclude as much subprofessional work form scientific and engineering jobs as possible. (This would hold true for other categories of professional employment as well, including medicine, nursing, finance, etc.) Studies cited earlier found that most engineers and scientists believe their skills are not being utilized properly. Further, when questioned about the percentage of time spent in different kinds of activities, the average professional reported that about two-thirds of her or his time was spent on routine work not requiring a professional-technical background.[29]

One partial solution found by a governmental agency was to assign "technical-program coordinators" and "administrative officers" to research and engineering groups with the specific assignment of relieving scientists and engineers of administrative details.[30] Other suggested partial solutions include assistance to scientists in finding information, increased efficiency in the planning and conducting of meetings and conferences, and more use of subprofessionals

[27] Gene W. Dalton and Paul H. Thompson, "Accelerating Obsolescence of Older Engineers," *Harvard Business Review,* 49:57–67 (September-October 1971).
[28] Ibid., p. 63.
[29] Hirsch, Milwitt, and Oakes, "Increasing Productivity of Scientists," pp. 67–68.
[30] Robert F. Mello, "Engineers and Scientists: We Found How to Use Them Better," *Personnel Journal,* 36:407–410 (April 1958).

and liberal arts graduates to assist scientists and engineers.[31] More extensive use of subprofessionals, then, suggests the need for pervasive job enrichment efforts in scientific or professional departments along with the creation of new jobs.

PERFORMANCE STANDARDS AND WORK RULES

As suggested in Chapter 10, the more complex the nature of the job and the further removed it is from the actual production process, the more difficult it is to establish performance standards. Nevertheless, cooperation between the professional and the manager in developing reasonable and realistic performance standards, either through formalized written standards or, indirectly, through traditional merit-rating procedures, are likely to result in a closer relationship between scientific activities and the enterprise's goals and in more realistic perceptions by both manager and the professional of the latter's job. Such efforts can emphasize those activities likely to contribute most to attaining the enterprise's goals and can point out activities that are extraneous and need curtailment. Furthermore, if approached on a problem-solving basis, the development of formal or informal performance standards can also pinpoint obstacles to achievement that the manager can assist in removing. Periodic distractions and irritations are serious obstacles to creativity, and the manager can do much to remove them from the environment.

The development of guides to expected performance will also point out the degree of freedom or restriction appropriate to the job. If scientific innovations or technical publication are the goals, a requirement that the scientist work precise hours from eight until five may be entirely unrelated to productivity. Some firms have found that under flexible conditions research scientists do not abuse freedom in working hours, but that, more typically, they work many additional hours and weekends.[32] On the other hand, an engineer assigned to trouble-shooting on manufacturing problems may be required to be available at more predictable hours. Similarly, team-research and team-engineering assignments may require the close coordination of working schedules.[33] (See also the discussion of flextime, Chapter 10.)

RECRUITMENT AND SELECTION

Additional efficiency can be gained by thoughtful recruitment and selection. In the first place, job specifications should be carefully developed so that the recruiter or interviewer has a clear understanding of the qualifications really needed. Secondly, information about job openings should be communicated as accurately as possible so that the candidate can do a more effective job of selection. Jobs that are oversold or glamorized often lead to disillusionment later on, and eventually this can result in either resignation or undesirable defensive behavior.

Since some discrepancy between the recruiter's expectations and the applicant's expectations tends to be typical, the recruiter must be particularly careful to avoid distorting the facts. For example, Marcson found that scientists recruited into laboratories expect to do basic research, but the laboratory may expect the recruit to produce devices.[34]

[31] Hirsch, Milwitt, and Oakes, "Increasing Productivity of Scientists," pp. 71–76.

[32] See Stanford University, *Motivation of Scientists and Engineers* (Stanford, Calif.: Graduate School of Business, Stanford University, April 1959), pp. 33–34.

[33] Although the Wage and Hour Laws exempt companies from paying professionals overtime pay, many companies do so when the overtime work is scheduled or expected for extended periods. Some nonscheduled overtime is usually expected of the professional, however, but the professional typically expects fewer constraints on reporting-in time and more liberal time-off policies as the *quid pro quo*.

[34] Simon Marcson, "Role Adaptation of Scientists in Industrial Research," *IRE Transactions on Engineering Management*, Vol. EM–7:159–166 (December 1960).

Attempts to assess the value orientation of the candidate also seem useful. A scientist who has a strong need for the approval of fellow scientists in other organizations might appropriately be employed in a laboratory doing basic research, but that person might be grossly misassigned as a technical assistant in a pilot plant, or in manufacturing, or in administration.[35]

TRANSFERS

One study found that the most frequently stated reason given by engineers for recent job changes was a wish to change the direction of their careers.[36] Therefore, it follows that when the nature of the particular scientist's capabilities becomes more evident, the intelligent use of transfers and/or promotions into different career paths can result in the retention of useful skills. For example, although ill-suited or uninterested in research and development, a person's technical experience and training might make her or him invaluable in patent work.

In addition, since individual interests shift—frequently from basic research to applied research—management can often profitably transfer scientists when such changes in interests occur. Further, since many scientists are keenly interested in the outcome of their discoveries, some firms have profitably used the device of transferring the scientist out of the laboratory into the pilot plant at the next stage of product development, then into manufacturing until the "bugs" have been ironed out,

and then back into the laboratory to start on a new research project.

PROMOTION

The strong orientation of a high percentage of scientists and engineers toward continued technical work rather than supervisory or administrative assignments has led a number of firms in recent years to establish parallel promotional opportunities. That is, the professional-technical employee can advance to such positions as "senior research scientist," as well as to such positions as "director of inorganic research."[37] One survey of twenty-two companies found three-fourths with some kind of parallel ladder system, although it appeared that the ladders in some companies did not go very high and that they were not comparable to the administrative ladder in certain cases.[38] Another study found that seven out of ten cooperating companies had dual hierarchies.[39]

According to a study in one organization—a division of an electronics company—the use of a dual ladder was not accomplishing what it was assumed to be doing. Questionnaires to both technical and managerial people found that 75 percent of the technical group did not perceive their pay to be as high for "comparable" managerial positions, and 80 percent believed their jobs carried less prestige than managerial jobs. Responses from the managerial group indicated that the managers thought pay scales for both groups were comparable, but 81 percent agreed with the technical people that technical positions carried less prestige. Both groups, however, had fairly high overall

---

[35] Research suggests that an analysis of the background of scientists may predict whether they will aspire to stay in research or to move into administration. See Lewis E. Albright and J.R. Glennon, "Personal History Correlates of Physical Scientists' Career Aspirations," *Journal of Applied Psychology*, 45:281–284 (October 1961). This research suggests a number of useful questions that could be used in an interview to assess the applicant's orientation.

[36] Arthur Gerstenfeld and Gabriel Rosica, "Why Engineers Transfer," *Business Horizons*, 13:43–48 (April 1970).

[37] See Peter F. Drucker, *The Practice of Management* (New York: Harper & Brothers, 1954), pp. 335–338.

[38] Stanford University, *Motivation of Scientists and Engineers*, pp. 14–16.

[39] John W. Riegel, *Administration of Salaries and Intangible Rewards for Engineers and Scientists* (Ann Arbor: Bureau of Industrial Relations, University of Michigan, 1958), p. 23.

morale; both groups derived satisfaction from their titles; and both groups believed that higher management was giving recognition to their contributions.[40]

Whether the creation of such additional technical titles has been accompanied by broader responsibilities in research or higher standards of performance is not clear from some of the reports. Such titles, in many cases, may reflect belated recognition of the worth of the technical person and thus of the necessity of increasing the maximum salary, or they may reflect recognition of a more symbolic nature, or they may reflect both types of recognition. Either is probably a legitimate move by management, unless management's attitude implies that the new title is purely an attempt to pacify restless engineers and scientists and that the title means little.[41]

That some corporations are creating bona fide technical positions involving unusually high expectations of performance is suggested by the creation of the position of "corporate fellow" in one company. Assigned to this post is a scientist who has shown "promise of notable contribution to knowledge and thought" and who is freed from managerial direction and from administrative responsibilities. The underlying assumptions seem to be that such a scientist, if well selected, will contribute substantially to the enterprise's goals in the long run.[42]

It should be kept in mind, however, that avenues of advancement in organizations employing scientific personnel have not been exclusively in research. In addition to moving into the managerial ranks within research, many scientists and engineers have moved up the managerial ladder via developmental operations, manufacturing, maintenance, quality control, purchasing, sales, technical service, advertising, personnel and industrial relations, and other phases of the company's operations.

The parallel-ladder concept is not without its problems. One problem occurs when a coordinator or director of research feels unfairly treated because of being paid less than the senior scientists whose work he or she "coordinates."[43] If there is no good reason for the discrepancy, the obvious solution, of course, is to correct the inequity. If there is a good reason, a partial solution to misunderstanding is better communication of the reasons for the discrepancy. It may be that the complexities and responsibilities of the particular administrative job are less than those of the research position. Perhaps the greater the latitude given the scientist in research, the less supervisory direction and control are needed. Much more research needs to be done on these matters.

Another problem is that the position of senior scientist may become a convenient place for "shelving" scientists who have not performed adequately in administration. This practice, of course, distorts the purpose of the position and minimizes its effectiveness as a goal in careers of research scientists.

APPRAISAL AND COACHING

An analysis of rating forms from sixty-nine research laboratories found that fifty-seven applied a graphic rating scale usually resulting in an overall point score (see Chapter 15 for a description of this and other appraising devices); five used a method involving a narrative response to general questions; four used "totem

[40] Bertram Schoner and Thomas W. Harrell, "The Questionable Dual Ladder," *Personnel*, 42:53–57 (January-February 1965). For further discussion of the dual ladder concept, see Fred H. Goldner and R.R. Ritti, "Professionalization as Career Immobility," *American Journal of Sociology*, 72:489–502 (March 1967).

[41] See Charles D. Orth III, "More Productivity from Engineers," *Harvard Business Review*, 35:57 (March-April 1957); and Stanford University, *Motivation of Scientists and Engineers*, p. 16.

[42] See *Industrial Relations News*, February 24, 1962.

[43] See Kornhauser, *Scientists in Industry*, p. 148.

pole" rankings, that is, rank-order ratings; and three used a performance standard and coaching method. Apparently, most or all of the responding companies followed the rating procedure with an interview in which the results were communicated. The popular graphic rating scales typically included items about job performance, personal characteristics, supervisory abilities, and promotional possibilities.[44]

An interesting development by the organization making the above survey was a "dual-evaluation" procedure in which both subordinate and superior rated the subordinate's performance and then met to discuss the results. The form developed for this purpose combined the features of the graphic rating scale and the narrative response.[45]

As emphasized in Chapter 15, the more precisely appraisals can measure the degree to which behavior contributes to the enterprise's goals, the greater the validity of the appraisals. It appears, however, that a high percentage of firms may be placing undue emphasis on the personal traits of their engineers and scientists,[46] a practice that is of doubtful validity. The engineer or scientist is no more likely to be an eccentric than anyone else, and penalizing mild forms of antisocial behavior by low ratings may be a serious mistake. Although brusque and undiplomatic mannerisms in a salesperson might well have a harmful effect on sales, the same mannerisms in a research scientist may be of little consequence when viewed in terms of overall contribution to the enterprise. On the other hand, behavior seriously curtailing the productivity of colleagues cannot be tolerated.

Also, as discussed in Chapter 15, rank-order comparisons or totem pole rankings may create a zero-sum kind of climate in which, by definition, half of all the scientists or engineers in a given unit are "below average." To give one person a higher ranking as a reward for good performance means that another's ranking is lowered, frequently creating a serious morale problem.[47] One way the organization can avoid such occurrences is for managers to refrain from direct peer comparisons and to focus on the extent to which targets and goals are achieved and on collaborative problem solving.

COMPENSATION

The job evaluation systems and salary administration devices that will be described in Chapter 19 are probably used by a vast majority of firms in determining the compensation of professional-technical employees. Although the complexities described earlier in this chapter require that such systems and devices be modified appropriately, nevertheless they are applicable and are widely used. Chapter 19 will also discuss the use of the "maturity curve," a salary administration technique frequently used for professional-technical employees.

DEVELOPMENT

There are at least three reasons why attention to the continued professional development of scientists and engineers is important to the en-

[44] A. Addison, T.B. Derr, and H.L. Yeagley, "A Method of Performance Evaluation for Engineers and Scientists," *IRE Transactions on Engineering Management,* Vol. EM–8:179–181 (December 1961). For a description of a rating method that focuses mainly on accomplishment, see Irwin W. Krantz, "Evaluating the Technical Employee: A Results Approach," *Personnel,* 41:47–58 (January-February 1964).

[45] Ibid., pp. 183–190. Upon use, it was found that subordinates tended to rate themselves lower than the supervisor's rating. For the experience of another organization, see Alexander G. Grasberg, "Merit Rating and Productivity in an Industrial Research Laboratory: A Case Study," *IRE Transactions on Engineering Management,* Vol. EM–6:31–37 (March 1959).

[46] Stanford University, *Motivation of Scientists and Engineers,* pp. 16–17.

[47] See Paul H. Thompson and Gene W. Dalton, "Performance Appraisal: Managers Beware," *Harvard Business Review,* 48:149–157 (January-February 1970); and Dalton and Thompson, "Accelerating Obsolescence of Older Engineers," pp. 57–67.

terprise. In the first place, scientific knowledge is developing so rapidly that the knowledge and skills of an individual may easily become obsolete without frequent updating. Second, the rapid increase in the number of subspecialties and the steady trend toward specialization require people who can establish an effective liaison among specialties. Third, many scientists and engineers will move into part-time or full-time managerial jobs, so that they must be educated in various aspects of administration.

Some of this developmental need can be fulfilled by careful job rotation. Many companies bring young engineers into training programs and transfer them among departments for a year or so, thus broadening the engineer's knowledge and providing an opportunity to assess more carefully personal interests and aspirations for a career. Transfers of experienced scientists or engineers can also partly serve the objective of additional training and development, as illustrated by the practice I have already mentioned of transferring the research scientist into the pilot plant and then into manufacturing until the problems with a new product are solved.

Avoiding the tempting practice of typically assigning the young engineer to projects involving new technology can also contribute to the development of engineers of all ages and help avoid the problem of obsolescence. As Dalton and Thompson have noted, "If a manager has two projects, one requiring existing technology and one requiring new technology, the obvious approach for short-term 'efficiency' is to assign an experienced man to the former and a new man to the latter."[48] Such practices may have a negative impact on the older engineer's motivation, willingness to learn new approaches, and, in the long run, on performance ratings and salary.

Time-off and tuition programs that permit the engineer-scientist to continue formal education at a nearby university are also in widespread use. In cooperation with colleges and universities, many industrial firms make it possible for the professional to obtain an advanced degree while working essentially full-time. Leaves of absence or sabbaticals are often granted under such programs to fulfill the university's residence requirements.

Advanced seminars, subscriptions to journals, and the maintenance of a company's libraries are other ways in which the continual development of the scientist-engineer can be facilitated.[49] Encouraging attendance at professional meetings and the writing of articles and books are also important devices in further development and training. The encouragement of writing not only stimulates the learning process of the writer, but also serves to increase and disseminate scientific knowledge and to provide recognition for the contributor.[50]

Another practice, used in at least a few firms, serves both to supplement programs of personal development and to present the possibility of furthering technological innovation. This practice allows the researcher, artist, engineer, or artisan to devote some proportion of paid working time—either on a daily or cumulative basis—to pursue research of particular personal interest. Scientists, engineers, and other employees are usually enthusiastic about such programs,[51] but to my knowledge the usefulness of these programs beyond their impact on morale has not been systematically investigated.

[48]Dalton and Thompson, "Accelerating Obsolescence of Older Engineers," p. 55.

[49]Scientists and engineers want the opportunity to attend seminars, but do not want to be required to attend. See Sidney L. Jones, "Meeting the Development Needs of R & D Personnel," *Personnel*, 39:61 (November-December 1962).
[50]For a discussion of company policies with respect to employee authorship, see Geneva Seybold, "When Employee Turns Author," *Management Record*, 20:42–46ff. (February 1958).
[51]Jones, "Meeting Development Needs," pp. 62–63. See also D.E. Hibsman, "Why Do Engineers Want MBA's?" *Personnel Administration*, 31:52–55 (January-February 1968).

LEADERSHIP AND SUPERVISION

Although Chapter 7 has gone into detail on the subject of which leadership patterns tend to further the enterprise's goals, some mention of supervisory patterns effective in promoting engineering and scientific productivity will be made here. Some studies in the social sciences bear directly on the question.

Research by the Michigan Institute for Social Research indicates that the scientists and engineers who perform the best are the ones who (a) set their own technical goals or have considerable influence on their supervisor in setting goals, (b) consult with their supervisor frequently, and (c) are deeply involved in their work. If involvement is not deep, however, better results are obtained when the scientist is permitted only moderate self-determination. In addition, performance is enhanced by frequent communication within the organization and among colleagues with different points of view.[52]

Research also indicates that the rate of publication among scientists is influenced by the available funds and freedom to choose problems. Neither additional funds alone nor increased freedom by itself produces the best results. A marked increase in productivity occurs when both freedom and funds are substantially increased.[53]

Research also suggests that relatively new research groups perform better in terms of several criteria than groups consisting of members who have been together for three, four, or five years.

These results were found consistently whether scientists rated their own groups or whether research executives rated the groups. Rank-order ratings were obtained on productivity, creativity, responsiveness to challenge, and other criteria. As a result, the researchers quite naturally raised the question of whether members of research groups should be reassigned every two or three years, and they cite such reassignment as a deliberate practice in one research laboratory in England.[54]

Shepard concludes that these and other studies "... point in the same direction: the effective research group leader is a creative, dynamic, enthusiastic person who relates easily to others." Shepard further concludes that research points to the fact that such people are relatively rare among scientists and engineers.[55] This conclusion demonstrates the importance of carefully identifying managerial talent among professional-technical employees and the importance of sound managerial training for those selected.

AFFIRMATIVE ACTION

As shown in Figure 11-4, Chapter 11, the proportion of blacks and other minority groups in professional-technical occupations more than doubled between 1950 and 1975. However, their representation is still below their proportion in the total labor force.[56] In 1974, the representation of women in professional occupations slightly exceeded the proportion of women employed in the labor force (see Figure 11-5, Chapter 11) but were disproportionately distributed among the occupations, e.g., they were heavily represented in elementary school teaching and nursing. The engineering field is

[52] Donald C. Pelz, "Motivation of the Engineering and Research Specialist," in *Improving Managerial Performance*, General Management Series Number 186 (New York: American Management Association, 1957), pp. 25–46. See also Rensis Likert, "Supervision," *International Science and Technology*, March 1962, pp. 57–62. Performance criteria are not discussed in the latter article with the exception of publication rate.

[53] Pelz, "Motivation of Engineering and Research Specialist," pp. 31–32.

[54] Ibid., pp. 43–45.

[55] Herbert Shepard, "Nine Dilemmas in Industrial Research," p. 304.

[56] U.S. Department of Labor, *Employment and Training Report of the President*, 1976, p. 153.

still essentially dominated by men.[57] These data, of course, indicate the importance of affirmative action by employers and by engineering and professional schools.

THE PERSONNEL DEPARTMENT

In addition to affirmative action and the traditional responsibilities of recruitment, salary administration, and the like, the personnel department has a number of important functions to perform relative to the management of the engineer, the scientist, and other professionals. It seems particularly necessary for this department to insure that professionals who are transferred from project to project are given careful and continuing consideration in terms of salaries, promotional opportunity, and their own career aspirations. Furthermore, the personnel department must work closely with the scientific-technical divisions of the enterprise so that it can develop salary structures, supplemental plans of compensation, and work rules that make sense in terms of the unique nature of both the technical-professional jobs and their incumbents. The personnel department may also be in a position to diagnose the need for and to assist in developing job enrichment programs and/or programs to restructure jobs and to utilize paraprofessionals.

It would appear that the personnel department should also have the difficult but challenging assignment of correlating such policies and practices with policies and practices affecting other segments of the work force. Management must be able to explain and justify differences in policy and treatment if people are to feel fairly treated. As stated earlier, the differences between technical-professional employees and other employees are differences only in degree, and management must maintain perspective in dealing with this group relative to all other groups.

SUMMARY

The demands of businesses and other organizations for rapid technological innovation, coupled with a rapid upgrading of the skill-mix in many firms, makes careful and systematic attention to the effective management of the engineer, scientist, and other professionals mandatory. Although American enterprise has been relatively successful in creating a climate for professionals that has resulted in rapid technological advance, research in the social sciences and reports of successful practice have identified areas where improvement is desirable. Performance rating, compensation practices, working conditions, and the avoidance of obsolescence are areas that need much more attention by managers and researchers. Research cited in Chapters 5, 7, and 26 suggests that an "organic-adaptive" type of organization may have considerable promise for enhancing the human and technical skills of individuals and teams in the scientific, engineering, or professional setting.

REVIEW AND DISCUSSION QUESTIONS

1. In what ways, if any, should scientists and engineers or other professionals be treated differently from other employees, and why? What unique problems occur in the management of these employees?

2. What do scientists and engineers want from their jobs?

3. In what ways does the research scientist in the laboratory have values different from those of the engineer in a managerial position in manufacturing? Discuss the implications.

[57] Rudolph C. Blitz, "Women in the Professions, 1870–1970," *Monthly Labor Review*, 97:34–39 (May 1974); and Stuart H. Garfinkle, "Occupations of Women and Black Workers, 1962–74," *Monthly Labor Review*, 98:25–29 (November 1975).

4. If you were to establish a dual ladder concept of salary administration, should a senior scientist having research assignments in a pharmaceutical company but no supervisory or administrative responsibilities draw as much salary as the company's (a) vice president—manufacturing, (b) vice president—marketing, or (c) vice president—research and development? Discuss each.

5. Describe Gouldner's concepts of cosmopolitans and locals as they relate to technical positions.

6. Discuss the relevance of job enrichment for (a) engineering departments and (b) scientific research departments.

7. What are some of the management practices contributing to the obsolescence of scientists and engineers? What changes would you recommend in these practices?

SUPPLEMENTAL REFERENCES

Aun, Emil M., "New Horizons for Aerospace Professionals," *Manpower,* January 1973, pp. 3–8.

Barnes, Louis B., *Organizational Systems and Engineering Groups* (Boston: Division of Research, Graduate School of Business Administration, Harvard University, 1960).

Blood, Jerome W., ed. *The Management of Scientific Talent* (New York: American Management Association, Inc., 1963).

Brooks, Harvey, "Science and the Allocation of Resources," *American Psychologist,* 22:187–201 (March 1967).

Danielson, Lee E., *Characteristics of Engineers and Scientists* (Ann Arbor: The University of Michigan, Bureau of Industrial Relations, 1960).

Eaton, B. Curtis, "Defense Engineers: Do They Have Special Reemployment Problems?" *Monthly Labor Review,* 94:52–54 (July 1971).

Goldner, Fred H., and R.R. Ritti, "Professionalization as Career Immobility," *The American Journal of Sociology,* 72:489–502 (March 1967).

Gooding, Judson, "The Engineers are Redesigning Their Own Profession," *Fortune,* June 1971, pp. 72–75ff.

———, *The Job Revolution* (New York: Walker & Company, 1972).

Graen, George B., Rene V. Dawes, and David J. Weiss, "Need Type and Job Satisfaction among Industrial Scientists," *Journal of Applied Psychology,* 52:286–289 (August 1968).

Hainer, Raymond M., Sherman Kingsbury, and David B. Gleicher, eds., *Uncertainty in Research, Management and New Product Development* (New York: Reinhold Publishing Company, 1967), Chapter 8.

Hansen, W. Lee, "The Economics of Scientific and Engineering Manpower," *The Journal of Human Resources,* 2:191–215 (Spring 1967).

Ladinsky, Jack, "The Geographic Mobility of Professional and Technical Manpower," *The Journal of Human Resources,* 2:477 (Fall 1967).

Marcson, Simon, *The Scientist in American Industry* (New York: Harper & Brothers, 1960).

Mitchell, William A., "Engineer Turnover—Back to the Basics," *Personnel,* 44:27–33 (July-August 1967).

Naughton, Kathleen, "Characteristics of Jobless Engineers," *Monthly Labor Review,* 95:16–21 (October 1972).

Pelz, Donald C., and F.M. Andrews, *Scientists in Organizations: Productive Climates for Research & Development* (New York: John Wiley & Sons, 1966).

Prandy, Kenneth, *Professional Employees: A Study of Scientists and Engineers* (London: Faber and Faber, 1965).

Rosenzweig, James E., "Managers and Management Scientists (Two Cultures)," *Business Horizons,* 10:79–86 (Fall 1967).

Saxberg, Borje O., and John W. Slocum, Jr., "The Management of Scientific Manpower," *Management Science,* 14:B473–B489 (April 1968).

Smith, Clagett G., "Consultation and Decision Processes in a Research and Development Laboratory," *Administrative Science Quarterly*, 15:203–215 (June 1970).

————, "Scientific Performance and the Composition of Research Teams," *Administrative Science Quarterly*, 16:486–495 (December 1971).

Taguiri, Renato, "Value Orientations and the Relationship of Managers and Scientists," *Administrative Science Quarterly*, 10:39–51 (June 1965).

Thompson, Paul H., and Gene W. Dalton, "Performance Appraisal: Managers Beware," *Harvard Business Review*, 48:149–157 (January-February 1970).

Wagner, William B., and M. Sami Kassem, "Scientists Who Migrate in Teams—And How to Manage Them," *Technology Review*, 73:29–33 (December 1970).

Zaleznik, Abraham, Gene W. Dalton, and Louis B. Barnes, *Orientation and Conflict in Career* (Boston: Division of Research, Graduate School of Business, Harvard University, 1970).

PART 7
THE COMPENSATION PROCESS

19. Administration of Wages and Salaries

20. Supplementary Benefits

21. Incentive Systems

The process of compensation is a complex network of subprocesses directed toward remunerating people for services performed and motivating them to attain desired levels of performance. Among the intermediate components of this process are wage and salary payments; the awarding of other cost items, such as insurance, vacations, and sick leave; and the provision of essentially noncost rewards, such as recognition, privileges, and symbols of status.

A wide variety of devices, systems, and policies is typically used to facilitate the administration of this complex process. Among these devices are job analysis, job descriptions, job evaluation, wage- and fringe-benefit surveys, compensation plans, merit rating, and many policies pertaining to the level and administration of wages and benefits.

Three chapters will examine the broad subject of compensation. Chapter 19 will be devoted to wage and salary administration, Chapter 20 to supplementary (fringe) benefits, and Chapter 21 to incentive systems.

Although these chapters contain no detailed discussion of nonmonetary rewards, it should be stressed here that financial rewards alone do not satisfy many of our human needs (see Chapter 6). For example, a high salary does not guarantee sleep and relaxation to a harassed and overworked executive. A high wage does not guarantee immunity from accidents to workers building a dam. Being on the payroll does not insure cooperation and acceptance from coworkers, and wage and salary payments may not necessarily carry with them recognition or prestige. Similarly, a "high" salary does not necessarily ensure that the individual feels fairly treated, nor does it guarantee that a person's desire for self-fulfillment will be satisfied. Thus, management needs to be concerned about many kinds of rewards in addition to financial rewards, including recognition, appreciation, participation, authority and power, privileges, information, interesting and challenging work, promotions, safe and pleasant working conditions, job security, and latitude for initiative.

CHAPTER 19
ADMINISTRATION OF WAGES AND SALARIES

CURRENT PRACTICES AND PROBLEMS

In general, wage payments within the organization are determined by a flow of events including job analysis, writing of job descriptions, job specifications, job evaluation, surveys of wages and salaries, analysis of relevant organizational problems, structuring of wages (which must exceed minimum-wage laws), establishing rules for administering wages, and finally, wage payments to individual employees. This flow of events is roughly diagrammed in Figure 19-1.

Not included in the diagram is collective bargaining, which, in the unionized firm, plays a major role in determining the price of labor. With collective bargaining, any events in the diagram that involve elements of personal judgment are likely to be bargained about, including job evaluation, various organizational problems, the wage structure, rules of administration, and appraisal of employees. Even for the nonunionized firm, collective-bargaining agreements reached elsewhere have an indirect, but important, impact on wage determination.[1]

JOB ANALYSIS AND JOB DESCRIPTIONS

As discussed in Chapter 10, job analysis is the systematic investigation of a job in order to identify its essential characteristics and to

---

[1] Although I use the words *wages* and *salaries* interchangeably, these terms have slightly different meanings in popular usage. Wages usually refer to the hourly rate paid to such groups as production and maintenance employees (blue-collar workers); salaries normally refer to the weekly or monthly rates paid to clerical, administrative, and professional employees (white-collar workers). In recent years, there has been growing pressure from labor unions to put production workers on a salaried basis—a matter I will discuss later in this chapter.

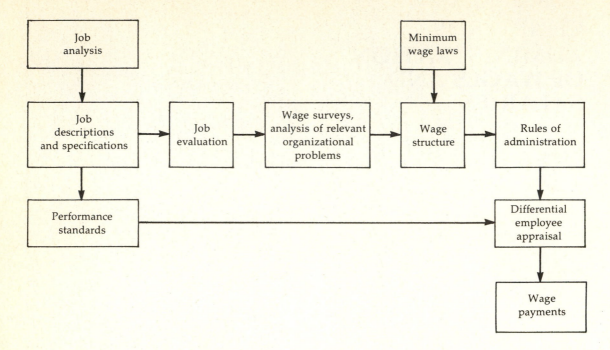

Figure **19-1**   The wage-determination process

translate these characteristics into writing in the form of a job description. Although job analysis can have other purposes, such as the development of hiring specifications and the clarification of duties, job analysis serves to provide the essential data for job evaluation. Job analysis, then, provides the data for writing job descriptions that, in turn, are used as references in job evaluation.

Job analysis should not be confused with time-and-motion study, which has as its purpose improvement in work methods or the establishment of production standards. At one time, however, time-study engineers were called "job analysts," and some confusion has thus arisen over the meaning of the term.

There are three commonly used techniques of job analysis, and they are largely self-explanatory: observation, the interview, and the ques-

tionnaire. Many companies use a combination of these techniques in obtaining information about the job.[2] In many situations company officials might use the simple procedure of having job incumbents or their superiors, or both, write job descriptions on the basis of their knowledge of the job, without any further attempt to collect or analyze job data.

Two problems in job analysis and in the writing of job descriptions are (a) accuracy and completeness and (b) acceptance by the people affected. If the information recorded in the job description is inaccurate or incomplete, the job evaluation will then be inaccurate. For ex-

[2] For a detailed discussion of job analysis methods, see Ernest J. McCormick, "Job and Task Analysis," in Marvin D. Dunnette, ed., *Handbook of Industrial and Organizational Psychology* (Chicago: Rand McNally College Publishing Company, 1976), pp. 651–696.

ample, a job description may present an inflated picture of the actual job, or it may not do justice to some of the important functions performed.

In addition, if employees or their superiors do not believe that job descriptions are an accurate reflection of the job, they will feel that job evaluation and the resulting wage structure are unfair. The first problem can be minimized by careful and systematic job-data collection; the second, by attempting to secure agreement among employees and supervisors as to the accuracy of the job description. In addition, job descriptions should be rewritten frequently enough to reflect changes in individual jobs.

Another problem stems from a lack of planning for the multiple uses of the data developed in job analysis. Without thorough planning, a number of different job analyses may be made of the same jobs in order to get different kinds of information. Multiple investigations are obviously inefficient and can understandably lead to resentment among employees and supervisors.

JOB EVALUATION

Job evaluation is the process of determining the relative worth of the various jobs within the organization, so that differential wages may be paid to jobs of different worth. Job evaluation assumes that (a) it is logical to pay the most for jobs contributing the most to attaining organizational goals, (b) people feel more fairly treated if wages are based on the relative worth of jobs, and (c) the goals of the enterprise are furthered by maintaining a job structure based on relative job worth.[3] As we shall see, job

evaluation also assumes that (d) there is considerable consistency between the resulting structure of wage rates and the structure of wage rates in the broader community. The latter assumption is the one most open to question.

Presumably, "relative worth" of jobs means relative value produced; but since the contributions of a specific job to the goals of the enterprise are difficult to measure, other variables are examined that are assumed to be related to value produced. Such factors as "responsibility," "skill," "effort," and "working conditions" are typical factors considered in formal job evaluation systems, and presumably the higher the degree of such factors in performance required by the job, the greater the contribution to the goals of the enterprise. (This question of validity will be discussed later in the chapter. See also the discussion of investments and costs in the chapter on organizational justice.)

Job evaluation of some kind is a universal phenomenon in organizations paying wages. For example, if the owner of an insurance brokerage firm decides that the receptionist should be paid more than a typist, the jobs have been evaluated. Thus, job evaluation occurs whenever decisions are made about relative worth of jobs, and it is inescapable in organizational life.

A high percentage of firms use formal job-evaluation plans. In one study, 74 percent of the firms surveyed reported the use of one or more formal job evaluation plans. In more than half of those firms using such plans, two or more separate plans were being used covering different groups of employees. Job evaluation plans were in use relative to technical employees (66 percent of responding companies), office and clerical employees (65 percent), professional employees (64 percent), supervisors

[3] The importance of job evaluation is illustrated by the following newspaper item: Romford, England, May 17 (United Press)—"An office equipment factory here was strike-bound today. The employees walked out to back demands that two men at opposite ends of a conveyor belt get the same pay. The man who unloaded the finished article from one end was getting more than the man who was putting on the raw mate-

rial at the other. Management promised to consider the issue." (From the *St. Louis Post-Dispatch*, May 18, 1958.)

(62 percent), middle managers (61 percent), and sales personnel (54 percent). The groups least likely to be covered were top managers (49 percent) and production and maintenance workers (42 percent.)[4]

Most formal job evaluation plans use the job data recorded in job descriptions. Job evaluation, of course, may be based on an understanding of various jobs without reducing this information to writing, but in organizations with a large number of positions, the job description serves as a helpful reminder to management of differences and changes within and among jobs.

There are four general types of formal job evaluation methods or devices in wide usage. In order of popularity over two or more decades, they are (1) the point method—by far the most widely used, (2) the factor-comparison method, (3) the classification method, and (4) the ranking method.[5] Each method features the application of a certain type of device or yardstick to various jobs in order to determine relative worth.

One study found the point method applied by 53 percent of the firms using job evaluation, the factor-comparison method by 33 percent, the job classification method by 24 percent, and some form of ranking system by 14 percent. This relative order of usage held for both office and plant jobs.[6]

The *point method* of job evaluation examines several factors common to the jobs being evaluated, and then rates each job along a scale of each factor. The scales are divided into point distances—thus, the name "point" method. For example, if it is determined that "responsibility," "skill," "effort," and "working conditions" are four important factors in determining relative job worth, a scale is devised that assigns different numbers of points to different degrees of these factors. In applying these scales to different jobs, the points are tallied up for each job to determine relative worth.[7]

Figure 19-2 shows the scale of points for the factor "latitude of responsibility" in a point system of job evaluation that has three major "areas"—"responsibility," "know-how," and "relationships"—and six subareas, or "factors" (see Figure 19-3). This particular system provides a total of 2,000 points, of which 800 points are allocated to "responsibility," 800 to "know-how," and 400 to "relationships." For an illustration of how points were allocated relative to the job of "accounting clerk" using this system, see Figure 19-4.

This general scheme is identical to that of the graphic rating scale, which, the reader will recall, is the most widely used device in the appraisal of employees. (See Chapter 15). The only difference is that the latter is designed to rate people and the point method of job evaluation is designed to rate jobs.

Although the four factors mentioned above—responsibility, skill, effort, working conditions—are included in most point methods of

---

[4] Bureau of National Affairs, "Job Evaluation Policies and Procedures," *Personnel Policies Forum*, Survey No. 113, June 1976, pp. 1–3.

[5] Bureau of National Affairs, "Job Evaluation Policies and Procedures," p. 4; William R. Spriegel, John R. Beishline, and Alfred G. Dale, *Personnel Practices in Industry*, Personnel Study No. 8, rev., (Austin: Bureau of Business Research, The University of Texas, 1958), p. 47; and Karl O. Mann, "Characteristics of Job Evaluation Programs," *Personnel Administration*, 28:45–47 (September-October 1965).

[6] Bureau of National Affairs, "Job Evaluation Policies and Procedures," p. 4.

[7] For a detailed description of this and other methods of job evaluation, see David W. Belcher, *Compensation Administration* (Englewood Cliffs, N.J.: Prentice-Hall, Inc., 1974), pp. 142–198; Joseph J. Famularo, ed., *Handbook of Modern Personnel Administration* (New York: McGraw-Hill Book Company, 1972), pp. 28–1 through 31-17; J.D. Dunn and F.M. Rachel, *Wage and Salary Administration: Total Compensation Systems* (New York: McGraw-Hill Book Company, 1971), Chapter 10; Leonard R. Burgess, *Wage and Salary Administration in a Dynamic Economy* (New York: Harcourt, Brace & World, 1968), Chapter 3; and Robert E. Sibson, *Wages and Salaries: A Handbook for Line Managers*, rev. ed. (New York: American Management Association, Inc., 1967).

Figure **19-2**   "Latitude of responsibility" scale of a point method of job evaluation

A. *Latitude:* Freedom to act as measured by the existence or absence of personal or procedural control over position.

	20	95	67	115	120	305	400

Prescribed	Controlled	Standardized	Generally regulated	Directed	Broad guidance
Directed & detailed instructions; close supervision.	Established work routines; close supervision.	Basic practices & procedures are regulated; general work instructions; supervision of progress & results.	Practices & procedures covered by precedents or well defined policy; supervisory review.	Broad practice & procedures covered by functional precedents & policies; managerial direction.	Subject only to broad policy and general management guidance.

Used with permission.

Figure **19-3**   System total—2,000 points

Areas		Factors		
Responsibility 40% (800 points)	50%	Latitude	(20% of whole)
	50%	Authority	(20% of whole)
Know-how 40% (800 points)	30%	Diversity	(12% of whole)
	30%	Degree	(12% of whole)
	40%	Application	(16% of whole)
Relationships 20% (400 points)	100%	Human-relations skill	(20% of whole)

Used with permission.

Figure **19-4**   Points allocated to an accounting clerk position

Responsibility

   Latitude   120

   Authority   83

Know-how

   Diversity   97

   Degree   126

   Application   120

Relationship

   Human relations skill   100

   TOTAL SCORE   646

   SALARY GRADE   7

DATE SCORED _____   BY: _____

                                                                 CHECKED: _____

Used with permission.

job evaluation, a wide variety of additional factors is commonly used by this method as well as by others. As few as three and as many as twenty-five or more are found in use, with the national average at about ten.[8] Other factors might be "complexity of job," "education and experience required," "mental requirements," "Supervisory responsibility," "responsibility for equipment," "outside contacts," and so forth.

Upon inspection, many of the additional factors are seen to be subdivisions of the four factors mentioned above or to be closely overlapping. Statistical research verifies this apparent intercorrelation of factors, with one author citing more than twenty studies indicating that two to four factors will determine the relative

worth of jobs just as well as a large number of factors.[9]

The *factor-comparison method* is far more complicated than the point method, and I shall not attempt to describe its intricacies. Its essential features involve ranking "key" jobs[10] in relation to other key jobs on the basis of each of several factors, determining what part of the present rate of pay for the specific job is allocated to each factor, and then ranking the remainder of the jobs to be evaluated in their proper places in the framework thus established. In this method, the points tallied to determine relative worth emerge as cents per

[8]E. Lanham, *Job Evaluation* (New York: McGraw-Hill Book Company, 1955), pp. 76–77.

[9]David W. Belcher, "Employee and Executive Compensation," in H.G. Heneman et al., eds., *Employment Relations Research* (New York: Harper & Brothers, 1960), pp. 89–118.
[10]Jobs that are commonly understood and about which there is little disagreement as to the appropriateness of the current rate of pay.

hour. The chief problems with the factor-comparison method stem from its complexity, which requires considerable training of raters and time spent in rating and which creates the possibility of resentment and suspicion among employees who may not understand the method.

The *classification method* of job evaluation starts with one-paragraph verbal descriptions of a number of levels, grades, or "classes" of jobs. These descriptions feature gradations of job responsibility, skill required, and the like. Job descriptions are then examined, and jobs are classified into the grades or levels that seem to be the most appropriate.

In contrast with the point and factor-comparison methods, the classification method requires a decision at the outset on the number of pay grades to be included in the wage and salary plan. Actual amounts to be assigned to the pay grades, of course, may be made after the job evaluation is completed.

The *ranking method* of job evaluation simply lists the relative worth of the various jobs examined. No attempt is made to determine the critical factors of the job; only an overall judgment of the relative worth of the job is made.

Because of the difficulties in ranking a large number of jobs at one time, the "paired comparison" technique of ranking is sometimes used. (See Chapter 15 for a description of this technique.) With this technique, decisions are made about the relative worth of only two jobs at a time.

The chief disadvantage of the ranking method is that there are usually no agreed-upon guides to what elements or aspects of jobs the organization considers valuable; thus, there are no "yardsticks" for the job, and, obviously, the underlying assumptions of those doing the ranking cannot be examined. There is also a further danger that ranking will be done in a very subjective fashion and will be based on impressions rather than fact. The method thus contrasts with the first three methods discussed where the factors used are at least open to perusal and challenge by those applying the technique. These deficiencies can be minimized, of course, by agreement about the elements to be considered in ranking and by referring to job descriptions, as in the other methods.

A number of additional problems arise in job evaluation. We have already mentioned the problem of gaining acceptance by employees and management of the job evaluation concept and the particular plan to be used. Another problem is whether to have one plan for all jobs or two or more plans to cover different employee groups. For example, the factors and scales used for production and maintenance jobs are usually not adequate yardsticks when it comes to evaluating sales, office, or executive positions.[11]

Another problem is selecting managers to participate in job evaluation committees. Broad understanding and acceptance requires considerable participation by the managers whose subordinates are affected; on the other hand, large committees are expensive and sometimes unwieldy. Still another question is the frequency with which jobs should be reevaluated and the procedure for evaluating newly created jobs.

A particularly difficult problem arises when jobs involve unusually hazardous work, such as dealing with radioactive materials, toxic substances, and the like. Typical practice is to avoid paying premium rates for the hazard itself, but to require safety practices and equipment that increase the complexity of the job and thus increase the job's worth as reflected in job

[11] For a discussion of job evaluation as applied to management jobs, see Philip H. Dutter, "Compensation Plans for Executives," in Famularo, *Handbook of Modern Personnel Administration*, pp. 32-1 through 32-14.

evaluation.[12] Another difficult problem is what to do if the relative worth of a job, as determined by job evaluation, is not consistent with the going wage in the labor market.

WAGE SURVEYS

Once the relative worth of jobs has been determined by job evaluation, the actual amounts to be paid must be determined. A major factor in making such decisions is the survey of wages and salaries. Since wage and salary practices of other firms have an effect on the selection, morale, and retention of employees, attention is ordinarily given to prevailing wage levels in the community or industry.

Most firms either participate in wage surveys and receive copies of results, or else they conduct their own. These surveys may be carried out by mail, telephone, or interview. In addition, wage surveys are periodically published by such organizations as the American Society for Personnel Administration, the American Management Association, the U.S. Bureau of Labor Statistics, and various trade and professional associations. One study found over 95 percent of responding firms using wage surveys in their programs of wage and salary administration.[13]

One of the main problems in wage surveys is making between-company comparisons of jobs. Unless careful investigation is made of the actual scope and responsibility of the jobs surveyed, job titles or brief descriptions can be misleading. Another problem is the statistics

to be used in collecting and analyzing data. Simple averages of wages paid by firms for a certain job do not take into account total numbers of employees. On the other hand, averages weighted with number of employees may be distorted by including large firms whose practices may be atypical or impossible to emulate. Other questions are whether to include suburban rates of pay in the same study with urban rates and the extent to which fringe benefits should be surveyed along with wage levels.

ANALYSIS OF RELEVANT ORGANIZATIONAL PROBLEMS

Numerous dimensions or problems must be considered in establishing the wage structure in addition to the results of job evaluation and wage surveys. For example, are there well-established and well-accepted relationships among certain jobs that would be upset by job evaluation? Or is the lack of job evaluation perpetuating discrimination against women? Using the revised structure, will the organization be able to recruit new employees? Are there certain skills in such short supply that the prevailing rates in the community or industry are not consistent with the results of job evaluation? What if job evaluation shows that certain jobs are underpaid compared to others, but the labor market makes it relatively easy to recruit people into these jobs anyway? What pressures will be brought to bear on the employer if job evaluation results in certain jobs being paid significantly more than going community rates? What will happen to the wages of employees found to be overpaid through job evaluation? What should be the relationship between the wage structure and the fringe-benefit structure?[14] These and other problems must be con-

---

[12] See Francis D. Harding, "Incentives for Hazardous Work: A Survey," *Personnel*, 36:72–79 (May-June 1959).

[13] Bureau of National Affairs, "Wage and Salary Administration," *Personnel Policies Forum*, Survey No. 97, July 1972, pp. 1–6. Some firms find themselves so deluged with surveys requesting information that they have been forced to develop criteria by which to choose the surveys in which they will participate. See Orval R. Grigsby and William C. Burns, "Salary Surveys—The Deluge," *Personnel Journal*, 41:274–280 (June 1962).

[14] One author lists 108 variables that can affect levels of compensation and the wage structure. See David W. Belcher,

sidered in establishing the wage structure of an organization. Some of these problems will be discussed under the next topic; others will be discussed later in the chapter.

DETERMINING THE WAGE STRUCTURE

Decisions about the actual structure of wages and salaries are typically made after the relative worth of jobs has been decided (job evaluation), after prevailing wage and salary practices have been ascertained (surveys),[15] and after relevant organizational problems have been considered. Several decisions must then be made, including (a) whether the organization wishes, or is able, to pay amounts above, below, or equal to the averages in the community or industry; (b) whether wage ranges should provide for merit increases or whether there should be single rates; (c) the number and width of pay grades and the extent of overlap; (d) which jobs are to be placed in each of the pay grades; (e) the actual dollar amounts to be assigned to various pay grades; (f) differentials between pay plans; and (g) what to do with salaries that are out of line once these decisions have been made.

Although there are no rules for making such decisions, one procedure commonly used is the two-dimensional graph on which job evaluation points for key jobs are plotted against actual amounts paid or against desired levels. (In the case of the ranking or classification methods of job evaluation, the rank number or grade number can be used as points.) Plotting the remaining jobs then reveals which jobs seem to be improperly paid with respect to the key jobs

and to each other. Any clustering of jobs can also be observed and will thus suggest which jobs may be grouped in different pay grades. Lines are sometimes drawn through the key jobs on these graphs to suggest the approximate contour that the remaining jobs should follow. A "least squares" or regression line is sometimes computed mathematically to represent more accurately the present relationship between points and dollars on key jobs.[16]

Figure 19-5 shows the points obtained through a point method of job evaluation plotted against actual salary levels in a hypothetical situation. A trend line has been drawn by inspection, and two jobs that appear overpaid and underpaid are identified.

Most organizations probably pay a standard rate for all jobs in the same pay grade in the case of production and maintenance workers, although it appears that a sizable minority of firms makes use of wage ranges. About 29 percent of firms surveyed in one study used merit rating for wages of blue-collar workers, which suggests that at least this percentage provided ranges for the various grades or classes of jobs. In the case of nonexempt salaried employees, about 48 percent of the firms surveyed used merit rating for salary administration, which suggests that at least this percentage of firms used salary ranges for such employees.[17] Since progression in salaries based on length of service or a combination of seniority and merit is used in many situations, the percentage of

---

Wage and Salary Administration, 2nd ed., (Englewood Cliffs, N.J.: Prentice-Hall, Inc., 1962).

[15] Competitive wages in the area are the most important factor in determining general wage levels for nonmanagement jobs, while industry comparisons are the most important for determining management salary levels. See Bureau of National Affairs, "Wage and Salary Administration," p. 2.

[16] For a description of some of the mathematics and techniques used in establishing pay grades, see Belcher, *Compensation Administration,* pp. 257–272; Allan N. Nash and Stephen J. Carroll, Jr., *The Management of Compensation* (Monterey, Calif.: Brooks/Cole Publishing Company, 1975), Chapter 5; Burgess, "Wage and Salary Distribution," Chapter 3; and Edward N. Hay, "How to Create Salary Grades," in M. Joseph Dooher and Vivienne Marquis, eds., *The AMA Handbook of Wage and Salary Administration* (New York: American Management Association, 1950), pp. 212–225.

[17] Interpretation of Bureau of National Affairs, "Employee Performance: Evaluation and Control," *Personnel Policies Forum,* Survey No. 108, February 1975, pp. 1–9.

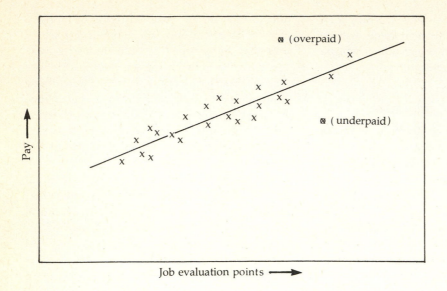

Figure **19-5** Job evaluation points plotted against pay, showing "overpaid" and "underpaid" jobs

firms using ranges is probably considerably higher than those figures. Most pay plans for exempt salaried employees provide for salary ranges, with the width of ranges as a percentage of the base of the range significantly higher in the case of top-management jobs than in middle-management jobs.[18]

The number of pay grades within a particular pay plan will depend partly on the number of such plans in a given firm. In any event, the number of pay grades found in industry is not standardized; the number in any one plan probably varies from as few as five to as high as thirty.

Like the number of pay grades, the width of pay grades is not standardized. In the case of

hourly jobs, the maximums of individual pay grades may vary from 10 percent to 20 percent above the minimums, while in the case of salaried employees the maximums of pay grades may vary from 15 percent to 75 percent above the minimums.[19] One study of supervisory pay ranges found a fairly consistent spread of about 33 percent between maximums and minimums.[20] Practices with respect to overlap of ranges also vary, although typical practice is to have some overlap.

Some authors have argued that there should be only one comprehensive pay plan for each organization, but it is probably more realistic to have several pay plans. A large number of factors, including pressures from the labor market and the diversity of jobs within the organization, makes the adoption of several such plans almost mandatory. This fact has been acknowl-

[18]One study found 6 out of 301 firms, that is, 2 percent providing supplemental pay or special maximum job rates for the specific purpose of rewarding length of service. Thirty-four, or 13 percent, provided cash bonuses for length of service. National Industrial Conference Board, "Recognition for Long Service," *Studies in Personnel Policy,* No. 106, 1950, pp. 21–23. See also "Wage Increases for Long Service," *Management Record,* 15:166–168 (May 1953).

[19]Belcher, *Compensation Administration,* p. 345.
[20]Dean H. Rosensteel, "Supervisory Compensation—An Interim Report," *Personnel,* 33:356 (January 1957).

edged in the *cluster concept* of wage-determination theory. Dunlop describes the cluster concept as follows.

A job cluster is defined as a stable group of job classifications or work assignments within a firm . . . which are so linked together by (1) technology, (2) the administrative organization of the production process, including policies of transfer, layoff and promotion, or (3) social custom that they have common wage-making characteristics. . . .

Thus the employees on a furnace or a mill and the crew of a train or plane may constitute a job cluster (technology); so also may employees in a department (administrative organization), or the salesgirls in a department store or the stenographers in an office (social custom). . . . Certain job clusters may be more closely related to some rather than to other clusters. In this sense, clerical rates as a whole may be more closely related to other clerical rates than to managerial or factory rates. . . .[21]

Livernash further describes job clusters in the same book:

. . . Broad groups may be illustrated within manufacturing as (1) managerial-executive, administrative, professional, and supervisory; (2) clerical, and (3) factory. Within each broad group, narrower groups are obvious. Within the factory group are maintenance, inspection, transportation, and production. Within production are certain smaller groups, varying with the nature of the industry.[22]

As a consequence, several pay plans for each organization are probably necessary. However, job clusters in which women are predominantly employed need to be carefully compared with others in order to avoid the perpetuation of customs that are discriminatory.

It is important, however, that these different pay structures be kept in some meaningful and explainable balance with each other. For example, it is important that there be adequate differentials between superiors and subordinates whether they are paid under the same pay plan or under different ones. Obviously, serious repercussions will occur if the pay of subordinates is allowed to exceed that of superiors. When the pay of one group is changed, attention must be given to the pay level of the other.

Significant differences in salary between subordinates and superiors is common practice. One study reports typical differentials between rank-and-file jobs and supervisory jobs ranging from 15 to 25 percent.[23] Other studies have found differentials between the company's chief executives and their immediate subordinates varying widely by industry, with the second-highest-paid executives receiving salaries of from 60 to 95 percent of the chief's salary, depending upon the industry.[24] In a third study, the after-tax earnings of the number-two executive averaged 67 percent of the president's after-tax earnings.[25]

More broadly, appropriate differentials must be maintained between the "exempt" and "nonexempt" groups. Exempt employees are those in executive, administrative, professional, or outside sales jobs as defined by the Wage and Hour Administrator and exempt from the overtime provisions of the Fair Labor Standards and the Walsh-Healy Acts. Through lack of attention, inadequate differentials between this

[21] John T. Dunlop, "The Task of Contemporary Wage Theory," in George W. Taylor and Frank C. Pierson, eds., *New Concepts in Wage Determination* (New York: McGraw-Hill Book Company, 1957), pp. 129–130.

[22] Robert Livernash, "The Internal Wage Structure," in Taylor and Pierson, eds., *New Concepts in Wage Determination*, p. 148. For research on equity theory that tends to confirm the wisdom of having different compensation plans for different employee groups, see D.W. Belcher and T.J. Atchison, "Equity Theory and Compensation Policy," *Personnel Administration*, 33:22–33 (July-August 1970).

[23] Bureau of National Affairs, "Wage Policies in an Inflationary Period," *Personnel Policies Forum*, Survey No. 56, March 1960, p. 4.

[24] See Arch Patton, "Top Executive Pay: New Facts and Figures," *Harvard Business Review*, 44:94–97 (September-October 1966); and Wilbur G. Lewellen, "Executives Lose Out, Even with Options," *Harvard Business Review*, 46:127–142 (January-February 1968).

[25] Lewellen, "Executives Lose Out," p. 138. See also National Industrial Board, "Top Executive Compensation," *Studies in Personnel Policy*, No. 204, 1966.

group and the nonexempt employees may develop, thus producing serious morale problems for the exempt employees.[26]

A particularly difficult problem arises when scientists or engineers work under the supervision of nonscientists. Competition in the labor market has sometimes tended to force salaries of technical employees upward at a faster rate than managerial salaries in general, and drastic narrowing of differentials—and sometimes reversals—have occurred in many companies. There is no easy solution to this problem, but it demonstrates the importance of paying constant attention to relative job worth and maintaining a meaningful and explainable balance among "job clusters."

Because of the continuous rise in wage and salary levels experienced in this country, a rise resulting from a variety of environmental pressures, considerable thought must be given to handling upward changes in the wage and salary structure. Some firms meet the problem by giving general percentage or across-the-board pay increases shortly after wage increases are negotiated in the unionized part of the firm and keeping such adjustments separate from merit or length-of-service increases. Other companies include a general adjustment factor in merit or length-of-service raises, although the organization may not label it as such. Since most employees recognize the gradual upward movement of wage and salary levels, the wisest course seems to be to identify general adjustments clearly and not attempt to disguise them as merit increases.

According to one study, a high percentage of personnel directors prefer doing away with general wage adjustments.[27] In my opinion,

general adjustments are inevitable in an inflationary period. If general adjustments are given under the guise of merit increases, it can lead to the employees' accusation that management is trying "to pull the wool over our eyes." One solution to the problem of keeping a wage structure in line with living costs during an inflationary period is to move the structure in proportion to changes in the Consumer Price Index published by the Bureau of Labor Statistics. This practice was adopted in many union-management agreements after escalator provisions were negotiated in the automobile industry in 1948 to protect the purchasing power of agreements.[28] However, cost-of-living increases have been attacked as contributing factors in the inflationary spiral.

RULES OF ADMINISTRATION

Other rules of administration need to be developed in addition to rules pertaining to general adjustments, overpaid and underpaid employees, and differentials between subordinates and superiors. For example, it must be determined to what degree advancement will be based on length of service rather than merit, with what frequency pay increases will be awarded, how controls over wage and salary costs can be maintained, and what rules will govern promotion from one pay grade to another. (See Figure 21-2, Chapter 21, for the proportion of plant and office workers under pay plans with progression based on merit. See also Chapter 15.)

One of the difficulties in wage administration is the problem of relating merit-rating decisions to actual dollar increases. Although some com-

[26]For an elaboration of this problem, see William G. Hoke, "Equity for Exempt Personnel," *The Personnel Administrator*, 21:41–46 (July 1976).
[27]See Bureau of National Affairs, "Wage Policies in an Inflationary Period," pp. 1–13. See also George W. Torrence, "Individual vs. General Salary Increases," *Management Record*, 23:18–20 (May 1961).

[28]By 1958 there were 4,500,000 workers under escalation, but three years later the figure had dropped to about 2,500,000. See Evan Clague, "Some Relationships of Productivity to Wages," in *Profit Sharing and Productivity Motivation* (Madison, Wisc.: Center for Productivity Motivation, School of Commerce, the University of Wisconsin, 1961), pp. 10–11.

panies have attempted to relate merit rating to pay increases on a mathematical basis, procedures allowing for more judgment about specific situations are probably wiser. In any event, decisions must be made in translating merit ranking of employees into meaningful decisions about the size and frequency of pay increases.[29]

Another problem arises from a change in wage and salary practices and structure that affects the relative wages of employees. What should be done about individual employees who appear to be overpaid or underpaid after such a change? Typical practice is to avoid reducing any salaries but to withhold general adjustments or merit increases until the company's pay structure catches up with the employee's rate of pay through inflationary pressure on overall wage levels. Sometimes overpayment is perpetuated until that particular employee retires. In contrast, typical practice when employees are found to be underpaid after job evaluation is to bring their salaries quickly up to the appropriate rate. These policies in relation to overpaid and underpaid employees, of course, make job evaluation and revision of an existing pay structure much more acceptable to employees.

More variables are ordinarily operating in pay increase decisions than most employees realize. Figure 19-6 shows many of the variables that are probably operating in most merit increase decisions. While a number of variables pertaining to individual performance typically enter into merit rating, another set of variables has little to do with individual performance. Some of the variables associated with individual performance might be the superior's perception of the person's goal attainment including whether high- or low-priority goals were

reached and the quantity and quality of work performed; the extent to which the person's skills are important to the future of the organization; unusually superior or deficient performance; day-to-day impressions; and the perceptions of others whose impressions are valued, such as the superior's opinion. Other dimensions might be the anticipated reaction of the employee or others to a given rating and any biases held by the superior about personality, age, sex, race, or the degree of compliance shown by the subordinate. These variables range from fairly objective dimensions to those that are highly subjective.

Some of the variables that have little to do with differential performance—but nevertheless are typically powerful dimensions in pay increase decisions—are budgetary considerations (these have produced wide fluctuations in salary increases in some industries, e.g., in the public schools and in universities), the need to maintain differentials between nonexempt and exempt employees, first-level supervision and middle management, etc.; the current state of morale among different groups of employees; the extent to which the organization chooses to have salary levels correspond with inflation or cost-of-living levels; labor market competition; affirmative action requirements. (For example, the organization may be under considerable pressure, if not a court order, to raise salary levels of women.) Educational, training, and/or seniority attainment will also be factors if the organization has policies of moving employees to higher pay brackets if they complete a particular academic degree or training requirement, or if pay plans have an automatic progression based on length of service. Some of these variables are forces largely internal to the organization; others are directly attributable to external events. Thus, merit increases are frequently a compromise between a number of variables operating simultaneously, many of which have little to do with differential performance.

[29] For a plan that features more frequent pay raises for superior performers, see Arthur A. Handy, Jr., "Pay-for-Performance," *The Personnel Administrator*, 17:27–29 (May-June 1972).

Figure **19-6**   Probable variables affecting pay increase decisions

Superior's perceptions of performance based on	Pay increase decisions based on
Subjective — **Objective**	

Goal attainment
   Priority of accomplishments
   Quantity and quality	

Observed skills, and projected future value of these skills to organization	
Critical incidents (unusually superior or deficient performance)	Merit rating (differential rating of subordinates)
Impressions from day-to-day inter-actions, observations	
Perceptions of others (superior's superior, etc.)	
Biases (personality, age, sex, race, compliance, etc.)	
Anticipated reaction (positive and negative from the individual, work group, union, etc.)	

Pay increase decisions

Forces internal to the organization	Budgetary considerations
	Need for differentials be-tween groups, levels, etc.
	Educational/training/ seniority policies
	Morale levels
Forces external to the organization	Inflation/cost-of-living
	Labor market competition
	Affirmative action require-ments

Rules are also needed to maintain some control over wage and salary expenditures by the firm. One technique used successfully is the *compa-ratio*. This is simply a calculation that tells to what degree the jobs within a pay grade will average out near the midpoint of the range. Since a figure of 100 is established as the midpoint value, a compa-ratio of 105 would mean that the average salary paid for the jobs in that pay grade is 5 percent above the midpoint.[30] Compa-ratios are used as controls by requiring departmental managers to stay within certain percentage limits in the case of each job grade or for all job grades combined. Other indexes

[30]See Edward N. Hay, "A Program of Salary Administration," in *The AMA Handbook of Wage and Salary Administration,* pp. 233–234.

that can be used in wage and salary control are budgets, comparisons among departments or divisions, total payroll, and unit labor costs.

Additional rules are needed for handling promotions and demotions from one pay grade to another or from one pay plan to another. Since managers are tempted to exert pressure to obtain more money for persons who have reached the top of a range—particularly long-service employees—control must be maintained to resist such pressures, or else, people are moved into higher pay brackets when there has been no genuine promotion. Such practices tend to subvert the meaning and usefulness of job evaluation, and salaries begin to reflect age or length of service instead of worth to the organization.

MATURITY CURVES

Many firms use a device called the "maturity curve" in salary administration programs pertaining to engineers and scientists, which either supplements or replaces job descriptions, job evaluations, and pay ranges. Its most widespread use is in making comparisons with other companies.[31] This device is simply a graph that plots salaries against age or against years of relevant experience. As a rule, the vertical axis is salary, and the horizontal axis represents age or years of experience. Median salaries for each age group (or for each group of different years' experience) are usually plotted, resulting in a curve against which individuals can be compared.

As shown in Figure 19-7, additional statistics can be plotted, including percentiles, medians for different salary groups within age groups, and the like. Using Figure 19-7 merely as an example, because these curves are not intended to represent current salary levels, the median monthly salary for the thirty-year-old group is about $1,450 and for the fifty-year-old group, about $2,050. Among the top 10 percent, the median salary for the age-thirty group is almost $2,000, and about $2,950 for the age-fifty group.

Criticisms of the maturity curve have been that too much emphasis is placed on age or length of experience,[32] that it is not tied closely enough to actual responsibilities and performance, and that it gives employees the notion that they are on a "salary escalator" that increases salary with age without any change in performance. Another criticism is that it is an "easy way out" and that technical-professional jobs can, and should be, evaluated with traditional job evaluation methods.[33] Those arguing for the maturity curve include those who would use it as a substitute for job evaluation and other salary-administration devices, as well as those who would use it only as one device supplementing more traditional methods.

In my opinion, the maturity curve can be a useful device as a supplemental tool, but care must be exercised to insure that the main emphasis in compensating scientists and engineers is on the contribution of the professional to the enterprise's goals. No doubt the assumption that age and years of experience are correlated with contribution to the enterprise's goals has some validity, but the assumption is not always true, and it ignores other, more relevant variables, such as drive, intelligence, and

[31] This discussion draws extensively from George W. Torrence, "Maturity Curves and Salary Administration," *Management Record*, 24:14–17 (January 1962). See also E.L. Reynard, "Updating Salary Information for Scientific and Technical Positions: A Statistical Approach," *Compensation Review*, 8:36–43 (First Quarter 1976). The term *career curve* is also sometimes used. See Robert E. Sibson, "Establishing Formal Pay Programs," in *Optimum Use of Engineering Talent* (New York: American Management Association, 1961), p. 219.

[32] Grigsby and Burns, *Salary Surveys—The Deluge*, pp. 276–277; and William F. Dinsmore, "The Case for Evaluating Professional Jobs," *Personnel*, 41:54–64 (November-December 1964).

[33] See Torrence, "Maturity Curves," p. 17.

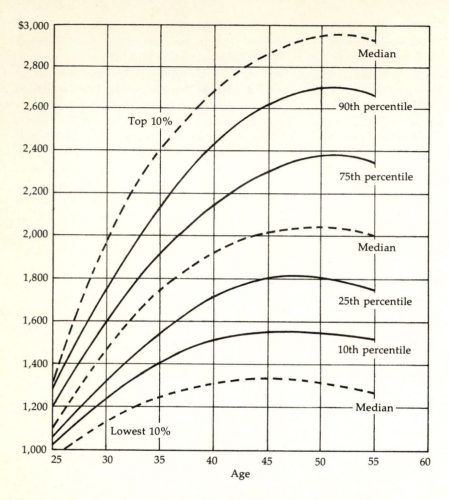

Figure 19-7 Maturity curve with percentiles and medians for top and bottom 10 percent

judgment.[34] Furthermore, the assumption that performance tapers off and/or that compensation should peak or perhaps decline in a per-

son's late forties or early fifties is open to serious question. In a study of 2,500 design and development engineers in six companies, Dalton and Thompson found, on the average, performance ratings declined *in their early thirties* and salary increases dropped dramatically at about age thirty-seven.[35]

[34] For detailed criticisms of the age-value assumption, see Grigsby and Burns, *Salary Surveys—The Deluge*, pp. 276–277. For further discussion of the maturity curve concept, see Thomas H. Patten, Jr., "Maturity-Pay Curves in a Floating Labor Market: The Case of Southern California," *The Quarterly Review of Economics and Business*, 7:57–72 (Fall 1967); and James Tait Elder, "Salary Comparison Method for Experienced Technical Personnel," *Personnel Journal*, 47:467–474 (July 1968).

[35] Gene W. Dalton and Paul H. Thompson, "Accelerating Obsolescence of Older Engineers," *Harvard Business Review*, 49:57–67 (September-October 1971).

From my experience, the classification method of job evaluation also seems to be widely used by aerospace firms and other firms employing relatively large numbers of technical-professional employees. Since the details of technical jobs are likely to change frequently, the classification method, which compares jobs against general descriptions of categories that are really levels of professional work, is readily applicable.[36]

As I have implied, no magic formulae are available for converting differences in performance to differences in paychecks, and management must consider a variety of factors in making such judgments, including the company's ability to pay and labor-market competition. However, there are those who believe that differentials in salary among below average, average, and outstanding performers are generally inadequate. One author states that productivity of scientists and engineers in governmental research varies by a factor of nearly 100, but their compensation varies by a factor of only about $2\frac{1}{2}$.[37] That is, the scientist producing 100 times as much as the poorest performer might make only $2\frac{1}{2}$ times the salary of the latter.

The extent to which employees are informed of the details of wage and salary programs varies with type of job, with companies, and with aspects of the wage programs. Although most hourly paid workers are informed through the wage contract about the details of wage programs, including wages paid to individuals, probably a substantially smaller percentage of salaried workers have such information about their jobs. Salaried workers are more likely to have information about ranges than about specific salaries.

One study of fifty-five companies found 95 percent of the firms giving general oral explanations of the salary program to the lower- or middle-level exempt employees. Information conveyed included a statement that there was a job evaluation program, that salaries reflected both the requirements of the job and the performance of the employee, that salary surveys were conducted periodically, and that individual performance was reviewed regularly. In 71 percent of the companies, the employee was informed of the maximum salary for her or his own position, but usually only upon request. In 85 percent of the companies, the employee was informed when at or near the maximum salary he or she could expect to earn on the particular job.[38]

A serious drawback to distributing information about actual salaries paid to individuals is the friction that seems to result from such disclosures. Though management may be prepared to defend its overall program, it often has difficulty justifying the legitimacy of minor differentials among employees. Since people are likely to make judgments about their own performance compared to that of their peers and these judgments are likely to differ from those made by higher management, disagreement over relative ranking is bound to occur. Most managements minimize this problem by trying to maintain secrecy about salary data. Secrecy becomes a control assumed to reduce the time and effort management must spend in dealing with complaints. Paradoxically, although I sometimes hear managers complaining that "everyone knows what everyone else is making," I know of no research that has studied the extent of employees' knowledge about specific salaries.

Some research, however, suggests that secrecy about average salaries and ranges in the

---

[36] See Sibson, "Establishing Formal Pay Programs," pp. 216–217.

[37] Robert M. Page, "Motivations of Scientists and Engineers," *Personnel Administration*, 21:32 (September-October 1958).

[38] George W. Torrence, "Explaining Salary Programs to Salaried Employees," *Management Record*, 23:15–17 (July-August 1961).

salaries of groups (not necessarily actual salaries) may create dissatisfaction rather than prevent it. It may also vitiate the potential motivating effects of disclosure. Lawler surveyed 563 middle and lower managers in seven organizations and found that managers tended (a) to underestimate the salaries of their superiors, (b) to overestimate the salaries of subordinate levels, and (c) to overestimate the salaries of their peers. Associated with these inaccuracies in perception was dissatisfaction about the differentials among themselves and both superiors and subordinates.[39] However, Schuster and Colletti queried 575 professional employees in an organization and found that only about half were willing to have their salaries known to others. This held true by occupational group, by self-assessed performance level, and by age. There was some tendency for the more highly paid persons to prefer to have salaries kept confidential.[40]

GUARANTEED ANNUAL WAGES

An interesting concept relative to the rules of administering wage payments is that of the guaranteed annual wage (GAW). Not at all widespread, GAW plans are found in only a few companies. GAW plans first appeared in the late 1880s at the initiative of each company's management and have only gradually grown in number.[41] A 1964 study reported that 2.8 percent of responding firms guaranteed wages or employment to hourly paid workers for a definite period.[42] Although union demands for such plans increased in the late 1940s and early 1950s, these demands have diminished with union successes in obtaining supplemental unemployment benefits (SUB), which substantially decrease financial hardships upon layoff.[43] (See also Chapters 14 and 17.)

Actually, the word *guaranteed* in GAW plans may be a misnomer, since many plans may be terminated at short notice and are not backed by reserve funds. In addition, it would be more accurate to speak of guaranteed *employment*, since most plans guarantee so many hours or days of work.[44]

One study reports that two-thirds of GAW plans "guarantee" full employment at full pay for one year, and that one-third of all plans cover most workers in the organizations using them.[45] Beginning in 1968, under a contract negotiated with the United Auto Workers, Ford Motor Company workers with seven years' seniority were entitled to 95 percent of normal pay for up to a year during a layoff.[46] Most plans limit eligibility to those who have been on the payroll for a certain length of time.

GAW plans typically require extra managerial attention to planning and work scheduling so that the work force can be productively utilized and idle time minimized. Changes in marketing, maintenance, construction, transfers, and

[39] Edward E. Lawler III, "The Mythology of Management Compensation," *California Management Review*, 9:11–12 (Fall 1966).

[40] Jay Schuster and Jerome Colletti, "Pay Secrecy: Who Is For and Against It?" *Academy of Management Journal*, 16:35–40 (March 1973).

[41] Murray W. Latimer, "Guaranteed Wages," in E. Wight Bakke, Clark Kerr, and Charles W. Anrod, eds., *Unions, Management, and the Public*, 2nd ed. (New York: Harcourt, Brace & Company, 1960), p. 403. The most frequently mentioned plans are those of George A. Hormel & Co., the Nunn-Bush Shoe Company, and Procter & Gamble.

[42] National Industrial Conference Board, "Personnel Practices in Factory and Office: Manufacturing," *Studies in Personnel Policy*, No. 194, 1964, p. 113.

[43] For a history and description of such plans, see Dorothy R. Kittner, "Supplemental Unemployment Benefit Plans," *Unemployment Insurance Review*, 4:1–10 (August 1967).

[44] Sumner H. Slichter, "Guaranteed Annual Wage Plans and Supplementary Unemployment Compensation," in *Industry at the Bargaining Table*, Personnel Series, No. 156 (New York: American Management Association, 1954), p. 3.

[45] Latimer, "Guaranteed Wages," p. 404.

[46] *Monthly Labor Review*, 91:III (January 1968). See also V.E. Lunardi, "The Push for a Guaranteed Annual Wage," *Factory*, 125:82–85 (November 1967).

many other aspects of the company's operations are likely to be made.[47] Unless the number of employees can be stabilized, such plans entail major cost risks for employers. Thus, such plans may be impractical in cyclical industries or in marginal companies that are the first to feel cutbacks in demand for their products.[48] It is likely, however, that the use of operations research and electronic data-processing equipment can significantly increase management's ability to stabilize employment.

WAGE STATUS VERSUS SALARIED

In recent years, usually at the initiative of management, but sometimes as a result of collective bargaining, a few companies have placed production and maintenance workers on salaried status. A variety of motives has probably prompted this move, but, in general, the change has been based on a perception that (a) the particular company had a stable work situation with only minor daily or weekly fluctuations; (b) many blue-collar jobs were not much different from white-collar jobs; (c) the economic implications of placing workers on salaried status were not great; (d) differences between the salaried and wage payroll in terms of sick-pay eligibility, time off with pay for personal business, and so forth, were irritating to the hourly paid employees and difficult to justify; (e) salaried status carried greater prestige; and (f) salaried status would probably result in better relations with employees and greater identification of employees with organizational goals. Some of the companies initiating this change include the Gillette Safety Razor Company, IBM, and the Cannon Electric Company

of Los Angeles.[49] Approximately 25,000 hourly employees at TI were paid on a salaried basis, beginning in 1968.[50]

Salaried status does not guarantee job security, however, although historically the salaried employee has been less subject to layoff or intermittent reduction in paid working time. Furthermore, computations of overtime pay for nonexempt salaried employees are usually identical with the computations for wage employees, since salaries are reduced to an hourly rate for such purpose.[51] In addition, salaried status does not necessarily imply higher basic wages, since many blue-collar workers are paid a higher hourly rate than many white-collar workers.

The major problems involved in shifting large groups of employees from wage to salaried status relate to the consequent changes in fringe benefits. The shift is sometimes accompanied by increasing supplemental benefits, such as sick leave, major medical insurance, severance pay, group life insurance, and time off for personal business.[52] Therefore, management must carefully examine the total cost implications and think through the purposes of such a move.

Another problem may be the reaction of those employees presently on the salaried payroll. If part of their "income" has been

[47]See Jack Chernick and George C. Helleckson, *Guaranteed Annual Wages* (Minneapolis: University of Minnesota Press, 1945), pp. 23–56.
[48]Slichter, "Guaranteed Annual Wage Plans," p. 5.
[49]See Paul G. Kaponya, "Salaries for *All* Workers," *Harvard Business Review*, 40:49–57 (May-June 1962); and Thomas R. Brooks, "Bleaching the Blue Collar," *Dun's Review and Modern Industry*, January 1962, pp. 58–64.
[50]*Monthly Labor Review*, 91:73 (February 1968).
[51]See administrative ruling under the Fair Labor Standards Act for regulations about pay computation. Since the number of hours varies with the number of days in the month, the hourly rate of monthly salaried employees is based on the average number of hours worked per month. Under a forty-hour week, the hourly rate of employees paid on a weekly basis is simply the weekly salary divided by forty.
[52]David A. Weeks, "Salaries for Blue Collar Workers," *The Conference Board Record*, 11:15 (November 1965), pp. 22–25; and "A Push for Blue-Collar Salaries," *Business Week*, February 5, 1967, pp. 135–136.

higher status and more liberal privileges and fringe benefits than those of hourly paid employees, they may react by agitating for re-establishment of some kind of differential or for higher wages—either through individual complaint or unionization. This reaction may be particularly evident in situations where (a) employees have rationalized their relatively lower wages in terms of better fringes or privileges, or (b) management has emphasized the "advantages" of the white-collar worker in communications with this group of employees.

IMPACT ON NEED FULFILLMENT

It seems a reasonable hypothesis that wage payments can enhance the fulfillment of most needs in the need hierarchy, but not completely, as we observed in relation to nonfinancial rewards. Wages are obviously used for filling physiological needs, such as food, shelter, and the like, although governmental and private agencies attempt to insure minimum levels of subsistence for those who are unemployed. Even with a broad-based public welfare program, however, there are probably many isolated cases where unemployment results in serious impairment of physiological well-being. For example, although a person may not be starving, lack of financial resources may seriously postpone or prevent proper medical or psychological treatment.

The frequency of wage payments can also enhance or frustrate the need for security. The desire for orderliness and predictability is certainly not furthered when wage payments are terminated through layoffs. The need for understanding and consistency is probably more affected by the methods used in determining wage and salary structure and levels than by the actual amounts paid. That is, if the procedures used result in a wage structure internally consistent or consistent except for unusual situa-

tions that are explainable and can be accepted, the need for wholeness is furthered. Furthermore, the need for understanding is enhanced when the methods of wage determination are explained to employees in understandable terms.[53]

Wage payments also affect the fulfillment of the needs for belonging and esteem. For example, in the case of merit pay, the degree of pay increase can be interpreted as one indication of the employee's worth to, and acceptance by, those in higher authority. Salary levels themselves have value for prestige and status, and they indicate relative worth, at least within broad occupational areas. In addition, salaried status tends to carry more prestige than wage status, since it is usually assumed that the former connotes more job security, better working conditions, and greater privileges.

Some authors have theorized that traditional merit-rating practices have an adverse impact on meeting needs for self-esteem. As discussed in Chapters 15 and 18, Thompson and Dalton believe that identifying "above average," "average," and "below average" performers tends to be demoralizing to those placed in the latter two categories. Placing more emphasis on a goals or results approach and using many kinds of feedback are seen as possible ways out of this dilemma.[54]

Meyer discusses the same dilemma and believes that pay based on merit rating frequently

[53] One of the reasons that labor unions have resisted job evaluation so strenuously in some situations has been the complexity of the particular plan promoted by management. For example, according to one labor leader: "Much of the complicated job evaluation technique is just hocus-pocus which prevents workers from understanding the pay system under which they work. Yet thorough understanding by workers of their rates is essential to a sustained high production and satisfactory worker-management relations." Boris Shishkin, "Job Evaluations, What It Means to Unionists," *American Federationist*, 54:21–22 (August 1947).

[54] Paul H. Thompson and Gene W. Dalton, "Performance Appraisal: Managers Beware," *Harvard Business Review*, 48:149–157 (January-February 1970).

Figure 19-8   Self-rating distributions for several employee groups

	Employee groups			
Self-ratings	Blue-collar group Plant A	Blue-collar group Plant B	Engineers in research laboratory	Accountants in several companies
Top 10%	46%	40%	29%	37%
Top 25%	26	28	57	40
Top 50%	26	28	14	20
Bottom 50%	1	2	0	3
Bottom 25%	0	0	0	0
Bottom 10%	0	0	0	0
No response	1	2	0	0
	100%	100%	100%	100%

Reprinted by permission of the publisher from Meyer, Herbert H., "The Pay for Performance Dilemma," *Organizational Dynamics*, Winter 1975, © 1975 by AMACOM, a division of American Management Associations.

demotivates rather than motivates because of the impact of average and below average appraisals on employees' self-esteem. Consistently, Meyer and other researchers have found that most people rate their own performance as well above average, and only 1 or 2 percent rate themselves below average when compared with their peers. (See Figure 19-8.) Supervisors, however, tend to rate these same people lower and, following the guidelines of most pay plans, cannot rate most people as superior. This, Meyer believes, ". . . lies at the root of most of our problems with merit plans. . . . The majority feel discriminated against because it appears that management does not recognize their true worth." Consequently, Meyer would give "all employees judged to be performing at a satisfactory level the same percentage increase whenever salaries are adjusted upward." Pay increases could be withheld from a small percent, and only after prior warning of inadequate performance.[55]

[55] Herbert H. Meyer, "The Pay-for-Performance Dilemma," *Organizational Dynamics*, 3:39–50 (Winter 1975).

Lawler counters that "[t]here is a great deal of research evidence that when pay is effectively tied to performance a number of good outcomes occur: employees are motivated, turnover occurs primarily among poor performers, and pay satisfaction is higher . . . pay satisfaction is highest when pay is based on performance." He goes on to say, ". . . you cannot satisfy everybody—but with merit pay, you can at least try to satisfy those who are the best performers and whom you wish to retain."[56] Lawler was undoubtedly citing his review of the research on individual merit plans, most of which appear to be incentive schemes tied directly to output in contrast to ratings by superiors.[57] There appears to be a dearth of research studies that focus on merit rating as it relates to subsequent job satisfaction and performance.

[56] Edward E. Lawler III, "Comments on Herbert H. Meyer's 'The Pay for Performance Dilemma,'" *Organizational Dynamics*, 4:73–75 (Winter 1976).
[57] See Edward E. Lawler III, *Pay and Organizational Effectiveness: A Psychological View* (New York: McGraw-Hill Book Company, 1971), pp. 118–128.

Figure **19-9**   Managers' mean ratings of criteria that are and should be used to determine the size of their salary increases

Criteria	Mean ratings are used	Mean ratings should be used	Difference
1. Level of job performance	5.35[a]	6.23[a]	.88*
2. Budgetary considerations	5.09[a]	4.53[b]	−.56*
3. Nature of job	4.77[a]	5.91[a]	1.14*
4. Amount of effort expended	4.71[a]	5.56[a]	.85*
5. Training and experience	4.50[a]	5.15[a]	.65*
6. Increases inside	4.42[a]	3.69[c]	−.73*
7. Increases outside	3.93[b]	4.64[b]	.71*
8. Cost of living	3.62[b]	5.21[a]	1.59*
9. Length of service	3.34[b]	3.31[d]	−.03

[a-d] Mean a values greater than b, mean b values greater than c, and so on ($p < .05$).
*$p < .01$.
Lee Dyer, Donald P. Schwab, and Roland D. Theriault, "Managerial Perceptions Regarding Salary Increase Criteria," *Personnel Psychology*, 29:237 (Summer 1976). Used with permission.

There are some studies, however, that show that managers want performance to be a major variable in pay determination. For example, Dyer et al. found that level of job performance was the item ranked highest by managers in terms of the importance they felt should be given to various items in determining their own pay increases. It was also the item ranked highest in terms of the criteria they believed to be actually used in determining their pay. (See Figure 19-9.) However, they believed that the nature of the job and the amount of effort expended should be given more weight than budgetary considerations, which in terms of criteria actually used was second only to job performance.[58] I conclude from this study that managers want ratings of their job performance to be tied to their pay, but that other factors are also important, and, if ignored, can lead to dissatisfaction.

Finally, wage payments are probably related to the fulfillment of the self-actualization needs, since financial resources open many avenues for self-actualization off the job. As one author puts it, ". . . money is the only form of incentive that is wholly negotiable, appealing to the widest possible range of seekers.[59] Thus, wage and salary payments make possible the fulfillment or the frustration of a wide variety of human needs. Monetary payments, then, can be expected to act as motivators and satisfiers interdependently with other job factors.

RELATIONSHIP TO OTHER ORGANIZATIONAL PROCESSES

The process of determining wages and salaries within the organization is interrelated with

[58] Lee Dyer, Donald P. Schwab, and Roland D. Theriault, "Managerial Perceptions Regarding Salary Increase Criteria," *Personnel Psychology*, 29:233–242 (Summer 1976). See also Edward E. Lawler III, "The Multitrait-Multirater Approach to Measuring Managerial Job Performance," *Journal of Applied Psychology*, 51:369–381 (1967).

[59] Crawford W. Greenewalt, *The Uncommon Man* (New York: McGraw-Hill Book Company, 1959), p. 38.

most of, if not all, the various organizational processes. In particular, it is related to the financial management process, since payments of wages and salaries are obviously one important area of finance. For example, commitments to pay a certain level of wages and salaries may result in a serious drain on financial resources and may thus limit the ability of the organization to invest in capital equipment, research and development, raw materials, and the like.[60] Similarly, commitments in these other areas limit the wages and salaries that can be paid. In addition, the process of compensation can obviously affect the quality of the administration of all organizational processes, since wage levels and the method of allocation will affect the quality of human resources that can be attracted to the organization, as well as the attitudes of the personnel assisting in the management of the various organizational processes.

Similarly, the compensating and staffing processes overlap in certain events, such as making salary offers to job applicants or to candidates for promotion. (In previous chapters, mention was made of the major impact on the salary structure of high beginning salaries paid new recruits when certain specialties are in short supply.)

Since job evaluation is based on job descriptions, which are in turn a reflection of the task-specialization process, the wage and salary structure will partly stem from the latter. Furthermore, the process of appraisal is a component of the compensating process whenever an attempt is made to evaluate the relative contribution of individuals and to reward them accordingly. In addition, the process of compensation can be considered an aspect of the training and developmental process, since the training and growth of individuals will be closely related to the organizational practices in rewards.

As I have discussed in Chapter 8, probably all allocations of rewards or penalties are interpreted as either fair or unfair, and thus the process of compensation is inseparable from the process of determining justice. And, as I have already suggested, the collective-bargaining process has a major impact on the allocation of rewards within the organization. Thus, the compensating process is intertwined with a complex network of other organizational processes.

IMPACT OF ENVIRONMENT

PREVAILING WAGES

As suggested by our discussion of wage and salary surveys, prevailing patterns in wages and salaries have an important impact on the wage and salary structure and the overall level of wage payments within most firms. Even firms that do not undertake surveys of wages and salaries are affected by these environmental pressures. For example, it would be impossible to staff an organization in a period of continuous inflation without giving some recognition to the upward movement of both wages and living costs. Thus, even in the absence of formal wage and salary surveys, organizations are eventually going to respond to signals from either the internal or external environment that all is not well with the structure of wages and salaries. The firm that waits too long to act on these signals, of course, will find itself in trouble.

---

[60] At least one firm, General Radio, has experimented with a pay plan for managers and professionals under which salaries fluctuate from month to month depending upon orders and shipments. See David A. Weeks, "A Fluctuating Paycheck for Managers," *The Conference Board Record*, 5:32–36 (April 1968). For an article on estimating the costs of proposed wage increases, see Thomas A. Mahoney, "The Real Cost of a Wage Increase," *Personnel*, 44:23–32 (May-June 1967).

FEDERAL AND STATE LAW

Federal and state legislation have an impact on basic wage payments, particularly through minimum wage laws. Under the Fair Labor Standards Act of 1938, as amended, employees "engaged in commerce or in the production of goods for commerce" must be paid wages of at least $2.30 per hour.[61] The law provides for even higher minimum wages in certain industries, as prescribed by the administrator of the Wage and Hour Division of the Department of Labor.[62] In addition, forty-one states had minimum wage laws by mid-1976.[63] Further, the Davis-Bacon Act of 1931 and its various amendments affect wage payments by requiring the secretary of labor to set minimum wage and fringe benefit levels for employees of private contractors doing construction work financed in part or whole by the federal government. These are set at the *prevailing rates* in the particular area.[64]

The Fair Labor Standards Act has an additional impact on wage payments through its encouragement of GAW plans. This law exempts companies from paying overtime beyond 40 hours in a week if the following conditions are met: The union-management agreement must provide that no employee will be required to work more than 1,040 hours during any twenty-six consecutive weeks, or 2,240 hours during a fifty-two-week period, but the employee must be guaranteed no less than 1,840 hours of employment. Under such plans, however, the law requires overtime payments beyond 12 hours in one day, 56 in one work week, and 2,080 in one year.[65] The same exemptions are provided by the Walsh-Healy Public Contracts Act.[66] The net effect is to permit companies having GAW plans to work employees extra-long hours during peak or rush periods, and to spread their pay over slack seasons.

The Equal Pay Act of 1963, effective June 1964, which amends the Fair Labor Standards Act, prohibits discrimination in wage payments on the basis of sex. According to this law, "No employer . . . shall discriminate . . . between employees on the basis of sex by paying wages . . . at a rate less than the rate at which he pays wages to employees of the opposite sex . . . for equal work on jobs the performance of which requires equal skill, effort, and responsibility, and which are performed under similar working conditions. . . ."[67] Thus, four major job evaluation factors are explicit in the law. As a consequence of the Equal Pay Act and the Civil Rights Act, many corporations have been faced with lawsuits on behalf of women employees and in a large number of instances have been required to pay sizable sums in back pay and to increase wage scales for women employees. In the Corning Glass case, the first to reach the Supreme Court, the court held that the Corning

[61] The 1974 amendments extended the Act to federal, state, and local government employees and to domestic workers, but a 1976 Supreme Court decision held that the federal government could not impose minimum wage and overtime requirements on state and local governments. *Business Week*, July 12, 1976, p. 27.

[62] Commerce Clearing House, *New 1974 Minimum Wage Law*, No. 82, April 9, 1974.

[63] The Bureau of National Affairs, *Labor Relations Reporter*, 4:SLL 1:19, August 7, 1976. Investigators visited only 4 percent of covered establishments in 1973 and found almost $83 million in unpaid minimum wages and overtime compensation due employees. American Society for Personnel Administration, "What to Do When the Wage-Hour Investigator Calls," p. 3 (no date).

[64] Russell L. Greenman and Eric J. Schmertz, *Personnel Administration and the Law* (Washington, D.C.: The Bureau of National Affairs, 1972), pp. 57–59. The Economic Stabilization Act of 1970 enables the President to issue executive orders to stabilize wages in the construction industry. If such controls are inadequate, presumably the Davis-Bacon Act would be suspended as it was, briefly, in 1941 and 1971.

[65] Section 7, Fair Labor Standards Act of 1938, as amended 1974.

[66] Section 42, Fair Labor Standards Act of 1938, as amended 1974.

[67] "Equal Pay for Equal Work under the Fair Labor Standards Act," U.S. Department of Labor, Interpractices Bulletin, Title 29, Part 800, 1967.

Glass Works had discriminated against women by paying a higher base wage rate to male night shift operators than to female operators on the day shift.[68] As another example, a U.S. circuit court ruled against the employer in the *Schultz v. Wheaton Glass Company* case concerning alleged discrimination against women inspector-packers, and awarded nearly $1 million in back pay. Upon appeal, the U.S. Supreme Court refused to hear the case, thus confirming the decision.[69] (See also the cases cited in Chapter 11.) One obvious implication of these cases is that organizations must be meticulous about writing job descriptions and conducting job evaluations without regard to any historical clustering of male versus female jobs in pay schemes.[70]

TECHNOLOGY AND SCIENCE

Technology and science affect the wage and salary structure of a firm in at least two important ways: (a) changes in job content and (b) increased ability to pay because of higher productivity. In the chapter on the task-specialization process, I discussed the impact of technology on job content and skill-mix. Such changes affect the relative worth of jobs and require new jobs to be fitted into the structure. Historically,

technological changes have also resulted in increased productivity, which in turn has tended to result in higher real wages.

COLLECTIVE BARGAINING AND UNION ATTITUDES

Collective bargaining has also had a major impact on wage structures and wage levels. It is within the unionized firm that the impact of collective bargaining on wages and salaries is most evident. Besides negotiating the wages to be paid specific jobs, rules of administration and any methods for determining relative worth of jobs are also subject to negotiation. Obviously, the nonunionized firm is ultimately affected by collective-bargaining agreements made elsewhere, since nonunionized firms are competing with the unionized firms for the services and loyalties of human resources. In addition, wages and benefits negotiated under union agreements have had the effect of increasing the "package" of compensation in nonunionized firms where managers have attempted to avoid unionization.

Notwithstanding a number of exceptions, labor leaders in general have questioned many devices and procedures used in wage determination and particularly in job evaluation. The following statement by William Gomberg, later a professor of management, probably reflects the prevailing attitude of organized labor toward job evaluation:

The trade unionist looks upon job evaluation as a subordinate tool in collective bargaining. It does not determine what a job is worth, it determines a limited concept of job content.

The final evaluation rates can only be one factor in determining what the relative wage structure should be.

Most job evaluation plans are exceedingly defective in measuring job content. Most abbreviated plans perform the same function more economically but are equally defective.

The most useful work in job evaluation is research

[68] George S. Roukis, "Protecting Workers' Civil Rights: Equality in the Workplace," *Labor Law Journal*, 26:3–16 (January 1975).

[69] *Business Week*, November 25, 1972, p. 44. The circuit court also ruled that jobs must be "substantially equal" and not "identical" to warrant equal pay. According to a Bureau of Labor Statistics study, the average earnings of men employed in metropolitan areas is almost always higher than those of women employed in the same occupations. However, the differential is much less in companies that employ both men and women in the same job. John E. Buckley, "Pay Differences between Men and Women in the Same Job," *Monthly Labor Review*, 94:36–39 (November 1971). See also Victor R. Fuchs, "Differences in Hourly Earnings between Men and Women," *Monthly Labor Review*, 94:9–15 (May 1971).

[70] For an elaboration, see George R. Wendt, "Should Courts Write Your Job Descriptions?" *Personnel Journal*, 55:442–445ff. (September 1976).

designed to isolate the factors that have governed the intuitive operation of collective bargaining as each party sought its own concept of equity. These factors can then be used for future guidance.[71]

Some of the additional factors to be considered in determining relative worth, according to the same author, are (a) irregularity of employment, (b) the career prospects of the job, (c) supply and demand, and (d) the traditional prestige carried by the job in the plant's social system.[72]

In the words of Boris Shishkin:

Labor denies the most fundamental assumption of job evaluation, that job content alone is an adequate measure of the value of a particular job and its proper relation to the values of other jobs. . . . There are many other factors affecting the value of each job, either alone or in relation to other jobs. Among such factors are: wage rates paid for comparable work in other sections of the industry; the comparable wages paid in the locality; labor market conditions; the complex patterns of traditions and past history of the wage structure; and various other elements affecting specific wage rates, such as irregularity of employment, opportunity for advancement, and provision made for vacations, rest periods, purchase of tools or uniforms, and so forth.[73]

As a consequence of such union attitudes about job evaluation, either job evaluation is likely to be rejected entirely in the unionized firm, or the union will insist on bargaining over the details of the method to be used and using job evaluation results as only one dimension of relative job worth.

MANAGERIAL ATTITUDES

Management attitudes, of course, will have a major impact on the wage structure and wage

level of the firm. Since judgment is exercised in many areas of wage and salary administration, including whether the firm should pay below-average, average, or above-average rates, what job factors should be used to reflect job worth, the weight to be given performance or length of service, and so forth, both the structure and level of wages are bound to be affected accordingly. In the unionized firm, of course, these attitudes will come into a dynamic interplay with the attitudes of the union rank and file and their leaders.

Top management's desire to maintain or enhance the company's prestige has been cited as a major factor in the wage policy of a number of firms acknowledged as wage leaders. Desires to improve or maintain morale, to attract high-caliber employees, to reduce turnover, and to provide as high a living standard for employees as possible also appear to be factors in management's wage-policy decisions.[74]

LABOR MARKET CONDITIONS

Labor market conditions, as has been suggested, play a major role in determining organizational wage structure and level. If the demand for certain skills is high and the supply is low, the result tends to be a rise in the price paid for these skills. When prolonged and acute, these labor market pressures probably force most organizations using job evaluation to reclassify hard-to-fill jobs at a higher level than that currently suggested by job evaluation, or their reclassification may be accomplished by deliberately distorting job content in *sub rosa* decisions. Such *sub rosa* practices, if found out by employees, would obviously reduce confidence in both job evaluation and the evaluators. On the other hand, if understood and accepted by all concerned, such practices are merely an acknowledgement of the variables in

---

[71] William Gomberg, "A Trade Unionist Looks at Job Evaluation," *Journal of Applied Psychology*, 35:7 (February 1951). See also William Gomberg, *A Labor Union Manual on Job Evaluation* (Chicago: Roosevelt College, 1948).
[72] Gomberg, "A Trade Unionist," p. 3.
[73] Boris Shishkin, "Job Evaluation, What It Means to Unionists," *American Federationist*, 54:21–22 (August 1947).

[74] Lester, *Company Wage Policies*, pp. 23–32.

addition to job evaluation that must be considered in pricing jobs.[75]

Other alternatives have been used to avoid subverting the job evaluation plan, however, including contracting out work formerly done on such jobs, eliminating the job by distributing parts of it within the organization, raising all wages, intensifying training efforts, and establishing separate pay plans. Problems created by short-run changes in the labor market have been minimized by emphasizing the advantages of employment with a particular firm in an attempt to retain employees who could obtain higher wages elsewhere.[76]

The labor market has an additional impact on the pay practices of an organization through pressure from managers outside the firm. To illustrate, if job evaluation or other variables result in wages paid that are significantly out of line with the rest of the community, informal pressures—for example, the implicit threat of loss of cordial relations—to bring rates back in line are sometimes applied by other managers whose job structures are thus threatened.[77] Once this occurs, managers may be reluctant in the future to deviate too far from the community's patterns.

Whether the company is a multiplant or a single-plant organization can have an impact on the wage structure and levels within the firm. One study found that thirteen out of seventy-nine multiplant companies having plants in more than one labor market area used a uniform wage structure throughout the company regardless of location of plant.[78] Such policies reject local labor market considerations and are likely to result in "premium" wages being paid by the firm in some communities, since it is likely that such a wage policy is designed to permit the managers of plants in the highest-priced labor market areas to meet competition.

AUTHORITY AND ACCOUNTABILITY

Most of the major components of the wage-determination process involve a cooperative relationship between the personnel department and the other departments of the organization. In the first place, any overall plans to undertake job analysis, the writing of job descriptions, and the evaluation of jobs are likely to be submitted for approval not only to the chief executive of the organization but to the other top executives as well. The chief executive and the personnel director will want a broad base of support if the plans are to be carried out. In addition, analyzing jobs and collecting data for job descriptions will involve both the job incumbent and the supervisor, and their cooperation is also important.

Like data gathering, job evaluation is a cooperative endeavor and is typically concluded by committee, although consultants are sometimes used to assist in the process. On the other hand, wage surveys are usually made independently by the personnel department in cooperation with outside organizations.

After the preliminary draft of the pay structure and rules of administration have been developed—based on job evaluation, wage surveys, and an analysis of pertinent organizational problems—the personnel department is likely to discuss the suggested plan

[75] For a discussion of a variety of solutions to the problem of labor-market pressure including the above, see Preston P. Le Breton, "Must Market Pressure Wreck the Company's Salary Structure?" *Personnel*, 36:34–45 (July-August 1959); Clark Kerr and Lloyd H. Fisher, "Effect of Environment and Administration on Job Evaluation," *Harvard Business Review*, 28:77–96 (May 1950); and Walter Fogel, "Wage Administration and Job Rate Ranges," *California Management Review*, 7:77–84 (Spring 1965).

[76] Le Breton, "Must Market Pressure Wreck Salary Structure?" See also Kerr and Fisher, "Effect of Environment and Administration," p. 82.

[77] Lester, *Company Wage Policies*, pp. 8, 43.

[78] See Kerr and Fisher, "Effect of Environment and Administration," p. 91.

with various top managers for their comments and suggestions before final approval is given by the chief executive of the organization. Department heads will want to anticipate problems that a new structure or new rules might create in the morale and retention of individual employees; the treasurer and/or controller will want to evaluate the impact of any increases in wage and salary costs; and so forth.

Once the chief executive has concurred on the wage and salary structure and the rules for administration, the implementation of the plan becomes a joint effort by both the personnel department and department heads, with the exception of those jobs in which the president takes a particular interest. The actual appraisal of the performance of subordinates is carried out by the various managers, who in turn submit their recommendations to higher authority and the latter, in turn, to the personnel department. The personnel department ordinarily reviews recommendations to ensure compliance with established rules of administration.[79]

Thus, although the details will vary from firm to firm, authority is normally shared in wage and salary administration. The basic planning in wage and salary administration is usually performed by the personnel department, advice is obtained from the top-management group, and final approval of wage and salary plans is granted by the chief executive. The day-to-day administration of the plans involves recommendations by department heads and monitoring and final approval by the personnel department. In unusual cases of serious disagreement, the CEO will make the final decision.[80]

UTILITY OF SYSTEMS

Although there may be no *best* method of job analysis or writing job descriptions, systematic collection of data is essential if decisions are to be made on the basis of job descriptions that accurately reflect the actual job. Inaccurate job analysis and job descriptions can lead to invalid job specifications and invalid job evaluation.

Research suggests that the particular system of job evaluation makes little difference in the results. One study found that raters in six different companies, using a variety of job evaluation systems but the same job descriptions and specifications, obtained essentially the same results. The different systems were the factor-comparison method, the point-rating method, and a combination of the ranking and grade-classification methods. None was identical to the other. The intercorrelation between the use of different systems varied from .89 to .97, with an average of .94.[81] Another study found that the classification method, the "time span of discretion," and the maturity curve resulted in a similar ranking of jobs.[82]

Research also suggests that abbreviated job evaluation systems produce about the same results as more complicated ones. One study of three firms found that the total points for various jobs using an abbreviated system and the total points for the same jobs using a more

[79] Typical practice is to have salary increases approved at least two levels higher than the individual involved. See George W. Torrence, "Who Approves Salary Increases?" *Management Record,* 22:11–13 (July-August 1960).

[80] For additional discussion of the role of the personnel department in wage and salary administration, see Maynard N. Toussaint, "Salary Administration in the Multi-Plant Firm," *Management of Personnel Quarterly,* 1:20–25 (Summer 1962);

and Wendell French and Dale Henning, "The Authority-Influence Role of the Functional Specialist in Management," *Academy of Management Journal,* 9:187–203 (September 1966).

[81] David J. Chesler, "Reaiability and Comparability of Different Job Evaluation Systems," *Journal of Applied Psychology,* 32:465–475 (October 1948). For similar results, see David D. Robinson, Owen W. Wahlstrom, and Robert C. Mecham, "Comparison of Job Evaluation Methods: a 'policy-Capturing' Approach Using the Position Analysis Questionnaire," *Journal of Applied Psychology,* 59:633–637 (October 1974).

[82] Thomas Atchison and Wendell French, "Pay Systems for Scientists and Engineers," *Industrial Relations,* 74:44–56 (October 1967). For an explanation of "time span of discretion," see section on "Validity of Systems" in this chapter.

complicated system resulted in an average correlation of about .95.[83]

There may be no best method of job evaluation, but it does seem essential that systematic attention be given to (a) what job aspects are considered to be of value, (b) what degree of these aspects are found in each job, and (c) what is the relative worth of jobs based on (a) and (b). Since organizations universally make decisions on relative worth, the question is one of how systematic (a), (b), and (c) are going to be. Although formalized methods of job evaluation serve to improve decision making about the relative worth of jobs, highly complicated methods contribute little to additional accuracy.

Again, there are no best structures and formulas for wage payments, but it is quite clear that wage payments must be systematic and planned and must be explainable if defensive behavior in the work force is to be avoided. We can imagine the resulting chaos if the frequency and amount of wage payments were completely random.

It should also be emphasized that any wage determination device or plan, including guaranteed annual wage plans or shifting employees from wage to salaried status, requires systematic attention to a wide number of organizational variables if the plan is to succeed. In short, the total context in which a given device or plan is to operate is as important as the plan itself.

RELIABILITY OF SYSTEMS

Little, if any, research seems to have been undertaken on the reliability of job analysis and the writing of job descriptions. Thus the extent to which different investigators arrive at the same set of job facts and the same descriptions has apparently not been studied.

There has been considerable research on the reliability of job evaluation systems, however, and the overwhelming evidence indicates a very high degree of consistency among trained raters in the application of job evaluation systems. Correlations among raters averaged .91 in one study,[84] about .90 in another,[85] and .97 in still a third study.[86] When trained in how to use the "yardstick" of a particular job evaluation system, then, raters applying the yardstick have a very high agreement. Time spent in rating does not seem to be associated with reliability.[87]

However, research suggests less agreement on some job evaluation factors than on others. For example, one study found very high agreement in the use of "skill-demand" factors but less agreement among raters when they applied factors relating to working conditions and job hazards.[88] Another study found greatest agreement on such factors as "working conditions," "physical effort," and "responsibility for safety" but very little agreement on intangible factors dealing with leadership or supervision.[89] Still another study showed a high degree of agreement among raters on some factors but much less agreement on others.[90] Since re-

[83] Milton K. Davis and Joseph Tiffin, "Cross Validation of an Abbreviated Point Job Evaluation System," *Journal of Applied Psychology*, 34:225–228 (August 1950).

[84] C.H. Lawshe and Patrick C. Farbro, "Studies in Job Evaluation: VIII. The Reliability of an Abbreviated Job Evaluation System," *Journal of Applied Psychology*, 33:158–166 (April 1949).

[85] Philip Ash, "The Reliability of Job Evaluation Rankings," *Journal of Applied Psychology*, 32:313–320 (June 1948).

[86] Chesler, "Reliability of Job Evaluation Systems," p. 472. See also Leonard Cohen, "More Reliable Job Evaluation," *Personnel Psychology*, 1:457–464 (Winter 1948).

[87] Joe T. Hazel, "Reliability of Job Ratings as a Function of Time Spent on Evaluation," *Journal of Industrial Psychology*, 4:16–19, No. 1 (1966).

[88] Lawshe and Farbro, "Studies in Job Evaluation," p. 160.

[89] Francis D. Harding, Joseph M. Madden, and Kenneth Colson, "Analysis of a Job Evaluation System," *Journal of Applied Psychology*, 44:354–357 (October 1960).

[90] Ash, "Reliability of Job Evaluation Rankings," p. 317.

liability is an essential component of validity, the validity of job evaluation could apparently be increased by eliminating factors that chronically result in high disagreement among raters.

There has been practically no research on the reliability of wage surveys. One study provided some useful insight into the question of reliability, however, by discovering that generalized, ambiguous job descriptions led responding companies to report widely diverse salary ranges for these jobs in contrast to the "spread" of salaries reported for jobs more clearly and specifically described.[91] (See Chapter 15 for a discussion of the reliability and validity of merit rating.)

VALIDITY OF VARIOUS COMPENSATION PRACTICES

Theoretically, the validity of various methods of determining wages and salaries may be judged by the extent to which they contribute to attaining the goals of the organization. Practically, however, this contribution is almost impossible to measure since a large number of variables need to be held constant in order to measure the effect of any one variable, such as job evaluation. The problem is further complicated by the criterion problem. Organizational goals are usually multiple, and devising an adequate measure of organizational success is, in itself, a difficult problem. Because of these complexities, it is understandable that practically no direct research on the validity of different systems of wage allocation has been undertaken.

To date, the best experimental research relating to the question of validity centers on the concept of perceived equity in pay. (For a theoretical treatment of equity, see Chapter 8.)

Adams describes an experimental study conducted by himself and Rosenbaum in which two groups of students were hired to conduct interviews at a fixed rate of $3.50 per hour. The experiment was conducted so that one group felt fairly paid and one group felt overpaid. The result: The group that felt overpaid displayed a much higher input in terms of effort and conducted more interviews in the allocated time.[92]

To test whether or not the members of the overpaid group were especially exerting themselves from fear of losing their jobs, Adams further cites a study by Arrowwood in which overpaid subjects outproduced the equitably paid subjects even though under the impression the experimenter would never know the results.[93]

In a further study, Adams and Rosenbaum again found that subjects who felt overpaid were outproducing subjects who were paid the same but felt merely equitably compensated. In addition the researchers hypothesized that, on a piecework basis, overpaid subjects would restrict their production. In other words, the hypothesis was that, since the degree of overpayment would increase as their production increased, they could minimize the inequity only by restricting output. The research supported the hypothesis.[94]

Since it was possible that the overpaid piece workers were reducing dissonance (see Chapter 8 for a discussion of cognitive dissonance) by increasing the quality of each unit, a further study tested this hypothesis, which turned out

[91] See John B. Harker, "Making Sense out of Salary Surveys," *Personnel Journal*, 31:131–134 (September 1952). See also William A. Groenekamp, "How Reliable Are Wage Surveys?" *Personnel*, 44:32–37 (January-February 1967).

[92] J. Stacy Adams, "Toward an Understanding of Inequity," *Journal of Abnormal and Social Psychology*, 67:422–424 (1963). For the original study, see J.S. Adams and W.B. Rosenbaum, "The Relationship of Worker Productivity to Cognitive Dissonance About Wage Inequities," *Journal of Applied Psychology*, 46:161–164 (1962).

[93] Ibid., p. 433. See A.J. Arrowwood, "Some Effects on Productivity of Justified Levels of Reward under Public and Private Conditions (Unpublished doctoral dissertation, University of Minnesota, Department of Psychology, 1961).

[94] Ibid., p. 434. See J. S. Adams and W.B. Rosenbaum, "Worker Productivity to Cognitive Dissonance," pp. 161–164.

to be true. That is, the restrictors of output were actually increasing their personal input by improving quality.[95] In a later study, in which striving for higher quality by overpaid subjects would not necessarily lead to lower productivity, the overpaid subjects clearly lowered their output, presumably in an effort to reduce their pay.[96] In another study, underpaid subjects (their salaries were less than their authority would suggest) produced work of a lower quality level than those paid equitably.[97] In a study that simulated the allocation of pay to subordinates, those managers who perceived their own pay to be inequitably low were the most "tight-fisted" with their own subordinates.[98]

One of the difficulties in such research is the impact of the research simulations on self-esteem and how this, in turn, affects performance. Campbell and Pritchard point out that the simulation of overpayment usually has involved a gruff statement to the overpaid subjects that they were less-than-qualified but would nevertheless receive more than they were worth. These authors cite a research study by Andrews and Valenzi that confirmed that impact on self-esteem might, indeed, be a major variable operating.[99]

In general, it appears that perceived equity in pay is associated with performance.[100] Although we should be cautious about generalizing from these studies, such research is making a significant contribution to an emerging body of knowledge about compensation practices.

In general, the concepts of job analysis, job descriptions, job specifications, job evaluation, and merit rating are valid when their logic is examined. Wage surveys also have a kind of validity in that they provide an index of what wage levels are necessary to recruit and retain needed talent and what wage levels would be higher than necessary and would lead to unnecessary costs. The validity of a specific device

[95] Ibid., pp. 434–435. A further study investigated the possibility that the results were due to overpaid workers having less job security. The study permitted a rejection of this explanation. See J. Stacy Adams and Patricia R. Jacobsen, "Effects of Wage Inequities on Work Quality," Journal of Abnormal and Social Psychology, 69:19–25 (1964).

[96] Ian Wood, and Edward E. Lawler III, "Effects of Piece-Rate Overpayment on Productivity," Journal of Applied Psychology, 54:234–238 (June 1970).

[97] William M. Evan, and Roberta G. Simmons, "Organizational Effects of Inequitable Rewards: Two Experiments in Status Inconsistency," Administrative Science Quarterly, 14:224–237 (June 1969).

[98] Paul S. Goodman, "Effect of Perceived Inequity on Salary Allocation Decisions," Journal of Applied Psychology, 60:372–375 (June 1975).

[99] John P. Campbell and Robert D. Pritchard, "Motivation Theory in Industrial and Organizational Psychology," in Marvin D. Dunnette, ed., Handbook of Industrial and Organizational Psychology (Chicago: Rand McNally College Publishing Company, 1976), pp. 104–110. See also I.R. Andrews and

E. Valenzi, "Overpay Inequity or Self-Image as a Worker: A Critical Examination of an Experimental Induction Procedure," Organizational Behavior and Human Performance, 53:22–27 (1970).

[100] See also David W. Belcher and Thomas J. Atchison, "Compensation for Work," in Robert Dubin, ed., Handbook of Work, Organization and Society (Chicago: Rand McNally College Publishing Company, 1976), pp. 567–611; H.R. Finn and Sang M. Lee, "Salary Equity: Its Determination, Analysis, and Correlates," Journal of Applied Psychology, 56:283–292 (August 1972); I.R. Andrews, "Wage Inequity and Job Performance: An Experimental Study," Journal of Applied Psychology, 51:39–45 (February 1967); and Edward E. Lawler III, and Paul W. O'Gara, "Effects of Inequity Produced by Underpayment on Work Output, Work Quality, and Attitudes toward Work," Journal of Applied Psychology, 51:403–410 (October 1967). Other studies that may be relevant are Jaques' experiments in England with the "time-span of discretion" concept as a method of arriving at equitable pay. Jaques believes (1) that at a given time "[t]here exists shared social norms of what constitutes a fair or equitable payment for any given level of work, these norms being intuitively known by each individual," and (2) that these norms about level of work can be identified with a measuring device which he calls "time-span of discretion." Time-span of discretion is defined as ". . . the maximum period of time during which the use of discretion is authorized and expected, without review of that discretion by his superior." Jaques states that his investigations have found that imbalances between level of work (as measured by time-span of discretion) and pay are associated with turnover, dissatisfaction, depression, anxiety, or guilt, or all five elements, depending upon the extent and direction of the imbalance. See Elliott Jaques, Equitable Payment (New York: John Wiley & Sons, 1961), pp. 9, 17, 131–133; and Elliott Jacques, Time Span Handbook (London: Heinemann Educational Books, Ltd., 1964).

and practice in wage determination, however, must be examined in the context of its particular environment.

Another test of validity, although a tenuous one, might be the extent to which managers believe compensation systems and devices actually work. The popularity of the various systems and devices described thus far can be ascertained by the statistics on usage quoted above. It is evident that most managers feel job analysis, job description, job evaluation, pay plans with rules of administration, and merit rating are useful devices and systems. One survey found job evaluation well established in terms of managerial support. Ninety-seven percent of firms using job evaluation reported they would install a job evaluation program if they had to do it all over again, and 91 percent reported their job evaluation plans ranged from "rather successful" to "highly successful." Only 9 percent indicated that their plans were "mildly satisfactory" or "unsatisfactory." [101]

What little evidence is available on guaranteed annual wage (GAW) plans suggests that managers in companies using them believed their plans were contributing to increased productivity. They expressed this belief even in the case of discontinued plans. [102]

What little information there is about the consequences of changing hourly paid employees to salaried status suggests that there is little abuse of extra privileges, that absenteeism has not increased, and that in some cases absenteeism has been reduced. [103] One survey, in which thirty-one firms made "before and after" comparisons, found twenty of the firms experiencing no change in absenteeism, five firms a reduction, three firms a slight rise and then a return to normal, and only three firms an increase in absenteeism. [104] Giving extra opportunity for time off with pay is apparently not abused and perhaps serves as a positive motivator when (a) individual employees and unions are conscious of their responsibility, (b) management has a basic belief in the integrity and good will of the employees, (c) meticulous records on absenteeism are kept and reported to supervisors, (d) rules are clearly spelled out, and (e) supervisors do a good job of managing. [105] Thus, increasing privileges and benefits is neither inherently valid nor invalid; it is the total organizational environment that determines the degree to which such changes contribute to or detract from organizational goals.

There is some research evidence that employee participation in salary administration has beneficial results. In an experimental program in a small manufacturing plant, employees participated in establishing a job evaluation plan and a salary structure, and actually assigned salaries. The results were increased job identification and satisfaction with pay administration, along with reduced turnover. Although there was about an 8 percent increase in the cost of salaries to the organization, a significant realignment of salaries occurred, and the researchers concluded that salaries came much more into line with what workers perceived to be fair. Although the workers were given wide latitude in setting salaries, they set their wages at the 50th percentile of their particular labor market. [106]

SUMMARY

The process of wage determination is one of the most significant aspects of personnel manage-

[101] George Fry & Associates, *Job Evaluation Survey*, 1960, pp. 1–18. See also Patton, "Top Executive Pay: New Facts and Figures," p. 73.

[102] Latimer, *Guaranteed Wages: Report to the President by the Advisory Board*, pp. 170–171, 306ff.

[103] Kaponya, "Salaries for *All* Workers," pp. 51–52.

[104] Weeks, "Salaries for Blue Collar Workers," p. 21.

[105] Kaponya, "Salaries for *All* Workers."

[106] Edward E. Lawler III, "Pay, Participation and Organizational Change," in Eugene L. Cass and Frederick G. Zimmer,

ment, since it has a profound effect on the recruitment, the retention, the satisfaction, and the motivation of employees and on the survival of the organization. There is a clear need for careful job analysis, job evaluation, and design of the wage and salary structure and rules of administration if organizations are to be managed effectively.

Many forces typically affect pay increase decisions in addition to merit rating, and attempting to focus only on differential performance is usually unrealistic. Variables such as inflation, cost of living, and the need for maintaining differentials between groups and levels usually need to be considered. The use of maturity curves can be a helpful device in administering salaries of engineers, scientists, and other professionals, but assumptions that performance tapers off as age progresses into the late forties or early fifties is open to serious question.

Secrecy relative to the actual amounts paid has been challenged by some authors, but the dysfunctional consequences of disclosure in many instances may outweigh advantages.

Some firms have adopted salaried status for all employees; the significance may be more symbolic than tangible, although salaried status may carry with it additional fringe benefits in some situations. Salaried status for all employees may intensify dissatisfaction of some groups of white-collar workers if appropriate differentials are not maintained.

The use of merit rating for determining "average," "below average," and "above average" performers may be statistically appropriate, but some authors theorize that this practice may have a serious impact on the self-esteem and motivation of employees, as well as on peer cooperation. This may be an insoluble dilemma, but the avoidance of direct peer comparisons and a focus on goals and collaborative

problem solving may be partial answers. Different semantics might assist in defusing the problem, particularly if management is convinced that all employees are "above average."

Behavioral scientists have only recently begun to examine the impact of various compensation practices and have focused primarily on the consequences of perceived inequity in pay and on the impact of secrecy in salary administration. A major difficulty in examining the degree to which a particular plan of reward contributes to organizational objectives is interdependency with many other variables in a complex organizational environment. This fact will become increasingly evident as we examine fringe benefits and incentive systems in the following chapters.

REVIEW AND DISCUSSION QUESTIONS

1. What is the purpose of job evaluation? What are its underlying assumptions?

2. What is the classification method of job evaluation?

3. What are *job clusters*, and how can they be taken into account in salary administration.

4. If you were a personnel director and wanted to conduct a survey of salaries, how could you make sure that the data you collected were based on comparable jobs?

5. How do the Fair Labor Standards Act and the Walsh-Healy Act relate to compensation?

6. In the light of Maslow's need hierarchy, how do wage payments relate to need fulfillment?

7. Discuss job evaluation and merit rating in the context of the concepts explained in Chapter 8.

8. What seem to be the underlying assumptions in the use of the maturity curve? What are some of the pros and cons of using this device?

eds., *Man and Work in Society* (New York: Van Nostrand Reinhold Company, 1975), pp. 142–143.

9. What does research say about the relationship between perceived inequity in wage payments and performance?

10. Do money payments motivate? Review the discussion of Herzberg's theory in Chapter 6.

11. What has been the impact of the Equal Pay Act and the Civil Rights Act on compensation practices?

12. Discuss the advantages and problems associated with awarding differential pay increases based on merit.

SUPPLEMENTAL REFERENCES

Andrews, Robert, ed., *Managerial Compensation* (Ann Arbor, Mich.: Foundation for Research in Human Behavior, 1965).

Atchison, T.J., and D.W. Belcher, "Equity, Rewards and Compensation Administration," *Personnel Administration*, 34:32–36 (March-April 1971).

Bassett, Glenn A., and Harlow A. Nelson, "Keys to Better Salary Administration," *Personnel*, 44:23–30 (March-April 1967).

Beal, Edwin F., "In Praise of Job Evaluation," *California Management Review*, 5:9–16 (Summer 1963).

Belcher, David W., *Compensation Administration* (Englewood Cliffs, N.J.: Prentice-Hall, Inc., 1974).

——, "Ominous Trends in Wage and Salary Administration," *Personnel*, 41:42–50 (September-October 1966).

——, "Toward a Behavioral Science Theory of Wages," in Michael T. Matteson, Roger N. Blakeney, Donald R. Domm, eds., *Contemporary Personnel Management* (San Francisco: Canfield Press, 1972), pp. 177–189.

——, and T.J. Atchison, "Compensation for Work," in Robert Dubin, ed., *Handbook of Work, Organization, and Society* (Chicago: Rand McNally College Publishing Company, 1976), pp. 567–611.

Berg, J. Gary, *Managing Compensation* (New York: Amacom, 1976).

Burgess, Leonard R., *Wage and Salary Administration in a Dynamic Economy* (New York: Harcourt Brace & World, Inc., 1968).

Crosley, W.D., "Progressive Wage and Salary Programming in the Hospital," *Personnel Journal*, 49:655–661 (August 1970).

Crystal, Graef, *Financial Motivation for Executives* (New York: American Management Association, 1970).

Deci, Edward L., "The Hidden Costs of Rewards," *Organizational Dynamics*, 4:61–72 (Winter 1976).

Dunlop, John T., "Wage and Price Controls as Seen by a Controller," in James L. Stern and Barbara Dennis, eds., *Proceedings of the 1975 Annual Spring Meeting*, Industrial Relations Research Association, pp. 457–463.

Dunnette, Marvin D., Edward E. Lawler III, Karl E. Weick, and Robert L. Opsahl, "The Role of Financial Compensation in Managerial Motivation," *Organizational Behavior and Human Performance*, 2:175–216 (May 1967).

Famularo, Joseph J., ed., *Handbook of Modern Personnel Administration* (New York: McGraw-Hill Book Company, 1972).

Gellerman, Saul, "Motivating Men with Money," *Fortune*, 77:144–146ff. (March 1968).

Ginsburg, Barry M., "The Impact of Automation on Wage and Salary Administration," *ILR Research*, 9:3–9, No. 1 (1963).

Gitelman, H.M., "An Investment Theory of Wages," *Industrial and Labor Relations Review*, 21:323–352 (April 1968).

Goetz, Billy E., "A Fair Day's Pay," *Advanced Management Journal*, 32:46–50 (January 1967).

Hinrichs, J.R., "Correlates of Employee Evaluations of Pay Increases," *Journal of Applied Psychology*, 53:1–489 (December 1969).

Howard, Cecil, "Overseas Compensation Policies of U.S. Multinationals," *The Personnel Administrator,* 20:50–62 (November 1975).

Hughes, Charles, "Existentialism in Personnel Management," *The Personnel Administrator,* 21:11–15 (July 1976).

Jaques, Elliott, "Objective Measures for Pay Differentials," *Harvard Business Review,* 40:133–138 (January-February 1962).

Kerr, Steven, "On the Folly of Rewarding A, While Hoping for B," *Academy of Management Journal,* 18:769–783 (December 1975).

Lawler Edward E., III, "Effective Pay Programs—An Interview with Edward E. Lawler III," *Compensation Review,* 8:14–27 (Third Quarter 1976).

————, "How Much Money Do Executives Want?" *Transaction,* 4:23–29 (January-February 1967).

————, "Participation and Pay," *Compensation Review,* 7:62–66 (Third Quarter 1975).

————, *Pay and Organizational Effectiveness: A Psychological View* (New York: McGraw-Hill Book Company, 1971).

————, and Lyman W. Porter, "Predicting Managers' Pay and Their Satisfaction with Their Pay," *Personnel Psychology,* 19:363–373 (Winter 1966).

Lester, Richard, "Pay Differentials by Size of Establishment," *Industrial Relations,* 7:57–67 (October 1967).

Lewellen, Wilbur G., and Howard P. Lanser, "Executive Pay Preferences," *Harvard Business Review,* 51:115–122 (September-October 1973).

Livy, Bryan, *Job Evaluation: A Critical Review* (London: George Allen & Unwin, Ltd., 1975).

Lupton, Tom, ed., *Payment Systems* (Middlesex, England: Penguin Books, Inc., 1972).

McCormick, Robert L., "A New Method for Fitting Salary Curves," *Personnel Journal,* 46:589–595 (October 1967).

Marshall, Don R., "Merit Pay without Headaches: How to Design a Plan for Nonexempts," *Compensation Review,* 7:32–41 (Second Quarter 1975).

Moore, Russell F., ed., *Compensating Executive Worth* (New York: American Management Association, 1968).

Nash, Allan N., and Stephen J. Carroll, Jr., *The Management of Compensation* (Monterey, Calif.: Brooks/Cole Publishing Co., 1975).

Orth, Charles D., III, and Frederick Jacobs, "Women in Management: Pattern for Change," *Harvard Business Review,* 49:139–147 (July-August 1971).

Patton, Arch, "Government's Pay Disincentive," *Business Week,* January 19, 1974, pp. 12–13.

Patten, Thomas H., Jr., *A Bibliography on Compensation Planning and Administration, 1960–1974* (Scottsdale, Ariz.: American Compensation Association, 1975).

Petrie, Donald J., "Executive Financial Planning—A New Fringe Benefit," *Personnel,* 48:17–25 (November-December 1971).

Porter, Lyman W., and Edward E. Lawler III, *Managerial Attitudes and Performance* (Homewood, Ill.: Richard D. Irwin, Inc., 1968).

Pursell, Robert B., "R & D Job Evaluation and Compensation," *Compensation Review,* 4:21–31 (Second Quarter 1972).

Riegel, John W., *Administration of Salaries and Intangible Rewards for Engineers and Scientists* (Ann Arbor: Bureau of Industrial Relations, University of Michigan, 1958).

Sakurabayashi, Makoto, "How a Japanese Firm Sets Salaries for Its Clerical Employees," *Compensation Review,* 7:42–49 (Second Quarter 1975).

Sangerman, Harry, "A Look at the Equal Pay Act in Practice," *Labor Law Journal,* 22:259–265 (May 1971).

Sibson, Robert E., *Wages and Salaries: A Handbook for Line Managers* (New York: American Management Association, Inc., 1960).

Suskin, Harold, "Personal Competence Rating," *Personnel Administration*, 35:62–66 (May-June 1972).

Tolles, N. Arnold, *Origins of Modern Wage Theories* (Englewood Cliffs, N.J.: Prentice-Hall, Inc., 1964).

Weick, Karl, "The Concept of Equity in the Perception of Pay," *Administrative Science Quarterly*, 11:414–439 (December 1966).

Zollitsch, Herbert G., and Adolph Langsner, *Wage and Salary Administration* (Cincinnati: South-Western Publishing Company, 1970).

CHAPTER 20
SUPPLEMENTARY BENEFITS

DESCRIPTION

In addition to basic wages and salaries, organizations typically pay for a wide variety of supplementary items—often called "fringe benefits." These payments take the form of time off with pay, programs to provide security against various contingencies in employees' lives, deferred wages like retirement pay, and numerous services.[1]

The determination of supplementary benefits usually involves fewer devices and systems than the determination of the basic wage structure. For example, job analysis, job evaluation, and merit rating are not directly used in connection with fringe benefits. As shown in Figure 20-1, the approximate flow of events that normally determines the supplementary benefit package includes basic-wage determination, supplementary benefit surveys, and analysis of relevant organizational problems. Labor legislation is included because of its major impact on fringe payments. Collective bargaining is also included, because it directly affects the determination of supplementary benefits in the unionized firm.

CURRENT PRACTICES AND PROBLEMS

Costs of fringe benefits are a significant part of total labor costs and, on a percentage basis,

---

[1] It should be noted here that there are many "unofficial," *sub rosa* fringes doled out in some organizations, including those that are condoned and those that are outright theft. Dalton describes many such fringes, including the making of storm windows on company time in the company's carpentry shop for use at home, the use of the company's vehicles for private purposes, the marking down of retail items for employees' purchase, and the theft of hams and canned goods. See Melville Dalton, *Men Who Manage* (New York: John Wiley & Sons, Inc., 1959), pp. 198–213.

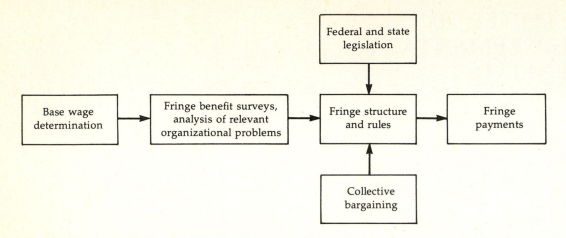

Figure **20-1**   Process of determining supplementary benefits

have been increasing substantially faster than basic wages in recent years. A 1976 report indicated that the average cost of fringe benefits in 152 companies surveyed periodically since 1955 had increased from 22.7 percent of payroll in 1955 to 40.3 percent in 1975 (see Figure 20-2). On a cents-per-payroll-hour basis, fringe benefits increased from 46.7¢ per hour in 1955 to 230.9¢ per hour in 1975. In terms of dollars per employee per year, the cost of fringes increased from $970 in 1955 to $4,731 in 1975.[2]

Relative costs and trends in costs among different fringe benefits can be seen in Figures 20-2 and 20-3. The reader will note from Figure 20-3 that payments for time not worked constitute 10.1 percent of payroll in 1975, or 13.7 percent if such items as paid rest periods, lunch periods, wash-up time, and clothes-changing time are included. Pension plans (11.6 percent), legally required payments (8.0 percent), and paid vacations (5.2 percent) loom large as major costs in the typical fringe benefit program (all companies, Figure 20-3).

However, wide variations in fringe benefits exist among different companies, industries, and regions. In the study cited above, fringes varied among the firms from less than 18 percent to more than 60 percent of payroll.[3] Some of this variation is between industries and between regions, but the variation *within* industries and *within* regions is much more evident. Differences between industries are most conspicuous in the case of hospitals and the chemical and allied products industry where fringe benefits in 1975 were respectively 24 percent and 42.2 percent of payroll.[4] There were some regional differences, with payments being highest in the states of the Northeast and somewhat lower in those of the Southeast.[5] Larger firms tended to have higher payments than smaller firms.[6]

---

[2]*Employee Benefits 1975* (Washington, D.C.: Chamber of Commerce of the United States, 1976), p. 27.

[3]Ibid., p. 6.
[4]Ibid., p. 9. This differential can be expected to narrow with the rapid emergence of collective bargaining in the health care field (see Chapter 22).
[5]Ibid., p. 14.
[6]Ibid., p. 15.

Figure **20-2**   Comparison of 1955–1975 employee benefits for 152 companies

Item	1955	1957	1959	1961	1963	1965	1967	1969	1971	1973	1975
All industries (152 companies)											
1. As per cent of payroll, total	22.7	24.8	25.5	26.9	27.8	28.0	30.2	31.9	34.4	36.5	40.3
a. Legally required payments (employer's share only)	2.8	3.1	3.5	4.0	4.6	4.2	4.9	5.3	5.6	6.6	7.1
b. Pension and other agreed-upon payments (employer's share only)	8.2	8.8	9.4	9.4	9.5	9.9	10.4	11.1	12.4	13.1	14.7
c. Paid rest periods, lunch periods, etc.	2.2	2.3	2.1	2.5	2.5	2.6	3.1	3.3	3.5	3.5	4.1
d. Payments for time not worked	7.6	8.5	8.7	9.2	9.3	9.4	9.8	10.2	10.8	11.1	11.9
e. Profit-sharing payments, bonuses, etc.	1.9	2.1	1.8	1.8	1.9	1.9	2.0	2.0	2.1	2.2	2.5
2. As cents per payroll hour	46.7	55.5	63.1	71.8	79.6	86.6	102.0	119.1	145.9	178.2	230.9
3. As dollars per year per employee	970	1142	1299	1476	1646	1793	2114	2460	2990	3677	4731

From *Employee Benefits 1975* (Washington, D.C.: Chamber of Commerce of the United States, 1976), p. 27. Used with permission.

FRINGE BENEFIT SURVEYS

A study made some years ago suggested that companies were not paying much attention to fringe benefits in their wage surveys.[7] It is very likely, however, that because of rising costs managers are now paying more and more attention to fringe benefit surveys. Furthermore, fringe benefits for unionized employees are usually surveyed by both management and the union prior to contractual negotiations.

Since fringes and wages are part of the total compensation package, fringe benefit surveys should be made simultaneously with wage surveys if wage data are to be really meaningful. To make external wage surveys or establish the level of wages and salaries within a firm without considering both external and internal fringe benefit practices is to ignore an important and costly area of compensation.

[7] Richard A. Lester, *Hiring Practices and Labor Competition* (Princeton, N.J.: Industrial Relations Section, Department of Economics and Sociology, Princeton University, 1954), p. 13.

ANALYSIS OF RELEVANT ORGANIZATIONAL PROBLEMS

Although there has been little research on the subject, the nature of the work force probably has an important bearing on fringe benefit decisions. For example, if an organization's work force consists of a high percentage of young people just out of high school who remain with the firm an average of three years, there may be little demand for a pension plan and little interest on the part of top management in establishing one. On the other hand, there may be two rest periods per day and meticulous attention to good cafeteria services. If the work force includes a high percentage of employees with families, both employees and management may be greatly interested in group medical and life-insurance plans, severance-pay plans, and other plans to increase family security.

There have been a few studies on fringe benefit preferences. For example, Chapman and Ottemann found that age and/or seniority, marital status, number of dependents, and occupational category (operating versus clerical work)

Figure **20-3** Employee benefits by type of payment, 1975

Type of benefit	Total, all companies	Total, all manu-facturing	Total, all nonmanu-facturing
Total employee benefits as per cent of payroll	35.4	36.1	34.4
1. Legally required payments (employer's share only)	8.0	8.8	6.9
a. Old-Age, Survivors, Disability and Health Insurance	5.7	5.8	5.4
b. Unemployment compensation	1.0	1.2	0.8
c. Workmen's compensation (including estimated cost of self-insured)	1.2	1.7	0.6
d. Railroad Retirement Tax, Railroad Unemployment and Cash Sickness Insurance, state sickness benefits insurance, etc.**	0.1	0.1	0.1
2. Pension and other agreed-upon payments (employer's share only)	11.6	11.6	11.4
a. Pension plan premiums and pension payments not covered by insurance type of plan (net)	5.5	4.9	6.4
b. Life insurance premiums, death benefits, accident and medical insurance premiums, hospitalization insurance, etc. (net)	5.2	6.1	3.8
c. Salary continuation or long term disability	0.2	0.2	0.2
d. Dental insurance premiums	0.1	0.1	0.1
e. Discounts on goods and services purchased from company by employees	0.2	*	0.3
f. Employee meals furnished by company	0.2	0.1	0.3
g. Miscellaneous payments (compensation payments in excess of legal requirements, separation or termination pay allowances, moving expenses, etc.)	0.2	0.2	0.3
3. Paid rest periods, lunch periods, wash-up time, travel time, clothes-change time, get-ready time, etc.	3.6	3.7	3.5
4. Payments for time not worked	10.1	10.1	10.3
a. Paid vacations and payments in lieu of vacation	5.2	5.4	4.8
b. Payments for holidays not worked	3.3	3.5	3.2
c. Paid sick leave	1.2	0.8	1.8
d. Payments for State or National Guard duty, jury, witness and voting pay allowances, payments for time lost due to death in family or other personal reasons, etc.	0.4	0.4	0.5
5. Other items	2.1	1.9	2.3
a. Profit-sharing payments	1.1	1.1	1.1
b. Contributions to employee thrift plans	0.3	0.2	0.4
c. Christmas or other special bonuses, service awards, suggestion awards, etc.	0.4	0.4	0.4
d. Employee education expenditures (tuition refunds, etc.)	0.1	0.1	0.2
e. Special wage payments ordered by courts, payments to union stewards, etc.	0.2	0.1	0.2
Total employee benefits as cents per payroll hour	193.2	191.3	195.8
Total employee benefits as dollars per year per employee	3984	3954	4025

*Less than 0.05%
**Figure shown is considerably less than legal rate, as most reporting companies had only a small proportion of employees covered by tax.

From *Employee Benefits 1975* (Washington, D.C.: Chamber of Commerce of the United States, 1976), p. 8. Used with permission. Figure 20-3 is not strictly comparable with Figure 20-2, since the data in Figure 20-2 are based on a smaller sample.

seemed to be factors in fringe benefit choices. As one illustration of the results of their study, it was found that younger employees were significantly more in favor of a four-day workweek and a family dental plan than older workers, and preference for a pension increase was significantly associated with age.[8] Ability to finance fringe benefit programs will be a factor in their adoption. A young, struggling firm will not be able to afford an extensive fringe benefit program, nor will a firm in a profit slump want to expand its fringe benefits.

FRINGE STRUCTURE AND RULES

Detailed rules of administration are usually developed before fringe benefit programs are implemented. For example, in the case of sick-leave benefits, rules must be established on the length of time salaries or wages will be continued, when benefits will start, the relationship between the benefits and length of service, the maximum that will be granted in any one year, whether a physician's statement will be required as proof of illness, and so forth.

If careful attention is not given to the development of such rules, policy must be decided the first time problems arise. Probably the most serious consequence of not spelling out rules in detail is the lack of realistic cost-forecasts when a particular plan is installed. In short, without detailed rules, the organization will not know what the plan is going to cost. Detailed rules are also necessary to prevent inequitable or capricious treatment of employees.

RELATIONSHIP TO OTHER ORGANIZATIONAL PROCESSES

Many fringe benefit payments stem indirectly from the process of determining basic wages. For example, once time-off-with-pay benefits such as vacation, sick leave, and holidays are awarded, the costs will be partly determined by basic wages as derived from job evaluation, surveys, and the like, since the basic wages are carried over into nonworking hours. The period of time over which nonworking pay is continued, however, is separately determined and subject to many of the forces and factors discussed earlier.

As in the case of basic wages, the method of payment and amount of fringe benefits will be an important aspect of the collective-bargaining and justice processes and, of course, inseparably related to the financial-management process. A notable difference between wage determination and fringe benefit determination is that fringe benefits are almost completely unrelated to the appraising process. Very rarely are fringe benefits awarded on the basis of differences in employees' performance as measured by merit rating. The only exceptions of which I am aware are rare situations where time off with pay for personal reasons is given on the basis of employee-attendance records.[9]

Supplementary compensation may also have an important impact on the staffing process, since fringes may affect the company's ability to recruit and may have a significant bearing on whether employees remain with the firm. As will be discussed later, it has been argued that supplementary benefits tend to "trap" employees into remaining with a particular firm in that they cannot afford to leave once they have accumulated such benefits as sizable pensions, long annual vacations, or extensive sick-leave benefits. Vesting regulations in the 1974 pension law, however, are likely to make it somewhat easier to leave a particular organization. (See the discussion of ERISA later.)

[8] J. Brad Chapman and Robert Otteman, "Employee Preference for Various Compensation and Fringe Benefit Options," *The Personnel Administrator*, 20 (November 1975), special insert, 6 pp.
[9] It is possible for fringe benefits to be *inversely* related to performance—e.g., if a sick-leave plan is not administered properly, marginal employees may take advantage of it.

IMPACT OF ENVIRONMENT

Fringe benefits are directly affected by certain environmental forces in addition to the practices of competitors, including federal and state legislation and collective bargaining. Science and technology, managerial attitudes, and labor-market conditions probably also affect fringe payments. That the type of industry is a variable in the level of fringe payments has already been indicated.

Federal and state laws require most employers to provide fringe benefits in the form of Social Security (Old Age, Survivors and Disability Insurance), unemployment compensation, and workmen's compensation. The cost of these programs to employers averages about 8 percent of payroll. (See Figure 20-3.)

Under the Social Security Act of 1935, as amended, employers and employees each contribute 5.85 percent of the first $15,300 earned annually by each employee and, by 1978 each will contribute over 6 percent. The employee's share is collected by the employer through payroll-deduction and, along with the employer's contribution, is paid to the federal government on a quarterly basis.

The Federal Unemployment Tax Act of 1935, as amended, requires employers of four or more employees in work covered by the Act to pay an unemployment insurance tax to the federal government. Amendments in 1970 set the rate at 3.2 percent of the first $4,200 in wages paid to each worker during each calendar year.[10]

State laws on workmen's compensation provide payments to workers or dependents in the case of job-incurred injuries, diseases, or death. Medical care and rehabilitation services are also provided. The total cost is borne by employers, although the method of insuring may vary from state to state and may involve a state fund, approved insurance companies, or special funds set up by employers.[11] More than 85 percent of both wage and salaried workers in the United States are covered by state and federal programs. However, while thirteen states cover more than 85 percent of their workers, fifteen states cover less than 70 percent.[12] The total system supports the families of approximately 14,500 employees killed at work each year and 2.2 million workers injured, the latter including about 90,000 who are permanently disabled.[13]

Federal income tax laws have probably increased fringe benefit coverage, since the employee obtains certain tax advantages when receiving compensation in the form of fringes. For example, benefits from a hospital-surgical plan are not taxed, and benefits from a retirement plan are subject to tax only when the benefit is paid, which is likely to be in a period of relatively low income for the individual affected. As a result, many employees may prefer that a relatively high proportion of their compensation package consist of fringe benefits.

During World War II, the National War Labor Board gave impetus to fringe benefit programs by ruling that employers could contribute to pension and other welfare plans if the cost was not greater than 5 percent of payroll. Since wages were essentially frozen, such benefit programs were fostered by employers in order to attract scarce labor. The Supreme Court's deci-

[10] Bureau of National Affairs, *Labor Policy and Practice: Pay Policies*, 356:25. See also Joseph A. Hickey, "A Report on State Unemployment Insurance Laws," *Monthly Labor Review*, 95:40–50 (January 1972).

[11] This insurance differs from sickness-benefits insurance required in some states. The latter is also employer-financed, but all sickness is covered, not just job-incurred sickness.
[12] *The Report of the National Commission on State Workmen's Compensation Laws*, Washington, D.C., 1972, p. 15. For further discussion see Florence C. Johnson, "Changes in Workmen's Compensation in 1971," *Monthly Labor Review*, 95:51–55 (January 1972).
[13] U.S. Department of Labor, *Manpower Report of the President*, April 1968, pp. 42–44.

sion in the *Inland Steel* case of 1949 further stimulated the growth of fringe benefit programs by stating that employers were obliged to bargain with unions about pension plans under Section 8 of the Taft-Hartley Act.[14]

Another law, the Welfare and Pension Plans Disclosure Act of 1958, with subsequent amendments, placed a record-keeping and report-submitting burden on employers and unions who administer pension and welfare plans. Under this law, organizations administering welfare and pension funds are required to submit reports to the secretary of labor, must have bonded officials to handle such funds, and are subject to legal action in the event that they misuse such funds.[15]

The Employee Retirement Income Security Act of 1974 (ERISA) has had a huge impact on private pension plans in the United States. The Act is of direct benefit to millions of employees because it (a) prohibits eligibility rules that require a minimum age of twenty-five or more than one year of service, whichever is later; (b) establishes minimum vesting standards; and (c) establishes an insurance program to protect pension funds. (Vesting means that the employee ultimately receives the employer's contributions even if the employee terminates that particular employment.) However, the Act has created extensive extra costs because of auditing charges and the reporting burden placed on employers. It should be noted that the Act does not require a company to establish a pension plan nor require any particular level of benefits. "Portability," that is, the ability of an employee to have the assets related to vested benefits transferred to another employer or to an individual retirement account, requires the agreement of the employer.[16]

The Equal Pay Act has also had a major impact on fringe benefits. Under this law, it is "an unlawful employment practice for an employer to discriminate between men and women with regard to fringes." In particular, fringe benefits designed to assist the "head of the household" or "principal wage earner" are considered discriminatory when the effect is to favor male employees. Similarly, it is unlawful to have pension or retirement plans that provide for different benefits or that set different compulsory or optional retirement ages based on sex.[17]

Under the Civil Rights Act, companies must provide maternity leave. The EEOC has ruled that employers must treat disabilities caused or contributed by pregnancy as temporary disabilities, must grant leaves of absence to pregnant employees, and must reinstate them without loss of seniority or other benefits.[18] However, this does not mean that the employer must provide insurance to cover pregnancy-related costs. The Supreme Court has held that GE did not violate the Civil Rights Act by excluding pregnancy from its disability insurance program. The Court held that "the plan . . . is nothing more than an insurance package which covers some risks but excludes others . . . there is no risk from which men are protected and women are not. Likewise, there is no risk from which women are protected and men are not."[19]

A federal law pertaining to holidays for gov-

---

[14] Edwin F. Beal and Edward D. Wickersham, *The Practice of Collective Bargaining*, rev. ed. (Homewood, Ill.: Richard D. Irwin, Inc., 1963), p. 488.
[15] Bureau of National Affairs, *Bulletin to Management*, March 22, 1962, p. 8. See also "Amendments to the Welfare and Pension Plans Disclosure Act," *Monthly Labor Review*, 85:535–536 (May 1962).

[16] This discussion is based on Donald G. Carlson, "Responding to the Pension Reform Law," *Harvard Business Review*, 52:133–144 (November-December 1974), and "Pension Reform's Expensive Ricochet," *Business Week*, March 24, 1975, pp. 144–155.
[17] "Equal Employment Opportunity Commission Guidelines on Discrimination Based on Sex," amended April 4, 1972, Section 1604.9, Fringe Benefits.
[18] "Maternity Leaves: A Look at Company Policies," *A P-H Survey*, Prentice-Hall, 1974, p. 3.
[19] *Honolulu Star-Bulletin*, December 7, 1976, p. 1.

ernment employees is having a major effect on holiday practices throughout the country. Under this law, federal employees observe the following holidays on Monday: George Washington's birthday, Memorial Day, Columbus Day, and Veterans Day. As a result, most states adopted similar laws pertaining to state employees, and a large proportion of private employers subsequently moved the observance of these holidays to Monday.[20]

Technology and science have also had an impact on fringe benefits. When technological changes dislocate workers, unions or management—or both—may attempt to minimize the problem of layoffs through severance pay, retraining programs, or supplemental unemployment benefit plans (SUB). SUB plans typically provide for a company's payments to workers who are laid off and are designed to supplement payments from state unemployment compensation funds. Originally negotiated in the auto industry in 1955, SUB benefits combined with state unemployment compensation pay approximate 95 percent of workers' regular weekly pay after taxes.[21]

Technological changes may have an even more direct impact on fringe benefits. For example, the introduction of toxic chemicals or hazardous equipment may require new kinds of protective clothing or equipment for employees.[22]

Collective bargaining, of course, has had a major impact over the years on the number and

worth of fringe benefits provided unionized employees. Furthermore, when fringe benefits are negotiated between a management and a union, similar benefits are often extended to the nonunionized employees in the same organization. In addition, unions typically call attention to fringe benefits negotiated elsewhere to support arguments for increasing fringe benefits in a particular firm.

Union efforts to increase fringe benefits are sometimes motivated by factors other than a desire to increase benefits for workers. For example, assuming that premium pay on Sundays or holidays is a "fringe benefit," double or triple time for work on Sundays or holidays may be sought in order to discourage management from scheduling work on those days. Additional vacation time or other time off may be sought to reduce unemployment, since longer vacations require additional workers to operate plants. (This was an objective of the United Auto Workers in the 1976 negotiations with the Ford Motor Company.)

Managerial attitudes will also affect the fringe benefit structure, just as they affect the organization's wage levels. Many fringe benefits have been introduced at the initiative of the employer from a wide variety of motives, including desires to increase the security and living standards of employees, to avoid unionization, to enhance morale, or to compete with other firms in recruiting and retraining people.

Labor market conditions are also likely to affect the fringe benefits paid by organizations. Shortages of certain skills and competition for these skills will probably be a factor in increasing fringe benefits. For example, if competition for engineers is keen, a company may endeavor to attract employees by initiating a tuition-payment and time-off program that permits engineers to work on advanced degrees at nearby universities.

Thus, a wide variety of environmental forces influence the fringe-benefit programs of organi-

[20]Bureau of National Affairs, *Personnel Management,* BNA Policy and Practice Series, 223:351.

[21]Constance Sorrentino, "Unemployment Compensation in Eight Industrial Nations," *Monthly Labor Review,* 99:23 (July 1976). There were 700 such plans covering 2.5 million workers in 1968. See U.S. Department of Labor, *Manpower Report of the President,* April 1968, p. 41.

[22]It may be inaccurate to consider protective clothing and equipment as fringe benefits when these are required to protect the employee from injury or ill health. When such benefits extend beyond the minimum health and safety requirements, however, probably they are then properly labeled as fringes.

zations. Federal and state laws, governmental agency rulings, court decisions, technology and science, collective bargaining, managerial attitudes, labor market conditions—all these forces, and probably others, influence the kind and level of fringe benefits provided employees in a given organization.

EFFECT ON NEED FULFILLMENT

Many fringe benefits serve to meet certain needs relating to physiology and safety. Depending upon their extent, these benefits may range from a minimum level of need fulfillment to maintaining essentially normal living standards of employees or their dependents in case of illness, injury, or death. Examples of benefits that contribute to fulfilling the needs of physiology and safety are sick pay, unemployment compensation, SUB plans, workmen's compensation, pension plans, life insurance, medical-hospital plans, protective clothing and equipment, and rest periods. Vacations contribute in part to fulfilling physiological needs.

A number of benefits may be construed as helping to meet self-actualization needs. Examples would be holidays, vacations, and pensions. These benefits permit the employee to be away from the job and participate in other life experiences while enjoying continued wages. These fringe benefits also probably contribute to the need for esteem in that they may be interpreted as indications of personal worth.

The way in which benefits are administered, however, can jeopardize need fulfillment. For example, when sick benefits are not payable until after one day of illness, employees may interpret this to mean a lack of confidence and trust by management and this certainly does not help fulfill an employee's need for esteem from others. Similar negative effects are produced by erratic administration of benefits and unjustifiably "stingy" programs.

The reader will recall from Chapter 6 that fringe benefits rank last in importance to the employees' job satisfaction. I interpreted this ranking to mean that fringe benefits ranked last in terms of what employees *want* relative to other rewards or environmental conditions.

The reason for this low ranking may be that basic needs, at least those of the employee, are taken care of fairly well in our society because of fringe benefits and public-welfare programs and that other unfulfilled needs loom higher in importance. This observation may be particularly true with respect to job security.[23] Another reason, or partial reason, for the low ranking of fringes may be that employees do not understand and appreciate the economic and tax advantages of their fringe benefits.[24]

AUTHORITY AND ACCOUNTABILITY

To our knowledge, practices in the planning and implementing of fringe benefit structures have not been systematically studied. In the nonunionized firm, it is likely that suggestions for increasing fringe benefits come from various sources, including the president, the personnel director, and the board of directors. In the unionized firm, constant pressure for increasing fringe benefits will come from the union. Because of the impact on financial resources, review and concurrence by top management, including the chief financial officer, is probably typical practice.

[23] Peter Drucker cites a case of a company where workers would have preferred job security to many of their fringe benefits, yet the fringes were costing far more than job security would have cost. Peter F. Drucker, *The New Society* (New York: Harper & Brothers, 1950), p. 293.

[24] In a study of over 36,000 employees in fifteen companies, more than 30 percent of the respondents had a poor understanding of the fringe benefits provided. David A. Harrington, "How to Improve the Return from Your Fringe Benefit Program," *Personnel Journal*, 49:604 (July 1970). For a discussion of the tax advantages of fringe benefits versus wages and salaries see Floyd F. Florey, "Fringe Benefits for All," *Taxes*, 39:870–888 (November 1961).

Ideally, it seems wise to hold the personnel department accountable for coordinating the planning of any changes in the fringe benefit structure since fringe benefits are an organizationwide matter and since fringe programs should be correlated with wage and salary administration. It also seems wise in fringe benefit planning for the personnel department to seek the advice of various department heads in order to obtain suggestions and anticipate possible problems. Further, the use of attitude surveys to obtain employees' reactions to different compensation items can be productive. Final approval of fringe benefit plans of any consequence should remain the prerogative of top management.

UTILITY OF SYSTEMS

As we have suggested, formalized systems and devices are not used in determining fringe benefits to the extent that they are used in determining basic wages. Ideally, however, fringe benefit and attitude surveys should be planned and conducted carefully, with meticulous attention to the statistical computations used and to the interpretation of the surveys. Furthermore, careful attention must be given to analyzing the costs of fringe benefits, since fringes are such significant costs in the reward-structure of most organizations.[25]

RELIABILITY OF SURVEYS

The reliability of fringe benefit surveys appears not to have been studied directly, but it may be inferred that the lack of standardized computa-

tional procedures and the apparent lack of thoroughness in such surveys causes different people seeking the same information to obtain different results. Discrepancies are probably even greater in the collective-bargaining situation, in which both parties may attempt to interpret results in such a way as to justify their particular positions.

VALIDITY OF FRINGES

The validity of fringe benefits would be the extent to which they contributed to the goals of the enterprise. If one organizational objective is the security and welfare of employees, fringe benefits are obviously valid. Relating fringe benefits to such objectives as productivity or profits, however, is much more difficult. Obviously, if fringe benefits are too costly, the organization will spend itself into financial difficulty. In addition, some fringe items, like workmen's compensation, are required by laws that, if violated, would place heavy burdens on offending organizations, including fines, injunctions, or imprisonment of executives.

Some fringe benefits, such as vacations and holidays, probably must be given in order to attract and retain employees. Additional fringes may be necessary for other reasons. For example, pension plans may not be necessary for recruiting employees into a new firm, but a pension plan may be necessary to hold key employees as they approach middle age.

Thus, it is possible that many fringe benefits are much more useful in retaining employees than in recruiting them—an opinion held by companies' officials, according to one study. The same study reported that new production workers, particularly unmarried youths and women, tended not to inquire about fringe benefits.[26]

[25] For suggestions and a discussion of some of the problems in computing and controlling costs of fringe benefits, see Michel T. Wermel and Geraldine M. Beidman, *How to Determine the Total Cost of Your Employee Benefit Programs* (Pasadena: California Institute of Technology, March 1960), BIRC Publication No. 12.

[26] Lester, *Hiring Practices and Competition*, pp. 88–92.

A number of authors have speculated that the holding power of fringe benefits, such as pensions, tends to "freeze" apathetic or marginal employees in their jobs. Still another argument suggests that pension funds may be creating labor obsolescence because accumulated pension funds are likely to be invested in new capital equipment that may make many workers obsolete. The solution proposed by the authors is to divert some of the money going into pension funds into training programs.[27] Others have argued that higher labor mobility may be good for the economy and that there should be "portable pensions" that the worker can take from job to job. Such plans have tended to occur within industries, including coverage of employees transferring among Bell Telephone System companies, coverage of some members of the International Association of Machinists, the Teamsters, the United Auto Workers, the International Brotherhood of Electrical Workers, and many college and university faculty members participating in the Teachers Insurance and Annuity Insurance plan. However, the vesting standards required by ERISA (e.g., full vesting after ten years of service) means that the employee ultimately receives the vested funds even though the employer does not agree to a transfer of the funds to another employer. Increased vesting should mean that pensions have less of a "freezing" effect on employees.

In general, fringe benefits probably contribute proportionately less to productivity and profits than wages. As stated earlier, one reason may be that employees do not understand the cost of fringes or the tax advantages of fringes in contrast to wages, but more subtle reasons may provide the explanation.

For one thing, most fringes are not *perceived*

as being related to job worth or performance, although, as we have seen, some are directly related to job worth when the benefit takes the form of continuing a salary. Some are awarded to large groups of employees or to the total work force, with the most obvious variable being length of service. Examples are sick pay, vacations, and severance pay. Others such as holidays and jury-pay allowance, may be awarded without any obvious differentiation among employees except that the recipients must be beyond the probationary period. Some are awarded on the basis of events or conditions over which neither the organization nor the employee has much control. Sick pay, hospitalization, and death benefits are examples.

It is not being suggested that fringes be awarded on the basis of merit rating, but it is suggested that most fringes may have inherent limits as motivating devices. However, a fringe benefit "package" that is too thin may serve as a negative motivator. On the positive side, a good fringe benefit program contributes to an environment in which management can insist on high levels of performance.

To enhance the potentiality of fringes as motivators, a number of authors in recent years have advocated the idea of a *flexible benefits plan* (or "compensation cafeteria" or "flexible compensation") through which the employee can choose a particular mix of benefits adding up to a given amount. However, because of the complexities involved in administration and the difficulties in pricing out various benefits as they relate to the different income tax levels of employees, such plans have not been adopted widely. At least one firm, TRW Systems Group, has inaugurated a "Flexible Benefits Plan." The company ran into policy, tax, and administrative problems in the more than three years it took to design and implement the plan, but successfully launched the program and has

[27] Henry I. Kester and Harold A. Wolf, "Pension Funds: Creator of Labor Obsolescence?" *Business Horizons*, 3:70–76 (Fall 1960).

consistently found a large majority of employees endorsing the concept.[28]

Some benefits, if extended too far, can clearly interfere with organizational productivity. As examples, time off for personal business, for jury duty, for political or community activities, and for attending school can seriously cut into the productivity of the organization if not kept within reasonable bounds. If these benefits are carried too far, the enterprise may be subsidizing productivity off the job instead of productivity on the job.[29] When carried to the extreme, such benefits can be justified only in terms of the employer's desire to contribute to the community's welfare. Within reason, of course, such activities as community and political service may contribute to the long-range potentiality of the employee as well as to the welfare of the community. A balanced approach, therefore, is necessary.

SUMMARY

Fringe benefits assist employees in meeting some of life's contingencies, contribute to meeting the social obligations of employers, assist in helping to attract and retain employees, and meet the minimum welfare programs as pre-

scribed by law. Up to a point, fringes undoubtedly contribute to the financial objectives of organizations. Beyond this point, however, and depending upon many other variables, returns become negative. Only careful analysis and reasoning can determine the probable location of this point in individual situations. Once a reasonable competitive fringe program has been developed, additional money would seem to be better spent on rewarding superior performance.

REVIEW AND DISCUSSION QUESTIONS

1. Which fringes have increased the most in recent years as a percentage of the payroll dollar? What are the implications?

2. Which fringes are indirectly affected by job evaluation?

3. What are the pros and cons of the portable pension concept?

4. What is your assessment of the advantages and disadvantages of the compensation cafeteria idea?

5. How does federal legislation affect fringe benefit payments?

6. What is the difference between SUB plans and GAW plans? (See also Chapter 19.)

7. Analyze each of the fringes in Figure 20-3 in terms of their probable strengths as motivators.

8. What has been the impact of the Equal Pay Act on fringe benefit programs?

9. How does ERISA affect pension plans?

[28] Berwyn N. Fragner, "Employees' 'Cafeteria' Offers Insurance Options," *Harvard Business Review*, 53:7–10 (November-December 1975). For a discussion of some of these complexities plus some of the advantages in a flexible benefits plan, see J. Taylor, "A New Approach to Compensation Management," *Compensation Review*, 1:22–30 (First Quarter 1969); L.M. Baytos, "The Employee Fringe Benefit Smorgasbord: Its Potential and Limitations," *Compensation Review*, 2:16–28 (First Quarter 1970); and George W. Hettenhouse, "Compensation Cafeteria for Top Executives," *Harvard Business Review*, 49:113–119 (September-October 1971). Research by Milkovich and Delaney suggests that the methods used in obtaining data about employee preferences may influence the results. See George T. Milkovich and Michael J. Delaney, "A Note on Cafeteria Pay Plans," *Industrial Relations*, 14:112–116 (February 1975).

[29] Baby bonuses have been a fringe benefit in at least one company. See *Industrial Relations News*, March 24, 1962, p. 3.

SUPPLEMENTAL REFERENCES

Allen, Donna, *Fringe Benefits: Wages or Social Obligation?* (Ithaca, N.Y.: New York State School of Industrial and Labor Relations, Cornell University, 1969).

Baytos, Lawrence M., "Employee Participation in Compensation Planning," *Compensation Review*, 8:25–38 (Second Quarter 1976).

Burck, Gilbert, "That Ever Expanding Pension Balloon," *Fortune*, 84:130 (October 1971).

Burgess, Leonard R., *Wage and Salary Administration in a Dynamic Economy* (New York: Harcourt, Brace & World, 1968), Chapters 7 and 8.

Famularo, Joseph J., ed., *Handbook of Modern Personnel Administration* (New York: McGraw-Hill Book Company, 1972), Part 7.

Foegen, J.H., "Is It Time to Clip the Fringes?" *Personnel*, 49:36–42 (March-April 1972).

——, "Far-Out Fringe Benefits," *Personnel*, 44:65–71 (May-June 1967).

Gordon, T.J., and R.E. LeBleu, "Employee Benefits, 1970–1985," *Harvard Business Review*, 48:93–107 (January-February 1970).

Greenewalt, Crawford, *The Uncommon Man* (New York: McGraw-Hill Book Company, 1959).

Griffes, Ernest J.E., "What's Happening to the Private Pension System?" *The Personnel Administrator*, 16:29–32 (September-October 1971).

Hickery, Joseph A., "Workmen's Compensation: Administration and Provisions," *Monthly Labor Review*, 90:29–39 (December 1967).

Mabry, Bevars, "The Economics of Fringe Benefits," *Industrial Relations*, 12:95–106 (February 1973).

Matthies, Mary T., "The Developing Law on Equal Employment Opportunity," *Journal of Contemporary Business*, 5:29–46 (Winter 1976).

Nealey, Stanley M., and James G. Goodale, "Workers Preferences among Time-off Benefits and Pay," *Journal of Applied Psychology*, 51:357–361 (August 1967).

Patton, Arch, "The Hidden Costs of Federal Pensions," *Business Week*, April 27, 1974, pp. 26–28.

Schreiber, Irving, ed., *Proceedings of First Annual Conference on Employee Benefits* (New York: Dornost Publishing Company, 1967).

CHAPTER 21
INCENTIVE SYSTEMS

GENERAL DESCRIPTION AND PURPOSES

Broadly conceived, the term *incentive systems* could include all forms of compensation and benefit plans that tie rewards to performance. Thus, a pay plan basing pay on merit would be an incentive system.

More narrowly, however, the term *incentive systems* is frequently used to describe wage-payment plans that tie wages directly or indirectly to standards of productivity of individuals, some to the productivity of groups, and some to the productivity or profitability of the total organization. Thus, the term sometimes has a limited meaning that excludes many kinds of inducements offered people to perform work or to work up to or beyond acceptable standards. For example, in a narrower usage, it does not include wage and salary payments of the kind discussed in the previous two chapters, including merit pay. In addition, the term in its narrower meaning ordinarily does not in-

clude overtime payments, pay for holiday work, pay for hazardous work, or differentials paid according to shifts—all payments that could be considered incentives to perform work at undesirable times.

Since merit pay and other forms of compensation have been discussed in the previous two chapters, this chapter will focus on certain specialized forms of incentive systems. In particular, four major types of plans will be discussed: (a) individual incentive plans, including piece-rates, commissions, and suggestion systems; (b) group plans, essentially individual plans modified to apply to group performance; (c) plantwide productivity plans; and (d) profit-sharing plans. Notwithstanding considerable overlapping among the categories, they will help us point out some important differences among these various methods of compensating people. Overtime payments and positive reinforcement programs will also be discussed briefly.

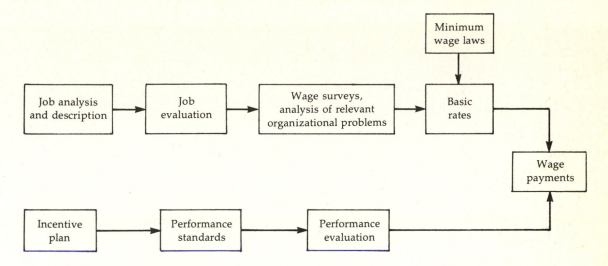

Figure **21-1**   Wage-determination process under incentive systems

The purpose of incentive plans, in general, is to increase the motivation of employees to contribute to the goals of the organization by offering financial inducements above and beyond basic wages and salaries. As we shall see, different types of incentive plans are aimed at different kinds of employees' behavior.

For a variety of reasons, including labor market competition and minimum wage laws, almost all individual and group incentive plans applying to production jobs guarantee a basic hourly wage. In addition, it appears that a majority of sales-commission plans feature a base salary.[1] A notable exception is found in the real estate industry. One study found that 73 percent of real estate firms surveyed paid straight commissions.[2]

These basic rates accompanying incentive systems tend to be established through job analysis, job evaluation, wage and salary sur-

veys, and other factors described in the wage-determination process in Chapter 19. For example, one survey reports that 84 percent of the firms with incentive systems have a formal job evaluation system.[3] Thus, incentive systems tend to be an extension of, or supplement to, the wage-determination process, and the flow of events is something like that shown in Figure 21-1. Collective bargaining is not shown in the diagram but will have an important impact on all these events. In the case of individual and group incentive plans, performance standards are based on time-and-motion studies. In the case of plantwide productivity and profit-sharing plans, performance standards are established for a plant or a company as a whole and may be based upon some ratio of production to payroll costs or a percentage of profit.

CURRENT PRACTICES AND PROBLEMS

As shown in Figure 21-2, 14 percent of plant workers in U.S. metropolitan areas were paid

[1] National Industrial Conference Board, "Incentive Plans for Salesmen," *Studies in Personnel Policy*, No. 217, 1970, p. 3.
[2] Warren R. Seyfried, "Characteristics of Real Estate Sales Firms in Seattle, Washington, 1962," *University of Washington Business Review*, 22:27 (June 1963).

[3] National Industrial Conference Board, "Wage Paymen Systems," *Studies in Personnel Policy*, No. 91, 1948, p. 14.

Figure **21-2** Percent distribution of plantworkers and officeworkers in all metropolitan areas, by method of wage determination, industry division, and region, July 1961 through June 1963, and July 1968 through June 1970

Method of wage determination	1961–63	1968–70	Industry division						Region[1]			
	All	All	Manufacturing	Public utilities[2]	Wholesale trade	Retail trade	Finance[3]	Services	North-east	South	North Central	West
	Plantworkers											
All workers	100	100	100	100	100	100	—	100	100	100	100	100
Paid time rates	79	86	80	99	95	90	—	94	82	89	83	94
Formal rate policy	65	73	74	96	69	61	—	66	71	63	76	85
Single rate[4]	37	36	40	43	35	18	—	40	32	32	38	46
Range of rates[5]	28	37	34	54	34	43	—	26	38	31	38	39
Progression based on automatic advancement according to length of service	—	16	14	39	11	14	—	8	17	12	16	19
Progression based on merit review	—	9	9	4	10	12	—	9	11	7	9	8
Progression based on a combination of length of service and merit review		12	11	11	13	16	—	10	10	12	14	12
No formal rate policy	14	13	6	4	26	29	—	29	11	25	7	9
Paid by incentive methods[6]	20	14	20	(7)	5	10	—	6	18	11	17	6
Piece rate	8	6	10	(7)	(7)	(7)	—	3	10	6	5	2
Individual	7	5	9	(7)	(7)	(7)	—	3	9	5	4	2
Group	1	1	1	(7)	(7)	(7)	—	1	1	1	1	(7)
Production bonus	8	6	10	(7)	(7)	1	—	1	8	2	10	1
Individual	4	3	5	(7)	(7)	1	—	1	3	1	5	(7)
Group	4	3	5	(7)	(7)	(7)	—	(7)	4	1	4	1
Commission	3	2	(7)	(7)	5	8	—	1	1	3	2	3

	All workers							Officeworkers				
	100	100	100	100	100	100	100	100	100	100	100	100
Paid time rates	99	99	99	99	100	99	100	100	100	99	99	100
Formal rate policy	64	72	75	86	52	59	76	50	71	61	74	81
Single rate[4]	4	3	2	13	3	2	[7]	2	3	3	3	4
Range of rates[5]	60	69	73	73	49	57	75	48	68	58	71	77
Progression based on automatic advancement according to length of service	—	11	10	39	3	9	4	4	9	10	7	20
Progression based on merit review	—	36	43	14	29	25	45	26	41	26	40	33
Progression based on a combination of length of service and merit review	—	22	20	21	17	23	27	18	18	22	24	24
No formal rate policy	35	28	25	14	48	41	24	50	29	38	26	19
Paid by incentive methods[6]	[7]	[7]	[7]	[7]	[8]	[7]	[8]	[8]	[8]	[7]	[7]	[8]

[1] The regions in the study are: Northeast—Connecticut, Maine, Massachusetts, New Hampshire, New Jersey, New York, Pennsylvania, Rhode Island, and Vermont; South—Alabama, Arkansas, Delaware, District of Columbia, Florida, Georgia, Kentucky, Louisiana, Maryland, Mississippi, North Carolina, Oklahoma, South Carolina, Tennessee, Texas, Virginia, and West Virginia; North Central—Illinois, Indiana, Iowa, Kansas, Michigan, Minnesota, Missouri, Nebraska, North Dakota, Ohio, South Dakota, and Wisconsin; and West—Arizona, California, Colorado, Idaho, Montana, Nevada, New Mexico, Oregon, Utah, Washington, and Wyoming. Alaska and Hawaii are not included in the program.

[2] Transportation, communication, and other public utilities.

[3] Finance, insurance, and real estate. Data are not shown separately for plantworkers in real estate establishments in this industry group. Plantworkers in real estate are included in the all areas data.

[4] Single-rate plans provide the same rate to all experienced workers in the same job classification. Learners, apprentices, and probationary workers may be paid according to rate schedules which start below the single rate for the job classification and permit achievement of the full rate over a period of time.

[5] Range-of-rate plans specify the minimum or maximum rates, or both, paid experienced workers for the same job classification.

[6] Incentive methods include wage payment plans which incorporate piecework, production bonuses, or commissions. Piecework is work for which a predetermined rate is paid for each unit of output. Production bonuses are based on production in excess of a quota or on completion of a job in less than standard time. Commissions are payments based on a percentage of value of sales or on a combination of salary plus a percentage.

[7] Less than 0.5 percent.

[8] No workers reported.

NOTE: Sums of individual items may not equal totals because of rounding. Dashes indicate information not available.

From John H. Cox, "Time and Incentive Pay Practices in Urban Areas," Monthly Labor Review, 94:54 (December 1971).

under individual or group incentive plans in the period 1968–1970 in contrast to the 20 percent paid under such plans seven years earlier. Payments by paid time rates increased from 79 percent of those covered in 1961–1963 to 86 percent covered by such plans in 1968–1974. The most likely explanations for this shift in numbers of employees away from incentive systems to paid time rates, according to Cox, are shifts in employment among employers with no change in the type of wage payment plan, and shifts in the proportion of direct to indirect workers due to the introduction of new work methods. Less than half of one percent of office workers were paid by incentive methods during both periods.[4]

This study does not include profit-sharing plans, which typically do not relate rewards directly to individual or group productivity. A 1964 study found that 26 percent of manufacturing firms with 250 employees or more had profit-sharing plans; 15 percent had plans pertaining to both white- and blue-collar employees; and 10 percent had plans pertaining to white-collar employees only.[5] Thus, profit-sharing plans almost always include white-collar workers, with blue-collar workers less likely to be included.

As suggested, a high percentage of sales people are under some kind of incentive plan. A 1964 study of outside sales staff of 665 firms found that a salary plus commission was paid to 67 percent of these sales forces.[6] A 1967 study involving 444 firms found a comparable percentage of firms, 65 percent, paying a salary plus some incentive compensation.[7] The figure is probably much higher in real estate sales.[8]

Supervisors participated in bonus plans in about 39 percent of the firms surveyed in one study. In still another study, middle- and top-management executives participated in bonus plans in about 45 percent of the firms surveyed.[9] Thus, participation in some kind of incentive plan that permits earning above and beyond basic wages and salaries appears to vary with type of job, with industry, and with organizational rank. Salespeople, followed by executives and supervisors, participate in some kind of incentive plan more frequently than nonexempt blue-collar or other white-collar employees.

INDIVIDUAL INCENTIVE PLANS

The purpose of individual incentive plans, according to Louden, ". . . is to offer a financial incentive for a worker or group of workers to produce work of an acceptable quality over and above a specified quantity."[10] According to Wolf, "Their primary purpose is to aid in obtaining minimum unit costs, thereby contributing to enterprise profits."[11] These two quotations emphasize the dual purpose of incentive compensation for individuals, namely (a) to reduce unit costs and (b) to maintain standards of quality.

It should be stressed that most individual incentive plans are designed to *assist* in increasing efficiency, not to accomplish it alone. As Louden has observed, incentive plans serve to

[4] John H. Cox, "Time and Incentive Pay Practices in Urban Areas," *Monthly Labor Review*, 94:53–54 (December 1971).

[5] National Industrial Conference Board, "Personnel Practices in Factory and Office: Manufacturing," *Studies in Personnel Policy*, No. 194, 1964, p. 110.

[6] National Industrial Conference Board, "Compensating Field Sales Representatives," *Studies in Personnel Policy*, No. 202, 1966, p. 19.

[7] Richard L. Smyth, "Financial Incentives for Salesmen," *Harvard Business Review*, 46:110 (January-February 1968).

[8] Seyfried, "Characteristics of Real Estate Sales Firms."

[9] Dean Rosensteel, "Supervisory Compensation—An Interim Report," *Personnel*, 33:354–362 (January 1957).

[10] J.K. Louden, *Wage Incentives* (New York: John Wiley & Sons, 1944), p. 13.

[11] William B. Wolf, *Wage Incentives as a Management Tool* (New York: Columbia University Press, 1957), p. 6.

make changes in work methods that are acceptable to employees and to sustain efficiencies gained by time-and-motion studies or by work-simplification.[12] In short, industrial engineering serves to organize tasks more efficiently or to simplify them, while individual incentive systems are designed to motivate the worker to carry out these industrial engineering plans for increased efficiency.

Most incentive plans for production workers are of two types: (a) *piece-rate plans* that provide for wage payments based on the quantity of units produced, or (b) *production-bonus plans* that provide for wage payments based on production that exceeds the standard rate or on the completion of tasks in less than standard time. Some years ago, piece-rate plans appeared to be the most popular form of incentive compensation,[13] but in more recent times the proportion of production bonus plans has equaled that of piece-rate plans. (See Figure 21-2.)

Some of the production-bonus plans found in a significant number of companies some years ago were the Halsey, Barth, and Rowan plans (5.8 percent of all firms surveyed used one of these plans), the Bedaux or Haynes point premium plan (5.5 percent), and the Gantt Task and Bonus plan (4.3 percent).[14]

Another type of plan is the *measured-day-rate plan*. Under this plan, employees are rated every two or three months on several factors, such as productivity, quality of work, depend-ability, and versatility and, if rated high, may make as much as 20 percent above the job rate. This merit rating fixes the wage until the next merit rating, at which time the individual's pay may be changed upward or downward. The essential differences between the measured-day-rate plan and most ordinary merit-rating plans are that productivity is given significantly higher weight under the former type of plan and that wages can be reduced if the rating falls.[15] This plan was used in 6.2 percent of firms surveyed in one study.[16]

Sales-pay plans featuring commissions or bonuses based on the number of items or dollar volume sold can also be considered in the category of individual incentive plans. The NICB 1964 study of sales forces cited earlier found that a straight salary was paid to 22 percent of the sales forces, a straight commission with no minimum guarantee to 11 percent, and a combination of salary and commission to 67 percent. (The word *commission* as used here includes payments based on net sales, gross wages, profits, and the like, and it includes the term *bonus*.) Quotas as a basis for the computation of bonuses were used in about one-third of the situations in which a bonus "pool" was used. Other factors in some of the plans were profitableness of different product lines, the question of whether the sale was new or repeat, and the type of customer.[17]

[12] Louden, *Wage Incentives*, p. 20.

[13] William R. Spriegel, John R. Beishline, and Alfred G. Dale, *Personnel Practices in Industry*, Personnel Study No. 8, rev. (Austin, Texas: Bureau of Business Research, 1958), pp. 26–29.

[14] Ibid., p. 27. For descriptions of these and other plans, see David W. Belcher, *Compensation Administration* (Englewood Cliffs, N.J.: Prentice-Hall, Inc., 1974), pp. 314–324; Adolph Langsner and Herbert G. Zollitsch, *Wage and Salary Administration* (Cincinnati: South-Western Publishing Company, 1961); and Robert E. Gibson, *Wage and Salaries: A Handbook for Line Managers*, rev. ed. (New York: American Management Association, 1967), Chapter VI.

[15] See Mary Cook, "Piecework vs. Daywork: The Big Dilemma," *The Personnel Administrator*, 18:2–4 (November-December 1973) (special insert); and Anne Shaw, "Measured Daywork: One Step towards a Salaried Workforce," in Tom Lupton, ed., *Payment Systems* (Middlesex, England: Penguin Books, Ltd., 1972), pp. 143–165.

[16] Spriegel, Beishline, and Dale, *Personnel Practices in Industry*, p. 27.

[17] National Industrial Conference Board, "Compensating Field Sales Representatives," pp. 21–23. For an article that recommends providing sales personnel with choices from a wide range of incentives, see David Gardner and Kenneth M. Rowland, "A Self-Tailored Approach to Incentives," *Personnel Journal*, 49:907–912ff. (November 1970).

Incentive plans emphasizing quality of performances are seldom mentioned in the literature, but, occasionally, they are found. Examples of job situations that provided appropriate conditions for such plans are aircraft-maintenance jobs or jobs involving custom-built electronic equipment requiring high reliability. The "Zero Defects" plans discussed in Chapter 10 typically do not include financial compensation as a form of reward.

Problems in the use of individual incentive systems are numerous. Obtaining the employees' acceptance of an incentive system may be a problem at the outset. Fears that the plan will lead to a "speed-up," layoffs, or reduced wages can cause worker resistance. One of the most difficult problems is the establishment of standards. No matter how skilled and fair the industrial engineer or whoever establishes standards may be, standards always involve value judgments. As one author puts it: "Disputes involving productivity standards cannot be separated from job values and human values."[18] I shall discuss this problem further under the subject of reliability.

Another problem may arise from the effect on productivity of forces over which the worker has no control. Obviously, workers will resent reduction in pay due to machine breakdown, defective raw materials, and so forth. Sales people on commissions will resent a sales decline because of ineffective advertising, inferior manufacture or generally poor business conditions. Productivity on some jobs is so clearly a function of variables other than the performance of the individual that most incentive systems are not applicable.

Numerous other problems arise from the natural tendency of the worker to "beat the system"—that is, to get the system to pay off in the rewards the worker wants. For example, unless standards of cooperation and quality are built into the system, some workers may attempt to maximize earnings at the expense of quality, and some at the expense of the production of other workers. A sales clerk may "push" easy-to-sell items that may not be the most profitable ones. Or, depending upon the particular type of plan, workers may perform rapidly at times and then hide surplus production to cover periods when they wish to slow down or to cover periods of setup or breakdown in machines.[19] While engineers are studying the job, the worker may deliberately slow down in order to obtain a low standard that will later yield a high bonus.[20] Restriction of output because of social pressures or fear that standards will be raised are additional problems.[21]

SUGGESTION PLANS

Ordinarily, the primary purpose of suggestion plans is to elicit workers' ideas on reducing costs. Other typical purposes include the obtaining of suggestions for increasing safety or improving quality. Some companies, however, promote suggestion plans so that employees may have the opportunity to participate more broadly in company matters. In other words, some companies use these plans as devices for improving communications and morale.[22]

The typical suggestion plan features boxes placed at convenient locations throughout the plant, with appropriate forms available. Em-

[18]James J. Foley, "How *Not* to Handle Productivity Disputes," *Harvard Business Review*, 37:79 (September-October 1959).

[19]See Robert H. Roy, "Do Wage Incentives Reduce Costs?" *Industrial and Labor Relations Review*, 5:207 (January 1952).
[20]For a case description of this "guessing game" played by time-study people and workers, see William Foote Whyte et al., *Money and Motivation* (New York: Harper & Brothers, 1955), pp. 14–19.
[21]For a discussion of a variety of these problems, see Frances Torbert, "Making Incentives Work," *Harvard Business Review*, 37:81–92 (September-October 1959).
[22]National Industrial Conference Board, "Suggestion Systems," *Studies in Personnel Policy*, No. 135, 1953, p. 6.

ployees may use one of the forms to write out a suggestion for cost-reduction or safety and deposit it in the box for subsequent evaluation. If the suggestion is accepted, a cash award based on some percentage of the first year's savings is usually paid, or a flat amount is paid for intangible suggestions, such as safety ideas. If suggestions are rejected, an explanation is usually given. Supervisory and professional employees are usually excluded from these plans on the assumption that cost-control is part of their jobs.

Suggestion plans have moderately wide usage in American industry. A 1964 survey reported that 29 percent of responding manufacturing firms had active systems for suggestion. Typical practice is to pay an award based on a percent of the savings to the company over the first year. [23]

Systems for suggestions have a number of inherent problems. One problem is that suggestions may result in the elimination of jobs or an increase in incentive standards and thus may come into conflict with other goals of workers. Another problem relates to the origin of the idea. Since many ideas originate as bits and fragments of ideas supplied by others, a claim for an award by one worker may be resented by others who believe they had a hand in its formulation. Conversely, many ideas probably do not mature because of fears that someone will steal them. Another problem is making the rejection of an idea acceptable to the suggesting employee. Still another problem is convincing the suggester that his or her idea has already been suggested and is being studied.

A particularly serious problem with many suggestion systems is that they bypass the supervisor. Supervisors may interpret suggestions as a reflection on their competence and may retaliate in some way, or else workers may

fear that their suggestions will result in retaliation of some kind. [24]

Certain of these problems are minimized or avoided under plantwide productivity plans, such as the Scanlon Plan to be discussed later. Although this plan grants individual recognition for suggestions, all employees, including supervisors, stand to gain from accepted suggestions, since bonuses are distributed to all employees. [25]

GROUP INCENTIVE PLANS

The purpose of group incentive plans is the same as that of individual plans except for the additional emphasis on cooperation within the group. Actually, most group incentive plans are individual plans applied to a small group of workers, with piece-rate compensation being the most prevalent incentive plan. These plans are particularly applicable to situations in which several workers must cooperate in performing a single task and the contribution of particular individuals is difficult to measure.

Although individual incentive plans cover twice as many employees, the Cox study cited above reported that 4 percent of workers were paid under group incentive methods in the 1968–1970 period. This was a slight decline over seven years earlier. (See the second column of Figure 21-2.)

One possible reason for the decline in these plans is that unusually excellent or unusually deficient individual performance cannot be rewarded directly and proportionately. Furthermore, individual incentive probably decreases as the size of the group increases. On the other

[23] National Industrial Conference Board, "Personnel Practices," p. 58.

[24] Many of these problems are discussed by Whyte et al., *Money and Motivation*, pp. 171–173.

[25] See Russell W. Davenport, "Enterprise for Everyman: A Case History of How the Scanlon Plan, as Applied by Union and Management at Lapointe Machine Tool, Has Raised Productivity, Profits, and Pay," *Fortune*, 41:55–59ff. (January 1950).

hand, such plans should encourage cooperation and should result in group pressures toward high production.

PLANTWIDE PRODUCTIVITY PLANS

The major purpose of plantwide productivity plans is to increase efficiency in production through workers' participation in committees on production. These committees process suggestions about methods, machines, scrap-reduction, plant-layout, materials, and other matters.

One of the most famous incentive plans of this type is the Scanlon Plan. This plan features a standard based on the ratio between the adjusted payroll and the dollar sales volume of production for some historical period. When this ratio for current operations declines—that is, when labor costs go down in relationship to productivity—the employees share all or part of the savings, depending upon the particular company. When labor costs do not go down, of course, there are no savings to share. Ordinarily, all employees are involved, including production, clerical, sales, and supervisory personnel.

Major features of the Scanlon Plan emphasize union-management cooperation and cooperation among employees at all levels by means of committees. The originator of the plan, Joseph Scanlon, would not institute the plan without union consent and participation. A committee on production in each department, consisting of a union-elected or appointed representative and a foreman, meets regularly to consider ways of increasing production and to evaluate suggestions from employees. Suggestions are thoroughly discussed, and the results of the meeting are referred for further consideration to a companywide screening committee consisting of union officials and top manage-

ment.[26] Other group plans of a similar nature are the Rucker Share-of-Production Plan and the Nunn-Bush Shoe Company Plan.[27]

Under the Kaiser Steel Union Sharing plan, employees share in cost reductions stemming from increased efficiency. Savings in labor, supplies, or materials are distributed between company and employees, with the company receiving 67.5 percent of the savings. The 32.5 percent that goes to the employees is paid in the form of monthly bonuses. Under the Plan, increases in wages and benefits are equal to, or greater than, those granted in the steel industry generally.[28]

Lack of workers' understanding and willingness to focus on problems of production can cause serious difficulties under Scanlon-type plans. The necessity for increased effectiveness in communications by both management and the union, the danger of leaving out middle-management people, and the possibility of decreased effectiveness in the grievance procedure are the problems. A particularly serious problem with such plans is the opportunity given

[26] Frederick G. Lesieur, "Worker Participation to Increase Production," *Management Record*, 21:38–41ff. (February 1959); Elbridge S. Puckett, "Measuring Performance under the Scanlon Plan," in Frederick G. Lesieur, ed., *The Scanlon Plan: A Frontier in Labor-Management Cooperation* (Boston and New York: The Technology Press of Massachusetts Institute of Technology and John Wiley & Sons, 1958), pp. 65–79; George Strauss and Leonard R. Sayles, "The Scanlon Plan: Some Organizational Problems," *Human Organization*, 16:15–22 (Fall 1957); and Daniel Katz and Robert L. Kahn, *The Social Psychology of Organizations* (New York: John Wiley and Sons, 1966), pp. 380–388.

[27] See Belcher, *Compensation Administration*, pp. 331–335.

[28] National Industrial Conference Board, "The Kaiser Steel Union Sharing Plan," *Studies in Personnel Policy*, No. 187, 1963. See also Leonard R. Burgess, *Wage and Salary Administration in a Dynamic Economy* (New York: Harcourt, Brace & World, 1968), pp. 123–25. This plan was the focal point of a strike in 1972 at Kaiser's Fontana plant, largely due to declining bonuses in contrast to payments made under piece-rate plans elsewhere in the steel industry. The strike was settled on the basis of a minimum guarantee in addition to a base hourly wage. *Monthly Labor Review*, 95:65 (May 1972).

workers or union officials to criticize management in any area, including sales. Unless such criticism is responsible and accepted in a mature manner, relationships between the parties may deteriorate.[29]

A plan combining the features of plantwide productivity plans, group incentive plans, and individual piece-rate plans is the Lincoln Incentive Compensation Plan of the Lincoln Electric Company.[30] At Lincoln Electric each employee works on piece rate, but all work together to decrease costs and to increase profitability. Each employee is rated by superiors on quality and quantity of production, and a bonus is calculated accordingly. Since 1934, bonuses have ranged between 50 percent and 150 percent of the total wage bill; the typical worker's take-home pay is about double that for competitors.[31] (For profitability and productivity results, see later in the chapter.)

"POSITIVE REINFORCEMENT" AND INCENTIVE PLANS

"Positive reinforcement programs," based on operant conditioning or behavior modification theories, have emerged in a number of companies. While most individual and group incentive plans are based on positive reinforcement of desirable behavior (productivity, quality, etc.) through wage payments, most so-called positive reinforcement approaches tend to emphasize praise and the avoidance of punishment in contrast to an emphasis on wage payments. As used at Emery Air Freight Corporation, the steps involved in establishing such a program are (a) defining the behavioral aspects of performance and conducting a performance audit, (b) the establishment of specific goals for each worker (participatory approaches are recommended), (c) allowing employees to keep records of their own work, and (d) praising the positive aspects of the employee's performance and withholding praise for substandard work.[32]

In addition to Emery Air Freight, organizations adopting such an approach include Michigan Bell (operator and maintenance services), GE (training relative to supervising minority and women employees), B.F. Goodrich Chemical Company, and Emerson Electronics. Programs at the Weyerhaeuser Company (clerical workers, tree planters, middle-level managers, and scientists) and the city of Detroit (garbage collection) include monetary payments among the positive reinforcers used. A program at Connecticut General Life Insurance Company includes earned time off as a positive reinforcer.[33]

While at the outset monetary payments have not been included in the majority of these programs, there are some indications that management will be obliged to move in this direction

---

[29] For case descriptions of successful use of this plan, see Nicholas L.A. Martucci, "Productivity and Incentive Pay," *Management Record,* 19:346–349ff. (October 1957); and Davenport, "Enterprise for Everyman." For a case history of an unsuccessful experience with the Scanlon Plan, see Thomas Q. Gilson and Myron J. Lefcowitz, "A Plant-Wide Productivity Bonus in a Small Factory: Study of an Unsuccessful Case," *Industrial and Labor Relations Review,* 10:284–296 (January 1957). For descriptions of both successful and unsuccessful applications of the Scanlon Plan, see Joseph N. Scanlon, "Profit Sharing under Collective Bargaining: Three Case Studies," *Industrial and Labor Relations Review,* 2:58–74 (October 1948).

[30] See Council of Profit Sharing Industries, *Profit Sharing Manual* (Akron: Council of Profit Sharing Industries, 1958), pp. 33–34; James F. Lincoln, *A New Approach to Industrial Economics* (New York: The Devin-Adair Company, 1961); and James F. Lincoln, *Incentive Management* (Cleveland, Ohio: Lincoln Electric Company, 1969).

[31] David Jenkins, *Job Power* (London: William Heinemann, Ltd., 1974), pp. 216–219; and Mitchell Fein, "Motivation for Work," in Robert Dubin, ed., *Handbook of Work, Organization*

and Society (Chicago: Rand McNally College Publishing Company, 1976), p. 52.

[32] W. Clay Hamner and Ellen P. Hamner, "Behavior Modification on the Bottom Line," *Organizational Dynamics,* 4:8–9 (Spring 1976).

[33] Ibid.

in a number of instances. Theoretically, it is not stretching equity theory too far to speculate that increased profitability of an organization based on the performance of employees will create considerable tension among employees if the rewards are not shared in some way. The avoidance of some disaster such as bankruptcy may be perceived by employees as the quid pro quo for improved productivity, but the emergence of higher and higher profits without a return to employees will ultimately be perceived, I believe, as inequitable. (I advanced the same argument in Chapter 9 relative to job enrichment. See also the discussion in Chapter 6 on the "Law of Effect and Operant Conditioning.") Indeed, in the Michigan Bell positive reinforcement program involving maintenance service employees, satisfaction with pay decreased. At Emery Air Freight, managers have begun to search for additional reinforcers such as a letter home, time off, and company-hosted luncheons. The explanation is that the effect of praise is dulled when used frequently and sometimes becomes an irritant.[34] Another explanation might be that employees begin to perceive the "outcomes" as inadequate relative to their "inputs" (see Chapter 8).

PROFIT-SHARING PLANS

Companies report a variety of purposes for profit-sharing plans. The stated purposes listed in decreasing order of frequency are (1) to encourage a sense of partnership between employee and employer and to stimulate the employee's interest in the enterprise; (2) to encourage employees to direct additional effort and imagination toward increasing company profits; and (3) to increase the financial security of employees.[35]

There are three general types of profit-shar-ing plans: (a) current-distribution (or cash) types, (b) deferred-distribution types, and (c) combined types that involve both current and deferred distribution. Under current-distribution plans, some percentage of profits is distributed in cash at intervals of one year or less. Under deferred-distribution types, some percentage of profits is deposited in an irrevocable trust and credited to the account of individual employees, with the money becoming available at retirement, death, or termination. In the case of termination, the most typical practice is for the employee to receive 10 percent of accumulated credits per years of service. Thus, at the end of ten years, an employee terminating employment is eligible for all the profits credited to his or her account. Some plans feature contributions of employees in addition to those of the employer, in which case the employee's contribution is invariably fully recoverable.[36]

By the end of 1970, there were approximately 101,842 deferred profit-sharing plans operating in this country and approved by the U.S. Treasury Department. This represents almost a fourfold increase over the decade from 1960 to 1970.[37] This did not include some 75,000–85,000 cash (current-distribution) plans in existence.[38] Approximately 7 to 8 million employees were covered by deferred (and combination) plans.[39] Among companies having profit-sharing plans, very small companies (0–19 employees) predominantly use cash plans, while a majority of the larger companies (20–500 employees and up) use deferred or combined plans.[40]

[34] Ibid.
[35] P.A. Knowlton, *Profit Sharing Programs* (Evanston, Ill.: Profit Sharing Research Foundation, 1954), pp. 55–56.

[36] Ibid., p. 53. See also B.L. Metzger, *Profit Sharing in Perspective*, 2nd ed. (Evanston, Ill.: Profit Sharing Research Foundation, 1966).
[37] B.L. Metzger and J.A. Colletti, *Does Profit Sharing Pay?* (Evanston, Ill.: Profit Sharing Research Foundation, 1971), p. 28.
[38] Ibid., p. 28.
[39] Ibid., p. 26.
[40] B.L. Metzger, *Profit Sharing in Perspective*, p. 31; and Industrial Conference Board, "Sharing Profits with Employees,"

One study found that most profit-sharing plans (86 percent) applied to all the company's employees meeting certain length-of-service or age requirements. Merit rating was a factor in only 6 percent of the current-distribution plans and in none of the deferred plans.[41]

The most difficult problem in profit-sharing plans is determining a formula to be used in distributing profits to employees. Such critical matters as payments to stockholders, taxes, and investment capital must be taken into account.[42] Questions of differentiation among employees on the basis of rank, length of service, and even plant or department must also be answered.

Another problem is the lack of immediate relation between the employee's efforts and rewards. Under the deferred type of plan, the employee may not enjoy these rewards until retirement. Other problems may be employee's dissatisfaction when profits decline or employees' taking the plan for granted.[43] However, it is significant that *not a single profit-sharing company abandoned its profit-sharing plan during the period* 1952–1969.[44]

The employee stock-ownership plan (ESOP) is not necessarily a profit-sharing plan, because it may emerge as a way of raising capital for the employer. Advocates of ESOP's, however, point out the potential morale and incentive value of stock being owned by employees. ESOP's were given a boost by favorable clauses in the Employee Retirement Income Security Act of 1974.[45]

IMPACT OF ENVIRONMENT
FEDERAL AND STATE LAWS

Federal and state laws have some impact on incentive systems in that they put a floor under such plans through minimum wage provisions. Furthermore, laws set forth rules for the computation of basic rates and overtime pay, and they make certain requirements with respect to records that must be maintained.

In addition, to comply with federal income tax laws, profit-sharing plans must be approved by the U.S. Treasury Department. Furthermore, reports to the government on deferred-distribution profit-sharing plans are required under the Employee Retirement Income Security Act of 1974.

During World War II, the federal government encouraged incentive plans for individuals and groups in order to stimulate production. Incentive systems made wage increases possible under otherwise stringent wartime controls, thus making incentives desirable from the workers' standpoint.[46] Similarly, profit sharing was encouraged during the same period because of tax laws, a tight labor market, and governmental wage controls.[47]

If overtime payments are considered incentive payments for working during undesirable

---

Studies in Personnel Policy, No. 162, 1956, p. 10. In March 1968, Xerox Corporation distributed more than $23 million to 17,000 salaried and production workers. Approximately 60 percent of the money was applied to the retirement plan and the rest was paid in cash or invested in company stock. *Monthly Labor Review*, 91:76 (June 1968).

[41]National Industrial Conference Board, "Sharing Profits with Employees," pp. 21, 25.

[42]Ibid., pp. 16–21.

[43]Ibid., pp. 55–61. For further discussion of profit-sharing plans, see John Dearden, "How to Make Incentive Plans Work," *Harvard Business Review*, 50:117–124 (July-August 1972).

[44]Metzger and Colletti, *Does Profit Sharing Pay?* p. 7.

[45]See Charles G. Burk, "There's More to ESOP Than Meets the Eye," *Fortune*, March 1976, pp. 128–133ff.; and "Stocks for Workers," *U.S. News & World Report*, August 16, 1976, pp. 68–70.

[46]Sumner H. Slichter, James J. Healy, and E. Robert Livernash, *The Impact of Collective Bargaining on Management* (Washington, D.C.: The Brookings Institution, 1960), p. 494.

[47]Edwin B. Flippo, *Profit Sharing in American Business* (Columbus, Ohio: Bureau of Business Research, College of Commerce and Administration, The Ohio State University, 1954), p. 9.

hours or for working unusually long hours, federal and state laws directly affect this type of incentive payment. (Overtime can also be considered an incentive to management to limit overtime and/or to hire more employees.) Under the Fair Labor Standards Act, employers in interstate commerce must pay time and a half—one and one-half times the regular hourly rate of pay—for any work in excess of forty hours in any one week. Exempted from this law are executive, administrative, professional, and outside sales employees, as well as employees in certain industries, such as agriculture, food processing, and forestry. In addition, the Walsh-Healy Act, as amended, requires employees in government contract work to be paid one and one-half times the regular rate of pay for work beyond eight hours in any one day,[48] except those employees exempt from its provisions. However, some organizations pay overtime to exempt employees; the most frequent practice is straight-time payments for scheduled work.[49]

TECHNOLOGY, PRODUCT, AND OTHER INFLUENCES

Technology and science, in particular, have had a major impact on the application and use of incentive systems. For example, new equipment, new materials, new methods, and new products can drastically change the nature of individual jobs and may thus require changes in standards or in the incentive system itself. Then, too, the more that productivity is governed by technological innovations, such as production lines and automatic equipment, the less incentive systems are applicable. Conversely, the more that worker-handling governs production, the more incentive systems are appropriate. And, since industrial engineering is an integral part of individual incentive systems, the technical capabilities of the industrial engineer will play an important part in the success of these plans.

That there are wide differences in the application of incentive systems among various types of industries is evident. For example, Figure 21-2 shows that 20 percent of plant workers in manufacturing were paid by incentive methods in 1970, only 5 percent in wholesale trade, and less than .5 percent in public utilities such as transportation and communications. In general, these differences reflect the extent of materials handling by the workers.

The use of profit-sharing plans also varies by industry. One study found a high incidence of profit-sharing plans in companies manufacturing photographic materials, soap, instruments, fabricated metal products, electrical goods, tools, and petroleum, and in store chains and banks. Profit-sharing plans tended to be infrequent or absent in companies manufacturing automobiles, chemicals, and agricultural machinery and in mining, building trades, transportation, public utilities, hotels, laundries, and motion pictures.[50]

There also seems to be some variation according to a company's size in the use of profit-sharing plans. In general, current-distribution plans are much more prevalent in small companies than in large ones.[51] Economic cycles have also affected profit-sharing plans. A high rate of failure for such plans has been reported dur-

[48]Some of the exemptions provided in the Fair Labor Standards Act also apply to the Walsh-Healy Act. Since these laws are amended from time to time, see the latest bulletins of the Wage and Hour and Public Contracts Division, U.S. Department of Labor.

[49]Some exempt employees were paid overtime in approximately half the manufacturing and utility companies surveyed in one study. See National Industrial Conference Board, "Overtime Pay for Exempt Employees," Studies in Personnel Policy, No. 208, 1967, p. 7. For the pros and cons of paying exempt employees overtime, see Robert A. Sbarra, "Exempt Employee Overtime," Compensation Review, 8:44–49 (First Quarter 1976).

[50]Knowlton, Profit Sharing Programs, pp. 10, 11.
[51]Ibid., p. 12.

ing periods of recession, and a very low rate during periods of prosperity.[52]

UNION, MANAGEMENT, AND EMPLOYEE ATTITUDES

No general labor movement policy toward incentive systems has been adopted; the attitudes of union leaders vary from opposition to enthusiasm. Some incentive plans have been established at the insistence of unions; some have been discontinued at the insistence of unions. Historically, the trend of union attitude has moved from unqualified opposition to a desire to bargain over the details of such plans.

In general, cooperation of the union is based upon an assurance that the union participate in setting standards and rates. For example, Gomberg states:

The logical solution of the rate setting problem consists in this recognition of rate setting as essentially a bargaining arrangement that takes place in the factory when new products go into production. The function of the time study engineer is to keep this bargaining within rational bounds.[53]

According to Barkin:

In the absence of any objective measure of human application and any scientific formulae to relate output and earnings, the problem of developing standards of machine assignments, production quotas, or incentive systems must necessarily rest on evaluative procedures derived from judgments and agreements reached by the partners in industry-management and workers.[54]

Similarly, no uniform trade union policy exists with respect to profit sharing, although union attitudes have gradually shifted toward cooperation.[55] There is general resistance to any plan that tends to eliminate collective bargaining over basic wage levels.[56]

Some research has been conducted on workers' attitudes toward incentive systems. A study by University of Michigan researchers of a large steel-fabricating company found that workers generally preferred the pay system under which they worked. Seventy-five percent of workers under an individual incentive system preferred to stay under such a system; a majority of those on straight hourly rates preferred to remain on this system; and the most frequent attitude expressed by those under a group incentive system was that they preferred what they had, although less than a majority expressed this view. Thirty-two percent of those under group incentives favored individual incentives,[57] a finding consistent with a study conducted by Opinion Research Corporation.[58]

Union-management relations and employee-management relations, in general, have a powerful impact on the adoption and success of incentive systems. One variable that stands out clearly in analyzing case studies of successful and unsuccessful incentive plans is the degree of confidence which employees have in the good intentions of management. If confidence is high, there is a good chance of success; if it is low, the plan is doomed to failure unless the situation can be corrected.

Managerial attitudes and abilities, of course, are important factors in securing the confidence of employees. If managers are unwilling to take the time and trouble to explain thoroughly

[52] Flippo, *Profit Sharing in American Business*, pp. 105-107.
[53] William Gomberg, *A Trade Union Analysis of Time Study*, 2nd ed. (New York: Prentice-Hall, Inc., 1955), p. 249.
[54] Solomon Barkin, "The Bench-Mark Approach to Production Standards," *Industrial and Labor Relations Review*, 10:235 (January 1957).

[55] I.B. Helburn, "Trade Union Response to Profit-Sharing Plans: 1886–1966," *Labor History*, 12:69–80 (Winter 1971).
[56] National Industrial Conference Board, "Sharing Profits with Employees," p. 63.
[57] Alfred G. Larke, "Worker Attitude on Incentives," *Dun's Review and Modern Industry*, December 1953, p. 61–62.
[58] Morris S. Viteles, *Motivation and Morale in Industry* (New York: W.W. Norton, 1953), pp. 46, 47.

and discuss proposed changes, an atmosphere of mutual confidence cannot be expected to develop. Managerial attitudes toward the concept of incentive systems will obviously affect whether or not incentive plans are adopted in the first place. Attitudes vary from high enthusiasm to downright opposition.[59]

EFFECT ON NEED FULFILLMENT

The context in which the incentive system emerges and the quality of its administration will have a major impact on need fulfillment. For example, if the plan relies upon a good deal of workers' participation, and constructive participation produces results in the form of higher wages, considerable fulfillment of self-actualization needs is likely to take place. Similarly, if employees are given enough information for a thorough understanding of the particular plan or system, the needs for integration or wholeness can be fulfilled. Again, if their participation results in recognition, a sense of affiliation, and so forth, needs for esteem and belonging will be satisfied. Also, if the plan results in higher wages, needs partially dependent upon purchasing power will be fulfilled to that extent.

Incentive systems can result in serious conflicts among needs. For example, if the incentive system rewards production obtained at the expense of fellow workers, then needs for affiliation with the group and for the cooperation and esteem of others may go unfulfilled, and the result may be detrimental to the employee's psychological security. Research by Dalton and others has shown that under certain incentive systems some workers are motivated to make extra money, but they keep their production

within the limits established by the group. Those who exceed the norm are called "rate busters" and are essentially ostracized from membership in the informal group consisting of the conformers.[60]

In general, it would seem that plantwide incentive systems like the Scanlon Plan, which emphasizes workers' participation on production problems, give more opportunity for fulfilling a variety of human needs than do individual incentive systems.[61] The reason for this conclusion is that plantwide plans tend to provide esteem from others and meet the need for cooperation as well as give opportunity for individual expression, ingenuity, and so forth.

AUTHORITY AND ACCOUNTABILITY

An analysis of the authority exercised by different managers in the installation and administration of incentive plans would probably show that suggestions for the establishment of such plans have come from a variety of sources within the firm, especially from the top executives in manufacturing and industrial engineers. Top management is undoubtedly involved in the approval of most plans that are adopted, with treasurers and controllers having a particular interest in the financial aspects.

Typically, industrial engineers will conduct the time-and-motion studies or work-simplification programs and will be involved in setting standards. One study reported central time-study departments being held accountable for time study in 86 percent of 286 companies

[59] For a discussion of different management attitudes, see Solomon Barkin, "Management's Attitude toward Wage Incentive Systems," *Industrial and Labor Relations Review*, 5:92–107 (October 1951).

[60] William Foote Whyte, *Men at Work* (Homewood, Ill.: The Dorsey Press and Richard D. Irwin, 1961), pp. 99–102. See also Orvis Collins, Melville Dalton, and Donald Roy, "Restriction of Output and Social Cleavage in Industry," *Applied Anthropology*, 5:1–14 (Summer 1946). See also F.J. Roethlisberger and William J. Dickson, *Management and the Worker* (Cambridge, Mass.: Harvard University Press, 1956), Chapter 18.

[61] Douglas McGregor, "The Scanlon Plan Through a Psychologist's Eyes," in Lesieur, *The Scanlon Plan*, p. 95.

having incentive systems. The personnel department is rarely involved in time study.[62]

The personnel department may advise on the system to be used; it will participate in negotiations with the union about the plan to be used, the standards, and the basic rates; and it will be deeply involved in any grievances that emerge. The personnel department will also conduct the wage surveys and participate in the job evaluation that serves as the floor under most incentive systems. The coordinator of any suggestion system will probably be a member of the personnel department, although the adoption of suggestions for reducing costs by changes in methods, materials, or equipment must necessarily remain the prerogative of the departmental head concerned.

Unions also have assumed considerable responsibility in administering incentive plans in some situations. For example, the Amalgamated Clothing Workers and the Ladies' Garment Workers have departments of staff engineers who participate in time-and-motion studies and in setting standards.[63] Under group incentive systems such as the Scanlon Plan, union stewards, officers, and committee representatives may assume considerable responsibility in the screening and processing of suggestions related to production problems.

UTILITY OF SYSTEMS

There is considerable agreement among researchers that certain environmental variables must be present to maximize the usefulness of particular pay plans. For example, the following conditions tend to make individual and group incentive plans impractical, although they do not necessarily preclude such plans:

1. Units of production are difficult to distinguish and measure.

2. Production is essentially placed by machines, conveyors, or automatic equipment.

3. Quality of work, in contrast to quantity, is of overriding importance.

4. Changes in technology frequently alter job content.

Individual and group incentive systems tend to be more practical when some of or all the following conditions are present:

1. Units of production are readily measured.

2. Handling or processing by workers is a major determinant of productivity.

3. Time-and-motion study or simplification of work can increase efficiency of jobs.

4. Technological changes affecting jobs are relatively infrequent.

5. Competition requires better predictability of unit labor costs.

6. The company employs experienced time-study personnel.

7. Close supervision is impractical.

8. Employees trust management not to change standards arbitrarily.[64]

It appears that neither set of conditions described above as handicapping or facilitating the adoption of incentive plans would preclude the use of Scanlon-type plantwide productivity systems. However, it is probable that the necessity for frequent and close communications between workers and management under a Scanlon-type plan would pose serious problems for an extremely large organization. Furthermore, the Scanlon Plan requires managerial and

[62] National Industrial Conference Board, "Wage Payment Systems," p. 16.
[63] Slichter, Healy, and Livernash, *Impact of Collective Bargaining*, pp. 496–497.
[64] For additional discussions of the factors affecting the applicability of different wage-payment systems, see Slichter, Healy, and Livernash, *Impact of Collective Bargaining*, pp. 490–557; and Belcher, *Compensation Administration*, pp. 309–311.

union leaders who are willing and able to cooperate in solving production problems.

Profit sharing tends to be impractical when the profits of a particular firm or industry are especially sensitive to economic cycles or other factors over which rank-and-file employees have no control. Some of these other factors might be the effectiveness of the company's research and developmental programs or the shrewdness of purchasing agents and those in charge of inventories.[65] Of course, these conditions argue for profit sharing by the company's key personnel who can exercise an influence on profits.

It should be remembered that time-and-motion study, work simplification, improved plant layout, and other improvements in managerial practices are applicable under any type of wage-payment plan unless workers' insecurities or hostilities have frozen the organization so that changes are difficult to make. Scanlon-type plans, in particular, seem to have the potentiality for creating an environment in which a variety of methods can be used to improve production.

Suggestion plans seem to be workable in organizations producing practically any kind of product or service, including governmental agencies.[66] They tend not to be appropriate for certain categories of employees, however. For example, if it is assumed that research chemists or industrial engineers are already being compensated for their ideas, a suggestion plan for these employees would not be appropriate.

It should be pointed out that many aspects of successful incentive systems cannot by systematized. That is, mutual respect and confidence,

effectiveness in interpersonal relationshps, and a desire to cooperate in the solution of organizational problems are all qualitative matters that cannot be insured by the adoption of any wage-payment plan. On the other hand, when incentive plans are adopted, a high degree of attention must be given to refining and administering all aspects of the particular system.

RELIABILITY

The question of reliability is particularly pertinent to incentive systems based on time-and-motion study. Although industrial engineers and organizations, such as the Society for the Advancement of Management, have made improvements in the reliability of time-and-motion study, the question of reliability continues to be an area of continuing conflict.[67] A major difficulty is that there are no universally agreed-upon measuring scales backed by an accepted standard as is the case with weights and linear measuring devices.[68] Even with such agreed-upon scales, there would still be room for different results when different people use them, and there would be differing opinions on what rates of production should be considered "standard," "normal," or "average." Research has shown enough discrepancy between the time measurements of different industrial engineers and the measurements made on different occasions by the same engineer to provide considerable room for argument about the accuracy of the measurements.

This is not to deny that time study is a highly useful device in work simplification and methods improvement and a guide for establishing production standards, but the prob-

---

[65] See Torbert, "Making Incentives Work," pp. 91–92.

[66] In 1954, Congress approved the Government Employees' Incentive Awards Act, which provides not only for cash awards for accepted suggestions, but also substantial cash awards for "superior accomplishments" or "special acts or services." See Felix A. Nigro, *Public Personnel Administration* (New York: Henry Holt and Company, 1959), p. 395.

[67] The Society for the Advancement of Management has developed films that are used extensively in training time-study personnel and union officers. See Langsner and Zollitsch, *Wage and Salary Administration*, p. 448.

[68] E.S. Buffa, "Time Study Rating as Measurement," *Advanced Management*, 18:20–22 (March 1953).

lems of reliability and of agreeing on standards are not automatically solved by this technique. According to one author:

. . . thus far modern industrial time study techniques can make no claims to scientific accuracy. *They are at best empirical guides to setting up a range within which collective bargaining over production rates can take place.*[69]

According to Wolf:

. . . in actual practice time study is little more than a systematic method of guiding judgment. Jobs are seldom standardized. A study taken at one time may not be representative of job conditions at a future date. Human errors enter into the reading of the stopwatch. The calculation of a representative sample of observed times involves arbitrary selection of statistical techniques. Leveling (the adjusting of average observed times to represent the time taken by a "normal" worker) is an attempt to use subjective judgment to attain an indefinite goal. . . .[70]

VALIDITY

INDIVIDUAL AND GROUP SYSTEMS

The validity of incentive systems may be judged by the extent to which they contribute to such organizational objectives as increased profits, increased productivity, lowered costs, and the like. The extent to which management believes incentive systems are useful is another index of validity, although more subject to bias.

A 1944 study of 302 installations of incentive plans in the New England region showed that the average installation, after three months' operation, resulted in a 14 percent decrease in unit labor costs, a 29 percent increase in production, and a 15 percent increase in wages.[71] A governmental survey in 1945 of 514 incentive

plan installations reported an average reduction in unit labor costs of about 12 percent, an average increase in production of about 39 percent, and an average increase in take-home pay of about 18 percent.[72]

A 1959 survey of plant executives showed that wage incentive installations had resulted in reduced costs in 96 percent of the plants using them, had improved employees' morale in 77 percent of the plants, and had improved the quality of output in 35 percent of the plants. Costs increased in 4 percent of the plants; grievances increased in 44 percent of the plants; and quality decreased in 20 percent of the plants.[73]

A 1959 study of the results of 2,500 wage incentive plans reported an average reduction in unit labor costs of about 26 percent and an average increase in productivity of about 64 percent. Employees' earnings increased an average of about 21 percent.[74] Lawler's research on equity theory indicates that subjects who are working under a piece-rate system will produce about 20 percent more than those working under an hourly wage system.[75]

There is general agreement that workers paid under incentive systems achieve higher earnings than workers on comparable jobs who are paid hourly rates. For example, an examination of the average hourly earnings in 1956 of workers in selected occupations in machinery-manufacturing companies reveals that the earnings of those under incentive plans were significantly higher than those on time rates.[76]

[69]Gomberg, *A Trade Union Analysis*, p. 246.
[70]Wolf, *Wage Incentives*, p. 83. For a further discussion of the reliability of time and motion studies, see Whyte, *Men at Work*, pp. 104–108; and Viteles, *Motivation and Morale in Industry*, pp. 30–39.
[71]Slichter, Healy, and Livernash, *Impact of Collective Bargaining*, p. 494.
[72]Viteles, *Motivation and Morale in Industry*, p. 27.
[73]"The Truth about Wage Incentives and Work Measurement Today," *Factory*, 117:79 (April 1959).
[74]"Wage Incentives and Productivity," *Personnel*, 36:4–5 (May-June 1959). See also Mitchell Fein, "Motivation for Work," pp. 521–522.
[75]Edward E. Lawler III, *Pay and Organizational Effectiveness: A Psychological View* (New York: McGraw-Hill Book Company, 1971), p. 124.
[76]Louis E. Badenhoop and A. N. Jarrel, p. 912. This effect of incentive plans seems to have persisted over the years. A

Not all authors will agree that the evidence cited thus far overwhelmingly proves the validity of incentive systems. One describes a number of cases in which costs of incentive systems were higher than they would be under ordinary hourly wages. In addition, the same investigator believes that incentive systems have hidden costs which are seldom considered, including the costs of preliminary studies, record-keeping, accounting, negotiations, grievances, and arbitration and the expense of policing to prevent mistakes and dishonesty.[77]

It should be recognized that a particular incentive plan is only a device in a network of variables generally affected by the installation and administration of incentive systems. The installation of the systems is usually accompanied by closer attention to improved methods and work simplification and perhaps by improved managerial practices in selecting, training, and other areas. Therefore, increases in productivity and reduction in unit labor costs should be attributed to the combination of environmental changes, and the question can properly be raised as to whether the same gains might have been made without the incentive plans but with improvements in other environmental variables.

This reservation, of course, does not question the validity of incentive *systems;* it merely questions the validity of the wage determination formulae, that is, the plans. Perhaps the same gains could be made by substituting straight hourly wages or wage ranges plus merit rating. Further research is needed on this question.

Although most are not incentive systems in the sense of involving wage payments, favorable results have been reported from "positive reinforcement" programs using self-recording of performance and praise as reinforcers. Some of the results, as reported by Hamner and Hamner, include cost savings at Emery Air Freight; attendance improvements of 50 percent at Michigan Bell (operator services); improved cost efficiency, safety, and service, but decreased satisfaction with pay, at Michigan Bell (maintenance service); cost savings and increased productivity at GE; an increase in production of over 300 percent at B.F. Goodrich Chemical Company; and substantial cost reductions and increased profits at Emerson Electronics. Among firms using wage payments or fringe benefits in addition to other positive reinforcers, Weyerhaeuser found an increase in productivity of 33 percent with one group of workers, an 18 percent increase with another, and an 8 percent decrease in a third group. Improved performance among the city of Detroit garbage collectors resulted in a significant decrease in citizen complaints, substantial savings, and an average annual bonus of $350 per employee.[78] Again, it should be noted that these programs typically involve added attention to many variables in the work situation, e.g., more attention to training, labor-management relations, and/or selection, etc.

SUGGESTION SYSTEMS

Reports on savings in costs resulting from suggestion systems have generally been favorable. A survey of all of the member firms of the National Association of Suggestion Systems in the mid-1970s found that, on the average, for each $1 spent on the suggestion system, organizations realized $5.70 in tangible net cost savings. In the aggregate, the 1,000 members of

1943 study reported workers paid under incentive plans having a wage advantage of 12 to 18 percent over nonincentive workers. *Monthly Labor Review*, 55:849–857 (May 1943).

[77]Robert H. Roy, "Do Wage Incentives Reduce Costs?" *Industrial and Labor Relations Review*, 5:195–208 (January 1952). For a discussion of some of the conflicting evidence as to the validity of incentive systems, see Garth L. Mangum, "Are Wage Incentives Becoming Obsolete?" *Industrial Relations*, 2:73–93 (October 1962).

[78]Hamner and Hamner, "Behavioral Modification on Bottom Line," pp. 11–19.

the NASS saved some $470 million during the year of the survey, and that figure was based on first-year savings alone.[79] On the average, the life of each accepted suggestion is considered to be about 3½ years.[80]

Tatter cites a number of examples of employees making suggestions that resulted in considerable savings to the employer and a significant reward to the employee. One example was the case of a flight officer for an airline who suggested that air cargo be shifted slightly to the rear of the aircraft, thereby altering the center of gravity and reducing the fuel required for takeoff. The suggestion saved the airline $458,500 over the first year, and earned the employee $45,850. As another illustration, a technologist at the Center for Disease Control in Atlanta developed a test for rabies that could be performed in one day, thus replacing the twelve-day waiting period that had been previously required. The idea saved the Center $50,000 over the first year, as well as saving lives and reducing anxiety. The amount of the reward to the employee was not reported. At a General Tire & Rubber Company plant, a master mechanic made a suggestion to modify equipment used in the manufacture of latex, and earned a $25,000 award.[81] In addition to cost savings, there is some evidence that suggestion programs that encourage ideas on safety are often associated with reduced accidents.[82]

The high mortality rate of suggestion systems, however, indicates that more than just the installation of a plan is necessary for success. According to a 1953 estimate, a majority of plans that were initiated in the previous two decades had been abandoned or were practically defunct.[83]

Executive opinion stresses the following conditions as necessary for success:

○ Full and continued support by top management

○ Clear-cut assignment of responsibility for the plan's administration

○ Indoctrination of each member of management in his or her part in the plan's procedure

○ Adequate schedule of awards

○ Detailed determination of eligibility

○ Companywide coordination of the plan

○ Skillfully designed forms

○ Employees' understanding of the plan

○ Prompt and competent processing of suggestions

○ Prompt and complete replies to suggestions not adopted or not given awards

○ Publicity appropriate to the plan

○ Adequate permanent records of suggestions[84]

Thus, we see that successful administration of suggestion systems requires careful and continuous linking of the system to the broad network of systems within the organization. A suggestion system that is permitted to drift will quickly begin to decline.

Rewarding employees simply for making suggestions, whether accepted or rejected, is a particularly questionable practice. For example, during a contest, one firm gave gifts for the first suggestion submitted by any employee, and as a result the number of suggestions increased from 280 weekly to 2,074.[85] As a device to improve morale, call attention to the

[79] Milton A. Tatter, "Turning Ideas into Gold," *Management Review*, 64:5 (March 1975).

[80] John E. Hein, "Employee Suggestions Pay," *Personnel Journal*, 52:218 (March 1973).

[81] Tatter, "Turning Ideas into Gold," pp. 5–6.

[82] William J. Kerr, "Complementary Theories of Safety Psychology," in Harris W. Karn and B. von Haller Gilmer, *Readings in Industrial and Business Psychology*, 2nd ed. (New York: McGraw-Hill Book Company, 1962), pp. 264–270.

[83] National Industrial Conference Board, "Suggestion Systems," p. 7. See also Tatter, "Turning Ideas into Gold," pp. 8–10.

[84] O'Meara, "How to Keep a Suggestion Plan Useful," p. 42.

[85] See *Industrial Relations News*, May 5, 1962, p. 3.

suggestion system, or dramatize some theme, such as cost reduction, these expenditures for gifts may have been justified. But as a general rule, awards based on the *contribution* of an idea to reduced costs or increased profits appear to be much more valid.

One of the most important questions with regard to the validity of suggestion systems is the following: Would the suggestions resulting in savings have been made without the formalized suggestion plan? Investigation of this question requires a carefully controlled experiment involving matched groups, with the only variables being the alternative methods used to encourage the upward flow of constructive suggestions. To our knowledge, no such study has been made. Obviously, this research would be highly complicated and perhaps impossible to conduct in the industrial situation.

Another way to investigate the question of whether the suggestions would have been made in the absence of a special system is to measure the flow of constructive ideas before and after the installation of plans. Here again, no such study has been made. Obviously, opinions will vary as to "before and after" differences, reflecting diverse experiences in various situations. Suggestion systems are only one means of obtaining constructive suggestions from employees.

Logically, any reasonable plan would be better than no plan, providing the plan were carefully integrated into the network of sytems in the organization. Consultation between subordinates and superiors, Scanlon-type incentive plans, the inclusion of "initiative" or some such category in merit rating, union-management cooperation in cost reduction or safety—these and others are all means of eliciting constructive ideas from employees. In short, the logic of the suggestion system is essentially valid, provided attention is given to minimizing the problems mentioned earlier, such as management support, adequate compensation, etc.

PLANTWIDE PRODUCTIVITY INCENTIVE PLANS

The literature on the validity of Scanlon-type incentive plans is much less extensive than that pertaining to individual incentive plans. One study of ten installations of the Scanlon Plan found improvements in productivity for the first two years of operation varying from a minimum of 10.3 percent in one company to a maximum of 39.2 percent in another, with an average increase in productivity of 23.1 percent for the 10 firms.[86] In addition, grievances are reported to have declined significantly under Scanlon Plans.[87] On the other hand, several unsuccessful applications have occurred.

One author believes that some Scanlon Plans have broken down because the basic method of measuring productivity is unsound. Fein states that the ratio of payroll dollars to sales volume dollars is ". . . not a valid measurement of work output . . ." since the ratio is affected by technology, production processes, product, and market conditions.[88]

Worker attitudes toward the Scanlon Plan appear to be generally favorable. In a study involving twenty-one plants and 2,638 respondents, employees thought it was worthwhile to make cost reduction suggestions to the plant committees, that the committees were important mechanisms for improving efficiency, and that the plan helped employees to perform better on their jobs and to know more about the company. The higher the respondents were in the organization's hierarchy, the more favorable were their attitudes.[89]

In general, the success of Scanlon-type incen-

[86] Elbridge S. Puckett, "Productivity Achievements—A Measure of Success," in Lesieur, *The Scanlon Plan*, pp. 112–115. See George Sherman, 'The Scanlon Concept: Its Capabilities for Productivity Improvement," *The Personnel Administrator*, 21:17–20 (July 1976).
[87] Gilson and Lefcowitz, "Plant-Wide Productivity Bonus"; and Scanlon, "Profit Sharing under Collective Bargaining."
[88] Fein, "Motivation for Work," pp. 518–519.
[89] Robert R. Goodman, J.H. Wakeley, and R.H. Ruh, "What Employees Think of the Scanlon Plan," *Personnel*, 49:22–29 (September-October 1972).

tive plans seems to depend upon the following factors:

1. Mutual trust among management, the union, and employees.

2. Careful planning and installation to insure both understanding and acceptance.

3. Sincere and diligent efforts of all parties to make the plan work.

4. Extensive and real participation in production problems by union officials, employees, and management at all levels and assumption by all parties of the responsibilities that accompany constructive and cooperative problem solving.

These factors seem to be operating at the Lincoln Electric Company where a combination of individual and group incentives is used. Productivity rose at an average of 15 percent per year between 1934 and 1950 compared with 3 percent in all U.S. manufacturing, and sales doubled between 1962 and 1971. While bonuses to employees were 90 percent of wages in 1971, the company still earned almost 11 percent on net worth.[90]

PROFIT SHARING

Since deferred-distribution profit-sharing plans are essentially retirement plans, the discussion of the validity of fringe benefits in Chapter 19 also applies to these plans. Since profit-sharing plans may have the advantage of focusing workers' attention and effort on the problem of profits, these plans may contain more validity than most other fringe benefits. Furthermore, since deferred-distribution plans are tied to profits, they are not fixed costs, as are many conventional plans. Consequently, they may reduce the company's economic burden in bad times and thus enhance its ability to survive. Although the effects on relations with em-

ployees during low-profit years must be considered, at least one study suggests that this problem may not be too serious.[91]

Because of the greater immediacy of the rewards, a cash or current-distribution plan would probably serve as a greater incentive to employees in achieving organizational goals than the deferred type of plan. However, a survey of managerial opinion on the contribution of profit-sharing plans to increased efficiency showed practically no difference between types of plans.[92]

In general, firms having profit-sharing plans believe that they are beneficial. In the study cited earlier, the management of 58 percent of the firms surveyed believed that their profit-sharing plans had resulted in some "important benefits," the management of 36 percent of the firms believed there were "some general benefits," and the management of 6 percent believed there were "no very noticeable benefits." There were no significant differences in opinion between firms having current-distribution plans and those having deferred-distribution plans. Improved employer-employee relationships, improved production, greater efficiency, lower turnover, increased interest in the company, better teamwork and cooperation, and reduction in costs were the principal benefits believed derived from profit sharing.[93] In addition, one study claims that fewer strikes result from profit-sharing plans.[94]

[90] Jenkins, *Job Power*, pp. 216–218.

[91] See National Industrial Conference Board, "Sharing Profits with Employees," p. 57. A survey of more than four hundred companies with profit-sharing plans showed that the average payment into employee accounts in 1972 was about 12 percent of salary. *U.S. News & World Report*, January 28, 1974, p. 72.

[92] National Industrial Conference Board, "Sharing Profits with Employees," p. 54.

[93] Ibid., pp. 52, 53. See also Metzger and Colletti, *Does Profit Sharing Pay?* pp. 80–81.

[94] Council of Profit Sharing Industries, *Profit Sharing Manual*, pp. 14–15. Another study reported a profit sharing plan in a company to be more successful than a Scanlon Plan in use in the same organization. See J.J. Jehring, "A Contrast Between Two Approaches to Total Systems Incentives," *California Management Review*, 10:7–14 (Winter 1967).

According to one study, employees' attitudes toward their companies and the free-enterprise system tend to improve as a result of profit-sharing plans. A higher percentage of employees under such plans, in contrast to workers without profit sharing, believe that (a) they are receiving a fair share of the company's prosperity, (b) they gain when they find ways to cut costs and save money, (c) their management is "outstanding," and (d) such plans are a good opportunity for people with ability to get ahead.[95] Further, profit-sharing companies have tended to have better financial records than non-profit-sharing firms in terms of net income to net worth, net income to sales, company earnings per employee, dividends per common share, etc. This trend appeared in the 1950s and continued through the 1960s.[96] While we should be cautious in drawing conclusions about a cause and effect relationship, it is probable that profit-sharing plans are symptomatic of a goal-oriented and cooperative work climate and that profit sharing tends to be congruent with and reinforce these organizational characteristics. As Metzger and Colletti say, ". . . profit sharing, as a partnership/incentive philosophy, can go to work for a company to bring about a 'unity of purpose' and a 'synergistic spirit of cooperation'—ingredients which hold everything together and pave the road to high achievement."[97]

EMPLOYEE PARTICIPATION AS A MAJOR VARIABLE

Experiences with the Scanlon Plan suggest that the degree of worker participation in the design and/or operation of incentive plans can be a key variable in determining their success or failure. This hypothesis was tested experimentally and continued in one study involving a small company employing part-time workers who cleaned buildings at night. The firm was experiencing high absenteeism and turnover among employees, and top management permitted the researchers to experiment with incentive plans in an effort to correct the situation. Briefly, nine groups participated in the experiment. Three were permitted to design their own incentive plans in collaboration with the researchers. Their plans were subject to final approval by top management (top management made only minor changes in the plans to make them equivalent; basically, the plans featured a $2.50 per week bonus for perfect attendance; one involved payment on a monthly basis, the other two on a weekly basis). Identical plans (one involving a weekly bonus and the other a monthly bonus) were imposed on two groups, but with explanations provided by a top manager. The researchers met with two other groups and discussed the problems of absenteeism and turnover, but no changes were made in their pay plans. Two other groups had their attendance monitored, but there was no employee involvement of any kind in the experiment.

The results: attendance on the part of the participative groups increased from 88 percent to 94 percent of scheduled hours over a sixteen-week period (the odds of this occurring by chance were one in a thousand); attendance of the groups in which a bonus plan was imposed did not improve (attendance for a sixteen-week period remained at 83 percent of scheduled hours); and data from the control groups showed no significant changes. The researchers concuded that ". . . participation in the development and implementation of a plan may have more of an impact on the effectiveness of a plan than the mechanics of the plan itself."[98]

[95] Robert D. Best, "Profit Sharing and Motivation for Productivity," in *Profit Sharing and Productivity Motivation* (Madison, Wisc.: Center for Productivity Motivation, School of Commerce, The University of Wisconsin, 1961), pp. 47–51.

[96] Metzger and Colletti, *Does Profit Sharing Pay?* pp. 72, 82.

[97] Ibid., p. 85.

[98] Edward E. Lawler III and J. Richard Hackman, "Impact of Employee Participation in the Development of Pay Incentive

SUMMARY

Properly planned, installed, and administered incentive plans of the individual, group, and plantwide variety can greatly increase efficiency and productivity, decrease costs, and increase workers' take-home pay. Refinements in plans and industrial-engineering practices are increasingly making it possible to include nonproduction jobs under such plans. Profit sharing also produces a number of desirable results, in the opinion of managers in firms using such plans.

Managers, unions, and employees alike, however, should recognize that most incentive plans involve a number of major changes in the work environment and may alter prevailing structures of authority and patterns of relationships. Furthermore, successful utilization of such plans requires careful and constant attention.

A major problem with all incentive systems is the necessity for mutual respect and confidence between management and employees. Unless these attitudes are achieved, no amount of technical refining of an incentive plan will ensure its success. Hastily installed or poorly understood plans, or plans launched under an atmosphere of suspicion and ill will, can have serious long-range consequences for both profits and labor relations.

Plantwide systems of productivity seem to have many of the same advantages as the individual systems and the additional advantage of stimulating employees' participation and cooperation in production problems that are broader than individual tasks. Such plans seem to offer additional possibilities of fulfilling self-actualization needs.

Positive reinforcement programs involving praise and the avoidance of criticism, and without wage incentives, appear to have had favorable results, but experience is beginning to show that compensation cannot be ignored indefinitely when productivity goes up. Further, additional variables are frequently changed in these programs, e.g., more attention to job methods and training.

It should be recognized that many practices that may be improved under incentive systems may also be improved in the absence of formalized incentive plans. It should also be recognized that merit rating is a type of incentive plan and that there are rewards in the working environment additional to increased wages. For example, opportunity for advancement, a new and challenging assignment, or opportunities to attend seminars on managerial development may be considered rewards.

Since most research and innovation relative to incentive plans have been in manufacturing, this chapter has emphasized incentive plans pertaining to plant workers. With exceedingly high distribution costs in our economy, however, it is important that careful attention be given to the incentives of sales people and to those in other distribution jobs vis-à-vis productivity and efficiency. Furthermore, the rapid increase in white-collar employment in contrast to employment in production and maintenance jobs provides more and more reason for careful attention to the potential application of incentive plans for sales, office, technical, and other white-collar occupations in both industry and government.

In general, organizationwide incentive or profit-sharing plans that feature committees on production or efficiency, coupled with merit-rating or individual incentive plans that are carefully tied into a network of other motivating devices, including employee participation in the design and administration of the plan(s),

Plans: A Field Experiment," *Journal of Applied Psychology,* 53:467–471 (December 1969). For an interesting follow-up to this study one year later, which confirmed the original conclusions and which emphasized the importance of managerial as well as employee involvement, see Kenneth C. Scheflen, Edward E. Lawler III, and J. Richard Hackman, "Long-Term Impact of Employee Participation in the Development of Pay Incentive Plans: A Field Experiment Revisited," *Journal of Applied Psychology,* 55:182–186 (June 1971).

have an optimal chance of success in many situations. In short, it is suggested that there should be high participation at all levels and rewards for *both* cooperation and individual performance. Further, *it is clear that successful incentive programs are characterized by careful attention to a wide range of organizational variables.*

REVIEW AND DISCUSSION QUESTIONS

1. What is the difference between a group incentive plan and a plantwide productivity plan as described in this chapter?

2. What are some of the administrative problems in the use of individual incentive systems?

3. In what kinds of situations is the Scanlon Plan most applicable?

4. What are some of the problems in using plantwide productivity plans?

5. What are the pros and cons of suggestion systems?

6. Analyze the various types of incentive plans in terms of how you think each would meet the several kinds of needs discussed in Chapter 6.

7. What are the advantages and disadvantages of (a) current-distribution and (b) deferred-distribution profit-sharing plans?

8. Which kinds of incentive systems require the most trust between management and employees? The least?

9. Discuss positive reinforcement and behavior modification approaches vis-à-vis individual and group incentive plans.

10. What are some of the possible reasons for the decline in proportion of plant workers covered by incentive plans? For the dearth of plans pertaining to office workers?

SUPPLEMENTAL REFERENCES

Aldis, Owen, "Of Pigeons and Men," *Harvard Business Review*, 39:59–63 (July-August 1961).

Bofenkamp, Larry, "Executive Compensation: Today and Tomorrow," *The Personnel Administrator*, 20:56–60 (October 1975).

Bright, James R., "Automation and Wage Determination," in John H.G. Crispo, ed., *Industrial Relations: Challenges and Responses* (Toronto: University of Toronto Press, 1966), pp. 19–59.

Brown, Wilfred, *Piecework Abandoned* (London: Heinemann Educational Books, 1962).

Burgess, Leonard R., *Wage and Salary Administration in a Dynamic Economy* (New York: Harcourt, Brace & World, 1968), Chapter 7.

Campbell, H., "Group Incentive Payment Schemes: The Effects of Lack of Understanding and of Group Size," *Occupational Psychology*, 26:15–21 (1952).

Cassell, Frank H., "Management Incentives and Management Style," *Personnel Administration*, 31:4–7ff. (July-August 1968).

Clark, Peter B., and James Q. Wilson, "Incentive Systems: A Theory of Organizations," *Administrative Science Quarterly*, 6:129–166 (September 1961).

Crandall, Richard E., "De-Emphasized Wage Incentives," *Harvard Business Review*, 40:113–116 (March-April 1962).

Czarnecki, Edgar R., "Effect of Profit-Sharing Plans on Union Organizing Efforts," *Personnel Journal*, 49:763–773 (September 1970).

Dalton, Melville, "Unofficial Incentives," in *Men Who Manage* (New York: John Wiley & Sons, Inc., 1959), pp. 198–206.

Dunn, J.D., and Frank M. Rachel, *Wage and Salary Administration: Total Compensation Systems* (New York: McGraw-Hill Book Company, 1971), Chapters 14 and 15.

Famularo, Joseph J., ed., *Handbook of Modern Personnel Administration* (New York: McGraw-Hill Book Company, 1972), Chapters 29–32.

Fottler, Myron D., and F. William Schaller, "Overtime Acceptance Among Blue-Collar Workers," *Industrial Relations*, 14:327–336 (October 1975).

Geare, J.A., "Productivity from Scanlon-type Plans," *The Academy of Management Review,* 1:99–108 (July 1976).

Greenman, Russell L., and Eric J. Schmertz, *Personnel Administration and The Law* (Washington, D.C.: The Bureau of National Affairs, 1972).

Gross, Edward, *Industry and Social Life* (Dubuque, Iowa: Wm. C. Brown Company, Publishers, 1965), Chapter 8.

Hethy, Lajos, and Csaba Mako, "Obstacles to the Introduction of Efficient Money Incentives in a Hungarian Factory," *Industrial and Labor Relations Review,* 24:541–553 (July 1971).

Jaffe, William A., "Paying Salesmen Properly," *The Personnel Administrator,* 17:30–32 (May-June 1972).

James, Charles F., and Philip V. Rzasa, "A Pricing Analysis of the One-for-One Incentive Plans," *Personnel Journal,* 47:398–401 (June 1968).

Jehring, J.J., "The Effects on Productivity of Dropping Industrial Incentives: A Case Study," *Personnel Journal,* 45:87–89 (February 1966).

Lawler, Edward E., III, "New Approaches to Pay: Innovations that Work," *Personnel,* 53:11–23 (September-October 1976).

Locke, E.A., and J.F. Bryan, *Goals and Intentions as Determinants of Performance Level, Task Choice, and Attitudes* (Washington, D.C.: American Institute for Research, 1967).

McKersie, Robert B., "Wage Payment Methods of the Future," *British Journal of Industrial Relations,* 1:191–212 (June 1963).

Mangum, Garth L., "Are Wage Incentives Becoming Obsolete?" *Industrial Relations,* 18:73–96 (October 1962).

Marriott, R., *Incentive Payment Systems,* rev. ed. (London: Staples Press, 1961).

Metzger, B.L., and J.A. Colletti, *Does Profit Sharing Pay?* (Evanston, Ill.: Profit Sharing Research Foundation, 1971).

National Industrial Conference Board, "Administration of Cost Reduction Programs," *Studies in Business Policy,* No. 117, 1965.

——, "Employee Stock Purchase Plans," *Studies in Personnel Policy,* No. 206, 1967.

——, "The Kaiser-Steel Union Sharing Plan," *Studies in Personnel Policy,* No. 187, 1963.

Nord, Walter R., "Beyond the Teaching Machine," *Organizational Behavior and Human Performance,* 4:352–377 (1969).

Patton, Arch, "Why Incentive Plans Fail," *Harvard Business Review,* 50:58–66 (May-June 1972).

Pedalino, Ed, and Victor V. Gamboa, "Behavior Modification and Absenteeism," *Journal of Applied Psychology,* 59:694–698 (December 1974).

Pizam, Abraham, "Some Correlates of Innovation within Industrial Suggestion Systems," *Personnel Psychology,* 27:63–76 (Spring 1974).

Recent Initiatives in Labor-Management Cooperation (Washington, D.C.: National Center for Productivity and Quality of Working Life, February 1976), 90 pp.

Salerno, A.A., "An Incentive Plan for Foremen," *Compensation Review,* 4:15–20 (Second Quarter 1972).

Skinner, B.F., "The Steep and Thorny Way to a Science of Behavior," *American Psychologist,* 30:42–49 (January 1975).

Smith, Elizabeth A., and Gerald F. Gude, "Reevaluation of the Scanlon Plan as a Motivational Technique," *Personnel Journal,* 50:916–919 (December 1971).

Trowbridge, Charles L., "ABC's of Pension Funding," *Harvard Business Review,* 44:115–126 (March-April 1966).

Weeks, David A., "A Fluctuating Paycheck for Managers," *The Conference Board Record,* 5:32–36 (April 1968).

Whyte, W.F., *Money and Motivation: An Analysis of Incentives in Industry* (New York: Harper & Row, 1955).

——, "Pigeons, Persons and Piece Rates: Skinnerian Theory in Organizations," *Psychology Today,* April 1972, pp. 67–68ff.

PART 8
THE COLLECTIVE-BARGAINING PROCESS

From a broad social standpoint, the collective-bargaining process may be thought of as a complex network of event-flows that serve to establish the price of labor, to fix hours and working conditions, to introduce an additional element of democracy into the relationship between employees and employers, and to build what Slichter called a "system of industrial jurisprudence." This phrase means the creation of rules governing the working situation that are established with the participation of the employee, in contrast to unilateral rule and decision making by the employer.[1]

The flow of events in collective bargaining serves to reconcile the conflicting demands and requirements of organized labor, management, and the public—the last having voiced, through the election of its representatives, its insistence

[1] See Sumner H. Slichter, *Union Policies and Industrial Management* (Washington, D.C.: The Brookings Institution, 1941), pp. 1–2.

on some degree of orderly proceedings in union-management relationships. Thus, this process has broad social, economic, and political purposes transcending the boundaries of single organizations. In that sense, the collective-bargaining process is different from most of the other processes in personnel management analyzed thus far, since they have been described as having purposes or consequences primarily related to individual organizations.

Relative to a particular firm, however, the collective-bargaining process consists essentially of the following two subprocesses: (a) the negotiation of the contract—negotiations between the union and the employer relative to wages, hours, and working conditions; and (b) the administration of the contract—primarily grievance proceedings and arbitration. The first subprocess—negotiating the agreement—will be discussed in Chapter 23; and the second—the administration of the agreement—will be discussed in Chapter 24. Before discussing these subprocesses, however, it would be well to examine the current status of the American labor movement, the reasons that prompt workers to join unions, and the implications of the emergence of a union in a particular organization. These topics will be discussed in Chapters 22 and 23.

CHAPTER 22
CURRENT STATUS AND PROBLEMS OF THE AMERICAN LABOR MOVEMENT

UNION MEMBERSHIP IN THE UNITED STATES

By 1972, membership in unions and employee associations in the United States totaled 23,100,000. Union membership constituted about 21.8 percent of the total labor force and about 26.7 percent of the employees in nonagricultural establishments. When employee associations engaging in collective bargaining are included, the figures become 24.3 percent, and 29.8 percent respectively.[1]

Although, in 1972, some 79 percent of the unionized workers in the United States belonged to unions affiliated with the AFL-CIO,[2] two of the three largest American unions are not part of the affiliation. The largest union, the International Brotherhood of Teamsters, Chauffeurs, Warehousemen and Helpers of America, representing some 1,855,000 workers in 1972,[3] has not been affiliated with the AFL-CIO since 1957. The United Auto Workers (UAW), the third largest American union, with a 1972 membership of about 1.4 million, withdrew from the federation in 1968.[4]

In 1972, the five largest unions in the AFL-CIO, listed by order of size, were (1) the United Steelworkers of America, 1,400,000 members; (2) the International Brotherhood of Electrical Workers, 957,000; (3) the United Brotherhood of Carpenters and Joiners of America, 820,000; (4)

---

[1] U.S. Department of Labor, *Directory of National Unions and Employee Associations 1973*, Bureau of Labor Statistics, 1974, pp. 66–67.
[2] Ibid., p. 86.

[3] Ibid., p. 74.
[4] In July 1968, the UAW and the Teamsters formed the Alliance for Labor Action as a step toward coordinating the activities of the two unions. *Business Week*, July 27, 1968, p. 28.

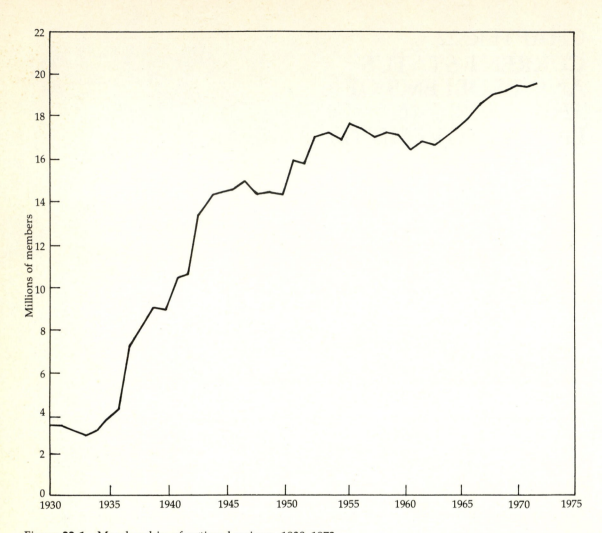

Figure **22-1**   Membership of national unions, 1930–1972

Excludes Canadian membership but includes members in other areas outside the United States. Members of AFL-CIO directly affiliated local unions are also included. For the years 1948–52, midpoints of membership estimates, which were expressed as ranges, were used.

From U.S. Department of Labor, *Directory of National Unions and Employee Associations 1973*, Bureau of Labor Statistics, 1974, p. 71.

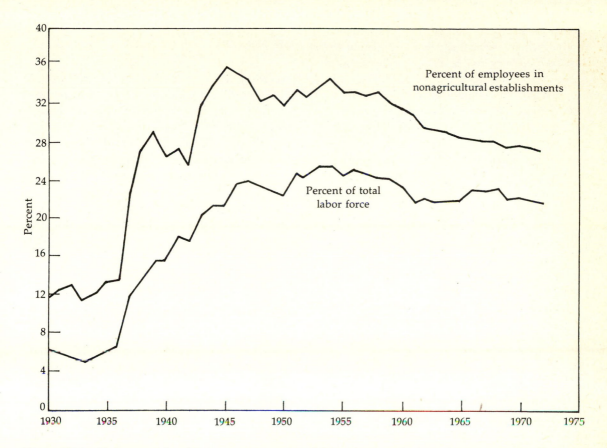

Figure 22-2   Union membership as a percent of total labor force and of employees in nonagricultural establishments, 1930–1972

Excludes Canadian membership.

From U.S. Department of Labor, *Directory of Unions and Employee Associations, 1973*, Bureau of Labor Statistics, 1974, p. 72.

the International Association of Machinists, 758,000; and (5) the Retail Clerks International Association, 633,000.[5]

It should be noted that there are significant numbers of workers belonging to unions with only a local or regional membership. A few years ago, approximately 400,000 workers belonged to single-firm unions independent of

any national or international union. There were approximately 1,400 such unions in the fifty states.[6]

TRENDS IN UNION MEMBERSHIP

Trends in union membership since 1930 can be traced in Figures 22-1 and 22-2. Figure 22-1 in-

[5] U.S. Department of Labor, *Directory*, p. 74. These figures include Canadian membership.

[6] Arthur P. Shostak, *America's Forgotten Labor Organization* (Princeton, N.J.: Industrial Relations Section, Department of

dicates that union membership rose dramatically after the enactment of the National Industrial Recovery Act of 1933 and the Wagner Act of 1935, continued to rise until 1956, and dropped off only slightly during the economic recessions of 1957–1958 and 1960–1961. As Figure 21-1 indicates, union membership has risen each year since 1964. Figure 21-2, however, indicates that union membership as a percentage of the total labor force and as a percentage of employees in nonagricultural establishments started declining about 1953.

WOMEN MEMBERS

Female membership in unions has grown slowly but steadily in recent years. Between 1962 and 1972 women members increased from 3.3 million to 4.5 million, or from 18.6 percent to 21.7 percent of all union members.[7] This represents 12.6 percent of the women in the labor force.[8] Another 1,200,000 women members are added, however, when we include women who belong to employee associations that engage in collective bargaining.[9]

Only a small proportion of union officials are women. In 1972, approximately 7 percent of the members of elected governing boards of unions and employee associations were women. These boards generally consist of the president, secretary, treasurer, and vice presidents of labor organizations.[10]

INDUSTRIAL DISTRIBUTION OF UNION MEMBERSHIP

According to the industrial classifications used by the Bureau of Labor Statistics, the three industries with the largest number of union members in 1972 were (1) contract construction, 2.7 million; (2) transportation, 2.4 million; and (3) wholesale and retail trade, 1.3 million. In terms of broader categories, of the total of 23.1 million union and association members, nearly 9 million were in manufacturing, 9.6 million were in nonmanufacturing and 4.5 million were employed in federal, state, and local governments.[11]

WHITE-COLLAR UNIONIZATION

Although some unions have been primarily or exclusively white-collar, such as the Retail Clerks International Association, the American labor movement has traditionally consisted of mostly blue-collar workers. However, this pattern is gradually changing. In 1972, unionized white-collar workers in the United States numbered approximately 3,434,000; this was 16.5 percent of the total membership of U.S. national and international unions. These figures are in contrast to the 2,463,000 white-collar union members in 1956, or 13.6 percent of total union membership. When employee associations are added to the 1972 data (for a total of 5,202,000), we find that white-collar workers comprise 22.6 percent of the total membership of unions and employee associations in the United States.[12]

Economics, Princeton University, 1962), p. 1. Two organizations of independent unions merged in 1963 forming the National Federation of Independent Unions. See *Business Week*, June 1, 1963, p. 50. For further information on union mergers, see Lucretia M. Dewey, "Union Merger Pace Quickens," *Monthly Labor Review*, 94:63–70 (June 1971).

[7] U.S. Department of Labor, *Directory*, p. 75.

[8] Virginia A. Bergquist, "Women's Participation in Labor Organizations," *Monthly Labor Review*, 97:3 (October 1974).

[9] U.S. Department of Labor, *Directory*, p. 75.

[10] Bergquist, "Women's Participation in Labor Organizations," p. 430.

[11] U.S. Department of Labor, *Directory*, p. 80.

[12] U.S. Department of Labor, *Directory*, p. 76. There is no precise definition of "white-collar," but the Bureau of Labor Statistics includes professional, technical, managerial, sales, and clerical workers in this category, a practice that indicates the general meaning of the term implied in this book.

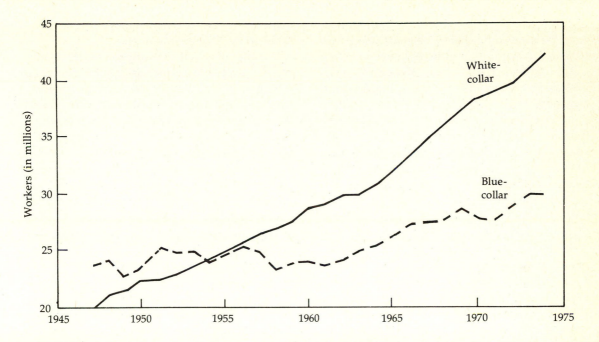

Figure **22-3**   Employment has shifted toward white-collar occupations

U.S. Department of Labor, *Occupational Outlook Handbook, 1976–1977 Edition*, Bulletin 1875, 1976, p. 16.

SIGNIFICANCE FOR LABOR MOVEMENT

With a gradual increase in white-collar jobs relative to those in production and maintenance, unions are naturally focusing more and more attention on the white-collar group. It was not until 1956 that white-collar workers outnumbered blue-collar workers,[13] and the trend toward a higher and higher proportion of white-collar workers appears likely to continue for the foreseeable future. (See Figure 22-3.) The proportions of workers in professions, technical and kindred occupations, service, and clerical employment are expected to continue to in-

crease. An average growth rate is expected among sales workers and artisans, while growth in the number of operatives—a major segment of American union membership—is expected to proceed at a much slower pace.[14] These shifts in proportions mean that unions could gradually lose their relative membership strength unless they are successful in organizing the white-collar worker. Obvious competitors to union organizing efforts are the nonaffiliated employee associations that are beginning to bargain with employers on behalf of their membership.

As examples of the changes in white-collar

[13] Carol A. Barry, "White Collar Employment, Trends and Structure," *Monthly Labor Review*, 84:17 (January 1961).

[14] U.S. Department of Labor, *U.S. Manpower in the 1970's* (Washington, D.C.: U.S. Government Printing Office, 1970).

versus blue-collar employment, the United Auto Workers could claim 85 percent of the employees at North American Aviation in 1941, but by 1962 the UAW could claim only 37 percent even though total company employment had increased.[15] In the steel industry, blue-collar employment per ton of shipped steel has declined dramatically, and the ratio of white-collar workers to blue-collar employees rose from one-ninth in 1934 to one-fourth in 1964.[16] Overall, the proportion of union membership to the total nonfarm labor force declined from 33.2 percent in 1958 to 26.7 percent in 1972.[17] (See Figure 22-2.)

Because of these trends, the AFL-CIO and many of its affiliated unions as well as such nonaffiliated unions as the Teamsters and United Auto Workers are seriously concerned about their relative strength and have launched extensive drives toward organizing the white-collar worker. Drives to organize those blue-collar workers presently not organized are also being stepped up.

Recent organizing efforts have produced substantial successes. From 1961 to 1975, the number of elections supervised by the National Labor Relations Board in white-collar units increased from 395 per year to 1,219. The number of elections won by unions increased from 177 to 706, and the number of new members increased from 4,660 in 1961 to 23,885 in 1975. These figures do not include successes in organizing public employees nor elections supervised by state agencies. Almost all categories of white-collar, nonmanagerial employees, according to the election results, appear to be vulnerable, including employees in business and industry, education and health care fields. Organizing of professionals in health-related areas accelerated after the Taft-Hartley Act was

extended in 1974 to cover employees in nonprofit hospitals and nursing homes.[18]

Outside of NLRB jurisdiction, public employees appear to be increasingly interested in collective action, a trend that has been stimulated by favorable administrative rulings and state legislation. In 1970, about one of every nine union members in the United States was a state or federal government employee. By 1972, the State, County, and Municipal Employees counted 529,000 members and had moved from twenty-first to tenth place in terms of size in the United States within a decade.[19]

Typical managerial resistance to unionization in business and industry contrasts with the position taken by the executive branch of the federal government under Executive Order 10988 of January 17, 1962, issued by President Kennedy (revised in 1969 by President Nixon's Executive Order 11491), which embarked on an active program to encourage organization among federal employees. This executive order, as has been suggested by Prasow and others, has ". . . provided somewhat the same impetus for public sector labor relations that the Wagner Act of 1935 did in the 1930's for private sector labor relations."[20] As a result, approximately 94,000 governmental workers joined unions within the first fifteen months after the directive was first issued.[21] Between 1964 and 1966, membership in governmental unions grew by 264,000, of which 127,000 were white-collar workers.[22] Between 1966 and 1972 total union membership among federal employees grew from 835,000 to 1,400,000. By 1972, 1.1

[15]*Business Week*, December 8, 1962, p. 127.
[16]*Business Week*, August 14, 1965.
[17]U.S. Department of Labor, *Directory*, p. 70.

[18]*White Collar Report*, April 2, 1976, pp. B–1, B–2. Decertification elections were held in seventy units, with unions losing fifty-four. Ibid., p. B–4.
[19]U.S. Department of Labor, *Directory*, p. 74.
[20]Paul Prasow et al., *Scope of Bargaining in the Public Sector—Concepts and Problems*, report submitted to Division of Public Employee Labor Relations, U.S. Department of Labor, 1972, p. 2.
[21]*White Collar Report*, April 18, 1963, p. B-3.
[22]*White Collar Report*, March 21, 1968, p. B-5.

million state and local government employees belonged to unions, and another 2.1 million belonged to employee associations, mostly in state and local jurisdictions.[23]

It should be noted, however, that collective bargaining between government employees and their superiors is somewhat different from the industrial union-management relationship. For example, federal employees are forbidden to strike under Section 305 of the Taft-Hartley Act, the penalties being discharge, forfeiture of civil-service status, if any, and a three-years loss of eligibility for re-employment. In addition, federal workers may bargain only on conditions of work and on procedures for grievance and arbitration, not on wages and hours or other matters established by law.[24] However, work stoppages by federal, state, and local government employees increased from 28 in 1950 to 142 in 1966.[25] This includes both police and firefighters.

Increasing numbers of teachers also appear interested in collective action. Some 249,000 teachers belong to the AFL-CIO affiliated American Federation of Teachers, but 1.2 million belong to the independent National Education Association,[26] which more and more is taking

on union functions, including those of collective bargaining and strikes. In 1974, for example, there were 133 work stoppages by teachers in the United States involving 60,000 employees.[27]

This conversion of a professional association into an instrument for collective bargaining has also taken place in many nurses' organizations in recent years.[28] The same phenomenon has also occurred to some extent among college professors, with the National Council of the American Association of University Professors adopting the position that the AAUP would "pursue collective bargaining as a major additional way of realizing the Association's goals in higher education. . . ."[29] By 1975 faculty collective bargaining legislation had been passed in twenty-three states, and faculties on almost four hundred campuses had voted to unionize.[30]

With the exception of the renewed interest among professionals that was sparked by the recession of the early 1970s, unions have typically found it very difficult to organize engineers and scientists in private employment in spite of their chronic frustrations (see Chapter 18). Nor have many professional groups become certified as bargaining agents, a situation exemplified by the demise in 1960 of the Engineers and Scientists of America, the only national federation of engineers' unions in the United States.[31] Plagued by internal political problems, decertification of member unions,

[23]U.S. Department of Labor, *Directory*, p. 67.
[24]See Executive Order 11491, Section 11. For a discussion of both federal and state labor laws as applied to government employees, see Joseph P. Goldberg, "Public Employee Developments in 1971," *Monthly Labor Review*, 95:56–66 (January 1972). As of 1970, forty states had passed laws authorizing public employees to participate in some form of union activity (p. 63).
[25]James E. Young and Betty L. Brewer, "State Legislation Affecting Labor Relations in State and Local Government," *Labor and Industrial Relations Series*, No. 2, Bureau of Economical Business Research, Kent State University, 1968, p. 1.
[26]Data from U.S. Department of Labor, *Directory*, pp. 73–74. The AFT claims 450,000 members. See Dennis Chamot, "Professional Employees Turn to Unions," *Harvard Business Review*, 54:120 (May-June 1976). Conventions of the AFT and the NEA in 1972 discussed a possible merger of the two organizations. For a further discussion of collective action by teachers, see William R. Hazard, "Collective Bargaining in Education: The Anatomy of a Problem," *Labor Law Journal*, 18:412–419 (July 1967).

[27]*Analysis of Work Stoppages*, 1974, U.S. Department of Labor, Bureau of Labor Statistics, 1976, p. 29.
[28]John Schmidman, "Nurses and Pennsylvania's New Public Employee Bargaining Law," *Labor Law Journal*, 22:725–733 (November 1971); and Ronald L. Miller, "Development and Structure of Collective Bargaining Among Registered Nurses," *Personnel Journal*, 50:218–225 (March 1971).
[29]*Academe*, November 1971, p. 1.
[30]*The Chronicle of Higher Education*, September 2, 1975, p. 1; and Martha A. Brown, "Collective Bargaining on the Campus: Professors, Associations and Unions," *Labor Law Journal*, 21:167–181 (March 1970).
[31]*Industrial Relations News*, December 1960, p. 1. See also *White Collar Report*, December 5, 1960, pp. A-9, A-10.

and difficulties in recruiting members, the organization finally disbanded. Even at its peak in 1956, the Engineers and Scientists of America had a membership of only 25,000 or approximately 4 percent of the engineers in the work force.[32] In 1967, Kleingartner estimated that unions represented approximately 45,927 engineers and 49,334 technicians. Given that at the time there were an estimated 850,000 engineers employed in the United States, only 5.4 percent of the total employed engineering population was unionized.[33]

Overall, in view of changes in the composition of the labor force, and the propensity of many professionals to turn their employee associations into bargaining instruments, leaders in the union movement consider the large numbers of white-collar employees a major challenge to their recruiting efforts. No categories of white-collar employees, with the exception of the top executive ranks, should be considered immune from collective action. Even some dentists and resident interns (physicians) have organized and, in some instances, have taken strike action.

Middle managers and supervisors, while excluded from protection by the Taft-Hartley Act,[34] showed a surprising interest in unionization during the recession of the early 1970s. A survey by the American Management Association of more than five hundred firms found about three-fourths of the middle managers surveyed were experiencing substantially more job frustration and discontent than in prior years, and almost half were in favor of laws permitting supervisors and middle managers to organize for collective bargaining purposes in organizations where a majority of supervisors and managers deemed it desirable. About 18 percent would join a union of managers if the law and corporate attitudes would permit it, and another 17 percent would seriously consider unionization as a means of regaining what they perceived as a diminished voice in their organizations. Many others indicated they would give unionization a second thought under different circumstances. Seventy percent believed middle managers should be allowed to organize informal groups to discuss conditions of employment with top management representatives on a company-by-company basis.[35]

[32] See "Engineer Union Fights for Life," *Fortune*, May 1960, pp. 246ff. However, see "Organization Drive: Ired by Unemployment, the Nation's Engineers Move Toward Unionism," *The Wall Street Journal*, February 22, 1972, p. 1. Strauss classifies seven types of associations available to engineers: "(1) learned societies, which seek only to advance knowledge; (2) technical societies, which aim to advance both knowledge and the professional interests of those who wish this knowledge; (3) professional organizations (such as the National Society of Professional Engineers), which are concerned purely with professional advancement; (4) 'sounding boards,' which meet with management to discuss personnel problems, but which are not certified collective bargaining agents; (5) certified unions which admit only professional engineers and are not affiliated with AFL-CIO unions; (6) unaffiliated unions which admit both engineers and technicians; and (7) unions affiliated with the AFL-CIO." George Strauss, "Professionalism and Occupational Associations," *Industrial Relations*, 2:27 (May 1963). The last three categories, which are units certified by the NLRB, are particularly relevant to our discussion. In some instances, however, members of such organizations disclaim the label of "union" although they bargain collectively.

[33] Archie Kleingartner, "Unionization of Engineers and Technicians," *Monthly Labor Review*, 90:30 (October 1967). A survey in a major Air Force installation in the Midwest found 53 percent of the responding scientists and engineers indicating that they would not join a union, 29 percent saying they were undecided, and 18 percent saying they would join a union. T. Roger Manley and Charles W. McNichols, "Attitudes of Federal Scientists and Engineers toward Unions," *Monthly Labor Review*, 98:57–60 (April 1975).

[34] Excluded from protection is any supervisor defined as ". . . any individual having authority, in the interest of the employer, to hire, transfer, suspend, lay off, recall, promote, discharge, assign, reward, or discipline other employees, or responsibly to direct them, or to adjust their grievances, or effectively to recommend such action, if in connection with the foregoing the exercise of such authority is not of a merely routine or clerical nature, but requires the use of independent judgment." See Russell L. Greenman and Eric J. Schmertz, *Personnel Administration and the Law* (Washington, D.C.: Bureau of National Affairs, 1972), p. 231.

[35] Dale Tarnowieski, "Middle Managers' New Values," *Personnel*, 50:47–53 (January-February 1973).

INDUSTRY VARIATIONS IN WHITE-COLLAR UNIONIZATION

White-collar unionization varies greatly by industry. For example, while a high proportion of white-collar employees in the railroad and the telephone and communications industries belong to unions, insurance companies and banks are relatively nonunionized. Only 34,000 union or association members were reported in the "finance, insurance, and real estate" industry group in 1972.[36]

PROBLEMS AND ISSUES CONFRONTING THE LABOR MOVEMENT

Many early problems of recognition and survival faced by the union movement have been essentially solved. Chapter 2 pointed out that the Wagner Act of 1935 established as public policy the encouragement of collective bargaining, and the subsequent amendments to that act by the Taft-Hartley Act of 1947 reaffirmed the workers' right to organize and bargain collectively. Public-opinion surveys in recent years have shown that about three-fourths of the general public favor laws guaranteeing workers the right to organize unions and bargain collectively with their employers. Furthermore, most surveys show that the overwhelming majority of rank-and-file union members are strongly loyal to their unions.[37] Thus, survival of the union and public acceptance of the union are accomplished facts, as is member loyalty. However, as we will see later, recent polls indicate that people believe unions should be more closely regulated.

Although Archibald Cox may be correct in stating that ". . . the most exciting and challenging part of the job facing labor unions and collective bargaining during the past quarter century has now been substantially accomplished,"[38] certain important problems remain. It has been pointed out previously that a major problem is maintaining and increasing relative strength as a portion of the work force. Other important problems faced by the labor movement have to do with governmental intervention in collective bargaining and union affairs, the so-called right-to-work laws, the rapidly changing nature of technology and world trade, and a chronic decline in the nation's increase in productivity relative to other major industrial countries. The latter two problems are the most serious, in my opinion. As I.W. Abel, president of the United Steelworkers, told union members, "You don't get anything by dropping a bucket into an empty well."[39]

GENERAL AND GOVERNMENTAL INTEREST IN COLLECTIVE BARGAINING

During the last twenty years or so, Congress and the executive branch of the government have shown increased interest in the regulation of union-management relations and in the conduct of union affairs. Evidence of this interest can be found in the passage of the Taft-Hartley Act, which outlawed certain practices on the part of unions in their dealings with management, including secondary boycotts and jurisdictional strikes. This legislation was passed after a serious wave of strikes and labor unrest following World War II.

More recent legislation, the Labor-Management Reporting and Disclosure Act of 1959 (Landrum-Griffin Act), was designed essentially to protect the individual worker and management from abuses of union power.

---

[36] U.S. Department of Labor, *Directory*, p. 80.
[37] See Derek C. Bok and John T. Dunlop, *Labor and the Community* (New York: Simon and Schuster, 1970), p. 12.

[38] Archibald Cox, "The Future of Collective Bargaining," *Monthly Labor Review*, 84:1210 (November 1961).
[39] *Business Week*, September 9, 1972, p. 100.

This legislation largely resulted from the investigations by the Senate McClellan Committee of corruption in the labor movement.[40]

A particularly notable feature of the Landrum-Griffin Act is governmental surveillance over the internal conduct of union affairs, including procedures for insuring secret-ballot election of officers, the right of free speech, protection against embezzlement of union funds by union officials, and restriction on the use of trusteeships. Thus, in addition to protecting and encouraging workers in bargaining collectively with management (Wagner Act), the government is now concerned with protecting employers against union tactics (Taft-Hartley Act) and with protecting individual employees and employers against arbitrary union power (Landrum-Griffin Act).

Public opinion tends to favor governmental regulation of union-management relations. The Opinion Research Corporation (ORC) reported in 1972 that 71 percent of the general public believed that unions had grown enough or were too big, and that 55 percent (including 41 percent of the union members who were polled) felt that unions had excessive power and that this power should be reduced. Sixty-two percent believed that it was necessary for unions to be more closely regulated, 68 percent thought strikes and labor disputes were doing serious harm to the country (61 percent of union members agreed), and a high percentage (59 percent of the general public and 68 percent of union members) believed that "the wages paid in this country make it difficult for the United States to compete in world markets."[41]

Direct intervention by the secretary of labor and the president of the United States in contract negotiations and labor disputes increased dramatically during the Kennedy administration. Early in its history this administration embarked on a program that would, in the words of Arthur Goldberg, then secretary of labor, "define and assert" the national interest in matters of collective bargaining. It very actively encouraged noninflationary settlements and urged quick settlements in major industries that were engaged in defense work.[42] Other examples of the Kennedy administration's involvement in collective bargaining include intervention in the steel industry negotiations in 1962 and the appointment by the president of a Missile Sites Labor-Management Committee to advise the Defense Department in any labor disputes.[43]

President Johnson, who also actively asserted the government's point of view, urged the "utmost restraint" in wage and price increases. For example, in the summer of 1968, he ordered that the Defense Department restrict purchases of steel to those companies holding the line on prices in the aftermath of substantial wage increases granted during 1968 labor negotiations. The most dramatic interventions of the Nixon administration into union contract regulations were the wage-price freeze of August 1971 and the subsequent wage and price controls that emerged from the freeze.

The reaction of labor leaders to such governmental intervention has been mixed. In general, however, the labor movement has been seriously concerned about increased governmental intervention in the collective-bargaining process.

---

[40] See U.S. Congress, "Final Report of the Select Committee on Improper Activities in the Labor or Management Field, United States Senate," 86th Congress, 2d Session, Report No. 1139, Parts 1–4.

[41] "The Public Looks at Unions Today," Opinion Research Corporation, 1972 (pamphlet, 24 pp); and "Trouble Plagues the House of Labor," *Business Week*, October 28, 1972, p. 67.

[42] See *Business Week*, March 17, 1962, p. 25.

[43] After an early signing of what appeared to be a noninflationary contract with the Steelworkers, U.S. Steel raised its prices, thereby precipitating the publicly expressed wrath of President Kennedy. The price increase was rescinded. See also, Glenn H. Parker, "The Missile Site Labor Commission," *ILR Research*, 8:8–15, No. 1 (1962).

RIGHT-TO-WORK LAWS AND UNION SECURITY

Another problem faced by the labor movement is created by the so-called state right-to-work laws. In essence, these laws outlaw both (a) the closed shop—a situation in which the employer may hire only union members, a practice declared illegal under the Taft-Hartley Act—and (b) union-shop provisions in contracts—clauses that make union membership mandatory for all workers in a bargaining unit once the majority votes for the union. Right-to-work laws also prohibit "maintenance of membership" provisions—clauses requiring workers belonging to the union at the beginning of a contract's term to remain members through the period of the contract but permitting withdrawal during a specified interval near the time the contract expires. The unions, of course, feel that those being represented should assume the financial and participative responsibilities of membership and that anything less than the union shop weakens the union.

Unless prohibited by state law, this financial problem is minimized by agency shop provisions under which nonunion members of the bargaining unit must contribute to the support of the union, usually the equivalent of union dues. Clauses establishing the agency shop are relatively rare, and they have been declared illegal in some right-to-work states.[44] A 1975 report found only about 9 percent of labor contracts containing such provisions. In contrast, 4 percent of the contracts examined contained provisions for maintenance of membership.

In 1976, twenty states had right-to-work laws. The first such law was passed in Florida in 1943. Eleven more states passed right-to-work laws in 1947, the same year as the Taft-Hartley

Act, presumably as a public reaction to the exercise of union power during the postwar period. Five were passed from 1950 through 1955, only two between 1956 and 1958,[45] one in 1963,[46] and one in 1976.[47] The law in Indiana was repealed in 1965.[48] Thus, there is either less and less governmental support for such legislation, or the saturation point has nearly been reached in terms of general support. Most of the states that have passed these laws are states in the South, Midwest, or West that are not heavily industrialized.

In 1966, the Johnson administration urged Congress to repeal Section 14(b) of the Taft-Hartley Act permitting state right-to-work laws, but the effort was defeated. At the present time, repeal of Section 14(b) appears unlikely, but a national right-to-work law is equally improbable. While such state legislation constitutes a threat to union security and a constant irritant to organized labor, approximately 97 percent of all union contracts contain union-security provisions, with 81 percent providing for one or more of the principal forms of union security—the union shop, modified union shop, maintenance of membership, or agency shop.[49]

TECHNOLOGICAL CHANGES, WORK RULES, AND PRODUCTIVITY

Probably the most serious problems confronting the American labor movement stem from rapid technological change, but these are occurring along with a declining rate of productivity improvement relative to other major industrial

---

[44] In 1963 the U.S. Supreme Court ruled that agency-shop clauses were legal under the Taft-Hartley Act (*NLRB* v. *General Motors*) but that individual states might ban this form of union security (*Retail Clerks, Local 1625* v. *Schermerhorn*).

[45] See David A. Swankin, "State 'Right-to-Work' Legislation in 1958," *Monthly Labor Review*, 81:1380–1381 (December 1958).
[46] *Industrial Relations News*, February 23, 1963, p. 1.
[47] Bureau of National Affairs, *Labor Relations Reporter*, July 19, 1976, pp. 1–2.
[48] Bureau of National Affairs, *Collective Bargaining Negotiations and Contracts*, 87:12 (1976).
[49] Bureau of National Affairs, *Basic Patterns in Union Contracts*, 87:1 (January 16, 1975).

nations. In order to meet economic competition both at home and abroad, a problem intensified by rising labor costs, high taxes, and the high cost of energy, managements are constantly seeking new machines, new tools, and new methods to increase efficiency. Consequently, human resource needs in terms of both skills and numbers are bound to shift rapidly, and the temporary dislocation of workers becomes inevitable. The union may have a number of different reactions to such changes, varying from (a) resistance to all such changes, to (b) support of change coupled with attempts to minimize problems of dislocation, to (c) cooperation with management in the solution of production and quality-of-worklife problems.

Union reaction to technological change and the introduction of new work methods has varied greatly from union to union and from situation to situation. In general, craft unions have tended to resist change in a higher proportion of situations than industrial unions. Because the former have memberships based on a particular craft, efficiencies resulting in layoffs are likely to reduce the number of dues-paying members. In the case of industrial unions, however, technological changes often create new occupations which may remain in the bargaining unit, and resistance to change is likely to be lower in such situations. Competition faced by the unions may also stimulate change in some situations, since it may be obvious that new equipment and methods are required for a particular craft to survive.

There are many examples of unions protecting the status quo and resisting change. Several instances, all of which occurred at one time or another through work rules at the local level, follow.[50] Such work rules typically give rise to the charge of "featherbedding," and a number of them have since been modified.

° Electrical workers performing unnecessary rewiring on apparatus purchased from another manufacturer

° Painters requiring paint brushes to be limited in width and rollers banned unless there is premium pay

° Compositors performing unnecessary resetting of advertisements run in another paper

° Plasterers requiring three coats of plaster when the building code requires only two

° Operating engineers employed to merely push buttons or turn switches

° More brakemen riding trains in some states (the number written into law) than in others

° Unnecessary stage hands in theaters

° Dock workers refusing to use pallets that would increase efficiency in loading and unloading

° Meatcutters refusing to handle precut and prepackaged meats

° Union electricians required when light bulbs need replacing

° Airline employees who can unload baggage, and some who can unload cargo, but not both

° Thirteen separate crafts required to install bathrooms in a hotel or apartment house in New York City

Similarly, many instances of union cooperation in technological change have occurred. the following list includes a few examples.[51]

---

[50] Examples drawn from Sumner H. Slichter, James J. Healy, and E. Robert Livernash, *The Impact of Collective Bargaining on Management* (Washington, D.C.: The Brookings Institution, 1961), pp. 318–337; *Business Week,* August 28, 1971, pp. 54–55; and *Business Week,* September 9, 1972, pp. 100–101ff.

[51] Slichter, Healy, and Livernash, *Impact of Collective Bargaining,* pp. 355–361; *Monthly Labor Review,* 95:68–69 (September 1972); and Gerald Somers, Arvid Anderson, Malcolm Denise, and Leonard Sayles, eds., *Collective Bargaining and Productivity* (Madison, Wisc.: Industrial Relations Research Association, 1975).

° Needle-trade unions' industrial engineering departments assisting companies in making technological changes necessary for company survival

° Plasterers' union encouraging its locals to use plaster gun to meet competition from dry-wall construction

° The Central States Conference of Teamsters encouraging the use of sleeper cabs in order to enable companies to compete with railroads

° Lithographers naming a director of technology to assist manufacturers in developing new machinery and processes

° Unions in Scanlon-plan companies cooperating to reduce costs and increase efficiencies

° United Mineworkers agreeing to a sweeping mechanization of coal mines

° Glass Bottle Blowers' Association encouraging technological improvements to protect employment opportunities

° International Longshoremen's and Warehousemen's Union agreeing to the introduction of large cargo containers to expedite handling

° United Transportation Union agreeing to the eventual elimination of the job of fireman on diesel freight locomotives

° Communications Workers of America working with the Bell System to minimize the impact of automation on employees

° Retail Clerks negotiating with Washington, D.C., stores to permit installation of electronic checkouts but to protect full-time workers.

Thus, at the local level there has been no general trade union policy toward technological change; policies vary from situation to situation. As a powerful determinant in the nation's standard of living, in its ability to meet foreign competition, and in its capacity to assist underdeveloped countries, the labor movement as a whole needs to adopt a policy of strongly sup-

porting technological advance while at the same time working with management and the government to find means of minimizing the impact of change on individual workers. While many labor leaders have stated strong support of such a philosophy at the national level, collective bargaining approaches at the local level are frequently in opposition.

A number of interesting experiments have taken place in recent years in an attempt to solve some of the employment problems created by technological change while at the same time minimizing obstructions to the change itself. For example, the Pacific Maritime Association and the International Longshoremen's and Warehousemen's Union agreed to permit introduction of labor-saving methods and devices in exchange for payments to the union which would represent a share of the savings. The work force would be reduced gradually by not replacing those quitting or retiring.[52]

An example of minimizing the impact of changes on workers is provided by the moving allowances that were negotiated in the automobile industry with the Auto-Workers Union in the case of employees who qualified for transfer to another company plant located more than fifty miles from the workers' present location. A similar agreement was made between the Meatcutters Union and Swift and Company. Armour and Company and the Meatcutters and Packinghouse Workers agreed to guarantee earnings during a ninety-day period after notice was given of plant shutdowns and to grant "technological adjustment pay" for laid-off employees with five or more years experience. The same parties also agreed to establish an automation fund for studying

[52] Slichter, Healy, and Livernash, *Impact of Collective Bargaining,* pp. 359–381; and S. Paul St. Sure, "Labor Unions and the Changing Technology," in Lafayette G. Harter, Jr., and John Keltner, *Labor in America* (Corvallis, Oregon: Oregon State University Press, 1966), pp. 48–49.

the problem of workers dislocated by technological changes and for paying the expenses of retraining and transfer.[53] The New York Typographical Union No. 6 signed an eleven-year agreement with New York newspapers to give management a free hand in automating plants and making job assignments in return for guarantees of lifetime employment for present employees, annual cost-of-living adjustments, and other benefits.[54]

These examples reflect a trend in policy toward which the unions are moving—a trend of encouraging technological change while minimizing the impact on individuals. This trend cannot help but boost the nation's productivity, raise its living standards, enable it to participate in a rapidly increasing volume of foreign trade, and at the same time allow it to meet the requirements of national defense.

Implementing the policy, however, requires managerial cooperation and assistance from federal, state, and local governments and agencies in facilitating worker relocation or retraining, or both. A problem so broad makes such cooperation essential, with the solution involving a combination of methods, including training programs, moving allowances, severance pay, Supplemental Unemployment Benefits, extended unemployment compensation, and aggressive counseling and placement programs.[55] Some of these methods are more practical than others, depending upon the time and circumstances. (For more on productivity bargaining, see Chapter 24.)

MINORITY MEMBERSHIP

In addition to the wide variety of managerial problems faced by any organization—organized labor employed more than 110,000 people in the United States in 1966[56]—the union movement faces the problem of integrating its membership. Title VII of the Civil Rights Act of 1964 made the following acts unlawful for a labor union (1972 amendments made it clear that these provisions also applied to applicants for union membership):

1. To exclude or to expel from its membership, or otherwise to discriminate against, any individual because of his race, color, religion, sex, or national origin;

2. To limit, segregate, or classify its membership, or to classify or fail to refuse to refer for employment any individual, in any way which would deprive or tend to deprive any individual of employment opportunities, or would limit such employment opportunities or otherwise adversely affect his status as an employee or as an applicant for employment, because of such individual's race, color, religion, sex, or national origin; or

3. To cause or attempt to cause an employer to discriminate against an individual in violation of this section.[57]

Discrimination against minorities in the construction industry appears particularly prevalent in recent years. According to Marshall, the construction crafts with the fewest black members have been electricians, sheet metal workers, plumbers, glaziers, iron workers, pipe

[53] Phyllis Groom, "A Review of American Labor in 1961," *Monthly Labor Review*, 85:2 (January 1962). For a history of contractual agreements between Armour and the Packinghouse Workers and the Meatcutters, see *Wage Chronology: Armour and Co., 1914–67*, Bulletin No. 1481, Bureau of Labor Statistics, U.S. Department of Labor, 1966.

[54] Joseph P. Goldberg, "Bargaining and Productivity in the Private Sector," in Somers et al., *Collective Bargaining and Productivity*, pp. 35–36.

[55] Federal efforts in this direction include the Comprehensive Employment and Training Act of 1973, increased efforts on the part of the U.S. Employment Service to assist in the relocation of workers, and extension of unemployment compensation benefits. (See Chapter 16 on skill training.)

[56] Robert A. Bedolis, "Labor Union Employment: The Total and the Trend," *The Conference Board Record*, 10:38–39 (October 1966).

[57] *Civil Rights Act of 1964*, Title VII, Section 703(c).

fitters, steam fitters, and elevator constructors. There also appears to have been little employment of blacks among the printing trades and the railroad unions.[58] In 1974, only two of the thirty-five members of the executive council of the AFL-CIO were black.[59] At the same time, however, major strides toward effective integration appear to have been made in the labor movement as a whole. Further progress probably lies partly in pressure from union headquarters on their locals, in federal and state law enforcement,[60] and in pressure from the members of minority groups themselves. The most effective solutions will come through affirmative action programs in which the unions and employers cooperate to identify and change patterns of discrimination.[61]

SUMMARY

The 1980s will find a strong American labor movement—well established through strength of members and through governmental policy and general public opinion. The unions, however, are faced with certain challenges and problems, including a membership that is declining in proportion to the total work force because of rapid growth in the service, trade, and professional occupations. Union policy states that one answer to this problem is to conduct vigorous recruiting drives among white-collar workers. These drives have been the most suc-

cessful among clerical workers, and unionization among federal and state employees has been given a major stimulus by favorable federal executive rulings and state legislation. While scientists and engineers have been difficult to unionize, the activities of nurses' and teachers' professional associations have increasingly expanded into collective bargaining activity. Recent stimulus to unionization has occurred through the extension of Taft-Hartley Act coverage to nonprofit hospitals and nursing homes.

Managerial pressure for rapid technological changes has presented a major problem to the union movement. The unions have been faced with the choice of resisting change, a position which may have short-run advantages for isolated groups of workers, or of encouraging change while minimizing the immediate problems of worker displacement and thereby reaping inevitable long-run gains. Having already followed the latter course in many instances, the trade union movement is tending toward the adoption of this policy on a broad basis.

Other problems of concern to the labor movement include increasing governmental intervention in labor-management relations and public insistence that the rights of the public be protected, particularly with respect to the impact of wage increases on prices and the impact of strikes. At this moment, the so-called right-to-work laws do not present a critical problem to the union movement, and a period of status quo with respect to such laws is likely. On the other hand, problems of racial and sex discrimination within the labor movement comparable to those within the broader society appear to constitute a major challenge for the next decade.

[58] Roy Marshall, "Labor Unions and Equal Opportunity: Collective Bargaining and Minority Employment," in *Labor in America*, pp. 49–73.

[59] *Business Week*, May 18, 1974, pp. 72–73.

[60] During the first year of operation of the Equal Employment Opportunity Commission, some 1,347 charges of discrimination by unions were filed, in contrst to 5,284 charges filed against employers. See *Newsletter from the Equal Employment Opportunity Commission*, 1:3 (July-August 1966).

[61] See Herbert Hammerman and Marvin Rogoff, "Unions and Title VII of the Civil Rights Act of 1964," *Monthly Labor Review*, 99:34–37 (April 1976).

REVIEW AND DISCUSSION QUESTIONS

1. Discuss shifts in patterns of employment that have had an impact on union membership.

2. Which white-collar workers have been the most susceptible to organization? What are the likely reasons?

3. How does collective bargaining in the federal government differ from collective bargaining in private employment?

4. What are the different kinds of affiliations and collective action open to professionals?

5. What has been the response of the union movement to technological change?

6. What are some of the major problems faced by the American labor movement?

7. What are the implications for the AFL-CIO and nonaffiliated unions of the growing tendency of professional associations to become collective bargaining agents? For employers?

8. What are some of the reasons supervisors and middle managers might become interested in collective action?

SUPPLEMENTAL REFERENCES

Adams, Alan E., "Unions to Step Up White Collar Organizations," *Banking,* 66:12–13 (January 1974).

Aronson, Robert L., "Automation—Challenge to Collective Bargaining?" in Harold W. Davey, Howard S. Kaltenborn, and Stanley H. Ruttenberg, eds., *New Dimensions in Collective Bargaining* (New York: Harper & Brothers, 1959), pp. 55–57.

Barbash, Jack, *American Unions: Structure, Government and Politics* (New York: Random House, Inc., 1967).

———, "The Tensions of Work: Can We Reduce the Costs of Industrialism?" *Dissent,* Winter 1972, pp. 240–248.

"Bargaining on an International Scale," *Business Week,* October 1975, pp. 38–40.

Berkwitt, George J., "Management—Sitting on a Time Bomb?" *Duns,* July 1972, pp. 38–41.

Cimini, Michael, "Government Intervention in Railroad Disputes," *Monthly Labor Review,* 94:27–34 (December 1971).

Cohen, Sanford, *Labor in the United States,* 3rd ed. (Columbus, Ohio: Charles E. Merrill Publishing Company, 1970).

Conway, Jack T., and Woodrow L. Ginsburg, "The Extension of Collective Bargaining to New Fields," *Proceedings of the Nineteenth Annual Winter Meeting,* Industrial Relations Research Association, 1966, pp. 303–311.

Couturier, Jean, "The Quiet Revolution in Public Personnel Laws," *Public Personnel Management,* 5:150–167 (May-June 1976).

Davey, Harold W., *Contemporary Collective Bargaining,* 3rd ed. (Englewood Cliffs, N.J.: Prentice-Hall, Inc., 1972).

DeMaria, Alfred T., Dale Tarnowieski, and Richard Gurman, *Manager Unions?* (New York: American Management Association, 1972).

Doherty, Robert E., and Walter E. Oberer, *Teachers, School Boards, and Collective Bargaining: A Changing of the Guard* (Ithaca, N.Y.: Cornell University), ILR Paperback No. 2, May 1967.

Gitlow, Abraham L., "The Trade Union Prospect in the Coming Decade," *Labor Law Journal,* 21:131–158 (March 1970).

Goldberg, Joseph P., "Public Employee Developments in 1971," *Monthly Labor Review,* 95:56–66 (January 1972).

Hammerman, Herbert, and Marvin Rogoff, "How to Live with Title VII: An Opportunity for Unions," *Employee Relations Law Journal,* 2:13–23 (Summer 1976).

Harvey, Michal G., and Roger A. Kerin, "Multinational Corporations Versus Organized Labor: Divergent Views on Domestic Unemployment," *California Management Review,* 18:5–13 (Spring 1976).

Imundo, Louis V., Jr., "Federal Government Sovereignty and Its Effect on Labor-Management Relations," *Labor Law Journal,* 26:146–151 (March 1975).

Kleingartner, A., "The Organization of White-Collar Workers," *British Journal of Industrial Relations*, 6:79–93 (March 1968).

Koziara, Karen S., "Collective Bargaining on the Farm," *Monthly Labor Review*, 91:3–9 (June 1968).

Loewenberg, J. Joseph, "Labor Relations for Policemen and Firefighters," *Monthly Labor Review*, 91:36–40 (May 1968).

Miller, Robert W., Frederick A. Zeller, and Glen W. Miller, *The Practice of Local Union Leadership: A Study of Five Local Unions* (Columbus: The Ohio State University Press, 1965).

Moore, William J., and Robert J. Newman, "On the Prospects for American Trade Union Growth: A Cross-Section Analysis," *Review of Economics and Statistics*, 62:435–445 (November 1975).

National Industrial Conference Board, "White Collar Unionization," *Studies in Personnel Policy*, No. 220, 1970.

Northrup, Herbert R., *Compulsory Arbitration and Government Intervention in Labor Disputes* (Washington, D.C.: Labor Policy Association, 1966).

"No Welcome Mat for Unions in the Sunbelt, *Business Week*, May 17, 1976, pp. 108–111.

Palombo, Raymond N., "The Agency Shop in a Public Service Merit System," *Labor Law Journal*, 26:409–416 (July 1975).

Pierson, Frank C., *Unions in Postwar America* (New York: Random House, Inc., 1967).

Purcell, Theodore V., S.J., *The Worker Speaks His Mind on Company and Union* (Cambridge, Mass.: Harvard University Press, 1953).

Ranks, Olive, *The Attitudes of Steelworkers to Technical Change* (Liverpool: Liverpool University Press, 1960).

Raphael, Edna E., "Working Women and Their Membership in Labor Unions," *Monthly Labor Review*, 97:27–33 (May 1974).

Seidman, Joel, "State Legislation on Collective Bargaining by Public Employees," *Labor Law Journal*, 22:13–22 (January 1971).

Sloane, Arthur A., and Fred Whitney, *Labor Relations* (Englewood Cliffs, N.J.: Prentice-Hall, Inc., 1967).

Snell, William, "Labor Trends: Bargaining in the U.S. Public Sector," *Personnel*, 49:60–67 (September-October 1972).

Stanton, Erwin S., "White Collar Unionization: New Challenge to Management," *Personnel Journal*, 51:118–124 (February 1972).

Ulman, Lloyd, *The Rise of the National Trade Union* (Cambridge, Mass.: Harvard University Press, 1966).

U.S. Department of Labor, *A Directory of Public Employee Organizations*, Labor Management Services Administration, November 1971.

Waiser, Kenneth O., and Mary L. Hennessy, *Public Management at the Bargaining Table* (Chicago: Public Personnel Association, 1967).

CHAPTER 23
THE UNIONIZATION PROCESS

Chapter 2 discussed some of the forces and factors that resulted in public acceptance and legalization of the labor union movement. Chapter 22 reviewed the status of current membership in the union movement and some of its current problems and challenges. This chapter directs attention toward the issues of why workers join unions, how a collective-bargaining unit comes into existence, some of the environmental variables affecting the unionization process, and the impact of unionization upon a firm.

WHY WORKERS JOIN UNIONS

Much has been written about the underlying reasons for workers joining unions, and it is generally accepted that sociological and psychological as well as economic factors are in-

volved. Bakke, for instance, describes unionization as a process arising from the feeling of workers that belonging to a union will facilitate the achievement of goals or conditions to which most people aspire, namely:

1. The society and respect of others

2. The degree of comfort and economic security possessed by the most favored of one's customary associates

3. Independence in, and control over, one's own affairs

4. Understanding the forces and factors at work in one's world

5. The maintenance of personal integrity—to be treated fairly; to have oneself and others treated justly.[1]

[1] Paraphrased from E. Wight Bakke, "To Join or Not to Join," in E. Wight Bakke, Clark Kerr, and Charles W. Anrod, eds.,

If Bakke's observations are still valid, and I believe they are, a desire to improve wages and fringe benefits is an important aspect, but only one aspect, of the reasons behind unionization. This conclusion has been dramatized by one group of researchers who found that, in interviewing workers about why they joined a union, not one worker stated he joined the union *primarily* to obtain higher wages.[2] It seems quite clear, however, that wages or salaries that are perceived as substantially below those paid to comparable occupations may be a major factor.[3]

Joining or forming a union may be a defensive move on the part of employees, or it may be a positive effort to enhance need fulfillment, or both. Probably more often than not, unionization is a manifestation of ego-defending behavior, i.e., a reaction against treatment perceived as being unfair or capricious. Much unionization, then, is an attempt by workers to inject more justice and orderliness into the work situation. (This, of course, was the intent of Congress in passing the Wagner Act of 1935, although there was also a broader purpose, that of facilitating the flow of commerce.)

In general, unionization seems largely an expression of dissatisfaction, a statement confirmed by a number of studies. For example, a study of workers in a Milwaukee "discount" department store found that twenty out of the thirty-nine workers who voted for a union were dissatisfied with various aspects of their employment, but only six out of the thirty-nine who voted against the union expressed general dissatisfaction.[4]

Unionization, therefore, attempts to enhance the fulfillment of a variety of human needs not being satisfied through the work situation—in particular, the needs for security, belonging, esteem, integration, and self-actualization. Undoubtedly, union membership has served at least partially to meet these needs for the vast majority of union members. If this was not true, decertification of bargaining units would have had a much higher incidence than has been the case over the years. Indeed it is a question of whether there would have been much successful union organizing in the first place, even under protective legislation.[5]

It should be recognized, however, that a minority of workers in a bargaining unit under a union-shop agreement and some of the newly hired who must join as a condition of employment may prefer not to be represented by a union. Consequently, for these employees unionization is not voluntary. The low incidence of decertified bargaining units, nevertheless, attests that once a union has been certified as the bargaining agent, the majority of union members tend to prefer the union to other alternatives.

THE UNIONIZATION PROCESS

THE DRIVE BEGINS

The initiative for organizing workers into a union may come from the employees themselves, from a union already representing some of the employees of a firm, or from a union representing workers elsewhere. In some instances, unions have been formed by collusion between an employer and union agents—

Unions, Management and the Public, 3rd ed. (New York: Harcourt, Brace and Company, 1967), pp. 85–92.
[2] Joel Seidman, Jack London, and Bernard Karsh, "Why Workers Join Unions," *The Annals of the American Academy of Political and Social Science,* 274:84 (March 1951).
[3] See "Education in America: On the Causes of Teacher Discontent," *Saturday Review,* October 21, 1967.
[4] Irving Brotslaw, "Attitude of Retail Workers Toward Union Organization," *Labor Law Journal,* 18:164 (March 1967).

[5] The Taft-Hartley Act empowers the NLRB to conduct elections to decertify bargaining units as well as to conduct elections for representation. In the fiscal year 1917, for example, the NLRB conducted 8,976 secret elections, of which 490 were decertification elections. *Thirty-Ninth Annual Report of the Labor Relations Board,* 1974, p. 2.

Figure **23-1**   Handbill used in unionization drive

ATTENTION! ALL OFFICE AND LABORATORY PERSONNEL OF THE XYZ COMPANY

Recently a large number of non-union employees in the labs and offices have contacted the Local 1 of the Plant Workers in regard to representation for wages, hours and working conditions. They are interested in representation which provides the know-how in dealing with the Company for working conditions and other Contract provisions as they affect monthly salaried office and laboratory employees.

This Union has been the bargaining agent for the wage personnel at XYZ Company for almost 20 years, and has been very successful in meeting all the situations peculiar to the XYZ Company, and has obtained for its members a broader range of benefits than has been obtained by other unions in this area.

Why stake YOUR job-security, YOUR opportunity for advancement, on the whims of your boss or supervisor? Make him follow the rules for advancement, wage progression, and job-security as set forth by a Labor Organization of your own choosing.

Why should your rates, rate ranges, and wage progressions be controlled solely by the vagaries of a capricious boss? Why not have a definite rate range, with automatic progression, as set forth in a bona-fide Union Contract? It is a protection you do not have now, but which you *will* have if you fill in and sign the attached card and drop it in the mail TODAY! Signing this card does not obligate you in any way. It merely indicates your desire to be represented by a progressive Union of your own choosing—Local 1 of the Plant Workers.

All Names Will Be Held In the Strictest Confidence! Sign it—and mail it—Today!

NOTICE . . . . NOTICE

In order to acquaint you more fully with the benefits obtainable with your organization, there will be a MASS MEETING of all eligible personnel, to be held in the ballroom of the Johnson Hotel, Monday evening, March 3rd, at 8:00 P.M.

---

a "sweetheart contract"—although such collusion is illegal under present labor laws. Typically, union drives start with an aggressive campaign of some union already representing part of a company's work force or with a campaign conducted by an outside union.

The first phases of a drive for organization are likely to be relatively quiet. Workers may be contacted initially at their homes or in restaurants or amusement places near work, and a good deal of soliciting and campaigning may take place between fellow workers on the job. Sometimes an outside union will contact workers on the job, as is often the case in retail stores. The first indication to management that a unionization drive is underway may be such signals as rumors or handbills. (See Figure 23-1 for an example of a handbill used in a unionization drive. The wording is authentic; the location has been disguised.)

THE NLRB ELECTION

Typically, the union will attempt to sign up 30 percent or more of the employees in the particular bargaining unit sought, at which point the appropriate regional office of the National Labor Relations Board will be petitioned to supervise an election.

The NLRB is empowered to determine the employees' choice of a bargaining representative and the appropriateness of a bargaining unit in most industries engaged in interstate commerce, with the exception of railroads, airlines, agriculture, and governmental agencies.[6]

A majority vote of the ballots cast by the employees in the unit is necessary for the Board to certify the union as the bargaining agent. This vote is not mandatory, since a company may recognize a union and bargain with it in the absence of an election, but it leaves the situation open for challenge by employees or by a rival union. From a practical standpoint, most employers will insist on an election to insure that a majority of the employees in a bargaining unit wish to be represented by the campaigning union.[7]

If the NLRB deems that a particular bargaining unit is appropriate, an election will be held, but the employer may challenge the nature of the unit, thus precipitating a separate NLRB ruling. If a majority of the workers in the unit who vote in the election cast their ballots for the union, the union involved will be certified as the exclusive bargaining agent for all the workers in the unit. The issue of a union shop will be a subject for future negotiations between the union and the employer, unless the union shop is prohibited by state law.

Determining the appropriateness of a unit for collective bargaining is an exceedingly complicated matter. Although the NLRB is empowered to make these decisions, few guidelines have been written into the Taft-Hartley Act, with the exception of four provisions in Section 9(b): (1) the Board is to attempt to ". . . assure to employees the fullest freedom in exercising the rights guaranteed by this Act . . . ," (2) a bargaining unit will not be considered appropriate if the unit sought contains both pro-

fessionals and nonprofessionals, unless a majority of the professionals vote for inclusion in such unit, (3) plant guards cannot be included in a unit with other types of workers, and (4) the Board may not decide that a craft unit is inappropriate on the grounds that the Board has made a different prior determination. In practice, some of the other variables examined by the NLRB are the bargaining practices historically used by parties in similar situations elsewhere. For example, the following issues are examined: the extent to which the proposed unit represents a distinct community of interest among the employees of the unit, the question of whether distinct crafts are involved, the relationship of the proposed unit to the organizational structure of the company, the scope of the required unit, and the scope of the employer's bargaining practices, i.e., whether the employer bargains as part of an employers' association.[8]

THE EMOTIONAL NATURE OF THE DRIVE

As suggested by the handbill in Figure 23-1, the unionization drive is likely to make use of emotional appeals. As Selekman stated years ago:

. . . When the organizer approaches the workers of any shop, he concentrates from start to finish upon appeals to emotion. Rational, logical arguments are part of the kit, but an exceedingly minor part. The organizer uses colorful and highly charged phrases for transmitting his message. He fortifies sentiments already inclining workers toward unionism. He neutralizes fears. He overcomes indifference and beats down opposition. He galvanizes positive feelings and transmutes negative feelings into the loyalty that will make workers join up. . . .[9]

[6] See Sections 2 and 9 of the Taft-Hartley Act, as amended. Amendments in 1974 removed the exemption on nonprofit hospitals.
[7] For a discussion of union authorization cards in elections, see H. Stephen Gerder, "Union Authorization Cards and the Duty to Bargain," Labor Law Journal, 19:201–223 (April 1968).

[8] For more detail on the criteria of the appropriateness of bargaining units, see Commerce Clearing House, 1972 Guidebook to Labor Relations, Labor Law Reports, 1972, pp. 78–88.
[9] Benjamin M. Selekman, Labor Relations and Human Relations (New York: McGraw-Hill Book Company, 1947), p. 15. For more on the organizing drive, see Edward R. Curtin, White-Collar Unionization, National Industrial Conference Board,

Thus, feelings are likely to run high during the campaign. One consequence may be to provoke defensive behavior on the part of superiors and higher management, particularly in the form of promises or threats. As we shall see later, such behavior can result in charges of unfair labor practices being brought against the union. We shall also have more to say about other implications of the emotional aspects of organizing drives.

IMPACT OF THE LAW ON THE UNIONIZATION PROCESS

Numerous provisions of the Taft-Hartley Act, including amendments to that Act by the Labor-Management Reporting and Disclosure Act of 1959 (Landrum-Griffin), regulate the conduct of a unionizing campaign. Some rules and regulations apply to the union; some apply to management. These regulations are enforced through NLRB hearings, subpoenas of evidence and witnesses, court orders and injunctions, and fines or imprisonment or both. More specifically, Section 10 of the Taft-Hartley Act empowers the NLRB to require persons to "cease and desist" from unfair labor practices, to reinstate employees with or without back pay, to require reports showing the extent to which parties have complied with orders, and to petition federal courts to enforce its orders. However, NLRB orders are subject to review by the courts. They may be appealed to a Federal Circuit Court of Appeals and may ultimately be appealed to the United States Supreme Court.

Studies in Personnel Policy, No. 220, 1970; and Rose Clavering, "The Unionization Drive: What's Fair, What's Legal?" *Supervisory Management*, 20:25–34 (September 1975). For a case history of a unionization drive, see William Foote Whyte, *Men at Work* (Homewood, Ill.: The Dorsey Press and Richard D. Irwin, 1961), pp. 249–267.

LEGAL CONSTRAINTS ON THE UNION

Some of the major restrictions on unions during a unionization campaign that are written into the Taft-Hartley Act are as follows:

Unions may not coerce workers in their right to refrain from union activity (Section 8), except that a contract may be signed making union membership a condition of continued employment after thirty days' employment (Section 8). Such mandatory membership (union shop) may be prohibited by state law, however (Section 14).

A union may not strike against an employer to compel the employer to recognize or bargain with that union when another union has already been certified as representative of the employees of that employer (Section 3).

No election may be held within a bargaining unit when a valid election has been held within the previous twelve months (Section 9).

Before a union may ask for a representation election by the NLRB, the union must submit certain information including its constitution and by-laws, a financial report, and affidavits certifying that none of the officers of the union is a Communist or advocates the overthrow of the U.S. government by force or illegal means (Section 9).

The following restrictions on unions were added to the Taft-Hartley Act by the Labor-Management Reporting and Disclosure Act of 1959:

Picketing in an attempt to organize a unit must be followed by the union's filing for an election within one month after the start of the picketing. If the election goes against the union, the union must desist from picketing for at least twelve months (Section 8).

Picketing where the employer has lawfully recognized another union, or where a valid election has been held during the previous twelve months, is illegal (Section 8).

Picketing to inform the public that a company is non-union is legal, unless the picketing stops deliveries to and from the company or causes other employees to withhold their services (Section 8).

Picketing to extort money from an employer is illegal. (Section 602 of the Landrum-Griffin Act.)

LEGAL CONSTRAINTS ON MANAGEMENT

Management is also constrained in its activities during an organizing drive. Most of the following restrictions were written into the Wagner Act and subsequently became part of the Taft-Hartley Act.

Employers may not interfere with, restrain, or coerce employees in the exercise of their rights to organize a union and bargain collectively or to refrain from union activity (Section 8). This prohibits such activities as direct or implied threats to employees of what might happen if they joined a union, prohibits promises of rewards for refraining from joining a union, and prohibits granting of wage increases or other benefits to thwart an organizing drive.

Employers may not dominate or interfere with the formation or administration of a union (Section 8).

Employers may not discriminate against any employee for union activity. This applies to such matters as initial hiring, conditions of employment, or retention on the payroll (Section 8).

Employers may not discriminate against workers for filing unfair labor practice charges or for testifying in an NLRB hearing (Section 8).[10]

In addition, the Landrum-Griffin bill added certain restrictions, including the following:

Employers must file reports with the Secretary of Labor as to expenditures for outside labor relations consultants concerning organizational campaigns, the influencing of employees in the exercise of their rights under the law, or the obtaining of information about the progress of an organizing drive (Section 203).[11]

Money payments (or of things of value) between management or its representatives and an official of a union seeking to organize a company's employees is illegal (added to Section 302 of the Taft-Hartley Act).

[10] For further discussion of constraints on management, see Peter A. Davis, "Before the NLRB Election: What You Can and Can't Do," *Personnel*, 44:8–18 (July-August 1967).
[11] This requirement is probably aimed partly at the now occasional practice of hiring detectives to spy on employees—a fairly prevalent practice during the early part of this century. See Eugene Emerson Jennings, *The Executives* (New York: Harper & Row, 1962), pp. 39–40.

Acceptance of such payments or demands for payments is also illegal.

These legislative provisions that indicate an extensive array of constraints include NLRB determination of the appropriateness of units, NLRB supervision of elections, and restrictions of both management and union.

IMPACT OF OTHER VARIABLES ON THE UNIONIZATION PROCESS

WORKERS' ATTITUDES

Attitudes about union membership may vary according to community, region, sex, or occupation. For example, we may expect a high proportion of production workers in a highly industrialized and highly unionized metropolitan area in the northeast United States to accept unionization as a matter of course. The majority of workers in such communities are likely to be imbued with labor-union philosophy and attitudes. To them, union activity is part of a way of life.

On the other hand, workers leaving the farm for jobs in industrial plants in predominantly agricultural trading towns are not steeped in the culture of trade unionism, nor are they so likely to look toward the union to fulfill their particular wants and desires. Trade-union membership may even be contrary to their desires for independence and may threaten them with loss of prestige in the eyes of their customary associates. Such attitudes tend to prevail in rural communities in the South and Southwest. For example, only 8 percent of nonfarm workers were unionized in South Carolina in 1974, while 38 percent were unionized in New York.[12]

White-collar workers have been generally reluctant to join unions although the pattern is gradually changing, as was pointed out in the

[12] *Business Week*, May 17, 1976, p. 109.

previous chapter. Some of the factors which seem to have been associated with this reluctance are closer identification than other workers with management, the expectation of opportunities for promotion, more varied and less routine jobs than those of most production workers, lack of particular craft-consciousness, and working conditions and benefits—not necessarily wages—superior to those for the plant workers.[13]

Although basic wages of many plant workers have normally exceeded the wages of lower-level clerical jobs, the median increases of clerical workers have stayed slightly ahead of production workers—that is, operatives, excluding craftsmen—over the years,[14] with the white-collar worker traditionally enjoying more job security, job freedom, and greater fringe benefits. For example, sick leave and vacation policies have tended historically to be more liberal for the white-collar group than for production workers. These factors have undoubtedly contributed to the reluctance of the white-collar group to join a union. As wages and benefits of the two groups converge in specific organizations, however, white-collar workers are more prone to unionization.

As the previous chapter pointed out, engineers, scientists, and professionals in general have been reluctant to join unions, although in recent years, there has been a substantial increase in collective bargaining among teachers and nurses. Moreover, professionals in city, state, and federal employment are increasingly participating in collective bargaining. For the most part, however, the professional seems to regard unionization as contrary to ideals held about individual initiative, creativity, and professional status. On the other hand, it also appears that professionals can change their attitudes drastically if they are provoked into defensive behavior by management and/or are faced with curtailed pay increases or loss of job security. Unionization of teachers and nurses and the willingness of these groups to engage in strike activities are dramatic examples.[15]

MANAGERIAL BEHAVIOR AND ATTITUDES

Thus, attitudes about unionization are based on predetermined attitudes which are brought to the job or developed within an occupational group or profession as well as on the behavior of management. Gross ineptitude by management can probably so alter even the most anti-union attitudes that unionization will appear to be a desirable alternative.

The evidence strongly suggests that effective management is a deterrent to unionization and that inadequate attention to the human aspects of administration quickly precipitates a collective-bargaining situation. This observation seems to be a sociological fact and, of course, is frustrating to union officials attempting to recruit new members when confronted with a particularly well-managed firm. However, these union leaders might take considerable comfort in realizing that a strong labor movement is an effective deterrent to widespread

[13] It is doubtful if "class-consciousness" is a major factor in white-collar workers being difficult to organize. In one study, although 67 percent perceived themselves as being more educated than plant workers and 53 percent saw themselves as more ambitious, only 35 percent felt they moved in a "higher social group." See *Can Management Hold White-Collar Employee Loyalty?* (Princeton, N.J.: Opinion Research Corporation, 1957), p. 10 (pamphlet).

[14] See Arthur Sackley and Thomas W. Gavett, "Blue-Collar/White-Collar Pay Trends: Analysis of Occupational Wage Differences," *Monthly Labor Review*, 94:5–12 (June 1971). In 1969 the median income for the following groups was in this rank order, from higher to lower: sales workers, artisans, clerical workers, operatives, and laborers. Robert L. Stein and Janice N. Hedges, "Blue-Collar/White-Collar Pay Trends: Earnings and Family Income," *Monthly Labor Review*, 94:14 (June 1971).

[15] See, for example, "Teacher Walkouts End," *Monthly Labor Review*, 94:88–89 (June 1971); Dennis D. Pointer and Harry Graham, "Recognition, Negotiation, and Work Stoppages in Hospitals," *Monthly Labor Review*, 94:54–58 (May 1971).

mismanagement (of human resources) through-out business and industry. The individual worker, of course, benefits from this check-and-balance system in the industrial community.

The varying personal attitudes of managers toward unionization also have an impact on the process of unionization. Some managers encourage and welcome unionization; others use every possible direct or indirect method to discourage the unionization of employees.[16] As we have learned from the previous chapter, most managers are not antiunion, but as a rule they prefer not to have workers join a union. In some instances, even union leaders have resisted unionization, as we shall see later.

TECHNOLOGY AND SCIENCE

Although technological changes are precipitating an increase in the proportion of white-collar workers in the labor force (particularly evident is a rapid increase in the proportion of professionals, who are not easily organized), there are those who argue that increased mechanization of many jobs will accelerate unionism. Kassalow, for example, has stated that organizers find it easier to recruit groups of white-collar employees working on machines, such as keypunch or comptometer machines, than to organize those on less routine and less mechanized jobs.[17] In general, however, rapid advances in technology have resulted in a much faster rate of growth in occupations traditionally not unionized, a situation which presents an organizing challenge of major proportions to the unions.

IMPACT OF UNIONIZATION ON ORGANIZATIONAL PROCESSES AND ON MANAGEMENT

It was suggested earlier that the unionization drive has an immediate impact on communications within an organization. During the campaign, managers are restricted in what they can and cannot say regarding the drive. In addition, the compensation process relative to the group of employees involved in the drive is partially suspended. Management may not grant pay increases or fringe benefits that may be interpreted as interfering with the union's drive.

The implications of the unionization drive are even broader. As managers know, collective bargaining, which comes in the aftermath of the certification of a collective-bargaining unit, has an impact on most organizational processes. Decisions related to the organization of work, staffing, appraisal, and compensation are no longer determined by the unilateral action of management. To a great extent, a labor contract now governs the work situation, and management is severely restricted in the areas where it can make decisions about human resources independently of the union.[18] Typically, contract provisions are extensive and may cover most or all of the items shown in Figure 23-2, or even more. It is no wonder that management typically resists the entry of a union. Furthermore, the coming of the union alters the authority-power structure of the organization. This occurs because there is a tendency for organizations to centralize direct contact with the union in one official, typically the personnel

[16]The Landrum-Griffin Act was designed to correct some of the most insidious practices, such as the employment of detective agencies to spy on union organizers. Practices such as this are probably rare in the late 1970s.
[17]Everett M. Kassalow, "Occupational Functions of Trade Unionism in the United States," White Collar Report, January 9, 1961, p. C-7.

[18]For a detailed treatment of the restrictions on management discretion that coincide with the advent of the union, see Sumner H. Slichter, James J. Healy, and E. Robert Livernash, The Impact of Collective Bargaining on Management (Washington, D.C.: The Brookings Institution, 1960); and Russell L. Greenman and Eric J. Schmertz, Personnel Administration and the Law (Washington, D.C.: The Bureau of National Affairs, 1972), pp. 245–279.

Figure 23-2 Examples of typical items in union-management agreements

Absenteeism	Management rights	Supplemental unemployment
Apprenticeship and training	Meal periods	compensation
Arbitration	Merit rating	Supplementary benefits
Call-in pay	Overtime pay	Tardiness
Contract length	Overtime rules	Tests
		Time off for union business
Discipline, discharge	Pensions	Tools
Discrimination	Premium pay (Saturday)	Transfers
Dues checkoff	Premium pay (Sunday)	Travel allowances
	Premium pay (holidays)	
Grievances	Promotions	Union literature, distribution of
		Union security
Holidays	Recall	
Hours (daily)	Rest periods	Vacations
Hours (weekly)	Retirement	
		Wages
Incentive rates or standards	Safety	Work clothes
Insurance, health	Seniority	Work load
Insurance, life	Severance pay	Work rules
	Shift differentials	
Job posting and bidding	Sick leave	
	Strikes, lockouts	
Labor-management committees	Subcontracting	
Layoff		
Leave of absence		

and industrial relations manager. Management can no longer deal unilaterally with employees—either individually or as a group—on matters of wages, hours, and working conditions. Loss of flexibility in dealing with employees is frequently mentioned by employers as a major disadvantage stemming from unionization.[19]

There are other and more personal reasons as to why managers resist unionization. If managers have been trying to do their best for employees, workers' interest in a union may be interpreted as a lack of gratitude and an injustice. Furthermore, managers may feel that interest in a union is a direct reflection on their competence in management and are then likely to

react defensively. Thus, the union is a threat to management's self-esteem.[20]

Dramatic evidence of the almost universal tendency for management to resist unionization is shown in the few reported instances where union officials have opposed the unionization of their own subordinates. For example, when union organizers working for the AFL-CIO decided they wanted to form an organizers' union called the "Field Representatives Federation," union officials declined to recognize the group on the grounds that the organizers were repre-

[20]Although unionization is often a result of mismanagement, caution should be exercised in drawing this conclusion. As our discussion of the reasons workers join unions suggests, the unionization drive is a result of a complex set of forces and factors in which the quality of first-line supervision and the aggressiveness of a union loom high in importance. To point to any one person or to any one factor is likely to be unrealistic.

[19]See National Industrial Conference Board, "White-Collar Unionization," pp. 59–68.

sentatives of management; their resistance forced an NLRB determination of the question.[21] Also, when organizers employed by the International Ladies' Garment Workers Union formed a union, ILGWU officials resisted recognition of this group.[22] When Local 2 of the Office Employees Union sought to represent professionals of the International Union of Electrical Workers, officials of the IUE declined to recognize the group and challenged the appropriateness of the unit in an NLRB hearing.[23]

Managerial resistance to the union does not ordinarily persist to a strong degree once the period of threatened egos and defensive behavior is past. Once the contract is signed, both parties usually find they can live reasonably amicably with each other and, indeed, often find there are many areas where mutual cooperation helps everyone concerned. Furthermore, unionization does not necessarily imply disloyalty to the company. In a study in which 385 packinghouse workers were interviewed, 73 percent expressed favorable sentiments toward *both* the company and the union. Thus, dual allegiance is a very possible phenomenon.[24]

A survey of several firms that had recently been unionized found most respondents seeing this as a real disadvantage to their organizations, but about 40 percent of the company spokesmen saw some advantage to the firm. For example, statements like the following were made:

We gained insight into a group of dissatisfied employees . . . a group so small it would have been ignored if they hadn't organized.

[Unionization] forced us to formalize and administer properly a merit review program.

The presence of the union has made the company much more sensitive in the handling of employee relations matters.[25]

Further, dealing through the union structure may provide a convenient mechanism for raising broad issues with employees, such as declining productivity.

THE UNION DRIVE AND THE PERSONNEL DEPARTMENT

The emotional, legal, and power aspects of the unionization drive require that management responses be coordinated by one individual and one department within the company. If there is a centralized personnel or industrial relations department, this assignment typically falls to the personnel director or labor relations director, respectively.

As our discussion has implied, a number of matters must be coordinated during the drive for unionization. Someone in management needs to be the point of contact for union representatives; someone needs to protect the company's interests by watching for unfair labor practices or illegal infringements on management's property rights, etc.; and someone needs to advise first-line supervisors and other managers about what they can and cannot do during the unionization campaign. Furthermore, a great deal of information may have to be compiled in the event the appropriateness of the bargaining unit is challenged by the employer in an NLRB hearing.

[21] The FRF subsequently won recognition. See *Business Week*, January 14, 1961, p. 99.
[22] *Business Week*, January 14, 1961, p. 99; *Fortune*, April 1961, p. 217; and *White Collar Report*, May 2, 1963, p. A-5.
[23] *White Collar Report*, April 19, 1962, p. A-1. For further discussion, see Karl F. Treckel, "The Unionization of Union Organizers and International Representatives," *Labor Law Journal*, 22:266–277 (May 1971). See also Karl F. Treckel, "The Unionization of Union Employees and Staff Members," *Labor and Industrial Relations Series No. 1*, Bureau of Economic and Business Research, Kent State University, Kent, Ohio (pamphlet, 37 pp., no date).
[24] Theodore V. Purcell, "Dual Allegiance to Company and Union Packinghouse Workers," *Personnel Psychology*, 7:48–58 (Spring 1954).
[25] Edward R. Curtin, *White-Collar Unionization*, National Industrial Conference Board, Studies in Personnel Policy, No. 220, 1970, pp. 63–66.

Because of the emotional aspects of the drive for unionization, efforts by the personnel department to minimize the defensive behavior of both supervisors and employees may, once the union is recognized, result in dividends during the early stages of the collective-bargaining relationship. The sooner hostile feelings diminish, the sooner both parties can work constructively toward establishing a compatible relationship. The personnel director may also be very defensive about a drive for unionization. If the personnel director and other managers do not keep their defensive behavior in check, the consequence may be additional defensive behavior on the part of employees and organizers, resulting in a "vicious spiral" that can make the early stages of a contractual relationship very difficult for both parties.

The compatibility of the personnel director's role as a bargaining agent with the role as an applied behavioral scientist will be explored in Chapter 27. Reasonable congruency in these two roles would probably require movement in the direction of integrative bargaining as contrasted with distributive bargaining (to be discussed in Chapter 24).

SUMMARY

Workers join unions for a variety of reasons, including those that are economic, social, and psychological. In general, unionization expresses dissatisfaction and appears to be an attempt to meet unfulfilled needs for security, belonging, esteem, integration, or self-actualization. Since unionization comes into conflict with relationships of authority and power established in the enterprise and since managers perceive collective bargaining as impinging on established organizational processes, managerial resistance to organization tends to be almost universal. Such resistance has been evident in instances where employees of unions have attempted to bargain with their union employers.

An extensive array of legal constraints surrounds the process of unionization, and both unions and employers are restricted in their activities during an organizational campaign. Most of these limitations stem from the Taft-Hartley Act and amendments to it in the Landrum-Griffin Act.

The personnel department typically conducts the employer's response to the drive for unionization. That department is in a position to minimize conflict and tension that otherwise can interfere with the early stages of collective bargaining following union recognition.

In the next two chapters, problems and practices related to the negotiation of the labor agreement and its administration will be discussed. Chapter 24 will be devoted to contract negotiations, and Chapter 25 to administering the agreement, with particular reference to the grievance-arbitration process.

REVIEW AND DISCUSSION QUESTIONS

1. What are the factors that cause workers to join unions? Discuss these factors in terms of (a) need fulfillment and (b) the concepts in the chapter on organizational justice (Chapter 8).

2. What concerns might management have about the scope of a collective bargaining unit?

3. What constraints are applied to management during a unionization campaign?

4. What constraints are applied to the union?

5. How does a union become certified as a bargaining unit?

6. From the perspective of the president of a small firm, what might be some of the disadvantages of your firm being unionized? Advantages?

7. Do you believe "dual allegiance" is a possible phenomenon? If so, what are its implications for management?

SUPPLEMENTAL REFERENCES

Bureau of National Affairs, *Major Labor-Law Principles Established by the NLRB and the Courts* (December 1963–February 1968), published 1968.

Chamot, Denis, "Professional Employees Turn to Unions," *Harvard Business Review*, 54:119–127 (May-June 1976).

Cohen, Frederick C., "Labor Features of the Postal Reorganization Act," *Labor Law Journal*, 22:44–50 (January 1971).

Curtin, Edward R., "Union Initiation Fees, Dues and Per Capita Tax," *The Conference Board Record*, 4:9–13 (August 1967).

Gitelman, Morton, *Unionization Attempts in Small Enterprises* (Chicago: Callaghan & Company, 1963).

Goldberg, Joseph P., "Public Employee Developments," *Monthly Labor Review*, 95:56–66 (January 1972).

Imberman, Woodruff, "How Expensive is an NLRB Election?" *MSU Business Topics*, 23:13–18 (Summer 1975).

Kassalow, Everett M., "What Happens When Everyone Organizes?" *Monthly Labor Review*, 95:27–32 (April 1972).

Lombardi, Vincent, and Andrew J. Grimes, "A Primer for a Theory of White-Collar Unionization," *Monthly Labor Review*, 90:46–49 (May 1967).

Mills, C. Wright, *White Collar* (New York: Oxford University Press, 1951), Chapter 14.

Moskow, Michael H., J. Joseph Loewenberg, and Edward Clifford Koziaro, *Collective Bargaining in Public Employment* (New York: Random House, 1970).

National Industrial Conference Board, "White-Collar Unionization," *Studies in Personnel Policy*, No. 220, 1970.

Pepe, Stephen P., "Certification Year Rule and the Mar-Jac Poultry Extension," *Labor Law Journal*, 19:335–351 (June 1968).

Perl, Arnold E., "Granting of Benefits During a Representation Election: Validity of NLRB General Rule," *Labor Law Journal*, 18:643–648 (November 1967).

Prasow, Paul, et al., *Scope of Bargaining in the Public Sector—Concepts and Problems*, report submitted to Division of Public Employee Labor Relations, U.S. Department of Labor, 1972.

Purcell, Theodore V., *Blue Collar Man* (Cambridge, Mass.: Harvard University Press, 1960).

Rose, Joseph B., "What Factors Influence Union Representation Elections?" *Monthly Labor Review*, 95:49–51 (October 1972).

Rosen, Hjalmar, and Ruth A. H. Rosen, *The Union Member Speaks* (Englewood Cliffs, N.J.: Prentice-Hall, Inc., 1955).

Sayles, Leonard R., and George Strauss, *The Local Union*, rev. ed. (New York: Harcourt, Brace & World, Inc., 1967).

Steiber, Jack, "Collective Bargaining in the Public Sector," in Lloyd Ulman, ed., *Challenges to Collective Bargaining* (Englewood Cliffs, N.J.: Prentice-Hall, Inc., 1967), pp. 68–69.

CHAPTER 24
THE NEGOTIATION PROCESS

Once a union has been certified as the exclusive bargaining agent for a group of employees, management and the union are required by the Taft-Hartley Act to bargain collectively with each other over matters pertaining to wages, hours, and other conditions of employment. This bargaining typically takes the form of private conference-room discussion and debate over proposed clauses in the contract. The clauses proposed for the first contract may be based on contracts in existence elsewhere, on present practice plus desired changes, or on combinations of these. Subsequent negotiations will be concerned with changing the existing contract.

The purpose of such bargaining is to reach agreement on a contract that both parties are willing to sign, and abide by, for a stipulated period. As Archibald Cox states it, the contract becomes the ". . . basic legislation governing the lives of workers in the plant."[1]

Traditional collective bargaining is not unlike the bargaining that goes on between a vendor and shopper in the open-air produce markets in certain parts of the United States, or between a car salesperson and customer. Both parties try to achieve the best settlement, and although the result is less beneficial than either party would have liked in an ideal situation, usually the agreement is generally satisfactory. On the other hand, as the following discussion indicates, some emerging contemporary relationships in collective bargaining are closer to a joint solution of problems than this description implies.

[1] Archibald Cox, "Rights Under a Labor Agreement," *Harvard Law Review*, 69:606 (February 1956).

Collective bargaining is often a much more complex process than the examples suggest, because union-management relationships are regulated by many governmental constraints, and because collective bargaining usually takes place between two parties wielding considerable power, as manifested in the strike and the lockout. In addition, mediation and conciliation, governmental fact-finding boards, court injunctions, and arbitration are sometimes an integral part of collective bargaining.

NUMBER AND SCOPE OF COLLECTIVE AGREEMENTS

In 1972, it was estimated that approximately 165,000 collective-bargaining agreements were in existence in the United States. Approximately 60 percent of these agreements involved ten unions, each negotiating 5,000 or more agreements. These ten unions were the Teamsters, Retail Clerks, Electrical (IBEW), Operating Engineers, Machinists, Meat Cutters, Service Employees, Steelworkers, Laborers, and Theatrical Stage unions.[2]

The 165,000 collective bargaining agreements represent a wide variety of bargaining patterns. These different patterns include single locals bargaining with single employers, several locals bargaining with a single employer, employers' associations bargaining with single locals, employers' associations bargaining with locals of several unions, and employers' associations bargaining with both internationals and locals. It is not uncommon for a company to bargain with a half-dozen or more different unions representing different parts of the work force, nor is it uncommon for these same unions to deal with a large number of different employers.

"Coalition bargaining" (or "coordinated bargaining"), which involves several national or international unions bargaining as a united front with one employer or with an industry group, is seen with increasing frequency.[3]

TYPES OF BARGAINING RELATIONSHIPS

SELEKMAN'S CATEGORIES

For purposes of contrast, and for their historical aspects, I will first comment briefly on eight different types of bargaining relationships as seen by Selekman. These are (1) containment-aggression, (2) conflict, (3) power, (4) deal, (5) collusion, (6) accommodation, (7) cooperation, and (8) ideological.[4] Selekman and others later added a ninth category: racketeering.[5] Although these categories were not intended to be mutually exclusive, they demonstrate the variety of possible bargaining relationships.

Selekman's *containment-aggression* is characterized by a union aggressively trying to extend its voice in the company's operations, with management trying equally as hard to keep the union in check. *Conflict* is characterized by the employer who never really accepts the union and attempts to get rid of the union at every opportunity. *Power* is characterized by both parties attempting to wring every possible advantage from the situation, depending upon economic conditions. *Deal* features secret negotiations between union leaders and top management, with minimum involvement of rank-and-file workers or lower management. *Collusion* has a much less desirable connotation

[2] U.S. Department of Labor, *Directory of National Unions and Employee Associations, 1973,* Bureau of Labor Statistics, 1974, pp. 87–88.

[3] See Abraham Cohen, "Union Rationale and Objectives of Coordinated Bargaining," *Labor Law Journal,* 27:75–83 (February 1976).

[4] Benjamin M. Selekman, "Varieties of Labor Relations," *Harvard Business Review,* 27:177–185 (March 1949).

[5] Benjamin M. Selekman, Sylvia K. Selekman, and Stephen H. Fuller, *Problems in Labor Relations,* 2nd ed. (New York: McGraw-Hill Book Company, 1958), pp. 7–8.

than "deal" bargaining, and involves conni-
vance to gain or maintain some mutual advantage over the public or competitors by controlling the market, prices, or raw materials, or by
some other practice.

A relationship of *accommodation* is characterized by tolerance and compromise on the part
of both parties. Although watchful of their respective rights, neither party is overly dogmatic
when confronted with demands. *Cooperation* is
characterized by mutual concern over matters
above and beyond wages, hours, and working
conditions, including matters of efficiency,
waste, and technological change. Both accommodation and cooperation are characterized by
an avoidance of extreme displays of power.

In his earlier essay, Selekman characterized
the *ideological* relationship as one involving
labor leaders committed to the ideologies of socialism or communism and dedicated to class
conflict.[6] In his later discussion of this relationship, Selekman emphasized the dangers of
communist and left-wing unions taking direction from the Soviet-dominated Communist
Party. He held that such "ideological" relationships occurred infrequently in the American labor movement, but that they inevitably
led to conflict in industrial relations.[7] He
regarded the *racketeering* type of relationship—
one involving corrupt union leaders, sometimes
aided and abetted by employers and sometimes
by the criminal element—as a pathological and
sordid blight on American industrial relations.[8]

[6]Selekman, "Varieties of Labor Relations," p. 179.
[7]Selekman, Selekman, and Fuller, *Problems in Labor Relations*,
p. 8. The threat of Communist influence in the labor movement diminished greatly with the expulsion of the Com-
munist-line unions from the CIO from 1950 on, and in the
formation of strong anti-Communist groups within these
unions. Ibid.; and F.S. O'Brien, "The 'Communist-
Dominated' Unions in the United States since 1950," *Labor
History*, 9:184–209 (Spring 1968).
[8]Selekman, Selekman, and Fuller, *Problems in Labor Relations*,
pp. 7–8. In the late 1950s the McClellan Committee of the
U.S. Senate investigated racketeering in the labor movement,
with the result that a number of antiracketeering provisions

The prevalent types of bargaining relationships found today are probably containment-aggression, conflict, power, deal, accommodation, and cooperation, with the
ideological, collusive, and racketeering types on
the wane. Of course, many bargaining relationships feature combinations of the more
prevalent types, and some shift from one type
to another depending upon the behavior of the
bargaining parties, upon the attitudes and personalities of the union leaders and managers involved, and upon economic conditions.

WALTON AND McKERSIE'S ANALYTICAL FRAMEWORK

In more recent years, Walton and McKersie
have advanced a fourfold analytical framework
somewhat different for Selekman's constructs.
These authors note four hypothetical types of
bargaining—distributive, integrative, attitudinal structuring, and intraorganizational
bargaining—defined as follows:

1. *Distributive bargaining* refers to situations in
which the goals of the two parties are in conflict
and in which it is assumed that the total values
are fixed, so that "one person's gain is another's
loss."

2. *Integrative bargaining* refers to situations in
which goals are not perceived as conflicting,
but in which there is a problem or area of common concern.

3. *Attitudinal structuring*, which is part of either
distributive or integrative bargaining, refers to
the activities in, and surrounding, negotiations
that serve to change attitudes and relationships.

were featured in the Landrum-Griffin Act of 1959. For an interesting behind-the-scenes account of the activities of this
committee, see the book by the late Robert F. Kennedy, *The
Enemy Within* (New York: Harper & Brothers, 1960).

4. *Intraorganizational bargaining* refers to the activities which take place within the union or within the company to bring "the expectations of principals into alignment with those of the chief negotiator." In short, there is a good deal of bargaining that goes on *within* unions and *within* companies about the positions to be taken by the respective chief negotiators in the actual collective-bargaining sessions.[9]

EXAMPLES OF DISTRIBUTIVE BARGAINING

Distributive bargaining is the most common strategy in the United States. This strategy, which I tend to think of as "horse trading," seems to have evolved as a reasonably satisfactory way for the two parties to accommodate each other in the collective-bargaining process. It is a bilateral or mutual strategy, and the progress of negotiations goes something like this:

1. Before the start of negotiations, the union presents in written form its initial demands for contract changes. These demands may constitute a long list far exceeding what the union expects to obtain. Some may indicate the demands which the union intends to press in years to come. By mentioning them now, the union hopes to get both management and the public accustomed to the ideas.

2. Management may or may not present a list of its own demands. The practice of presenting a list has grown in recent years, but more than likely the list will be shorter than that of the union. Management may also have in mind a few desirable contractual changes to which it will agree but which it prefers to have suggested by the union.[10]

3. The initial bargaining sessions are devoted to a union explanation of its demands for nonwage and nonfringe benefits and to its presentation of arguments and data supporting these demands. Similarly, management explains its position. Many of these sessions may be slow-moving and frustrating to the participants. Furthermore, much haggling may occur over procedural matters.

4. Management presents arguments against the union proposals, expresses agreement with some items in a noncommittal way, and then counters with the suggestion that the union trim its list to reasonable proportions. During any of these stages, either party may be prone to argue eloquently about "principles." Although the arguers may sincerely believe in the principles they are advocating, most such arguments mask a specific advantage that one party wants or would like to retain.[11] This is not to suggest the undesirability of principles, but it does suggest the desirability of assessing the underlying reasons for advocacy of a principle.

5. The parties proceed to hard bargaining on the noneconomic demands, with the provision that any agreements will be tentative until the entire contract has been negotiated. Management concedes certain items provided the union drops certain others or provided the union agrees to certain of management's desired contract changes.[12] This "horse trading" goes on until the noncost items are cleared away. During this stage and others, members of the negotiating teams may encounter periods of considerable hostility from the opposing sides.

---

[9] Richard E. Walton and Robert B. McKersie, *A Behavioral Theory of Labor Negotiations* (New York: McGraw-Hill Book Company, 1965), pp. 4–6.

[10] Although it is an unusual occurrence, managements have succeeded in negotiating substantial wage cuts in some instances when high costs made plant closures imminent.

[11] See Paul Diesing, "Bargaining Strategy and Union-Management Relationships," *The Journal of Conflict Resolution*, 5:373 (March 1961).

[12] Clark Kerr calls this "an exercise in graceful retreat. . . ." See Clark Kerr, "Bargaining Processes" in E. Wight Bakke, Clark Kerr, and Charles W. Anrod, eds., *Unions, Management, and The Public,* 2nd ed. (New York: Harcourt, Brace & Company, 1960), p. 284.

6. Negotiating the cost items—wages and fringe benefits in particular—becomes most tedious, with the company starting from the position that the wage structure is already satisfactory and the union asking an exorbitant increase. Both sides face the problem of getting the other to move in the direction of its demands and of finding out what the opponent's "final" position is likely to be without giving away its own "final" position. "Horse trading" really goes on in earnest at this stage, with management agreeing to a few fringe benefit increases if the union will drop its demands significantly. Meanwhile, the company's wage position moves up a few cents from zero, and the union's wage demand may drop off much further.

7. This procedure continues until the company has essentially revealed the maximum cents-per-hour it will grant, including both wages and fringe benefits, and the union has essentially revealed the minimum it will tolerate. If the positions are close, e.g., within one or two cents per hour, settlement is likely; the two parties "split the difference" and sign the new contract. If the positions are significantly far apart, the contest becomes one of finding out who is less willing to accept a strike. (By this time, the union negotiating committee has probably long since secured a strike authorization vote from the union membership and, if a member of a national or international union, authorization from headquarters.) If both parties are adamant, the use of a mediator from the Federal Mediation and Conciliation Service or from a state mediation service may assist the parties in further "horse trading" so that agreement can be reached.

8. If the union resorts to a strike, the contest becomes one of economic pressure and willingness to make sacrifices. One or both parties may by this time have advertised their positions and supporting arguments through the newspapers or other media.

9. When agreement is finally reached, usually after concurrence by the union membership, both parties may switch from a belligerent to a festive mood, shaking hands, joking, and making statements about the contract being "fair and just" to employees, management, and stockholders. This ritual eases the tension and serves mutual notice that the parties must now cooperate in administering the contract during the ensuing year.[13]

Not only is the signing of the agreement a ritual, but the entire process of collective bargaining under the distributive approach has its ritualistic aspects. For example, in addition to finding points of compromise tolerable to both parties, collective bargaining serves the purpose of making the terms of the agreement acceptable to those not participating in the negotiations. If a settlement is reached too quickly, rank-and-file workers, foremen, and other non-participants in the negotiations may not have time to assimilate and accept the "real position" of the other party.[14]

A less common form of distributive bargaining has been called *Boulwarism*—a label given to the type of strategy followed by the former director of employee relations in the General Electric Company, Lemuel R. Boulware.[15] Because of its unique strategy, it could also be

---

[13] For a description of this ritual see Robert Dubin, *Working Union-Management Relations* (Englewood Cliffs, N.J.: Prentice-Hall, Inc., 1958), pp. 163–165.

[14] See Albert A. Blum, "Collective Bargaining: Ritual or Reality?" *Harvard Business Review*, 29:63–69 (November-December 1961). For further discussion of the ceremonial aspects of the collective bargaining process, see William Foote Whyte, *Men at Work* (Homewood, Ill.: The Dorsey Press and Richard D. Irwin, 1961), pp. 324–351.

[15] For an article by Boulware and a short account of his background, see Lemuel R. Boulware, "Everybody's New and Larger Personnel Job—Part I," *The Personnel Administrator*, 8:4–8ff. (March-April 1963).

called the *take-it-or-leave-it approach*, and since it has been used by unions as well as management, the broader level is perhaps more appropriate.[16] As practiced at GE under Boulware, "Boulwarism" featured essentially a final offer made by the company at the beginning of negotiations. This offer, in the form of the total contract, was based on careful research into what constituted a good and fair offer in the opinion of the company, with nothing held in reserve for "horse trading." The company often agreed to minor modifications in its position if the union could present convincing evidence to support them, but the basic position of the company ordinarily remained the same in the face of both strikes or threats to strike. By 1973, this strategy appeared to be defunct at GE.[17]

EXAMPLES OF INTEGRATIVE BARGAINING

Integrative bargaining is probably far less prevalent than distributive bargaining, but more and more examples are appearing. The integrative strategies require a change in attitude on the part of both union and management from an offensive-defensive position to a genuine interest in and concern for joint exploration of problems, fact gathering,[18] and problem solving. This suggests that integrative bargaining should be a way of life for the two parties rather than a negotiating style adopted at the time negotiations begin. In particular, the elements differentiating these relationships from more traditional distributive approaches include:

1. Continued efforts to improve relationships, including frequent mutual discussions of problems at all levels, quarterly meetings at the national level, and attempts to settle problems without arbitration.

2. Special committees for study and joint fact finding to work on difficult problems.

Examples of bargaining that approach the integrative model are found in the instances cited in Chapter 22 of unions and employers agreeing on the adoption of more efficient technology and practices while agreeing on means of minimizing the impact on employees and sharing in the gains. Other illustrations are United Airlines and the Air Line Pilots Association jointly studying a number of problems pertaining to jet aircraft, and General Motors and the United Auto Workers jointly studying problems pertaining to pensions.[19] Other topics that have been productively discussed through the use of special committees are technological change and workers' retirement in the longshoring industry, automation and worker retraining in the meat-packing industry, job evaluation and "industrial sabbaticals" in the steel industry, and programs for alcoholics in various industries.[20] In the railroad industry, a joint labor-

---

[16] This strategy has been used occasionally in the building trades, by the Musicians Union, and the International Typographical Union. See C. Wilson Randle, *Collective Bargaining—Principles and Practices* (Boston: Houghton Mifflin Company, 1951), p. 196.

[17] *Business Week*, May 26, 1973, p. 26. Use of these tactics by GE in the 1960 negotiations caused the International Union of Electrical Workers to file a charge of unfair labor practice; and in 1963 a National Labor Relations Board trial examiner upheld the union. In 1964, the full Board held GE guilty of bargaining in bad faith. The case was then appealed to the Second Circuit Court of Appeals in New York City, and in 1969 the Board decision was upheld. Ultimately, the U.S. Supreme Court refused to disturb the appeals court decision. Arthur A. Sloan and Fred Witney, *Labor Relations*, 2nd ed. (Englewood Cliffs, N.J.: Prentice-Hall, Inc., 1972), pp. 182–183.

[18] For a discussion of "coordinated fact gathering" in decision making, see Rensis Likert, *New Patterns of Management* (New York: McGraw-Hill Book Company, 1961), pp. 216–217.

[19] From James J. Healy, ed., *Creative Collective Bargaining* (Englewood Cliffs, N.J.: Prentice-Hall, Inc., 1965), pp. 60–77.

[20] See "Revitalization of Bargaining: The Committee Approach," *Industrial Relations News*, Special Report, June 1963,

management team studied the St. Louis terminal of the Missouri Pacific Railroad and made recommendations for a series of experiments in terminal operations.[21] (Other examples of integrative bargaining will be cited under the topic of productivity bargaining.)

THE NEGOTIATIONS

MEMBERSHIP ON BARGAINING TEAMS

The union bargaining team typically includes the officers of the local, several shop stewards (or committee members), and a representative of the district or national organization. The size of the union team typically ranges from five to eleven members; a committee of seven members appears to be most common.[22]

Managerial teams are usually slightly smaller, with typical membership of from two to six persons and an average membership of three or four.[23] Personnel directors (the specific title may vary among companies) are almost always found on managerial teams and are typically the chief spokesmen for the team. Plant managers or works managers and superintendents are also normally found on the company's negotiating teams and are the next most likely representative for the company. Presidents of companies are occasionally found on negotiating teams, although seldom in firms of more than 5,000 employees.[24] As firms grow, the task of negotiating contracts is ordinarily turned over to the personnel department or the operating departments, or both, although the president typically retains considerable authority in negotiations. Although a majority of firms utilize lawyers for legal advice during negotiations, only in about one out of eight situations is a lawyer an active member of the negotiating team.[25]

AUTHORITY AND ACCOUNTABILITY IN NEGOTIATIONS

The authority of the management negotiating team is generally limited by guidelines established prior to negotiations by the top management of the company, including the president. The negotiating team will usually keep the president informed of progress and, before any concessions are made, union demands requiring a major financial commitment or major changes in plant operations will have to be cleared by the president.[26]

In one study involving eighteen firms, the presidents of each company exercised a high degree of authority over collective-bargaining decisions. In thirteen of the companies, vice presidents also made major decisions in contract negotiations, but major decision making below this level was rare.[27] In another study of twenty-five firms, the personnel director was typically not given unilateral authority over maximum bargaining concessions.[28]

Thus we find considerable authority delegated to the negotiating team but with limits established prior to negotiations. Such limits seem logical, given the impact which contract

---

pp. 1–4; Marion Sadler and James F. Horst, "Company/Union Programs for Alcoholics," *Harvard Business Review,* 50:22–24ff. (September-October 1972).
[21] Edgar Weinberg, "Labor-Management Cooperation: A Report on Recent Initiatives," *Monthly Labor Review,* 99:18 (April 1976).
[22] Paul V. Johnson, "Decision-Making Under Collective Bargaining," *Monthly Labor Review,* 80:1061–1062 (September 1957).
[23] James J. Bambrick and Marie P. Dorbandt, *Preparing for Collective Bargaining* (New York: National Industrial Conference Board, 1959), pp. 26–31.
[24] Ibid., pp. 28–30.

[25] Ibid., p. 30.
[26] Ibid., pp. 32–33; and Johnson, "Decision-Making under Collective Bargaining," p. 1060.
[27] Johnson, "Decision-Making under Collective Bargaining," p. 1060.
[28] Wendell French and Dale Henning, "The Authority-Influence Role of the Functional Specialist in Management," *Academy of Management Journal,* 9:187–203 (September 1966).

negotiations have on the entire enterprise. They also seem wise from a psychological standpoint. In the heat of argument, particularly under distributive bargaining, and perhaps to demonstrate his or her importance or authority, the negotiator might make concessions dangerous to the welfare of the organization unless limits and guidelines are established by higher authority. This danger is one of the reasons that many presidents of companies do not participate directly in negotiations as a member of a negotiating team.

A problem that seems to be occurring with increasing frequency is rejection by the union membership of agreements made by union negotiators at the bargaining table. In 1974, rank-and-file unionists declined to ratify 12 percent of all negotiated settlements, up from 9.6 percent in the previous year.[29] In such circumstances, the negotiators return to the bargaining table in an effort to win larger settlements.

CURRENT BARGAINING ISSUES

Although a wide range of topics is usually discussed during collective-bargaining sessions, the issues receiving the most publicity tend to be those that reflect a new and major goal of either party. In recent years, such matters as the assignments of crews and the introduction of new equipment and methods have given rise to the issue of so-called work rules—a problem with which bargainers in such industries as steel and railroad transportation have had to wrestle. Governmental and managerial demands for noninflationary wage settlements and union demands for a shorter workweek[30]

have also been recent issues attracting considerable publicity. Union demands for cushioning the impact of technological change on the individual worker and union interest in having blue-collar workers achieve "salaried" status have also been well-publicized issues. Pensions, early retirement provisions, and other fringe benefits are recurring issues. "Humanization" of assembly line jobs is an issue that is beginning to emerge in collective bargaining.[31] (See also Chapter 9.) One of the most recent demands by the UAW has been more days off with pay during the year. The United Steelworkers are seeking "a life-time security program for steelworkers" through a combination of job and income guarantees and a reduction in working days per year.[32] And requests for flextime are appearing in more and more contract talks.

PRODUCTIVITY BARGAINING

Productivity bargaining has become more conspicuous in the United States, largely in response to foreign competition, inflation, and continued wage demands. Rosow defines this process.

In productivity bargaining, management and labor write an agreement that establishes a set of *quid pro quos* whereby (a) labor agrees to scrap old work habits for new and more effective ones desired by management, and (b) management returns some of the gains of modernization and increased efficiency to labor in the form of new and better work incentives.[33]

One of the most successful examples of productivity bargaining stems from the contract concluded in England between Imperial Chemical Industries (ICI) and the Transport and General

[29]*Business Week*, July 20, 1974, p. 28.
[30]AFL-CIO President George Meany announced as early as 1962 that labor would soon start a concentrated campaign for a thirty-five-hour week. See *Time*, August 17, 1962. The UAW included a shorter workweek in 1976 demands and indicated it was aiming for a four-day week over the next several years. *Honolulu Sunday Star Bulletin and Advertiser*, September 19, 1976, p. A-14.

[31]*Business Week*, October 28, 1972, p. 70.
[32]*Business Week*, September 13, 1976, p. 82.
[33]Jerome M. Rosow, "Now Is the Time for Productivity Bargaining," *Harvard Business Review*, 50:78 (January-February 1972).

Workers Union. In this contract, wage increases were based on measurable productivity improvements enhanced by the elimination of many restrictive practices and the additional autonomy given to rank-and-file employees. For example, plant workers were permitted to do simple maintenance work, and maintenance engineers could do welding under the new contract.[34] Probably a major reason for the success of this program was its planned congruency with other programs, including job enrichment, management training, compensation, and organization development.

In the United States in 1971, the United Steelworkers and the steel industry agreed on the formulation of joint advisory committees on productivity for each plant in the industry (Experimental Negotiating Agreement). These committees were continued when the union concluded in 1973 that

. . . after three years of experience under the joint productivity program, a great many tangible results became apparent. No speedup measures have been instituted by management. None of the feared job rearrangements materialized. Slowly the process of building up mutual trust set in after the plant committees began functioning.[35]

Another illustration of productivity bargaining is the Work Improvement Program agreed to in 1973 between the Harmon International Company, a producer of automobile mirrors, and the United Automobile Workers. After an attitude survey was used to identify major problems, a labor-management committee was established to review the results and to plan and organize work improvement experiments. Small groups of workers, along with their su-

pervisors, were given latitude to change work methods with the objective of improving both job satisfaction and productivity. One project included a new system of rewards in which workers exceeding production standards in less than eight hours could have the option of taking off some time or earning more money. Two results were increased productivity and a request for more in-plant training.[36]

In another instance, the Garden State Paper Company and the United Paperworkers and the Operating Engineers negotiated a ten-year plan in which productivity bonuses will be paid on the basis of the tonnage of newsprint produced, but only in years in which no strike occurs. Problems that cannot be resolved will be submitted to arbitration.[37]

VALIDITY OF VARIOUS NEGOTIATING SYSTEMS

Other than case descriptions, little or no research has been undertaken on the degree to which the various approaches to collective bargaining contribute to organizational goals. The vast majority of firms use the distributive type of bargaining rather than the integrative type. Of the two styles in distributive bargaining described above, the "horse trading" approach is generally considered more valid than the Boulware style. From a psychological point of view, the Boulware approach appears to provide little opportunity for fulfilling the needs of union negotiators and rank-and-file employees. Thus, it is likely to cause defensive behavior.

Recent success with the use of committees as an adjunct to negotiation of contracts suggests that a mere integrative approach has considerable validity. However, it appears workable only in an environment in which (a) the two parties have a strong desire to solve problems by joint consultation, (b) they have carefully

[34] "ICI Breaks Its Bottlenecks," *Business Week,* September 9, 1972, p. 119.

[35] As quoted in Joseph P. Goldberg, "Bargaining and Productivity in the Private Sector," in Gerald Somers, Arvid Anderson, Malcolm Denise, and Leonard Sayles, *Collective Bargaining and Productivity* (Madison, Wisc.: Industrial Relations Research Association, 1975), pp. 30–31.

[36] Weinberg, "Labor-Management Cooperation," pp. 17–18.
[37] *Monthly Labor Review,* 98:70 (May 1975).

explored alternative solutions, and (c) each party makes sincere attempts at understanding the problems faced by the other party. In short, the strategy must be one of understanding rather than gaining an advantage over the other party.

Research suggests that some issues are more suitable to integrative bargaining than others. Based on a questionnaire to union officials, joint programs with management outside of collective bargaining were seen as the best way to deal with such issues as interesting work, control of work, and productivity, while formal collective bargaining was seen as the best instrument for dealing with such issues as earnings, fringe benefits, job security, and hours of work.[38]

Attitudes of the chief executive, the personnel director, and other key executives are important determinants of whether an integrative or a distributive approach will prevail during collective bargaining sessions. Their basic assumptions about people, their perceptions of what constitutes effective leadership, and their notions about effective problem solving are major ingredients in the type of collective bargaining that will emerge.

MEDIATION AND CONCILIATION

Mediation-conciliation is the process whereby a third party helps labor and management reach close enough agreement to sign a labor contract. The terms mediation and conciliation are essentially synonymous, although conciliation connotes helping the parties to develop and adhere to an agenda and encouraging them to address

the issues as objectively as possible. Mediation connotes a more active role, including suggesting alternatives for the parties to consider.[39] Arbitration, on the other hand, is a process involving an impartial third party who hands down a decision binding on both parties. Arbitration will be discussed in the next chapter.

The Federal Mediation and Conciliation Service (FMCS) was created by the Taft-Hartley Act in 1947 as an independent agency, with a director appointed by the president. This agency superseded the Department of Labor's Conciliation Service, which employers felt was too likely to reflect the pro-labor bias of that department.[40] The Taft-Hartley Act specifically states ". . . the Director and the Service shall not be subject in any way to the jurisdiction or authority of the Secretary of Labor or any official or division of the Department of Labor." The Act further establishes a National Labor-Management Panel to advise the director of the service concerning the use of mediation in controversies affecting the nation's welfare. This panel is comprised of six managerial and six labor representatives appointed by the president.[41]

The major responsibility of the Mediation and Conciliation Service is to assist unions and managements in reaching agreements and avoiding work stoppages. Another function is to assist in settling grievances arising under the administration of collective-bargaining agreements, but the Taft-Hartley Act is quite explicit that this latter function is to be exercised ". . .

[38]Thomas A. Kochan, David B. Lipsky, and Lee Dyer, "Collective Bargaining and the Quality of Work: The Views of Local Union Activists," in James L. Stern and Barbara D. Dennis, *Proceedings of the Twenty-Seventh Annual Winter Meeting*, Industrial Relations Research Association Series, 1975, pp. 150–162.

[39]See Walter Maggiolo, "Traditional Approaches to Dispute Resolution—Mediation, Arbitration, and Fact Finding," in A. Eliot Berkeley and Ann Barnes, eds., *Labor Relations in Hospitals and Health Care Facilities* (Washington, D.C.: The Bureau of National Affairs, 1976), p. 73.
[40]See Section 201 and 202 of the Taft-Hartley Act; and Gordon F. Bloom and Herbert R. Northrup, *Economics of Labor Relations*, 4th ed. (Homewood, Ill.: Richard D. Irwin, 1961), pp. 812–814.
[41]Labor Management Relations Act (as amended, 1959), Sections 202(d) and 205.

only as a last resort and in exceptional cases."[42] This provision of the Act is obviously designed to encourage arbitration clauses in collective-bargaining agreements.

Although the Federal Mediation and Conciliation Service may not force itself on unwilling parties, the Service may take the initiative in offering assistance. Either or both parties to a dispute may also request the help of the Service if a deadlock or strike appears imminent. The Federal Mediation and Conciliation Service is automatically notified of a potential dispute, since the Taft-Hartley Act requires that the party wishing to terminate or modify a labor contract notify the Service at least thirty days before the expiration date of the contract.[43] The same party must also notify the other party to the contract sixty days before the expiration date.

In my experience, the mediator's essential techniques are (1) meeting with both parties together and then singly to ascertain the nature of the disagreement and the last positions of the parties, and (2) then meeting alternately with each party to explore possible areas in which the parties can move from their present positions. To be effective, the mediator obviously must be neutral and interested only in a settlement—not the quality of it. If either party believes the mediator to be serving the cause of the other side, the parties will no longer confide in him or her. Such confidence is essential if the mediator is to help the parties reconcile their differences and to assist them in moving from what appears to be an impasse.[44]

The importance of mediation in the American economy is reflected by the fact that the use of

federal or state mediators was reported in 45 percent of the work stoppages ending in 1974. Federal mediators participated in 40 percent of all work stoppages.[45]

Beginning about 1973, the FMCS started an experimental program, called "Relations by Objective," a problem-solving or conflict resolution process involving the use of mediators to assist a union and a management group in improving their relationship. As an illustration, FMCS staff members helped the five unions and management at the Woodland, Maine, pulp and paper mill of the Georgia-Pacific Corporation sort out the reasons for a decade of poor labor-management relations and to analyze what goals they had in common. As a result, some long-standing problems were solved, and communications greatly improved.[46] Similar procedures have been used by the FMCS at Rodman Industries, a particle-board manufacturer, and Tempo Stores, a chain of retail department stores.[47] The process appears to be very similar to the "organization development" consultancy mode described in Chapter 26, and probably stems from that approach.

FACT FINDING

In fact finding, an outside neutral or a panel of neutrals is appointed to seek out the facts in a dispute and to make a report. The assumption is that the parties will more likely reach agreement after the facts are known, or that the public will apply pressure on the parties to settle the conflict. However, according to Maggiolo, who is pessimistic about the value of fact find-

[42]Labor Management Relations Act (as amended, 1959), Section 203(d).

[43]Labor Management Relations Act (as amended, 1959), Section 8(d) (3).

[44]In many respects the role of the mediator is much like the role of the real-estate broker who acts as a go-between in the negotiations between seller and buyer, except that the broker extracts a fee based on price.

[45]Analysis of Work Stoppages, 1974, Bulletin No. 1902, United States Department of Labor, Bureau of Labor Statistics, 1976, p. 58.

[46]Business Week, April 21, 1975, p. 108.

[47]"FMCS Fosters Cooperation at Three Companies," in Recent Initiatives in Labor-Management Cooperation (Washington, D.C.: National Center for Productivity & Quality of Working Life, 1976), pp. 23–30.

ing as an approach to dispute settlement, ". . .
the parties often knew the facts but chose to ignore them in the bargaining process . . ." and
". . . experience soon revealed that unless the
dispute involved great public inconvenience,
the marshaling of public opinion did not take
place."[48]

Fact finders have no authority to make recommendations unless this authority is specifically
given to them. For example, under the national
emergency disputes section (206) of the Taft-
Hartley Act, the board of inquiry appointed by
the president may not make recommendations;
under the newer Section 213 pertaining to the
health care field, the fact-finding board appointed by the Federal Mediation and Conciliation Service is given the express power to make
recommendations.[49]

STRIKES AND LOCKOUTS

Strikes and lockouts, or the threat of them, are
an integral part of the collective-bargaining process. Through the strike, labor's "ultimate
weapon," economic pressure is brought to bear
on the employer in the form of workers withholding their services. Since a strike seriously
interrupts the company's operations, the threat
of a strike and the strike itself become major
tools in the hands of the union negotiators. Selective strikes—strikes against only selected
plants of a large employer—are sometimes used
by unions to lessen the impact on union strike
funds and to reduce the number of employees
taken off the company payroll.

In the lockout, the managerial counterpart of
the strike, workers are literally locked out of a
plant. The lockout is exceedingly rare these
days, with its use confined generally to in-

stances when the union strikes against one
member of an employer's association, and all
members of the association retaliate with the
lockout.[50]

Another managerial device is the "mutual-
aid fund." The airlines have used this device,
paying struck companies sums based on increased revenues derived from passengers
switching to the non-struck firms.[51]

EXTENT OF WORK STOPPAGES

Although strikes are highly publicized in the
press, over a period of years they constitute a
relatively small percentage of total working time
on a nationwide basis. In 1974 the time spent
on work stoppages represented 0.24 percent of
total working time exclusive of private household, forestry, and fishery employment. The
average duration of strikes in 1974 was 27.1
days, although the median length of strikes was
14 days.[52] Trends in work stoppages since 1927
can be seen in Figure 24-1.[53]

MAJOR ISSUES IN STRIKES

The major issues precipitating strikes in 1974
are reflected in the statistics shown in Figure
24-2. It should be recognized, however, that
these categories reflect only judgments about
what constituted the predominant issues and
that in many situations the real issues may have
been obscured. Furthermore, the parties themselves often do not agree on what constitutes
the major issues.

As shown in Figure 24-2, demands for general wage changes, either by themselves or in
conjunction with other demands, represented

[48]Maggiolo, "Traditional Approaches to Dispute Resolution,"
p. 74.
[49]Ibid., p. 75.
[50]See *Monthly Labor Review*, 99:52 (June 1976).
[51]See *Business Week*, October 7, 1972, p. 28.
[52]*Analysis of Work Stoppages*, 1974, p. 2.
[53]For comparison with other countries, see *Yearbook of Labour
Statistics* (Geneva: International Labour Office, 1975), Part IX.

Figure **24-1** Work stoppages in the United States, 1927–1974 (workers and days idle in thousands)

Year	Work stoppages			Workers involved		Days idle during year		
	Number	Duration (days) Mean[2]	Median	Number	Percent of total employed[3]	Number	Percent of est. total working time[3]	Per worker involved
1927	707	26.5	3	330	1.4	26,200	(4)	79.5
1928	604	27.6	(4)	314	1.3	12,600	(4)	40.2
1929	921	22.6	(4)	289	1.2	5,350	(4)	18.5
1930	637	22.3	(4)	183	.8	3,320	(4)	18.1
1931	810	18.8	(4)	342	1.6	6,890	(4)	20.2
1932	841	19.6	(4)	324	1.8	10,500	(4)	32.4
1933	1,695	16.9	(4)	1,170	6.3	16,900	(4)	14.4
1934	1,856	19.5	(4)	1,470	7.2	19,600	(4)	13.4
1935	2,014	23.8	(4)	1,120	5.2	15,500	(4)	13.8
1936	2,172	23.3	(4)	789	3.1	13,900	(4)	17.6
1937	4,740	20.3	(4)	1,860	7.2	28,400	(4)	15.3
1938	2,772	23.6	(4)	688	2.8	9,150	(4)	13.3
1939	2,613	23.4	(4)	1,170	3.5	17,800	.21	15.2
1940	2,508	20.9	(4)	577	1.7	6,700	.08	11.6
1941	4,288	18.3	(4)	2,360	6.1	23,000	.23	9.8
1942	2,968	11.7	(4)	840	2.0	4,180	.04	5.0
1943	3,752	5.0	(4)	1,980	4.6	13,500	.10	6.8
1944	4,956	5.6	(4)	2,120	4.8	8,720	.07	4.1
1945	4,750	9.9	(4)	3,470	8.2	38,000	.31	11.0
1946	4,985	24.2	(4)	4,600	10.5	116,000	1.04	25.2
1947	3,693	25.6	(4)	2,170	4.7	34,600	.30	15.9
1948	3,419	21.8	(4)	1,960	4.2	34,100	.28	17.4
1949	3,606	22.5	(4)	3,030	6.7	50,500	.44	16.7
1950	4,843	19.2	8	2,410	5.1	38,800	.33	16.1
1951	4,737	17.4	7	2,220	4.5	22,900	.18	10.3
1952	5,117	19.6	7	3,540	7.3	59,100	.48	16.7
1953	5,091	20.3	9	2,400	4.7	28,300	.22	11.8
1954	3,468	22.5	9	1,530	3.1	22,600	.18	14.7
1955	4,320	18.5	8	2,650	5.2	28,200	.22	10.7
1956	3,825	18.9	7	1,900	3.6	33,100	.24	17.4
1957	3,673	19.2	8	1,390	2.6	16,500	.12	11.4
1958	3,694	19.7	8	2,060	3.9	23,900	.18	11.6
1959	3,708	24.6	10	1,880	3.3	69,000	.50	36.7
1960	3,333	23.4	10	1,320	2.4	19,100	.14	14.5
1961	3,367	23.7	9	1,450	2.6	16,300	.11	11.2
1962	3,614	24.6	9	1,230	2.2	18,600	.13	15.0
1963	3,362	23.0	8	941	1.1	16,100	.11	17.1
1964	3,655	22.9	8	1,640	2.7	22,900	.15	14.0
1965	3,963	25.0	9	1,550	2.5	23,300	.15	15.1
1966	4,405	22.2	9	1,960	3.0	25,400	.15	12.9

Figure 24-1   Work stoppages in the United States (*cont.*)

Year	Work stoppages			Workers involved		Days idle during year		
	Number	Duration (days) Mean[2]	Median	Number	Percent of total employed[3]	Number	Percent of est. total working time[3]	Per worker involved
1967	4,595	22.8	9	2,870	4.3	42,100	.25	14.7
1968	5,045	24.5	10	2,649	3.8	49,018	.28	18.5
1969	5,700	22.5	10	2,481	3.5	42,869	.24	17.3
1970	5,716	25.0	11	3,305	4.7	66,414	.37	20.1
1971	5,138	27.0	11	3,280	4.6	47,589	.26	14.5
1972	5,010	24.0	8	1,714	2.3	27,066	.15	15.8
1973	5,353	24.0	9	2,251	2.9	27,948	.14	12.4
1974	6,074	27.1	14	2,778	3.5	47,991	.24	17.3

[1]The number of stoppages and workers relate to those stoppages that began in the year; average duration, to those ending in the year. Days of idleness include all stoppages in effect. Workers are counted more than once if they were involved in more than 1 stoppage during the year.

Available information for earlier periods appears in *Handbook of Labor Statistics,—1975—Reference Edition*, BLS Bulletin 1865 (1975), tables 159–164. For a discussion of the procedures involved in the collection and compilation of work stoppage statistics, see *Handbook of Methods for Surveys and Studies*, BLS Bulletin 1711 (1971), ch. 19.

[2]Figures are simple averages; each stoppage is given equal weight regardless of its size.

[3]Agricultural and government employees are included in the total employed and total working time; private household, forestry, and fishery employees are excluded. An explanation of the measurement of idleness as a percentage of the total employed labor force and of the total time worked is found in 'Total Economy Measure of Strike Idleness,' by Howard N. Fullerton, *Monthly Labor Review*, Oct. 1968.

[4]Not available.

[5]Does not include an undetermined number of jurisdictional disputes for which identifying information was not available.

From U.S. Department of Labor, *Analysis of Work Stoppages, 1974*, Bureau of Labor Statistics, Bulletin 1902, 1976, p. 2.

issues in about 60 percent of all strikes in 1974. Matters of plant administration, including discipline, work load, work rules, and safety, ranked second in frequency. Union organization and security issues constituted the third most frequent category of work stoppages.[54]

[54]*Analysis of Work Stoppages, 1974*, p. 15. One author states that strikes have often been a result of workers feeling themselves ignored and that the strike served as ". . . an emphatic demand for attention. . . ." See Glenn Gilman, "Culture, Society, and Industrial Development," in W. Lloyd Warner and Norman H. Martin, eds., *Industrial Man* (New York: Harper & Brothers, 1959), p. 417. See also Arnold M. Zack, "Why Public Employees Strike," *The Arbitration Journal*, 23:69–84, No. 2 (1968).

STRIKE PREPARATION AND PROBLEMS

Strikes typically involve a good deal of preparation by both parties and, paradoxically, a certain amount of cooperation. For example, the unions have usually cooperated in a gradual shutdown of furnaces and other equipment in steel plants in order to minimize damage. Furthermore, unions tend to permit maintenance crews to maintain and repair equipment during a strike. The striking union expects to be back on the job eventually and is anxious to protect the employing capacity of the struck company.

A number of matters require careful planning by management in the face of a threatened

Figure **24-2**   Major issues involved in work stoppages, 1974

Major issues	Stoppages beginning in 1974		Man-days idle during 1974 (all stoppages)	
	Number	Percent	Number (in thousands)	Percent
General wage changes	3,638	59.9	38,924.4	81.1
Plant administration	1,120	18.4	2,340.8	4.9
Union organization and security	348	5.7	1,841.4	3.8
Job security	248	4.1	1,543.0	3.2
Interunion or intraunion matters	240	4.0	188.1	.4
Wage adjustments	148	2.4	445.2	.9
Other contractual matters	97	1.6	818.6	1.7
Other working conditions	91	1.5	256.4	.5
Supplementary benefits	70	1.2	1,104.3	2.3
Hours of work	7	.1	443.8	.9
Not reported	67	1.1	84.7	.2

From U.S. Department of Labor, *Analysis of Work Stoppages, 1974*, Bureau of Labor Statistics, Bulletin No. 1902, 1976, p. 15.

strike: relations with customers and suppliers, protection of the plant, the question of whether to try operating the plant with nonstriking or new employees, the continuation or suspension of employee benefits, and many other subjects. As one author states, "Running a plant during a strike is much like operating a city under siege."[55] To illustrate the complexity of the plans that must be made, one study reports forty-six major items typically covered in companies' strike manuals.[56] Strike plans in hospitals are particularly complicated. When doctors (interns and residents) struck in twenty-three New York City hospitals in 1975, the hospitals immediately set emergency procedures in motion to care for patients.[57]

To insure that such plans are made, strike committees are ordinarily established in organizations having had experience with strikes. One study of 106 recently struck U.S. and Canadian companies found that about 90 percent had strike committees. Among the company's executives, personnel directors are the most likely to be on these committees, with various vice presidents in charge of such major functions as sales, manufacturing, purchasing, and engineering also usually serving as members.[58]

How to treat the nonunionized segment of the work force—usually white-collar workers—during a strike is a major problem of management. If the strike is of short duration, typical practice is to keep white-collar workers on the payroll and on the job. In the study cited above, forty-five of the fifty-seven firms with numerous office workers request such employees to remain on the job. The majority of

[55] John G. Hutchinson, *Management Under Strike Conditions* (New York: Holt, Rinehart and Winston, 1966), pp. 136–138.
[56] James J. Bambrick and Willard A. Lewis, *Preparing for Collective Bargaining—II* (New York: National Industrial Conference Board, 1962), pp. 14–15. For a strike manual, see American Society for Personnel Administration, *Strike Preparation Manual* (Berea, Ohio: ASPA, 1974).
[57] *Seattle Times*, March 17, 1975.

[58] Bambrick and Lewis, *Preparing for Collective Bargaining—II*, p. 12.

these companies apparently expected white-collar workers to be permitted to cross picket lines as a matter of legal right but usually urged them to avoid physical resistance.[59]

Although there has been much less violence during strikes in recent years than in the early days of the union movement (see Chapter 2), violence occasionally does erupt. Emotions can run high, particularly on the picket line when nonstriking employees are seen entering the plant. When rocks are thrown, if fist fights break out, or in the rare instance when shots are fired, the problem becomes one for the local police, whose duty it is to maintain law and order. In general, however, most strikes and picket lines are relatively free from physical violence.

Another major problem is whether to replace strikers. Although it is legal to do so in economic strikes (in contrast to unfair-labor-practice strikes), and it is occasionally done, such managerial action tends to transform a strike into a bitter struggle for union survival. A number of undesirable consequences may result, including picket line violence, difficult problems in settling the status of replacements relative to returning strikers, and problems related to worker morale and harmony once the strike is over.[60]

IMPACT OF ENVIRONMENTAL FACTORS

FEDERAL LAW AND GOVERNMENTAL RULING

OBLIGATION TO BARGAIN In addition to making the services of the Federal Mediation and Conciliation Service available in labor disputes, federal labor law establishes, or gives a legal basis to, a wide range of constraints on the parties during the negotiating process. For ex-

ample, the Taft-Hartley Act also requires the employer and the representative of the employees ". . . to meet at reasonable times and confer in good faith with respect to wages, hours, and other terms and conditions of employment . . . but such obligation does not compel either party to agree to a proposal or require the making of a concession. . . ."[61]

What constitutes "good-faith" bargaining has long been a problem for the National Labor Relations Board and the courts. Over the years, however, the NLRB and the courts have established some general guidelines pertaining to the positive signs of good-faith bargaining, including intent to reach an agreement, active participation, and the making of counterproposals. Negative indications include stalling tactics, sudden shifts in position when agreement is close, rejection of clauses found routinely in most contracts, and refusal to sign once an agreement is reached.[62]

Refusal to furnish data necessary for bargaining has also been regarded as an unfair labor practice. Subjects requiring company-supplied information are individual earnings, job rates and classifications, pensions, operations of the incentive system, merit increases, time-study data, incentive earnings, and piece rates. Furthermore, when a company attempts to justify a refusal to grant a wage increase on economic grounds, good-faith bargaining requires that the company furnish the union with enough data to enable it to bargain intelligently.[63]

WHAT IS BARGAINABLE The problem of what is bargainable constitutes an extension of the good-faith problem and a similarly difficult

[59]Ibid., pp. 17–19.
[60]See Walter H. Uphoff, *Kohler on Strike: Thirty Years of Conflict* (Boston: Beacon Press, 1966).

[61]Labor Management Relations Act, 1947 (as amended, 1959), Section 8(d).
[62]Robben W. Fleming, "The Obligation to Bargain in Good Faith," in Joseph Shister, Benjamin Aaron, and Clyde W. Summers, *Public Policy and Collective Bargaining* (New York and Evanston: Harper & Row, 1962), p. 63.
[63]Cox, "The Duty to Bargain," pp. 1427, 1431.

one. To grapple with this problem, the NLRB has established three categories of demands: illegal, mandatory, and voluntary. *Illegal demands* are those that would come into conflict with some law; *mandatory demands* include wages, hours, and working conditions; and *voluntary demands* involve topics outside the mandatory category. In general, the board has held that a refusal to bargain over demands that are contrary to law is not an unfair labor practice, that insistence upon bargaining to an impasse over voluntary subjects *is* an unfair practice, and that a refusal to bargain to a genuine impasse over mandatory subjects is an unfair practice.[64]

The difficulty is that the borderline between mandatory and voluntary demands is not distinct and remains fluid, shifting and changing with NLRB and court decisions. An increasingly wide range of subjects appears to be mandatory, however, including the moving, streamlining, or closing down of a company's operations and the subcontracting of work. This seems to be the implication of the Supreme Court's decision in the *R.R. Telegrapher's* case, in which the Court held that the Northwestern Railroad was obliged to bargain with the union if the company wished to close down some of its stations.[65] In the subsequent *Town and Country* and *Fibreboard* cases, the Supreme Court held that it was mandatory for management to bargain with a union over plans for letting out work under a subcontract.[66]

The broad implications of these cases are obvious when we consider the rapid changes taking place in the labor force because of technological innovations. Neglecting or refusing to bargain about technological changes that affect employees may well result in such NLRB or court orders as the requirement that closed-down operations be reopened, the payment of back wages, and the payment of travel and moving costs. Apparently, the effect of these court rulings is to place management's plans for changes in the company's operations face to face with economic power of the union—the right to strike—should negotiations on such matters reach an impasse. The NLRB, however, has taken the point of view that such negotiations may prove fruitful, with the union often agreeing to assist management in making such changes.[67]

The Taft-Hartley Act specifically forbids certain kinds of agreements between the parties. For example, employers or unions are forbidden to agree to cease handling the products of, or to cease doing business with, other firms or persons. Such "hot cargo" agreements are illegal except in the garment industry and at the site of construction or repair in the construction industry. In addition, clauses agreeing to a closed shop or discriminatory hiring practices are also illegal.[68]

MANAGERIAL RIGHTS Most managements and most arbitrators assume that management retains whatever rights it has not bargained away under the so-called *residual-rights* or *reserved-rights* theory. This theory, however, is occasionally overturned by arbitration rulings and court decisions, and it is constantly challenged by the labor movement. For example, Arthur Goldberg argues that the theory of reserved rights is in error because it does not recognize the many inherent rights of labor that exist

[64] Fleming, "Obligation to Bargain in Good Faith," pp. 63, 64.
[65] Ibid., p. 70.
[66] Elihu Platt, "The Duty to Bargain as Applied to Management Decisions," *Labor Law Journal*, 19:148–150 (March 1968).
[67] Platt, "The Duty to Bargain," pp. 157–159.
[68] Labor Management Relations Act (as amended, 1959), Section 8(e) and Section 8(a)(3). For more on "hot cargo" cases, see Paul A. Brinker, "Hot Cargo Cases in the Construction Industry Since 1958," *Labor Law Journal*, 22:690–707 (November 1971).

whether or not management has recognized them.[69]

The apparent vulnerability of the reserved-rights theory has prompted many companies to negotiate into contracts clauses on *managerial rights*. Almost two-thirds of the labor agreements in one study reported such clauses.[70] The assumption underlying these clauses is that they will be useful in reminding the union of "managerial prerogatives" and that they will protect against arbitrators who do not adhere to the "reserved-rights" theory. Regardless of such clauses, however, the fact is that so-called managerial prerogatives have been steadily encroached upon by unions. Conversely, bilateral decision making in increasingly wide areas of a company's operations has been the trend and appears to be the prospect for the immediate future. (See the next chapter for more on this subject.)

STRIKES Federal law and NLRB rulings place certain constraints on both management and labor during a strike. For example, the party desiring to terminate or modify a contract must give written notice at least sixty days before the terminating date. A strike or lockout in this period is an unfair labor practice.

In addition, although management may replace strikers—except in a strike that involves an unfair labor practice on the part of the employers[71]—management may not refuse to reinstate employees because they took part in a lawful strike, provided a job for which they qualify is open. Furthermore, management may not refuse to deal with the union because its members are on strike.[72]

Constraints relative to strikes are also placed on the union. The following stem from Section 8 of the Taft-Hartley Act:

° Unions or their agents may not threaten employees with bodily injury or loss of jobs for failure to support the union's activities.

° Secondary boycotts are forbidden. An example would be a union's picketing of a retail store that handles the products of the manufacturer with which the union had a dispute.[73]

° Mass picketing and force and violence on the picket-line are forbidden. Jurisdictional strikes are forbidden. That is, unions may not strike to force an employer to assign work to one union, trade, or craft instead of another union, trade, or craft unless the employer is failing to comply with an order of the NLRB relative to such work.

The Landrum-Griffin Act amended the Taft-Hartley rules pertaining to decertifying elections held during a strike. Striking employees who had been replaced and were thus not eligible for reinstatement had been previously excluded from voting. The Landrum-Griffin amendment to the Taft-Hartley Act, however,

---

[69] Arthur J. Goldberg, "Management Rights and the Arbitration Process," in *Proceedings of the Ninth Annual Meeting of the National Academy of Arbitrators*, January 1956, pp. 118–25.

[70] Bureau of National Affairs, "Basic Patterns in Union Contracts," *Collective Bargaining Negotiations and Contracts*, Vol. 2, 65:1, January 16, 1975.

[71] In an unfair labor-practice strike, management may be required to release replacements and reinstate strikers. In 1976, the NLRB approved a settlement between the Kellwood Company and the International Ladies' Garment Workers Union that provided $1.5 million in back pay to 753 workers who had been replaced in an unfair labor-practice strike.

Bureau of National Affairs, *Labor Relations Reporter*, "Summary of Developments," March 29, 1976, p. 1.

[72] National Labor Relations Board, "Summary of the Labor Management Relations Act as Amended through 1959," pamphlet, pp. 5, 6.

[73] Some of the loopholes in the secondary boycott provisions of the Taft-Hartley Act were closed through amendments to the act by the Labor-Management Reporting and Disclosure Act of 1959 (Landrum-Griffin). For a review of the results of these amendments, see Philip Ross, "An Assessment of the Landrum-Griffin Act's Secondary Boycott Amendments to the Taft-Hartley Act," *Labor Law Journal*, 22:675–689 (November 1971).

expressly permits replaced employees to vote in an election held within twelve months after the start of the strike. The consequences of this change is to make the decertification of a striking union more difficult. Prior to this amendment, the employment of replacements who were not sympathetic with the union cause could readily build up a majority vote against the union.

NATIONAL-EMERGENCY DISPUTES Sections 206 through 210 of the Taft-Hartley Act empower the president of the United States to initiate action that can result in an eighty-day postponement of a strike or lockout likely to ". . . imperil the national health or safety. . . ." The procedure is as follows:

1. The president appoints a board of inquiry to investigate the problem and to make a report to him on the issues. The report is also filed with the Mediation and Conciliation Service and is made public.

2. The president may then direct the attorney general to petition the appropriate United States district court to prohibit the strike or lockout.

3. If the court finds the dispute to be of such significance that a court order is warranted under the law, the court will enjoin the strike or lockout. This order is subject to review by the appropriate court of appeals and the Supreme Court.

4. The parties to the dispute are expected ". . . to make every effort to adjust and settle their differences . . ." with the assistance of the Federal Mediation and Conciliation Service.

5. Having been reconvened at the time of the court order, the board of inquiry reports to the president at the end of sixty days on the current position of the parties and the employer's last offer, unless the dispute has been settled.

6. Within the next fifteen days, the NLRB takes a secret ballot of the employees in the bargaining unit on the question of whether they are willing to accept the employer's final offer. The results of this vote, which are not binding on the union negotiating team, are filed within five days after the election.

7. Upon receipt of the results, or upon the dispute being settled, the attorney general requests the court to remove the injunction.

8. When the injunction is discharged, the president submits a full report to Congress with recommendations for the appropriate action to be taken.[74]

How well this procedure has worked since its enactment into law is a controversial matter. Between 1947 and the end of 1965, the emergency machinery was invoked by the president in twenty-four disputes. Injunctions were requested and obtained in twenty out of the twenty-four instances, and in all but one of the twenty situations, the dispute was effectively stopped for the period of the injunction. "Final offer" balloting supervised by the NLRB resulted in rejection by employees in all fourteen disputes in which balloting was conducted, and in one other case the election was boycotted by employees. Full agreement was reached between the parties within the statutory eighty-day period in ten of the injunctive situations, and one agreement was reached before the injunction was issued.[75]

On the surface, the record would show that the Taft-Hartley strike vote procedure is essen-

[74] The provisions of the Taft-Hartley Act are not applicable to matters under the jurisdiction of the Railway Labor Act and Executive Order 10988. Thus, different procedures are used for disputes in the railroad and airline industries, and in federal employment.
[75] U.S. Bureau of Labor Statistics, *National Emergency Disputes Under the Labor Management Relations (Taft-Hartley) Act, 1947–65*, Bulletin No. 1482, U.S. Department of Labor, March 1966, pp. 1–2.

tially useless. Employees are not likely to weaken the position of the union negotiating committee after having once authorized it to call a strike. On the other hand, the general Taft-Hartley procedures appear to have substantially reduced the potential work stoppage time inherent in national emergency disputes. It might be assumed, however, that the procedures simply prolonged the negotiations. It has been argued that, since the parties expect the government to step in, there is less last-minute pressure to come to an agreement, and the pressure simply gets postponed eighty days. Furthermore, it has been argued that a board of inquiry interferes with the bargaining process.[76]

As a partial solution, an independent study group recommends that the president be given wide discretion and more flexibility in emergency disputes, including the use of the boards of inquiry as mediators and the ordering of only partial operation of struck facilities when closure of the entire facility would endanger the requirements of the emergency situation. The same group also recommends that the strike vote procedure be eliminated from the law.[77]

OTHER ENVIRONMENTAL FACTORS

From our discussion thus far, it is obvious that a large number of factors have an impact on the process of collective bargaining. Federal law, NLRB rulings, court orders, the Federal Media-

tion and Conciliation Service, the offices of the president and the secretary of labor, the requirements of national defense, the pattern of recent contractual settlements, arbitrational awards, and technological change—these and other factors have a major impact on collective bargaining in specific situations. In addition, and implicit in the various types of bargaining relationships discussed earlier, is the fact that the attitudes of the two parties toward each other and their skill in dealing with each other have powerful effects.[78]

Interwoven with these factors and modifying many of them is the prevailing economic condition of the particular enterprise, the particular industry, and the entire economy. It is unlikely that employers will knowingly bargain themselves out of business or that union members will accept a marginal subsistence wage to keep a sick organization alive—particularly if the cause is poor management. Furthermore, the public is less and less inclined to accept the repercussion of major strikes in the form of layoffs in nonstruck companies and the dampening effect on the economy as a whole. Some labor leaders are also concerned about the costs of long strikes to union members, to union treasuries, and to the economy.[79]

Other economic factors also affect collective bargaining. Large inventories of finished goods may make an employer less reluctant to accept a strike, as will an agreement with other firms to share losses due to strikes, as among the airlines. Strike insurance is also extensively used in the newspaper and railroad industries. On the other hand, heavy investments in model

[76]See Charles C. Killingsworth, "Emergency Disputes and Public Policy," *Monthly Labor Review*, 94:42–45 (August 1971).
[77]An Independent Study Group, *The Public Interest in National Labor Policy* (New York: Committee for Economic Development, 1961), pp. 95–104. See also Arthur A. Sloane, "Presidential Boards of Inquiry in National Emergency Disputes: An Assessment after 20 Years of Performance," *Labor Law Journal*, 18:665–675 (November 1967).

[78]For a discussion of the consequences of inept management practices in dealing with unions, see Sumner H. Slichter, James J. Healy, and E. Robert Livernash, *The Impact of Collective Bargaining on Management* (Washington, D.C.: The Brookings Institution, 1960), pp. 809–813.
[79]See "Trouble Plagues the House of Labor," *Business Week*, October 28, 1972, p. 76.

changeovers and advertising may make the employer extremely reluctant to see operations shut down. Similarly, large sums in the union's strike fund, accumulated individual savings from overtime work, or the availability of unemployment compensation or food stamps may make a strike less undesirable than usual to the rank-and-file worker. High employment and shortages of skilled labor may also make workers less fearful of the possibility of being replaced in the event of a strike and less anxious about finding a new job if they are replaced. For these reasons, the timing of negotiations and of a strike is exceedingly important in collective-bargaining strategy. Thus, the collective-bargaining process is affected by a wide range of environmental factors.

RELATIONSHIP TO OTHER ORGANIZATIONAL PROCESSES

As we have discussed in previous chapters, collective bargaining is closely interrelated with most, if not all, of the various personnel processes in the unionized firm. For example, the general nature of the jobs to be performed—the task-specialization process—will influence a good deal of the discussion during negotiations, and, reciprocally, collective bargaining will modify the nature of the jobs to be performed. Similarly, the labor agreement will govern transfers, promotions, and layoffs—the staffing process—within the bargaining unit. Furthermore, collective bargaining will have an obvious impact on the level of wages and fringe benefits and the procedures for allocating rewards—the compensation process—within the organization.

Other processes within the organization are similarly interrelated with the process of negotiating the agreement. It is obvious that both wage settlements and strikes affect the flow of money in the enterprise—the financial management process—and that the financial status of the organization will affect management's attitude during negotiations. Similarly, the production-management process can be drastically affected by slowdowns and completely stopped by a strike, and the attitudes of the union negotiators will be affected by the treatment employees are receiving in the day-to-day operations of the plant. Finally, adjustments will have to be made in the marketing-management process if wage increases force prices up or if a strike precludes deliveries of products to customers.

EFFECT ON NEED FULFILLMENT

The process of negotiating the agreement provides an outlet for many needs of employees. The union negotiating team in particular finds much opportunity for self-actualization and expression of its needs for information, attention and recognition from others, independence, dominance, and achievement. Given a reasonably democratic union, participation in union meetings and the establishment of policy for negotiations provides rank-and-file members similar opportunity for satisfying their needs. Thus, through collective action workers can have a major impact on the operations of the enterprise and can insure that their interests are considered.

Strikes often can be interpreted as a deliberate effort to obtain more satisfaction of needs—a positive move on the part of the union. Many strikes have strong overtones of ego-defending behavior, however, and are negative in this sense. Indeed, the duration of many strikes cannot be explained only on economic grounds, since the participants are obviously losing money, but must be understood in terms of a wide range of human wants and needs.

UTILITY OF SYSTEMS

There are apparently two major areas where substantial systematization is appropriate in negotiating contracts. One area is that of compiling data and calculating costs. Very careful assembling of data relevant to collective bargaining is essential to ensure that no concessions are made that will seriously handicap the organization's ability to survive.[80] Furthermore, negotiations focused on facts and figures that can be replicated are less likely to produce destructive conflict. Jointly obtained data, in particular, can greatly facilitate negotiations.

The second area where extensive systematization seems appropriate is the preparation of bargaining goals. Unless the company knows where it is headed in the bargaining process, its strategy can only be a defense against, or an acquiescence to, union demands.

A high degree of unilateral systematization in the actual conduct of negotiations is probably impossible in most situations. Unless one of the parties is much weaker than the other, neither will long tolerate the other's dictating procedural matters. Collective bargaining involves accommodation, not only with respect to the rules governing wages, hours, and working conditions, but also with respect to the conduct of the discussions about these subjects.

SUMMARY

Contract negotiations obviously present considerable opportunity for cooperation, accord, and industrial statesmanship. It is equally obvious that negotiations are fraught with possibilities for ego-aggrandizement, conflict, defensive behavior, and short-sighted economic advantage. Both unions and managements have much to gain by sending mature, intelligent, well-trained, and well-prepared negotiators and problem solvers to the committee rooms and bargaining tables, and much to lose by not doing so. Similar attributes are required of any governmental officials or other third parties who find themselves involved in the complex negotiation process. Finally, "integrative" approaches to the collective-bargaining process show great promise of solving problems in such a way as to enhance the objectives of both parties, particularly with respect to such issues as productivity, job interest, and employee control over work.

REVIEW AND DISCUSSION QUESTIONS

1. Compare Selekman's categories with those of Walton and McKersie. How are they similar and how do they differ?

2. Discuss the "take-it-or-leave-it" approach to collective bargaining relative to (a) need theory and (b) leadership research.

3. What are some of the ritualistic aspects of collective bargaining? What purpose do these aspects have?

4. What governmental constraints are applied to management's conduct of negotiations with a union?

5. Describe the process of mediation.

6. Describe the National Emergency Disputes procedure and its controversial aspects.

7. What are the major issues in contemporary strikes?

8. What are some of the constraints imposed on (a) management and (b) the union during a strike?

9. What are some factors that would influence a union to strike? To avoid a strike?

---

[80] Unions are beginning to use computers to make comparative analyses of union contracts. See "Bargaining by Electronics," *Business Week,* June 5, 1971, pp. 78–80.

10. Describe several collective-bargaining situations that have occurred in recent years that could be called "distributive bargaining."

SUPPLEMENTAL REFERENCES

Aaron, Benjamin, "Employee Rights Under an Agreement: A Current Evaluation," *Monthly Labor Review*, 94:52–56 (August 1971).

————, "How Other Nations Deal with Emergency Disputes," *Monthly Labor Review*, 95:37–43 (May 1972).

Bakke, E. Wight, Clark Kerr, and Charles W. Anrod, *Unions, Management, and the Public*, 3rd ed. (New York: Harcourt, Brace & World, Inc., 1967).

Bartsell, John M., *Airline Industrial Relations: Pilots and Flight Engineers* (Boston: Harvard University, Graduate School of Business Administration, 1966).

Beal, Edwin F., Edward D. Wickersham, and Philip Kienast, *The Practice of Collective Bargaining*, 5th ed. (Homewood, Ill.: Richard D. Irwin, Inc., 1976).

Bell, Daniel, "The Racket-Ridden Longshoremen: A Functional Analysis of Crime," in Walter Galenson and Seymour Martin Lipset, eds., *Labor and Trade Unionism* (New York: John Wiley & Sons, 1960).

Blake, Robert R., and Jane S. Mouton, "Reactions to Intergroup Competition under Win-Lose Conditions," *Management Science*, 7:420–435 (July 1961).

Bok, Derek C., and John T. Dunlop, *Labor and the American Community* (New York: Simon and Schuster, 1970).

Cimini, Michael, "Government Intervention in Railroad Disputes," *Monthly Labor Review*, 94:27–33 (December 1971).

Commerce Clearing House, *1972 Guidebook to Labor Relations*, Labor Law Reports, 1972.

Crump, Michael W., and Harvey Kahalas, "Civil Law Traditions and Industrial Relations Systems," *Labor Law Journal*, 26:243–249 (April 1975).

Davey, Harold W., *Contemporary Collective Bargaining*, 3rd ed. (Englewood Cliffs, N.J.: Prentice-Hall, Inc., 1972).

"Emergency Stoppages in the Private Sector," *Labor Law Journal*, 22:452–480 (August 1971).

Gilroy, Thomas P., and Anthony V. Sincropi, *Dispute Settlement in the Public Sector: The State of The Art*, report submitted to Division of Public Employee Labor Relations, U.S. Department of Labor, 1972.

Jehring, J.J., *A New Approach to Collective Bargaining? Progress Sharing at American Motors* (Madison: University of Wisconsin, 1962).

Levin, Richard A., "National Emergency Disputes Under Taft-Hartley: A Legal Definition," *Labor Law Journal*, 22:29–43 (January 1971).

Levinson, Harry, "Stress at the Bargaining Table," *Personnel*, 42:17–23 (March-April 1965).

Marshall, Howard D., and Natalie J. Marshall, *Collective Bargaining* (New York: Random House, 1971).

Morton, James E., "Union-Management Consultation in the Federal Government: Problems and Promise," *Labor Law Journal*, 27:11–17 (January 1976).

Murphy, Betty Southard, "The Chairman Looks at the NLRB," *The Personnel Administrator*, 21:22–26 (May 1976).

Perline, Martin M., and Kurtis L. Tull, "The Impact of Arbitration on Collective Bargaining Agreements," *Labor Law Journal*, 19:112–116 (February 1968).

Pondy, Louis R., "Organizational Conflict: Concepts and Models," *Administrative Science Quarterly*, 12:296–320 (September 1967).

Ross, Irwin, "How to Tell When the Unions Will Be Tough," *Fortune*, July 1975, pp. 100–104ff.

Rubin, Jeffrey Z., and Bert R. Brown, *The Social Psychology of Bargaining and Negotiation* (New York: Academic Press, 1975).

Sloane, Arthur A., and Fred Whitney, *Labor Relations*, 2nd ed. (Englewood Cliffs, N.J.: Prentice-Hall, Inc., 1972).

Stagner, Ross, and Hjalmar Rosen, *Psychology of Union-Management Relations* (Belmont, Calif.: Wadsworth Publishing Company, 1965).

Straus, Donald B., "Alternatives to the Strike," *Labor Law Journal*, 23:387–397 (July 1972).

Tagliaferri, Louis E., "Plant Operation During a Strike," *Personnel Administration*, 35:47–51ff. (March-April 1972).

U.S. Department of Labor, *Exploring Alternatives to the Strike*, reprints of 18 articles from *Monthly Labor Review*, September 1973.

Walton, Richard E., and Robert B. McKersie, *A Behavioral Theory of Labor Negotiations* (New York: McGraw-Hill Book Company, 1965).

CHAPTER 25
THE GRIEVANCE-ARBITRATION PROCESS

The day-to-day administration of the labor-management agreement is an integral and significant part of the broad collective-bargaining process. The grievance-arbitration process in particular, along with the use of any joint problem-solving committees, is the focal point for union-management relationships during the period between the signing of a contract and the time for its renegotiation. The grievance-arbitration process will be the main subject of this chapter.

DESCRIPTION AND PURPOSE

The grievance-arbitration process involves systematic union-management deliberation of a complaint at successively higher organizational levels. The problem may be settled at any of these levels, and if not, the complaint may be submitted to an impartial outside party whose decision is final and binding. The complaint is usually one made by an employee. Though management sometimes uses grievance procedures to process a complaint about the union, such use is rare. Almost all contracts contain grievance procedures, and about 95 percent contain provisions for arbitration as a final step.[1]

Typically, the first step of the grievance procedure in a labor contract occurs when an ag-

[1] W.J. Usery, Jr., "Some Attempts to Reduce Arbitration Costs and Delays," *Monthly Labor Review*, 95:3 (November 1972). A study of 620 labor agreements each covering 2,000 workers or more found 595 (96 percent) with grievance and/or arbitration provisions. Of the 595, only 19 did not provide for arbitration as a last step. "Characteristics of Agreements Covering 2,000 Workers or More," Bulletin 1729, Bureau of Labor Statistics, U.S. Department of Labor, 1972. For a discussion of what happens when there is no arbitration clause, see Bob Repas, "Grievance Procedures without Arbitration," *Industrial and Labor Relations Review*, 20:381–390 (April 1967).

grieved employee or a union steward on behalf of the employee brings a verbal or written complaint to the employee's immediate supervisor. About 60 percent of labor contracts require that the grievance be presented in writing at the first step.[2]

If the problem is not handled to the satisfaction of the employee at the first step, he or she may then take the problem (almost always in writing at this step and almost always processed by a union official or committee) to the next higher managerial level designated in the contract, and so on through a total of three, four, or five steps. The most common practice is for the contract to provide for three steps, exclusive of arbitration.[3]

The managerial people concerned will ordinarily seek the advice of the industrial relations department at some point in the process, and that department will usually be involved in the managerial decision at the final step within the organization. Sometimes a contract will specify participation by the general manager or the president of a company at the final step in the process.

Finally, a problem that cannot be settled between the parties to the contract is submitted to an arbitrator. The arbitrator conducts a hearing and hands down a decision which both parties have agreed in advance to accept as final and binding.

Grievance-arbitration procedures in federal employment are similar to those mentioned except for the less prevalent use of binding arbitration. However, a survey of contracts negotiated since Executive Order 11616 of 1972 (which required contracts to include some grievance procedure for resolving disputes arising over the interpretation or application of the contract) found the most common procedure to have either three or four steps with some kind of arbitration as a final step.[4]

The central purpose of the *grievance-arbitration* process is to seek an application of the contract with a degree of justice for both parties that makes a resort to strikes or lockouts unnecessary. (See also organizational due process in Chapter 8.) There are some related, secondary purposes as well. One purpose is to interpret the language of the agreement. Since life in an organization is dynamic, problems frequently arise during the period of the contract which were not anticipated by the parties involved and consequently not provided for in the contract. When a grievance is filed, the parties must reach an agreement on applying the contract to the particular problem, or they must submit the matter to an outsider for a decision.

Another purpose of the grievance procedure is to provide a communicative device from the rank-and-file workers to higher management. The grievance procedure tends to "take the pulse" of the organization, notifying management of potential trouble spots and areas of discontent, and indicating places where managerial attention is needed. It sometimes also serves a political purpose within the union in that stewards or other officers push employee's grievances to demonstrate the usefulness of the union hierarchy.

Still another purpose of the grievance-arbitration procedure is that of suggesting to the union, to management, or to both, those parts of the contract requiring clarification or modification in subsequent negotiations. Contractual clauses under which grievances constantly seem to arise usually need careful examination and correction.

Arbitration is sometimes used to settle disputes stemming from wage negotiations—in

[2] Bureau of National Affairs, *Collective Bargaining Negotiations and Contracts*, Vol. 2, 51:2, February 27, 1975.
[3] Ibid.

[4] William J. Kilberg, Thomas Angelo, and Lawrence Lorber, "Grievance and Arbitration Patterns in the Federal Service," *Monthly Labor Review*, 95:23–30 (November 1972).

particular, under wage-reopening clauses—but such use is very uncommon. Arbitration is also used occasionally to settle unresolved issues after the end of a strike.[5]

CURRENT PRACTICES AND PROBLEMS

EXTENT OF USE

As shown, grievance and arbitration procedures are set forth in most labor union contracts. In contrast, formal grievance procedures are found in only a small minority of nonunionized organizations. According to one study, only 22 percent of responding companies had grievance procedures for hourly workers not represented by a union, and only 9 percent had such procedures for nonexempt salaried employees not represented by a union. Rarely did such procedures include arbitration.[6] According to another study, only 11 percent of responding organizations had a formal appeal procedure for nonunionized employees.[7]

There appear to be no statistics on the total number of labor arbitration cases occurring each year, but statistics from the American Arbitration Association and the Federal Mediation and Conciliation Service indicate to some extent the widespread use of arbitration in labor disputes.[8] In 1972 the Federal Mediation and Conciliation Service submitted 13,842 panels of arbitrators to parties requesting this service (a "panel" is a list of several arbitrators from which the union and the employer select one); 6,263 appointments were made from these panels, and 3,438 awards ultimately resulted.[9] The same year, cases processed through the American Arbitration Association resulted in 3,829 awards.[10] (The major reason that the number of panels far exceed the number of awards is the high incidence of parties resolving the dispute before the total process unfolds.) Since many private arbitrations are not processed by these agencies, however, the total number of actual hearings and awards is probably in the neighborhood of 20,000 each year.[11]

For every case that went to arbitration, several were undoubtedly settled at earlier steps in the grievance procedure. As a conservative estimate, there must be close to one million separate formal grievances settled under grievance and arbitration procedures in the United States each year. Since there are about 165,000 collective bargaining agreements in effect, it would require only about six grievances per year to reach that total. Thus, a great deal of industrial conflict in the United States is minimized each day through this voluntary machinery.

PROBLEMS IN HANDLING GRIEVANCES

Many grievances stem from perceived injustices or injured feelings rather than from contract violations on the part of supervisors. When such grievances arise, the union has the difficult problem of deciding whether to process the complaint and face the possibility of rebuffs during the successive stages of the grievance procedure or whether to attempt pacification of the aggrieved employee. Management also has the problem of how to handle such grievances.

---

[5] See Richard V. Miller, "Arbitration of New Contract Wage Disputes: Some Recent Trends," *Industrial and Labor Relations Review*, 20:250–264 (January 1967).

[6] "Personnel Practices in Factory and Office," *Studies in Personnel Policy*, No. 145, 5th ed. (New York: National Industrial Conference Board, 1954), pp. 56, 109.

[7] William G. Scott, *The Management of Conflict: Appeal Systems in Organizations* (Homewood, Ill.: Richard D. Irwin, 1965), pp. 56–61.

[8] Arbitration is also used to resolve controversies in other commercial areas, including those stemming from commercial contracts and insurance policies.

[9] James F. Power, "Improving Arbitration: Roles of Parties and Agencies," *Monthly Labor Review*, 95:15–22 (November 1972).

[10] Joseph Krislov, "The Supply of Arbitrators: Prospects for the 1980's," *Monthly Labor Review*, 99:27–30 (October 1976).

[11] Ibid., p. 28.

Selekman has suggested a partial solution through a "clinical approach," in contrast to a "legalistic" one. With a clinical approach, the shop steward or supervisor attempts to assess the emotional and social aspects of the complaint and deal with the problem at that level. Simply permitting the employee to "blow off steam" may provide a partial solution. In any event, careful listening and analysis may permit the steward or supervisor to identify the "real" problem.[12] (See the discussion in Chapter 12 on nondirective interviewing.)

Another difficulty in the use of the grievance procedure is the possibility of its becoming a vehicle for the respective parties to test their relative strengths. The union may file grievances at every opportunity in order to wring every possible concession from management, or management may fight every grievance in an attempt to contain the union. Under such circumstances, the grievance procedure can hardly adjust problems at the lowest possible organizational level. On the other hand, the use of the grievance machinery, including arbitration, under such circumstances does serve to clarify the limits of the contract for both parties.

TYPES OF ISSUES GOING TO ARBITRATION

In recent years, the issues upon which arbitrators have most frequently ruled pertain to the following: discharge and disciplinary actions; seniority in demotion, promotion, transfer, layoff, and recall; job evaluation; overtime; and the scope of the contract agreement. As shown in Figure 25-1, disciplinary cases topped the list in 1972, as they typically have for many years.

NUMBER OF MEMBERS ON PANELS

About 72 percent of all labor contracts provide for a single arbitrator, and most of the remaining contracts provide for tripartite boards, consisting of union and company representatives plus an impartial chairman.[13] The latter practice has been criticized, since the important third member of three-member boards tends to act as a sole arbitrator.[14] When one member is appointed by the union and another by management, these two members will naturally sympathize with their respective sides.

DURATION OF ARBITRATOR'S APPOINTMENT

Arbitrators, sometimes called "umpires," are appointed to hand down an award for a single case—ad hoc arbitration—in about 80 percent of labor contracts.[15] Although the same arbitrator may handle cases for many different firms and unions during a year and perhaps several for the same two parties, under ad hoc procedures in a contract, the arbitrator is appointed on a case-by-case basis.

"Permanent" arbitrators are appointed under about 13 percent of labor agreements.[16] In this situation, the parties agree to use a particular individual, or several individuals in rotation, for the period of the agreement. The chief advantage claimed for the system of permanent arbitration is that the arbitrator develops an understanding and familiarity with the particular and unique problems of the parties involved.

SELECTION AND COMPENSATION OF ARBITRATORS

About 24 percent of contracts provide that an impartial agency select an arbitrator. The vast majority of contracts, however, state that the parties will try to agree on an arbitrator but if

[12] Benjamin M. Selekman, *Labor Relations and Human Relations* (New York: McGraw-Hill Book Company, 1947), Chapter 5.

[13] Bureau of National Affairs, *Collective Bargaining*, Vol. 2, 51:8.
[14] See Harold W. Davey, *Contemporary Collective Bargaining*, 3rd ed. (Englewood Cliffs, N.J.: Prentice-Hall, 1972), p. 176.
[15] Bureau of National Affairs, *Collective Bargaining*, Vol. 2, 51:7.
[16] Ibid.

Figure 25-1 Frequency of occurrence of issues in cases in which arbitrators selected from FMCS panels made awards, fiscal year 1972

Issue[1]	Frequency of occurrence
General issues:	
New or reopened contract terms	29
Contract interpretation or application	2,586
Specific issues:	
Discharge and disciplinary actions	1,226
Incentive rates or standards	77
Job evaluation	387
Seniority[2]	646
Overtime[3]	363
Union officers—superseniority and union business	21
Strike or lockout issues	18
Vacations and vacation pay	132
Holidays and holiday pay	101
Scheduling of work	182
Reporting, call-in, and call-back pay	77
Health and welfare	51
Pensions	21
Other fringe benefits	92
Scope of agreement[4]	211
Working conditions, including safety	48
Arbitrability of grievance[5]	261
Miscellaneous	237

[1] Compilations based on the number of arbitration awards for which data were available; that is 3,414 of the 3,432 awards. Some awards involved more than one issue.
[2] Includes promotion and upgrading (137), layoff, bumping, recall (327), transfer (96), and other matters (86).
[3] Includes pay (172), distribution of overtime (172), and compulsory overtime (19).
[4] Includes subcontracting (92), jurisdictional disputes (17), foreman, supervision, and so on (61), mergers, consolidations, accretion, other plants (11).
[5] Includes procedural (141), substantive (68), procedural/substantive (32), and other issues (20).

From James F. Power, "Improving Arbitration: Roles of Parties and Agencies," *Monthly Labor Review*, 95:21 (November 1972).

they cannot agree, they must turn to an impartial agency for the selection.[17]

Those impartial agencies that are most widely utilized in the selection of arbitrators are the Federal Mediation and Conciliation Service and the American Arbitration Association. Both

agencies maintain rosters of qualified arbitrators and will submit lists from which an arbitrator can be chosen by the parties. If desired, these agencies will select the arbitrator.[18]

[17] Ibid., 263:503.

[18] For a description of these procedures see "Rules of American Arbitration Association," *Labor Policy and Practice*, 263:411 (1965); and "Federal Mediation and Conciliation Ser-

However, many arbitrators are selected directly by the parties without going through an intermediary.

Labor arbitrators come from many walks of life, but according to a 1970 survey of the National Academy of Arbitrators, professors and lawyers constitute the majority among their ranks. About 36 percent were found to have degrees in law, and 29 percent had a Ph.D. degree. The average age was fifty-seven.[19]

The average per diem rate charged by arbitrators in 1971 was $163.88 and the average fee charged was $480.88, indicating that the average arbitration case took about three days of the arbitrator's time.[20] This time would include studying the submission agreement—a document prepared by the union and management stating what issue or general problem the arbitrator is expected to decide—conducting the hearing, and writing the decision. Additional expenses charged by arbitrators averaged $85.71, which brought the average total charged to $566.59.[21] The parties generally agree ahead of time to share these expenses.

THE ROLES OF THE ARBITRATOR AND THE COURTS

The arbitrator's role is generally considered quasi-judicial, that is, analogous to, or approaching the role of, a judge. He or she is expected to listen to evidence, weigh it impartially and objectively, and make a decision based on the labor contract.

There are some important differences between the arbitrator's role and that of a judge, however. In the first place, arbitrational hearings tend to be much more informal than courtroom proceedings. The parties may or may not have legal counsel present at the hearings, and the proceedings are not bound by the rules of evidence as in a court of law. However, the proceedings are expected to be conducted with dignity and fairness, and they are likely to include the cross-examination of the parties or witnesses and the submission of documents as evidence.[22]

Secondly, since both parties have agreed to submit a problem to an impartial third party for a final and binding solution, they have agreed in advance not to appeal the decision. Since the parties have signed a contract to this effect, both federal and state courts will ordinarily enforce arbitrational awards and will not disturb an arbitrational decision, unless there is evidence of fraud, corruption, incorrect calculations, or misconduct on the part of the arbitrator, such as refusal to hear evidence.[23] Further, in the famous *Trilogy* cases, the Supreme Court held that an award must be enforced if the arbitrator remained within the limits of the *submission agreement* and if the arbitration based the decision on an interpretation of the labor contract.[24] In short, courts ordinarily will not review the substance of an arbitrator's award. Whether a case should go to arbitration, however, often becomes a question for a court to decide, as we shall see later.

vice: Arbitation Policies, Functions, and Procedures," text of Regulations, Part 1404, effective January 8, 1957.

[19]Maurice S. Trotta, *Arbitration of Labor-Management Disputes* (New York: Amacom, 1974), p. 65. Because acceptable younger arbitrators are tending not to fill vacancies in the ranks of arbitrators due to retirements and death, the U.S. Department of Labor has undertaken a number of projects designed to train arbitrators. The training involves university classes and apprenticeship with experienced arbitrators. See Usery, "Attempts to Reduce Arbitration Costs," pp. 4–6; and Power, "Improving Arbitration," pp. 17–20.

[20]*Twenty-Fourth Annual Report, Fiscal Year 1971*, Federal Mediation and Conciliation Service, 1972, p. 55.

[21]Ibid.

[22]For more details on the expected conduct of the arbitrator, see "Code of Professional Responsibility For Arbitrators of Labor-Management Disputes," approved by the National Academy of Arbitrators, the American Arbitration Association, and the Federal Mediation and Conciliation Service, April 1975. Reprinted in Bureau of National Affairs, *Collective Bargaining*, Vol. 1, 17:51 through 17:59, May 22, 1975.

[23]Clarence M. Updegraff and Whitley P. McCoy, *Arbitration of Labor Disputes* (Washington, D.C.: The Bureau of National Affairs, 1961), p. 216.

[24]See Thomas J. McDermott, "Arbitrability: The Courts vs. the Arbitrator," *The Arbitration Journal*, 23:18–27, No. 1 (1968).

Thirdly, the role of the arbitrator differs from that of the judge in that the arbitrator is not bound by precedent to the extent that the judge is—by the principle of *stare decisis*.[25] Although the arbitrator may study decisions of other arbitrators in order to sharpen understanding of the issues and although both parties may cite arbitrational decisions in support of their positions, an arbitrator is not *bound* by the decisions of other arbitrators. On the other hand, following precedents established in arbitration awards earlier in the relationship between the parties is recommended in order to give consistency to the particular relationship and to minimize unnecessary grievances.[26] Nevertheless, the degree to which precedent should be followed and actually is followed in arbitration is highly controversial.

A major problem faced by the arbitrator is whether to hand down a decision based on a personal concept of the arbitrator's role or whether to behave in a way expected by the parties. The quasi-judicial role is ordinarily expected; but the arbitrator is sometimes expected to be, in Davey's words, a "mutual friend," a "father-confessor," a "labor relations psychiatrist," or a mediator, and is sometimes expected to use a "split-the-difference" approach.[27] Most arbitrators tend to carry out the quasi-judi-

cial role, although many variations of this role and many exceptions can be found, depending upon the convictions of the arbitrator and other factors discussed later.

In general, the authority of the arbitrator is limited by the submission agreement. This agreement, sometimes called a "stipulation" or an "agreement to arbitrate," describes the dispute and the authority that can be exercised by the arbitrator, and is signed by both parties.

PRECEDENT IN ARBITRATION AWARDS

As indicated above, an arbitrator is not bound by the decisions of arbitrators in other union-management relationships, or, for that matter, by previous arbitration decisions under the contract in question, although precedent is usually followed in the latter case. However, arbitrators' decisions are widely reported and carefully studied by other arbitrators, managements, and unions.[28] One survey found that 77 percent of 238 responding arbitrators believed that precedent, including awards under other contracts, should be given some weight in decision making.[29]

Although the use of previous arbitrational awards in preparing and analyzing new cases is recommended by the American Arbitration Association, a number of authors are alarmed by what they feel is excessive perusal of previous cases. These authors assert that such use may encourage the belief that there are "universal" principles in labor-management relations and may minimize the wide differences among spe-

[25] The entire maxim is *stare decisis et non quieta movere*: "to adhere to precedents and not unsettle things which are established." From *Black's Law Dictionary*, 3rd ed. (St. Paul, Minn.: West Publishing Co., 1933). It should not be assumed that the judge is completely bound by the principle of *stare decisis*. For essays on *stare decisis*, see Walter F. Murphy and C. Herman Pritchett, eds., *Courts, Judges, and Politics* (New York: Random House, 1961), pp. 376–381; William O. Douglas, "Stare Decisis," *Columbia Law Review*, 49:735–737 (June 1949); and Frank Elkouri and Edna Elkouri, *How Arbitration Works*, 2nd ed. (Washington, D.C.: The Bureau of National Affairs, 1960), pp. 248–251.

[26] Harold W. Davey, *Contemporary Collective Bargaining*, 2nd ed. (Englewood Cliffs, N.J.: Prentice-Hall, Inc., 1959), pp. 149, 150.

[27] Ibid., p. 38. For further discussion of the role of the arbitrator, see Trotta, *Arbitration of Labor-Management Disputes*, p. 71ff.

[28] In addition to "significant" decisions reported in books, journals, and magazines, arbitrational awards are published systematically in such publications as *Labor Arbitration Reports* (Washington, D.C.: Bureau of National Affairs), and *American Labor Arbitration Awards* (Englewood Cliffs, N.J.: Prentice-Hall). Management's bulletins and reports in magazines tend to comment on arbitrational awards like this: "You may be required to . . . if you don't . . ."—thus implying that the award establishes, or almost establishes, precedent.

[29] Elkouri and Elkouri, *How Arbitration Works*, p. 247.

cific situations, including the particular contract. Other authors defend the increasing reliance on precedent, orderly procedures, and a "common law" of arbitration.[30] The question of the proper application of precedent and "universal principle" is the central problem in labor arbitration today. In coming to a conclusion about this problem, it is helpful to make a distinction between *authoritative precedent* and *persuasive precedent* relative to a court of law. Decisions establishing authoritative precedent must be followed by the judge in making his award. For example, a federal district court judge must follow decisions of the U.S. Supreme Court. Decisions establishing persuasive precedent are those that the judge need not follow but that may be considered and given whatever weight the case merits.[31] As an example, a state court need not follow a decision of a federal district court. To apply this distinction to the field of arbitration, arbitration awards do not establish authoritative precedent, but in practice they can and do establish persuasive precedent.

Although conflicting arbitration awards can be found on almost any subject, an analysis of trends in arbitration awards clearly suggests that a body of "industrial-relations common law" is evolving through the persuasive weight of arbitration decisions. For example, in disciplinary cases, arbitrators almost universally hold that the burden of proof is on the company to show "just cause," and that the punishment must "fit the crime."[32] When the case involves the discharge of an employee and the employee is reinstated, arbitrators award none, some, or all back pay and will avoid substitute penalties, such as forfeiture of overtime work.[33] Discharge or other disciplinary action for not meeting production standards is often upheld by arbitrators, provided the company can demonstrate that the standards exist and that adequate records are kept on employees' performance. On the other hand, precipitate tightening of discipline without adequate warning is not likely to be upheld by arbitrators.[34]

In my opinion, the evolution of an industrial-relations common law is proper and desirable *up to a point*, provided that it is evolved from persuasive precedent rather than authoritiative precedent. Arbitrators and the parties to a contract are wise to study arbitration awards, to benefit from the analysis of the issues and the reasoning behind awards in similar situations, and then to utilize the relevant aspects of such awards in analyzing the immediate problem. But it is imperative that the weight given such decisions be appropriate, depending upon the degree of similarity in the contracts, the intent of the parties in agreeing on the contract's language, and the past practice of the parties. Each situation involving a grievance is unique and must be evaluated on its own merits.

DIFFERENT TYPES OF ARBITRATION

Thus far, the most frequently used form of arbitration has been discussed, but there are other forms and/or nuances which should be mentioned. In particular, expedited arbitration, interest arbitration, and final-offer arbitration will be described briefly.

Expedited arbitration is simply an accelerated

---

[30]See, for example, Paul H. Tobias, "In Defense of Creeping Legalism in Arbitration," *Industrial and Labor Relations Review*, 13:596–607 (July 1960).

[31]This discussion is based on Elkouri and Elkouri, *How Arbitration Works*, pp. 248–265; and Murphy and Pritchett, *Courts, Judges, and Politics*, pp. 376–381.

[32]Harold W. Davey, "The Arbitrator Speaks on Discharge and Discipline," *The Arbitration Journal*, 17:98, No. 2 (1962).

[33]This example is given in Morris Stone, *Labor-Management Contracts at Work* (New York: Harper & Brothers, 1961), pp. 290–291.

[34]Lawrence Stessin, "Is the Arbitrator Management's Friend in Discipline Cases?" *Monthly Labor Review*, 82:374 (April 1959).

arbitration procedure. Under the rules for expedited arbitration as recommended by the American Arbitration Association, the two parties to the dispute do not file prehearing or posthearing briefs, there is no stenographic record taken, awards are made within five days from the end of the hearing, and the arbitrator's opinions, when required, are very short. The major advantages to this procedure are savings in time and costs. Experience since 1972, when this alternative approach was initiated by the American Arbitration Association, has generally been positive.[35]

Interest arbitration involves submitting to an arbitrator any point the parties cannot agree on relative to a future contract. For example, under the Experimental Negotiation Agreement between the United Steelworkers and ten steel companies, points of dispute in bargaining are submitted to an arbitrator, thus avoiding a strike or lockout.[36] (See also Chapter 24.)

Final-offer arbitration is sometimes called "last-offer ballot," or "forced-choice arbitration." Under this procedure, when the two parties cannot agree, the final package as proposed by each of the two parties is submitted to an arbitrator who *must make a choice*. The usual procedure is for the arbitrator to choose one total package or the other, but some contracts permit the arbitrator to make choices, item by item.[37] Final-offer arbitration has been used in Eugene, Oregon, relative to city employees; Minnesota and Iowa adopted it for public employees; and Wisconsin, Michigan, and Massachusetts adopted the procedure for police and firefighters as an alternative to strikes. The procedure has also been agreed to by the Major

League Baseball Players Association and the club owners.[38] In 1974, as reported by Staudohar, fifty-four out of about five hundred players submitted salary disputes to arbitration and twenty-nine awards were made. Arbitrators chose the club's offer in sixteen cases and the player's offer in thirteen. For example, McNally of the Orioles requested $115,000, the club offered $105,000, and the arbitrator ruled for the player. Bahnsen of the White Sox requested $82,500 in contrast to the club's offer of $70,000, the case went to arbitration, and the arbitrator ruled in favor of the club.[39]

Proponents of final-offer arbitration argue that the procedure is a strong motivator to bargain at least close to agreement in fear that the arbitrator will see one's position as unreasonable and make the award to the other side. Critics argue that it has no greater strike-deterrent effect than interest arbitration, and that the awards are ordinarily very one-sided. Further, arbitrators are frequently frustrated by being required to choose one package or the other when each party's proposal may have some desirable aspects. On the other hand, if the arbitrator is permitted to choose item by item, the parties may be tempted to submit extraneous items in hope of acceptance by the arbitrator.[40]

IMPACT OF ENVIRONMENTAL FACTORS
LAW

THE GRIEVANCE PROCEDURE Although grievances are typically processed with union help and under a clause on grievance negotiated by the union and management, the Taft-Hartley Act specifically permits individual employees or groups of employees to present grievances to the employer without the intervention of the

[35]Michael F. Hoellering, "Expedited Arbitration of Labor Grievances," *Monthly Labor Review*, 98:51–53 (April 1975).
[36]Betty Southard Murphy, "The Chairman Looks at the NLRB," *The Personnel Administrator*, 21:26 (May 1976).
[37]Paul D. Staudohar, "Results of Final-Offer Arbitration of Bargaining Disputes," *California Management Review*, 18:57–61 (Fall 1975).

[38]Ibid., p. 58.
[39]Ibid., p. 60.
[40]Charles Feigenbaum, *Industrial Relations*, 14:311–317 (October 1975); and Staudohar, "Results of Final-Offer Arbitration," pp. 57–61.

bargaining representatives. The adjustment must not be inconsistent with the agreement, however, and the bargaining representative must be given the opportunity to be present when the adjustment is made.[41]

ARBITRABILITY   Arbitration also comes under the surveillance of the federal government. In addition to enforcing arbitrators' awards, the courts are empowered to determine the question of the arbitrability of an issue arising under a labor agreement. In the past, although some states had laws making an agreement to arbitrate enforceable, in some states refusal by one of the parties to arbitrate a question ended the matter.[42] Since the 1957 Supreme Court decision in the *Lincoln Mills* case, however, agreements to arbitrate have been held enforceable under Sections 203 and 301 of the Taft-Hartley Act, regardless of state law, when the contract includes a no-strike provision.[43] The Supreme Court considers arbitration a *quid pro quo* for an agreement not to strike.[44] The *Trilogy* cases further defined the role of the courts and set forth general guidelines for determining arbitrability.[45]

MANAGEMENT'S RIGHTS   Furthermore, it now appears that, unless the contract specifically excludes some topics from arbitration, all disputes are arbitrable. Exclusionary clauses written in general terms do not suffice. In the case of the *Warrior and Gulf Navigation Company*, the Supreme Court stated that courts must compel arbitration unless the arbitrational clause clearly did not cover the situation.[46] Furthermore, in the *American Manufacturing* case, the Supreme Court has ruled that courts "have no business weighing the merits of a grievance" and that even "frivolous claims" are arbitrable.[47] The net effect of such decisions most likely will be to increase the number and variety of disputes going to arbitration and the number of cases going to arbitrators for determining arbitrability of the issue. Some contracts provide that the question of arbitrability be submitted to an arbitrator, thus avoiding the necessity for court action.[48] Furthermore, managements are likely to attempt negotiation of very specific areas excluded from arbitration, rather than rely on general management-rights clauses.[49]

DAMAGE SUITS   The administration of the agreement may also be affected by Sections 301 and 303 of the Taft-Hartley Act. Section 301 states that either party may bring suit in a U.S. district court for violation of a labor contract and that any monetary judgments against unions are enforceable against the union and its assets as an entity, but not against individuals. Section 303 states that a union may be sued for secondary boycotts and other illegal activities injuring a business or property.

OTHER ENVIRONMENTAL FACTORS

PAST PRACTICE AND INTENT OF THE PARTIES   A survey of ninety leading arbitrators indicated that

---

[41]Labor Management Relations Act, 1947 (as amended), Section 9(a).

[42]Updegraff and McCoy, *Arbitration of Labor Disputes*, pp. 26–27.

[43]Russell A. Smith, "Arbitrability—The Arbitrator, the Courts, and the Parties," *The Arbitration Journal*, 17:5, No. 1 (1962); and Updegraff and McCoy, *Arbitration of Labor Disputes*, p. 26.

[44]Updegraff and McCoy, *Arbitration of Labor Disputes*, p. 26.

[45]See McDermott, "Arbitrability—The Courts vs. the Arbitrator," p. 22.

[46]See *Fourteenth Annual Report of the FMCS*, p. 40. In the *Warrior and Gulf* case, Justice Douglas stated that the arbitrator should not only decide a case on the basis of the contract but on the potential effect on productivity, shop morale, and whether tensions will be heightened or diminished. See Smith, "Arbitrability—Arbitrator, Courts and Parties," p. 9.

[47]"Labor Arbitration in the Federal Courts," *The Arbitration Journal*, 15:114, No. 3 (1960).

[48]Sam Kagel, *Anatomy of a Labor Arbitration* (Washington, D.C.: Bureau of National Affairs, 1961), p. 9.

[49]For an article recommending this approach, see James C. Center, "The Strange New Doctrine of Arbitration," *Personnel Journal*, 39:260 (December 1960).

arbitrators are inclined to give considerable weight to consistent past practice in the particular union-management relationship when the contract is silent or ambiguous with reference to a particular problem.[50] Although arbitrators differ as to the scope of application of this "principle," nevertheless past practice tends to become part of the labor contract, and unilateral changes by management in the interim between negotiations are likely to be challenged through the grievance procedure and through arbitration.

The intent of the parties when they negotiated the contract is also given considerable weight if the contract is ambiguous. Thus, the arbitrator often makes inquiry into the meaning of the contract language at the time the contract was negotiated.[51]

SOCIAL CUSTOMS AND MORES I have already pointed out that the arbitrator's own perception of his or her proper role may have an impact on the decision rendered. If arbitrators think of themselves as interpreters of a contract, one kind of decision may be handed down; if they think of themselves as dispensers of fairness or justice, another kind of decision may be forthcoming. In general, however, arbitrators are not immune to the impact of the broader cultural environment of which they are a part. Thus, the prevailing sense of justice and fair play tends to be given expression in their awards, as shown, for example, in the belief that the "punishment should fit the crime."

PRESSURES ON THE GRIEVANCE PROCEDURE AND THE ARBITRATOR During the processing of a grievance, shop stewards or members of the union grievance committee may be subjected to considerable pressure from the aggrieved worker to push a grievance to further steps or to arbitration. Likewise, union officials may wish to press the case as a test of strength or to "get back" at management. Similarly, supervisors and higher managerial officials may be pressured by other members of management to settle or not to settle the grievance, depending upon the current labor-relations climate in the organization.

Arbitrators are also subject to considerable pressure of a different sort. Articles featuring criticism of decisions appear in both union and managerial journals and magazines, and both parties are likely to keep a "box score" of the awards of particular arbitrators. An arbitrator deciding too many cases in favor of the union may soon fall out of favor with management, and vice versa. Such pressures are likely to have an impact on individual arbitrators, although undoubtedly the vast majority of arbitrators make a conscientious effort to remain impartial and objective when rendering their decisions.

MANAGERIAL SKILLS AND ATTITUDES Supervisory skills in dealing with subordinates obviously play a major role in minimizing the number of grievances and arbitration cases. Supervisors unfamiliar with the contract or prone to alienate and antagonize workers are likely to be focal points for a disproportionate share of grievances. Similarly, the quality of relationship between higher management and union officials will affect the degree to which the union is disposed to press cases to arbitration. And, of course, inordinate pressures to get out production, or capricious or too restrictive work rules may result in hostilities and friction on the shop or plant floor. Thus, the frequency of use of the grievance-arbitration process is a function of the training and effectiveness of management at all levels of the organization and of the personalities and militancy of union members and officers.

---

[50]Charles T. Doyle, "Past Practice as a Standard in Arbitration," *Personnel*, 39:63–69 (May-June 1962).
[51]Elkouri and Elkouri, *How Arbitration Works*, pp. 203–204.

RELATIONSHIP TO OTHER PROCESSES

It is apparent that the grievance-arbitration process is inextricably interrelated with the process of contract negotiations. What the parties intended when they negotiated the contract may become an important element in an arbitration decision, and the arbitrator's decision may prompt one or both parties to seek a revision in the contract. Similarly, ambiguous or vague contractual clauses may precipitate grievances to test the meaning of the contract's language. In addition, if a high degree of controversy and hostility characterize negotiations, a similar spirit may carry over into the administration of the contract, and vice versa.

The grievance-arbitration process is also inseparable from the broader process of justice within the organization. Although a grievance may take on overtones of politics and power, the grievance-arbitration process is in large measure the instrument through which the rank-and-file unionized worker seeks a degree of justice in the work situation.

Like negotiations of contracts, the grievance-arbitration process may have a profound effect on management's freedom to manage both the personnel management subprocesses and the broader general processes. For example, the process of task specialization—the organization of work and shop rules—can be shaped and molded by arbitration rulings. This impact on the specializing process, in turn, affects the broad materials-management process. That is, arbitration rulings may affect management's freedom in redesigning the flow of materials to the extent that the rulings restrict the scope of jobs, the number of men or crews, and standards of output. Similarly, the broad financial- and marketing-management processes may be affected if arbitration rulings prevent desired efficiencies and reductions in costs, a situation which in turn can affect the price of the products offered for sale.

This is not to say that the grievance-arbitration process inevitably has a restrictive effect on the management of the enterprise's processes—in general, the opposite is probably true, as will be shown later under the topic of "validity"—but the grievance-arbitration process may have such an impact on specific situations. Although arbitrators are generally of the opinion that "management must manage," loose contractual clauses and loose administrative practices may set the stage for unfavorable arbitration rulings.

EFFECT ON NEED FULFILLMENT

As in unionization and negotiating contracts, the grievance-arbitration procedure may give expression to a variety of human wants and needs. The self-esteem needs—independence, dominance, and achievement, in particular—and the need for the esteem of others—recognition, attention—find expression in filing a grievance against management and pushing the complaint to a satisfactory conclusion. The assistance of the steward and the union officers enhances the fulfillment of the needs for belonging and cooperation. Even if the grievance is eventually denied, the employee involved may feel that he or she has had a fair hearing, and the probability of a perception of justice is increased if the grievance is submitted to an impartial arbitrator.

The grievance-arbitration process also establishes orderly machinery for the airing of pent-up emotions which otherwise might be turned toward sabotage, work stoppages, and other forms of defensive behavior. Although a grievance may be denied, careful handling of the problem by both union and management may permit the aggrieved worker to "save face" through a friendly—yet firm—processing of the case. Belligerent and legalistic arguments by the parties may do just the opposite, increasing hostility and magnifying the problem.

AUTHORITY AND ACCOUNTABILITY

Under a grievance-arbitration procedure, either party may agree to the recommended decision of the other party. Disagreement will automatically send the grievance to a higher level, with this process culminating in arbitration. As has been shown earlier, the courts have authority to enforce the procedure since both parties have signed a contract to this effect.

Once a grievance is filed, its processing is likely to be entirely out of the hands of the aggrieved rank-and-file employee, and union and managerial officials will determine how far the matter is pursued. Supervisors and middle managers are not likely to be given unlimited authority in settling grievances, but they will be expected to try to solve problems within the confines of the contract or to make only those concessions in which higher management concurs. Typically, the industrial-relations department will be consulted at various steps of the grievance procedure and will carefully assess the implications of alternatives. Depending upon the particular company, top operating officials or the industrial-relations department, or both, will decide the company's position concerning whether a case will go to arbitration. Ordinarily, the industrial-relations department is heavily involved in this decision.

When a case goes to arbitration, the industrial-relations director is likely to be the chief strategist for the company, unless the firm is represented by an attorney. The immediate supervisor involved in the case and other members of management are likely to participate in planning the arbitration presentation, however, and may be used as witnesses.

CONSEQUENCES OF SYSTEMATIZATION

Establishing grievance and arbitration procedures produces two important consequences:
(1) a tendency to insure careful attention to employee's and union complaints, and (2) if no agreement is reached, a solution that the parties have agreed to abide by. Thus, the use of more costly procedures, such as lockouts and strikes, is precluded during the term of the agreement.

Criticism has been directed toward too high a degree of systematization in arbitration, however. Many feel that excessive reliance on courtroom procedures and previous decisions is not the best way to achieve a satisfactory accommodation between the union and management. They believe such oversystematization establishes unnecessary "ritual" which handicaps the arbitrator in making an award in the best interests of labor-management relations. This question is much debated, but the trend seems to be toward greater systematization, not less.

VALIDITY AND RELIABILITY OF GRIEVANCE-ARBITRATION PROCEDURES

RELIABILITY

As a communicative device, the grievance procedure is considered by Dunlop and Healy to be more reliable than the usual chain-of-command procedures in both the union and managerial hierarchy. Since the claims and arguments of either side are immediately subjected to scrutiny by the other side, these authors believe that the grievance procedure is less likely to tolerate self-serving statements than most communications in the chain of command.[52]

Reporting of arbitration awards and the concept of persuasive precedent serve to increase the consistency (reliability) of arbitration. That is, what arbitrators have said before indicates future decisions in similar cases. That the de-

---

[52] John T. Dunlop, and James J. Healy, *Collective Bargaining: Principles and Cases* (Homewood, Ill.: Richard D. Irwin, 1955), p. 79.

sirability of this trend is highly controversial has been pointed out.

VALIDITY

In general, grievance-arbitration procedures would seem to contribute to organizational goals by minimizing the possibility of sabotage and work stoppages. The Congress that passed the Taft-Hartley Act evidently believed this to be the case, because the law, directed toward minimizing "industrial strife which interferes with the normal flow of commerce," contains a section stating that "final adjustment by a method agreed upon by the parties is hereby declared to be the desirable method for the settlement of grievance disputes arising over the application or interpretation of an existing collective bargaining agreement."[53] Thus, Congress believed, and presumably still believes, that arbitration effectively minimizes industrial conflict and therefore interferences in commerce.

Grievance-arbitration procedures probably also serve to check those supervisory practices that may lead to lowered morale and defensive behavior. Furthermore, the grievance-arbitration procedures give both union and management a respite between the annual, or less frequent, renegotiation of the contract. In a sense, they permit both parties to take a vacation from the threat of a strike or lockout.

The grievance-arbitration process cannot be said to contribute to organizational goals without qualification, however. When an arbitration decision severely restricts the flexibility of management in subcontracting work or when an arbitration award reinstates an employee clearly attempting to frustrate management's objectives, the grievance-arbitration process obviously does not contribute to organizational

goals. On the other hand, the defect may not be in this process but in the wording of the contract or in management's loose disciplinary practices. Sometimes arbitrators do make mistakes, but more often an absence of managerial foresight and a lack of meticulousness in managing is at the root of the problem. Unions, too, must assume their share of responsibility for pressing grievances that, although they may be "won," are not in the best interests of both parties.

Joint, long-range problem solving of major issues is likely to be much more satisfactory to both parties than reliance on either crisis bargaining or the grievance-arbitration process. The author of a study on bargaining in the glass industry, for example, concludes that issues surrounding incentive systems, crew sizes, and seniority rules are much better resolved through ". . . extended treatment of workplace issues by the parties themselves. . . ."[54] As discussed in the previous chapter, however, this requires a shift in the attitudes of leaders in both parties toward an integrative concept of bargaining.

SUMMARY

Grievance-arbitration procedures are found almost universally in labor-management arrangements and are supported by public policy. Although most would agree that such procedures are vital in effective day-to-day administration of the labor contract, many observers are concerned about recent court decisions on what is arbitrable and about the apparently growing tendency of arbitrators to give weight to persuasive precedent. In short, the grievance-arbitration process is being molded by a growing body of law and "arbitration common law,"

---

[53] Labor Management Relations Act, 1947, Sections 1 and 203(d).

[54] Trevor Bain, "Arbitration: An Alternative to Crisis Bargaining," *The Arbitration Journal*, 23:109, No. 2 (1968).

and its ultimate form cannot be ascertained at this time.

It can be generally said that grievance-arbitration procedures have been effective in solving day-to-day problems under a labor agreement, in identifying areas where contract language and supervision require improvement, and in minimizing work stoppages and sabotage. These procedures are such a vital part of the broad collective-bargaining process that both labor and management would be wise to assess periodically the external influences described above. In addition, the more the parties can use a joint problem-solving approach aimed at reaching creative solutions where everyone "wins," the less likely the grievance-arbitrarion process will be the focal point of a win-lose conflict. In the ideal situation, grievance-arbitration procedures are safety valves and guarantees of a substantial level of organizational justice, with managers and subordinates working toward a climate of sufficient responsiveness to each other so that the formal procedures play a secondary, although significant, role in problem solving.

REVIEW AND DISCUSSION QUESTIONS

1. Describe a typical grievance procedure.

2. What is the difference between authoritative and persuasive precedent?

3. What weight do arbitrators give to precedent in arbitration decisions, and what weight, in your opinion, *should* they give?

4. Discuss the role of the arbitrator. How does it differ from the role of a mediator?

5. What is expedited arbitration? Interest arbitration? Final-offer arbitration?

6. What role does the court system play with respect to arbitration?

7. Discuss arbitration in the light of the discussion of distributive and integrative collective bargaining in Chapter 24.

8. What is the validity of labor arbitration from the standpoint of organizational goal attainment?

9. With reference to Chapter 8 and this chapter, is the principle of the grievance procedure applicable to nonunionized employees, or is it mainly workable in the unionized situation? Discuss its application to (a) production employees, (b) office employees, (c) professional employees, and (d) supervisors.

SUPPLEMENTAL REFERENCES

Aaron, Benjamin, "The Individual's Legal Rights as an Employee," *Monthly Labor Review*, 86:666–673 (June 1963).

Amis, Lewis R., "Due Process in Disciplinary Procedures," *Labor Law Journal*, 27:94–98 (February 1976).

Bakke, E. Wight, Clark Kerr, and Charles Anrod, *Unions, Management, and the Public*, 3rd ed. (New York: Harcourt, Brace & Company, 1967).

Beal, Edwin E., Edward D. Wickersham, and Philip Kienast, *The Practice of Collective Bargaining*, 4th ed. (Homewood, Ill., Richard D. Irwin, Inc., 1972).

Cahn, Sidney L., "Some Ways to Control Arbitration Costs: An Arbitrator's View," *Monthly Labor Review*, 98:31–35 (June 1975).

Colfax, J. David, "Labor Responds to Compulsory Arbitration: Organizational Correlates of Protest and Acquiescence," *Industrial and Labor Relations Review*, 20:76–87 (October 1966).

Coulson, Robert, "Experiments in Labor Arbitration," *Labor Law Journal*, 17:259–265 (May 1966).

Davey, Harold W., *Contemporary Collective Bargaining*, 3rd ed. (Englewood Cliffs, N.J.: Prentice-Hall, Inc., 1972).

Gershenfold, Walter J., "Compulsory Arbitration Is Ready When You Are," *Labor Law Journal*, 23:153–166 (March 1972).

Handsaker, Morrison, "Grievance-Arbitration and Mediated Settlements," *Labor Law Journal,* 17:579–583 (October 1966).

Jennings, Kenneth, "Arbitrators, Blacks, and Discipline," *Personnel Journal,* 54:32–37ff. (January 1975).

Jones, Dallas L., ed., *The Arbitrator, the NLRB, and the Courts* (Washington, D.C.: Bureau of National Affairs, 1967), Proceedings of the Twentieth Annual Meeting, National Academy of Arbitrators.

Kagel, S., and J. Kagel, "Using Two New Arbitration Techniques," *Monthly Labor Review,* 95:11–14 (November 1972).

King, Geoffrey R., "Seniority, Technological Change, and Arbitration," *The Personnel Administrator,* 19:23–27 (September 1974).

Kuhn, James S., "The Grievance Process," Chapter 10 in John T. Dunlop and Neil W. Chamberlain, eds., *Frontiers of Collective Bargaining* (New York: Harper & Row, Publishers, 1967).

Laffer, Kingsley, "Compulsory Arbitration: The Australian Experience," *Monthly Labor Review,* 95:49–53 (May 1972).

Lythgoe, R.F., "On Improving Arbitration: The Transcript Trauma," *Monthly Labor Review,* 97:47–50 (June 1974).

Menard, Arthur P., "The National Labor Relations Board—No Longer a Threat to the Arbitral Process?" *Labor Law Journal,* 23:140–152 (March 1972).

Prasow, Paul, and Edward Peters, *Arbitration and Collective Bargaining: Conflict Resolution in Labor Relations* (New York: McGraw-Hill Book Company, 1970).

Rehmus, Charles M., "Legislated Interest Arbitration," in James L. Stern and Barbara D. Dennis, *Proceedings of the Twenty-Seventh Annual Winter Meeting* (Madison, Wisc.: Industrial Relations Research Association, 1975), pp. 307–314.

Sayles, Leonard R., and George Strauss, *The Local Union,* rev. ed. (New York: Harcourt, Brace & World, Inc., 1967), Chapter 2.

Scott, William G., "An Issue in Administrative Justice: Managerial Appeal Systems," *Management International Review,* 6:37–53, No. 1 (1966).

Silver, Isidore, "The Corporate Ombudsman," *Harvard Business Review,* 45:77–78 (May-June 1967).

Trotta, Maurice S., *Arbitration of Labor-Management Disputes* (New York: Amacom, 1974).

Wallen, Saul, "Arbitrators and Judges Dispelling the Hay Haze," *California Management Review,* 9:17–24 (Spring 1967).

PART 9
ORGANIZATION DEVELOPMENT AND THE PERSONNEL DEPARTMENT

26. Organization Development: Organizational Improvement through Action Research

27. The Personnel Department: Its Emerging Role

This final section of the book will deal with two topics that, in my view, are of great importance to personnel management. The first, organization development (Chapter 26), has to do with a unique organization improvement strategy growing out of the behavioral sciences that has major implications for managing the various personnel subsystems, for labor-management problem solving, and for managing the culture of an organization. The second (Chapter 27) will largely focus on the personnel department.

This chapter will discuss some of the factors associated with the creation of a personnel department, its structure, typical functions, and the role of the corporate personnel director. In addition, the chapter will discuss a major challenge confronting the corporate personnel executive and staff—a challenge stemming from the applied behavioral sciences. Finally, the chapter will examine the emerging role of the personnel department for the 1980s.

CHAPTER 26
ORGANIZATION DEVELOPMENT: ORGANIZATIONAL IMPROVEMENT THROUGH ACTION RESEARCH

This chapter will describe an approach to organization improvement, organization development (OD), that has extensive implications for managing organizations and for personnel management. While on the surface it appears to focus on the "people" domain, this approach can serve as an "umbrella" strategy under which other kinds of improvement efforts, such as MBO (management by objectives) or the introduction of a computer, can emerge in a more participative, diagnostic way.

Before describing what organization development efforts look like in practice, I will first define the term, briefly discuss the history of OD, and then identify some of the assumptions and values underlying this approach. The chapter will then move on to a description of typical OD interventions.

A DEFINITION

Although a literal interpretation of the phrase *organization development* could refer to a wide range of strategies for improving organizations, the term has come to take on some fairly specific meanings in the behavioral science literature and in practice. I say "fairly specific" because the boundaries are not entirely clear, perceptions of different authors and practitioners vary, and the field is evolving rapidly.

As we have defined the process elsewhere, and in the behavioral science sense of the term,

. . . organization development is a long-range effort to improve an organization's problem-solving and renewal processes, particularly through a more effective and collaborative management of organization culture—with special emphasis on the culture of formal work teams—with the assistance of a change agent, or catalyst, and the use of the theory and technology of applied behavioral science, including action research.[1]

This definition recognizes certain features of organization development that, when included in a total strategy, differentiate organization development from other organization improvement strategies that have appeared in the past. These features are:

1. The use of an action research model

2. An emphasis on the work team as the key unit for learning more effective modes of organizational behavior (In contrast, management development focuses on the individual as the key unit.[2])

3. An emphasis on a collaborative management of the culture[3] of work teams and the total organization

4. The use of a change agent, or catalyst

5. Consultant emphasis, although not exclusively so, on group and organizational processes in contrast to making extensive recommendations for change

6. Attention to total system ramifications of the improvement effort

7. A view of the change effort as an ongoing process.

Organization development as I have defined it is relatively new, but such planned improvement programs are increasingly evident within the United States, Japan, England, the Netherlands, Norway, Sweden, and other countries. Among the growing number of organizations that have embarked to some degree on organization development are Union Carbide, Esso, TRW Systems Group, Humble Oil, Weyerhaeuser, American Airlines, IBM, Saga Foods, National Aeronautics and Space Administration (NASA), and Imperial Chemical Industries Limited. Other kinds of institutions undertaking such efforts include public school systems, churches, hospitals, federal and state agencies, and city governments.

HISTORY

Organization development began to emerge about 1957 as an attempt to apply some of the values and insights of laboratory training to total organizations. The late Douglas McGregor, working with Union Carbide,[4] is considered one of the first behavioral scientists to talk systematically about, and to implement, an organization-development program. In collaboration with McGregor, John Paul Jones established a small internal consulting group that in large part used knowledge from the behavioral sciences in assisting line managers. Other

[1] Wendell French and Cecil H. Bell, Jr., *Organization Development: Behavioral Science Interventions for Organization Improvement* (Englewood Cliffs, N.J.: Prentice-Hall, Inc., 1973), p. 15. While I will use the word *program* from time to time, ideally, organizational development is a *process*, not just another new program of temporary quality.

[2] For further elaboration, see W. Warner Burke, "A Comparison of Management Development and Organization Development," *The Journal of Applied Behavioral Science*, 7:569–579 (September-October 1971).

[3] By "culture" we mean prevailing patterns of activities, interactions, norms, sentiments, beliefs, attitudes, values, and products. Thus, culture would include both the formal organization and the informal organization as described in Chapter 5. See also French and Bell, *Organization Development*, p. 16.

[4] Richard Beckhard, W. Warner Burke, and Fred I. Steele, "The Program for Specialists in Organization Training and Development," p. ii, mimeographed paper, NTL-Institute for Applied Behavioral Science, December, 1967; and John Paul Jones, "What's Wrong with Work?" in *What's Wrong with Work?* (New York: National Association of Manufacturers, 1967), p. 8. For a history of NTL-Institute for Applied Behavioral Science, with which Douglas McGregor was long associated in addition to his professional appointment at M.I.T., and which has been a major factor in the history of organization development, see Leland P. Bradford, "Biography of an Institution," *The Journal of Applied Behavioral Science*, 3:127–143 (April-May-June 1967).

names associated with such early efforts are Herbert Shepard and Robert Blake, who in collaboration with the Employee Relations Department of the Esso Company, launched a program of laboratory training (sensitivity training) in the company's various refineries. This program emerged in 1957 after a division in human-relations research at headquarters began to view itself as an internal consulting group offering services to field managers rather than as a research group developing reports for top management.[5] As they gained experience, the consultants moved from a pure T-group mode to working with formal work teams (superiors plus subordinates) on problems that the teams were experiencing. In addition, the consultants began to work on intergroup problems that had developed between teams. Thus, a real organizational emphasis emerged, and organization development was born.[6]

Another significant part of the history of organization development was the emergence of *survey research and feedback methodology* at M.I.T. and later at the University of Michigan, which provided some of the important consulting technology and insights subsequently used by OD specialists. As one example, in 1948 in the accounting departments of the Detroit Edison Company, researchers began systematic feedback of data from an employee and management attitude survey. In this project, the attitude survey data were fed back to participating accounting departments in what Mann calls an "interlocking chain of conferences."[7]

Some of the insights that emerged have a very contemporary OD flavor. To illustrate, in drawing conclusions from the Detroit Edison study, Baumgartel stated:

> The results of this experimental study lend support to the idea that an intensive, group discussion procedure for utilizing the results of an employee questionnaire survey can be an effective tool for introducing positive change in a business organization. It may be that the effectiveness of this method, in comparison to traditional training courses, is that it deals with the system of human relationships as a whole (superior and subordinate can change together) and it deals with each manager, supervisor, and employee in the context of his own job, his own problems, and his own work relationships.[8]

OBJECTIVES OF TYPICAL ORGANIZATION DEVELOPMENT PROGRAMS

The specific objectives of organization development programs will vary according to the diagnosis of each organization's problems. Typically, these objectives have to do with major end-result goals such as increased productivity, efficiency, profitability, and/or morale. On the other hand, a number of concomitant objectives typically emerge, reflecting problems that are common to many organizations:

1. To increase the level of trust and support among organizational members

2. To increase the incidence of confronting organizational problems, both within groups and among groups, in contrast to "sweeping problems under the rug"

[5] Harry D. Kolb, in "Introduction" to *An Action Research Program for Organization Improvement* (Ann Arbor, Mich.: The Foundation for Research in Human Behavior, 1960), p. i.

[6] Based partly on French and Bell, *Organization Development*, Chapter 3.

[7] Floyd C. Mann, "Studying and Creating Change," in Warren Bennis, Kenneth Benne, and Robert Chin, *The Planning of Change* (New York: Holt, Rinehart and Winston, 1961), pp. 605–613. Another early project that had some characteristics of contemporary organization development but was not

published for many years was the "Tremont Hotel Project." See William Foote Whyte and Edith Lentz Hamilton, *Action Research for Management* (Homewood, Ill.: Richard D. Irwin, 1965), pp. 1–282.

[8] Howard Baumgartel, "Using Employee Questionnaire Results for Improving Organizations: The Survey 'Feedback' Experiment," *Kansas Business Review*, 12:2–6 (December 1959).

3. To create an environment in which the authority of an assigned role is augmented by personal authority based on expertise and knowledge

4. To increase the openness of communications laterally, vertically, and diagonally

5. To increase the level of personal enthusiasm and satisfaction in the organization

6. To find synergistic solutions to problems with greater frequency

7. To increase the level of self- and group-responsibility in planning and implementation.

DIFFICULTIES IN CATEGORIZING

Before describing some basic assumptions and strategies of organization development, it would be well to point out that one of the difficulties encountered in discussing this emerging field is that a wide variety of activities are subsumed under this label. These activities have varied all the way from inappropriate applications of "canned" managerial developmental programs to highly responsive and skillful joint efforts of behavioral scientists and their clients.

Thus, although labels are useful, they may gloss over a wide range of phenomena. The "human relations movement," for example, has been widely written about as though it were all bad or all good. To illustrate, some critics of the movement have accused it of being "soft" and a "hand-maiden of the Establishment," of ignoring the technical methods and systems of power in organizations, and of being naively too participative. Such criticisms have no doubt been warranted in some circumstances but, in other situations, may not have been at all appropriate. Paradoxically, some major insights of the human relations movement, e.g., that the organization can be viewed as a social system and that subordinates have substantial control

over productivity, have been assimilated by its critics. In short, the problem is to distinguish between appropriateness and inappropriateness of programs and between their effectiveness and ineffectiveness. The following discussion will attempt to describe the "ideal" circumstances for organization development programs as well as to point out some pitfalls and common mistakes in efforts at organizational change.

BASIC ASSUMPTIONS

Some basic assumptions about people that underlie programs for organization development are similar to the Theory Y assumptions described in Chapter 7 and will be repeated only briefly here. On the other hand, some assumptions about groups and total systems that seem to underlie these programs will be treated more extensively. The assumptions are as follows: [9]

ABOUT PEOPLE

1. Most people have drives toward personal growth and development, and these drives are most likely to be actualized in an environment that is both supportive and challenging.

2. Most people want to make, and are capable of making, a much higher level of contribution to the attainment of organizational goals than most organizational environments permit.

ABOUT PEOPLE IN GROUPS

1. Most people wish to be accepted and to interact cooperatively with at least one small ref-

[9]In addition to being influenced by the writings of McGregor, Likert, Argyris, and others, this discussion has been influenced by "Some Assumptions About Change in Organizations," *Program for Specialists in Organization Training and Development, 1967,* a reading notebook published by NTL-Institute for Applied Behavioral Science. It has also been influenced by staff members who participated in that program.

erence group and usually with more than one group, i.e., the work group, the family group, etc.

2. One of the most psychologically relevant reference groups for most people is the work group, including peers and the superior.

3. Most people are capable of greatly increasing their effectiveness in helping their reference groups solve problems and in working effectively together.

4. If a group is to optimize its effectiveness, its formal leader cannot perform all the functions of leadership in all circumstances at all times, and the members of the group must assist each other with effective leadership and behavior as members.

ABOUT PEOPLE IN ORGANIZATIONAL SYSTEMS

1. Organizations tend to be characterized by overlapping, interdependent work groups, and the "linking pin" function of supervisors and others needs to be understood and facilitated. (See Chapter 7.)

2. What happens in the broader organization affects the small work group and vice versa.

3. What happens to one subsystem (social, technological, or administrative) will affect and be influenced by other parts of the system.

4. The culture in most organizations tends to suppress the expression of feelings that people have about each other and about where they and their organizations are heading.

5. Suppressed feelings adversely affect problem solving, personal growth, and job satisfaction.

6. The level of interpersonal trust,[10] support, and cooperation is much lower in most organizations than is either necessary or desirable.

7. Although realistic and appropriate in some situations, "win-lose" strategies among people and groups do not provide optimal long-run solutions to most organizational problems.

8. Synergistic solutions—creative solutions in which two plus two equals more than four and by which all parties gain more through cooperation than through conflict—can be achieved with much greater frequency than is actually the case in most organizations.[11]

9. Viewing feelings as data important to the organization tends to open many avenues for improving goals, leadership, communications, problem solving, intergroup collaboration, and morale.

10. Improved performance stemming from efforts at organizational development needs to be sustained by appropriate changes in the appraisal, compensation, training, staffing, and task-specialization subsystems—in short, in the total personnel system.

VALUES AND BELIEFS OF CHANGE AGENTS

While scientific inquiry ideally is value free, the applications of science are not. Behavioral scientists acting as consultants in organization development tend to subscribe to a comparable set of values. On the other hand, we should avoid assuming that they constitute a completely homogenous group; they do not.

One value to which many change agents give high priority is that the needs and aspirations of human beings are the reasons for organized effort in society. They tend, therefore, to be developmental in their outlook and concerned with long-range opportunities for the personal growth of people in organizations.

[10] For research that suggests that lack of trust is a highly significant deterrent to effective problem solving, see Dale E. Zand, "Trust and Managerial Problem Solving," *Administrative Science Quarterly*, 17:229–239 (June 1972).

[11] Cattell defines synergy as "the sum total of the energy which a group can command." Daniel Katz and Robert L. Kahn, *The Social Psychology of Organizations* (New York: John Wiley & Sons, 1966), p. 33.

A second value is that work and life can become richer and more meaningful, and organized effort more effective and enjoyable if feelings and sentiments are considered more legitimate parts of the culture. A third value is a commitment to action along with a commitment to research in an effort to improve the effectiveness of organizations.[12] A fourth value—or perhaps a belief—is that improved competency in interpersonal and intergroup relationships will result in more effective organizations.[13] A fifth value is that research in behavioral science and an examination of the assumptions and values in behavioral science are relevant and important aspects of organizational effectiveness. While many change agents are perhaps overly oriented toward action in utilizing their time, nevertheless, as a group they are paying more and more attention to research and the examination of ideas.[14]

The value placed on research and inquiry raises the question of whether the assumptions stated earlier in the chapter represent values or theories that conform with "facts." In my judgment, a substantial body of knowledge, including the research cited in the chapter on leadership, suggests a considerable factual basis for these assumptions. Nevertheless, to conclude that they are facts, laws, or principles would be to contradict the value placed by behavioral scientists on continual research and inquiry. Thus, in my opinion, they should be considered theoretical statements based on provisional data.

These theories raise the paradox: The belief that people are important tends to result in their being important. The belief that people can grow and develop in terms of personal and organizational competency tends to produce this result. Thus, values and beliefs tend to be self-fulfilling, and the question becomes "What do you want to believe?" Although this position can become Pollyanna-ish in the sense of not seeing the real world, nevertheless, behavioral scientists (at least this one), who are change agents, tend to place a value on optimism. It is a kind of optimism that says people can do a better job of setting goals, facing up to problems, and solving problems, not an optimism that says the number of problems is diminishing.

Furthermore, it is important that the values and beliefs of each change agent be made visible both to that person and to the client. In the first place, neither can learn to adequately trust the other without much exposure—a hidden agenda handicaps both the building of trust and mutual learning. Secondly, and perhaps more pragmatically, efforts at organizational change tend to fail if a prescription is applied unilaterally and without proper diagnosis.

[12] Bennis sees three major approaches to planned organizational change, with the behavioral scientists associated with each approach having ". . . a deep concern with applying social science knowledge to create more viable social systems; a commitment to action, as well as to research . . . , and a belief that improved interpersonal and group relationships will ultimately lead to better organizational performance." Warren G. Bennis, "A New Role for the Behavioral Sciences: Effecting Organizational Change," *Administrative Science Quarterly*, 8:157–158 (September 1963); and Herbert A. Shepard, "An Action Research Model" in *An Action Research Program for Organization Improvement*, pp. 31–35.

[13] Bennis, "New Role for Behavioral Sciences," p. 158.

[14] For a discussion of some of the problems and dilemmas in behavioral science research, see Chris Argyris, "Creating Effective Relationships in Organizations," in Richard N. Adams and Jack J. Preiss, eds., *Human Organization Research* (Homewood, Ill.: The Dorsey Press, 1960), pp. 109–123; and Barbara A. Benedict et al., "The Clinical-Experimental Approach to Assessing Organizational Change Efforts," *The Journal of Applied Behavioral Science*, 3:347–380 (November 3, 1967).

STRATEGY IN ORGANIZATION DEVELOPMENT: AN ACTION RESEARCH MODEL

An almost universally used strategy in programs of organization development is based on what behavioral scientists call an *action research*

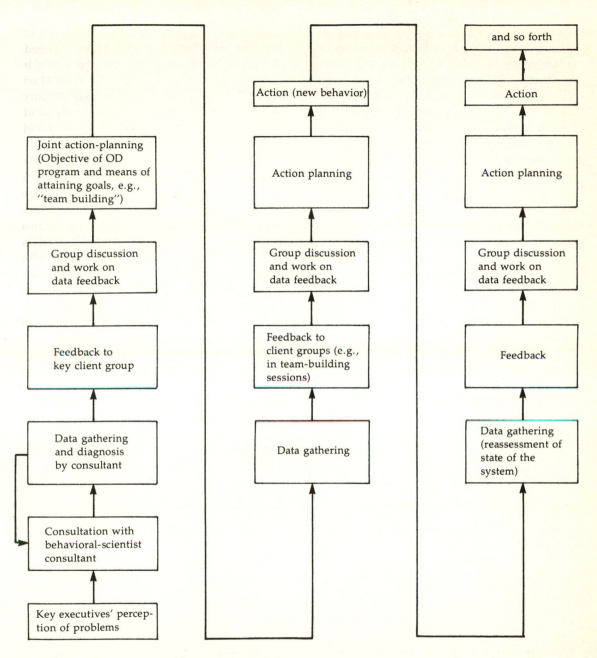

Figure 26-1 An action research model for organization development

model. This model involves extensive collaboration between the consultant (whether an external or an internal change agent) and the client-group in the gathering of data, the discussion of data, and planning. Although descriptions of this model vary in detail and terminology from author to author, the dynamics are essentially the same.[15]

Figure 26-1 summarizes some essential phases of the action research model, using an emerging organization development program as an example. The key aspects of the model are *the gathering of data, diagnosis, feedback to the client-group, discussion of data by the client-group, work by the client-group, action planning,* and *action.* The sequence tends to be cyclical, with the focus on new or advanced problems as the client-group learns to work more effectively together. Action research should also be considered a process since, as Whyte says, it involves ". . . a continuous gathering and analysis of human relations research data and the feeding of the findings into the organization in such a manner as to change behavior."[16] Action research is so pervasive in OD efforts that *organization development* could be defined as *organization improvement through action research.*

DIAGNOSIS

Ideally, the initial objectives and strategies of a program for organization development stem from a careful diagnosis of such matters as interpersonal and intergroup relationships, decision-making processes, and communication flows when they are currently causing problems in the client's organization. As a preliminary step, the behavioral scientist and the key client (the president of a company, the vice president in charge of a division, the works manager or superintendent of a plant, or a superintendent of schools, etc.), will make a joint, initial assessment of the critical problems. They may also interview subordinates in order to obtain supplemental data. The diagnosis may very well indicate that the central problem is technological or that the key client is not at all willing or ready to examine the organization's problem-solving ability or managerial behavior.[17] Either diagnosis may justify postponing organization development, although the technological problem may easily be related to deficiencies in interpersonal relationships or decision making. The diagnosis may also indicate the desirability of one or more additional specialists—in engineering, finance, or electronic data processing, for example—to simultaneously work with the organization.

This initial diagnosis, which focuses on the expressed needs of the client, is extremely critical. As discussed earlier, in the absence of a skilled diagnosis, the change agent would be imposing a set of assumptions and a set of objectives which may be hopelessly out of line with either the current problems of the people in the organization or their willingness to learn new modes of behavior. In this regard, it is extremely important that the consultant *hear and understand* what the client is trying to say. This requires a high order of skill.[18]

[15] For further discussion of action research, see Edgar H. Schein and Warren G. Bennis, *Personal and Organizational Change through Group Methods* (New York: John Wiley & Sons, 1966), pp. 272–274.
[16] William Foote Whyte and Edith Lentz Hamilton, *Action Research for Management* (Homewood, Ill.: Richard D. Irwin, 1964), p. 2.
[17] O'Connell appropriately challenges the notion that there is "one best way" of organizational change and stresses that the consultant should choose his role and strategies of intervention on the basis of "the conditions existing when he enters the client system." Jeremiah J. O'Connell, *Managing Organizational Innovation* (Homewood, Ill.: Richard D. Irwin, 1968), pp. 10–11.
[18] For further discussion of organizational diagnosis, see Richard Beckhard, "An Organization Improvement Program in a Decentralized Organization," *Journal of Applied Behavioral Science*, 2:3–4 (January, February, March 1966).

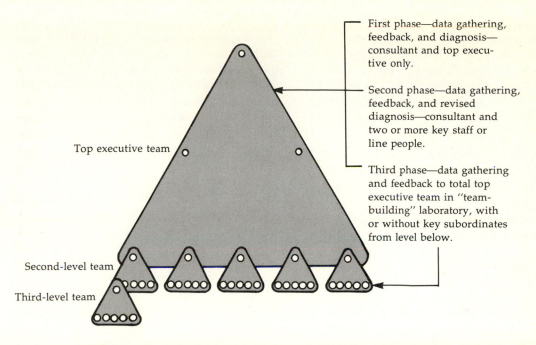

First phase—data gathering, feedback, and diagnosis—consultant and top executive only.

Second phase—data gathering, feedback, and revised diagnosis—consultant and two or more key staff or line people.

Third phase—data gathering and feedback to total top executive team in "team-building" laboratory, with or without key subordinates from level below.

Top executive team

Second-level team

Third-level team

Fourth and additional phases—data gathering and team-building sessions with second or third level teams.

Subsequent phases—sessions across groups in data gathering, feedback, and interface problem solving.

Simultaneous phases—(a) several managers may attend "stranger" T-groups; (b) courses in the management-development program may supplement this learning.

Figure 26-2   Organizational development phases in a hypothetical organization

DATA GATHERING

Interviews are frequently used for data gathering in organization development, because personal contact builds a cooperative relationship between the consultant and the client-group. The interview is also important because the behavioral-scientist consultant is interested in spontaneity and expressed feelings as well as in cognitive matters. Nevertheless, questionnaires are on occasion successfully used, in the context of what is sometimes called "survey feedback," to supplement data from interviews.

Sometimes a comprehensive survey feedback effort, without interviews, comprises the initial phases of an OD effort.[19]

Data gathering typically progresses through several phases. The first phase is related to

[19]See Floyd C. Mann, "Studying and Creating Change," in Timothy W. Costello and Sheldon S. Zalkind, eds., *Psychology in Administration—A Research Orientation* (Englewood Cliffs, N.J.: Prentice-Hall, 1963), pp. 321–324. For a description of procedures in feedback used by the Survey Research Center, University of Michigan, see Floyd Mann and Rensis Likert, "The Need for Research on the Communication of Research Results," in Richard N. Adams and Jack J. Preiss, eds., *Human Organization Research*, pp. 57–66.

diagnosing the state of the system and making plans for organizational change. It may take the form of a series of interviews between the consultant and the key client or between a few key executives and the consultant. Subsequent phases focus on problems specific to the top executive team and to subordinate teams. (See Figure 26-2).

Typically, questions in data gathering or *problem sensing* include the following:

1. What problems do you see in your group, including problems among people, that are interfering with getting the job done the way you would like to have it done?

2. What problems do you see in the broader organization?

Such open-end questions give respondents a wide latitude and encourage a reporting of problems *as the individual sees them*. The interviewing is usually conducted privately, with a commitment on the part of the consultant that the information will be used in such a way as to avoid undue embarrassment to anyone. The intent is to find out what common problems or themes emerge with the data in order to use them constructively for both diagnosis and feedback.

FEEDBACK, DISCUSSIONS OF DATA, AND THE CONSULTANT'S ROLE

Usually, two- or three-day off-site sessions in team building or group problem solving become a major focal point in programs of organization development.[20] Early in these meetings, the behavioral scientist typically provides "feedback" to the group in terms of the themes that emerged in the problem-sensing inter-

views. The consultant then typically encourages the group to rank items or themes according to what the group wishes to work on during the workshop. These themes usually provide substantial and meaningful data with which the group may begin its work. Interpersonal matters, both positive and negative, tend to emerge spontaneously as the participants begin to gain confidence from the level of support which is sensed in the group.

While the behavior of different consultants will vary in such sessions, they will typically serve as observers of the "process" and interpreters of the dynamics of the group's interaction, to the degree that the group expresses a readiness for such intervention. They also will typically encourage people to take calculated risks, a step at a time, and to experiment with new behavior, given the level of support in the group. Thus, the trainer-consultant(s) attempts not only to stimulate new behavior but also to protect members of the group. The climate I try to build in my consulting practice, for example, is: "Let's not tear down any more than we can build back together." Further, the trainer-consultant typically works with the group to help its members improve skills in diagnosing and facilitating the group's progress.[21]

It should be noted, however, that different groups will have different needs along a task-process continuum. For example, some groups may need intensive work on clarifying objectives; others may have the greatest need to work on furthering interpersonal relationships. Further, the consultant, or the chief consultant

[20] For a description of an OD effort that featured a series of half-day sessions, see Frank T. Paine, "A Conference Approach in Assessing Management," *Personnel Administrator,* 35:47–52 (June 1972).

[21] For a description of what goes on in team-building sessions, see Richard Beckhard, "An Organization Improvement Program in a Decentralized Organization," pp. 9–13; and Newton Margulies and Anthony P. Raia, "People in Organizations—A Case for Team Training," *Training and Development Journal,* 22:2–11 (August 1968). For a description of problem-solving sessions involving the total management group (about seventy) of a company, see Richard Beckhard, "The Confrontation Meeting," *Harvard Business Review,* 45:149–155 (March-April 1967).

in a team of consultants, involved in an organization development program will play a much broader role than serving as a T-group or team-building trainer. The consultant will also play an important role in periodic data gathering and diagnosis and in joint long-range planning of the efforts at change.[22]

MAJOR TYPES OF OD INTERVENTIONS[23]

The variety of OD interventions available to the practitioner and client is constantly evolving. Currently a wide range of activities constitutes the available technology of organization development programs and, as we see it, the following are the major contemporary "families" or types of OD interventions:

◦ *Diagnostic activities* These are fact-finding activities designed to ascertain the state of the system, the status of a problem, the "way things are." Available methods range from projective devices like "build a collage that represents for you your place in this organization" to the more traditional data collection methods described earlier in the chapter such as interviews, questionnaires, surveys, and meetings.

◦ *Team-building activities* Described above, these activities typically occur in off-site sessions and are designed to enhance the effective operation of teams. They may relate to task issues, such as the way things are done, the needed skills to accomplish tasks, the resource allocations necessary for task accomplishment; or they may relate to the nature and quality of the relationships between the team members or between members and the leader. Again, a wide range of activities is possible, and these activities are relevant to the various kinds of teams that may exist in the organization, such as formal work teams, temporary task force teams, newly constituted teams, and the like. These activities should not be equated with T-group activities. (See Figure 26-3 for a chart that differentiates team building from other group dynamics applications.)

◦ *Intergroup activities* These are activities designed to improve the effectiveness of interdependent groups. They focus on joint activities and the output of the groups is considered as a single system rather than as two subsystems. When two groups are involved, the activities are generally designated intergroup or interface activities; when more than two groups are involved, the activities are often called "organizational mirroring." A typical intervention in an intergroup session is to ask the members of each group to independently develop lists of (a) what problems they are experiencing with the other group, (b) how they see themselves as a group, and (c) their predictions as to what problems the other group is experiencing with them. The groups are brought together to explain the lists and to ask questions for clarification; they then meet independently to discuss the implications and come back together again for discussion, the resolution of issues, and action planning.

◦ *Survey feedback activities* Discussed earlier in the chapter, these are related and similar to the

[22] For a description of actual organization-development programs, see Paul C. Buchanan, "Innovative Organizations—A Study in Organization Development," in *Applying Behavioral Science Research in Industry* (New York: Industrial Relations Counselors, 1964), pp. 87–107; Sheldon A. Davis, "An Organic Problem-Solving Method of Organizational Change," *The Journal of Applied Behavioral Science*, 3:3–21, No. 1 (1967); Cyril Sofer, *The Organization from Within* (Chicago: Quadrangle Books, 1961); Alfred J. Marrow, David G. Bowers, and Stanley E. Seashore, *Management by Participation* (New York: Harper & Row, 1967); Robert R. Blake, Jane S. Mouton, Louis B. Barnes, and Larry E. Greiner, "Breakthrough in Organization Development," *Harvard Business Review*, 42:133–155 (November-December 1964); Alton C. Bartlett, "Changing Behavior as a Means to Increased Efficiency," *The Journal of Applied Behavioral Science*, 3:381–403, No. 3 (1967); and Robert R. Blake and Jane Mouton, *Corporate Excellence through Grid Organization Development* (Houston: Gulf Publishing Company, 1968).

[23] This section is based largely on French and Bell, *Organization Development*, pp. 102–105.

Figure **26-3**   Varieties of laboratory training and organizational applications: examples

	Individual emphasis ← →		Group emphasis ← →	Organizational emphasis ← →	
	Personal growth laboratories	Human relations laboratories	Group process laboratories	Team building	Organizational problem-solving conferences
Clients	Strangers (names may be kept anonymous)	Strangers	Strangers	Work team (superior plus subordinates)	Entire management group
Objectives	More awareness of own capacity for feeling, experiencing; for growth, creativity	Interpersonal competence: A. Increased awareness of own feelings B. Increased awareness of others C. More tolerance and respect for self, others D. Increased awareness of group and organizational phenomena (more emphasis in group process lab)	Interpersonal competence in group setting:	Increased organizational effectiveness and personal satisfaction; enhanced individual, team, and organizational competency A. Increased level of confrontation of problems B. Increased level of support and trust C. Increased openness of communications: vertically, diagonally, horizontally D. Increased level of enthusiasm and satisfaction E. Increase in frequency and quality of synergistic solutions F. Increase in shared leadership in teams	

Typical activities	T-groups
	Non-verbal exercises
	Phantasy
	Body awareness
	Art, music
	Lectures
		T-groups
		Lectures
		  Emotions
		  Communications
		  Trust
		  Constructive openness
		
		Exercises
		  Basic communication skills
			T-groups
			Lectures
			  Emotions
			  Communications
			  Trust
			  Constructive openness
			
			Task and maintenance behavior
			  Leadership
			  Decision making
			  Conflict
			Exercises
			  Communication skills
			  Decision making
			  Structure
			  Communication networks
			  Conflict
				Action research model
				  Preliminary diagnosis
				  Data gathering from client group
				  Data feedback to client group
				  Problem diagnosis by client group
				  Action planning
				Process consultation
				Lectures (minimal and when relevant to problems being worked on)
				  Force field analysis
				  Leadership
				  Systems theory
				  Communication, etc.	

Figure **26-4**   Two approaches to the use of attitude surveys

	Traditional	Survey feedback (organization development)
Data obtained from	Rank and file employees, perhaps first-line supervisors	Everyone in the system (or subsystem), including professionals and managers
Data presented to	Top management	Everyone who participated
Data worked on by	Top management (maybe)	Everyone in overlapping work teams (supervisors plus subordinates)
Consultant role	Design and administering questionnaire; development report	Collaboration on total strategy and questionnaire; workshop design and appropriate interventions; collaborative follow-up
Action planning by	Top management	Teams at all levels
Probable extent of improvement	Low	High

From Wendell L. French and Cecil H. Bell, Jr., *Organization Development: Behavioral Science Interventions for Organization Improvement*, © 1973, p. 131. Adapted with permission of Prentice-Hall, Inc., Englewood Cliffs, New Jersey.

diagnostic activities mentioned above. However, they are important enough in their own right to be considered separately. These activities center around actively working the data produced by a questionnaire survey and designing action plans based on the survey data. (For a description of how survey feedback differs from traditional use of attitude surveys, see Figure 26-4.)

∘ *Techno-structural   activities*   Although   not strictly OD activities unless they have the characteristics of OD described earlier, these activities are designed to improve the effectiveness of the technical or structural inputs and constraints affecting individuals or groups. The activities may take the form of experimenting with new organization structures and evaluating their effectiveness in terms of specific goals. The creation of semiautonomous work groups, job enrichment, and MBO are examples.

∘ *Process consultation activities*   These are activities on the part of the consultant ". . . which

help the client to perceive, understand, and act upon process events which occur in the client's environment."[24] These activities perhaps more accurately describe an approach, a consulting mode, in which the client is given insight into the human processes in organizations. Primary emphasis is on processes such as communications, leader and member roles in groups, problem solving and decision making, group norms and group growth, leadership and authority, and intergroup cooperation and competition. Emphasis is also placed upon learning how to diagnose and develop the necessary skills to be effective in dealing with these processes. One major aspect of the role of the consultant in team building is frequently to serve as a process observer.

∘ *Grid organization development activities*   These activities, invented and franchised by Robert

[24] Edgar H. Schein, *Process Consultation* (Reading, Mass.: Addison-Wesley Publishing Company, 1969), p. 9.

Blake and Jane Mouton,[25] comprise a six-phase change model involving the total organization. Internal resources are developed to conduct most of the programs which may take from three to five years to complete. The model starts with upgrading individual managers' skills and leadership abilities, moves to team-improvement activities, then to intergroup relations activities. Later phases include corporate planning for improvement, developing implementation tactics, and concluding with an evaluation phase assessing change in the organization culture and looking toward future directions.

◦ *Third-party peacemaking activities* These activities, conducted by a skilled consultant (the third party) are designed to ". . . help two members of an organization manage their interpersonal conflict."[26] They are based on confrontation tactics and understanding of the processes involved in conflict and conflict resolution.

◦ *Coaching and counseling activities* These activities entail the consultant or other organization members working with individuals to help them (1) define learning goals; (2) learn how others see their behavior; (3) learn new modes of behavior to help them to achieve their goals better. A central feature of this activity is the nonevaluative feedback given by others to an individual. A second feature is the joint exploration of alternative behaviors.

◦ *Life and career-planning activities* These activities may be an off-shoot of an OD effort, and are designed to enable individuals to focus on their life and career objectives and how they might go about achieving them. Structured activities lead to the production of life and career inventories; discussions of goals and objectives; and assessment of capabilities, needed additional training, and areas of strength and deficiency. (See also Chapter 17.)

◦ *Planning and goal-setting activities* These activities include theory and experience in planning and goal setting, utilizing problem-solving models, planning paradigms, ideal organization versus real organization "discrepancy" models, and the like. These activities frequently occur in a team-building setting.

◦ *Education and training activities* While not always OD activities in the sense of our definition of OD, these activities are usually complementary to OD interventions and frequently provide a cognitive or experiential base to an OD effort. Basically, these activities are designed to improve the skills, abilities, and knowledge of individuals. There are several activities available and several approaches possible. For example, the individual can develop skills in isolation from the work group (in a T-group comprised of strangers) or can develop skills in relation to the work group (e.g., when a work team learns how better to manage interpersonal conflict). The activities may be directed toward the acquisition of technical skills required for effective task performance, toward improving intertask performance, or toward improving interpersonal competence. The activities may be directed toward leadership issues, the responsibilities and functions of group members, decision making, problem solving, goal setting and planning, etc.

RELEVANCY TO DIFFERENT TECHNOLOGIES AND ORGANIZATIONAL SUBUNITS

The research by Joan Woodward (Chapter 5) and Lorsch and Morse (Chapter 7) suggests that

[25] R.R. Blake and J.S. Mouton, *Building a Dynamic Corporation through Organization Development* (Reading, Mass.: Addison-Wesley Publishing Company, 1969). This book is a treatise showing how grid organization development programs operate.

[26] R.W. Walton, *Interpersonal Peacemaking: Confrontation and Third-Party Consultation* (Reading, Mass.: Addison-Wesley Publishing Company, 1969), p. 1. This book is devoted to an explication of this specialized intervention technique.

efforts at organization development aimed at creating open, organic systems might be more relevant to certain kinds of technologies and organizational levels, and perhaps to certain work force characteristics, than to others. For example, OD efforts may be more appropriate in an organization devoted to prototype manufacturing than to an automobile assembly plant. *However, the dimension of group effectiveness was not a central part of these studies,* although dealt with indirectly by Lorsch and Morse. Theoretically, the more participative or laissez-faire the leadership, the more important become group member skills in leadership and group dynamics (see footnote 29). Moreover, experiments in such organizations as Texas Instruments and General Foods (see Chapter 9) suggest that some manufacturing efforts that appear to be inherently mechanistic may lend themselves to a more participative, organic managerial style than is often thought possible.

Given the necessarily narrower job structure for production employees, OD may be relatively more productive and relevant at the managerial and professional levels of the organization. Certainly OD efforts, as I have defined OD, are most effective when they start at the top. Research and development units—particularly those involving a high degree of interdependency and joint creativity among the group's members—also are particularly appropriate for OD if the members are currently experiencing problems in communicating or interpersonal relationships.

However, from my experience, if perceived by organizational members as relevant, OD can be a very useful process at all levels of organizations. Theoretically, if OD has to do with a collaborative management of organizational culture toward objectives that organization members have in common, OD should be relevant to all levels and all units of an organization. Paradoxically, through participation in OD effort, the members of a group or depart-

ment may decide that their culture needs to be more structured or mechanistic along some dimensions. This assertion is congruent with my experience and supported to some extent by Lorsch and Morse, who found the more effective container plants to be fairly high in structure *plus* having groups of people who were fairly high in the ability to expose and resolve underlying problems and conflicts.[27] The issue, then, may be whether or not there will be a collaborative effort to manage the culture of the unit (or total organization), rather than whether the unit should be organic or mechanistic.

CONDITIONS AND TECHNIQUES FOR SUCCESSFUL ORGANIZATION DEVELOPMENT

Theory, research, and experience to date suggest that successful OD programs tend to evolve approximately in accordance with the following sequence of conditions and techniques:

1. There is strong pressure for improvement both from outside the organization and from within,[28] or key executives wish to take a reading on the state of the system and to make whatever improvements are warranted.

2. An outside behavioral scientist is invited to consult with the top executives and to diagnose organizational problems.

3. A preliminary diagnosis suggests that a program of organization development designed in response to the expressed needs of the key executives is warranted.

4. A collaborative decision is made between the key group of clients and the consultant to

[27] Jay W. Lorsch and John J. Morse, *Organizations and Their Members: A Contingency Approach* (New York: Harper & Row, 1974), pp. 79–80.
[28] On this point, see Larry E. Greiner, "Patterns of Organization Change," *Harvard Business Review,* 45:119–130 (May-June 1967).

begin to work on organizational problems. The specific goals may be to improve communications, secure more effective participation from subordinates in problem solving, and move in the direction of more openness, more feedback, and more support. In short, a decision may be made to change the culture for the purpose of helping the company meet its organizational goals and providing organizational members with better avenues for initiative, creativity, and self-actualization.

5. Two or more top executives, including the chief executive, attend outside ("stranger") laboratory training sessions. While not necessary for an OD effort to evolve, experience in T-groups enhances skills and insights that can greatly enhance organization-development activities. Frequently, attendance at labs is one of the factors precipitating interest in obtaining an outside consultant. From my experience, one of the insights that frequently occurs from a T-group experience is that it is possible to collaboratively manage the culture of a group.

6. If people attend laboratory training programs, attendance is voluntary. Although it is difficult to draw a line between persuasion and coercion, OD consultants and top management should be aware of the dysfunctional consequences of coercion (see the comments on authentic behavior).

7. Team-building sessions are held with the top executive group or with the group at the highest point where the program is started. Ideally, the process is started at the top of the organization, but it can start at levels below the president as long as there is significant support from the chief executive and preferably from other members of the top power structure.

8. In a firm large enough to have a personnel executive, the personnel and industrial relations director becomes heavily involved at the outset.

9. One of two organizational forms emerges to coordinate efforts in organization development: (a) a coordinator reporting to the personnel executive (the personnel executive may fill this role) or (b) a coordinator reporting to the chief executive. The director of managerial development is frequently in an ideal position to coordinate OD activities with other activities in managerial development.

10. Ultimately, it is essential that the group in personnel and industrial relations, including people administering salaries, be an integral part of the organization-development program. Since OD groups have such potential as catalysts in rapid organizational change, the temptation is great for OD practitioners to see themselves as "good guys" and the other people in personnel as "bad guys" or simply ineffective. Any conflicts between a separate organization development group, on the one hand, and the personnel and industrial relations groups, on the other, should be faced and resolved. Such tensions can be the "Achilles' heel" for either the OD or personnel program. In particular, however, the change agents in the organization development program need the support of the other people heavily involved in administering human resources; and what is done in the OD program must be compatible with what is done in selection, promotion, salary administration, and appraisal, and vice versa. In terms of systems theory, it seems imperative that one aspect of the human resources function, such as any program for organization development, be managed in a congruent way with other aspects of the function. TRW Systems and Saga Foods exemplify organizations that involve top executives and make the personnel and industrial relations group an integral part of the OD program.[29]

[29] For TRW experience see Davis, *Organic Problem-Solving Method,* pp. 3–21. For a brief description of the OD effort at Saga Foods, see *Business Week,* July 22, 1972, pp. 48–49.

11. At the request of the various executives, team-building workshops—designed on the basis of careful data gathering and diagnosis of problems—are conducted at successively lower levels of the organization with the help of outside consultants plus that of internal consultants whose expertise is gradually developed. (See Figure 26-2.)

12. It is imperative that skill development is accompanied by good intentions. Openness in communications, for example, must be accompanied by constructive feedback and in learning how to deal with one's own feelings and attitudes with a minimum of inferential judgments about the motives of others. A desire to improve the effectiveness of planning and decision making in teams must be accompanied by skill development pertaining to various levels of group work.[30]

13. Ideally, as the program matures, members of the personnel staff and a few line executives are trained to do some work in organization development in conjunction with the external and internal professionally trained behavioral scientists. In a sense, then, external change agents try to work themselves out of jobs by developing internal resources.

14. The outside consultant(s) and the internal coordinator work very carefully together and periodically check on the fears, anxieties, or misunderstandings which may be developing as the effort progresses. Issues need to be confronted when they emerge. Not only does the organization need outside agents for their skills, but it needs someone to act as a "governor"—to keep the program focused on

real problems and urge authenticity in contrast to gamesmanship. The danger always exists that the organization will begin to punish or reward involvement in the OD activities per se rather than focus on improved performance.

15. The OD consultants constantly examine and try to improve their own effectiveness in interpersonal relationships and their own diagnostic skills. Consequently, they are not in a position of "do as I say, but not as I do." Further, both consultant and client work together to optimize the consultant's knowledge of the organization's unique and evolving cultural structure and web of interpersonal relationships.

16. Results must be continually audited, both in terms of the evolving attitudes about what is going on and in terms of the extent to which problems identified at the outset by the key clients are being solved through the program.

17. As implied above, the system of rewards and other personnel systems must be readjusted to accommodate changes in performance that are emerging in the organization. Substantially improved performance by individuals and groups is not likely to be sustained if financial and promotional rewards are not forthcoming. In short, management must have a "systems" point of view and must think through the interrelationships of the OD effort with the systems of reward and staffing and with other aspects of the total subsystem for human resources.

In the last analysis, the president and the line executives of the organization will evaluate the OD effort in terms of the extent to which it helps the organization to meet its human and economic objectives. For example, marked improvements in various indices from one plant, one division, one department, and the like will be important indicators of the program's success. Although indices for the administration of human resources are not yet perfected, some

---

[30] I see four levels of group work: (1) the task level, (2) the procedural level (how the agenda is decided upon, physical facilities, whether decision making is by consensus or voting, etc.), (3) the group "process" level (the various leadership and group maintenance roles that can be fulfilled by team members), and (4) the interpersonal level (usually involving dealing with feelings).

of the measuring devices being developed by Likert, Mann, and others show considerable promise.[31]

SUMMARY

Efforts at organization development have emerged through attempts to apply the values and assumptions of laboratory training to total systems and through the invention of survey feedback technology. Such efforts are organic in the sense that they emerge from, and are guided by, the problems being experienced by the people in the organization. The key to their viability and avoidance of becoming a passing fad lies in an authentic focus on problems and concerns of the members of the organization and in a confrontation of issues and problems.

Organization development is based on assumptions and values similar to Theory Y assumptions and values, but it includes additional assumptions about total systems and the nature of the client-consultant relationship. Strategies of intervention by the behavioral scientists as a change agent tend to be based on an action-research model and to be focused more on helping the people in an organization learn how to solve problems than on prescriptions of how things should be done differently.

Laboratory training is frequently an important adjunct to an organization development effort, but the extent and format of such training will depend upon the evolving needs of the organization. In contrast, team-building workshops (involving a superior and subordinates) that focus on the organizational problems being experienced by team members are usually viewed as central to OD efforts. Stranger labs,

however, can play a key role in efforts at change when used as part of the broader effort.

Successful organization development requires skillful intervention by behavioral scientists, a systems view, and support and involvement by top management. In addition, changes stemming from organization development must be linked to changes in the total personnel system. The viability of efforts at organization development lies in the degree to which they accurately reflect the aspirations and concerns of the participating members.

In conclusion, successful organization development tends to be (a) a total-system effort; (b) a continual process of planned improvements—not a temporary program; and (c) a plan aimed at developing the organization's internal resources for effective change in the future.

REVIEW AND DISCUSSION QUESTIONS

1. What are the underlying assumptions of organization development?

2. What appear to be some of the basic values of behavioral scientists who are change agents? How do these values agree with yours?

3. Discuss the role of the consultant in OD programs.

4. What are the basic elements of the action-research model?

5. How does organization development differ from laboratory training?

6. What seem to be the ingredients of successful OD efforts?

7. How did contemporary organization development emerge?

8. What are some of the techniques used in OD programs?

9. How is OD similar to or different from participative management?

10. What is meant by collaborative management of organizational culture?

[31]See Rensis Likert, *The Human Organization: Its Management and Value* (New York: McGraw-Hill Book Company, 1967); and R.L. Brummet, W.C. Pyle, and Eric G. Flamholtz, "Human Resource Accounting in Industry," *Personnel Administration*, 32:34–46 (July-August 1969).

SUPPLEMENTAL REFERENCES

Argyris, Chris, "Conditions for Competence Acquisition and Therapy," *The Journal of Applied Science*, 4:147–177, No. 2 (1968).

———, *Intervention Theory and Method* (Reading, Mass.: Addison-Wesley Publishing Company, 1970).

———, *Management and Organizational Development* (New York: McGraw-Hill Book Company, 1971).

Beck, Arthur C., Jr., and Ellis D. Hillmar, eds., *A Practical Approach to Organization Development Through MBO—Selected Readings* (Reading, Mass: Addison-Wesley Publishing Company, 1972).

Beckhard, Richard, "The Confrontation Meeting," *Harvard Business Review*, 45:149–155 (March-April 1967).

———, "An Organizational Improvement Program is a Decentralized Organization," *The Journal of Applied Behavioral Science*, 2:3–25 (January, February, March 1966).

———, *Organization Development: Strategies and Models* (Reading, Mass.: Addison-Wesley Publishing Company, 1969).

———, and Dale G. Lake, "Short- and Long-Range Efforts of a Team Development Effort" from Harvey A. Hornstein et al., eds., *Social Intervention: A Behavioral Science Approach* (New York: The Free Press, 1971), pp. 421–439.

Beer, Michael, and Edgar F. Huse, "A Systems Approach to Organization Development," *The Journal of Applied Behavioral Science*, 8:79–101 (January-February 1972).

Benne, Kenneth D., Leland P. Bradford, Jack R. Gibb, and Ronald O. Lippitt, eds., *The Laboratory Method of Changing and Learning* (Palo Alto, Calif.: Science and Behavior Books, Inc., 1975).

Bennis, Warren G., "Changing Organizations," *The Journal of Applied Behavioral Science*, 2:247–263, No. 3 (1966).

———, *Changing Organizations* (New York: McGraw-Hill Book Company, 1966).

———, *Organization Development: Its Nature, Origins, and Prospects* (Reading, Mass.: Addison-Wesley Publishing Company, 1969).

Blake, Robert R., and Jane S. Mouton, *Building A Dynamic Corporation Through Grid Organization Development* (Reading, Mass.: Addison-Wesley Publishing Company, 1969).

———, *Consultation* (Reading, Mass.: Addison-Wesley Publishing Company, 1976).

———, *Corporate Excellence through Grid Organization Development* (Houston: Gulf Publishing Company, 1968).

———, *Diary of an OD Man* (Houston: Gulf Publishing Company, 1976).

———, "Grid Organization Development," *Personnel Administration*, 30:6–14 (January-February 1967).

Blake, Robert R., Jane S. Mouton, Louis B. Barnes, and Larry E. Greiner, "Breakthrough in Organization Development," *Harvard Business Review*, 42:133–155 (November-December 1964).

Blake, Robert R., Jane S. Mouton, and Richard L. Sloma, "The Union-Management Intergroup Laboratory: Strategy for Resolving Intergroup Conflict," *Journal of Applied Behavioral Science*, 1:25–57, No. 1 (1965).

Bowers, David G., "OD Techniques and Their Results in 23 Organizations: The Michigan ICL Study," *The Journal of Applied Behavioral Science*, 9:21–43 (November 1, 1973).

Buchanan, Paul C., "Laboratory Training and Organization Development," *Administrative Science Quarterly*, 14:466–480 (September 1969).

Burke, W. Warner, "Organization Development in Transition," *Journal of Applied Behavioral Science*, 12:22–43 (January, February, March 1976).

———, "Training OD Specialists," *Professional Psychology*, 1:1–3 (Summer 1970).

———, ed., *Contemporary Organization Development: Conceptual Orientations and Interventions* (Washington, D.C.: NTL-Institute for Applied Behavioral Science, 1972).

Eddy, William B., W. Warner Burke, Vladimir A. Dupré, and Oron P. South, *Behavioral Science and the Manager's Role* (Washington, D.C.: National Institute for Applied Behavioral Science, 1969).

Ferguson, Charles K., "Concerning the Nature of Human Systems and the Consultant's Role," *Journal of Applied Behavioral Science*, 4:186–193 (1968).

French, Wendell, and Cecil H. Bell, Jr., *Organization Development: Behavioral Science Interventions for Organization Improvement* (Englewood Cliffs, N.J.: Prentice-Hall, Inc., 1973).

————, and Robert A. Zawacki, eds., *Organization Development: Theory, Practice, and Research* (Dallas: Business Publications, Inc., forthcoming).

Friedlander, Frank, and L. Dave Brown, "Organization Development," *Annual Review of Psychology*, 25:219–341 (1974).

Gardner, John W., "Can Organization Dry Rot Be Prevented?" *Personnel Administration*, 29:3–5ff. (May-June 1966).

Golembiewski, Robert T., and Stokes B. Carrigan, "Planned Change in Organization Style Based on the Laboratory Approach," *Administrative Science Quarterly*, 15:79-93 (March 1970).

Greiner, Larry E., "Patterns of Organizational Change," *Harvard Business Review*, 45:119–130 (May-June 1967).

Guest, Robert H., *Organizational Change: The Effect of Successful Leadership* (Homewood, Ill.: Ricard E. Irwin, Inc., 1962).

Harrison, Roger, "Choosing the Depth of Organizational Intervention," *Journal of Applied Behavioral Science*, 6:182-202 (1970).

————, "When Power Conflicts Trigger Team Spirit," *European Business*, Spring 1972, pp. 57–65.

Herman, Stanley M., "A Gestalt Orientation to Organization Development," in W. Warner Burke, ed., *Contemporary Organization Development: Conceptual Orientations and Interventions*,

(Washington, D.C.: NTL-Institute for Applied Behavioral Science, 1972), pp. 69–89.

————, "What Is This Thing Called Organization Development?" *Personnel Journal*, 50:595–603 (August 1971).

Hite, Anthony L., ed., *Organizational Development: The State of the Art* (Ann Arbor: Foundation for Research on Human Behavior, 1971). Proceedings of the Western Organizational Development Conference. 88 pp.

Hornstein, Harvey, Barbara Bunker, W. Warner Burke, Marion Gindes, and Roy Lewicki, eds., *Social Intervention* (New York: The Free Press, 1971).

House, Robert J., *Management Development: Design, Evaluation, and Implementation* (Ann Arbor: Bureau of Industrial Relations, Graduate School of Business Administration, University of Michigan, 1967).

Journal of Contemporary Business, Vol. 1 (Summer 1972).

Kahn, Robert L., "Organizational Development: Some Problems and Proposals," *Journal of Applied Behavioral Science*, 10:485–502 (1974).

Kuriloff, Arthur H., *Organization Development for Survival* (New York: American Management Association, 1972).

Lawrence, Paul R., and Jay W. Lorsch, *Developing Organizations: Diagnosis and Action* (Reading, Mass.: Addison-Wesley Publishing Company, 1969).

Leavitt, Harold J., "Suppose We Took Groups Seriously . . . ," in Eugene L. Cass and Frederick G. Zimmer, *Man and Work in Society* (New York: Van Nostrand Reinhold Company, 1975), pp. 67–77.

Lewin, Kurt, "Action Research and Minority Problems," *Journal of Social Issues*, 2:34–46 (November 1946).

Lippitt, Gordon L., *Organization Renewal* (New York: Appleton-Century, 1969).

Lippitt, Gordon L., and Warren H. Schmidt, "Crisis in a Developing Organization," *Harvard*

Business Review, 45:102–112 (November-December 1967).

Lippitt, Gordon L., Leslie This, and Robert Bidwell, Jr., *Optimizing Human Resources: Readings in Industrial and Organization Development* (Reading, Mass.: Addison-Wesley Publishing Company, 1971).

McGill, Michael, "Assessing the Effectiveness of Organization Development (OD) Programs," *Organization and Administrative Science*, 7:123–128 (Spring-Summer 1976).

Management 2000, "Implications of Behavioral Sciences in the Year 2000," (New York: The American Foundation for Management Research, 1968), pp. 98–133.

Margulies, Newton, and Anthony P. Raia, *Organizational Development: Values, Process and Technology* (New York: McGraw-Hill, Book Company 1972) (readings plus text).

Marrow, Alfred J., "Managerial Revolution in the State Department," *Personnel*, 43:8–18 (November-December 1966).

———, *Behind the Executive Mask* (New York: American Management Association, Inc., 1964).

Miles, Matthew B., *Learning to Work in Groups: A Program Guide for Education Leaders* (New York: Teacher's College Press, Teachers College, Columbia University, 1965).

Miles, Raymond E., "Organization Development," in George Strauss, Raymond E. Miles, Charles C. Snow, and Arnold S. Tannenbaum, eds., *Organizational Behavior: Research and Issues* (Madison, Wisc.: Industrial Relations Research Association, 1974), pp. 165–191.

Mosley, Donald C., "Professional Ethics and Competence in Management Consulting," *California Management Review*, 12:444–48 (Spring 1970).

Myers, M. Scott, "Overcoming Union Opposition to Job Enrichment," *Harvard Business Review*, 49:37–49 (May-June 1971).

Paine, Frank T., "A Conference Approach in Assessing Management," *Personnel Administration*, 35:47–52 (June 1972).

Patten, Thomas H., Jr., "OD, MBO and the R/P System: A New Dimension in Personnel Administration," *Personnel Administration*, 35:14–23 (March-April 1972).

Raia, Anthony P., "Organizational Development—Some Issues and Challenges," *California Management Review*, 14:13–20 (Summer 1972).

Schein, Edgar H., *Process Consultation: Its Role in Organization Development* (Reading, Mass.: Addison-Wesley Publishing Company, 1969).

Schmuck, Richard A., and Matthew B. Miles, eds., *Organization Development in Schools* (Palo Alto, Calif.: National Press Books, 1971).

Schutz, William C., "The Effects of T-group Laboratory on Interpersonal Behavior," *The Journal of Applied Behavioral Science*, 2:265–286, No. 2 (1966).

Seashore, Stanley E., and David G. Bowers, *Changing the Structure and Functioning of an Organization* (Ann Arbor: The University of Michigan, 1963).

———, "Durability of Organization Change," *American Psychologist*, 25:227–233 (1970).

Shepard, Herbert A., "An Action Research Approach to Organization Development," *Management Record*, 22:26–30 (June 1960).

———, "Rules of Thumb for Change Agents," *OD Practitioner*, 7:1–5 (November 1975).

Steele, Fred I., "Physical Settings and Organizational Development," in Harvey A. Hornstein, Barbara B. Bunker, W. Warner Burke, Marion Gindes, and Roy J. Lewicki, eds., *Social Intervention: A Behavioral Science Approach* (New York: The Free Press, 1971), pp. 244–254.

Steele, Fritz, *The Open Organization: The Impact of Secrecy and Disclosure on People and Organizations* (Reading, Mass.: Addison-Wesley Publishing Company, 1975).

Strauss, George, "Organization Development," in Robert Dubin, ed., *Handbook of Work, Organization, and Society* (Chicago: Rand McNally College Publishing Company, 1976), pp. 617–685.

Walton, Richard E., "Interpersonal Confrontation and Basic Third-Party Functions: A Case Study," *The Journal of Applied Behavioral Science*, 4:327–344, No. 3 (1968).

——, *Interpersonal Peacemaking: Confrontations and Third-Party Consultation* (Reading, Mass.: Addison-Wesley Publishing Company, 1969).

White, Sam E., and Terence R. Mitchell, "Organization Development: A Review of Research Content and Research Design," *Academy of Management Review*, 1:57–73 (April 1976).

Zand, Dale E., "Collateral Organization: A New Change Strategy," *Journal of Applied Behavioral Science*, 10:63–89 (1974).

——, "Trust and Managerial Problem Solving," *Administrative Science Quarterly*, 17:229–39 (June 1972).

Zaner, Theodore, "Action Research in Management Development," *Training and Development Journal*, 22:28–33 (June 1968).

CHAPTER 27
THE PERSONNEL DEPARTMENT: ITS EMERGING ROLE

If personnel management is the recruitment, selection, development, and utilization of, as well as accommodation to, human resources by organizations, any person at any level in any kind of organization is involved in personnel management when planning the use of human resources or influencing, directing, or controlling their use. Thus, the president, the supervisor, the industrial engineer, the controller, and the sales manager of a business organization are all deeply engaged in personnel management, although personnel management may not be considered their primary responsibility. Similarly, superintendents of schools, principals, and teachers spend a high proportion of their time immersed in personnel management. The same holds true for managerial/supervisory people in hospitals, military organizations, clubs, churches, colleges and universities, and

for those in national, state, and local governments—in other words, for managers in all goal-seeking enterprises. Personnel management processes are inherent in organizations of any kind and of all sizes and complexities.

One particular department in medium-sized and large organizations spends such a high percentage of its time in the area of human resources that it is aptly called the "personnel" department or some similar name, such as the "industrial relations" or "human resources" department. In small enterprises, there may be no such department, since the various centralized components of the personnel management function may be managed by the chief executive and/or other members of the top management group. As Chapter 1 implies, the establishment of a personnel department does not departmentalize the entire personnel function.

561

No one individual or department can possibly exercise exclusive jurisdiction over this function as we have defined and described it.

One theme of this book is that it is useful to analyze the broad personnel management function from an overall systems approach, not solely from the standpoint of the personnel department's role or solely from the standpoint of the manager's role. What the personnel department does and what the supervisor does are both important, but neither by itself adequately describes personnel management.

Consequently, this book has described personnel management as a broad network of interdependent processes within the enterprise and as a complex network of interdependent systems designed to facilitate these processes. It has also presented a way of analyzing these processes and systems that provides a medium for understanding their interrelatedness, what impact they have on people, who typically has authority and responsibility over which components, the impact of environmental forces, and the degree to which different personnel devices and systems contribute to the goals of the enterprise. I hope such an analysis has made it clear that *all managers, including the personnel manager, have highly important roles in the effective utilization of human resources* and that the assignment of specific authority and responsibility over particular aspects is an arbitrary matter, a consequence of the particular design of the systems within particular organizations.

THE EVOLVING PERSONNEL DEPARTMENT

WHEN THE DEPARTMENT EMERGES

Studies suggest that personnel departments, presumably containing more than one full-time employee, begin to appear when companies reach a size of 200 or more employees, and sometimes earlier. They also provide evidence that before this stage some personnel activities are assigned full-time to at least one employee. A study in the automobile parts manufacturing industry found the average company using a full-time personnel specialist by the time there were 77 production employees, or about 107 employees in all.[1]

A study by Wickesberg of 106 firms, ranging from those with fewer than 10 employees to those with 400 to 499 employees, found that no firms with fewer than 200 employees had personnel departments but that two out of eight firms with 200 to 299 employees did have them, as did one out of three firms with 300 to 399 employees and five out of six firms with 400 to 499 employees. Considered in terms of annual dollar sales, only firms with sales of $3 million or more had personnel departments.[2]

It is interesting that the study by Wickesberg found personnel departments beginning to appear at about the same stage in the company's growth as departments in production planning and control, industrial engineering, and market research. However, personnel departments evidently emerged with somewhat greater frequency than those other departments in companies with more than 200 employees or $3 million annual sales.[3]

A study by Baker found that only 4 percent of firms with less than 25 employees had part-time personnel managers, but about 3 percent had full-time personnel managers; 15 percent of firms with 25 to 74 employees had part-time personnel managers, but 3 percent had full-time personnel managers; and 29 percent of firms

[1] Bruce Erwin DeSpelder, *Ratios of Staff to Line Personnel* (Columbus: Bureau of Business Research, College of Commerce and Administration, The Ohio State University, 1962), Research Monograph No. 106, p. 45.

[2] Albert K. Wickesberg, *Organizational Relationships in the Growing Small Manufacturing Firm* (Minneapolis: University of Minnesota, 1961), pp. 25, 33–34.

[3] Ibid. This same study found personnel departments in small companies to be a post–World War II phenomenon, although the sizes of the companies at the time of the emergence of the personnel department were not reported.

with 75 to 149 employees had part-time personnel managers, while 18 percent had full-time
personnel managers. In 11 percent of firms with
150 to 299 employees, there were part-time personnel managers, but the full-time specialist
now appeared in 65 percent of the firms.[4]
Thus, personnel functions exist in firms of any
size, but when the firm begins to grow, certain
aspects of these functions are assigned to one
employee or manager, first on a part-time basis
and then full-time as the firm reaches approximately 200 employees.

THE MANAGER'S TITLE

A study by the National Industrial Conference
Board of 249 large companies, mostly in manufacturing, found that the majority (126 companies) of personnel executives had the title of
vice president. Approximately one-third (92)
had the title "director of" or "corporate director
of." The units that these executives headed
were most frequently called "industrial relations" (90 out of 249), "personnel" (64), "employee relations" (42), or "personnel and public
relations" (20). The word "personnel" appeared in 30 additional units. Overall, the
name "personnel" appeared in 114 of the 249
units.[5]

TO WHOM THE PERSONNEL EXECUTIVE REPORTS

The above study found 65 percent (161 companies) of the corporate personnel executives reporting to the president or chairman of the
board. In another 29 percent (74 companies),
the corporate personnel executive reported to
an executive vice president, vice president of

administration, etc.[6] Trends in recent years
suggest that in the future, the personnel executive will report to the president and hold the
title of vice president in an even higher percentage of firms.

The personnel director, of whatever title, can
serve the goals of the enterprise more effectively by reporting to the chief executive. Since
personnel policies, processes, and systems tend
to cut across all organizational subdivisions, an
organizationwide viewpoint is needed in personnel planning, coordinating, and controlling.
Furthermore, the personnel director can serve
all executives and departments more effectively
if not subordinate to any one section of the enterprise.

THE ORGANIZATION AND ASSIGNED FUNCTIONS OF THE PERSONNEL DEPARTMENT

In most companies, staffing, appraisal, training
and development, compensation, collective
bargaining, and health and safety are included
in the purview of the personnel department.
Only a few firms have departments which specialize in some of these functions and which are
separate from the personnel department. The
practice of separating "personnel" from "labor
relations," for example, has declined in recent
years. Today, in the vast majority of companies, the personnel department is expected to
be concerned about all major "people aspects"
of the enterprise.[7]

The principal categories of functions performed by personnel departments may include
many subfunctions. For example, the administration of employee-benefit programs may include representing the company's interests in
unemployment compensation and workmen's
compensation. Occasionally, the personnel department may be involved in such matters as

[4] Alton W. Baker, *Personnel Management in Small Plants* (Columbus: Bureau of Business Research, College of Commerce
and Administration, The Ohio State University, 1955), p. 31.
[5] National Industrial Conference Board, "Personnel Administration: Changing Scope and Organization," *Studies in Personnel Policy*, No. 203, 1966, p. 14.
[6] Ibid., p. 15.
[7] See National Industrial Conference Board, "Personnel Administration: Changing Scope and Organization."

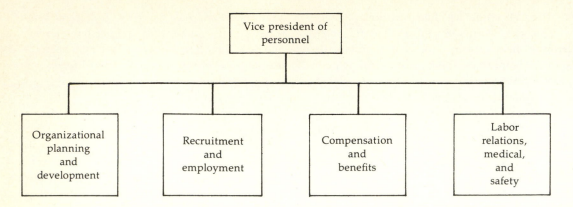

Figure **27-1**   Example of personnel-department organization in a large company

managing parking lots, preparing the annual report to stockholders, or running the annual United Fund or United Good Neighbor drive.

McFarland calls this tendency to assign such miscellaneous functions to the personnel department the "trashcan hypothesis." He believes, and cites evidence for his conclusions, that indiscriminate assignment of functions to the personnel department weakens the potential impact of the personnel program and diverts the energies and attentions of the department's members from those functions that should be their central concern. Furthermore, McFarland finds that chief executives believe there should be little restriction on what is assigned to the personnel department, while personnel directors resent the tendency to make the personnel department a "dumping ground" of miscellaneous functions. Thus, conflict and frustration result from neglecting to clearly define the role of the personnel department.[8]

The organization of the personnel department will reflect not only the functions assigned to it, but also the size of the enterprise. When a company is small, the personnel department may consist of one person and a secretary. In a large company, several subordinate managers may report to the personnel director, including a safety director, a medical director, who is usually an M.D., a wage-and-salary administrator, an employment manager, a training director, and a labor-relations director. Such a structure is shown if Figure 27-1. Many firms may group two or more of these subfunctions under subordinate administrators, as shown in Figure 27-2. Although these examples are similar to the actual structure of the personnel departments in many firms, the details of the personnel department's structure will vary from firm to firm.

Which functions belong to the personnel department is probably a more important question than the actual design of the department. There can be no precise formula, but the following questions provide useful guides when assigning functions to the personnel department once an enterprise has grown too complex for the chief executive to handle the major responsibilities in personnel management:

○ Does the particular function require a total-enterprise philosophy about the utilization of human resources?

[8] Dalton E. McFarland, *Cooperation and Conflict in Personnel Administration* (New York: American Foundation for Management Research, 1962), pp. 48–69.

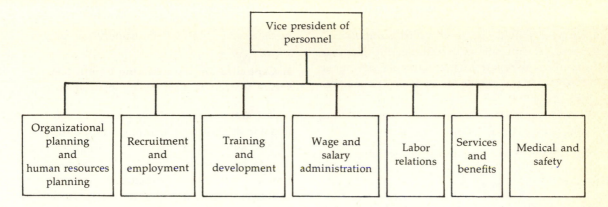

Figure 27-2   Broader grouping of personnel-department functions

○ Do any activities related to the selection, utilization, and development of human resources necessitate centralized attention?

○ Does the administration of human resources demand specialized skills which would be impractical for subdivisions of the enterprise to recruit or develop?

Such criteria help identify the most important functions belonging to the personnel department. Of course, some functions are so near the borderline that it may not make much difference where they are assigned, so long as the chief executive insures that they are administered effectively.

EMERGING FUNCTIONS

Organization development, human-resources planning, organizational planning, EEOC and OSHA compliance, and administration of salaries are probably going to receive substantially more attention by top management during the next decade, and personnel executives will be expected to assume substantial leadership in these areas. There is some evidence for these predictions. McFarland, for example, in a study of some 400 firms found that company presidents and personnel executives were expecting more changes in managerial development, training, and organizational planning than in any of the other personnel functions.[9] As another example, the National Industrial Conference Board's study of 249 firms cited earlier found "a vastly greater emphasis" on human-resources planning, organizational development, and compensation than was the case in earlier studies.[10] Chapter 10 discussed the impact of OSHA, and various chapters throughout this book have documented the accelerating effort that is being made to remedy the effects of previous discrimination and to avoid new instances. Dilemmas posed by some of these trends will be discussed later in this chapter.

PERSONNEL MANAGEMENT IN MULTIUNIT ORGANIZATIONS

The multiplant or multidivisional company introduces additional problems in personnel

[9] Dalton E. McFarland, *Company Officers Assess the Personnel Function* (New York: American Management Association, 1967), A.M.A. Research Study 79, pp. 81–88.
[10] National Industrial Conference Board, "Highlights for the Executive," in "Personnel Administration: Changing Scope and Organization."

management. For example, how much local autonomy should be given the subdivision? Should the personnel director in the plant or subdivision report to the corporate personnel director, to the plant's (or division's) manager, or to both?

Arguments for headquarters' coordination and control run as follows:

1. The personnel and industrial-relations function is so important that top-management attention should be given to it.

2. Uniform practices are necessary so that people throughout the organization may feel they are treated fairly.

3. Multiplant bargaining requires centralized attention to this function. When contracts are negotiated with different unions, centralization of direction is needed in order to avoid "whip-sawing" tactics—the argument that "plant X has this benefit, why can't we?"

4. Labor legislation and administrative ruling require central administration to insure appropriate standards.

5. Centralization provides economies through specialization.

6. Many personnel and industrial-relations matters cut across departmental and divisional boundaries, particularly such matters as insurance and retirement programs.

7. Insuring optimum selection and use of human resources by an enterprise requires central coordination and control of such matters as recruitment, promotion, and transfer among subunits.

Arguments that tend to be advanced against headquarters' coordination and control of personnel and industrial relations are as follows:

1. Local conditions and problems must be taken into account.

2. Since personnel management is inseparable from managing people, the function of personnel and industrial-relations management should be as close to the first-line supervisors as possible.

3. Centralization increases the time it takes to secure answers to local personnel problems.

The arguments for headquarters' coordination and control are the stronger of the two positions, although the argument about local conditions has particular merit. For example, in companies with widely scattered plants located in different labor markets, it may be economically unwise to pay uniform wage rates throughout the company. On the other hand, an overall rationale for whatever differentials exist seems imperative, and this requirement means central planning and coordination. An exception might be the subsidiary that has had a tradition of local autonomy and in which employees tend to identify with the local organization rather than the parent company. If the subsidiary is unionized, however, and the parent company pays better wages or has better fringe benefits, the union is likely to make a strong effort to have these advantages extended to the subsidiary.

Opinions and practices also differ about the question of to whom the personnel director of the division or plant should report. Although most personnel or industrial-relations directors of plants or divisions report to the manager of the plant or division, some companies have used a structure in which personnel officers of these subunits report directly to a corporate personnel director. Probably in the vast majority of multiunit companies the personnel director of the plant or division looks to the manager of the plant or division for day-to-day direction, but operates within the framework of overall company policy in personnel and industrial relations.

The real question then is whether the corporate personnel director exercises coordination and control *directly* with the personnel director in the division or plant, or whether this coordination and control is exercised *indirectly through the manager* of the plant or division. In any event, the subunit's personnel director must work closely with the top executive of the subunit in order to be effective. At the same time, however, the plant or divisional personnel director must make decisions within the context of overall company policy. In most situations, a modus operandi probably evolves in which some matters are decided by the corporate personnel director in consultation with both the manager of the plant or division and the subordinate personnel director. In practice, there is likely to be a good deal of direct communication between the corporate personnel office and the personnel office in the plant or division about the planning and administration of overall company policy, while the manager of the division or plant and the personnel office confer frequently about day-to-day decisions within the framework of company policy.

THE PERSONNEL GENERALIST CONCEPT

The *personnel generalist* in essence extends the concept of the *plant's* personnel director in multiplant enterprises to smaller subdivisions, such as departments or laboratories. In other words, instead of having specialists in such fields as training and the administration of wages and salaries serve an entire company or major division, the personnel function is broken up geographically, with "generalists" assigned to major departments. Each generalist then handles all specialized personnel activities for his or her assigned area, including wage and salary administration, training, transfers, etc., with coordination and control from a central office.[11]

The terminology *personnel generalist*, then, has evolved to promote the idea of more diversified responsibilities for the various subordinate members of personnel departments and to counteract some presumed disadvantages of specialization. In a sense, the personnel generalist applies the concept of job enrichment to the personnel function.

At what size an enterprise should be subdivided and served by personnel directors subordinate to a corporate personnel director rather than by various personnel specialists is a question not easily answered. Part of the answer lies in the overall structure of the enterprise. If the enterprise has subdivisions headed by managers to whom different functional specialists—controllers and purchasing agents, for example—report, it seems that personnel directors who are generalists should also report at this level and that they should receive direction both from the enterprise's headquarters and from their particular subdivision. In short, the degree of specialization or generalization within personnel management is part of the broader question of how the total enterprise is to be organized.

PERSONNEL DEPARTMENT'S ROLE IN THE VARIOUS PERSONNEL SUBSYSTEMS

Any discussion about the role of the personnel department in managing the various personnel subsystems is made difficult because assumptions and practices vary so widely among organizations. I will, however, try to describe in a general way what is probably the typical role of the personnel department in a majority of organizations and then the role that appears to be emerging in some of the more progressive organizations.

---

[11] For a description of the use of personnel generalists in one company, see Harry R. Knudson, Jr., "Enter the Personnel Generalist," *Personnel*, 37:33–41 (March-April 1960). For a discussion of regional personnel offices in multinational firms, see David A. Heenan and Calvin Reynolds, "RPO's: A

Step toward Global Human Resources Management," *California Management Review*, 18:5–9 (Fall 1975).

LEADERSHIP AND ORGANIZATION CLIMATE

CONTEMPORARY ROLE   It is likely that the typical role of the personnel department relative to the leadership style(s) and climate existing in the organization is one of accommodation. The typical personnel department works hard at designing and administering personnel systems and special programs that are acceptable to the chief executive and to other top managers, with the chief executive officer's style and managerial philosophy typically a dominant and pervasive dimension. Day-in and day-out activities—such as recruitment, screening, monitoring wage and salary programs, supervising transfers, and dealing with the union— occupy a high proportion of the time of the personnel department staff.

New programs—such as testing, orientation, MBO, job enrichment, and preretirement programs—are frequently negotiated with top managers after the personnel director or other executives hear of successes in other organizations. Sometimes a personnel department will be inventive in the development of a particular approach and will be a pacesetter for other firms.

Most of this is as it should be, with the personnel department carrying out many activities vital to the ongoing life and success of the organization. But there are some activities that are frequently not very evident. These dimensions have to do with leadership and organizational climate.

EMERGING ROLE   I believe it is a fair statement to say that probably only a small minority of personnel directors act in a *catalyst* role to help the organization articulate and evolve an internally consistent organizational climate, including the broad boundaries of the preferred leadership style. However, I see this role emerging in more and more organizations and, to be prescriptive, I believe this to be one of the most important functions a personnel director

can perform. Ideally, the crystallization of managerial philosophy with regard to human resources would be a reflection of input from all organizational members; at a minimum it should involve several layers of management. The development of a clear philosophy in which most organizational members concur requires, of course, effective diagnostic techniques, such as the use of questionnaires and/or interviews, and the feeding of data back for discussion and resolution of issues.

One of the reasons that this emerging role for the personnel director is so important is that organizational climate and leadership style are greatly affected by the design and administration of the various personnel systems and vice versa. Each new personnel program, including how it evolves and how it is managed, carries with it an implicit leadership style and/or set of assumptions about managing people. An example, as described in Chapter 15, is MBO, which can be autocratic or participative. It can reinforce a one-on-one or a team-leadership style. In turn, organization climate and leadership style have major consequences in terms of morale and job performance. (Other examples of implicit leadership style or management philosophy will be given in the following discussion of the role of the personnel department in the various personnel subsystems.)

And why is it important that the leadership style or managerial philosophy implicit in various personnel systems be internally consistent, i.e., congruent? Because incongruency leads to confusion, cynicism, and wasted effort. If the management development program is teaching the merits of participation while the job enrichment program is highly unilateral and autocratic, what new and desired behaviors are likely to emerge? Probably nothing but cynicism and additional resistance to new ideas will result.

It should be emphasized that while a great deal of research tends to indicate the efficacy of a participative mode, participation per se is not a universal solution. Not only does participation need to be perceived as relevant to solving significant organizational problems, but participation carries with it the need for *participatory skills*. The greater the participation, the greater the need for interpersonal and group skills, including skills in the sharing of leadership activities.

The major point I want to make is that the personnel director and staff are in a key position to help the top management and other key organizational members develop and articulate the desired organizational climate and leadership style. This role is not an easy one. It means leadership on the part of the personnel director, and it requires the earning of a high degree of acceptance in the eyes of peers at the executive level, including the CEO. It may also mean drawing on outside consultants for assistance (see Chapter 26).

TASK SPECIALIZATION/JOB DESIGN

CONTEMPORARY ROLE The personnel department usually is not involved in establishing the economic, technical, or service objectives of the enterprise that mainly determine the nature of the tasks to be performed. Typically outside the personnel department's purview is the planning of the technology to be used, the plant's layout, work simplification, time-and-motion study—in short, the technical design of work and work flow.

Once technological changes have been planned, however, the personnel department, as a rule, becomes heavily involved in helping the enterprise adapt these technological aspects to the human aspects of the organization, and vice versa. To put it another way, the personnel department usually has a high degree of responsibility for integrating the technical system of the enterprise with its social system.

The personnel department typically furthers this integration through helping to design personnel subsystems for such areas as staffing, appraisal, training and development, and compensation in order that people will use the technical aspects of the enterprise to the best advantage. For example, the personnel department is likely to coordinate the writing of job descriptions, which reflect the objectives and technology of the organization and which, in turn, are used in developing job specifications necessary for controlling quality in employment. These job descriptions are also used in job evaluation, which is essential to a program of compensation considered fair and equitable by employees. Similarly, the personnel department is likely to work closely with various top managers in developing and formalizing work rules necessary to insure that tasks are carried out efficiently and safely. In the area of performance standards, the personnel department may work with various managers to develop the system, but it will not be involved in actually establishing specific standards. In the unionized organization, however, the performance-standard system may become a problem for the personnel department during negotiations.

Thus, the activities of the personnel department to a great extent reflect the technical side of the enterprise as designed by the chief executive, the various technical specialists, and others. The personnel department, then, is more involved in the "after-the-fact" aspects of the specialization process than in its initial aspects. Much of what the personnel department does, however, stems from this process.

EMERGING ROLE Various illustrations cited earlier in the book from such organizations as Texas Instruments and TRW Systems suggest that the corporate personnel executive in some organizations may well be emerging as one of the central advocates of placing high priority on both task/economic goals and creating a more humanistic work environment. Relative to these objectives, the personnel director and his or her staff may be involved in encouraging participative management or job enrichment, either of which may have a major impact on job design. As stated before, there is also substantial indication that the corporate personnel staff is becoming increasingly concerned with organizational planning, preparation of organizational manuals, and advice to the chief executive on overall organizational structure. In addition to working with line managers in developing organizational plans, personnel departments frequently assist in implementing plans of reorganization.

One of the dilemmas posed by these trends is whether the personnel department should act as an *advocate* of particular organizational or job structures: as an *advocate of experiments* with various selected approaches such as flextime, the compressed workweek, or the use of permanent part-time employees; or as a *consultant-catalyst*. In the long run, the role of consultant-catalyst is likely to be the most effective. Too often, programs like job enrichment are "solutions in search of a problem" instead of suggestions emerging from a careful diagnosis of the present state of affairs. I am assuming that organic changes that result from managers' and their subordinates' perception of significant problems will release more creativity and collaboration than prescriptive changes designated by the top managers. In part, I am suggesting that the personnel department will become more active in *problem diagnosis* in the future. This has relevance, of course, to all of the personnel subsystems.

STAFFING

CONTEMPORARY ROLE The typical personnel department is deeply involved in the staffing process. That department is likely to be very active in intermittent human-resources planning, in developing sources of applicants, in preliminary screening of candidates, and in induction and orientation. As a rule, it also exercises important controls over staffing. For example, the staffing system usually includes authorization by the personnel department before new employees may be hired or before transfers and promotions may be finalized. This authorization insures that staffing decisions have taken into account the total staffing needs of the organization and that they reflect a total organizational viewpoint. Similarly, the staffing system usually includes the personnel department's screening out of candidates who fall below minimum specifications. This insures that a work force of appropriate quality is obtained.

Another important control exercised by the personnel department is that of authorizing beginning salaries and increases for promotions. By reviewing proposed compensation before making offers to hire or promote, the total structure of wages and salaries can be taken into account, thereby avoiding inequities which could lead to internal dissension and/or to excessive costs. Similarly, through watching proposed discharges, the personnel department can make certain that the total interests of the organization are being considered and that the employee is being treated fairly. Obviously, these staffing controls are also components of the processes of compensation, financial management, and justice determination.

EMERGING ROLE Potentially, the central personnel staff of an organization holds a position of tremendous influence in selecting employees and assisting in their career growth at all levels of the organization, up to and including those reporting to the chief executive. These potentialities are natural correlates of an expanded role in job design, organizational planning, and managerial development.

Such a role, however, assumes expertise and a commitment to the idea that the personnel department ought to be concerned about the total human resources of the organization. It means that the personnel staff is not a service group responding solely to requests or stimuli from other departments. The staff must seek opportunities to be heavily involved in organizational and human-resources planning, initial selection, orientation, promotion decisions, affirmative action, and career planning. By career planning I mean working with managers to identify the extent of growth- and promotion-potential in their subordinates, and working with both subordinates and their superiors to make long-range plans for personal development. In addition, in many organizations, I see the personnel department having a major role in helping create a more open system in terms of transfer and promotion opportunities. This may mean creative adaptation of such devices as job posting, career ladders, and assessment centers, and the encouragement of a climate that will permit women and minorities to rise in management. I also see the personnel department and/or training people becoming more adept at using small group techniques in such matters as orientation, upward communication, and preretirement planning. The ability to conduct adequate test validation studies is a role that has not had high priority for many personnel departments in the past, but now must.

APPRAISAL

CONTEMPORARY ROLE The personnel department is extensively involved in designing and monitoring appraisal systems relative to promotions, transfers, discharges, pay increases, and job coaching, but not in the appraisals per se. In any organization large enough to have a separate personnel department, that department cannot possibly be close enough to the actual performance of all employees to do a very effective job of day-to-day appraising. It can, how-

ever, help establish merit-rating or performance-standard systems, and it can train and encourage managers in their proper use. An MBO effort, in particular, requires considerable coordination, training, and support, and these functions can be supplied by the personnel department. Furthermore, since some managers may chronically rate their subordinates much higher or lower than other managers, the personnel department often performs an important function in attempting to assess such discrepancies and correct them through persuasion and education.

EMERGING ROLE Two significant themes seem to be emerging from recent research on appraisal systems. First, appraisal systems must be designed in accordance with their purpose. Second, appraisal systems designed for the growth and development of subordinates must permit a much higher level of open and supportive dialogue between superior and subordinate, and substantially more subordinate participation, than is the typical practice. The personnel executive is challenged to help create a climate where such collaborative behavior is possible and where a zero-sum philosophy of human resources does not prevail. I also see the need for more awareness on the part of the personnel executives of the differences between various forms of MBO and of the implicit leadership style and organizational climate they represent.

COMPENSATION

CONTEMPORARY ROLE In addition to coordinating job descriptions, the personnel department is likely to undertake the tasks of developing and "selling" necessary to insure the effective operation of a job evaluation system. Moreover, a representative of the personnel department will probably be a member of the job evaluation committee and participate in decisions on the relative worth of jobs.

As a rule, the personnel department conducts surveys of wages and salaries and uses these data in planning revisions of the current pay structure. Once the general concurrence of top management to modify the overall plan on wages and salaries has been secured, the personnel department typically monitors compliance with the rules which have been established. Usually, individual managers will make decisions about pay within the framework of wage and salary plans, with the personnel department insuring that the limits are not exceeded and that the spirit and intent of the plans are carried out.

The personnel department is usually only one of many sources from which recommendations about fringe benefits originate. The board of directors, the president, the union, and various managers may take an active interest in supplemental compensation. The more effective personnel departments systematically study the costs of the different items in the compensation package and compare the total "package" with the total packages of other firms. The department then makes recommendations to top management accordingly.

Once top management has approved the programs of supplemental compensation, some of these programs are administered by the personnel department and others by the accounting or finance departments. Although practices vary from firm to firm, the personnel department is likely to monitor time-off-with-pay programs (sick leave, personal business, jury duty, etc.), while the accounting department may administer such matters as the life insurance and pension programs.

The moving force in the installation of incentive systems is likely to be the production or engineering departments and others immediately concerned with output, although the personnel department may occasionally assume the initiative. In all probability the personnel department is ordinarily asked for advice on such matters and is involved in planning such systems. Actual administration of incentive systems is likely to be a joint venture of the particular departments where the system is used, the payroll department, and the personnel department. In the unionized organization, the personnel department will also participate in negotiations over the details of incentive programs as well as over any grievances arising under such programs. Suggestion systems, whether considered part of the communicative system or a kind of incentive system, are typically administered by the personnel department.

EMERGING ROLE   A major challenge confronting top management and the top personnel executive in particular is how to design the total system of compensation in such a way as to optimize attainment of organizational goals. Many compensation plans, including wages and salaries, incentives, and the fringe-benefit package, have grown erratically without an overall rationale or any consistent set of assumptions. To an increasing extent, personnel executives are studying the total compensation system, diagnosing its dysfunctional aspects, and making recommendations for change.

The more an organization moves in the direction of managerial styles that indicate more creativity and productivity, the more it becomes necessary to look at the appropriateness of the particular compensation system. In a broad sense, managerial practices that are designed to increase the contribution of subordinates to the success of an organization and to the financial enhancement of its top management but do not proportionally increase the rewards to subordinates are hypocritical. This may mean more and more emphasis on the use of incentive programs, such as systems of profit sharing or bonuses. A pressing challenge in many organizations is the development of compensation plans that do not discriminate against women and a careful assessment of compensation practices to determine if older employees are being discriminated against.

The adoption of flexible benefit programs appears to be emerging only slowly, but recent successes suggest that more and more personnel staffs will need to develop expertise in this area.

COLLECTIVE BARGAINING

CONTEMPORARY ROLE   The personnel department is ordinarily the central point of contact between the union and the company when a union requests bargaining recognition, for the union's submission of initial demands during negotiations, for collective bargaining, and for the administration of the agreement during the life of the contract. In addition, the personnel department usually coordinates the company's responses to efforts at organizing currently non-affiliated employees, coordinates the company's planning in the face of threatened strikes, and both represents the company and coordinates the company's presentation in National Labor Relations Board and arbitration hearings. Furthermore, the personnel department is customarily designated in the labor contract as the company's final agency of review in the grievance procedure.

EMERGING ROLE   In some collective-bargaining situations, the personnel department is playing a key role in moving the company and union toward integrative bargaining. Integrative bargaining has been shown to be highly relevant across a wide range of problems, including health and safety matters, job design, the introduction of technological improvements, and associated problems of worker displacement and compensation. Such a shift from distributive bargaining requires a different set of skills—those of effective leadership and building trust in contrast to those of the protagonist.

Traditional collective bargaining poses a dilemma for the personnel executive who recognizes the need for a more participative and open managerial style in his organization. If there is no union, should unionization be resisted? Although this question has no simple answer, organizational members are probably much less interested in collective action when the environment is highly responsive to their drives toward personal and group effectiveness.

What if there is a union already? Are efforts to create a more organic system compatible with win-lose bargaining? Given such incongruity, management would probably confront the union with the issue in an attempt to alter the traditional bargaining relationship. In the event of union resistance or lack of understanding, long-range education by example would probably bring about a gradual change in union attitudes, but the tension from two styles of interpersonal relationships might persist for a time. That a more open, participative managerial style can be compatible with a unionized situation is evidenced by the experience of the Weldon Company, where a changing organizational environment gradually shifted union-management relations in the direction of joint problem solving.[12]

A willingness to explore optional forms of conflict resolution will also characterize the emerging role of many personnel departments. Examples would be expedited arbitration, or the use of a third party to assist the parties in exploring their relationship and making plans for improvement.

ORGANIZATIONAL JUSTICE

CONTEMPORARY ROLE   Not only is the personnel department of the unionized organization involved in the grievance process, but it is often also a designated agency where appeals may be taken by nonunion employees. Although formalized grievance procedures in the nonunionized organization are rare, the personnel department is frequently mentioned in the

[12] See Alfred J. Marrow, David G. Bowers, and Stanley G. Seashore, *Management by Participation* (New York: Harper & Row, 1967).

handbooks for employees as a place to which complaints may be taken when an aggrieved employee is dissatisfied after discussions with his immediate or higher superior, or with both superiors. Further, the personnel department typically takes an important part in developing an organizational "constitution," that is, personnel policies and formal or informal mechanisms of appeal that serve to encourage equitable treatment of employees. Probably the personnel department is used almost universally as a counseling or advising agency— a "sounding board" where employees of all ranks seek advice and perspective in dealing with superiors, subordinates, and peers. Through such counseling, the personnel department undoubtedly injects additional elements of justice into the work situation by advising against inequitable or unjust practices and, in some cases, by acting as an intermediary in remedying an injustice.

EMERGING ROLE The emerging role of the personnel department in determining organizational justice may lie in its emphasis on integrity and authenticity in human relationships and in its development and protection of systems of appeal. In particular, the personnel department may play a major role in protecting an organizational *pluralism*—a spectrum of opinions about effective managerial behavior— while at the same time promoting an atmosphere of inquiry. I am referring mainly to organization development efforts and the attendant necessity for candid exposure of concerns and feelings about different approaches. In short, the effectiveness of managerial philosophy and personnel practice should be subject to constant scrutiny, and constructive dissenters should be protected from punishment. In the long run, any really participative managerial philosophy must be based on a spirit of openness and inquiry.

Further, an emerging role for the personnel department would be that of acquiring a heightened sense of the variables perceived by employees to be relevant to equitable treatment, and their translation into day-to-day personnel administration. An example would be to understand how nonexempt employees view overtime practices, which are frequently perceived as exploitative.

TRAINING AND DEVELOPMENT

CONTEMPORARY ROLE Through training units, personnel departments in many large organizations run extensive educational programs. When needed skills are not available within the firm and cannot be obtained in the labor market, the personnel department may be called upon to organize and staff training efforts relative to those skills. The personnel department may also work with first-line supervisors in establishing effective procedures for induction and orientation. Similarly, the personnel department may be called upon to organize management-development programs with seminars on or off the company's premises, or it may be called upon to coordinate the sending of managers to special programs at universities, conferences, and institutes.

The personnel department may attempt to persuade managers of the desirability of certain kinds of skill-training and general-educational programs based on the department's assessment of the organization's needs. In neither training nor educational programs, however, is the personnel department likely to select the candidates nor is it likely to impose such programs on managers. The CEO's interest or pressure may, of course, be a major determinant in establishing such programs.

Although found in only a minority of firms, any formalized counseling activities conducted by the personnel department that have as their objective the personal growth and development of employees can also be considered part of the broader training and developmental function. Since increased personal effectiveness, insight, and creativity are inseparable from increased mental health, such counseling programs overlap a broader health-management program.

EMERGING ROLE   As discussed earlier, many organizations are beginning to devote more attention to identifying and developing both the professional-technical and managerial talents represented in their work forces. Dramatic shifts in the skill mix of employees and competitive pressures for a higher and higher level of technical and managerial skills are requiring a much broader perspective on the part of personnel departments than was previously warranted. One implication of this is that the personnel department will frequently become more proactive relative to the problem of mid-career obsolescence, a problem partly due to short-sighted assignment practices on the part of managers. Further, increased demand for the development of human resources is likely to be accompanied by insistence upon a program's relevance and avoidance of piling one new training program upon another. In short, the most effective training and development people are emerging as skilled diagnosticians as well as skilled educators.[13] In addition, I anticipate that training departments will devote more and more attention to training group process and conflict resolution skills in organizations where increased emphasis is placed upon participation.

ORGANIZATION DEVELOPMENT

The recent emergence of efforts to develop organizations and of other applications of behavioral sciences points up a major challenge for the corporate personnel director. Briefly stated,

innovations in the applied behavioral sciences are beginning to make line executives look toward the personnel director and his or her staff as the key persons in the organization to help them translate and adapt this new knowledge into successful managerial practice.

If the personnel executive has not developed personal knowledge and expertise or assisted personnel staff members in the development of new skills, he or she runs the danger of being considered obsolete, and the personnel department may be bypassed. One consequence of this eventuality may be the emergence of a separate unit as a source of behavioral science expertise. Unfortunately, however, this can lead to incompatibility between the efforts of organizational change and the management of the various personnel subsystems. As has been discussed, personnel policies and practices must be designed to support changes in the philosophy and style of leadership. If they are not, constructive changes may undergo a reversal. In short, the vice presidents of personnel and directors of industrial relations of the future, along with their subordinates, are likely to be faced with a choice between becoming effective applied behavioral scientists or being considered administrators of the status quo.

The positive side of this dilemma is that many personnel departments throughout the United States and abroad have made, or are making, this transition. To an increasing degree, such personnel departments will have a major impact on their organizations in terms of helping their organizations meet the challenges of a rapidly changing world.

SUMMARY

Personnel management and personnel departments are in a state of transition. Although the last two decades have witnessed an almost universal recognition and acceptance by top executives of the important role that personnel departments can perform in planning and

[13] Bennis expects the training and developmental director of the future (who usually reports to the personnel director) to fill several new functions, including "training for change," "systems counseling," "developing new incentives," and "building collaborative, problem-solving teams." Warren Bennis, "Organizations of the Future," *Personnel Administration*, 30:17 (September-October 1967).

administering systems of human resources, the remainder of this decade and the 1980s present a major new challenge.

The challenge is how able the personnel executive and staff can become in the role of behavioral scientists collaborating with the total managerial group and with formal work teams in improving organizational effectiveness. Increasingly, personnel executives are working with external and/or internal behavioral scientist consultants and with line managers in utilizing behavioral science knowledge in their organizations, and their efforts are creating exciting and profitable innovations. One part of the challenge lies in how to create and manage the various personnel subsystems in a way compatible with the thrust in many organizations toward more participative, results-oriented, adaptive, and humanistic organizations. Systems of job design, staffing, appraisal, compensation, collective bargaining, organizational justice, and training and development must all be examined and improved toward these ends.

This challenge is made all the more real and urgent by two sometimes seemingly contradictory imperatives that have overtaken us—the imperative toward more efficient production of quality goods and services, and the imperative toward a higher quality of life in our organizations. Personnel management must—and will—play a major role in furthering a creative synthesis of these two imperatives.

REVIEW AND DISCUSSION QUESTIONS

1. If you were the president of a company, how would you define the relationship between a divisional personnel director and the corporate personnel director in your company?

2. What criteria would be useful in determining the functions that should be assigned to the personnel department?

3. To whom does the plant personnel director in multiplant companies report? What tensions or problems does this produce?

4. What aspects of personnel management are beginning to receive more emphasis, at least in large corporations? Is there any common theme to this emphasis?

5. What appears to be the emerging role of the personnel department in the following areas?

a. Leadership style and organizational climate
b. Task specialization
c. Staffing
d. Appraisal
e. Compensation
f. Collective bargaining
g. Organizational justice
h. Training and managerial development
i. Organization development

6. What do you see as the major challenges faced by personnel directors and personnel departments today?

SUPPLEMENTAL REFERENCES

American Society for Personnel Administration, *1974–1975 Salary Survey* (Berea, Ohio: ASPA, 1975).

———, "Some Questions and Answers about the ASPA Accreditation Programs," ASPA Accreditation Institute, P.O. Box F, Berea, Ohio 44017.

Argyris, Chris, "Behavioral Scientist at Large . . . ," *The Conference Board Record*, 4:23–28 (May 1967).

Baker, John K., and Robert Schaffer, "Making Staff Consulting More Effective," *Harvard Business Review*, 47:62–71 (January-February 1969).

Bass, Bernard M., "Organizational Life in the 70's and Beyond," *Personnel Psychology*, 25:19–30 (Spring 1972).

Beavers, Wiley, "Accreditation: What Do We Need That For?" *The Personnel Administrator*, Vol. 20 (November 1975).

Berra, Robert, "An Interview with Bob Berra," *The Personnel Administrator*, 21:29–33 (February 1976).

Burack, Elmer H., and Edwin L. Miller, "The Personnel Function in Transition," *California Management Review*, 18:32–38 (Spring 1976).

Bureau of National Affairs, "The Personnel Department: Budgets and Staffing Policies," *ASPA-BNA Survey No. 31*, May 20, 1976 (4 pp.).

Cayer, N. Joseph, *Public Personnel Administration in the United States* (New York: St. Martin's Press, 1975).

Cheek, Logan M., "Cost Effectiveness Comes to the Personnel Function," *Harvard Business Review*, 51:96–105 (May-June 1973).

Coleman, Charles J., and Joseph M. Rich, "Why Not Fire the Personnel Manager?" *Human Resources Management*, 14:20–26 (Summer 1975).

Craft, James A., and Jacob G. Birnberg, "Human Resource Accounting: Perspective and Prospects," *Industrial Relations*, 15:2–12 (February 1976).

Daughtery, A.C., "A President Looks at the Personnel Function," *Personnel Journal*, 47:402–406 (June 1968).

Davis, Keith, "Some Basic Trends Affecting Management in the 1980s," Alumni Lecture Series, College and Graduate School of Business Administration, University of Minnesota, May 7, 1976.

Davis, Louis E., and Albert B. Cherns, eds., *The Quality of Working Life, Vol. I: Problems, Prospects, and the State of the Art*, and *Vol. II: Cases and Commentary* (New York: The Free Press, 1975).

Day, Virgil B., "Managing Human Resources in the Seventies," *Personnel Administration*, 33:4–7ff. (January-February 1970).

Famularo, Joseph J., ed., *Handbook of Modern Personnel Administration* (New York: McGraw-Hill Book Company, 1972).

Fischer, Frank E., "The Personnel Function in Tomorrow's Company," *Personnel*, 45:64–71 (January-February 1968).

Foulkes, Fred K., "The Expanding Role of the Personnel Function," *Harvard Business Review*, 53:71–84 (March-April 1975).

French, Wendell, and Dale Henning, "The Authority-Influence Role of the Functional Specialist in Management," *Academy of Management Journal*, 9:187–203 (September 1966).

Gardner, John W., "Can Organization Dry Rot Be Prevented?" *Personnel Administration*, 29:3–5ff. (May-June 1966).

Glueck, William F., "Where Organization Planning Stands Today," *Personnel*, 44:19–26 (July-August 1967).

Gross, Edward, "Sources of Lateral Authority in Personnel Departments," *Industrial Relations*, 3:121–133 (May 1964).

Gruber, William H., "Behavioral Science, Systems Analysis and the Failure of Top Management," *IMR*, 9:37–48 (Fall 1967).

Guion, Robert M., "Gullibility and the Manager," *The Personnel Administrator*, 20:20–23 (January 1975).

Hardin, Einar, "Interindustry Differences in the Size of the Industrial Relations Work Force," paper presented at American Statical Association, Business and Economic Statistics Section, Boston, August 24, 1976.

Harris, O. Jeff, "Personnel Administrators—The Truth about Their Backgrounds," *MSU Business Topics*, 17:22–29 (Summer 1969).

Herman, Georgianna, ed., *Personnel and Industrial Relations Colleges: An ASPA Directory* (Berea, Ohio: American Society for Personnel Administration, 1974).

Hill, V.A., "The President and His Personnel Man," *Business Review* (Australia), 11:21–22 (March 1968).

Jain, Harish C., "Training of Management Specialists in Labor Relations," in James L. Stern and Barbara D. Dennis, *Proceedings of the 1975 Annual Spring Meeting* (Madison, Wisc.: Industrial Relations Research Association, 1975), pp. 464–471.

Jennings, Ken, "Improving Line/Staff Relationships," *The Personnel Administrator*, 20:47–51 (October 1975).

Johnson, Rossall J., "The Personnel Administrator of the 1970's," *Personnel Journal*, 50:298–305ff. (April 1971).

Lanham, Elizabeth, "EDP in the Personnel Department," *Personnel*, 44:16–22 (March-April, 1967).

Levy, Seymour, "What is the Role of the Director of Personnel in Applying Theories of Organization Development?" *Personnel Administration*, 29:51–53 (March-April 1966).

McFarland, Dalton E., "Company Officers Assess the Personnel Function," *AMA Research Study 79* (New York: American Management Association, Inc., 1967).

Macy, Barry A., and Philip H. Mirvis, "A Methodology for Assessment of Quality of Work Life and Organizational Effectiveness in Behavioral-Economic Terms," *Administrative Science Quarterly*, 21:212–226 (June 1976).

Mahler, Walter R., *Diagnostic Studies* (Reading, Mass.: Addison-Wesley Publishing Company, 1974).

Meyer, Herbert E., "Personnel Directors Are the New Corporate Heroes," *Fortune*, February 1976, pp. 84–88ff.

Mills, Ted, "Human Resources—Why the New Concern?" *Harvard Business Review*, 53:120–134 (March-April 1975).

Miner, John B., "Levels of Motivation to Manage among Personnel and Industrial Relations Managers," *Journal of Applied Psychology*, 61:419–427 (August 1976).

Nash, Allan N., and John B. Miner, *Personnel and Labor Relations: An Evolutionary Approach* (New York: The Macmillan Company, 1973).

National Industrial Conference Board, "Personnel Administration: Changing Scope and Organization," *Studies in Personnel Policy*, Number 203, 1966.

Patten, Thomas H., Jr., "Is Personnel Administration a Profession?" *Personnel Administration*, 31:39–48 (March-April 1968).

———, "Personnel Administration and the Will to Manage," *Human Resource Management*, 11:4–9 (Fall 1972).

Petersen, Donald J., and Robert L. Malone, "The Personnel Effectiveness Grid (PEG): A New Tool for Estimating Personnel Department Effectiveness," *Human Resource Management*, 14:10–21 (Winter 1975).

Rhode, John G., Edward E. Lawler III, and Gary L. Sundem, "Human Resource Accounting: A Critical Assessment," *Industrial Relations*, 15:13–25 (February 1976).

Rico, Leonard, "Managerial Schizophrenia: The Personnel Function in Firm," *Management of Personnel Quarterly*, 3:11–23 (Winter 1965).

Ritzer, George, and Harrison M. Trice, *An Occupation in Conflict: A Study of the Personnel Manager* (Ithaca, N.Y.: New York State School of Industrial and Labor Relations, Cornell University, 1969).

Rush, Harold M.F., "Behavioral Scientist at Large . . . A Candid Conversation with Chris Argyris," *The Conference Board Record*, 4:23–28 (May 1967).

Scheer, Wilbert E., "Do We Throw The Book Away and Start Over?" *Personnel Journal*, 50:189–195 (March 1971).

U.S. Department of Labor, "Personnel and Labor Relations Workers," *Occupational Outlook Handbook, 1976–77 Edition*, pp. 143–146.

Whyte, William F., "Organizations for the Future," in Gerald G. Somers, ed., *The Next Twenty-Five Years of Industrial Relations* (Madison, Wisc.: Industrial Relations Research Association, 1973), pp. 129–140.

Yoder, Dale, and Herbert G. Heneman, Jr., *Planning and Auditing PAIR*, ASPA Handbook of Personnel and Industrial Relations, Vol. IV, (Washington, D.C.: The Bureau of National Affairs, 1976).

APPENDIX
A CHRONOLOGICAL HISTORY OF PERSONNEL MANAGEMENT IN THE UNITED STATES

1607 Jamestown, Virginia is founded.
Throughout 1600's, artisans from England, Sweden, Holland, Poland, France, Italy, Germany, Ireland, Scotland, Greece, Spain, and other countries come to America.

1619 First blacks brought to Virginia are treated as bound labor; were subsequently freed when terms expired. By the 1640s, practice began in colonies of selling imported blacks for life. During colonial period, many white Europeans bound themselves as servants, averaging four years of service in return for ship passage to America.

1636 Group of Maine fishermen protest the withholding of their wages.

1646 Virginia Colony provides that two children from each county be taught, at public cost, the arts of carding, knitting, and spinning.

1647 Massachusetts Bay Colony passes law requiring each town of fifty or more houses to contribute to support of a teacher.

1718 British parliamentary act authorizes sentences of seven years at bound labor in the colonies for lesser crimes and fourteen years for offenses punishable by death. An estimated ten thousand convicts were sent to the colonies from Old Bailey between 1717 and 1775.

1741 Bakers in New York strike to protest a municipal regulation on the price of bread.

1786 Strike conducted by Philadelphia journeymen printers against a wage-cut results in a minimum wage of $6 per week.
New York City Chamber of Commerce organizes an arbitration tribunal to hear dispute involving seamen's wages.

1790 Profit sharing is introduced in this decade by Albert Gallatin in his New Geneva, Pennsylvania, glassworks.

1791 Philadelphia carpenters strike unsuccessfully for a ten-hour day and for additional pay for overtime.

1792 First local craft union formed for collective bargaining in the United States is organized by Philadelphia shoemakers.

1794 Federal Society of Journeymen Cordwainers is formed in Philadelphia.
Typographical Society is organized by printers in New York.

1799 Attempt at collective bargaining by Philadelphia journeymen cordwainers (shoemakers) results in a lockout, followed by a settlement between union and employers' association.

1806 Cordwainers are found guilty of criminal conspiracy to raise wages.

1820 First attempt to measure working population of the United States is made in the taking of the Fourth Census.

1825 Boston House Carpenters, rebelling at their sunrise-to-sunset working hours, strike for ten-hour day and lose.
The United Tailoresses of New York is formed in New York City by and for women only.

1827 The Mechanics' Union of Trade Associations, composed of unions of skilled craftsmen in different trades, is formed in Philadelphia.

1828 The Workingmen's Party is organized in Philadelphia. It includes wage earners, craftsmen, farmers.

1829 *The Mechanics' Free Press* of November 21, 1829, reports "hundreds of boys, seven years old and upwards" working from dawn until 8 P.M. in suburban Philadelphia factories. Children under sixteen comprise one-third to one-half of factory labor force of New England.

1831 New England Association of Farmers, Mechanics, and Other Workingmen is formed in Rhode Island and spreads throughout New England.

1834 A federation of City Centrals, called the National Trades' Union, is formed—a first attempt at forming a national labor organization.

1835 Geneva Cordwainers' case: New York courts uphold a law based on a "conspiracy doctrine" making collective action to obtain raises in wages illegal.

1836 Similar case involving tailors likewise upholds conspiracy doctrine.
First national union of a single craft is organized: the National Cooperative Association of Journeymen Cordwainers.
The ten-hour day is introduced at the Philadelphia Navy Yard.

1840 President Van Buren establishes a ten-hour day for federal employees on public works, without reduction in pay.

1842 The Massachusetts Supreme Court overthrows the conspiracy doctrine and declares unions not illegal in the case of *Commonwealth v. Hunt.*
Connecticut and Massachusetts pass laws prohibiting child labor beyond ten hours a day.

1847 New Hampshire passes law fixing ten hours as the legal workday.

1848 Pennsylvania passes a state child-labor law setting the minimum age for workers in commercial occupations at twelve years.

1852 The Typographical Union is formed—the first national organization of workers that has continued to the present day.
Massachusetts passes nation's first safety law, establishing safety standards for steam engines.

1862 The "Molly Maguires," a secret society of Irish miners in the anthracite fields, comes to public attention because of its terrorist activities aimed at controlling relations with mine owners.
Morrill Act, providing grants of land to support state colleges devoted to agricultural and mechanical arts, signed by President Lincoln.

1863 Brotherhood of Locomotive Engineers is founded. Laws in Illinois and Minnesota are passed providing for fines and imprisonment of strikers who prevent others from working.

1866 National Labor Union, a federation of national craft federations, is established.

1868 Congress passes a federal eight-hour-day law applying to laborers, workers, and mechanics employed on behalf of the U.S. government.
Massachusetts establishes a state labor bureau.

1869 Knights of Labor is founded in Philadelphia, Pennsylvania.

1870 Coal miners and operators sign their first written contract. Contract provides for sliding scale of pay based on the price of coal.

1873 Brotherhood of Locomotive Firemen and Enginemen is organized.

1875 First industrial pension plan established by the American Express Company.

1876 Fourteen of the leaders of the Molly Maguires are imprisoned, and ten are executed, for criminal activity, including the murder of mine owners and mine bosses. Convictions are based primarily on evidence collected by an agent of the Pinkerton detective agency.

1877 Strikes on railroads, and clashes between strikers and federal troops in Baltimore and Pittsburgh, result in the death of more than one hundred people.
Massachusetts passes law requiring shields on dangerous parts of some machinery.

1878 Knights of Labor is organized nationally.

1880 Suggestion plan is started at Yale and Towne Manufacturing Company, Stamford, Connecticut.
Baltimore and Ohio Railroad establishes a relief association (insurance) for employees, incorporated 1882, but charter is revoked by Maryland in 1888.

1881 Delegates of craft unions meet in Pittsburgh to form Federation of Organized Trades and Labor Unions (forerunner of the AFL).

1882 New York City carpenter, Peter J. McGuire, cofounder of the American Federation of Labor, suggests setting aside one day of the year in honor of labor.

1883 Pendleton Act creates the U.S. Service Commission.
The Brotherhood of Railroad Trainmen is organized.

1884 U.S. Bureau of Labor Statistics is founded. Bureau of Labor is established in the Department of Interior.

1885 Frederick W. Taylor starts experiments in Midvale and Bethlehem Steel plants that lead to "scientific management."
Carroll Wright, formerly Director of Massachusetts Bureau of Statistics, is confirmed as first U.S. Commissioner of Labor.

1886 Thousands of workers across the United States go on strike for an eight-hour day. Chicago police kill four strikers at the McCormick Reaper Works. At a meeting in Haymarket Square, a bomb is thrown into police ranks with seven police and four workers killed in the resulting melee.
Failure of an attempt to merge the Federation of Organized Trades and Labor Unions with the Knights of Labor results in the Federation's holding a convention in Columbus, Ohio, which in turn results in formation of the American Federation of Labor (AFL). Samuel Gompers is elected president.
Henry R. Towne reads a paper, "The Engineer an Economist," to a meeting of the American Society of Mechanical Engineers, and thereby greatly influences F.W. Taylor.

1888 First federal labor relations law is passed. Law applies to railroads and provides for arbitration and presidential boards of investigation.

1889 "Social secretary" role is created by American League for Social Service. Appointments in industry spread rapidly and a conference of social secretaries is called in 1893.

1890 Term "mental test" is first used by Cattell, early industrial psychologist.
Sherman Antitrust Act is passed.
United Mine Workers is organized.
Workweek in manufacturing averages sixty hours; for unionized employees, fifty-four; for building trades, fifty-one; for postal employees, forty-eight.

1892 American Psychological Association is founded.
Homestead Steel strike leads to violence between strikers and armed Pinkerton men.
White scalemen and packers allied with black teamsters strike for ten-hour day on New Orleans waterfront; ultimately unions are convicted of violating the Sherman Antitrust Act.

1894 Pullman strike is suppressed by federal troops.

1894 Standard personal history blank in use at Georgia Association of Life Insurers.

1898 Congress passes the Erdman Act, providing for mediation and arbitration in the railroad industry. The Act makes dismissing or discriminating against employees for union activity a criminal offense.

1899 Nicholas Paine Gilman's book, *A Dividend to Labor: A Study of Employer's Welfare Institutions* is published in Boston and London. It includes a chapter on profit sharing and an appendix, "Some Dangers of Paternalism."

1900 International Ladies' Garment Workers' Union, AFL, is formed.
A few employment agents or employment clerks are found in business.
Employment department at the B.F. Goodrich Company starts at about this time.

1901 International Federation of Trade Unions is formed.

Labor department at the National Cash Register Company is formed at about this time.

1902 Maryland passes first state workmen's compensation law, but the law is declared unconstitutional.

1903 Department of Commerce and Labor is created by an act of Congress.
F.W. Taylor presents his paper "Shop Management" to a meeting of the American Society of Mechanical Engineers.
The magazine *System* publishes Herbert J. Hapgood's article, "System in Employment."

1904 National Child Labor Committee organized to press for limitations on child labor.

1905 Industrial Workers of the World is organized in Chicago.
Simon-Binet tests of mental ability are first published in France.
Supreme Court holds a maximum-hour law for bakery workers unconstitutional (*Lochner* v. *New York*).
Budgett Meakin's book, *Model Factories and Villages: Ideal Conditions for Labour and Housing* is published in London. Subtopics of its chapters include, "social relations," "medical attendance," "dangerous trades," "communications," "incentives," "rewards," "suggestion schemes," and "workmen's councils."

1906 The International Typographical Union strikes successfully for an eight-hour day.
Civil Service Assembly of the United States and Canada is founded in Chicago—name is changed in 1958 to the Public Personnel Association.

1908 Section 10 of the Erdman Act of 1898 is declared unconstitutional by the U.S. Supreme Court. This section had outlawed the "yellow dog" contract in the railroad industry and discharge of workers for union membership.
United Hatters of Danbury, Connecticut, is held responsible for a boycott against D.E. Lowe and Company and in restraint of trade under the Sherman Antitrust Act.

1910 A strike of the International Ladies' Garment Workers' Union is settled by providing for preferential union hiring, a board of grievances, and a board of arbitration.

Alice Hamilton, physician, begins study of lead poisoning in industry.

1911 Society to Promote the Science of Management is formed by Frank Gilbreth and others. It became the Taylor Society after Frederick Taylor's death in 1915.

The Triangle Waist Company fire, New York, causes the death of 146 workers and leads to the establishment of the New York Factory Investigating Commission.

Taylor's book, *The Principles of Scientific Management* and Frank B. Gilbreth's book, *Motion Study*, are first published.

1912 Massachusetts adopts a minimum-wage act for women and minors.

Congress appoints a U.S. Commission on Industrial Relations.

Strikers involved in a spontaneous strike in the textile mills in Lawrence and Lowell, Massachusetts, are organized by the Industrial Workers of the World (IWW). Nonviolent tactics result in a victory for the strikers.

National Safety Council starts.

This is approximate date of appearance of modern personnel departments.

First Employment Managers' Association is formed in Boston. It is sponsored by Meyer Bloomfield, Director of the Vocation Bureau of Boston.

Edward Cadbury's book, *Experiments in Industrial Organization*, is published in London. A forerunner of modern personnel texts, it includes chapters entitled, "The Selection of Employees," "Education of Employees," "Discipline," "Provisions for Health and Safety," and "Methods of Remuneration."

1913 The U.S. Department of Labor is established, including Bureau of Labor Statistics, Children's Bureau, and Conciliation Service.

Hugo Munsterberg's *Psychology and Industrial Efficiency* is published in the United States.

1914 Colorado Coal Commission is appointed by the president to investigate the Ludlow Massacre during a strike of the United Mine Workers in Colorado coal mines.

Clayton Act is passed, exempting unions from the provisions of the Sherman Act, limiting the use of injunctions in labor disputes, and making picketing legal.

Lillian Gilbreth publishes *The Psychology of Management*.

1914 to 1919 AFL supports World War I war effort.

National War Labor Board is created; it establishes in factories many "work councils" consisting of elected representatives of workers in the various departments.

World War I gives impetus to the employment-management function because of the scarcity of labor, the necessity of good labor relations, and governmental insistence on employment departments in plants manufacturing war materials.

1915 Tuck School of Dartmouth College offers the first training program for "employment managers."

First full-time psychiatrist in U.S. industry employed by Cheney Brothers Silk Manufacturing Company.

German army creates a psychological testing center to select motor-transport drivers.

1916 The federal Child Labor Law is passed.

The National Industrial Conference Board—an independent, nonprofit organization devoted to research on business practices and problems, including personnel management—is organized in New York.

Bureau of Salesmanship Research at Carnegie Institute of Technology is established; Walter Dill Scott is appointed to head Bureau.

Henri Fayol's classic, *General and Industrial Management*, is published in France.

1917   The International Workers of the World's strike in copper mines of Arizona ends with the sheriff deporting 1,200 strikers.

President appoints a mediation commission to assist with wartime labor problems.

Society of Industrial Engineers is organized.

U.S. Supreme Court upholds the "yellow dog" contract.

Walter D. Scott secures backing of Newton D. Baker, secretary of war, to establish a Committee on Classification of Personnel in the Adjutant General's Office. This committee establishes an Army Personnel Program, including records on the qualification of all military personnel, an index of civilian occupations useful to the military, a series of personnel specifications for military jobs, a series of trade tests, and a specialized army training corps program.

Robert M. Yerkes, president of the American Psychological Association and former assistant to Munsterberg at Harvard, calls governing council into session to discover ways in which psychologists can help with the war effort. Committee on the Psychological Examination of Recruits, with Yerkes as chairman, prepares two mental-ability tests—Test A for literates and Test B for illiterates. Yerkes is commissioned a major and made head of a section of psychology under the surgeon-general of the Army. This section then starts the first personnel research in the U.S. Army by developing the Army Alpha and Army Beta form the A and B tests.

Journal of Applied Psychology, devoted in part to research on selecting employees, is first published. A journal by the same name had been established in Germany in 1907.

The federal government takes control of the railroads from December 1917 until March 1920, resulting in an expansion of railroad unionism and the development of a system for handling labor disputes.

U.S. Supreme Court upholds the Workmen's Compensation Law of the state of Washington, which requires the employer to pay for lost time and injuries resulting from occupational accidents.

1918   Roy Kelly's pioneering book in personnel management, *Hiring the Worker,* is published; it includes discussion of job descriptions, job specifications, application blanks, interviews, medical examinations, placement, training, transfers, promotions, and discharges.

1919   The United Mine Workers strike against the Bituminous Coal Operators and subsequently agree to arbitration by a presidential commission.

Strikes occur in steel and other industries as employers withdraw recognition of many unions recognized during the war.

J. Coss and L. Outhwaite's topical outline and bibliography, *Personnel Management,* is published by the U.S. Army.

The magazine *Personnel* first published.

Henry Link's *Employment Psychology: The Application of Scientific Methods to the Selection, Training, and Grading of Employees* is published.

First firm of personnel consultants, the Scott Company of Philadelphia, is established.

1920   The Kansas Court of Industrial Relations is the first tribunal to experiment with compulsory arbitration in the United States. It is later held unconstitutional in part.

A published interview with Samuel Gompers states support of labor-saving machines providing they are regarded as "additions to intelligence and not as substitutes for intelligence."

O. Tead and H.C. Metcalf publish *Personnel Administration,* the first textbook in personnel management. Ordway Tead is teaching one of the first courses in personnel administration in the United States; it is being offered through the evening program at Columbia University. Henry Metcalf, experienced in vocational guidance and governmental personnel work, is to conduct an executive-development program in New York City in 1924.

The Transportation Act returns the railroads to private management and provides for a tripartite Railroad Labor Board, established to hear labor disputes and to make recommendations for settlement.

1921 The Personnel Research Federation—a cooperative effort to exchange information on research in personnel management—is founded. Robert Yerkes is first chairman, Samuel Gompers vice chairman.

The Supreme Court holds that the Clayton Act does not legalize secondary boycotts or protect unions against injunctions brought against them for conspiracy in restraint of trade.

1922 The United Mine Workers is not held responsible for local strikes, and the act of striking is not held a conspiracy to restrain commerce within the Sherman Act, although labor unions are held liable to suit for their acts.

Industrial Relations Section is established in the Department of Economics and Social Institutions at Princeton University.

National Personnel Association is formed by merger of National Safety Council, National Association of Corporation Training, and National Association of Employment Managers.

Journal of Personnel Research—now called *Personnel Journal*—is first published by the Personnel Research Federation.

1923 American Management Association, which assimilates the National Personnel Association, is founded.

E.K. Hall of the American Telephone and Telegraph Company is the first person to attain title of "Vice President in Charge of Personnel Relations."

1924 Experiments in illumination at the Hawthorne Works of the Western Electric Company in Chicago, with the collaboration

to

1932 of the National Research Council and

Massachusetts Institute of Technology and Harvard University, lead to investigations of group behavior and worker sentiments.

Merrill R. Lott develops one of first plans for evaluating jobs on the basis of job characteristics.

1925 Warner W. Stockberger is the first personnel director in the U.S. Department of Agriculture and in the U.S. government. He subsequently becomes the first president of the Society for Personnel Administration, Washington, D.C. (1937).

1926 Railway Labor Act is passed, establishing collective bargaining in the railway systems, establishing grievance and arbitration procedures, and providing for "cooling off" periods, fact finding, and mediation.

American Arbitration Association is founded.

1927 Mary Parker Follett's papers on "The Psychology of Control, Consent, and Arbitration" and "Conciliation and Arbitration"—early, pioneering essays in personnel management—are published in *Psychological Foundations of Business Administration*.

1929 Stock market crashes and the Great Depression and large-scale unemployment begins. Communist-inspired Trade Union Unity League is formed.

1931 The Davis-Bacon Act provides for the payment of prevailing wage rates to laborers and mechanics employed by contractors and subcontractors on federal contracts.

1932 Wisconsin adopts the first unemployment insurance act in the United States.

The Norris-LaGuardia Act is passed, outlawing the "yellow dog" contract and making difficult the use of injunctions in labor disputes.

1933 The National Industrial Recovery Act (NIRA) is passed, giving the workers the right to organize and bargain collectively without interference, coercion, or restraint from employers.

The Wagner-Peyser Act is passed, providing for social security.

1934 First National Labor Legislation Conference is called and convened by Secretary of Labor Frances Perkins with the objective of obtaining closer federal-state cooperation in working out appropriate national labor-relations laws.

The United States joins the International Labor Organization (ILO).

Society of Industrial Engineers is combined with the Taylor Society as the Society for the Advancement of Management.

U.S. Employment Service begins an occupational-research program.

1935 Social Security Act is passed.

The U.S. Supreme Court declares the National Industrial Recovery Act unconstitutional.

The National Labor Relations (Wagner) Act is passed, re-enacting the labor provisions of the NIRA and establishing the National Labor Relations Board. It establishes right of workers to organize and to elect representatives for collective bargaining.

Atlantic City Convention of the AFL results in dissatisfaction by industrial union advocates, who later meet to form the Committee for Industrial Organization (CIO).

1936 The United Rubber Workers (CIO) wins recognition at the Goodyear Tire and Rubber Company in the first large "sitdown" strike.

The Anti-Strikebreaking (Byrnes) Act makes it unlawful to transport or aid in transporting strikebreakers in interstate or foreign commerce.

The Public Contracts (Walsh-Healy) Act establishes labor standards on governmental contracts, including minimum wages, overtime compensation for hours over eight in one day or forty in one week. It also contains provisions on health and safety requirements for child and convict labor.

1937 Ten people are killed and eighty wounded in a Memorial Day clash between police and members of the Steelworkers' Organizing Committee at the Republic Steel Company plant in South Chicago.

The AFL expels unions connected with the CIO.

United Auto Workers (CIO) signs contract with General Motors and Chrysler.

American Association for Applied Psychology is formed. It is now the Division of Industrial and Organizational Psychology of the American Psychological Association.

Bureau of Apprenticeship in U.S. Department of Labor is established by National Apprenticeship Act.

The National Labor Relations Act is held constitutional in the case of *NLRB* v. *Jones and Laughlin Steel Corporation.*

Walter C. Langer's book, *Psychology and Human Living,* dealing with human needs, repression, and integration of personality, is first copyrighted.

American Medical Association establishes the Council on Industrial Health.

The Society of Personnel Administration is formed in Washington, D.C.

U.S. Supreme Court upholds state of Washington law authorizing fixing of minumum wages for women and minors.

1938 President Roosevelt signs Executive Order 7916 requiring main administrative branches of the government to establish personnel offices.

The CIO organizes on a permanent basis with John L. Lewis as its first president.

The Steelworkers' Organizing Committee is recognized as the bargaining agent for members of the union at the United States Steel Corporation. A 10 percent increase in wages, an eight-hour day, and a forty-hour week are negotiated.

The Fair Labor Standards Act is passed. For firms in interstate commerce, it provides minimum wages and time and a half when hours exceed forty in a week.

The Railroad Unemployment Insurance Act is passed.

The Merchant Marine Act of 1936 is amended to provide for a Federal Maritime Labor Board.

Chester Barnard's *The Functions of the Executive* is published.

1939 *Dictionary of Occupational Titles* is published by the U.S. Department of Labor.

F.J. Roethlisberger and W.J. Dickson publish *Management and the Worker*, describing the Hawthorne studies.

1940 In the case of *Apex Hosiery Company* v. *Leader*, a sitdown strike is held not to be an illegal restraint of commerce under the Sherman Act in the absence of an intent to impose market controls.

Personnel Procedures Section is established in the Adjutant General's Office in the War Department.

Training Within Industry Service (TWI) of the War Manpower Commission is established to assist industry in improving workers' productivity through better training.

1941 United States enters World War II. Unions give a no-strike pledge. United Auto Workers (CIO) wins recognition at the Ford Motor Company. After a ten-day strike, the union and the company sign a union-shop agreement.

1942 National Association of Suggestion Systems is organized.

National War Labor Board, representing labor, management, and the public, is set up to deal with wartime disputes.

First Psychological Research Unit is established in the U.S. Army Air Forces.

The National War Labor Board hands down the "Little Steel" formula for wartime adjustments in wages.

The Stabilization Act authorizes the president to stabilize wages and salaries.

Carl Rogers' book, *Counseling and Psycho-*

therapy, of significance in improving interviewing techniques, is published.

1943 A Committee on Fair Employment Practices is created by executive order of the president.

Abraham Maslow's essay, "A Theory of Human Motivation," appears in the *Psychological Review.*

The War Labor Disputes (Smith-Connally) Act authorizes seizure of plants in order to avoid interference with the war effort.

1945 Research Center for Group Dynamics is formed at the Massachusetts Institute of Technology by Kurt Lewin to perform laboratory and field experiments in group behavior. It is to be moved in 1948 to the University of Michigan.

First state Fair Employment Practices Act is adopted by New York.

1946 The American Sociological Society creates a section on industrial sociology.

Institute for Social Research is founded at the University of Michigan by Rensis Likert to conduct research in social science. It is later to have two divisions, the Survey Research Center and the Research Center for Group Dynamics.

Most extensive wave of strikes in U.S. history breaks out. The United Steel Workers (CIO) ends a one-month strike and obtains a wage increase of eighteen and one-half cents an hour. The United Automobile Workers (CIO) ends a three and one-half month strike against General Motors and obtains an hourly wage increase of eighteen and one-half cents.

1947 The Labor Management Relations (Taft-Hartley) Act is passed, amending the Wagner Act and making certain union practices unfair labor practices. The closed shop, the jurisdictional strike, the secondary boycott or sympathy strike, and refusal to bargain are outlawed. Law makes legal the right of states to pass "right-to-work" laws.

National Training Laboratory for Group Development is established at Bethel, Maine, for the purpose of experimentation and training in group behavior. It is now called NTL Institute for Applied Behavioral Science.

Industrial Relations Research Association—a professional association of professors, labor leaders, and others interested in advancing knowledge in personnel and industrial relations, labor economics, and related areas—is founded.

Nationwide telephone strike occurs.

The Portal to Portal Act is approved to "relieve employers and the Government from potential liability . . . in 'portal to portal' claims"—employers are exempted from paying wages for time used in washing up, changing clothes, walking from work place to plant gate, and so forth.

1948 *Personnel Psychology* is first published.

American Society for Personnel Administration is formed.

Mississippi is the forty-eighth state to enact workmen's compensation legislation.

The federal government holds its first national conference on industrial safety.

President Truman appoints a Commission on Labor Relations in the Atomic Energy Installations.

1949 The U.S. Supreme Court holds in the case of *Inland Steel Company* v. *United Steelworkers of America* that the Labor Management Relations Act requires employers to bargain with unions on retirement plans.

Two unions are expelled from the CIO in an anti-Communist drive, and nine other unions are expelled early in 1950.

The CIO and the Free Democratic Trade Unions of various other countries withdraw from the World Federation of Trade Unions, which is Communist dominated. A new worldwide labor organization, the International Confederation of Free Trade Unions (ICFTU), is formed in London, England, with participation of the American AFL, CIO, and United Mine Workers union.

The term *behavioral sciences* is coined by a group of scientists at the University of Chicago.

1950 A five-year contract with no reopening provisions is negotiated between the United Auto Workers and the General Motors Corporation, providing for pensions, automatic cost-of-living adjustments in wages, guaranteed annual increases and a modified union shop.

1953 Presidential order ends governmental controls on wages and salaries.

1955 AFL-CIO is formed by merger, representing approximately 16 million workers—over 85 percent of the U.S. union membership. George Meany is elected first president.

1957 AFL-CIO expels the Teamsters, Bakery Workers, and Laundry Workers on charges of domination by corrupt influences.

An organization-development (OD) program begins to emerge at Esso Standard Oil through the work of the Employee Relations Research Division, Herbert Shepard, and Robert Blake. Simultaneously, an OD program is emerging at Union Carbide through the efforts of Douglas McGregor, John Paul Jones, and others.

1958 Senate Select Committee on Improper Activities in the Labor or Management Fields (McClellan Committee) continues its activities.

Michigan Bell Telephone Company establishes an assessment center.

1959 Labor-Management Reporting and Disclosure Act of 1959 (Landrum-Griffin Act) is passed establishing certain rights of rank-and-file union members and requiring certain kinds of reports by both employers and labor unions. It amends Taft-Hartley Act to eliminate "no man's land" in NLRB cases and to close certain loopholes in law.

Longest major steel strike in history takes place.

1962   President Kennedy issues Executive Order 10988 encouraging unionization of federal employees.

Manpower Development and Training Act is signed by President Kennedy.

1963   Two organizations of independent unions merge to form the National Federation of Independent Unions.

U.S. Supreme Court upholds two lower court decisions that the railroads are entitled to change work rules and eliminate jobs once the procedures of the Railway Labor Act have been exhausted.

U.S. Supreme Court rules that the agency shop is legal under the Taft-Hartley Act (*NLRB* v. *General Motors*) but that individual states can ban this form of union security (*Retail Clerks, Local 1625* v. *Schermerhorn*).

The Congress passes a law providing for compulsory arbitration of a dispute between the railroads and the operating brotherhoods, a dispute centering on the desire of the railroads to abolish certain jobs.

More than 200,000 black and white Americans march in Washington, D.C., to demand equal opportunities in employment and other civil rights.

Equal Pay Act is passed by Congress.

Vocational Education Act provides assistance to the states for constructing vocational schools and broadening provisions of eligibility for training.

1964   Civil Rights Act is passed by Congress. Title VII prohibits discrimination based on race, color, religion, sex, or national origin.

1965   Philadelphia teachers (50,000) ratify their first contract with the Philadelphia Board of Education.

Social Security amendments provide partial hospital and medical care for elderly—"Medicare."

The *Journal of Applied Behavioral Science* is first published.

1967   Chicago Board of Education and American Federation of Teachers agree on a contract covering 23,000 teachers.

AFL-CIO forms Council of Professional, Scientific and Cultural Employees to further white-collar unionism.

Age Discrimination in Employment Act is passed by Congress protecting those aged forty to sixty-five.

1968   UAW leave AFL-CIO. It combines with the Teamsters to form Alliance for Labor Action.

Equal Employment Opportunity Commission rules that sex is not a bona fide occupational qualification for position of flight cabin attendant—steward or stewardess.

NLRB jurisdiction is extended to private hospitals and nursing homes.

1969   Council of Engineering and Scientific Organizations, representing 50,000 engineers in nine associations, is founded.

Four of five railway operating unions, Trainmen, Conductors and Brakemen, Switchmen, and Firemen and Enginemen merge into a new United Transportation Union.

Coal Mine Health and Safety Act is passed by Congress, stemming partly from a coal-mine explosion in which seventy-eight miners are killed, and partly from reports of extensive black lung disease among miners.

1970   Occupational Safety and Health Act is passed by Congress.

1972   First general strike in the history of baseball occurs and delays the start of the regular season.

Xerox Corporation appoints ombudsman for its largest division.

1973   The International Personnel Management Association is formed by a consolidation of the

Public Personnel Association and the Society of Personnel Administration.

Vocational Rehabilitation Act is passed, requiring federal contractors to establish affirmative action plans for the physically handicapped.

1974 Employee Retirement Income Security Act is passed; establishes government standards for private pension plans.

NLRB jurisdiction is extended to nonprofit hospitals and nursing homes.

1975 Eighteen-day strike by doctors ends when residents and interns at Chicago's Cook County Hospital agree to settlement with Cook County Health and Hospital Governing Commission.

1976 American Society for Personnel Administration begins accreditation program in personnel management.

United Transportation Union ends ten-year strike against Florida East Coast Railway (longest railroad dispute in history).

SOURCES

Beal, Edwin F., and Edward D. Wickersham, *The Practice of Collective Bargaining* (Homewood, Ill.: Richard D. Irwin, 1959).

Bellows, Roger M., *Psychology of Personnel in Business and Industry* (Englewood Cliffs, N.J.: Prentice-Hall, Inc., 1949 and 1954).

Benge, Eugene J., *Standard Practice in Personnel Work* (New York: H.W. Wilson Company, 1920).

Business Week.

Cadbury, Edward, *Experiments in Industrial Organization* (London: Longmans, Green, and Company, 1912).

Cohen, Sanford, *Labor in the United States* (Columbus, Ohio: Charles E. Merrill Books, 1960).

Commons, John R., et al., *History of Labour in the United States*, Vols. I and II (New York: The Macmillan Company, 1918).

Commons, John R., Don D. Lescohier, and Elizabeth Brandeis, *History of Labor in the United States, 1896–1932*, Vol. III (New York: The Macmillan Company, 1935).

Commons, John R., Selig Perlman, and Philip Taft, *History of Labor in the United States 1896–1932*, Vol. IV (New York: The Macmillan Company, 1935).

Crowther, Samuel, "If I Were an Employer: An Interview with Samuel Gompers," *System*, 37:722 ff. (April 1920).

Eilbirt, Henry, "The Development of Personnel Management in the United States," *Business History Review*, 33:345–364 (Autumn 1959).

Eitington, Julius E., "Pioneers of Management: Personnel Management," *Advanced Management—Office Executive*, 2:16–19 (January 1963).

Filipetti, George, *Industrial Management in Transition* (Homewood, Ill.: Richard D. Irwin, 1946).

Fortune.

Gilman, Nicholas Paine, *A Dividend to Labor: A Study of Employer's Welfare Institutions* (Boston and London: Houghton Mifflin Company and MacMillan and Company, Ltd., 1899).

Gilmer, B. von Haller, *Industrial Psychology* (New York: McGraw-Hill Book Company, 1961).

Ginzberg, Eli, and Hyman Berman, *The American Worker in the Twentieth Century* (New York: The Free Press of Glencoe, 1963).

Greenman, Russell L., and Eric J. Schmertz, *Personnel Administration and the Law* (Washington, D.C.: The Bureau of National Affairs, 1972).

Kelly, Eleanor T., ed., *Welfare Work in Industry* (London: Sir Isaac Pitman & Sons, Ltd., 1925).

Kelly, Roy W., *Hiring the Worker* (New York: The Engineering Magazine Company, 1918).

Kennedy, Robert F., *The Enemy Within* (New York: Popular Library, 1960).

Leavitt, Harold J., *Toward Organizational Psychology* (Pittsburgh: Carnegie Institute of Technology, 1962), Reprint No. 117.

Ling, Cyril C., *The Management of Personnel Relations: History and Origins* (Homewood, Ill.: Richard D. Irwin, 1965).

Lytle, Charles W., *Job Evaluation Methods* (New York: Ronald Press, 1946).

Meakin, Budgett, *Model Factories and Villages: Ideal Conditions of Labour and Housing* (London: T. Fisher Unwin, 1905).

Metzger, B.L., *Profit Sharing in Perspective*, 2nd ed. (Evanston, Ill.: Profit Sharing Research Foundation, 1966).

Miller, Delbert C., and William H. Form, *Industrial Sociology* (New York: Harper & Brothers, 1951).

Miller, James G., "Toward a General Theory for the Behavioral Sciences," *American Psychologist*, 10:513–524 (1955).

Monthly Labor Review.

Morris, Richard B., ed., *Bicentennial History of the American Worker* (Washington, D.C.: U.S. Department of Labor, 1976).

Nigro, Felix A., *Public Personnel Administration* (New York: Henry Holt and Company, 1959).

Okubayashi, Koji, "Personnel Management in the United States During the 1920's," *The Annals of the School of Business Administration*, Kobe University, 1975.

Patten, Thomas H., Jr., *Manpower Planning and The Development of Human Resources* (New York: John Wiley & Sons, 1971).

Rossi, William H., and Diana Rossi, *Personnel Administration, A Bibliography* (1925).

Scott, Walter Dill, Robert C. Clothier, and William R. Spriegel, *Personnel Management*, 5th ed. (New York: McGraw-Hill Book Company, 1954), Chapter 15.

Seimer, Stanley J., *Suggestion Plans in American Industry* (Syracuse, N.Y.: Syracuse University Press, 1959).

Spates, Thomas G., *Human Values Where People Work* (New York: Harper & Brothers, 1960).

———, *The Scope of Modern Personnel Administration*, Section III, Book 1, *Reading Course in Executive Technique* (New York: Funk & Wagnall Company, 1948).

Supreme Court Reporter.

Trotta, Maurice S., *Arbitration of Labor-Management Disputes* (New York: Amacom, 1974).

U.S. Department of Labor, *Employment and Training Report of The President, 1976.*

———, *Important Events in American Labor History*, 1960.

———, *Safety Standards.*

Van Riper, Paul P., *History of the United States Civil Service* (Evanston, Ill.: Row, Peterson and Company, 1958).

Viteles, Morris S., *Industrial Psychology* (New York: Norton, 1932).

Willoughby, William F., *Workingmen's Insurance* (New York: Thomas Y. Crowell and Company, 1898).

Wood, Norman J., "Industrial Relations Policies of American Management," *Business History Review*, 34:403–420 (Winter 1960).

Author Index

Subject Index

absenteeism: costs of, 88; fairness and, 131; group factors and, 91; and job dissatisfaction, 88; leadership style and, 106, 107, 109
accountability, defined, 48
achievement, need for, 75
"across the board" increases, 400
action research, 544–546
administrative processes, 38
affirmative action, 208–209, 268–271, 382
age: as a basis of discrimination, 209–210; and job satisfaction, 84; and productivity, 209–210
Age Discrimination in Employment Act, 209–210
agency shop, 477
Albermarle v. *Moody*, 238, 329
American Airlines, 540
American Arbitration Association, 524, 526, 528
American Manufacturing case, 529
American Oil Company, 290
American Society for Personnel Administration, 5
Ansul Chemical Company, 266, 310
applicants, developing sources of, 214–216
application blanks, 222–228; unfair inquiries on, 226–227
appraisal, 299–301, 303–317; defined, 299; *see also* merit rating
appraisal interview, 300, 317–321
appraisal process, defined, 299–300
apprenticeship training, 337
Apprentice Training Service, 342
appropriateness of bargaining units: *see* National Labor Relations Board
arbitration, 138, 141, 520–535; expedited, 527–528; final-offer, 528; interest, 528; issues in, 523–524; prec-

edent in, 526–527; types of, 527–528
arbitrators, 523–526
Armour & Company, 343, 479
assembly-line work, 153–155, 160–163
assessment center concept, 266–268
AT&T, 159, 164, 166, 207, 263, 267, 270
attitude surveys, 551
authority, defined, 52; types of, 52–53, 372
autocratic leadership: *see* leadership
automation: impact of, 153–154; union reaction to, 477–480; *see also* technological change

Bank of America, 207, 270
behaviorally anchored rating scales, 175, 315–317
behavioral sciences, definition of, 24
Bethlehem Steel Company, 17
Boeing Company, 182
Boise Cascade Corporation, 225
bidding, job, 285
"buddy" ratings: *see* merit rating, by peers
"bumping," 289
bureaucratic leadership: *see* leadership

Cannon Electric Company, 407
"capital punishment" in labor relations, 291; *see also* discharge
career ladders, 283–284
career planning, 363, 552
change agents, 543–544
Chesapeake and Potomac Telephone Company, 164

child labor, 14
Chrysler Corporation, 155, 158, 185, 186
Civil Rights Act, 204–209, 431, 480
Civil Service Commission, 20
civil service rules, 216, 245–246, 309
Classification Act of 1923, 309
Clayton Act, 16
climate, organizational, 118–121, 568
clinical approach: to discipline, 137; to grievances, 523
clinical-statistical approach to testing, 238
closed shop, 477
coaching, 348–349, 552
cognitive dissonance, 130
cohesiveness, group, and productivity, 91
collaborative management by objectives, 323–326, 328
colleague authority, 372
collective bargaining, 496–519
collective-bargaining process: defined, 46; types of relationships, 497–502
Combination Laws, 15
"common law": of arbitration, 527; of industrial relations, 527
Commonwealth v. *Hunt*, 15
company unions, 16
compa-ratio, 402
compensation "cafeteria," 435
compensation process, defined, 46
Comprehensive Employment and Training Act, 342–343
compressed workweek, 184–186
computers, impact of, 152–153, 200; *see also* technological change
conciliation, 505–506; defined, 505
Connecticut General Life Insurance Company, 447

605